CompTIA A+ E   jective

OBJECTIVE		
1.0 PC HARDWARE (40		
1.1	Configure and appl	2
1.2	Differentiate betwe	1, 2, 3
1.3	Compare and contr	3
1.4	Install and configur	5, 6
1.5	Install and configur	4
1.6	Differentiate amon	g method.	3
1.7	Compare and conti	4, 5, 6, 9, 19
1.8	Install an appropriate power supply based on a given scenario.	1
1.9	Evaluate and select appropriate components for a custom configuration, to meet customer specifications or needs.	10
1.10	Given a scenario, evaluate types and features of display devices.	6
1.11	Identify connector types and associated cables.	4, 5, 6, 19
1.12	Install and configure various peripheral devices.	5, 6, 7
2.0 NETWORKING (27 PERCENT)		
2.1	Identify types of network cables and connectors.	19
2.2	Categorize characteristics of connectors and cabling.	19
2.3	Explain properties and characteristics of TCP/IP.	20, 21, 24
2.4	Explain common TCP and UDP ports, protocols, and their purpose.	20, 21
2.5	Compare and contrast wireless networking standards and encryption types.	23
2.6	Install, configure, and deploy a SOHO wireless/wired router using appropriate settings.	22, 23
2.7	Compare and contrast Internet connection types and features.	9, 18
2.8	Identify various types of networks.	18, 19
2.9	Compare and contrast network devices and their functions and features.	18, 22
2.10	Given a scenario, use appropriate networking tools.	19, 24
3.0 LAPTOPS (11 PERCENT)		
3.1	Install and configure laptop hardware and components.	8
3.2	Compare and contrast the components within the display of a laptop.	8
3.3	Compare and contrast laptop features.	8
4.0 PRINTERS (11 PERCENT)		
4.1	Explain the differences between the various printer types and summarize the associated imaging process.	7
4.2	Given a scenario, install, and configure printers.	7
4.3	Given a scenario, perform printer maintenance.	7
5.0 OPERATIONAL PROCEDURES (11 PERCENT)		
5.1	Given a scenario, use appropriate safety procedures.	1, 6, 19
5.2	Explain environmental impacts and the purpose of environmental controls.	1, 10
5.3	Given a scenario, demonstrate proper communication and professionalism.	10
5.4	Explain the fundamentals of dealing with prohibited content/activity.	10

Exam Objectives   The exam objectives listed here are current as of this book's publication date. Exam objectives are subject to change at any time without prior notice and at CompTIA's sole discretion. Please visit the CompTIA Certifications webpage for the most current listing of exam objectives: *http://certification.comptia.org/getCertified /certifications.aspx*.

CompTIA A+ Exam 220-802 Objective Map

OBJECTIVE	CHAPTER
1.0 OPERATING SYSTEMS (33 PERCENT)	
1.1 Compare and contrast the features and requirements of various Microsoft Operating Systems.	12
1.2 Given a scenario, install, and configure the operating system using the most appropriate method.	11, 12, 15, 16, 18
1.3 Given a scenario, use appropriate command line tools.	14, 16, 17, 24
1.4 Given a scenario, use appropriate operating system features and tools.	7, 12, 13, 14, 15, 16, 17, 22, 25
1.5 Given a scenario, use Control Panel utilities (the items are organized by "classic view/large icons" in Windows).	6, 8, 13, 15, 22, 25
1.6 Setup and configure Windows networking on a client/desktop.	18, 19, 21, 22, 24
1.7 Perform preventive maintenance procedures using appropriate tools.	15, 16, 17, 26
1.8 Explain the differences among basic OS security settings.	25
1.9 Explain the basics of client-side virtualization.	10
2.0 SECURITY (22 PERCENT)	
2.1 Apply and use common prevention methods.	22, 25, 26
2.2 Compare and contrast common security threats.	26
2.3 Implement security best practices to secure a workstation.	25, 26
2.4 Given a scenario, use the appropriate data destruction/disposal method.	25
2.5 Given a scenario, secure a SOHO wireless network.	23
2.6 Given a scenario, secure a SOHO wired network.	24
3.0 MOBILE DEVICES (9 PERCENT)	
3.1 Explain the basic features of mobile operating systems.	9
3.2 Establish basic network connectivity and configure email.	9
3.3 Compare and contrast methods for securing mobile devices.	9
3.4 Compare and contrast hardware differences in regards to tablets and laptops.	9
3.5 Execute and configure mobile device synchronization.	9
4.0 TROUBLESHOOTING (36 PERCENT)	
4.1 Given a scenario, explain the troubleshooting theory.	10
4.2 Given a scenario, troubleshoot common problems related to motherboards, RAM, CPU and power with appropriate tools.	1, 2, 3, 24
4.3 Given a scenario, troubleshoot hard drives and RAID arrays with appropriate tools.	4, 14, 16, 17
4.4 Given a scenario, troubleshoot common video and display issues.	6
4.5 Given a scenario, troubleshoot wired and wireless networks with appropriate tools.	19, 23, 24
4.6 Given a scenario, troubleshoot operating system problems with appropriate tools.	12, 15, 17, 26
4.7 Given a scenario, troubleshoot common security issues with appropriate tools and best practices.	26
4.8 Given a scenario, troubleshoot, and repair common laptop issues while adhering to the appropriate procedures.	8
4.9 Given a scenario, troubleshoot printers with appropriate tools.	7

Exam Objectives   The exam objectives listed here are current as of this book's publication date. Exam objectives are subject to change at any time without prior notice and at CompTIA's sole discretion. Please visit the CompTIA Certifications webpage for the most current listing of exam objectives: *http://certification.comptia.org/getCertified /certifications.aspx*.

CompTIA A+
(Exam 220-801 and
Exam 220-802)

Training Kit

Darril Gibson

Acquisitions and Developmental Editor: Kenyon Brown

Production Editor: Kristen Borg

Editorial Production: nSight, Inc.

Technical Reviewer: Bill Talbott and Steve Buchanan

Copyeditor: nSight, Inc.

Indexer: nSight, Inc.

Cover Design: Twist Creative • Seattle

Cover Composition: Zyg Group

Illustrator: nSight, Inc.

To my wife, Nimfa. Thanks for all the support you've given me over the years. I'm grateful for my successes and I know that many of them are due to the support you provide on a daily basis.

—DARRIL GIBSON

Contents

Chapter 2   **Understanding Motherboards and BIOS**   **39**

Chapter 13 Using Windows Operating Systems   437

Chapter 14 Using the Command Prompt   473

Chapter 15   Configuring Windows Operating Systems   509

Chapter 16 Understanding Disks and File Systems 543

Chapter 17 Troubleshooting Windows Operating Systems   577

Chapter 20 Understanding Protocols   679

Chapter 26   Recognizing Malware and Other Threats 873

What do you think of this book? We want to hear from you!

Microsoft is interested in hearing your feedback so we can continually improve our books and learning resources for you. To participate in a brief online survey, please visit:

www.microsoft.com/learning/booksurvey/

Introduction

This training kit is designed for information technology (IT) professionals who want to earn the CompTIA A+ certification. It is assumed that you have a basic understanding of computers and Windows operating systems. However, the A+ certification is an entry-level certification, so you are not expected to have any in-depth knowledge to use this training kit.

To become an A+ certified technician, you must take and pass the 220-801 and 220-802 exams. The primary goal of this training kit is to help you build a solid foundation of IT knowledge so that you can successfully pass these two exams the first time you take them.

The materials covered in this training kit and on exams 220-801 and 220-802 relate to the technologies a successful personal computer (PC) technician is expected to understand. This includes PC hardware concepts, Windows operating system technologies, networking basics, and IT security. You can download the objectives for the 220-801 and 220-802 exams from the CompTIA website: *http://certification.comptia.org/Training/testingcenters/examobjectives.aspx*.

By using this training kit, you will learn how to do the following:

- Recognize hardware components used within a computer.
- Assemble a computer's hardware components.
- Install, configure, and maintain devices.
- Troubleshoot and repair hardware problems.
- Install, configure, and troubleshoot laptop computers.
- Describe, install, configure, and troubleshoot printers.
- Describe the features used in mobile operating systems.
- Configure and secure mobile devices.
- Describe the differences between common operating systems.
- Install and configure operating systems.
- Use various command line and operating system tools.
- Troubleshoot and repair operating system issues.
- Recognize common components used in a network.
- Connect a computer and configure it on a network.
- Troubleshoot basic networking issues.
- Recognize common prevention methods used to enhance security.

Refer to the objective mapping page in the front of this book to see where in the book each exam objective is covered.

About the Exams

The 220-801 exam is focused on skills required to install and maintain hardware. It includes objectives in the following five areas:

- PC Hardware (40 percent of exam)
- Networking (27 percent of exam)
- Laptops (11 percent of exam)
- Printers (11 percent of exam)
- Operational Procedures (11 percent of exam)

The 220-802 exam is focused on operating systems and troubleshooting. This includes troubleshooting operating systems, security issues, and hardware. It includes objectives in the following four areas:

- Operating Systems (33 percent of exam)
- Security (22 percent of exam)
- Mobile Devices (9 percent of exam)
- Troubleshooting (36 percent of exam)

These exams became available in late 2012 and are the fifth version of A+ exams. Previous versions came out in 1993, 2003, 2006, and 2009, and over the years, more than 900,000 people around the world have earned the A+ certification. IT professionals commonly start with the A+ certification to lay a solid foundation of IT knowledge and later move on to higher-level certifications and better-paying jobs.

As I write this, CompTIA has not published how many questions will be on each exam, how long you'll have to complete each exam, or what the passing scores are. You can look here for up to date information: *http://certification.comptia.org/aplus.aspx*.

In previous versions, each exam included 100 questions and you had 90 minutes to complete the exam. This gave you a little less than a minute to answer each question. Because of this, the questions were straightforward. For example, what's 10 + 10? Either you know it or you don't, and you won't need to spend a lot of time analyzing the question.

More than likely, you'll have the same number of questions, but you'll probably have longer to complete them due to the addition of performance-based questions. Most of the questions will be simple, but some will require you to perform a task.

Prerequisites

CompTIA recommends that test takers have a minimum of 12 months of lab or field work experience prior to taking the exams. That is, they expect that you have been studying computers (lab work) working in an IT job (field work) or a combination of both for at least 12 months.

This is different from what CompTIA has previously recommended. The 220-701 and 220-702 objectives recommended test takers have 500 hours of lab or field work, which equals about three months of 40-hour weeks.

Note that this is not a requirement to take the exams. Anyone can take the exams after paying for them, and if they pass, they earn the certification. However, you'll have the best chance of success if you have been studying and working with computers for at least 12 months.

Performance Based Testing

A significant difference in the 220-801 and 220-802 exams over previous versions is the introduction of performance-based testing. Instead of just using multiple choice questions, CompTIA is introducing questions that will require you to perform a task.

Imagine that you wanted to know if a person could ride a bike. You could ask some multiple choice questions, but you'll find that these questions aren't always reliable. A person might answer questions correctly but not be able to actually ride the bike. Put the person in front of a bike, ask the person to ride it, and you'll quickly know whether the person can or not. Performance-based testing uses this philosophy to see if someone has a skill.

Consider the following multiple choice question:

1. Which of the following commands will change a file to read-only?

   A. assoc -R study.txt

   B. attrib +R study.txt

   C. readonly -true study.txt

   D. ren -readonly study.txt

The answer is attrib, and the +R switch sets the read-only attribute to true, making it read-only.

This same knowledge might be tested in a performance-based testing question as follows:

1. "Navigate to the C:\Data folder and change the study.txt file to read-only." When you click a button, you'll be in a simulated Windows environment with a Command Prompt. You would then need to enter the following two commands:

```
cd \data
attrib +R studynotes.txt
```

When it's a multiple choice question, you have a 25-percent chance of getting it correct. Even if you didn't remember the exact syntax of the attrib command but knew the purpose of it, you would probably get the previous question correct. The performance-based testing method requires you to know the material and be able to enter the correct commands.

Throughout the book, with performance-based testing in mind, I've included steps and instructions for how to do many tasks. If you do these tasks as you work through the book, you'll be better prepared to succeed with these performance-based tests. I'll also be posting A+ notes and tips on Blogs.GetCertifiedGetAhead.com. Check it out.

Objective Changes

CompTIA includes a note in the objectives that states that, "Objectives are subject to change without notice." I don't know of any time they've changed the objectives without notice, but they have changed objectives.

For example, when the 220-701 and 220-702 objectives were published in 2009, Windows 7 wasn't available and the objectives didn't include any Windows 7 topics. However, the popularity of Windows 7 increased, and CompTIA decided to add Windows 7 topics. In September 2010, CompTIA announced objective modifications to include Windows 7. The changes became effective for anyone who took the exam after January 1, 2011.

The same timing is occurring with the 220-801/220-802 objectives and Windows 8. When the objectives were first published, Windows 8 was not available, so you won't see any Windows 8 topics on the exams.

Is it possible that Windows 8 will become popular and that CompTIA will announce changes to the objectives in 2013? Absolutely. If that happens, I plan on staying on top of the changes and will post updates on my blog at *http://blogs.getcertifiedgetahead.com*. I'll also include information on the following page: *http://getcertifiedgetahead.com/aplus.aspx*.

Study Tips

There's no single study method that works for everyone, but there are some common techniques that many people use to pass these exams, including the following:

- **Set a goal.** Pick a date when you expect to take the first exam, and set your goal to take it then. The date is dependent on how long it'll take you to read the chapters and your current knowledge level. You might set a date two months from now, four months from now, or another time. However, pick a date and set a goal.

- **Take notes.** If concepts aren't familiar to you, take the time to write them down. The process of transferring the words from the book, through your head, and down to your hand really helps to burn the knowledge into your brain.

- **Read your notes.** Go back over your notes periodically to see what you remember and what you need to review further. You can't bring notes with you into the testing area, but you can use them to review key material before the exam.

- **Use flash cards.** Some people get a lot out of flash cards that provide a quick test of your knowledge. These help you realize what you don't know and what you need to brush up on. Many practice test programs include flash cards, so you don't necessarily have to create them yourself.

- **Review the objectives.** This is what CompTIA says it will test you on. Sometimes just understanding the objective will help you predict a test question and answer it correctly.

- **Record your notes.** Many people record their notes on an MP3 player and play them back regularly. You can listen while driving, while exercising, or just about anytime. Some people have their husband/wife or boyfriend/girlfriend read the notes, which can give an interesting twist to studying.

- **Take the practice test questions on the CD.** The practice test questions on the CD are designed to test the objectives for the exam but at a deeper level than you'll have on the live exam. Each question includes detailed explanations about why the correct answer(s) is/are correct and why the incorrect answers are incorrect. Ideally, you should be able to look at the answers to any question and know not only the correct answer but also why the incorrect answers are incorrect.

System Requirements

The actual system requirements to use this book are minimal. The only requirement is a computer that you can use to install the practice tests on the Companion CD.

Ideally, you'll have an old computer that you can take apart and put back together. It isn't required, but actually removing and reinstalling a power supply, case fan, or hard drive is much more meaningful than just reading about doing it.

Starting with Chapter 11, "Introducing Windows Operating Systems," the objectives have a strong focus on Windows XP, Windows Vista, and Windows 7. As a PC technician, you should be familiar with these operating systems.

You will find that most of the tested material is the same in Windows Vista and Windows 7. Therefore, if you have Windows XP and Windows 7, it isn't important that you have Windows Vista.

Instead of having two or three separate computers, you can use a single PC with virtualization software hosting these operating systems. Chapter 2, "Understanding Motherboards and BIOS," introduces virtualization, and Chapter 10, "Working with Customers," discusses virtualization workstations. The following sections describe hardware and software requirements to set up a virtualization workstation.

Hardware Requirements for Virtualization

If you plan on using virtualization, your computer should meet the following requirements:

- A processor that includes hardware-assisted virtualization (AMD-V or Intel VT), which is enabled in the BIOS. (Note: you can run Windows Virtual PC without Intel-VT or AMD-V.) Ideally, the processor will be a 64-bit processor so that you can have more RAM.
- At least 2.0 GB of RAM, but more is recommended.
- 80 GB of available hard disk space.
- Internet connectivity.

Software Requirements

You should have a computer running Windows 7. The objectives heavily cover Windows 7, and if you have it, you can easily run Windows XP in a virtual environment.

Additional requirements include the following:

- **Windows Virtual PC and Windows XP Mode.** Windows Virtual PC allows you to run multiple virtual Windows environments. The following page introduces the Windows Virtual PC and Windows XP Mode: *http://www.microsoft.com/windows/virtual-pc/*. The following page includes the download link after you identify your operating system and the desired language: *http://www.microsoft.com/windows/virtual-pc /download.aspx*.
- **Windows 7 (32-bit).** You can download a 90-day trial copy of Windows 7 Enterprise here: *http://technet.microsoft.com/en-us/evalcenter/cc442495.aspx*.

After following the instructions to download and install Windows Virtual PC and Windows XP Mode, you will have Virtual PC installed on your system. You will also have a fully functioning copy of Windows XP that you can use for Windows XP Mode and to explore the functionality of Windows XP while you are studying.

Next, download the 90-day trial of Windows 7 and install it as a VM within Windows Virtual PC. If you haven't completed the exams by the time the 90-day trial expires, create a new VM and install it again. The experience is worth it.

As an alternative to Windows Virtual PC, you can use either VirtualBox or VMware. Oracle provides VirtualBox as a free download here: *https://www.virtualbox.org/wiki /Downloads*; and you can download a free version of VMware player here: *http://www .vmware.com/products/player/overview.html*. Both VirtualBox and VMware player support 64-bit host machines, but you can only run 32-bit hosts within Windows Virtual PC.

Using the Companion CD

A companion CD is included with this training kit. The companion CD contains the following:

- **Practice tests**   You can reinforce your understanding of the topics covered in this training kit by using electronic practice tests that you can customize to meet your needs. You can practice for the 220-801 and 220-802 certification exams by using tests created from a pool of 400 realistic exam questions, which give you many practice exams to ensure that you are prepared.

- **An eBook**   An electronic version (eBook) of this book is included for when you do not want to carry the printed book with you.

- **A list of video links**   Throughout the book, videos are pointed out to supplement learning. The CD includes a list of all the video links mentioned in the chapters and a few more. There are also links to a few more resources that you might find valuable during your studies.

- **The CPU-Z freeware utility**   Chapter 3 discusses how this utility can be used to provide information on the CPU, the motherboard, memory, and more.

> **NOTE**   Companion content for digital book readers
> If you bought a digital-only edition of this book, you can enjoy select content from the print edition's companion CD. Visit *http://go.microsoft.com/FWLink/?Linkid=265182* to get your downloadable content.

How to Install the Practice Tests

To install the practice test software from the companion CD to your hard disk, perform the following steps:

1. Insert the companion CD into your CD drive and accept the license agreement. A CD menu appears.

> **NOTE   IF THE CD MENU DOES NOT APPEAR**
> If the CD menu or the license agreement does not appear, AutoRun might be disabled on your computer. Refer to the Readme.txt file on the CD for alternate installation instructions.

2. Click Practice Tests and follow the instructions on the screen.

How to Use the Practice Tests

To start the practice test software, follow these steps:

1. Click Start, All Programs, and then select Microsoft Press Training Kit Exam Prep.

   A window appears that shows all the Microsoft Press training kit exam prep suites installed on your computer.

2. Double-click the practice test you want to use.

When you start a practice test, you can choose whether to take the test in Certification Mode, Study Mode, or Custom Mode:

- **Certification Mode** Closely resembles the experience of taking a certification exam. The test has a set number of questions. It is timed, and you cannot pause and restart the timer.
- **Study Mode** Creates an untimed test during which you can review the correct answers and the explanations after you answer each question.
- **Custom Mode** Gives you full control over the test options so that you can customize them as you like.

In all modes, the user interface when you are taking the test is basically the same but with different options enabled or disabled depending on the mode.

When you review your answer to an individual practice test question, a "References" section is provided that lists where in the training kit you can find the information that relates to that question and provides links to other sources of information. After you click Test Results to score your entire practice test, you can click the Learning Plan tab to see a list of references for every objective.

How to Uninstall the Practice Tests

To uninstall the practice test software for a training kit, use the Program And Features option in Windows Control Panel.

Acknowledgments

The author's name appears on the cover of a book, but I am only one member of a much larger team. First of all, thanks to Steve Weiss for originally reaching out to me and inviting me to write this A+ Training Kit. Several editors helped throughout this process, and I am grateful for all their work. I especially appreciate the copy editing by Richard Carey and the technical editing by Bill Talbott. I extend a huge thanks to José Vargas, who helped out with some writing on two of the hardware chapters. I especially appreciate my wife putting up with my long days and nights working on what she has nicknamed "the forever book" because it seems like I've been working on this book close to forever. Last, a special thanks to readers who have provided feedback to me over the years, letting me know what helps them learn and what things I can improve.

Support & Feedback

The following sections provide information about errata, book support, feedback, and contact information.

Errata & Book Support

We've made every effort to ensure the accuracy of this book and its companion content. Any errors that have been reported since this book was published are listed on our Microsoft Press site at oreilly.com:

http://go.microsoft.com/FWLink/?Linkid=265181

If you find an error that is not already listed, you can report it to us through the same page.

If you need additional support, email Microsoft Press Book Support at:

mspinput@microsoft.com

Please note that product support for Microsoft software is not offered through the addresses above.

We Want to Hear from You

At Microsoft Press, your satisfaction is our top priority, and your feedback is our most valuable asset. Please tell us what you think of this book at:

http://www.microsoft.com/learning/booksurvey

The survey is short, and we read every one of your comments and ideas. Thanks in advance for your input!

Stay in Touch

Let us keep the conversation going! We are on Twitter: *http://twitter.com/MicrosoftPress.*

Preparing for the Exam

Microsoft certification exams are a great way to build your résumé and let the world know about your level of expertise. Certification exams validate your on-the-job experience and product knowledge. While there is no substitution for on-the-job experience, preparation through study and hands-on practice can help you prepare for the exam. We recommend that you round out your exam preparation plan by using a combination of available study materials and courses. For example, you might use the training kit and another study guide for your "at home" preparation and take a Microsoft Official Curriculum course for the classroom experience. Choose the combination that you think works best for you.

Note that this training kit is based on publically available information about the exam and the author's experience. To safeguard the integrity of the exam, authors do not have access to the live exam.

CHAPTER 1

Introduction to Computers

In this chapter, you'll learn about some basic computer-related concepts that are important for any technician to understand. For example, different numbering systems are often unfamiliar to many people, but don't underestimate their importance in understanding how a computer works. The Numbering Systems section lays the foundation for topics in many future chapters. This chapter also includes information about cases, fans, and power supplies—core hardware computer components that often require periodic maintenance by technicians. Last, you'll learn about some basic safety issues and tools you can use when maintaining computers.

> **IMPORTANT**
> ### *Have you read page xliv?*
> It contains valuable information regarding the skills you need to pass the exams.

Exam 220-801 objectives in this chapter:

- 1.2 Differentiate between motherboard components, their purposes, and properties.
  - Power connections and types
  - Fan connectors
- 1.8 Install an appropriate power supply based on a given scenario.
  - Connector types and their voltages
    - SATA
    - Molex
    - 4/8-pin 12v
    - PCIe 6/8-pin
    - 20-pin
    - 24-pin
    - Floppy
  - Specifications
    - Wattage
    - Size
    - Number of connectors

- ATX
- Micro-ATX
- Dual voltage options
- 5.1 Given a scenario, use appropriate safety procedures.
  - ESD straps
  - ESD mats
  - Self-grounding
  - Equipment grounding
  - Personal safety
    - Disconnect power before repairing PC
    - Remove jewelry
    - Lifting techniques
    - Weight limitations
    - Electrical fire safety
  - Compliance with local government regulations
- 5.2 Explain environmental impacts and the purpose of environmental controls.
  - MSDS documentation for handling and disposal
  - Temperature, humidity level awareness and proper ventilation
  - Power surges, brownouts, blackouts
    - Battery backup
    - Surge suppressor
  - Protection from airborne particles
    - Enclosures
    - Air filters
  - Dust and debris
    - Compressed air
    - Vacuums
  - Component handling and protection
    - Antistatic bags
  - Compliance to local government regulations

Exam 220-802 objectives in this chapter:

- 4.2 Given a scenario, troubleshoot common problems related to motherboards, RAM, CPU and power with appropriate tools.
    - Common symptoms
        - No power
        - Overheating
        - Loud noise
        - Intermittent device failure
        - Smoke
        - Burning smell
    - Tools
        - Multimeter
        - Power supply tester

REAL WORLD   **DIRTY FANS MIGHT SOUND LIKE JET ENGINES**

Not too long ago, a friend was complaining to me about a computer she had. She said she was going to have to replace it because it was just too loud and slow. I took a look, or perhaps I should say a listen, and sure enough it reminded me of being next to a jet engine. However, I knew how to solve this problem.

I bought a can of compressed air, took the computer outside, and removed the case. There was dust gunked up in just about every vent and throughout the inside of the computer. I methodically blew out all the dust and put the computer back together. Sure enough, without the extra dust, the computer was quieter and quicker.

The extra dust in the vents was making the fans work harder, and louder. The extra dust on the central processing unit (CPU) and its fan was causing the CPU to quickly overheat, and it was running slower as a result. However, with all the dust gone, the computer was humming along quietly and returned to its previous speed.

It made me wonder how many people toss out perfectly good computers when all they need to do is clean them. I certainly understand how intimidating it can be for some users to open up a computer case and look inside. However, the A+ technician (you) with just a little bit of knowledge can be the hero for these people. You can help them restore their computer to its previous glory.

Computing Basics

At the most basic level, a computer has three functions: input, processing, and output. It accepts input, performs some processing, and provides an output, as shown in Figure 1-1. This is often shortened to just *input/output (I/O)*.

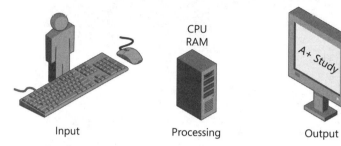

Input   Processing   Output

FIGURE 1-1 Input, processing, and output.

- **Input.** User-provided input comes from a keyboard, a mouse, or even a touch screen. Sometimes input is provided by other sources, such as a disk drive when opening files or a network interface card (NIC) when receiving data.

- **Processing.** The computer responds to the input by completing an action. The central processing unit (CPU) is the brain of the computer. It does the processing, and it uses random access memory (RAM) to store and manipulate data.

- **Output.** Output is commonly provided to a screen or a printer. However, computers also provide output to other destinations. These can include output to speakers or headphones to play sound, to disk drives when saving files, and to a NIC when transmitting data.

NOTE **LONG-TERM AND SHORT-TERM STORAGE**

Computers are unable to work with data or programs until the information is in memory. Disk drives provide long-term storage, but information must be moved to the memory before the CPU can work with it. This is often transparent to the user.

For example, imagine you wanted to open up a Microsoft Word document that has your A+ study notes. You would start by double-clicking the document, using the mouse as your input.

The computer processes your double-click with several actions:

1. It identifies the extension of the Microsoft Word file (.doc or .docx). It recognizes that this extension is associated with Microsoft Word.

2. It locates and retrieves the Microsoft Word program from the disk drive and begins moving the program from the disk drive to memory.

3. When the program is in memory, the computer can actually run it.

4. The computer begins sending results to the graphics card, showing the process of Microsoft Word starting.

5. When Microsoft Word is in memory and started, the computer locates the Word Study Notes file and moves it from the hard drive to memory.

6. When the file is in memory, the computer begins sending results to the graphics card.

> **NOTE** **IPO**
>
> Computer troubleshooting can often be reduced to identifying what is not working: input, processing, or output (IPO). When you identify this, it's much easier to troubleshoot and resolve the problem.

The preceding IPO process is constantly repeated. Consider typing your A+ notes about fans or power supplies into your study file. Each key press is another input that is processed and generates an output. The computer identifies what key you pressed, stores its value in memory, and displays it on the screen. When you save the file, it writes everything in its memory to the file on the drive.

Despite being able to do so much, it's worth pointing out that computers are pretty dumb. They can work only with numbers. Specifically, they can work only with ones and zeros. Everything that is written to a disk drive or to memory is a series of ones and zeros.

Admittedly, computers can work with these ones and zeros very quickly. Ask it to multiply two five-digit numbers, and a computer will do so in a flash. However, it must first translate any input you give it to a string of ones and zeros, process these strings, and then translate the result of ones and zeros into a usable display.

With this in mind, it's important for any A+ technician to have a rudimentary understanding of some basic numbering systems.

Numbering Systems

You and I count by using decimal numbers. We understand the meaning of the numbers 0 through 9. After you get up to 9, the next number is 10. This is also known as a numbering system with a base of ten, because there are ten digits in the numbering system.

If you see a number like 2,357, you know that its decimal parts are two thousand, three hundred, fifty, and seven. Table 1-1 shows the underlying math, which should make a lot of sense to you if you're familiar with decimal numbers.

TABLE 1-1 Decimal Values

	10^3	10^2	10^1	10^0
Decimal value	1000	100	10	1
Number	2	3	5	7
Calculated value	2,000	300	50	7

- The column on the far left is 10^3, or 10 cubed. The value of 10 x 10 x 10 is 1,000. The number 2,357 has 2 in this column, so it represents 2,000.

- The next column is 10^2, or 10 squared. The value of 10 x 10 is 100, and the number 2,357 has 3 in this column, so its value is 300.

- Any number raised to the one power is itself, so 10^1 is 10. The number 2,357 has 5 in this column, so its value is 50.

- Last, any number raised to the zero power is 1, so 10^0 is 1. The number 2,357 has 7 in this column, so its value is 7.

If you add 2,000 + 300 + 50 + 7, you get 2,357. When you see the number 2,357, you probably don't think of it this way, but you do recognize the value. For example, if I said I was going to give you your choice of $2,357 or $7,532, you'd easily recognize that the first choice is a little over $2 thousand and that the second choice is over $7 thousand. By reviewing what you know, it's easier to bridge that knowledge to something that might be new to you.

Base ten numbers aren't very efficient for computers. They result in a lot of wasted space. Because of this, computers use different numbering systems, such as *binary* and *hexadecimal*.

Binary

Binary numbers have a base of two. Instead of using numbers 0 through 9, they only use the numbers 0 and 1.

> **NOTE** **BINARY BIT**
>
> In binary, a single digit is referred to as a bit. A bit can have a value of 1 or 0. When it is a 1, it is considered to be on, or true. When the bit is a 0, it's considered to be off, or false.

Consider the binary number 1001. Table 1-2 shows how you can convert this number to a decimal value that has more meaning to you and me.

TABLE 1-2 Binary Values

	2^3	2^2	2^1	2^0
Decimal value	8	4	2	1
Binary number	1	0	0	1
Calculated value	8	0	0	1

- The column on the far left is 23, or 2 cubed. The value of 2 x 2 x 2 is 8. The number 1001 has 1 in this column, so it represents a calculated decimal value of 8.
- The second column is 2 squared. The value of 2 x 2 is 4, and the number 1001 has 0 in this column, so its value is 0.
- Any number raised to the one power is itself, so 21 is 2. The number 1001 has 0 in this column, so its value is 0.
- Last, any number raised to the zero power is 1, so 20 is 1. The number 1001 has 1 in this column, so its value is 1.

If you add 8 + 0 + 0 + 1, you get 9. Therefore, the binary number 1001 has a decimal value of 9.

Hexadecimal

Although binary and bits work well with computers, they aren't so easy for people to digest. If you need to tell someone to use the number 201, that's rather easy. But if you need to tell someone to use the binary equivalent, it's 1100 1001. That string of ones and zeros is a little difficult to communicate. However, you could also express the same number as C9 by using hexadecimal.

Hexadecimal uses the characters 0–9 and A–F, adding six extra digits to the base ten numbers of 0–9. Hexadecimal uses a base of 16. It is easier to express than binary and more efficient for computers than base 10 because it easily translates to binary.

> **NOTE** **BINARY GROUPING**
>
> When grouping several binary numbers, it's common to separate groups of four with a space. This is similar to adding commas to decimal numbers. For example, 135792468 is often expressed as 135,792,468 because the commas make it easier to see that it starts with 135 million. Similarly, 11001001 isn't as easy for most people to process as 1100 1001, although both numbers mean the same thing.

The binary number 1100 1001 can also be expressed as C9, because 1100 is C in hexadecimal and 1001 is 9 in hexadecimal. Table 1-3 shows the decimal, binary, and hexadecimal equivalent for the numbers up to hexadecimal F.

TABLE 1-3 Decimal, Binary, and Hexadecimal Values

Decimal	Binary	Hexadecimal	Decimal	Binary	Hexadecimal
0	0000	0	8	1000	8
1	0001	1	9	1001	9
2	0010	2	10	1010	A
3	0011	3	11	1011	B
4	0100	4	12	1100	C
5	0101	5	13	1101	D
6	0110	6	14	1110	E
7	0111	7	15	1111	F

> **NOTE HEXADECIMAL CASE**
>
> Hexadecimal numbers are not case sensitive. An uppercase C is the same as a lowercase c, and both equate to 1100 in binary. They are expressed both ways by different applications. Additionally, hexadecimal numbers are often preceded with 0x that to indicate that they are hexadecimal numbers. For example, if Windows 7 stops responding, the screen will display an error code such as STOP Error 0x0000002E, or hexadecimal code 2E. (This error code indicates a problem with memory.)

A common example of how hexadecimal numbers are used is with media access control (MAC) addresses. Network interface cards are assigned 48-bit MAC addresses, and these are commonly listed in six pairs of hexadecimal numbers like this: 6C-62-6D-BA-73-6C. Without hexadecimal, the MAC would be listed as a string of 48 bits.

Bits vs. Bytes

A single binary number is a *bit,* and eight bits makes up a *byte.* You can extend binary as far as you need to, but most computer technicians deal with numbers that do not go beyond a byte. This is not to say that computers can't work with more than eight bits. They certainly can. However, technicians and other Information Technology (IT) professionals still express the numbers as bytes.

Table 1-4 shows the value of each of the bits in a byte. The column on the far left is 2^7, or 2 x 2 x 2 x 2 x 2 x 2 x 2. If you convert this to decimal, it is 128.

TABLE 1-4 Bits in a Byte

2^7	2^6	2^5	2^4	2^3	2^2	2^1	2^0
128	64	32	16	8	4	2	1

Kilo, Mega, Giga, and Tera

Computers handle huge numbers of bytes, which are often expressed as *kilobytes (KB)*, *megabytes (MB)*, *gigabytes (GB)*, and *terabytes (TB)*. A KB is 1,024 bytes, but most technicians shorten this to "about a thousand" bytes.

Here's a comparison of these values:

- KB = about one thousand bytes (2^{10})
- MB = about one thousand KB or about a million bytes (2^{20})
- GB = about one thousand MB or about a billion bytes (2^{30})
- TB = about one thousand GB or about trillion bytes (2^{40})

✔ **Quick Check**

1. What is the decimal value of the hexadecimal character C?

2. How many bits are in a byte?

Quick Check Answers

1. 12

2. 8

Cases and Cooling

Computer cases house many of the components in the computer, and there are many different types, sizes, and shapes of cases. Standard *personal computers (PCs)* use desktop cases. Some cases are towers that stand up beside a desk, and others fit on top of a desk. The common purpose of a computer case is to house the components needed within a computer.

Figure 1-2 shows an opened computer case with several components highlighted.

FIGURE 1-2 Computer case.

1. **Power supply.** The wires coming out of the right side of the power supply are connected to different computer components.

2. **CPU fan.** This is a dedicated fan to keep the CPU cool. The CPU is directly beneath this fan and can't be seen.

3. **Case fans.** This case has two fans, a smaller one on the left and a larger one on the bottom right. These fans pull air into the case. Vents on the case are positioned so that air constantly flows over key components to keep them cool.

4. **Motherboard.** The large white square outlines the motherboard. Multiple components are located on the motherboard, including the CPU, RAM, and the graphics card. Chapter 2, "Understanding Motherboards and BIOS," provides more details on the motherboard, and Chapter 3, "Understanding Processors and RAM," covers RAM. Chapter 6, "Exploring Video and Display Devices," covers displays and graphics (including graphics cards) in more detail.

5. **Optical drive bays.** CD and DVD optical drives are located here. This system has two drives, with space for another one.

6. **Hard disk drive bays.** Hard disk drives are used for permanent storage of data. This system has two hard disk drives, with space for another one. Chapter 4, "Comparing Storage Devices," covers the different types of storage devices.

You can also see a variety of different cables within the case. The power supply cables are covered later in this chapter, and other cables and connectors are covered in future chapters.

Not all cases have this much space or this many components. However, Figure 1-2 does give you an idea of what you'll see within a computer case.

A quick exercise you can do is to open your computer's case and peer inside. Make sure you first power the computer down and unplug the power cable. One side of the case can normally be opened by removing two thumb screws on the back of the case and pulling off the side panel. There's no need to manipulate anything inside the case at this stage, but you can look at it and compare your case with the case shown in Figure 1-2.

EXAM TIP

A+ exam questions often expect you to be able to identify components within a computer. Looking at different computers will help you correctly answer these questions. If you don't have multiple computers handy, check out the pictures on *bing.com*. **Type in your search phrase (such as "computer case," "motherboard," or "power supply") and select Images.**

Motherboards

As you can see in Figure 1-2, the motherboard takes up a significant amount of space. The case shown in the figure is relatively large, and you will likely see other computers where the case is not much larger than the length and width of the motherboard. All the components are squeezed in. These smaller cases don't have as much room for expansion, such as adding hard drives.

An important consideration related to the motherboard and the case is ensuring that the case can adequately house it. If you ever replace a computer's motherboard with a different brand or model, you'll need to ensure that it fits within the case.

Chapter 2 covers motherboard form factors in more depth, but as an introduction, the Advanced Technology Extended (ATX) motherboard form factor is the most common. The ATX standard has been in use since 1995, with several improvements and modifications added over the years. Many cases are designed so that they will support ATX motherboards.

Case Fans

Computers can get very hot, so fans are used to keep cool air flowing over the components. They draw air in from the room, direct it over key components, and then the air exits from vents on the case.

Fans come in different levels of quality, and the most noticeable difference is in how much noise they make. Inexpensive fans have cheap bearings that are noisy, while quality fans have sophisticated bearings that are extremely quiet. Many quality fans include a thermistor, which automatically adjusts the speed of the fan based on the temperature.

Common Problems with Fans

When a case fan becomes clogged or dirty, it can be so noisy that people commonly complain it sounds like a jet engine. They never get quite that loud, but they can be a nuisance.

Even worse, if the case fan is clogged, the computer is often not getting enough air flow through it. Internal components become hotter, and it's common for the entire system to slow to a crawl. In some cases, problems with the fan can cause the system to fail.

EXAM TIP

Intermittent failures, such as random restarts, are often an indication of a heat-related problem. This is especially true if the fans are loud, indicating that they are working very hard.

The easy solution is to clean the fan along with the case as described in the Cleaning Cases section later in this chapter. This will often reduce the noise and increase the performance. If it doesn't solve the problem, you can replace it with a higher-quality fan.

If a fan fails completely, it should be replaced as soon as possible to ensure that other components do not overheat and fail.

Replacing a Fan

A fan is considered a *field replaceable unit (FRU)*, so if a fan is too noisy or has failed, you can replace it. Many companies sell case fans, and they are relatively easy to replace on a system. If you do replace the fan, make sure that the fan you're purchasing fits in your case. The two most common sizes for case fans are 80 mm and 120 mm.

Figure 1-3 shows the case fan within a system. Take a look at it as you follow the steps to remove the fan.

FIGURE 1-3 Removing a case fan.

> **IMPORTANT** **TURN OFF THE POWER**
>
> Ensure that the computer is turned off and that the power cable is removed before open-
> ing the case and replacing a fan. Power is still provided to the motherboard even if the
> system is turned off, and you can cause damage to the computer or yourself if the power
> cable is not removed.

1. **Remove four screws from the back of the case.** The arrows in Figure 1-3 point to
   two of the screws, and the other two screws are on the other two corners of the fan.

2. **Remove the power connector.** The power connector plugs into a specific jack on the
   motherboard. Take note of this jack, and ensure that you plug the new fan into the jack
   the same way. Fan connectors can use two, three, or four pins. The 4-pin connectors
   are commonly used with variable speed fans, allowing the computer to control the
   speed of the fan. You can also use adapters to connect some fans into a *Molex* type of
   connector from the motherboard.

After removing the old fan, you can install the new fan by reversing your steps. Attach the
four screws and plug it in.

Even with new fans, though, if the case vents become clogged with contaminants, the fans
will work harder to pull the air through the system. The easy solution is to clean the case.

Cleaning Cases

With all the air blowing into the computer case, it will gather some dust. In extreme work
environments, the inside of a computer can get quite dirty. For example, a computer within a
manufacturing plant will collect dirt and contaminants inside the case. Similarly, a computer
with dogs or cats in the area can collect fur and hair.

It's relatively easy to clean a case. The most common method is by using a can of compressed air, which you can purchase from electronics stores. Take the computer outside,
remove the cover, and use the compressed air to blow out the dust and other contaminants.

EXAM TIP

Cleaning a case and its fans can improve a computer's performance. Excessive dust creates
additional heat, and many computers include components that can automatically sense the
temperature. These components often increase the speed of the fans, making the system
louder, and also slow down the speed of the CPU to reduce the heat.

Notification Switch for Security

Many computer cases have a special push-button switch that detects whether the case has
been opened. This is also called a *biased switch,* and it stays depressed as long as the case
is closed. When the case is opened, the switch opens and the change is recorded in the

computer. The next time the system starts, it indicates that the system case has been opened. This is useful for detecting whether someone has been tampering with a computer.

> ✔ **Quick Check**
>
> 1. What are the two common sizes of a case fan?
>
> 2. A computer has become louder and slower. What is a common solution?
>
> **Quick Check Answers**
>
> 1. 80 mm and 120 mm.
>
> 2. Clean it.

Power Supplies

Computers run on electricity. Electricity is measured as voltage, and voltage is the difference in potential between two points. For example, an electrical signal can be 12 volts above a ground potential of zero volts, giving it a value of 12 volts. Power supplies within computers ensure that components within a system consistently have the correct voltages.

As an A+ technician, you might need to troubleshoot a system with a faulty power supply or even replace a power supply. With that in mind, you need to have a basic understanding of power supplies.

AC vs. DC

The two types of voltages are alternating current (AC) and direct current (DC). *AC voltage* alternates above and below zero volts, and *DC voltage* provides a steady voltage either above or below zero.

Commercial power companies traditionally provide power as AC, which looks like a sine wave. Power supplies within computers convert this AC voltage into DC voltage, as shown in Figure 1-4.

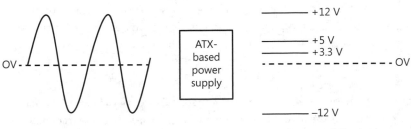

FIGURE 1-4 AC vs. DC.

Figure 1-4 isn't to scale. AC voltages vary about 115 VAC (volts AC power) above and below 0 volts in many regions, such as in the United States, and 230 VAC above and below 0 volts in other regions, such as in Europe. The key point is that AC voltage is an alternating or varying voltage, whereas DC voltage is a constant steady voltage. The DC voltages shown in the figure are common voltages used within computers, and are sometimes expressed as VDC, such as 12 VDC.

Wattage Power Ratings

Power supplies are rated based on the amount of power they can provide, and power is computed as a *watt (W)*. In simple terms, watts are computed by multiplying the voltage by the amperage. Amperage (A) refers to the rate of flow of the voltage. Higher amperage results in a higher rate of flow, and higher amperage with the same voltage provides more power.

Each individual component within a computer requires a certain amount of power. For example, it's not uncommon for a CPU to require as much as 100 W. Additionally, the motherboard, case fans, and disk drives all draw additional power. With this in mind, power supplies must not only convert AC to DC and supply the correct DC voltages, but they must also provide enough power to support all the components in the system.

When replacing a *power supply unit (PSU)*, you should look for the W within the specifications to identify the power output. For example, a 600-watt PSU would be listed as 600 W. The range of common current ATX-based PSUs is about 300 W to 1,000 W.

If a system requires 600 W and you put in a 300-W power supply, you'll have some problems. In most cases, the computer simply won't work. In other cases, the power supply won't be able to provide steady voltages and the variances might damage system components.

Rails

Power supplies provide separate lines (called *rails*) for the different voltages. The voltage that draws the most power is 12 V, used for CPUs, case fans, and disk drives, and a single 12-V rail provides 18 A of power. However, this single 18-A rail often isn't enough to power all the components that need the voltage.

Many current power supplies include at least two 12-V rails, with one rail dedicated to the CPU and the second rail dedicated to everything else. Some power supplies include three or four rails. When replacing a power supply, you need to ensure that you are replacing it with one that has at least the same number of 12-V rails as the original.

EXAM TIP

The 12-V rails provide primary power to disk drives. If these rails are overworked, they will frequently cause problems for the hard drives. In other words, if hard drives are frequently failing in a computer, consider replacing the power supply with one that has an additional 12-V rail.

Power Supply Connections

The ATX standard mentioned within the Motherboards section earlier in this chapter also identifies power supply requirements. Most current desktop systems include power supplies that support ATX-based motherboards, and they provide specific voltages defined in the ATX specifications.

Figure 1-5 shows the rear view of a power supply, along with its connectors. This power supply was removed from a computer with an ATX-style motherboard. Refer to the figure as you read the following descriptions.

FIGURE 1-5 Power supply.

1. **AC power jack.** The power cable connects from here to a power source providing AC power.

2. **Dual voltage power selection.** Select 115 or 230 based on the commercial power provided at your location. For comparison, commercial power provided in the United States is 115 VAC, and power provided in Europe is 230 VAC. Some systems can automatically sense the voltage, so the switch isn't needed.

3. **Power indicator.** When on, it indicates that the power supply has power. This does not indicate that the actual computer is turned on. Computers typically have a separate power button and power indicator on the front of the case.

4. **Molex connectors.** These provide 5 V and 12 V to different devices, such as Parallel Advanced Technology Attachment (PATA) disk drives.

5. **SATA power connector.** This 15-pin connector provides power to Serial Advanced Technology Attachment (SATA) disk drives. It includes 3.3-V, 5-V, and 12-V DC voltages.

6. **Secondary motherboard power connection.** Most current motherboards use a 4-pin connector that provides 12 VDC used by the CPU. This connector is formally called ATX12V but is also known as P4 because it was first used with the Pentium 4 CPUs. Systems with more than one CPU use an 8-pin connector (or two 4-pin connectors) to provide power for multiple CPUs. This is formally known as EPS12V.

7. **Floppy drive mini-connectors.** These are sometimes called Berg connectors or mini-Molex connectors. They provide 5-VDC and 12-VDC power to 3.5-inch floppy drives, when the system includes floppy drives.

8. **Primary power connector.** A 20-pin or 24-pin connector provides primary power to the motherboard. It's commonly called the P1 connector and provides 3.3 VDC, 5 VDC, and 12 VDC to the motherboard.

Many power supplies also have a PCI Express (PCIe) power connector. This was originally a 6-pin connector, but new systems use an 8-pin connector similar to the one shown in Figure 1-6. Some power supplies use a 6+2 connector, allowing you to plug it into an older system with only 6 pins, or a newer system with 8 pins.

FIGURE 1-6 PCIe power connector.

Cable Keying

Most cables are keyed. That is, they are designed to fit into a jack in one way, and one way only. However, these connectors and plugs are just plastic, so it is possible to force a connector onto a plug backwards. If you do, the wrong voltages or signals will be sent to a device.

In the worst case scenario, plugging a cable in backwards can destroy a device. If you're lucky, plugging the cable in wrong will just result in the device not working. Neither result is desirable, so it's best to look for the key and ensure that you plug in the connector correctly.

Figure 1-7 shows some common methods of how cables are keyed.

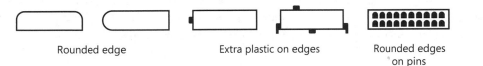

Rounded edge   Extra plastic on edges   Rounded edges on pins

FIGURE 1-7 Cable keying examples.

It might not be apparent in Figure 1-5 shown earlier, but several of the connectors have keyed connectors similar to that shown in Figure 1-7. The Molex connectors (item 4 in Figure 1-5) have rounded edges. The SATA power connector (item 5) has an extra edge. The mini-connector (item 7) has several extra edges. The primary power connector (item 8) has rounded edges on the individual pins.

IMPORTANT **NEVER FORCE A CONNECTOR**

Plugging in any connector the wrong way can damage the computer. Although the keying does help, the connectors are plastic and in some cases it is possible to force a connector onto a plug the wrong way. If a connector doesn't seem to fit, don't try to force it. Instead, double-check the keying to ensure that it is plugged in correctly.

ATX vs. Micro-ATX Power Supplies

ATX power supplies are the standard used in many computers today. However, some smaller PCs have lower power requirements and can be powered by using smaller power supplies. Micro-ATX power supplies provide a lower amount of wattage, often between 180 and 300 watts, though some special-purpose power supplies are as low 90 watts.

The micro-ATX power supplies are smaller in size and have fewer power connectors than a regular ATX-based power supply. Also, the primary power connector (P1) usually has only 20 pins on the micro-ATX power supply, rather than the 24 pins often found on ATX-based power supplies.

Replacing a Power Supply

Many components within a computer, including the power supply, are modular. When a module fails, you need to replace only the module, not the entire computer. This is similar to a car. If your car gets a flat tire, you replace the tire, not the entire car. If the power supply fails in a computer, you replace the power supply.

EXAM TIP

When power supplies fail, you can sometimes see smoke or smell burning components. New power supplies often give off an odor for a short burn-in period, but they aren't faulty. However, if you see smoke or hear sparks, remove power immediately.

The primary indicator that the power supply has failed is that the system doesn't have any lights or indicators. Of course, you'd want to verify that the computer is plugged in and turned on. Also, some systems have a power switch on the power supply that needs to be turned on in addition to turning on the power via a switch or button in the front of the system. If you've checked these but still have no power indications, it might be time to replace the power supply.

The power supply is relatively easy to replace, but you need to keep a few important concepts in mind:

- **Turn off and remove the power plug.** You should not attempt to replace computer components while the system is plugged in. The exception is "hot swappable" components such as USB flash drives that are designed to be inserted or removed while turned on.

- **Use a suitable replacement.** Ensure that the wattage of the replacement is at least as high as the original, if not higher. Also, ensure that the power supply has at least the same number of 12-V rails as, if not more, than the original.

- **Document cable placement.** Pay attention to the cables before you take them out. Draw a diagram showing where each cable goes, or take a couple of pictures with your cell phone. Without this documentation, when the old power supply is out and the new power supply is in, you might have trouble remembering where all the cables went. Also, ensure that you identify the keying of the cables and plug them in correctly.

When you're ready to replace the power supply, you'll find there are only four screws holding it on. Remove the cables and the screws, and you'll be able to remove the power supply. Occasionally, you might need to remove other components first to get to the power supply and remove it.

Protecting Systems from Power Problems

Commercial power isn't always stable, and it can sometimes cause problems to computers. However, there are some basic steps you can take to protect them. Some of the common problems you might see on commercial power lines are as follows:

- **Surge.** Commercial power can occasionally increase or *surge*. Instead of providing a steady 115 VAC, it can increase to 120 VAC or higher. Surges are usually short term and temporary but can sometimes be observed as lights become brighter.

- **Spike.** This is a quick, sharp increase in AC voltage. The voltage immediately returns to normal, but the *spike* can destroy unprotected equipment. Lightning strikes are a common source of spikes.

- **Sags and brownouts.** Commercial power can also reduce or *sag*. Instead of providing a steady 115 VAC, it can decrease to 110 VAC or lower. If this occurs for less than a second, it's called a sag, but if it lasts longer, it's referred to as a *brownout*. You can often see lights flicker or become dimmer during brownouts, and they can cause systems to restart.

- **Blackouts.** A *blackout* is the total loss of power (or the reduction of power to such a low level that the equipment is unable to operate). The following sections identify some of methods used to protect against power-related problems.

Surge Suppressors

A *surge suppressor* is a power strip with extra protection. It has built-in sensors that can detect when the power surges or spikes. Most surge suppressors have a circuit breaker that will pop when it detects surges or spikes. When the circuit breaker pops, the surge suppressor no longer provides voltage to any systems plugged into it. You can usually reset it by pressing a button on the surge suppressor or by turning it off and back on.

> *NOTE* **POWER STRIPS VS. SURGE SUPPRESSORS**
>
> A power strip is similar to an extension cord with extra power plugs. Many people assume it protects against surges and spikes, but it does not provide any protection. Surge suppressors include some type of tag or marking indicating that they are surge suppressors.

Battery Backup

An *uninterruptible power supply (UPS)* provides the benefits of a surge suppressor and also provides constant power to a system. It includes batteries, and if commercial power is lost or sags, it can continue to supply power to systems for a short time, for as much as 10 or 15 minutes or longer.

For example, I recently added an UPS rated at 900 watts. I plugged in my primary PC and flat screen monitor, but nothing else, to the UPS. During a power outage, the UPS continued to provide power for over an hour. If I had two PCs and two monitors plugged into it, the UPS would likely have lasted only about 30 minutes.

If power isn't restored within a certain time frame, the UPS can send a signal to the computer to perform a logical shutdown. This prevents hardware and software problems caused by unexpected power losses.

Figure 1-8 shows how the UPS is connected to the computer. The UPS plugs into the wall to receive commercial power. This power provides a continuous charge to the batteries within the UPS. The UPS provides AC power to the computer or to other systems plugged into it. If power fails, the UPS continues to provide power to the computer for a short time.

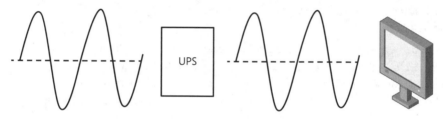

AC commercial power   AC power

FIGURE 1-8 UPS used to protect against short-term power loss.

EXAM TIP

An UPS can be used to provide power to computers for short-term power. Laser printers draw a significant amount of power, and they should not be plugged into an UPS.

It's important to ensure the UPS system can meet the power requirements of the systems you're trying to protect from power outages. Additionally, you should plug in only systems that you need to keep operational during short-term power failures. If you plug all your equipment into the UPS, they will draw additional power. This will reduce the amount of time that the UPS provides power to these systems during an outage. Other equipment should be plugged into a surge suppressor.

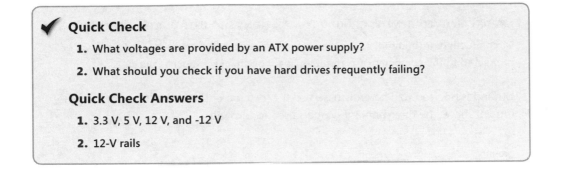

Safety Issues

When working on computers, it's important to pay attention to safety considerations. A basic premise to always keep in mind is that computers are just things that can be replaced, but we can't replace people. In other words, value people first when working with computers. By following basic safety precautions, you can prevent damage to people and to equipment.

Electrical Safety

Unless you're measuring voltages within a computer, you should never work on computers without first removing power. This includes turning the computer off and unplugging it.

Just turning off the power is not enough. ATX-based power supplies provide power to the motherboard even if the front power switch on the computer indicates that it is turned off. If you want to ensure that the computer does not have any power, unplug the power supply.

Most people consider PSUs modular units. In other words, if the PSU fails you simply replace it instead of trying to repair it. However, if you do open the power supply, don't forget the following two important warnings:

- Never open it when it is plugged in.
- Even after you unplug it, capacitors within the power supply will hold a charge. If you touch the capacitor, it can easily discharge and shock you. I learned this lesson first-hand when playing with one of my father's radio sets when I was about eight years old. It knocked me against the wall and left my mother white-faced for quite a while.

Equipment and Self-Grounding

In electronics, *ground* refers to a path to Earth. A copper cable is attached to a spike and hammered into the ground. The other end of this cable is available in the electrical system and identified as a ground. Most electrical equipment includes circuitry that will automatically redirect any dangerous voltages to ground to prevent shocks.

Ground is referred to differently based on the location of the connection. For example, Figure 1-9 shows the three primary symbols used for ground.

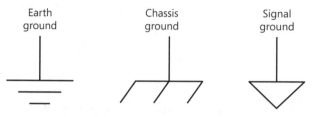

FIGURE 1-9 Ground symbols.

Earth ground is the path directly to Earth. *Chassis ground* refers to the path to the equipment case or chassis. *Signal ground* refers to the return path for a signal. Signal ground connections are commonly connected to the chassis. For example, some screws connecting a motherboard to a computer case connect the motherboard signal ground to the case. The chassis ground is then connected to the Earth ground via the power cable.

ESD

Static electricity builds up on different types of objects, and when one object touches another, the static discharges. You've probably experienced a static discharge after walking across a carpeted floor and touching a doorknob. This is also called *electrostatic discharge (ESD)*.

The shock you felt might have been unpleasant, but it wasn't harmful. However, it can be damaging to computers. If you felt it, at least 3,000 volts were discharged from your hand to the doorknob. If you actually saw the spark when it discharged, it was at least 8,000 volts. The good news is these voltages won't kill or hurt people, mostly because they aren't combined with current to generate power.

In contrast, computer components can be damaged by as little as 250 volts. You won't see it. You won't feel it. However, the damage will be real.

The primary way to prevent ESD damage is by ensuring that the worker and the equipment are at the same ground potential. Steps you can take to reduce ESD damage include the following:

- **Use an ESD wrist strap.** An ESD wrist strap wraps around your wrist and has a metal component touching your skin. A wire leads from the strap to an alligator clip that you can clip to the computer case. This results in you and the case being at the same potential, and it prevents static discharge. On work benches, ESD straps are used to connect the equipment case to a grounding bar that is connected to Earth ground. The technician can connect alligator clips from the wrist strap to the case or to the grounding bar.

- **Use antistatic bags.** When storing and transporting electronic components, they should be stored in antistatic bags. These bags help prevent static from building up and causing ESD damage to the components.
- **Use ESD mats.** Special ESD mats prevent static buildup, and they are commonly used on work benches. Technicians place computers on the antistatic mat while working on them. Larger antistatic mats can be placed on the floor in front of the technician's bench to reduce static.

EXAM TIP

Very small amounts of ESD can cause damage. This is especially true when handling sensitive components such as CPUs and memory. ESD protection such as antistatic wrist straps, antistatic component bags, and antistatic mats are valuable to protect against ESD damage when handling CPUs, memory, and other sensitive components.

- **Self-grounding.** If you touch the computer case before working on any components, built-up static will discharge harmlessly onto the case. This ensures that your body is at the same ground potential as the case. Additionally, if you keep your feet stationary after touching the case, it reduces the chances for static to build up.
- **Don't touch components or pins.** If you remove any circuit cards, don't touch the components or the pins. Instead, hold the outside edges or the plastic handles.
- **Control humidity.** When the humidity is very low, static builds up more quickly. If you live in a colder area, you'll notice that static is more common in the winter because heating systems remove humidity from the air. In contrast, when the humidity is higher, the static charges dissipate naturally. Ideally, humidity should be around 50 percent.
- **Don't place computers on carpets.** Static can build up on carpets more easily than on other floor surfaces. You've probably noticed that in a heated building you can shuffle your feet over a carpet to quickly build up static. This doesn't work on tile floors or other floor surfaces.

MSDS

Material Safety Data Sheets (MSDSs) are available for most products that have a potential to cause harm to people or equipment. This includes materials such as cleaning solutions, paints, and chemicals. The MSDS identifies important safety facts about the material including its contents, its characteristics, how to handle and store it safely, and how to dispose of it. It will also list first-aid steps to take if the material presents a danger.

As an A+ technician, you are likely to use products that have MSDS sheets. For example, you might use cleaning products that clean computer screens or keyboards. If any of these products is causing an adverse reaction to either people or the equipment, you can refer to the MSDS sheet for information about the product and additional steps to take after the exposure.

Compliance with Regulations

Any government regulations pertaining to safety or environmental controls must be followed. For example, the state of California has mandated that all batteries be disposed of as hazardous waste. Even if the batteries are the newer mercury-free alkaline batteries, the regulation still requires special handling.

> **NOTE   IGNORANCE IS NO EXCUSE**
>
> An old saying related to the law is that "ignorance is no excuse." With that in mind, organizations have a responsibility to learn what regulations apply to them where they operate, and to comply with those regulations.

Fire Safety

Fires are classified based on what is burning, and fire extinguishers are classified based on what fires they can safely extinguish. The four primary types of fires are as follows:

- **Class A.** This type of fire involves ordinary combustible material such as paper and wood. The fire can be extinguished with water or a Class A fire extinguisher.

- **Class B.** This type of fire involves flammable liquids and gases. Class B fire extinguishers use chemicals to disrupt the chemical reaction, or they smother the fire with a gas such as carbon dioxide. Spraying water on a Class B fire is dangerous because it will spread the fire instead of extinguishing it.

- **Class C.** An electrical fire is a Class C fire, and the best way to extinguish it is by removing the power source. For example, unplugging it or turning off the circuit breaker can stop the fire. Class C fire extinguishers use special chemicals such as Purple-K or carbon dioxide to extinguish a fire.

> **IMPORTANT   NEVER USE WATER TO EXTINGUISH CLASS C FIRES**
>
> Water is conductive. Electricity can travel up the water stream and electrocute you if you spray water onto an electrical fire.

- **Class D.** This type of fire involves combustible metals. A Class D fire extinguisher uses special chemicals to smother the fire. Water should not be used.

Lifting

When lifting equipment, it's best to lift with your legs, not your back. In other words, instead of bending down to pick up heavy equipment, you should squat, bending your knees, to pick it up.

There aren't any firm guidelines on safe weight limitations. However, it's generally recommended that individuals do not try to lift equipment weighing more than 70 pounds without help.

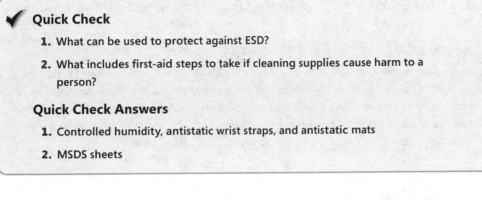

✔ Quick Check

1. What can be used to protect against ESD?

2. What includes first-aid steps to take if cleaning supplies cause harm to a person?

Quick Check Answers

1. Controlled humidity, antistatic wrist straps, and antistatic mats

2. MSDS sheets

Tools

If you're going to work on computers, you'll need some tools. The following sections identify some common tools you should have.

Screwdrivers

Case fans, power supplies, and motherboards are all secured with screws, so if you need to remove them, you'll need a screwdriver. Most screws are Philips, so you'll need one or two Philips screwdrivers in addition to one or two flat-blade screwdrivers in your toolkit.

Extension Magnet

It's not uncommon to drop a screw within a system, but your fingers often won't fit into the small spaces to retrieve it. You can retrieve it with an extension magnet. An extension magnet has a handle similar to a screwdriver, but it has an extendable wand with a magnet on the end. In some situations, the screw might fall onto other electrical components, such as the motherboard. Instead of using the extension magnet, you can use a pair of plastic tweezers to avoid possible damage to system components.

Compressed Air and Compressors

As mentioned previously, compressed air can be used to clean out a computer case. You can purchase cans of compressed air online or at computer and electronics stores. They usually have plastic straws that you can attach to the spray nozzle so that you can direct the air into the nooks and crannies of the case. Compressed air is also useful for blowing out keyboards, printers, and laptop cases.

Compressors are electronic motors that build up air pressure and allow you to blow out components with a hose. For example, many gas stations have compressors that you can use to add air to your tires. Unlike compressed air cans, a compressor will never run out of air.

> **IMPORTANT   BE CAREFUL WHEN USING AIR COMPRESSORS**
>
> Some compressors have very high air pressure, which can damage components within the computer if you're not careful. Additionally, some air compressors collect water that can spray into the computer. Technicians that use these often have a regulator that they use to keep the pressure below 20 pounds per square inch (psi), and they use filters to trap any water. Some technicians strongly oppose using air compressors at all.

Computer Vacuum

In some cases, it isn't feasible to take computers outside to blow out the dust. However, if you blow out the dust inside the building, you're going to make quite a mess. Instead, you can use a computer vacuum cleaner to clean out the computer.

You should use only vacuum cleaners designed for the job. Regular vacuum cleaners generate static electricity and can easily damage the sensitive components within the computer. Computer vacuums are made of special materials and often use batteries instead of AC power.

> **EXAM TIP**
>
> Regular vacuum cleaners and their attachments can cause ESD damage to systems. Computer vacuums are made of special material resistant to ESD.

Multimeter

Multimeters have multiple functions, and technicians commonly use them to measure power supply voltages.

For example, power supplies sometimes lose the ability to provide constant power. Instead of a steady 12 V, a power supply might waver between 10 V and 14 V. Even though a system has some tolerance for variations, generally anything beyond 5 percent can cause problems, such as random restarts. Therefore, the 12-V line should not waver more than plus or minus 0.6 V (11.2 V to 12.6 V). If you're experiencing random problems and suspect the power supply, you can use a multimeter to measure the voltages.

EXAM TIP

Random restarts can also indicate other problems. Overheating and in some cases faulty memory can cause a system to occasionally restart. Additionally, malicious software such as a virus can cause a system to randomly restart. Using a multimeter to verify that the voltages are stable can eliminate the power supply as a problem source.

Figure 1-10 shows a multimeter set to the V setting. It can measure both DC and AC voltages by using this setting. Additionally, this is an autorange digital multimeter (DMM), meaning that it can automatically sense the voltage range.

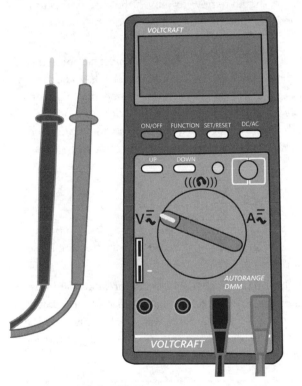

FIGURE 1-10 Digital multimeter.

Less expensive multimeters require you to set the range at the highest possible voltage to avoid damage. If you set it at a low voltage, such as 5 V, and then measure 12 V, you might damage the meter.

In Figure 1-10, you can see that the multimeter has two probes. It might not be apparent in the black-and-white picture, but one probe is red and one is black. You would connect the black probe to a ground pin of a connector (with a black wire) and connect the red probe to the voltage pin in the connector. For example, if you want to measure 12 V provided on a connector, connect it to the pin with the yellow wire. If you want to measure the 5-V line, connect the red probe to the pin with the red wire.

> **CAUTION** **SEVERE ELECTRICAL SHOCK POSSIBLE**
>
> You can measure the voltage only when the power is on and supplying voltage to the system. Because of this you can be exposed to voltages when taking measurements. You should ensure that you do not touch anything within the computer except the connector. This includes touching components with your hands or with the multimeter probes.

When taking voltage measurements, you should remove jewelry. If the jewelry touches a metal component that has voltage, it's possible to short it out and damage the equipment. It could also shock you.

Multimeters can also take other measurements. Besides voltage, the most common measurement is a continuity check. When the meter is set to do a continuity check, you can touch the probes together and the meter will beep, indicating a continuous connection. You can use this setting to check for a break in a cable. You touch one probe to the connector on one side of a cable, and the other probe to the other side. If it beeps, it indicates a continuous connection in the cable, indicating that the cable is good. If it doesn't beep, the cable has a break and should be replaced.

Power Supply Tester

Most power supplies will not provide voltages unless they are plugged into the component. For example, if you want to measure voltages on the motherboard P1 connector, the P1 connector needs to be plugged in. If it's not plugged in, the voltages are zero.

This can be a problem if you want to check a power supply but you don't have a motherboard or other components. However, a *power supply tester* simulates the load for a power supply and lets you know if you have a problem. You plug the power supply cables into the power supply tester and turn it on. The tester will display the voltages, and if any of the voltages are outside specifications, it will indicate the problem.

> ✔ **Quick Check**
>
> 1. What should you use to clean out a computer case?
> 2. What can you use to verify a power supply is providing 12 VDC to a system?

Chapter Summary

- The three functions of a computer are input, processing, and output. These are often shortened to I/O.

- Binary numbers use only ones and zeros. Hexadecimal numbers are created from four binary bits and include the characters 0–9 and A–F. Eight bits make up a byte.

- Large numbers of bytes are expressed as KB, MB, GB, and TB.

- Computer cases house key computer components, including motherboards, case fans, and power supplies.

- Case fans help keep a system cool by drawing air into the case. Cases and fans often get dirty. They can become quite loud, and the system can slow down or intermittently fail. The easy solution is to clean them.

- Case fans can be replaced. If a fan fails, the system can overheat, so the fan should be replaced as soon as possible.

- Power supplies convert commercial AC power to DC voltages. Power supplies are rated based on the power they provide, expressed as watts (W). Replacement power supplies need to meet or exceed the power requirements of the computer.

- Dual voltage power supplies have a switch identified as 115 or 230 to identify the source voltage. Ensure that it is set to the correct voltage supplied by commercial power.

- ATX-based power supplies provide 3.3 V, 5 V, 12 V, and -12 V to system components through various power connectors. These voltages can be measured with a multimeter or a power supply tester.

- The P1 power plug is the primary power connector for the motherboard and includes 20 or 24 pins. Many systems have a secondary power plug that includes 4, 6, or 8 pins.

- Molex connectors provide 5 V and 12 V to PATA disk drives. The SATA connector provides 3.3 V, 5 V, and 12 V to SATA disk drives. Power to disk drives is provided via 12-V rails, and desktop power supplies commonly have two rails but can have more. If disk drives are failing, you might need a power supply with an additional rail.

- PCIe connectors use 6 pins, 8 pins, or 6+2 pins.

- Surge suppressors protect components against spikes and surges in power. UPS systems protect systems against sags and short-term power losses.

- ESD damage can be prevented by using ESD wrist straps and ESD mats, and by controlling the humidity.

- Extension magnets can help retrieve screws that can't normally be reached. Compressed air or special antistatic vacuum cleaners can be used to clean computers.

- MSDS sheets document characteristics about potentially hazardous material used in a work center, including how to store and dispose of hazardous material. When local regulations exist, they take precedence.

- Electrical fires are Class C fires. You should never use water on an electrical fire.

- Compressed air is the preferred method of cleaning systems. If a vacuum is used, it should be a special antistatic vacuum.

- Multimeters measure voltages and can check cable continuity. Power supply testers can check voltages on power supplies without a motherboard.

Chapter Review

Use the following questions to test your knowledge of the information in this chapter. The answers to these questions, and the explanations of why each answer choice is correct or incorrect, are located in the "Answers" section at the end of this chapter.

1. A computer is making a lot of noise. Of the following choices, what is the likely problem?

    A. Faulty motherboard

    B. USB flash drive

    C. Power supply set to wrong voltage

    D. Case fan

2. Another technician ordered a fan for a computer case. It has arrived, and you need to install it. The original fan has been removed. Where should you connect the fan power connection?

    A. AC outlet

    B. P1 power supply connector

    C. Front panel power

    D. Motherboard

3. A power supply failed after a technician added some hard drives to a desktop computer. You need to purchase an additional power supply. What is a likely power rating
   you'll purchase to ensure that the power supply doesn't fail again?

   A. 600 W

   B. 600 V

   C. 300 W

   D. 250 V

4. Which of the following voltages are not provided by ATX-based power supplies?
   (Choose two.)

   A. 12 VDC

   B. -12 VDC

   C. 115 VAC

   D. 15 VDC

5. Molex connectors provide power to disk drives from ATX-rated power supplies. What
   voltages are supplied through the Molex connector?

   A. 3.3 V and 5 V

   B. 5 V and 12 V

   C. 5 V and 15 V

   D. 12 V and 15 V

6. A system is no longer booting to the SATA hard drive, and you suspect that the
   ATX-based power supply might not be providing the correct voltages. What voltages
   should you see on the SATA power connector?

   A. 3.3 VDC, 5 VDC, and 12 VDC

   B. 3.3 VDC, 12 VDC, and 15 VDC

   C. 5 VDC, 12 VDC, and 15 VDC

   D. 12 VDC, 15 VDC, and 24 VDC

7. Which of the following can you use to protect against power sags?

   A. Commercial power

   B. Power supply

   C. UPS

   D. MSDS

8. Which of the following can protect against ESD damage? (Choose all that apply.)

   A. ESD wrist strap

   B. Reducing humidity as much as possible

   C. Ensuring that computers are stored on carpets whenever possible

   D. ESD mat

9. You want to verify that a power supply is providing proper voltages while it's connected to the P1 connector on the motherboard. What would you use?

   A. Surge suppressor

   B. Multimeter

   C. Power strip

   D. Power supply tester

10. You open a computer to troubleshoot it and notice an excessive amount of dust inside it. Of the following choices, what is the best choice to clean it?

    A. Lint-free cloth

    B. Vacuum cleaner

    C. Glass cleaner

    D. Compressed air

11. Which of the following can contribute to ESD damage?

    A. Case fans

    B. Carpet

    C. Touching the computer case while working on a computer

    D. ESD mats

12. After cleaning a computer screen with a cleaning compound, your fingers start to develop a rash. What can you use to quickly identify what was in the cleaning compound?

    A. MSDS

    B. Internet

    C. Local hospital

    D. Coworkers

Answers

This section contains the answers to the chapter review questions in this chapter.

1. **Correct Answer:** D
   - **A.** **Incorrect:** When motherboards fail, they are not noisy.
   - **B.** **Incorrect:** Hard disk drives sometimes make a lot of noise when they are failing, but not USB flash drives.
   - **C.** **Incorrect:** If the power supply is set to the wrong voltage, it might make a single loud pop when it fails, or not work at all, but it won't make a lot of noise.
   - **D.** **Correct:** When case fans begin to fail, they are often noisy. They can also be noisy if they are dirty.

2. **Correct Answer:** D
   - **A.** **Incorrect:** Case fans do not get power from AC outlets.
   - **B.** **Incorrect:** The P1 connector provides power to the motherboard, not to fans.
   - **C.** **Incorrect:** Front panels do not have power for fans.
   - **D.** **Correct:** Fans get power from a connector on the motherboard.

3. **Correct Answer:** A
   - **A.** **Correct:** A 600-W power supply is common in desktop computers and is the best choice of those given.
   - **B.** **Incorrect:** Power supplies are rated in watts, not volts.
   - **C.** **Incorrect:** A 300-W power supply is on the low range found with desktop computers. If the original failed after adding an additional load with disk drives, a larger power supply is needed.
   - **D.** **Incorrect:** Power supplies are rated in watts, not volts.

4. **Correct Answers:** C, D
   - **A.** **Incorrect:** ATX-based power supplies provide 12 VDC.
   - **B.** **Incorrect:** ATX-based power supplies provide -12 VDC. They also provide 5 VDC and 3.3 VDC.
   - **C.** **Correct:** ATX-based power supplies use AC voltage as an input but do not provide AC voltage.
   - **D.** **Correct:** ATX-based power supplies do not provide 15 VDC.

5. **Correct Answer:** B

   A. **Incorrect:** 3.3 V is provided to the motherboard through the 20-pin or 24-pin P1 connector, but not on the Molex connector.

   B. **Correct:** Molex connectors supply 5 V and 12 V from the power supply to different drives in a computer.

   C. **Incorrect:** 5 V is provided through both Molex and the P1 motherboard connector, but 15 V is not used in ATX power supplies.

   D. **Incorrect:** 12 V is provided through both Molex and the P1 motherboard connector, but 15 V is not used in ATX power supplies.

6. **Correct Answer:** A

   A. **Correct:** The correct voltages on a SATA connector are 3.3 VDC, 5 VDC, and 12 VDC.

   B. **Incorrect:** ATX power supplies do not provide 15 VDC.

   C. **Incorrect:** ATX power supplies do not provide 15 VDC.

   D. **Incorrect:** ATX power supplies do not provide 15 VDC or 24 VDC.

7. **Correct Answer:** C

   A. **Incorrect:** A power sag occurs when the commercial power is lower than normal, so commercial power doesn't protect against it.

   B. **Incorrect:** Power supplies convert AC to DC, but they cannot protect against power sags.

   C. **Correct:** An uninterruptible power supply (UPS) uses a battery backup to protect against power sags. Flickering lights are an indication of power sags.

   D. **Incorrect:** Material Safety Data Sheets (MSDSs) provide safety-related information for items used within a work environment.

8. **Correct Answers:** A, D

   A. **Correct:** Electrostatic discharge (ESD) wrist straps protect against ESD damage.

   B. **Incorrect:** Low humidity generates more static. Ideally, humidity should be around 50 percent.

   C. **Incorrect:** Carpets generate static easily, so it's best not to store computers on carpets.

   D. **Correct:** ESD mats also protect against ESD.

9. **Correct Answer: B**

   A. Incorrect: A surge suppressor will prevent power spikes from reaching a computer, but it doesn't measure voltages.

   B. Correct: A multimeter can measure DC voltages provided to a motherboard on the P1 connector.

   C. Incorrect: A power strip provides unprotected power to a system but doesn't measure voltage.

   D. Incorrect: A power supply tester can test an unconnected power supply, but it isn't used for a power supply plugged into a system.

10. **Correct Answer: D**

   A. Incorrect: Lint-free cloths are used to clean screens but would not be used for an excessive amount of dust.

   B. Incorrect: An antistatic vacuum cleaner could be used but a standard vacuum cleaner can cause ESD damage.

   C. Incorrect: Glass cleaner includes ammonia and alcohol, which might damage internal components.

   D. Correct: Compressed air would be the best choice for blowing out the dust.

11. **Correct Answer: B**

   A. Incorrect: Case fans keep a system cool but do not contribute to ESD damage.

   B. Correct: Static builds up on carpet, so placing computers on carpets can contribute to ESD damage.

   C. Incorrect: Touching the computer case while working on a computer helps keep you at the same potential as the computer and reduces static buildup.

   D. Incorrect: ESD mats reduce the potential for ESD damage.

12. **Correct Answer: A**

   A. Correct: A Material Safety Data Sheet (MSDS) documents characteristics of materials used within a workplace.

   B. Incorrect: You might be able to find the information on the Internet, but an MSDS sheet should be readily available.

   C. Incorrect: Medical personnel will likely want to know what was in the cleaning compound, but they wouldn't know what was used.

   D. Incorrect: Coworkers wouldn't be the best source to identify the contents, but they can retrieve the MSDS.

CHAPTER 2

Understanding Motherboards and BIOS

In this chapter, you learn about motherboards, including the different types and how to identify different motherboard components. The motherboard includes a significant amount of supporting hardware for a system and is a primary component that determines the overall capabilities and speed of a system. The motherboard also includes firmware, commonly called Basic Input/Output System (BIOS), which is used to start the computer. The BIOS includes a program that you can use to view and configure hardware settings. This chapter shows how to start BIOS, view and manipulate the settings, and update the BIOS program through a process called flashing. You also learn about some basic troubleshooting related to the motherboard and BIOS.

Exam 220-801 objectives in this chapter:

- 1.1 Configure and apply BIOS settings.
  - Install firmware upgrades—flash BIOS
  - BIOS component information
    - RAM
    - Hard drive
    - Optical drive
    - CPU
  - BIOS configurations
    - Boot sequence
    - Enabling and disabling devices
    - Date/time
    - Clock speeds
    - Virtualization support
    - BIOS security (passwords, drive encryption: TPM, lo-jack)
  - Use built-in diagnostics
  - Monitoring

- Temperature monitoring
- Fan speeds
- Intrusion detection/notification
- Voltage
- Clock
- Bus speed

- 1.2 Differentiate between motherboard components, their purposes, and properties.
  - Sizes
    - ATX
    - Micro-ATX
    - ITX
  - Expansion slots
    - PCI
    - PCI-X
    - PCIe
    - miniPCI
    - CNR
    - AGP2x, 4x, 8x
  - RAM slots
  - CPU sockets
  - Chipsets
    - North Bridge
    - South Bridge
    - CMOS battery
  - Jumpers
  - Front panel connectors
    - USB
    - Audio
    - Power button
    - Power light
    - Drive activity lights
    - Reset button
  - Bus speeds

Exam 220-802 objectives in this chapter:

- 4.2 Given a scenario, troubleshoot common problems related to motherboards, RAM, CPU and power with appropriate tools.
    - Common symptoms
        - Unexpected shutdowns
        - System lockups
        - POST code beeps
        - Blank screen on bootup
        - BIOS time and settings resets
        - Attempts to boot to incorrect device
        - Continuous reboots
        - Fans spin—no power to other devices
        - Indicator lights
        - BSOD
    - Tools
        - POST card

REAL WORLD   **UNDERSTANDING THE BIOS BOOT ORDER**

I remember teaching a Windows class to several students at a corporate site where basic knowledge about BIOS turned out to be important. Early in the class, we discussed the installation of Windows, and then the students had an opportunity to install it on their system.

Each of the students had an installation DVD, and they needed to put the DVD into the drive, boot to the DVD, and begin the installation. About half the student computers were configured to boot to the DVD first, and these didn't give the students any trouble.

However, many of the computers in the company's training room were configured to boot to the hard drive instead of the DVD. Most of the students using these computers quickly recognized that they needed to reconfigure the BIOS to boot to the DVD, and they quietly did so.

Unfortunately, one of the students didn't understand why his system wouldn't boot to the DVD. He first thought his installation DVD was faulty, so he got another one and tried again and then became convinced his computer was faulty. We ended up working together to reconfigure the BIOS on his system. He remarked that this was the first time he had ever accessed this program. Lacking this basic knowledge didn't stop him from learning, but it did slow him down.

By the end of this chapter, you'll have an opportunity to access the BIOS and see exactly how to manipulate these settings. It is important knowledge, and you never know when you'll need it as a PC technician.

Motherboards

The motherboard is the primary circuit board within a computer, and it holds several key components, including the processor, random access memory (RAM), expansion slots, and more.

Motherboards are created by using form factors that define their size and the components on the motherboard. Similarly, cases are built to support one or more motherboard form factors. In Chapter 1, "Introduction to Computers," Figure 1-2 showed the inside of a computer with the motherboard highlighted. In this chapter, you'll learn more about the types of motherboards available and the individual components on a typical motherboard.

Identifying Motherboard Components

All of the relevant components of a motherboard are presented within this chapter. Figure 2-1 shows the outline of a motherboard with several key components identified. You won't find all of these components on every motherboard or in exactly the same location. However, the figure gives you an idea of common components and how to identify them.

EXAM TIP

When taking the exam, you should be able to identify different components on the motherboard based on their shape. You should also be able to identify their purposes and properties.

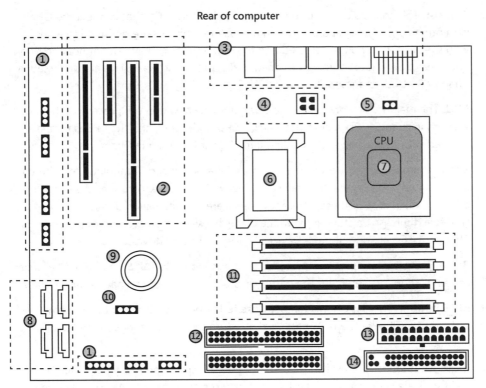

FIGURE 2-1 Motherboard outline.

1. **Miscellaneous connectors and jumpers.** Connectors are available to connect to a speaker, to fans, and to the front of the case for power and displays. They can be located in different places on the motherboard.

2. **Expansion slots.** Expansion slots allow you to add additional cards to a motherboard for additional capabilities. Several different types of expansion slots are available, including Peripheral Component Interconnect (PCI), Accelerated Graphics Port (AGP), and more.

3. **Rear connectors.** Several connectors are attached to the motherboard and are accessible via the rear of the computer. These include connectors for audio and video Universal Serial Bus (USB) devices and more. Chapter 5, "Exploring Peripherals and Expansion Cards," discusses common connectors.

4. **CPU 12-V power.** A 4-pin plug from the power supply plugs into here to provide power to the Central Processing Unit (CPU). On systems with multiple CPUs, this can be two 4-pin plugs or an 8-pin plug.

5. **CPU Fan.** CPUs generate a lot of heat, so it's common to attach a fan on top of them. A connection on the motherboard provides power for the fan. CPU fans are often variable speed so that they can spin faster when the CPU gets hotter.

6. **Chipset.** This consists of one or more integrated circuits (ICs) that connect the CPU with other components and devices on the system. Chipsets are designed to work with specific CPUs and are soldered into the motherboard. They can get hot and often have heat sinks on top of them designed to dissipate heat. Heat sinks are discussed in Chapter 3, "Understanding RAM and CPUs."

7. **CPU.** The majority of work done by a computer occurs within the processor. The motherboard includes a CPU socket into which a CPU is plugged, and the CPU is normally covered with a heat sink and a cooling fan. CPUs are covered in Chapter 3.

8. **SATA connectors.** Most computers support Serial Advanced Technology Attachment (SATA) drives. SATA connectors have a distinctive *L* shape. SATA connectors come in different versions, and these different versions are identified with different colors. However, there isn't a standard with the colors between motherboard manufacturers. Chapter 4, "Comparing Storage Devices," covers hard disk drives.

9. **Battery.** The battery provides power to the Basic Input/Output System (BIOS) so that certain settings are retained. The battery is often circular but can have a barrel shape.

10. **BIOS jumper.** There is often a jumper close to the battery. Shorting the two pins on this jumper will reset the BIOS password or return the BIOS settings to the factory defaults.

11. **RAM.** Motherboards usually have at least two RAM slots, and many have four or six. RAM slots are very specific and will accept only certain types of RAM based on the specifications of the motherboard. Chapter 3 covers RAM.

12. **IDE connectors.** Extended Integrated Drive Electronics (EIDE) connectors are used for EIDE devices such as hard drives and optical drives. Many systems have replaced EIDE drives with SATA drives, but you still might see the connectors. When the board includes them, you'll see two connectors labeled IDE1 and IDE2, or sometimes IDE0 and IDE1.

13. **P1 power connector.** The primary power connection from the power supply is either a 20-pin connector or a 24-pin connector.

14. **Floppy drive connector.** This is for 3.5-inch floppy drives. They are rare today, but if the system has a floppy connector, it is usually by the IDE connectors.

Sizes

While computer cases come in a wide variety of sizes, you'll find that most motherboards follow a form factor standard and conform to specific sizes. The following are some of the common motherboard form factors in use today:

- **Advanced Technology Extended (*ATX*).** This has been the standard used in many systems since 1995 and is still used today. It added capabilities and improved on the original AT motherboard design.

- **Micro-ATX (mATX or μATX).** This is a smaller version of the ATX and is very popular with desktop computers. It is designed to be backward-compatible with the ATX form factor so that it can fit in any ATX case and has the same power connectors. Because it is smaller, it has fewer expansion slots.

- **ITX.** ITX motherboards originated with VIA technologies and come in several different *small form factor* (*SFF*) designs, including mini-ITX, nano-ITX, and pico-ITX. They are referred to as embedded boards and consume very little power compared to ATX-based boards. They don't need to be cooled with fans.

    - **Mini-ITX.** These are envisioned for use in home theater systems. They can fit into any case by using standard ATX mount points.

    - **Nano-ITX.** These small boards are designed for smaller devices such as digital video recorders (DVRs) and set-top boxes.

    - **Pico-ITX.** These extremely small boards can be embedded in different types of mobile devices. The Pico-ITX has been adopted as an open standard by the Small Form Factor Special Interest Group, or SFF-SIG.

EXAM TIP

Although there are additional types of motherboards, the preceding list provides an idea of the types you might see on the exam. The ATX motherboard and ATX variants are still the most popular. Additionally, all the ATX variants are smaller than the ATX, and many will fit into a case designed for an ATX motherboard.

Table 2-1 shows the sizes of common motherboard standards, organized from the largest form factors to the smallest.

TABLE 2-1 Form Factor Sizes

Form Factor	Size in Inches	Metric Size
ATX	12 x 9.6	305 mm x 244 mm
Micro-ATX	9.6 x 9.6 largest 6.75 x 6.75 smallest	244 mm x 244 mm 171.45 mm x 171.45 mm
Mini-ITX (VIA)	6.7 x 6.7	17 cm x 17 cm
Nano-ITX (VIA)	4.7 x 4.7	120 mm x 120 mm
Pico-ITX	3.9 x 2.8	10 mm x 7.2 mm

NOTE **THE MICRO-ATX FORM FACTOR**

The Micro-ATX form factor is the only one that comes in different sizes. However, it is designed so that it will fit into any case that supports an ATX motherboard.

Busses

A *bus* within a computer refers to the connection between two or more components, and it is used to transfer data between these components. A computer has multiple busses that often work independently of each other. However, some busses work together.

As an example, computers have a data bus and an address bus, as shown in Figure 2-2. Data bytes are stored in RAM in separate memory locations, and each location is identified by an address. You can think of these locations as 1, 2, 3, and so on. A typical computer has billions of locations.

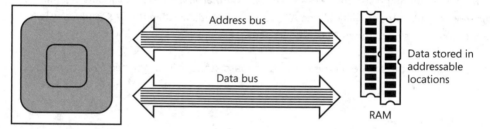

FIGURE 2-2 Address and data bus used to read and write memory data.

When a system wants to retrieve data from a specific location, it places the desired address on the address bus. The data in that memory location is then placed on the data bus for the system. Similarly, when a system wants to write data into a memory location, it simultaneously places the data on the data bus and the address on the address bus. These busses also have other signals that synchronize the activity and control whether data is read or written.

The size of the address bus determines how much memory can be addressed. A 32-bit address bus is limited to 2^{32} addressable locations, or 4 GB of RAM. A 64-bit bus can address 2^{64} addressable locations, or over 17 exabytes (EB) of RAM.

Similarly, the size of the data bus determines how much data can be transferred at a time. A 32-bit data bus can transfer 32 bits of data at a time (which equals 4 bytes). A 64-bit data bus can transfer 64 bits of data a time.

Some of the other types of busses you'll come across include the following:

- **Back side bus.** The *back side bus* is the connection between the CPU and its internal cache memory.

- **Front side bus (FSB).** The *front side bus* refers to the connection between the CPU and the supporting chipset on the motherboard. The speed of this is frequently used to identify the speed of the CPU. Newer systems have replaced the front side bus with a *Direct Media Interface (DMI)*.

- **Direct Media Interface (DMI) bus.** This connects the CPU and newer chipsets in place of the front side bus.

- **Expansion slot bus.** Expansion slots have their own dedicated busses, and these are implemented differently depending on the expansion slots included in the system.

- **Universal Serial Bus (USB).** This is used to transfer data between the computer and external USB devices such as USB flash drives.

Bus Speeds

Motherboards include one or more oscillator crystals, which vibrate at specific frequencies when a voltage is applied. The output is a sine wave that alternates at a specific frequency such as 66 MHz or 100 MHz.

NOTE **HERTZ, MHz, AND GHz**

A *hertz* (*Hz*) is a cycle and refers to how many times a signal can go up, down, and return to the starting point in one second. Alternating current (AC) power in North America runs at 60 Hz, meaning that it can finish 60 cycles a second. A 100-*MHz* signal completes 100 million cycles in a second, and a 1-*GHz* signal completes 1 billion cycles in a second.

A computer uses these cycles as a clock to transfer data. For example, when the cycle is rising (rising edge), the system interprets this as a clock tick and takes an action such as reading or writing data to RAM. Many systems use the rising edge as one clock tick and use the falling edge as another clock tick. Therefore, a system will commonly have two clock ticks for each cycle.

Computers can process data more quickly than the base frequencies of these crystals, and they use additional multiplier circuitry to increase the frequency. For example, if a crystal generates a 100-MHz signal and the motherboard uses a two-times (2X) multiplier, the output is 200 MHz, as shown in Figure 2-3.

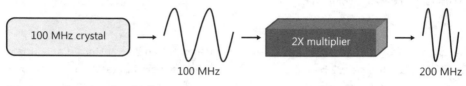

FIGURE 2-3 Crystal and multiplier.

An important point to remember is that the frequency of the bus directly impacts how much data a bus can transfer—the faster the frequency, the more data the bus can transfer.

Additionally, the amount of data a bus can transfer is dependent on how many bits can be transferred at a time. Two common data bus widths in use today are 32 bits and 64 bits. That is, for each clock cycle on a 32-bit bus, the system will send 32 bits of data. If it's a 64-bit bus, it can send 64 bits of data at a time.

> **NOTE** **DATA THROUGHPUT**
>
> Data throughput is commonly expressed as megabytes per second (MB/s) or gigabytes per second (GB/s). For example, some expansion boards can reach speeds of 16 GB/s.

Expansion Slots

Motherboards include expansion slots so that you can add expansion cards. For example, your motherboard can have basic video capabilities built into it, but you might want video that is faster and crisper. You can purchase a top-of-the-line video card with onboard RAM, install it in an expansion slot, and enjoy some awesome graphics.

Before you buy any expansion card, you should know what expansion slots are available in your computer. You don't want to buy a card only to find that it isn't supported by your computer or that the slot is already occupied by another expansion board.

The following sections cover the common types of expansion slots you should know about for the A+ exams. The standards are as follows:

- **Peripheral Component Interconnect (PCI).** This comes in 32-bit and 64-bit versions and reaches speeds up to 533 MB/s. Newer motherboards might still include a PCI slot.

- **Accelerated Graphics Port (AGP).** AGP was introduced as a dedicated slot for a graphics card. It allowed high-end graphics to transfer data at speeds up to 2,133 MB/s without competing with other PCI device data transfers.

- **PCI-Extended (PCI-X).** This was an improvement over PCI and could reach up to 1,064 Mb/s. It is primarily used in servers.
- **PCI Express (PCIe).** This is the primary standard in use today and replaces PCI, AGP, and PCI-X on many motherboards. It can reach speeds up to 2 GB/s on multiple lanes simultaneously.

PCI

The *Peripheral Component Interconnect (PCI)* standard was a replacement for earlier *industry standard architecture (ISA)* and extended ISA expansion cards. It originally used a 32-bit data bus but was later improved to use a 64-bit bus. Table 2-2 shows the data rates and frequencies available with 32-bit and 64-bit versions of PCI.

TABLE 2-2   PCI Data Rates and Frequencies

Standard	Data Rate	Frequency
PCI (32-bit)	133 MB/s	33 MHz
PCI (32-bit)	266 MB/s	66 MHz
PCI (64-bit)	266 MB/s	33 MHz
PCI (64-bit)	533 MB/s	66 MHz

Another difference in PCI cards is that early versions used 5 volts but newer versions used 3.3 volts. Lower voltages decrease the heat generated by the cards. They also increase the speed of the devices because it takes less time for a signal to reach 3.3 V than it does to reach 5 V. Each of these types is keyed differently, as shown in Figure 2-4, to prevent plugging a board into the wrong slot.

FIGURE 2-4 PCI slots.

> ***TIP* PCI CARDS**
>
> Some PCI cards are created as universal cards with keying that can fit into either a 3.3-V or a 5-V slot. However, only 32-bit PCI cards can plug into 32-bit PCI slots and only 64-bit PCI cards can plug into 64-bit PCI slots.

Even though PCI has been largely replaced by PCIe, you will likely still see some PCI expansion slots on motherboards. The two versions have different slots, so it is easy to tell the difference between PCI and PCIe expansion slots and cards.

AGP

Accelerated Graphics Port (AGP) is a dedicated expansion slot used for graphics. A huge benefit of AGP over PCI was that it used a separate bus for graphics data so it wasn't competing with data from other expansion cards. Before AGP, graphics cards were plugged into a PCI slot and all PCI devices shared the same data bus. Graphics-intensive applications such as computer-aided design (CAD) applications and some games were extremely slow without AGP.

AGP came in four versions, with each successive version doubling the data rate. Table 2-3 shows the data rates available with the different versions. Notice that AGP always uses a 66-MHz bus.

TABLE 2-3 AGP Data Rates and Frequencies

Standard	Data Rate	Frequency
AGP	266 MB/s	66 MHz
AGP 2X	533 MB/s	66 MHz
AGP 4X	1,066 MB/s	66 MHz
AGP 8X	2,133 MB/s	66 MHz

PCI-X

PCI-Extended (PCI-X) was developed as an enhancement over PCI. It came in 64-bit versions and was primarily used on servers. A benefit was that PCI-X was backward-compatible with PCI so the PCI-X expansion cards could plug into PCI expansion slots.

The most common frequency used with PCI-X is 133 MHz, giving a data throughput rate of 1,064 MB/s. PCI-X also came in versions with different frequencies and data rates, as shown in Table 2-4, but 133 MHz remained the most common.

TABLE 2-4 PCI-X Data Rates

Standard	Data Rate	Frequency
PCI-X	532 MB/s	66 MHz
PCI-X	1,064 MB/s	133 MHz
PCI-X	2.15 GB/s	266 MHz
PCI-X	4.3 GB/s	533 MHz

PCIe

PCI Express (PCIe) is the primary standard you'll see in use today in place of PCI, PCI-X, and AGP. Engineers designed this significantly differently from other busses. Three important differences are as follows:

- **Data sent in byte streams.** Previous expansion busses used 32 bit or 64-bit connections and would transfer these bits in parallel, as 32 bits at a time or 64 bits at a time. PCIe instead sends the data as a continuous stream of data bytes and achieves higher data throughputs. The stream is sent as serial data (one bit at a time) instead of parallel.

- **No external clock signal.** Because the data is sent as a stream of bytes, PCIe isn't tied to an external clock signal. This effectively allows it to transfer data much more quickly.

- **Multiple two-way lanes.** A PCIe expansion card includes one or more lanes used to transfer serial data streams. Because the lanes are two-way, a device can send data at the same time it is receiving data. These multiple lanes allow a PCIe card to send and receive more data at the same time. A PCIe can have 1, 2, 4, 8, 16, or 32 lanes (designated as x1, x2, x4, x8, x16, and x32).

Figure 2-5 shows a comparison of different PCIe slots related to a 32-bit PCI slot. There are two important points about these slots:

1. PCIe slots almost always have a plastic extension used to provide additional support for the card. This extension doesn't include any pins but does help the card fit snugly and prevent it from wiggling loose. Smaller cards have one extension, and larger cards often have two extensions.

2. The keying for each of the PCIe cards is the same. If you have a PCIe x1 card, you can plug it into the PCIe x1 slot, the PCI x4 slot, or the PCIx16 slot, as shown in Figure 2-5.

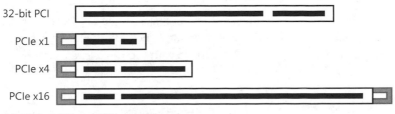

FIGURE 2-5 PCI and PCIe expansion slot comparison.

If you plug a smaller card into the larger slot, some of the pins aren't used, but these additional pins are used for additional lanes that aren't supported by the smaller PCIe x1 card. You can plug any smaller PCIe card into a larger PCIe slot. For example, you can plug a PCIe x4 card into a PCIe x8, PCIe x16, or PCIe x32 slot. However, you can't put a larger card into a smaller slot any more than you can put a round peg into a square hole. It just won't fit.

EXAM TIP

You can plug smaller PCIe expansion cards into larger PCIe expansion slots. However, you cannot mix and match PCI and PCIe expansion cards. PCIe is not backward-compatible with PCI.

PCIe has been steadily improving over the years, and there are currently three versions of PCI. The slots are the same, but each version supports faster speeds. Table 2-5 shows the different data rates you can get out of different PCIe versions. Because PCIe isn't using an external clock, the speed is measured in transfers per second, and all the PCIe versions achieve speeds in the gigatransfers per second (GT/s) range.

TABLE 2-5 PCIe Data Rates

Standard	Data Rate per Lane	Transfers per Second
PCIe v1	250 MB/s	2.5 GT/s
PCIe v2	500 MB/s	5 GT/s
PCIe v3	1 GB/s	8 GT/s
PCIe v4	2 GB/s	16 GT/s

Table 2-5 shows only the data rate per lane. If you have a PCIe x2 card, you'll get the same data rate in each of the two lanes, doubling the overall data rate. Similarly, x4, x8, x16, and x32 cards multiply the overall data rate.

MiniPCI

MiniPCI slots were developed for use in laptop computers. They are smaller and use a 32-bit, 33-MHz bus. They are commonly used to install a wireless network interface card into the slot so the laptop can connect to wireless networks.

MiniPCI Express (MiniPCIe) is an upgrade to MiniPCI similar to the way PCIe is an upgrade to PCI. The MiniPCIe slots and cards are smaller than the MiniPCI slots and cards, but they can carry larger amounts of data. Chapter 8, "Working with Laptops," covers laptops in more depth.

CNR

Some motherboards have a *Communications and Networking Riser (CNR)* expansion slot. It is about the size of a PCIe x1 slot, although it is not compatible with PCIe. The CNR slot is specifically designed to accept audio, modem, and network interface cards. These types of expansion cards have to be certified by the United States Federal Communications Commission (FCC), and by creating the cards separately from the motherboard, manufacturers can certify the motherboards separately from the CNR expansion cards. This allows motherboard manufacturers to create new motherboards more quickly and then just plug in the precertified CNR card. In contrast, when these FCC-governed devices are built into the motherboard, each new motherboard has to be certified separately.

End users rarely insert cards into the CNR slot. Instead, *original equipment manufacturers (OEMs)* would put the appropriate card into the motherboard as they are building a computer.

> **NOTE** **WHAT IS AN OEM?**
>
> An OEM is any company that resells another company's product using their own name and branding. For example, Dell uses motherboards it has purchased from Intel to build computers that it sells. These are marketed as Dell computers, and Dell is the OEM.

CNR slots aren't common in computers today. Instead, motherboards commonly integrate these capabilities within the motherboard. However, you might see them on smaller form factor motherboards, such as micro-ATX systems.

CPU Chipsets

A CPU *chipset* is one or more ICs that provide the primary interface between the CPU and the rest of the system. The two primary manufacturers of CPUs are Intel and Advanced Micro Devices (AMD). The two primary manufacturers of chipsets that work with these CPUs are also Intel and AMD. Older chipsets divided their functions into *north bridge* and *south bridge*. Newer CPUs take over the functions of the north bridge.

North Bridge and South Bridge

Recent versions of chipsets have used two chips called the north bridge and the south bridge. Figure 2-6 shows how a north bridge (NB) and south bridge (SB) chipset interact.

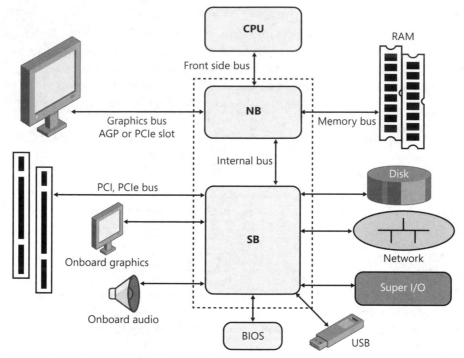

FIGURE 2-6 North bridge and south bridge chipset.

- **North bridge.** The north bridge, also called the *memory controller hub* (*MCH*), is the primary interface for high-speed devices such as the CPU, RAM, and, if it exists, a dedicated graphics slot. On newer processors, the north bridge functions have been taken over by the CPU, as you can see in Figure 2-7.

- **South bridge.** The south bridge provides an interface to low-speed devices, which is essentially everything else in the system. It is also called the I/O Controller Hub (ICH).

EXAM TIP

Features included on a motherboard are dependent on support from the chipset. When the feature is included, it is referred to as *onboard* or *built-in*. For example, the south bridge includes onboard graphics. Alternately, you can add a dedicated graphics card and not use the onboard graphics.

The Super I/O is a separate chip that provides connections to different types of legacy, or older, I/O devices via a serial port, a parallel port, the keyboard, or the mouse. It includes a *universal asynchronous receiver transmitter (UART)* chip needed to translate data between serial and parallel connections. Most new devices use USB, so the Super I/O chip isn't needed or included on many current systems.

Combining North Bridge onto the CPU

Understanding how the north bridge is used for high-speed devices and how the south bridge is used for lower-speed devices is useful background information. However, many newer motherboards using both Intel and AMD CPUs use a single chipset and have moved the functionality of the north bridge to the CPU.

Figure 2-7 shows the configuration for the Intel X79 Express Chipset. If you compare this to Figure 2-6, you can see the differences. Instead of using a single front side bus for graphics, RAM, and the chipset, the CPU has three separate busses: a PCIe bus for graphics, a data bus for RAM, and a Direct Media Interface (DMI) bus for the chipset. The chipset takes care of the rest.

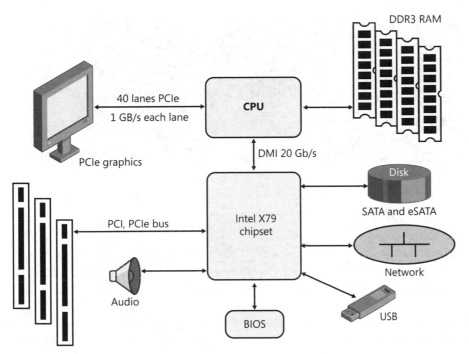

FIGURE 2-7 Newer chipset without north bridge and south bridge.

NOTE **POPULAR CHIPSET MODELS**

Two popular models of current chipsets that have moved the north bridge functions to the CPU are Intel's Sandy Bridge model and AMD's Fusion model.

Jumpers

Motherboards have a variety of different pins that can be connected with jumpers for different purposes. The most common reason to access a jumper is to reset the BIOS password. It's possible for a user to set the password for the BIOS so that only that user can access the BIOS settings. If the user forgets the password, you can clear it with a jumper so that you are able to manage the BIOS.

Figure 2-8 shows the connections to clear the password, with the jumper removed and lying to the left of the pins. The directions are printed directly on the motherboard (on the bottom left), and for clarity, the pins are labeled. If you want to clear the password, you connect the jumper to pins 1 and 2. By default, this jumper is connected to pins 2 and 3.

FIGURE 2-8 Motherboard outline.

> **NOTE JUMPERS**
>
> This motherboard also has a jumper labeled as CLEAR CMOS. This will reset all of the BIOS settings to the factory default. In Figure 2-8, this jumper is connected to pins 2 and 3, but moving the jumper to pins 1 and 2 will reset the BIOS settings.

Some motherboards include jumpers that affect the clock speed. By manipulating the jumpers, hobbyists can cause the CPU to run with a faster clock. This is commonly called overclocking and is mentioned in the "Clock Speeds" section later in this chapter.

Front Panel Connectors

Motherboards commonly have connectors that are used to run wires to the front panel. If you look again at Figure 2-8, you can see several front panel connectors on the motherboard (to the right of the password jumper). Wires are plugged into these connectors with the other ends going to the appropriate connection on the front panel. Some common connectors include the following:

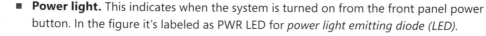

- **Power light.** This indicates when the system is turned on from the front panel power button. In the figure it's labeled as PWR LED for *power light emitting diode (LED)*.

- **Power button.** This turns the power on for the computer and is labeled as PWR BTN in the figure. This is different from a power switch on the back of the computer. If there is a power switch on the back of the computer, it turns on the power supply but not the computer.

EXAM TIP

ATX motherboards introduced soft power allowing the power to be controlled from the front panel. Plugging in and turning on the power supply provides power to the motherboard, but the computer isn't fully turned on until the front panel button is set to on. If you suspect this power button is faulty, you can remove the connection and connect the two pins on the motherboard connector by using a flat-blade screwdriver. This simulates pressing the button. If the system then turns on, you've verified the power button is faulty. If it doesn't turn on, the problem is elsewhere.

- **Drive activity lights.** When the disk drive is actively reading or writing data, these lights will blink. They are typically red LEDs. Figure 2-8 shows this labeled as HD LED for hard disk drive LED.
- **Reset button.** Many systems include a reset button that will force the computer to restart. Whenever possible, it's better to logically shut down and restart a computer, but if the computer isn't responsive to any keyboard or mouse commands, you can force a restart by pressing the reset button.
- **USB.** On the rear panel, motherboards commonly include USB connections that are connected directly to the motherboard. However, USB devices are very popular with users and users often want access to USB ports on the front panel. Wires run from the USB ports on the front panel to connectors on the motherboard.
- **Audio.** Many systems include one or more audio outputs on the front panel that are connected from the motherboard. A headphone or speaker jack is usually a lime green color and includes a headphones icon. Some systems also have a microphone jack, commonly a pink color, with a microphone icon.

✔ **Quick Check**

1. Is it possible to plug a PCIe x4 card into a PCIe x1 slot?
2. How can you reset the BIOS password?

Quick Check Answers

1. No. You can plug smaller PCIe cards into larger PCIe slots, however.
2. Connect the clear password jumper on the motherboard.

Viewing an Actual Motherboard

Earlier in this chapter, in Figure 2-1, you saw a line drawing of a motherboard with an explanation of many of the components. Figure 2-9 shows a picture of an Intel DX 79SI Extreme series motherboard with the individual components identified. It's a newer motherboard, so it doesn't have some of the older components, such as AGP slots or IDE connectors.

FIGURE 2-9 Intel motherboard. Photo provided by Intel. [Copyright © Intel Corporation. All rights reserved. Used by permission.]

1. **RAM slots.** This motherboard includes eight dual in-line memory module (DIMM) slots for double data rate type 3 (DDR3) memory.

2. **SATA ports.** Four SATA 3 GB/s ports and two SATA 6.0 GB/s ports are included. It's not apparent in the figure, but the 3 GB/s ports are black and the 6 GB/s ports are blue, so that they can be distinguished from each other.

3. **Intel X79 Express Chipset.** This chipset uses the Direct Media Interface (DMI) as an interface to the CPU.

4. **Voltage regulators covered by heat sinks.** The heat sinks keep the voltage regulators cool. One is providing power for the CPU, and one is providing power to the chipset.

5. **CPU socket.** This socket is for an Intel Core i7 processor with either four or six cores.

6. **One PCI expansion slot.** This is for earlier-version PCI cards.

7. **Three PCIe 3.0 x 16 expansion slots.** These are for newer PCIe boards.

8. **Power-on self test (POST) decoder.** This displays different numbers as the system progresses through the startup cycle. It can be used for troubleshooting the motherboard in place of a PCI or PCIe card used for providing the same information.

9. **USB ports 3.0 ports.** These are accessible via the back panel. Other connectors on the board can be routed to USB connectors on the front panel.

10. **Back panel ports.** This group includes two RJ-45 network interface connections, one IEEE 1394 firewall connection, and six USB 2.0 connections.

11. **Audio back panel ports.** This group includes multiple connections for different types of audio, including 7.1 systems.

12. **CMOS battery.** This motherboard is using a circular battery, but the battery is inserted sideways into a battery slot.

13. **PCIe x1 expansion slots.** These are for smaller x1 cards.

BIOS

The *Basic Input/Output System (BIOS)* includes software code that provides a computer with basic instructions so that it can start. When a computer is turned on, it runs the program within BIOS to do some basic system checks, locate the operating system on a disk, and start.

For example, most computers have the operating system on a hard disk, and BIOS provides the initial instructions on how to locate the hard disk and start the operating system. The programming provided by BIOS is referred to as the *bootstrap programming*, and starting a computer is commonly called *booting* a computer. The BIOS allows the computer to start without any user intervention other than turning it on.

The program within BIOS is stored in a chip on the computer that can be rewritten. Older computers used an *electrically erasable programmable read-only memory chip (EEPROM)* for the BIOS. *Read-only memory (ROM)* has gone through several iterations over the years, from *programmable read-only memory (PROM)*, to *erasable read-only memory (EPROM)*, and then to *EEPROM*. New computers use a type of flash memory similar to what is used with USB thumb drives.

> **NOTE   WHAT IS FIRMWARE?**
> The BIOS is often referred to as *firmware*. It is a hardware chip that you can physically see and touch, and it includes software that runs code on the computer. The combination of hardware and software is firmware.

BIOS also includes a BIOS setup application you can use to configure different settings for your computer. For example, you can set the time of the computer, identify which drive to boot to, configure the CPU to support virtualization technologies, and more. These settings are explored later in this chapter.

BIOS vs. CMOS

As you study computers, you're likely to come across the term *complementary metal oxide semiconductor (CMOS)*. When referring to BIOS and CMOS, there are differences.

- **BIOS.** This is the firmware. It stores the instructions for starting the computer and includes a program that can be used to change some settings. The firmware can be updated in a procedure referred to as *flashing the BIOS* (covered later in this chapter).
- **CMOS.** This holds only the user-configurable BIOS settings, such as the current time. Users can change these settings by accessing the BIOS application. CMOS is volatile, meaning that the data is lost if the system is turned off. Motherboards include a CMOS battery to retain the CMOS data even if the system is turned off.

That's probably clear to you: BIOS is the application, CMOS is the data, and a CMOS battery keeps CMOS powered to retain the settings. Unfortunately, it's misleading.

Technically, CMOS is a specific type of chip that you'll rarely find on any motherboard, but there is still a need to store the user-configurable settings. Instead of CMOS, the data can be stored on battery-powered static RAM. Sometimes, it's stored in the same chip as the *real-time clock* that is keeping time. Just like CMOS, these chips are powered by a battery when the system is turned off to ensure the system keeps these settings.

When the BIOS is using newer flash memory, the user-configurable data is often stored on the same chip as the BIOS application. Due to how flash memory stores data, it doesn't even need a battery. However, the real-time clock still needs a battery to keep time when the system is turned off.

Even though systems no longer have CMOS, and this battery isn't powering CMOS, it is still commonly called the *CMOS battery*. Even the CompTIA objectives refer specifically to CMOS and the CMOS battery.

BIOS Vendors

Just as you can purchase software developed by different vendors, motherboard manufacturers can use BIOS developed by different vendors. Two of the most popular BIOS vendors are American Megatrends (AMI) and Phoenix Technologies. Each vendor develops different versions of BIOS to meet the needs of different motherboard manufacturers.

The motherboard vendor chooses the BIOS to include with the motherboard, so you don't have to worry about which one to use. However, there are differences between versions, so it's important to realize that one system will look different from another.

Accessing the BIOS Application

When you first turn on a computer, you'll see one or more screens flash onto the screen, providing bits of information. One of these screens gives you a message to press a specific key to access the setup options or the setup utility.

> **NOTE BIOS CAN MEAN DIFFERENT THINGS IN DIFFERENT CONTEXTS**
>
> Primarily, BIOS refers to the bootstrap code used to start the computer without user intervention. However, technicians commonly use the term BIOS to refer to the setup application or setup utility. If you're asked to access the BIOS, you're being asked to get into the setup application or setup utility.

The only sure way of knowing what key to press is by reading the screen. For example, if the screen says to press the <F2> key to enter the setup utility, you'll need to press the F2 function key. Other common keys or key combinations are: F1, F10, Del (delete key), Ctrl+Alt+Esc keys (pressed at the same time), and Ctrl+Alt+Enter keys. On some laptops, you press the Fn+Esc or FN+F1 keys.

Admittedly, that's a lot of combinations. Just remember that what you really need to do is read the messages on the screen as the system starts.

I strongly encourage you to start up the BIOS on a computer and go through these settings. Your BIOS might not use the same words, but you'll be able to see the settings. You can change settings in the BIOS, and as long as you don't save your changes, they won't apply.

After the BIOS starts, it will look similar to Figure 2-10. The mouse cannot be used in most BIOS utilities; instead, you have to use the keyboard and arrows to navigate. Somewhere on the screen, each BIOS utility will have directions about how to navigate through the program, how to select individual settings, and how to change them. In the figure, these instructions are in the right pane.

```
                         BIOS SETUP UTILITY
  Main    Advanced    Power    Boot    Security    Exit

  Supervisor Password :          Not Installed      Install or Change the
  User Password       :          Not Installed      password.

  Change Supervisor Password
  Change User Password
  Clear User Password




                                                →      Select Screen
                                                ↑↓     Select Item
                                                Enter  Change
                                                F1     General Help
                                                F10    Save and Exit
                                                ESC    Exit


        v02.10 (C)Copyright 1985-2001, American Megatrends, Inc.
```

FIGURE 2-10 BIOS setup utility.

BIOS Component Information

You can use the BIOS to verify the different components that are installed on a system. This can be useful to ensure that the system is recognizing newly installed hardware. For example, if you install new RAM but it's not recognized, the BIOS can sometimes give you insight into the problem.

Figure 2-11 shows a screen from a different BIOS version with the system information page selected.

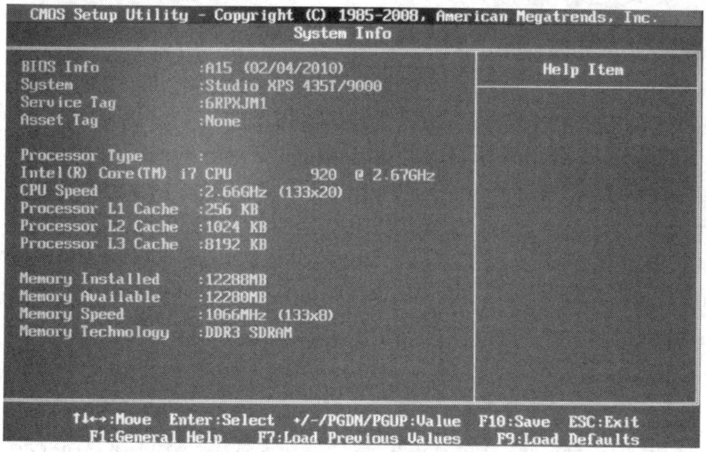

```
CMOS Setup Utility - Copyright (C) 1985-2008, American Megatrends, Inc.
                          System Info

BIOS Info          :A15 (02/04/2010)              Help Item
System             :Studio XPS 435T/9000
Service Tag        :6RPXJM1
Asset Tag          :None

Processor Type     :
Intel(R) Core(TM) i7 CPU          920  @ 2.67GHz
CPU Speed          :2.66GHz (133x20)
Processor L1 Cache :256  KB
Processor L2 Cache :1024  KB
Processor L3 Cache :8192  KB

Memory Installed   :12288MB
Memory Available   :12280MB
Memory Speed       :1066MHz (133x8)
Memory Technology  :DDR3 SDRAM




  ↑↓←→:Move  Enter:Select  +/-/PGDN/PGUP:Value  F10:Save  ESC:Exit
     F1:General Help      F7:Load Previous Values  F9:Load Defaults
```

FIGURE 2-11 BIOS setup utility.

This page shows information about the processor type, processor cache, and memory. You can see that the processor is an Intel Core i7, with a 133-MHz clock multiplied by 20, giving a CPU speed of 2.66 GHz.

You can also see that the system has 12 GB (12,288 MB) of RAM installed. The RAM has a speed of 1,066 MHz (using a 133-MHz clock multiplied by 8) and is DDR3 SDRAM.

Additionally, most BIOS systems will automatically detect the presence of different drives and report their presence within BIOS. This includes hard disk drives and different types of optical drives, such as DVD drives. Sometimes these settings are reported in the Standard CMOS Features page, if it exists, and other times the settings are on a dedicated page for the drives.

Drives might be reported as SATA1, SATA2, and so on if the system is using a SATA interface. If the system is using an EIDE interface, they might be reported as IDE, EIDE, or as hard disk drives.

This can be useful if you've installed a new drive but find that it's not recognized after starting. Go into BIOS, find the drive settings, and ensure that the new drive is recognized by BIOS. If it's not recognized, you need to check the hardware such as the cables or configuration.

BIOS Configuration

There are a few configuration settings that are important to understand. Changes you make in the configuration will remain in the system even after the system has been powered off.

Time and Date

A very basic setting for the BIOS is the time and date. You'll often see these settings on the very first page of BIOS, which is sometimes called the Main page or the Standard CMOS Features page.

The computer keeps time with a real-time clock, and the CMOS battery keeps the clock ticking even when the system is turned off. You rarely need to change this except when the CMOS battery is failing. If the battery is failing, the real-time clock is slow and needs to be reset often.

When replacing the battery, make sure that you replace it with the correct type. Motherboard manufacturers warn that the wrong battery could explode. Also, always follow local regulations when disposing of the original battery.

Boot Sequence

One of the most important BIOS settings for a PC technician to understand is the boot sequence. The boot sequence setting tells the computer the device from which it should try to boot first.

Figure 2-12 shows the boot sequence screen in BIOS. Currently, it's set to boot to the hard drive. If the hard drive doesn't have a bootable operating system, it will look for a bootable operating system on the CDROM, then on a floppy drive, and then by using PXE. As configured, it will never boot using the CDROM drive unless the hard drive failed. If you want to boot using a bootable CDROM drive, you need to change the configuration.

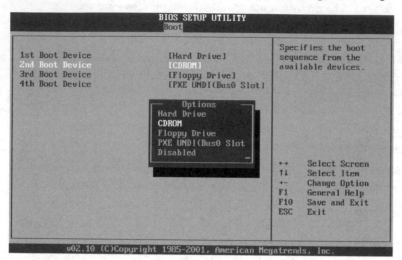

FIGURE 2-12 Configuring the boot sequence.

EXAM TIP

The BIOS on most systems is configured to boot to the hard drive first and will look at other drives only if there's a problem with the hard drive. To boot from a CD or DVD drive, you often have to modify the BIOS.

In Figure 2-12, I selected CDROM in the 2nd Boot Device row and pressed Enter. The Options box has appeared, and I can now use the arrows to change the order. For example, if I press the Up Arrow so that Hard Drive is highlighted and then press Enter, the CDROM and Hard Drive selections will change positions. The system will then attempt to boot to the CDROM first.

The BIOS uses the CDROM setting for any type of optical drive. These include CD drives and DVD drives.

The PXE (Preboot Execution Environment) selection shown in Figure 2-12 allows a system to boot by using a network interface card. A PXE-enabled system contacts a server on the network and can then download an operating system over the network. Chapter 12, "Installing and Updating Windows Operating Systems," discusses network installations using PXE.

Enabling and Disabling Devices

You can often enable and disable devices in BIOS. For example, in Figure 2-12, one of the selections in the Options menu is Disabled. If you want to disable any of the devices, you can select Disabled.

Different types of BIOS allow you to enable and disable devices from different menus. Other devices that can sometimes be enabled or disabled from a BIOS menu include the following:

- **USB controller.** Disabling this prevents USB devices from working.

- **Onboard 1394 (Firewire) controller.** Disabling this prevents Firewire devices from working.

- **Onboard graphics.** This disables graphics capabilities from the chipset. You would disable this on systems that have a dedicated graphics card.

- **Onboard audio.** This disables audio capabilities from the chipset. You would disable this on systems that have audio cards installed in an expansion slot.

- **Onboard network card.** This disables network capabilities from the chipset. You would disable this on systems that have a network interface card installed in an expansion slot.

EXAM TIP

Chipsets include a wide variety of onboard features and capabilities, but these are often basic. It's common to upgrade some features by adding an expansion card. If an expansion card is added, the related onboard feature should be disabled to prevent conflicts. For example, if a powerful graphics card is added, the onboard graphics should be disabled.

Virtualization Support

Virtualization allows you to run one or more operating systems in virtual machines (VMs) instead of physical systems. The VM runs as an application within the physical computer, often called the *host*.

For example, imagine that you wanted to master the details of how Windows 8 and Windows Server 2012 work, but you still want to use Windows 7 for your day-to-day work. Purchasing two additional physical computers and installing Windows 8 on one and Windows Server 2012 on the other would be expensive.

Instead, you can use virtualization software on your Windows 7 computer. You can then install Windows 8 as one VM and Windows Server 2012 as another VM. Figure 2-13 shows how the two VMs would run within Windows 7.

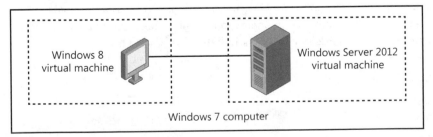

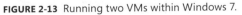

FIGURE 2-13 Running two VMs within Windows 7.

You can configure the VMs so that they can communicate with each other and share Internet access with the host machine. Any time you wanted to play around with a VM, you would start it by using your virtualization software.

EXAM TIP

Virtualization is popular technology frequently used by many IT professionals. It's important to understand the basics, the relevant BIOS settings, and the requirements. This section provides some basics and lists BIOS settings. Chapter 10, "Working with Customers," lists the requirements in a virtualization workstation and mentions virtualization software.

One of the core requirements for virtualization applications to run is CPU support. Most current CPUs include hardware-assisted virtualization (HAV) features, but they are identified differently depending on the CPU vendor:

- **VT-x.** Intel refers to its HAV features as VT-x.
- **AMD-V.** AMD refers to its HAV features as AMD-V, or AMD Virtualization.

Some Intel-based motherboards require you to enable virtualization in the BIOS before it's used. It's referred to differently depending on the BIOS vendor. However, two common names and locations are as follows:

- **Virtualization.** Locate the setting in the Virtualization Support menu and enable the Intel Virtualization Technology setting.
- **Virtualization Technology.** Locate the setting in the System Configuration menu.

Clock Speeds

Motherboards typically include a *serial presence detect* (*SPD*) chip that detects and stores the speed of the CPU and the RAM. The BIOS either reads the data from the SPD chip or automatically detects the clock speeds and reports them. For example, if you look again at Figure 2-11, you can see the CPU and memory speeds. These were detected from the SPD chip.

Some BIOS utilities allow you to manipulate these clock speeds by altering the frequency, the multiplier, or the voltage. For example, if a system has a 133-MHz clock and a 20x multiplier, the speed is 2.66 GHz. If you change the clock from 133 MHz to 148 MHz, you have a speed of 2.96 GHz. If you also change the multiplier from 20x to 24x, you have a speed of 3.55 GHz.

Manufacturers commonly warn that modifying these settings can cause additional heat or other damage, cause the CPU or other components to fail, and reduce system performance. However, for the promise of a quicker PC, many hobbyists are willing to take the risk.

The biggest danger of overclocking is heat. The more quickly a system runs, the hotter it gets. If it gets too hot, it can destroy components. Chapter 3 talks about some advanced methods of keeping systems cool, including liquid-cooled systems.

Security

Many BIOS utilities include security settings, and the most common security setting is related to BIOS passwords. Other possible settings are related to a *Trusted Platform Module (TPM)* and *LoJack*.

Looking again at Figure 2-10, you can see the settings for a supervisor password and a user password. When set, the supervisor password provides full control over any BIOS settings and is sometimes set by administrators to ensure that they can override any changes made by a user.

Depending on the BIOS, the user password provides varied access. It might allow the user to do anything except change the supervisor password, or it might allow the user to change only limited settings such as the date and time. In some systems, it requires a user to enter the password every time the system is started.

The TPM is a chip on the motherboard that is used with software applications for secu-rity. For example, many Windows-based systems include BitLocker Drive Encryption that can work with a TPM. Combined, they provide full-disk encryption and monitoring of the system. Encryption applies a cipher to the data so that it cannot be read.

If someone steals a drive from an unprotected PC, the thief might be able to install it as a secondary drive in another computer and read the data. However, if the drive is protected with a TPM and BitLocker, the thief will not be able to read data from the drive.

Many automobiles include a LoJack unit. It includes a small transceiver, and if the auto is stolen, it can send out signals used to locate it. Similarly, many laptops include a feature from

Computrace known as LoJack for Laptops, from Computrace. It is disabled by default in the BIOS but can be enabled after purchasing a license from Computrace.

POST and Other Diagnostics

When a computer boots, it will run some basic tests commonly known as *power-on self test* (*POST*). POST performs only rudimentary checks on a few core devices. It ensures that the CPU and system timer are both running, that the RAM and graphics are accessible, that the keyboard is working, and that BIOS is not corrupt.

If the computer passes these tests, it will continue to boot. If it fails one of these tests, it stops and gives you an indication of the failure. You'll usually see an error on the display, but POST can't rely on the display, so it uses different types of beep codes.

The POST routine is in the BIOS, and as you now know, there are many different types of BIOS. Similarly, there are just about as many versions of beep codes. The BIOS manufacturer or the motherboard manufacturer has documentation on each of their beep codes, but it is not feasible to list what every POST beep code means. The following are a few examples of what you might hear:

- **No beep.** This often indicates that a system has no power or has a problem with the power supply. However, some systems do not beep at all, and this is normal.
- **One short beep.** This usually indicates that the system has passed the POST. In some systems, it indicates that the RAM might have a problem.
- **Continuous beep or repeating beeps.** This often indicates a problem with the power supply, the motherboard, or the keyboard.
- **Buzz or quickly repeating beeps.** This often indicates a problem with RAM.

EXAM TIP

When the system gives a different indication than normal, look for what has recently changed. For example, if RAM was recently upgraded and it's now giving a different beep code than normal, check RAM. If nothing has recently changed, you should check the power supply voltages.

Many newer systems will display a message on the screen associated with the beeps. For example, if a key is stuck on the keyboard, you'll hear a different beep code and you'll see a message on the monitor indicating a problem with the keyboard.

Older systems displayed cryptic codes on the screen, such as Error 301 to indicate a stuck key on the keyboard. You had to look up the error code in a manual to determine the error. You'll rarely see messages with just an error code today. Instead, if a key is stuck, you'll see a display indicating that a key is stuck.

Some BIOS programs include other built-in diagnostics. For example, I have a laptop that has a Diagnostic menu that includes selections to run tests on memory and the hard drive. However, these tests are often very basic, and you can find better tools. For example, Chapter 3 covers the Windows Memory Diagnostic, which can be used to check for memory problems. Chapter 16, "Understanding Disks and File Systems," covers many tools, such as chkdsk, that can be used to check and repair disk problems.

POST Cards

Looking again at Figure 2-9, you can see that this motherboard has a POST decoder built into it. As the system boots, this LED display changes as POST enters various stages. By watching this LED as the system boots, you can identify what phases are succeeding and the point at which the system fails. The motherboard manual lists codes from 00 through F9 hexadecimal.

For systems that don't have this built into the motherboard, you can use a *POST card*. POST cards that you can plug into a PCI or PCIe expansion card are available, and they have an LED display that displays the POST code as the system is starting.

Monitoring

Some BIOS applications include the ability to monitor the system and provide feedback when issues are detected. The BIOS records the information, and when the system is restarted, it displays a message on the monitor describing the issue. Some common examples include the following:

- **Temperature monitoring.** Systems with temperature monitors will often shut down when the CPU gets too hot to protect them. When the system restarts, you'll see a message indicating that the system was previously shut down due to a thermal event. This is a clear indication to check all the fans.

- **Intrusion detection/notification.** If the case has a biased switch, as described in Chapter 1, opening the case causes the BIOS setting to change. Each time the system is restarted afterward, the CPU will indicate the detected intrusion.

- **Fan speeds.** The BIOS can monitor the speed of some variable-speed fans and report when the speed exceeds predefined thresholds.

- **Voltage.** Some voltages can be monitored. A variance of more than 5 percent of the specified voltage indicates a problem that can be reported by the BIOS.

Flashing the BIOS

As mentioned earlier, the BIOS is firmware, meaning that it includes software code installed on a hardware chip. This firmware can be upgraded through a process commonly known as *flashing the BIOS*. When you flash the BIOS, you're erasing the original firmware and writing new firmware onto the system.

A common reason to flash the BIOS is to add a capability to your system. For example, you might try to run a virtualization program on your system but get an error indicating that virtualization isn't enabled in the BIOS. When you look in the BIOS, you realize it doesn't have a setting to enable virtualization. However, a newer version of BIOS supports virtualization, so you first need to upgrade the BIOS.

If you need to flash the BIOS, go to the computer manufacturer's website. If the manufacturer doesn't maintain one, you'll need to go to the website of the motherboard manufacturer. One of these sites will provide free downloads of programs you can use to flash the BIOS. First you'll need to see what version of BIOS you have and compare it to available versions.

You can check the version of BIOS you have in your system with the System Information tool in Windows systems. You can access this on Windows 7 systems by clicking Start, typing **msinfo32** in the Search Programs And Files text box, and pressing Enter. It's also available via the Start, All Programs, Accessories, System Tools menu. Figure 2-14 shows the System Information dialog box with the BIOS data shown.

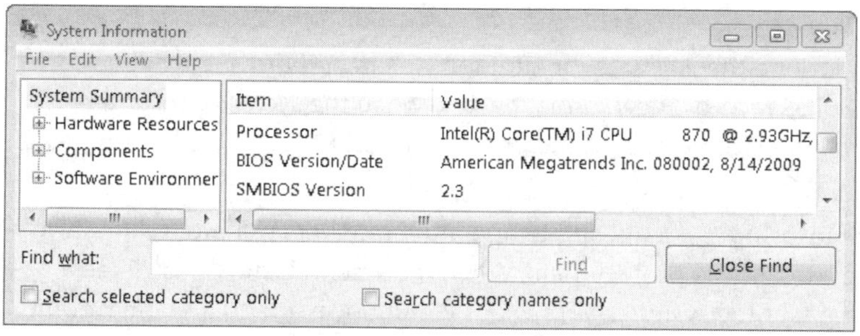

FIGURE 2-14 Viewing the BIOS version in System Information dialog box.

If your version is older than a version available from the manufacturer, you can update it.

Years ago, this was a tedious process. You had to download the program, copy it to a drive that could boot to a basic disk operating system (DOS), restart the computer, boot to this drive, and run the program. The bootable drive was often a floppy or a USB drive, so even creating this bootable drive was a challenge for some people.

The process is much easier today. Most manufacturers provide the update in an application you run from Windows. For example, I recently updated the BIOS on an HP laptop. I located the update on the HP website, downloaded it, and ran it from Windows 7. Figure 2-15 shows what it looks like.

It shows that the version of the current BIOS is slightly older than the new BIOS version (hexadecimal F.26 instead of hexadecimal F.2D). A dialog box appeared asking if I wanted to update the BIOS, and after I clicked Yes, it ran. It took a moment to update the firmware, and when it completed, the system shut down. That was it. The next time I started this computer, it started using the new BIOS.

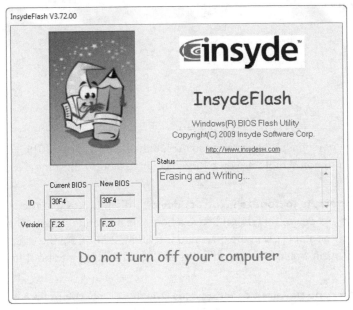

FIGURE 2-15 Flashing the BIOS with a program from the manufacturer.

IMPORTANT **DO NOT TURN OFF COMPUTER DURING UPDATE PROCESS**

If the system loses power before completing the update, the program in BIOS might be only partially written or corrupt. You will no longer be able to start the system, and usually the only option is to return the computer or motherboard to the manufacturer. Ideally, you should plug the computer into an uninterruptible power supply (UPS).

UEFI

BIOS is being replaced by Unified Extensible Firmware Interface (UEFI) on many systems. The functionality is largely the same as BIOS—it provides an interface between the hardware and the software so that the computer can start. However, the UEFI provides some enhancements.

One of the primary advantages of UEFI is the ability to boot from disks over 2 TB in size. Additionally, it is designed to be CPU-independent. That is, the same UEFI could potentially work with both Intel and AMD CPUs. Although the CompTIA objectives don't mention UEFI, you might see it, especially when working with larger disks.

Troubleshooting

Throughout this chapter, many potential problems and their solutions were addressed. This section reminds you of some common symptoms you might encounter, along with some details about what to check.

- **Invalid boot disk or attempts to boot to incorrect device.** This indicates that the system is trying to boot to a device that doesn't have a bootable operating system. The system might have a non-bootable CD in the drive and is trying to boot from the CD. Remove the CD and try again. You can also modify the BIOS boot sequence to boot to the hard drive first.

- **Fans spin, no POST beep, no power to other devices.** The most likely culprit here is that the CPU is not getting power. This is provided from a 4-pin or 8-pin power connector to the motherboard. It then goes through a regulator to the CPU. Measure the voltages with a multimeter. If the voltages to the motherboard are good, the problem is probably the regulator on the motherboard. It could also be the CPU, but this is less likely unless it was just replaced. The fans spin because the power supply doesn't need the CPU to power them.

> **NOTE SPINNING FANS, NO POWER**
>
> Spinning fans and no power to other devices can be a challenging problem. The most likely source is the power supply or the voltage regulator on the motherboard. However, if this symptom started soon after you replaced a component, check that component.

- **BIOS time and settings reset.** If the BIOS time or settings reset, it indicates that the battery has failed or is failing. You might also see an error from the BIOS on startup, such as CMOS Battery Error, CMOS Checksum Error, or CMOS Timer Error. The solution is to replace the battery.

- **Blank screen on startup.** If you don't see any display on the screen, make sure that everything is plugged in and turned on. Also, make sure that the system is plugged into the correct connection. Many systems have add-on graphics expansion cards and onboard graphics. The onboard graphics is disabled so that the screen will be blank if the display connection is plugged in here. Instead, plug the monitor into the expansion card.

- **No power.** Make sure that the power supply is plugged in and turned on and that the front panel power button is depressed. Then check the voltages from the power supply as mentioned in Chapter 1. If the voltages are out of tolerance, replace the power supply. If the voltages are good, the motherboard or an expansion board might be faulty.

- **Stop error.** This is commonly called a *blue screen of death* (*BSOD*). If hardware prevents the system from starting, this stop error screen gives an indication of the problem, which could be a faulty motherboard, faulty RAM, or a problem accessing the hard drives.

If you suspect a motherboard is faulty, there usually isn't much you can do. Motherboards themselves can't be repaired by technicians in the field. You can replace the CMOS battery, manipulate jumpers, and replace the CPU, RAM, and expansion cards. However, if the motherboard itself is faulty, you can either send it back to the manufacturer if it is under warranty or you can replace it with another motherboard.

Chapter Summary

- The most popular motherboard form factor is ATX. Smaller motherboard form factors are micro-ATX and different versions of ITX.

- The speed of the computer is determined by bus speeds, and a computer will have multiple busses for transferring information. Bus speeds are based on the speed of a crystal oscillator and a multiplier.

- Expansion slots are used to add expansion cards. Expansion cards expand the capabilities of the computer. Older AGP, PCI, and PCI-X expansion slots are replaced by PCIe in most current computers. PCIe cards cannot be plugged into an AGP, PCI, or PCI-X slot.

- AGP was used for dedicated graphics cards and came in 2x, 4x, and 8x versions. Each version doubled the data rate of the earlier version. AGP had a data rate of 266 MB/s at 66 MHz, and AGP 8x had a data rate of 2133 MB/s.

- PCIe supports multiple two-way lanes and can have 1, 2, 4, 8, 16, or 32 lanes, designated as x1, x2, x4, x8, x16, and x32. More lanes require larger slots. You can plug in smaller PCIe expansion cards (such as x2) into larger PCIe expansion slots (such as x8).

- Motherboards include a chipset to support the CPU and to provide additional features. The north bridge provides an interface for high-speed devices such as the CPU, RAM, and a dedicated graphics card when it's used. The south bridge provides an interface for everything else.

- Newer CPUs have taken over the function of the north bridge and directly access RAM and the PCIe graphics cards. The chipset provides an interface for everything else that is similar to the older south bridge.

- Motherboards include jumpers for different purposes, and almost all motherboards include jumpers that are used to clear the BIOS password and to clear all of the BIOS settings.

- Motherboards include connectors that are used to run wires to the front panel of a computer. These are used for LED indicators, a power button, audio, and USB connections.

- The BIOS includes software embedded on a motherboard chip (commonly called firmware). It includes the code accessed when a computer first starts and helps the computer start.

- BIOS also includes a program that can be used to view and modify configuration of a system. When the system starts, it shows a message indicating what key to press to access this program. Common keys are F2, F10, or Del.

- Common BIOS configuration settings that you can manipulate are the boot sequence, enabling and disabling devices, and the date and time. If the BIOS loses time, if time needs to be reset frequently, or if the system generates CMOS errors, replace the battery.

- BIOS includes power-on self test (POST), which performs basic checks on core hardware components. If it fails POST, it will display an error on the display and give a series of beeps to indicate the problem. These beep codes are different for different systems, so you'll need to consult a manual.

- POST cards are available as PCI or PCIe expansion cards to watch the progress of a system as it starts. It displays codes in an LED display for different phases of the startup.

- BIOS monitors, records, and reports abnormal events related to high temperatures, intrusion detection, fan speeds, and some voltages. These errors are reported when the system restarts.

- Flashing the BIOS is the process of updating it. You can obtain a program to flash the BIOS from the computer manufacturer or the motherboard manufacturer. Before running the program, plug the computer into an UPS to ensure that it doesn't lose power during the update.

Chapter Review

Use the following questions to test your knowledge of the information in this chapter. The answers to these questions, and the explanations of why each answer choice is correct or incorrect, are located in the "Answers" section at the end of this chapter.

1. Which of the following choices lists common motherboard form factors from the smallest to the largest?

   A. Pico-ITX, mini-ITX, micro-ATX, ATX

   B. Pico-ITX, micro-ATX, mini-ITX, ATX

   C. ATX, pico-ITX, mini-ITX, micro-ATX

   D. Mini-ITX, micro-ATX, pico-ITX, ATX

2. Of the following choices, what two components determine the speed of a bus?

   A. Bit size and multiplier

   B. Crystal frequency and bit size

   C. Crystal frequency and multiplier

   D. CPU capability and cache size

3. You have PCIe x2 card that you want to install into a computer. Of the following choices, where could you install it?

   A. PCIe x1 expansion slot

   B. PCIe X4 expansion slot

   C. PCI expansion slot

   D. PCI-X expansion slot

4. You are trying to start a system from a bootable DVD, but the system always boots to the hard drive instead. What should you do?

   A. Replace the DVD.

   B. Replace the DVD drive.

   C. Manipulate the start sequence in the BIOS.

   D. Flash the BIOS.

5. When starting a computer, you see a message indicating a CMOS error. What is the most likely solution?

   A. Flash the CMOS.

   B. Flash the BIOS.

   C. Replace the battery.

   D. Replace the CMOS.

6. After trying to run virtualization software, you realize that the BIOS doesn't support virtualization. What should you do?

   A. Upgrade the CPU.

   B. Upgrade the motherboard.

   C. Replace the CMOS battery.

   D. Flash the BIOS.

Answers

This section contains the answers to the chapter review questions in this chapter.

1. **Correct Answer:** A

   A. **Correct:** Pico-ITX form factors are 3.9 x 2.8 inches, Mini-ITX are 6.7 x 6.7 inches, micro-ATX are between 6.75 x 6.75 inches and 9.6 x 9.6 inches, and ATX form factors are 12 x 9.6 inches.

   B. **Incorrect:** Micro-ATX is smaller than mini-ITX.

   C. **Incorrect:** ATX is the largest, not the smallest.

   D. **Incorrect:** Pico-ITX is the smallest.

2. **Correct Answer:** C

   A. **Incorrect:** The bit size (such as 32-bit or 64-bit) determines the data throughput, not the speed.

   B. **Incorrect:** The bit size determines the data throughput.

   C. **Correct:** The frequency of the oscillator crystal and the multiplier combine to determine a bus speed.

   D. **Incorrect:** The CPU uses the clock speed, but it doesn't determine the speed.

3. **Correct Answer:** B

   A. **Incorrect:** A larger PCIe card will not fit in a smaller PCIe slot.

   B. **Correct:** You can plug smaller PCIe cards into larger PCIe slots, so a PCIe x2 card will fit in a PCIe x4 slot.

   C. **Incorrect:** PCIe cards are not compatible with PCI slots.

   D. **Incorrect:** PCIe cards are not compatible with PCI-X slots.

4. **Correct Answer:** C

   A. **Incorrect:** Replacing the DVD might be necessary, but you should check the BIOS first.

   B. **Incorrect:** Replacing the DVD drive might be necessary, but you should check the BIOS first.

   C. **Correct:** You can change the boot order in the BIOS so that the system tries to boot to the DVD first.

   D. **Incorrect:** You would flash the BIOS only if it needed to be upgraded. You should try to change the settings first.

5. **Correct Answer:** C

   A. Incorrect: The CMOS isn't flashed. Settings in the CMOS are configured by the user and retained by battery power.

   B. Incorrect: You'd flash the BIOS to upgrade it, but an upgrade wouldn't solve this problem.

   C. Correct: This error indicates that the settings in CMOS aren't being retained by the current battery.

   D. Incorrect: The BIOS is normally soldered into the motherboard, and it's rare to replace it.

6. **Correct Answer:** D

   A. Incorrect: The current CPU might support virtualization, but it must be enabled in BIOS.

   B. Incorrect: Upgrading the motherboard might not be necessary. The BIOS should be upgraded first.

   C. Incorrect: The battery doesn't determine whether virtualization is supported.

   D. Correct: If the BIOS doesn't support an option, you can often upgrade it by flashing the BIOS to get the new feature.

CHAPTER 3

Understanding RAM and CPUs

In this chapter, you'll learn about two important concepts for any A+ technician to understand: random access memory (RAM) and central processing units (CPUs). A CPU is the brain of the computer, performing most of the processing, and RAM is used to store applications and data being used by the CPU. Both continue to be steadily improved and include a significant amount of technical detail that can easily confuse a regular user. This chapter will help you understand many of the terms used when describing them.

Exam 220-801 objectives in this chapter:

- 1.2 Differentiate between motherboard components, their purposes, and properties.
    - CPU sockets
- 1.3 Compare and contrast RAM types and features.
    - Types
        - DDR
        - DDR2
        - DDR3
        - SDRAM
        - SODIMM
        - RAMBUS
        - DIMM
        - Parity vs. non-parity
        - ECC vs. non-ECC
        - RAM configurations
            - Single channel vs. dual channel vs. triple channel
        - Single sided vs. double sided
    - RAM compatibility and speed

- 1.6 Differentiate among various CPU types and features and select the appropriate cooling method.
    - Socket types
        - Intel: LGA, 775, 1155, 1156, 1366
        - AMD: 940, AM2, AM2+, AM3, AM3+, FM1, F
    - Characteristics
        - Speeds
        - Cores
        - Cache size/type
        - Hyperthreading
        - Virtualization support
        - Architecture (32-bit vs. 64-bit)
        - Integrated GPU
    - Cooling
        - Heat sink
        - Fans
        - Thermal paste
        - Liquid-based

Exam 220-802 objectives in this chapter:

- 4.2 Given a scenario, troubleshoot common problems related to motherboards, RAM, CPU and power with appropriate tools.
    - Common symptoms
        - Unexpected shutdowns
        - System lockups
        - Overheating

RAM

When technicians are talking about a computer's memory, they are primarily talking about *random access memory (RAM)*. RAM is used for short-term storage of applications or data so that the processor can access and use this information. In contrast, computers use hard drives for long-term storage of data.

Most RAM is volatile. This doesn't mean that it's explosive; it means that data in RAM is lost when power is removed.

As an introduction, the following list identifies commonly used types of RAM. All of these types of RAM are volatile.

- **Dynamic RAM (DRAM).** Dynamic refers to how bits are stored in an electrical component called a capacitor. The capacitor holds the bit as a charge, but the capacitor needs to be regularly refreshed to hold the charge. This configuration uses very few components per bit, keeping the cost low, but the constant refresh reduces the speed.
- **Synchronous DRAM (SDRAM).** *SDRAM* is synchronized with a clock for faster speeds. Almost all primary *DRAM* used in computers today is SDRAM, but it's often listed as DRAM to avoid confusion with *SRAM*.
- **Static RAM (SRAM).** Static RAM uses switching circuitry instead of capacitors and can hold a charge without a constant refresh. It requires more components per bit so it is more expensive, but due to how the switching works, it is quicker than DRAM. Due to the speed, SRAM is commonly used for CPU cache (described later in this chapter) but is rarely used as the primary RAM because of its cost.

> **NOTE** **SRAM VS. SDRAM**
>
> SRAM and SDRAM are often conflated; however, they are different, and the S makes the difference. The *S* in SRAM indicates *static*, but the *S* in SDRAM indicates *synchronous*. Because of its speed, SRAM is used for CPU cache. SDRAM is used as the primary RAM in computer (PCs). Almost all DRAM in personal computers is SDRAM.

Flash memory is very popular, but not as the primary RAM used in a system. USB flash drives, solid-state drives (SSDs), and memory cards used in cameras and other mobile devices all use flash memory. Flash memory is used for BIOS in many motherboards. Unlike DRAM and SRAM, flash memory is not volatile and retains data without power.

Double Data Rate SDRAM

While the original SDRAM versions were quick and efficient for their time, manufacturers have steadily improved them. *Double data rate* (*DDR*) is one of the improvements and is used in almost all SDRAM. As a reminder, SDRAM is tied to a clock, and when the clock ticks, data is transferred.

SDRAM uses only the leading edge for the clock. However, each of the *DDR SDRAM* versions uses both the leading and trailing edge of the clock. This is often called *double pumping*. Figure 3-1 compares the two over two cycles of a clock. You can see that SDRAM has two clocks from these cycles and that DDR has four clocks from the same two cycles.

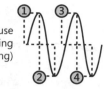

SDRAM uses only
leading edge

DDR versions use
leading and trailing
edge (double pumping)

FIGURE 3-1 SDRAM compared with double-pumping DDR.

The following list provides an overview of the different DDR versions:

- **Double Data Rate (DDR) SDRAM.** DDR uses double pumping to double the data rate of SDRAM.

- **DDR2.** DDR2 doubles the data rate of DDR. In addition to double pumping, it modifies the way that data is processed and can transfer twice as much data as DDR SDRAM.

- **DDR3.** DDR3 doubles the data rate of DDR2. It uses double pumping and further modifies the way that data is processed. It can transfer four times as much data as DDR and eight times as much data as SDRAM.

EXAM TIP

DDR3 SDRAM is the primary type of RAM you see in most systems today. It supersedes SDRAM, DDR SDRAM, and DDR2 SDRAM. However, some existing systems have older RAM, and the CompTIA objectives list each type of RAM, so you'll need to be aware of all of them.

DDR4 isn't included in the objectives, but it is on the horizon as a replacement for DDR3. It's expected to double the speed of DDR3.

DIMMs and SODIMMs

RAM comes on cards plugged into the slots in the motherboard. They are smaller than expansion cards, and technicians commonly call memory cards *sticks*. The two most common types of memory sticks are:

- **Dual in-line memory module (DIMM).** A *DIMM* is the circuit board that holds the memory chips.

- **Small outline dual in-line memory module (SODIMM).** *SODIMM* chips are smaller and are used in smaller devices such as laptop computers and some printers.

Figure 3-2 shows a DIMM (top) and a SODIMM (bottom).

IMPORTANT   AVOID ELECTROSTATIC DISCHARGE DAMAGE

The CPU and RAM are most susceptible to electrostatic discharge (ESD) damage. If you plan on touching the CPU or RAM, ensure that you use ESD wrist straps and other ESD protection as mentioned in Chapter 1, "Introduction to Computers."

FIGURE 3-2 Comparing a DIMM and a SODIMM.

DIMMs and SODIMMs have a different number of pins depending on the type used.

- **DDR SDRAM DIMM:** 184 pins
- **DDR2 SDRAM DIMM:** 240 pins
- **DDR3 SDRAM DIMM:** 240 pins
- **DDR SDRAM SODIMM:** 200 pins
- **DDR2 SDRAM SODIMM:** 144 or 200 pins
- **DDR3 SDRAM SODIMM:** 204 pins

Single Channel, Dual Channel, and Triple Channel

Many motherboards and CPUs support single-channel, dual-channel, and triple-channel memory architectures. Each *single channel* represents a separate 64-bit line of communication that can be accessed independently. With dual channel, the system can access 128 bits at a time; triple channel gives it access to 192 bits at a time.

Using dual and triple channels provides an additional performance enhancement to DDR, DDR2, and DDR3, in addition to double pumping and other enhancements provided by the DDR versions. If you use a dual-channel motherboard with DDR3, it doubles the throughput of DDR3, providing 16 times more data throughput than SDRAM.

If you are upgrading a computer's memory, it's important to understand these channels. You can purchase DIMMs in matched pairs. Where you install each DIMM determines how many channels your system will use and can affect the performance of RAM.

Single Channel vs. Dual Channel

Dual-channel motherboards are very common. If you look at a dual-channel motherboard, you see that it has four memory slots, two slots of one color and two slots of another color. Figure 3-3 shows a diagram of four memory slots labeled for a motherboard using an Intel-based CPU. Slots 1 and 3 are one color, and slots 2 and 4 are another color.

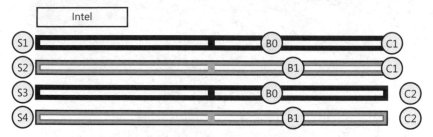

FIGURE 3-3 Intel-based DDR slots (S), banks (B), and channels (C).

- **Slots:** Each slot can accept one DIMM.
- **Banks:** A bank is composed of two slots. In Figure 3-3, Bank 0 includes slots 1 and 3 and these two slots are normally blue. Bank 1 includes slots 2 and 4 and these slots are normally black. This is standard for Intel CPU-based motherboards.
- **Channels:** Each channel represents a separate 64-bit communication path. Slots 1 and 2 make up one channel, and slots 3 and 4 make up the second channel.

EXAM TIP

On most motherboards, the slots are color-coded to identify the banks. Slots of the same color indicate the same bank, and matched pairs should be installed in these slots.

You can install a single DIMM in slot 1, and the system will have a single-channel RAM. You can purchase DIMMs in matched pairs, and it's important to know in which slots to install them. For the best performance, you should install matched DIMMs in the same bank. Looking at Figure 3-3, you should install the matched pair of DIMMs in slots 1 and 3 (Bank 0), leaving slots 2 and 4 empty. The system will take advantage of the dual-channel architecture by using two separate 64-bit channels.

What happens if you install the DIMMs in slots 1 and 2 instead? The system will still work; however, both DIMMs are installed in channel 1, so the system will work with only a single channel. RAM will be about half as fast as it could be if it were installed correctly to take advantage of the dual channels.

Figure 3-3 and the previous explanation describe the color coding, banks, and channels for Intel-based CPU motherboards. However, most motherboards designed for AMD CPUs are organized differently, as shown in Figure 3-4. On these motherboards, slots 1 and 2 make up Bank 0, and slots 3 and 4 make up Bank 1. Channel 1 includes slots 1 and 3, and channel 2 includes slots 2 and 4.

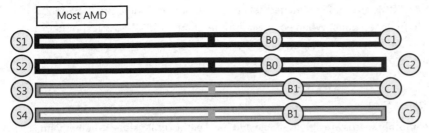

FIGURE 3-4 AMD-based DDR slots (S), banks (B), and channels (C).

While this can be confusing between different motherboards, the good news is that most motherboard manufacturers use the same color for each bank. For Intel-based motherboards, Bank 0 includes slots 1 and 3, and these will be the same color (often blue). Bank 1 includes slots 2 and 4, and they will be a different color (often black). AMD motherboards also use one color for Bank 0 (slots 1 and 2) and another color for Bank 1 (slots 3 and 4).

EXAM TIP

Many motherboards allow the use of different size DIMMs in different channels. However, for the system to use the multichannel capability, each DIMM within a bank must be the same size. If one DIMM in a bank is 1 GB and the second DIMM in the bank is 2 GB, the sizes are different and the system will use single channel. Also, you can use different speed DIMMs in the same bank, although this is not recommended. The speed of the bank will default to the lower-speed DIMM or, in some cases, to single channel.

Triple Channel

On some motherboards, you see six DIMM slots instead of four. This indicates the system supports *triple-channel* memory usage. Table 3-1 shows the configuration of the slots, banks, and channels for a motherboard using triple-channel RAM.

TABLE 3-1 Triple-Channel DIMMs

Slots	Banks	Channels
Slot 1	Bank 0	Channel 1
Slot 2	Bank 1	Channel 1
Slot 3	Bank 0	Channel 2
Slot 4	Bank 1	Channel 2
Slot 5	Bank 0	Channel 3
Slot 6	Bank 1	Channel 3

Slots in each bank are commonly the same color, so you might see a motherboard with Bank 0 slots (slots 1, 3, and 5) all blue and with Bank 1 slots all black.

Triple-channel DIMMs are sold in matched sets of three, similar to how dual-channel DIMMs are sold in matched pairs. When you install triple-channel DIMMs, you should install the matched set in the same bank. For example, if you bought one set, you'd install it in slots 1, 3, and 5.

> **NOTE QUAD CHANNEL**
>
> Quad-channel motherboards are also available and have eight DIMM slots. When buying RAM for a quad-channel motherboard, you buy the RAM in a matched set of four. Quad-channel RAM is not mentioned in the CompTIA A+ objectives.

Single Sided vs. Double Sided

You'd think that *single-sided* and *double-sided* RAM refers to how many sides of a DIMM have chips. That makes sense, but it's not entirely accurate. Instead, single sided or double sided refers to how a system can access the RAM.

In double-sided RAM, the RAM is separated into two groups known as ranks, and the system can access only one rank at a time. If it needs to access the other rank, it needs to switch to the other rank. In contrast, single-sided (or single-rank) RAM is in a single group; the system can access all RAM on the DIMM without switching.

If you have a DIMM with chips on only one side, it is most likely a single-sided (single-rank) DIMM. However, if it has chips on both sides, it can be single rank, dual rank, or even quad rank. You often have to dig into the specs to determine how many ranks it is using.

Usually, you'd think that *double* is better than *single*, but in this case, more rank is not better. Switching back and forth between ranks takes time and slows down the RAM. Single-sided RAM doesn't switch, and if all other factors are the same, single-sided RAM is faster than double-sided RAM.

> **NOTE DUAL-SIDED IS NOT DUAL CHANNEL**
>
> Dual-sided (or dual-ranked) is not the same as dual channel. Dual channel improves performance, but a dual-ranked DIMM doesn't perform as well as a single-ranked DIMM.

> ✔ **Quick Check**
>
> **1.** A system has six RAM slots. What does this indicate?
>
> **2.** Where should you install two new DIMMs on a dual-channel motherboard?
>
> **Quick Check Answers**
>
> **1.** Triple-channel RAM.
>
> **2.** In the same bank, identified by slots of the same color.

RAM Compatibility and Speed

An important point about DDR, DDR2, and DDR3 is that they aren't compatible with each other. You can't use any version in a slot designed for another type. For example, you can use DDR3 DIMMs only in DDR3 slots. From a usability perspective, that's not so great, but if you're trying to remember which types are compatible, it's a lot easier. You can't mix and match them.

Figure 3-5 shows a comparison of the keyings of DDR, DDR2, and DDR3, with a dotted line as a reference through the middle of each one. You can see that the notched key at the bottom of the circuit card is different for each. The standards aren't compatible, and this keying prevents technicians from inserting a DIMM into the wrong slot.

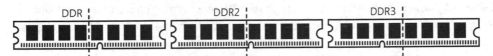

FIGURE 3-5 Comparing DDR versions.

Speeds

Some RAM is faster than other RAM, and with faster RAM you often see faster overall performance. As you'd expect, faster RAM is more expensive. If you're shopping for RAM, you want to ensure that you buy exactly what you need. This includes the correct DDR version, the correct number of channels if your motherboard supports multiple channels, and the correct speed.

The speed of RAM is expressed as the number of bytes it can transfer in a second (B/s) or, more commonly, as megabytes per second (MB/s). However, the speed of most RAM isn't listed plainly. Instead, it's listed using standard names and module names such as DDR3-800 or PC3-12800, respectively. These names indicate their speed, but not directly. If you need to shop for RAM, you need to understand these names and how they relate to the speed.

> **NOTE DIMM STICKERS**
>
> Most DIMMs have stickers on them that include the standard name, module name, or both. If you're working at a company that has stored excess DIMMs in static-free packaging, you can identify details from these names.

You can calculate the overall speed of any SDRAM DDR type by using a specific mathematical formula for that type. The formula includes the speed of the clock (Clk), a clock multiplier (Clk Mult) for DDR2 and DDR3, and doubling from double pumping (DP). The speed is calculated for a single channel, which is 64 bits wide, and then converted to bytes by dividing it by 8. The following formulas show how to calculate the speed of each of the DDR versions by using a 100-MHz clock:

- **DDR speed calculation:**
    - Clk × 2 (DP) × 64 (bits) / 8 (bytes)
    - 100 MHz × 2 × 64 / 8 = 1,600 MB/s
- **DDR2 speed calculation:**
    - Clk × 2 (Clk Mult) × 2 (DP) × 64 (bits) / 8 (bytes)
    - 100 MHz × 2 × 2 × 64 / 8 = 3,200 MB/s
- **DDR3 speed calculation:**
    - Clk × 4 (Clk Mult) × 2 (DP) × 64 (bits) / 8 (bytes)
    - 100 MHz × 4 × 2 × 64 / 8 = 6,400 MB/s

Table 3-2 shows how these speeds relate to the different naming conventions used with DDR types. You can see that the standard name is derived from the clock, the clock multiplier, and double pumping. For example, DDR3 uses a 4-times multiplier and double pumping. Therefore, it's eight times faster than SDRAM. The standard name is derived by multiplying the clock by 8. The module name is a little more cryptic, but if you calculate the speed by using the clock, you can see that the PC name indicates the calculated speed in MB/s. Also, you can see that the names include the version (DDR, DDR2, or DDR3).

TABLE 3-2 DDR Standard Names and Module Names

	100 MHz	166 2/3 MHz	200 MHz
DDR Standard Name DDR Module Name	DDR-200 PC-1600	DDR-333 PC-2700	DDR-400 PC-3200
DDR2 Standard Name DDR2 Module Name	DDR2-400 PC2-3200	DDR2-667 PC2-5300 PC2-5400	DDR2-800 PC2-6400
DDR3 Standard Name DDR3 Module Name	DDR3-800 PC3-6400	DDR3-1333 PC3-10600	DDR3-1600 PC3-12800

> **NOTE SOME ROUNDING ALLOWED**
>
> If you enjoy math, you can plug the fractional number 166 2/3 into the speed calculation formulas and see that they don't work out exactly. For example, DDR2-667 works out to about 5333.312 MB/s. Some manufacturers advertise this as PC2-5300, while others round it up to PC2-5400.

Each DDR version supports multiple clock speeds, and each newer version supports faster clocks. Some of the clock speeds supported by different DDR versions are as follows:

- **DDR:** 100, 133 1/3, 166 2/3, and 200 MHz
- **DDR2:** 100, 133 1/3, 166 2/3, 200, and 266 2/3 MHz
- **DDR3:** 100, 133 1/3, 166 2/3, 200, 266 2/3, and 400 MHz

A key consideration when purchasing RAM is to ensure that the RAM speeds are supported by the motherboard. If the speeds don't match, the motherboard defaults to the slower speed. For example, if your motherboard has a 100-MHz clock and you install PC3-12800 RAM, the RAM will run at 100 MHz instead of 200 MHz. It still works, but you won't get the benefit of the higher-speed RAM.

EXAM TIP

You might need to shop for memory, either to replace memory in your own system or to help someone else. If you can master how memory is named and marketed, you'll be able to identify the correct memory to purchase.

Compatibility within Banks

In addition to matching the RAM speed with the motherboard speed, you should also match the RAM speed within banks when using dual-channel and triple-channel configurations. If one DIMM in a bank fails, you should replace both with a matched set. However, if you have to replace the failed DIMM with a spare, look for a spare that uses the same speed.

For example, if Bank 0 currently has two PC3-12800 sticks and one fails, you should replace the failed stick with a PC3-12800 stick. PC3-12800 uses a 200-MHz clock. If you replaced it with a PC3-6400 (designed for a 100-MHz clock), both sticks would run at the slower speed or revert to single channel.

REAL WORLD **USING THE WRONG SLOTS RESULTS IN SLOWER RAM**

I once helped a friend troubleshoot the speed of a PC after a RAM upgrade. The system started with two 2-GB RAM sticks installed in slots 1 and 2, incorrectly using a single-channel configuration. These DIMMs were PC3-6400, using a 100-MHz clock, and they were working fine, but he wanted more RAM.

He purchased two new 2-GB PC3-12800 DIMMs designed to work with a 200-MHz clock. His motherboard supported 200 MHz, so it could take advantage of the faster RAM. However, after installing the RAM, he ran some tests and found that all the DIMMs were using 100 MHz, so he called me for some help.

Do you see the problem? It took a while to figure out and was exacerbated by the original RAM using the wrong slots. Bank 0 (in slots 1 and 3) now included one 100-MHz DIMM and one new 200-MHz DIMM, so it ran at the slower speed of 100 MHz. Similarly, Bank 1 (in slots 2 and 4) now included one 100-MHz DIMM and one 200-MHz DIMM, so it also ran at the slower speed.

Most users won't test the speed of the RAM after installing it. They're just happy that they have more memory. However, when speeds are mixed in the same bank, users won't get the higher performance.

Shopping for RAM

When shopping for RAM, you need to determine the clock speed of your computer and then determine the DDR name. You can boot into BIOS, as shown in Chapter 2, "Understanding Motherboards and BIOS," to identify the clock speed used by RAM and then plug it into the formula to determine the standard name and module name.

If you have access to the Internet, there's an easier way. You can go to one of the memory sites, such as *Crucial.com* or *Kingston.com*, and use one of their tools. You can enter the make and model of your computer, and the tool will tell you what memory is supported. *Crucial.com* also has an application that you can download and run to identify your motherboard, the type and speeds of supported RAM, how much RAM is installed, and recommendations for upgrading the RAM. Another tool that can help is CPU-Z (described at the end of this chapter).

> **EXAM TIP**
>
> When shopping for memory, you'll find that most memory resellers use the module name, such as PC3-6400. You'll need to match this with the speed of the clock on the target system. Also, remember that the DDR versions are not compatible. PC2-6400 indicates DDR2, and PC3-6400 indicates DDR3.

Parity and ECC

Desktop systems rarely need extra hardware to detect or correct memory errors, but some advanced servers need this ability. The two primary error-detection technologies are *parity* and *error correction code (ECC)*. When shopping for RAM on desktop systems, you'll almost always buy non-parity and non-ECC RAM.

> **NOTE   APPLICATIONS CHECK FOR ERRORS**
>
> Applications routinely check for errors and often detect and correct errors without the need for parity or ECC RAM.

Parity works by using 9 bits for every byte instead of 8 bits. It sets the ninth bit to a 0 or a 1 for each byte when writing data to RAM. Parity can be odd parity or even parity, referring to odd and even numbers.

Odd parity is common, and when used, it ensures that the 9 bits always have an odd number of 1s. For example, if the 8 data bits were 1010 1010, it has four 1s. Four is an even number, so the parity bit needs to be a 1. Whenever data is written to RAM, the parity bit is calculated and written with each byte.

When the data is read, the system calculates the parity from the 9 bits. If it ever detects an even number of 1s, it knows there is an error, meaning that the data isn't valid and should not be used. Parity can't fix the problem; it just reports the error.

ECC RAM uses additional circuitry and can detect and correct errors. This extra circuitry adds significantly to the cost of the RAM and should be purchased only when necessary. For example, spacecraft that might be exposed to solar flares commonly use ECC RAM. Additionally, some high-end scientific and financial servers need it to ensure that the data in RAM remains error-free.

Rambus and RDRAM

Another type of DRAM is *Rambus DRAM (RDDRAM)*. More commonly, you see it referred to as Rambus, Rambus DRAM, or RDRAM. RDRAM is not compatible with any of the DDR versions and is rarely used.

The circuit boards are called *Rambus in-line memory modules (RIMMs)* instead of DIMMs. When installing RDRAM, you must install it in pairs. In some cases, only one circuit card has memory and the second circuit card in the pair is needed to complete the circuit. The second card is called a *continuity RIMM (CRIMM)*.

EXAM TIP

Rambus and RDRAM are mentioned in the CompTIA objectives, but don't be surprised if you never see a RIMM. They aren't used in new computers, but you might see one in an older computer. You can identify RIMMs by the distinctive metal covering over the chips.

RDRAM generates quite a bit of heat. To dissipate the heat, the chips are covered with a piece of metal acting as a heat sink or heat spreader. This makes them easy to identify because DDR SDRAM is not covered with metal.

CPUs

The *processor*, or *central processing unit (CPU)*, is the brain of the computer. It does the majority of the processing work and is a key factor in the overall performance of a system. Over the years, CPUs have steadily improved, and as a computer technician, you're expected to know some basics about them.

There are two primary manufacturers of computers used in computers: *Intel* and *Advanced Micro Devices (AMD)*.

- **Intel.** Intel is the largest seller of CPUs, selling about 80 percent to 85 percent of all CPUs. It manufactures other products as well, including chipsets, motherboards, memory, and SSDs.

- **AMD.** AMD is the only significant competition to Intel for CPUs, and it sells about 10 percent to 15 percent of all CPUs. It also manufactures other products, including graphics processors, chipsets, and motherboards.

It's possible to purchase a new CPU and install it in a motherboard as part of an upgrade. An important question to ask is, "What should I buy?" When shopping, you'll see names like the following:

- Intel Core i7-960 Processor 3.2 GHz 8 MB Cache Socket LGA 1366
- Phenom II X4 965 AM3 3.4 GHz 512KB 45 NM

Will either of these fit in your motherboard? You might not know right now, but by the end of this chapter, you'll have the information to answer that question.

> **NOTE   RISC**
>
> You might hear about Advanced RISC Machine (ARM) processors. ARM uses a *reduced instruction set computer (RISC)* architecture and often runs more quickly and with less power than Intel and AMD-based CPUs, so these processors don't need fans. ARM processors are popular in tablets such as the iPad, but you can't replace CPUs in a tablet. You can replace CPUs in computers, so the Intel and AMD CPUs are more important to understand as a computer technician.

32-bit vs. 64-bit

CPUs are identified as either 32-bit or 64-bit. Similarly, operating systems and many applications are referred to as either 32-bit or 64-bit. Key points to remember include the following:

- Windows operating systems come in both 32-bit and 64-bit versions.
- A 64-bit CPU is required to run a 64-bit operating system.
- A 64-bit operating system is required for 64-bit applications.
- A 64-bit CPU will also run 32-bit software.

The numbers 32 and 64 refer to the address bus discussed in Chapter 2. As a reminder, the address bus is used to address memory locations. A 32-bit CPU supports a 32-bit address bus and can address 2^{32} memory locations, or 4 GB of RAM. A 64-bit CPU supports a 64-bit address bus and can address 2^{64} memory locations, or about 17 EB.

> **NOTE   NOT REALLY 4 GB**
>
> The CPU also uses this address bus to address devices in the system in addition to RAM. Because of this, a 32-bit system reserves some of the address space for the other devices. If you install 4 GB of RAM in a 32-bit system, you find that operating system can use only about 3.3 GB.

Operating systems and applications have gotten more sophisticated over the years. Developers have programmed extra features and capabilities, but all of these extras consume additional RAM. For many users, 4 GB of RAM simply isn't enough.

Due to the demand, developers such as Microsoft have created 64-bit versions of their operating systems. However, these 64-bit operating systems can run only on 64-bit CPUs. If you want to directly address more than 4 GB of RAM, you need both a 64-bit CPU and a 64-bit operating system.

- **32-bit and x86.** You often see 32-bit operating systems and software referred to as x86. This is a reference to the long line of Intel CPUs that ended in 86 and can run 32-bit software. AMD processors have different names but are also known to be x86-compatible.

- **64-bit.** Intel refers to its 64-bit processors as Intel 64, and AMD calls its 64-bit processors AMD64. Software makers often refer to 64-bit compatible software as x64.

EXAM TIP

If you want to use 64-bit operating systems, you must have a 64-bit CPU, but you do not need to have software designed specifically for a CPU model. For example, Windows operating systems will work with either Intel or AMD CPUs.

CPU Cores

Most CPUs today have multiple cores within them. Each *core* is a fully functioning processor. With multiple cores, the CPU can divide tasks among each core. The result is a faster system.

Operating systems view the multiple cores as individual CPUs. For example, a single eight-core processor will appear in Task Manager as though it is eight separate processors, as shown in Figure 3-6.

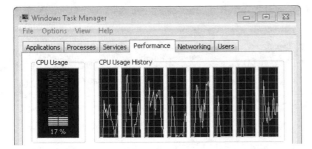

FIGURE 3-6 Task Manager showing eight cores of a single CPU.

MORE INFO **CHAPTER 13, "USING WINDOWS OPERATING SYSTEMS"**

Figure 3-6 shows a partial view of Windows Task Manager. You can start it on Windows systems by pressing Ctrl+Shift+Esc. Chapter 13 provides more details about Task Manager, including how to interpret the displays.

It's worth noting that Figure 3-6 is the same view you'd see if you had an Intel four-core processor with hyper-threading enabled. Hyper-threading is described later in this chapter.

A key point to remember is that even when a CPU has multiple cores, it is still a single chip that plugs into the motherboard. Motherboards are available that accept multiple CPUs, but they are more common on servers than on desktop systems. Most desktop systems have a single CPU, and it's common to see CPUs with multiple cores.

Hyper-Threading

Hyper-Threading Technology (HT) is used on some Intel CPUs to double the number of instruction sets the CPU can process at a time. Within a CPU, a thread is an ordered group of instructions that produce a result. When hyper-threading is used, a single CPU can process two threads at a time.

This is not physically the same as a multiple-core CPU. However, just as a dual-core CPU simulates two physical CPUs, a single-core CPU with hyper-threading simulates two physical CPUs. Operating systems can't tell the difference.

> **NOTE ENABLE IN BIOS**
>
> Hyper-threading needs to be enabled in the BIOS before the operating system is installed for it to work. This is usually listed as hyper-threading within a CPU Technology Support menu.

Intel makes use of both hyper-threading and multiple cores on some of its CPUs. For example, Figure 3-7 shows a screen shot of the System Information tool in Windows 7. It identifies the processor as an Intel Core i7 CPU with four cores and eight logical processors. Each core is using hyper-threading, and the operating system interprets it as eight CPUs.

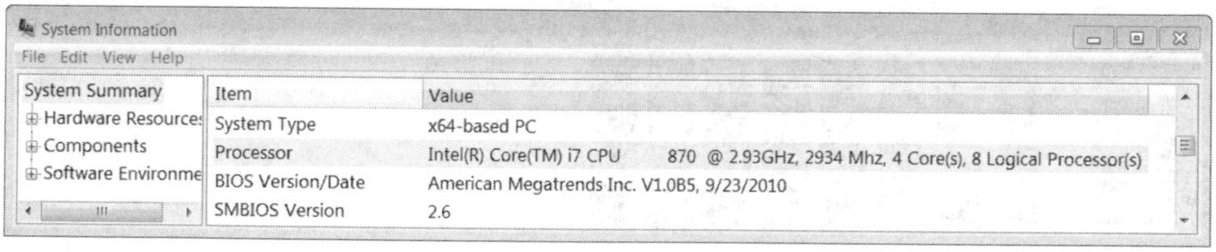

Item	Value
System Type	x64-based PC
Processor	Intel(R) Core(TM) i7 CPU 870 @ 2.93GHz, 2934 Mhz, 4 Core(s), 8 Logical Processor(s)
BIOS Version/Date	American Megatrends Inc. V1.0B5, 9/23/2010
SMBIOS Version	2.6

FIGURE 3-7 Msinfo32 showing that hyper-threading is enabled.

> **MORE INFO CHAPTER 2 AND CHAPTER 14**
>
> Chapter 2 introduced the System Information tool as a way to check your BIOS version. There are several ways to launch this tool, including entering **msinfo32** at the command prompt. Chapter 14, "Using the Command Prompt," covers how to start and use the command prompt.

CPU Cache

Many computer components and software applications use some type of *cache*. As a simple example, web browsers use a browser cache. When you go to a website, information is transmitted over the Internet and displayed in your web browser, and it is also stored in the browser cache. If you go to the website again, data can be retrieved from the browser cache rather than downloaded from the Internet again. The browser uses different techniques to ensure that it displays current data, but if that data is on your drive, it is displayed much more quickly than it would be if it had to be downloaded again.

The CPU has cache that it uses for fast access to data. If the CPU expects to use some type of information again, it keeps that information in cache. A significant difference between the web browser cache and the CPU cache is that the CPU cache is RAM and the web browser cache is stored as a file on a hard drive.

> **NOTE CACHE**
>
> Cache is commonly referred to as an area where data is stored for a short time for easy retrieval. It's important to realize that cache can be memory areas that are volatile or can be temporary files stored on hard drives that are kept after a system is powered down.

CPU Cache Types

The two primary types of cache used by CPUs are:

- **L1 cache.** This is the fastest, and it's located closest to the CPU. A multiple-core CPU has a separate *L1 cache* located on each CPU core.
- **L2 cache.** *L2 cache* is a little slower than L1 cache, and it is shared by all cores of the CPU. In older systems, L2 cache was stored on the motherboard, but today it is much more common for L2 cache to be part of the CPU.

> **NOTE L3 CACHE**
>
> *L3 cache* is used on some systems, but it isn't as common as L1 and L2. When used, it can be on the motherboard or on the CPU. It is slower than L2 cache and is shared among all cores.

Figure 3-8 shows the relationship of the CPUs to cache and RAM installed on the motherboard. In the diagram, the CPU is a two-core CPU, and you can see that the L1 cache is included on each core and that L2 cache is shared by each of the cores. When the CPU needs data, it will check the L1 cache first, the L2 cache next, and then the L3 cache if it exists. If the data isn't in cache, the CPU retrieves it from RAM.

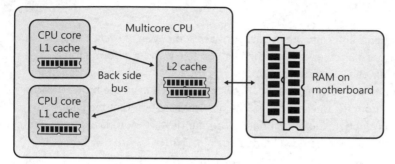

FIGURE 3-8 CPU and cache.

> **NOTE** **ACCESSING RAM WITHOUT NORTH BRIDGE.**
>
> As discussed in Chapter 2, newer CPUs access the motherboard RAM directly, as shown in Figure 3-8. On older CPUs, they access RAM through the north bridge portion of the chipset.

Many newer CPUs include L1 cache for each core, L2 cache for each core, and a single shared L3 cache—all on the same CPU chip.

Without cache, the CPU would have to store data in the motherboard RAM. The CPU cache is SRAM, which is much faster than the dynamic RAM used on the motherboard. Also, the motherboard RAM is physically farther away, adding more delays.

CPU Cache Size

The size of the CPU cache is small compared to the overall amount of memory in a system. For example, you might see cache sizes as low as 8 KB or as large as 20 MB. In contrast, most personal computers have 1 GB of RAM or more. The cache can be listed as just a total of all L1, L2, or L3 cache, or you might see it listed individually.

- **L1 is smallest.** L1 is sometimes stated as two numbers, such as 32 KB + 32 KB, to indicate it is using one cache for frequently used instructions and another cache for data. Sizes of 32 KB or 64 KB are common.

- **L2 is larger than L1.** When a CPU has separate L2 cache for each core, it is often identified as the amount per core. For example, a two-core CPU with 4 MB total L2 cache can be expressed as 2 × 2 MB, or just 2 MB per core. Sizes of 256 KB, 512 KB, and 1,024 KB are common.

- **L3 is larger than L2.** Sizes between 2 MB and 8 MB are common.

Speeds

The speed of a CPU is based on the speed of the crystal and the multiplier. For example, if the crystal speed is 100 MHz and the multiplier is 20, the CPU has a speed of 2 GHz (20 × 100). The faster the speed, the faster the CPU.

You commonly see the speed of the processor listed as only the multiplied speed. For example, in Figure 3-7 you can see that the processor is an Intel Core 7 CPU 870 and the clock is listed as 2.93 GHz. The system is using a 133.333-MHz clock (commonly listed as 133 MHz) and a 22-times multiplier.

> **NOTE   SPEEDS ARE VARIABLE**
>
> Most current processors can dynamically adjust the speed based on requests from the operating system or an application. When a boost in a CPU core is needed, the operating system can send a signal to make the core run faster. Intel refers to this as Turbo Boost, and AMD refers to it as Turbo Core.

Processors are rated based on the maximum speed they can handle, and more expensive processors can handle faster speeds. You can increase the speed by increasing the clock frequency, increasing the multiplier, or both. Most motherboards have this preselected, but it is sometimes possible to manipulate the clock or the multiplier to overclock the system. In some systems, the BIOS includes a Cell menu that enables you to increase the base frequency and increase the CPU Ratio (multiplier).

EXAM TIP

Overclocking a system is not recommended, but it is frequently done. If you overclock a system, you need to take extra steps to keep it cool, such as using liquid cooling. Liquid cooling is discussed later in this chapter.

Chapter 2 mentions the front side bus (FSB) and how it provides a direct connection between the CPU and the north bridge portion of the chipset. In the past, CPU speeds were stated as the FSB speed. Today, many CPUs have taken over the functionality of the north bridge. The CPU still needs to communicate with the chipset, and there are a few different ways this is done, including the following:

- **Intel Direct Media Interface (DMI).** The DMI can use multiple lanes, similar to Peripheral Component Interconnect Express (PCIe).
- **Intel's QuickPath Interconnect (QPI).** Each core in a processor has a separate two-way 20-lane QPI link to the chipset.
- **HyperTransport.** AMD uses *HyperTransport* with the FSB to increase the speed.

You still see CPUs advertised with a speed that you can use for comparisons. For example, one CPU might have a speed of 2.8 GHz and another might have a speed of 3.4 GHz. It's safe to assume that the 3.4-GHz CPU is faster, but the speed isn't always tied to the FSB.

Virtualization Support

Chapter 2 introduced virtualization concepts and instructions on how to enable virtualization in BIOS. As a reminder, virtualization software allows you to run multiple virtual machines (VMs) as guests within a single physical host computer. The CPU needs to support virtualization, and it usually needs to be enabled in BIOS. On many AMD-based systems, virtualization is enabled by default and cannot be disabled.

Most Intel and AMD CPUs include native support for virtualization. The exception is laptop computers, which sometimes include CPUs that do not support it. Intel refers to its virtualization support as VT-x, and AMD calls its support AMD-V. If you want to verify that a CPU or motherboard supports virtualization, look for those terms.

> **NOTE   COLD BOOT REQUIRED**
>
> If you change the virtualization setting in the BIOS, it's recommended that you do a cold boot. A cold boot completely powers down the computer. You should wait about 10 seconds and then restart the computer. In contrast, a warm boot shuts down the software and restarts it, but does not shut down the power.

Integrated GPU

Graphics is one of the areas of a computer that has been increasing as quickly as the CPU area, and the two are starting to merge. Early computers could display only letters on a screen 80 characters wide. Today, it's common to watch high-quality video streaming from a website or to play games with computer-generated graphics and amazingly realistic scenery.

The following list describes the progression of graphics capabilities on computers:

- **Onboard graphics.** Graphics capability was built into the chipset. This was often very basic but met most needs.

- **Expansion cards.** You could install a graphics card with a dedicated graphics processing unit (GPU) and plug it into an available expansion slot. Instead of the CPU doing the graphics calculations, the GPU would do them. Peripheral Component Interconnect (PCI) cards were an early version.

- **Dedicated graphics slots.** Accelerated Graphics Port (AGP) provided a single dedicated graphics slot that worked separately from PCI. AGP did not compete with PCI, so it provided better performance. Later, PCIe allowed graphics cards to use their own dedicated lanes, and it replaced AGP.

- **Direct access graphics.** The CPU interacted with the AGP slot via the chipset. Newer CPUs bypass the chipset and interact directly with a dedicated PCIe slot used for graphics. This is common in many systems today.

- **Integrated graphics processing unit (GPU).** A recent trend in newer CPUs is to include an *integrated GPU* on the CPU. GPUs can provide high-quality graphics without the additional cost of a graphics card. However, these are not as powerful as a dedicated card.

AMD refers to some chips with a GPU as an accelerated processing unit (APU) instead of a CPU. APUs can include a GPU or other specialized capability, and the AMD Fusion is an example.

CPU Versions

There is a dizzying number of different processors. You're not expected to know the characteristics of each individual CPU, but you should be able to recognize the names and know the manufacturers. The objectives specifically list the CPU socket types you should know, but for the sockets to make sense, you need to have a little bit of knowledge about the CPU versions.

Intel and AMD use code names related to the manufacturing process and then create different processor families with the process. The manufacturing process is stated as a measurement and refers to the distance between certain components within the chip. Many current CPUs have processes of 65 nanometers (nm), 45 nm, 32 nm, and 22 nm. A nanometer is one billionth of a meter and is often used to express atomic scale dimensions, such as the width of an atom or the width of a group of molecules. In this case, smaller is better.

> **NOTE MOORE'S LAW**
>
> One of the founders of Intel, Gordon Moore, predicted in 1965 that the number of transistors that could be placed on a chip would double about every two years. This miniaturization trend has been consistent since his prediction. With more transistors, chips are faster and more complex, and the process used to create them is smaller.

The following are recent Intel and AMD code names:

- **Intel**
  - Core—65-nm and 45-nm process
  - Nehalem—45-nm process
  - Sandy Bridge—32-nm process
  - Ivy Bridge—22-nm process
- **AMD**
  - K8—65-nm, 90-nm, and 130-nm processes
  - K9—processors were never released
  - K10—65-nm process
  - K10.5—45-nm process
  - Bulldozer—22-nm process

Table 3-3 shows a list of common Intel code names and some of their related CPUs. You can see that the Core i3, i5, and i7 family names are frequently repeated.

TABLE 3-3 Intel Code Names and Processors

Architecture Name	CPU Family names
Core	Core 2 Duo, Core 2 Quad, Core 2 Extreme
Nehalem	Intel Pentium, Core i3, Core i5, Core i7, Xeon
Sandy Bridge	Celeron, Pentium, Core i3, Core i5, Core i7
Ivy Bridge	Core i5, Core i7, Xeon

The Core i3, i5, and i7 series represents a Good, Better, Best philosophy, with the i3 versions representing the basic version and the i7 versions providing the most power. The number (such as i3 or i5) doesn't refer to the number of cores.

It's also important to realize that there are significant differences between a Nehalem Core i5 and an Ivy Bridge Core i5. The Ivy Bridge versions have smaller processes and are more powerful.

> **MORE INFO** **WIKIPEDIA**
>
> This chapter does not list all the existing Intel and AMD CPUs. If you want to see a list of Intel or AMD processors, check out these two Wikipedia pages: *http://en .wikipedia.org/wiki/List_of_Intel_microprocessors* and *http://en.wikipedia.org/wiki /List_of_AMD_microprocessors*.

Table 3-4 shows a list of common AMD code names and their related CPUs. The primary AMD CPUs that you find in desktop computers are Sempron, Athlon, and Phenom.

TABLE 3-4 AMD Code Names and Processors

Architecture Name	CPU Family names
K8	Opteron, Athlon 64, Athlon 64 FX, Athlon 64 X2, Sempron, Turion 64, Turion 64 X2
K10	Opteron, Phenom, Athlon, Athlon X2, Sempron
K10.5	Phenom II, Athlon II, Sempron, Turion II
Bulldozer	FX (Zambezi), Interlagos Opteron

EXAM TIP

Many AMD processor names give clues as to what they include. If the name includes 64, it is a 64-bit CPU. When the name has an X (such as X2), it indicates how many cores the processor has.

CPU Socket Types

A CPU plugs into a *socket* on the motherboard. There was a time when just about every motherboard had the same socket type, but that certainly isn't the case today. Instead, there are a wide variety of different socket types for different types of CPUs. If you ever need to replace a CPU, it's important to recognize that there are different types of sockets. The following sections talk about some sockets used by Intel and AMD, with information about how they are installed.

Zero Insertion Force

It's important that each of the pins on a CPU has a good connection to the motherboard. In early versions of CPUs, this was accomplished by creating a tight connection between the pins and the socket. This required technicians to use some force to plug the CPU into the socket. Unfortunately, it was easy to bend one or more pins, and bent pins would often break, making the CPU unusable.

Manufacturers came up with a great idea to eliminate the problem—*zero insertion force (ZIF)* sockets. A ZIF socket has a locking lever. You can place a CPU into a socket without any force other than gravity, and after the CPU is in place, you lock the lever to secure it. This lever ensures that the pins are making a solid connection to the motherboard.

Figure 3-9 shows a ZIF socket with the lever raised. The CPU is removed and standing up on the left. You can see that there are some areas on the CPU where there aren't any pins. These provide a key, and they match up to areas on the socket where there aren't any pin holes.

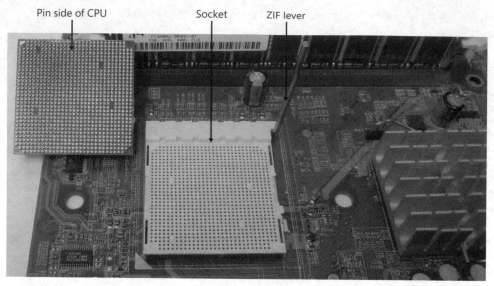

FIGURE 3-9 Processor and ZIF socket.

NOTE CPUS ARE KEYED

CPU sockets and CPUs are keyed so that the CPU fits into a socket in only one way. If you feel any resistance when putting a CPU into a ZIF socket, it indicates that the pins aren't lined up. You should double-check the keying and ensure that the CPU is lined up correctly. If you try to force it, you will likely bend some pins and ruin either the chip or the socket.

PGA vs. LGA

The socket shown in Figure 3-9 is a *pin grid array (PGA)* type of socket. It includes holes into which the pins can be plugged. A newer type of socket is a *land grid array (LGA)* socket. Instead of the processor having pins and plugging into a socket with holes, the socket has small pins, and the CPU has small pins created as bumps or pads. When the CPU is installed, the pins and bumps line up, making the connection.

When using an LGA socket, the CPU sits on top of the socket but is locked in place with a flip-top case. Figure 3-10 shows an example of a flip-top case used with an Intel processor.

This socket has a hinged top and a lever that locks the case when it's closed. You unlock the lever, open the case, and remove the CPU. When installing a new CPU, ensure that the keys line up, place the CPU in the case, close the top, and lock it with the lever. Remember to use ESD protection when handling the CPU.

FIGURE 3-10 Removing processor from a flip-top case. Diagram provided by Intel. [Copyright © Intel Corporation. All rights reserved. Used by permission.]

Another type of array you might run across is ball grid array (BGA). In a BGA chip, the pins on the CPU are replaced with balls of solder. The chip is mounted in the socket and then heated, often in an oven, to melt the solder. Manufacturers can fit more pins on a BGA CPU, and they are sometimes used in mobile devices.

Intel CPU Sockets

The following list describes recent Intel sockets:

- **LGA 775.** 775 pins. Also called Socket T. Replaced Socket 478.

- **LGA 1366.** 1,366 pins. Also called Socket B and designed to replace LGA 755 in high-end desktop computers.

- **LGA 2011.** 2,011 pins and released in 2011. Also called Socket R. It replaces LGA 1366 sockets in high-end desktop systems.

- **LGA 1156.** 1,156 pins. Also called Socket H or Socket H1.

- **LGA 1155.** 1,155 pins. Also called Socket H2 and replaces LGA 1156 in basic desktop systems. LGA 1,156 CPUs will work in LGA 1155, but the BIOS may need to be upgraded.

EXAM TIP

Notice that the numbers indicate the number of pins and are not a reflection of newer or older sockets. Also, each of these Intel sockets is an LGA socket.

Table 3-5 lists the common Intel sockets along with some CPUs used with them, busses they support, and supported DDR channels.

TABLE 3-5 Intel Sockets and Related CPUs

Type	CPUs, Busses, DDR Channels
LGA 775 (Socket T)	Pentium 4, Pentium D, Core 2 Duo, Core 2 Quad, Celeron, Xeon Front side bus, single channel DDR2 and DDR3 RAM
LGA 1366 (Socket B)	Core i7, Xeon, Celeron QPI, triple channel DDR3 RAM
LGA 2011 (Socket R)	Core i7, Xeon QPI, DMI, quad channel DDR3 RAM
LGA 1156 (Socket H or H1)	Core i3, Core i5, Core i7, Celeron, Pentium, Xeon DMI, dual channel DDR3 RAM
LGA 1155 (Socket H2)	Core i3, Core i5, Core i7, Celeron, Pentium DMI, dual channel DDR3 RAM

AMD CPU Sockets

The following list describes recent AMD sockets:

- **Socket 940.** 940 pins (PGA).
- **Socket AM2.** 940 pins (PGA). Not compatible with Socket 940.
- **Socket AM2+.** 940 pins (PGA). Replaces AM2. CPUs that can fit in AM2 can also fit in AM2+.
- **Socket AM3.** 941 pins (PGA). Replaces AM2+. Supports DDR3. CPUs designed for AM3 will also work in AM2+ sockets, but CPUs designed for AM2+ might not work in AM3 sockets.
- **Socket AM3+.** 942 pins (PGA). Replaces AM3. CPUs that can fit in AM3 can also fit in AM3+.
- **Socket FM1.** 905 pins (PGA). Used for accelerated processing units (APUs).
- **Socket F.** 1,207 pins (LGA). Used on servers and replaced by Socket C32 and Socket G34.

Table 3-6 lists the common AMD sockets along with some CPUs used with them, busses they support, and supported DDR channels.

TABLE 3-6 AMD Sockets and Related CPUs

Socket	CPUs, Busses, DDR Channels
940	Opteron and Athlon 64 FX FSB with HyperTransport version 1, single channel DDR2 RAM
AM2	Athlon 64, Athlon 64 X2, Athlon FX, Sempron, Phenom, Opteron FSB with HyperTransport version 2, single channel DDR2 RAM
AM2+	Athlon 64, Athlon 64 X2, Athlon II, Sempron, Phenom, Phenom II, Opteron FSB with HyperTransport version 3, single channel DDR2 RAM

AM3	Phenom II, Athlon II, Sempron, Opteron FSB with HyperTransport version 3, single channel DDR2 and dual channel DDR3 RAM
AM3+	Phenom II, Athlon II, Sempron, Opteron FSB with HyperTransport version 3, dual channel DDR3 RAM
FM1	Fusion and Athlon II APUs FSB with HyperTransport version 3, dual channel DDR3 RAM
F	Opteron, Athlon 64 FX FSB with HyperTransport version 3, single channel DDR2 RAM

Comparing Names

Earlier in this chapter, I listed two CPUs using common marketing names. To tie some of this together, here are the two CPUs with an explanation of the names. I'm hoping these names make a lot more sense at this point.

- **Intel Core i7-960 Processor 3.2 GHz 8 MB Cache Socket LGA 1366.** This name indicates that it is an Intel processor in the Core i7 family with a model number of 960 and a 3.2-GHz multiplied clock. The 8-MB cache phrase refers to the total amount of cache. Last, LGA 1366 indicates the type of socket into which the processor will plug.

- **Phenom II X4 965 AM3 3.4 GHz 512 KB 45 NM.** This indicates that it is an AMD Phenom II processor with a model number of 960. X4 indicates that the processor has four cores, and AM3 indicates the socket type. The 3.4-GHz clock speed is the internal speed of the processor. Cache size is indicated by 512 KB, and in this case, it indicates the L2 cache size for each of the cores. The process is 45 nm.

Cooling

CPUs have millions—and sometimes billions—of miniaturized transistors within them, all connected with extremely small wires. If these transistors or wires get too hot, they can easily break, rendering the CPU useless. Manufacturers spend a lot of time designing these chips, and one of their goals is to keep temperatures within acceptable limits. However, most of the cooling occurs externally.

Heat Sinks, Fans, and Thermal Paste

Common methods of cooling a CPU include using a *heat sink*, a fan, and *thermal paste*. Take a look at Figure 3-11 as you read about how these components work together.

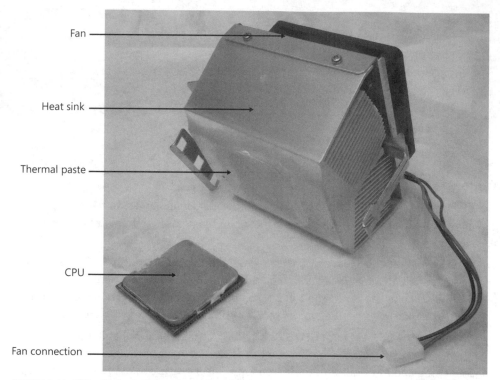

Fan

Heat sink

Thermal paste

CPU

Fan connection

FIGURE 3-11 CPU with heat sink and attached fan.

- **Heat sink.** A heat sink is a piece of metal that draws heat from the CPU and dissipates it into the air. Heat sinks have multiple fins to increase the surface area and to allow air to easily flow through them. The fins are usually flared to allow more air through.

- **Fan.** A fan is attached to the heat sink to increase the airflow around the fins. These are called CPU fans. They aren't attached to the CPU but usually plug into the motherboard close to the CPU. Many CPU fans have variable speeds and spin faster when the CPU gets hotter.

- **Thermal paste.** Heat sinks commonly have clamps to secure them to the motherboard and provide a better connection with the CPU. However, there are microscopic gaps in the metal on both the CPU and the heat sink, so it isn't possible to get 100 percent contact between the components. Thermal paste is used to improve this connection. This paste fills these microscopic gaps and also helps draw heat from the CPU into the heat sink.

 EXAM TIP

When replacing a CPU, ensure that you clean off the old thermal paste from the heat sink and apply new thermal paste.

If you are replacing a CPU, you'll need to clean off the old thermal paste from the heat sink. Some vendors sell specialized cleaning compounds to remove old paste, but you can often use cotton swabs and isopropyl alcohol to remove it.

After installing the new CPU into the socket and locking the ZIF arm, place a dab of the paste in the center of the CPU. When you attach the heat sink and clamp it down, the pressure will spread the paste evenly between the heat sink and the CPU. Be careful not to apply too much paste; you need only enough to fill the microscopic gaps between the CPU and the heat sink.

Liquid Cooling

An advanced method of keeping a system cool is using a liquid-based cooling system. Liquid-based cooling systems use water (most commonly) or some other liquid that is pumped through the cooling system.

For example, Figure 3-12 shows a basic diagram of a liquid-based cooling system. A specialized heat sink is attached to the CPU, using thermal paste just like a standard heat sink. However, this heat sink has channels so that the liquid can flow through it. Tubing is connected from the pump to the heat sink, and the pump constantly pumps the liquid through the heat sink.

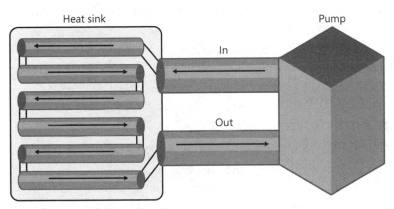

FIGURE 3-12 Liquid-cooled heat sink.

EXAM TIP

Liquid-based cooling can be used for any components that use a heat sink. This includes CPUs, GPUs, and chipsets.

One of the biggest challenges with a liquid-based cooling system is ensuring that the tubing connections do not leak. This is one place where you don't want to skimp on quality. The liquid is usually water, and if it leaks, it could easily destroy the system.

Liquid-based cooling systems are most common among gamers and hobbyists. These people often overclock the processors to get more power out of them, but overclocking generates more heat. Overclocking is sometimes possible by changing jumpers on the motherboard or by manipulating BIOS settings, but manufacturers discourage the practice.

> ✓ **Quick Check**
>
> 1. What is another name for Socket H2?
> 2. What's the best way to keep an overclocked CPU cool?
>
> **Quick Check Answers**
>
> 1. LGA 1155.
> 2. Liquid cooling.

Troubleshooting

You might occasionally run across a system that is having a problem with the CPU or RAM. Sometimes the problems are consistent, but more often they are intermittent; sometimes you'll see the problem, sometimes you won't.

Intermittent problems are frequently related to overheating, so a good first step is to ensure that the system has adequate airflow. Shut the system down, open the case, and either vacuum it with an ESD-safe vacuum or take it outside and blow it out with compressed air.

Common Symptoms

The following are some common symptoms and possible causes related to the CPU or RAM:

- **Unexpected shutdowns.** If the system is randomly shutting down or rebooting, the most likely cause is a heat problem. Check the ventilation and clean out the fans.

- **System lockups.** When a computer stops responding to inputs from the keyboard or mouse, technicians refer to it as frozen or locked up. This can also be due to heat issues. Check the ventilation.

- **Continuous reboots.** In some cases, a hardware issue can prevent the system from booting completely. It starts, gets so far, and then resets itself. This is more common after a faulty software update, but it can be due to a hardware problem. If you've just replaced hardware, double-check your steps. If that isn't the issue, boot into Safe Mode and troubleshoot the operating system using the steps provided in Chapter 17, "Troubleshooting Windows Operating Systems."

Tools

If you've cleaned out the system and you're still having intermittent problems, there are two primary things to check:

- **Power supply.** An overloaded or failing power supply can cause intermittent problems. Use a multimeter to verify the voltages. If the voltages are out of tolerance, replace the power supply.

- **RAM.** It is possible to have a certain area of RAM that is faulty. The system can work until it writes data to that area, and then it shuts down or freezes. In some cases, you receive a stop error or blue screen of death (BSOD) with an error code indicating a memory problem. If you suspect a RAM problem, use a memory checker to run memory diagnostics.

EXAM TIP

The two primary *hardware* sources of intermittent problems are the power supply and RAM. The primary *software* source of intermittent problems is a virus or some type of malicious software. Chapter 26, "Recognizing Malware and Other Threats," covers viruses in more depth, but running up-to-date antivirus software usually reveals and removes the problem. Occasionally, you'll need to boot into Safe Mode and run the up-to-date antivirus software.

Windows Memory Diagnostics

Windows Vista and Windows 7 include the Windows Memory Diagnostic tool, and steps later in this section show how to run it. It's easy to run and can perform in-depth testing of the system RAM and the cache within the CPU.

The diagnostics include three sets of tests (basic, standard, and extended). By default, it runs two passes of the standard set of tests, and this is usually good enough. If this passes but you still suspect you have memory problems, you can choose other options by pressing F1 to modify them. For example, if you have an intermittent problem and want to do detailed tests for a day or longer, you can set the pass count to 0 and it will run continuously.

You can use the following steps on a Windows 7 system to run the Windows Memory Diagnostics tool:

1. Click Start and type **Memory** in the Search Programs And Files text box.

2. Select Windows Memory Diagnostic.

3. Select Restart Now and check for problems. After the system reboots, the tests will start and you'll see a display similar to the following graphic. If any errors are identified, they will be displayed in the Status area, but they usually won't stop the diagnostic from running. After the test completes, the system automatically reboots.

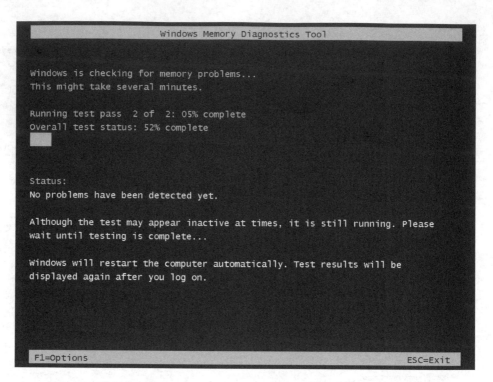

```
                    Windows Memory Diagnostics Tool

Windows is checking for memory problems...
This might take several minutes.

Running test pass  2 of  2: 05% complete
Overall test status: 52% complete


Status:
No problems have been detected yet.

Although the test may appear inactive at times, it is still running. Please
wait until testing is complete...

Windows will restart the computer automatically. Test results will be
displayed again after you log on.




 F1=Options                                                      ESC=Exit
```

4. About a minute or so after you log on, you'll see a balloon message appear in the system tray at the bottom right indicating the results. It appears and then fades out. If you miss it, you can also view the results in the System log via the Event Viewer. It's listed with a source of MemoryDiagnostics-Results and an Event ID of 1201.

If you're unable to boot into the operating system, you can access the Windows Memory Diagnostic by using several other methods. Each of the following methods will start the Windows Recovery Environment (Windows RE), showing the System Recovery Options, as shown in Figure 3-13. You can then select Windows Memory Diagnostic.

- Press F8 as the system is booting to access the Advanced Boot Options page and select Repair Your Computer.

- Start from a Windows Vista installation DVD, select the Language, and then click Repair Your Computer.

- Create a system repair disc and use it to boot directly into the Windows RE.

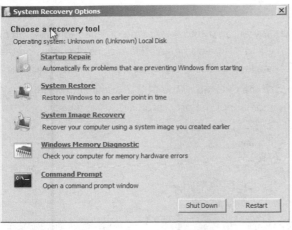

FIGURE 3-13 Running Windows Memory Diagnostic from boot DVD.

MORE INFO **CHAPTER 17**

Chapter 17 covers the Event Viewer, including how to launch it and access different log files. It also includes information on the other system recovery options and how to create a system repair disc in Windows 7.

If the memory diagnostic gives any errors, you might be able to do a quick fix by reseating the memory sticks. Power your system down and open it up. Hook up an ESD strap to ground yourself with the system and then locate the RAM. Press the tabs on each side to pop out each DIMM, and then push each back into the slot until the tabs lock. This same fix can also be used on any expansion card.

You might be wondering why this works. Electrical components expand and contract from heat and cold, causing some movement. Additionally, the electrical contacts can become tarnished, preventing a good connection. When you pop it out and push it back, the friction scrapes the tarnish off the contacts. With the tarnish removed, it has a good connection.

NOTE **CLEANING CONTACTS**

You can clean contacts with contact cleaner created specifically for this purpose. You can also use isopropyl alcohol and a lint-free cloth or cotton swab. You should not rub the contacts with a pencil eraser. The eraser removes the tarnish by scraping it off, but it leaves residue and can cause ESD damage.

CPU-Z

CPU-Z is a handy freeware utility that you can use to view some detailed information on your system. It's been around a long time and has helped many technicians. A copy is on the CD, and you can find a link about the installation here: *getcertifiedgetahead.com/aplus.aspx*.

Figure 3-14 shows a screen shot of the CPU tab of the CPU-Z application. You can see that this provides some detailed information about the processor, clocks, and cache.

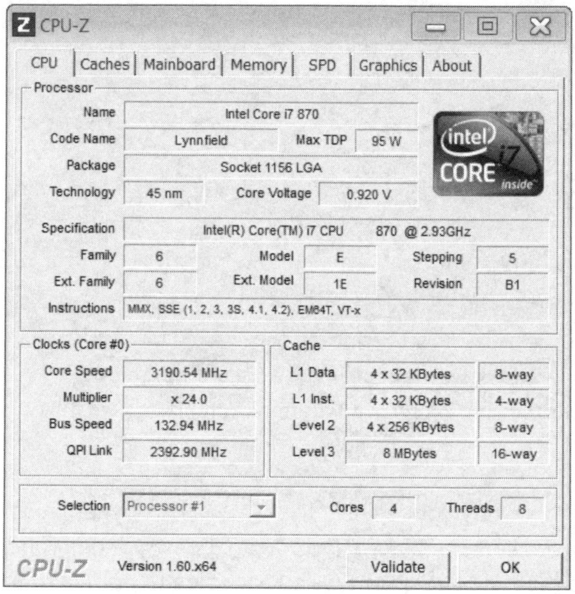

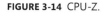

FIGURE 3-14 CPU-Z.

If you click the Mainboard tab, it gives you details about your motherboard and BIOS. The Memory tab provides overall information about installed memory, and the SPD tab enables you to select individual memory slots to determine what is installed. As you'd expect, the Graphics tab provides details about the graphics card. The About tab includes buttons you can use to save the details of the report as either a text file or an HTML file.

> ✔ **Quick Check**
>
> 1. What are two primary hardware problems that can cause system fails?
> 2. Where can you determine how much RAM is installed in a system?
>
> **Quick Check Answers**
>
> 1. Faulty power supply or faulty RAM.
> 2. BIOS or System Information (msinfo32).

Chapter Summary

- Systems use synchronous dynamic RAM (SDRAM) for primary memory. Static RAM (SRAM) is used for L1, L2, and L3 cache. Common versions of SDRAM are DDR, DDR2, and DDR3.

- Memory comes on circuit cards called DIMMs for desktop computers and SODIMMs for laptops. DIMMs and SODIMMs come in different sizes for different DDR versions.

- Dual-channel and triple-channel RAM provide additional 64-bit paths for transferring data to and from RAM. When installing multichannel DIMMs, install matched sets in the same bank. Banks are normally the same color. On an Intel dual-channel mother-board, Bank 0 includes slots 1 and 3.

- A triple-channel motherboard has six slots for RAM, and RAM should be purchased in matched sets of three DIMMs.

- The speed of RAM is tied directly to the clock. The formula to calculate DDR3 RAM speed is: Clk $\times$ 4 $\times$ 2 $\times$ 64 / 8. For a 200-MHz clock, the speed is 200 $\times$ 4 $\times$ 2 $\times$ 64 / 8, or 12,800 MB/s.

- The DDR3 standard name is derived from the clock $\times$ 8. For a 200-MHz clock, the DDR3 standard name is DDR3-1600. The module name is derived from the overall speed. The DDR3 module name with a 200-MHz clock is PC3-12800.

- If matched DIMMs are not used and a bank includes different speed DIMMs, the bank will default to the slowest speed.

- CPUs come in 32-bit and 64-bit versions, referring to how many bits they use to address memory. If you want to use more than 4 GB of RAM, you need a 64-bit CPU and a 64-bit operating system.

- Multiple-core CPUs include more than one fully functioning processor, and the operating system views each core as a separate CPU. Intel uses hyper-threading, which allows each core to process two threads at a time, and each core using hyper-threading is treated as a separate CPU by the operating system.

- CPUs use fast static RAM (SRAM) as cache to improve processing. They commonly include L1, L2, and sometimes L3 cache. L1 is fastest and closest to the CPU, and L3 is slowest and farthest away. L1 is smallest, and L3 is the largest. When the CPU needs data, it looks in L1, then L2, and then L3.

- The speed of the CPU is based on the speed of the clock and a multiplier. It is usually listed as the multiplied speed, such as 3.4 GHz. Intel uses Turbo Boost and AMD uses Turbo Core to modify these speeds during operation.

- Most CPUs support virtualization. Intel refers to its support as VT-x, and AMD calls its support AMD-V. These settings can be enabled in BIOS on most systems.

- An integrated GPU refers to a graphics processor embedded within a CPU. AMD calls some of its integrated GPU chips APUs.

- Common Intel CPUs are Core i3, Core i5, and Core i7 series. Most Intel CPUs use LGA sockets. Common Intel sockets are: LGA 775 (Socket T), LGA 1366 (Socket B), LGA 2011 (Socket R), LGA 1156 (Socket H or H1), and LGA 1155 (Socket H2).
- Common AMD CPUs are Sempron, Athlon, and Phenom. Most AMD CPUs use PGA sockets, and common sockets are: Socket 940, AM2, AM2+, AM3, AM3+, FM1, and Socket F.
- CPUs are commonly kept cool with heat sinks and fans. When replacing a CPU, use thermal paste between the CPU and the heat sink. Liquid cooling is an advanced cooling practice.
- Hardware problems that can cause unexpected shutdowns and intermittent fails include overheating due to failed fans or inadequate ventilation, faulty power supply, or faulty RAM.
- Use a software memory tester to test RAM.

Chapter Review

Use the following questions to test your knowledge of the information in this chapter. The answers to these questions, and the explanations of why each answer choice is correct or incorrect, are located in the "Answers" section at the end of this chapter.

1. You are replacing two DDR3 DIMMs in an Intel dual-channel motherboard. Into which slots should you put them?

    A. Two different-colored slots

    B. Two identical-colored slots

    C. Separate banks

    D. Slots 1 and 4

2. You are shopping for replacement DDR3 RAM. Your system has a 400-MHz clock. What should you buy?

    A. PC3-400

    B. DDR3-400

    C. PC3-25600

    D. PC3-12800

3. An Intel CPU has two cores, but the operating system shows it has four CPUs. What feature allows this to happen?

   A. Hyper-threading

   B. HyperTransport

   C. Dual-channel RAM

   D. L2 cache

4. Of the following choices, which is fastest?

   A. L1 cache

   B. L2 cache

   C. L3 cache

   D. Triple-channel DDR3

5. Which of the following replaces the Intel Socket H?

   A. LGA 775

   B. LGA 1366

   C. LGA 1156

   D. LGA 1155

6. You are asked to troubleshoot a computer that is randomly rebooting or failing. Of the following choices, what hardware can cause these symptoms? (Choose all that apply.)

   A. RAM

   B. Fan

   C. Power supply

   D. Virus

Answers

1. **Correct Answer: B**

   A. **Incorrect:** Different-colored slots indicate different banks.

   B. **Correct:** Dual-channel RAM should be installed in the same bank, which is the same color on most motherboards.

   C. **Incorrect:** If you place the RAM in different banks, it will be used as single-channel RAM instead of dual-channel RAM.

   D. **Incorrect:** Slots 1 and 4 are always in different banks.

2. **Correct Answer: C**

   A. **Incorrect:** PC3-400 indicates a clock speed of 50 MHz.

   B. **Incorrect:** If the DDR3 name is used, it is identified as the clock times 8. 400 × 8 = 3,200, or DDR3-3200.

   C. **Correct:** The calculation for DDR3 is Clk × 4 × 2 × 64 / 8. 400 MHz × 4 × 2 × 64 / 8 = 25,600, so it is PC3-25600.

   D. **Incorrect:** PC3-12800 indicates a clock speed of 200 MHz.

3. **Correct Answer: A**

   A. **Correct:** Hyper-threading is supported on Intel CPUs and allows each core to appear as two CPUs.

   B. **Incorrect:** HyperTransport is used on AMD processors in place of a front side bus.

   C. **Incorrect:** Dual channel RAM provides two paths to RAM, but it does not affect the CPU cores.

   D. **Incorrect:** L2 cache is fast RAM stored on the CPU for improved performance, but it does not affect the CPU cores.

4. **Correct Answer: A**

   A. **Correct:** L1 cache is a fast cache, close to the CPU.

   B. **Incorrect:** L2 cache is slower than L1 cache.

   C. **Incorrect:** L3 cache is slower than L1 and L2 cache.

   D. **Incorrect:** Any type of DDR RAM is slower than L1, L2, or L3 cache.

5. **Correct Answer: D**

   A. **Incorrect:** LGA 775 is Socket T and was replaced by Socket B.

   B. **Incorrect:** LGA 1366 is Socket B.

   C. **Incorrect:** LGA 1156 is Socket H.

   D. **Correct:** The LGA 1155 is also known as Socket H2 and replaces Socket H or H1.

6. **Correct Answers:** A, B, C

    A. **Correct:** Faulty RAM can cause these symptoms.

    B. **Correct:** Failing or dirty fans can result in overheating problems, causing these symptoms.

    C. **Correct:** A power supply providing varying voltages or voltages out of specifications can cause these symptoms.

    D. **Incorrect:** Viruses can cause these types of symptoms, but a virus is software, not hardware.

CHAPTER 4

Comparing Storage Devices

I n this chapter, you'll learn about the different types of storage devices, including hard drives, solid state drives, optical drives, and fault tolerant arrays. Many different types of interfaces are currently used to connect drives, and it's important to know what is available and how to connect them. This chapter covers the hardware elements of hard drives, and in Chapter 16, "Understanding Disks and File Systems," you'll build on this knowledge to configure and troubleshoot disks.

Exam 220-801 objectives in this chapter:

- 1.5 Install and configure storage devices and use appropriate media.
  - Optical drives
    - CD-ROM
    - DVD-ROM
    - Blu-Ray
  - Combo drives and burners
    - CD-RW
    - DVD-RW
    - Dual Layer DVD-RW
    - BD-R
    - BD-RE
  - Connection types
    - External
      - USB
      - Firewire
      - eSATA
      - Ethernet

- Internal SATA, IDE and SCSI
    - IDE configuration and setup (Master, Slave, Cable Select)
    - SCSI IDs (0 – 15)
- Hot swappable drives
- Hard drives
    - Magnetic
    - 5400 rpm
    - 7200 rpm
    - 10,000 rpm
    - 15,000 rpm
- Solid state/flash drives
    - Compact flash
    - SD
    - Micro-SD
    - Mini-SD
    - xD
    - SSD
- RAID types
    - 0
    - 1
    - 5
    - 10
- Floppy drive
- Tape drive
- Media capacity
    - CD
    - CD-RW
    - DVD-RW
    - DVD
    - Blu-Ray
    - Tape
    - Floppy
    - DL DVD

- 1.7 Compare and contrast various connection interfaces and explain their purpose.
    - Physical connections
        - SATA1 vs. SATA2 vs. SATA3, eSATA, IDE speeds
- 1.11 Identify connector types and associated cables.
    - Device connectors and pin arrangements
        - SATA
        - eSATA
        - PATA
            - IDE
            - EIDE
        - SCSI
    - Device cable types
        - SATA
        - eSATA
        - IDE
        - EIDE
        - Floppy
        - SCSI
            - 68pin vs. 50pin vs. 25pin

Exam 220-802 objectives in this chapter:

- 4.3 Given a scenario, troubleshoot hard drives and RAID arrays with appropriate tools.
    - Common symptoms
        - Read/write failure
        - Slow performance
        - Loud clicking noise
        - Failure to boot
        - Drive not recognized
        - OS not found
        - RAID not found
        - RAID stops working
        - BSOD
    - Tools
        - Screwdriver
        - External enclosures

Hard Drives

The *hard disk drive (HDD)* is the primary long-term storage device used in personal computers. A hard drive includes multiple *platters* that spin as fast as 15,000 revolutions per minute (rpm). These platters are covered with ferromagnetic material, and data can be written to the drive by magnetizing that material. The hard drive is not volatile. That is, even without power, data remains stored on the drive.

Figure 4-1 shows an open hard drive, with the physical components listed on the left and the logical components on the right.

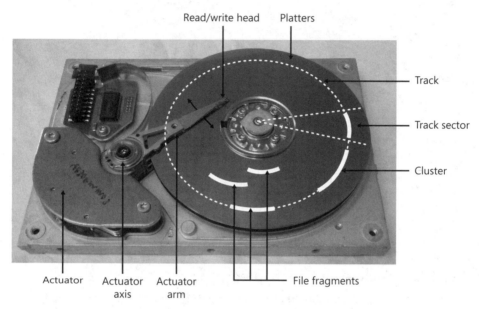

FIGURE 4-1 Looking inside a hard drive.

IMPORTANT **DON'T OPEN HARD DRIVES IF YOU WANT TO USE THEM AGAIN**

The heads are riding on a very thin pocket of air hundreds of times smaller than a human hair. They are sealed to prevent contaminants from getting inside, but if you open a hard drive and then try to use it, the heads can crash on these contaminants, making the drive useless.

- **Physical components:**
    - **Platters.** Hard drives have multiple spinning platters, and each platter can be written to on both sides.
    - **Read/write head.** A hard drive will have one read/write head for each platter side. This drive has two platters and four read/write heads.
    - **Actuator.** The *actuator* controls the movement of the arm.

- **Actuator arm and axis.** The actuator arm is moved back and forth by pivoting around the actuator axis. This positions the read/write head on different areas of the platter.
- **Logical components:**
  - **Tracks.** Each platter is logically divided into multiple tracks, which are circular areas on the disk. When the head is positioned over a *track*, it can read or write data on the track as the platter spins.
  - **Sectors.** Tracks are logically separated into track sectors. A *sector* can be between 512 bytes and 2 KB in size.
  - **Clusters.** A *cluster* is a group of multiple sectors. Clusters are also known as allocation units and are the smallest element of a drive to which an operating system can write.

> **NOTE** **HOW MANY SECTORS ARE ON A 1-TB DRIVE?**
>
> A 1-TB hard drive using 2-KB sectors would have about 500 million track sectors. The tracks, track sectors, and clusters shown in Figure 4-1 aren't shown in actual size, but the figure does accurately illustrate their relationships to each other.

  - **Files.** Files are written to clusters. If the file is bigger than a single cluster, the file is written to multiple clusters. Ideally, a file will be written to clusters that are next to each other, or *contiguous clusters*. However, if other data is already written on an adjoining cluster, the file is fragmented and written to another available cluster.

During normal hard disk operation, the platters spin at a constant rate. When data needs to be read or written, the actuator moves the actuator arm to position the head over a specific track. It waits for the target cluster to arrive under the head, and then it reads or writes the data. When you think about how fast the platters are spinning, you realize how amazing the technology has become.

Hard Drive Characteristics

It's relatively common to replace or add a hard drive to a system. For example, many people store enough data on the original drive that came with their computer that they fill up the drive. They can either buy a new computer or buy an additional hard drive, and the additional hard drive is much cheaper.

If you're shopping for a new hard drive, you'll want to remember the following important considerations:

- **Capacity or Size.** The size of the drive is listed as GB or TB—for example, 750 GB or 1 TB. Bigger drives hold more data but are more expensive.
- **Interface.** You can connect a drive internally or externally. Later sections in this chapter cover the different choices.

- **Rotational speed.** This is stated as rpm, and higher speeds generally result in a faster drive.

Hard Drive Speeds

The rotational speed of the drive helps determine how quick it will be overall. Common speeds are 5,400, 7,200, 10,000, and 15,000 rpm. Drives with 7,200 rpm are used in standard desktop computers.

Other factors also contribute to the speed. For example, *seek time* refers to the average amount of time it takes to move the read/write head from one track to another track, and lower seek times are better. If you find two drives of the same size with the same rpm speed but one is significantly cheaper, it might be due to a higher seek time, resulting in overall slower performance.

The interface can also limit the speed. Imagine a drive spinning at 15,000 rpm with a low seek time. It can read and write data to and from the hard drive, but it is limited as to how much data can actually be transferred between the hard drive and other computer components. The following sections describe common interfaces.

IDE/EIDE/PATA Drives

Hard drive interfaces have gone through several changes and improvements over the years. Even though you won't see many of the older versions, if you understand a little about them, it makes it easier to understand current versions. Also, many of the older versions are mentioned in the CompTIA A+ objectives. As a quick introduction, the following list provides a short history:

- **Integrated Drive Electronics (IDE).** These appeared in the 1980s and included drive controller electronics on the drive.
- **Advanced Technology Attachment (ATA).** *IDE* was standardized as ATA and later became known as ATA-1. The maximum drive size was 137 GB. In earlier drives, the maximum was 2.1 GB.
- **Extended IDE (EIDE) and ATA-2.** Modifications and enhancements of the original IDE were marketed as *EIDE* and later standardized as ATA-2.
- **ATA Packet Interface (ATAPI).** Originally IDE and ATA were designed only for hard drives. *ATAPI* provided standards so that EIDE and ATA versions could be used for other drives, such as CD-ROM and DVD-ROM drives.
- **Renamed to Parallel ATA (PATA).** ATA was upgraded regularly to ATA-7, which also introduced *Serial ATA (SATA)*. EIDE versions were renamed to *PATA* to differentiate it from SATA. (SATA is described later in this chapter.)

PATA Speeds

PATA drives use *direct memory access (DMA)* transfers. DMA allows a device to directly access memory without the central processing unit (CPU), freeing up the CPU for other tasks. *Ultra DMA (UDMA)* appeared in ATA version 4 (ATA-4) and supported data transfers as high as 44 megabytes per second (MBps).

ATA and UDMA were updated several times, and Table 4-1 identifies the speeds and names for the different versions.

TABLE 4-1 PATA Speeds

Type	Maximum Speed	Comments
ATA-4	33 MBps	Also called UDMA/33 and Ultra ATA/33
ATA-5	66 MBps	Also called UDMA/66 and Ultra ATA/66
ATA-6	100 MBps	Also called UDMA/100 and Ultra ATA/100 Maximum drive size increased to 144 PB
ATA-7	133 MBps	Also called UDMA/133 and Ultra ATA/133

PATA Connectors and Cables

All PATA connectors are 40-pin rectangular connectors, and they are the same on both the hard drive and the motherboard. Motherboards that support PATA typically have two connectors named IDE 1 and IDE 2 (or sometimes IDE 0 and IDE 1), as shown in Figure 4-2.

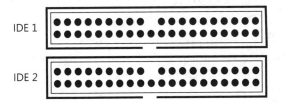

FIGURE 4-2 IDE connectors on a motherboard.

PATA drives use ribbon cables similar to the one shown in Figure 4-3. Each ribbon cable includes three connectors—one for the motherboard IDE connection and two for the drives. In the figure, the two IDE connectors (IDE 1 and IDE 2) are on the left, and the cable is lying on top of the motherboard. A typical PATA-based system would have two ribbon cables connecting a maximum of four drives.

Early versions of PATA cables used 40 wires, but this was switched over to 80-wire cables with ATA-4. These extra wires provided signal grounds within the cable and supported the higher UDMA speeds. Even though the number of wires in the cables doubled, the connectors still have 40 pins. The maximum length of an IDE cable is 18 inches.

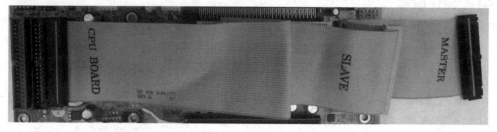

FIGURE 4-3 IDE ribbon cable to motherboard.

EXAM TIP
Most 80-wire UDMA cables are color-coded. The connector on the end (labeled master in the figure) is black, and the middle connector is gray. Also, ribbon cables have a red stripe on one side. The red stripe should match up with pin 1 on the IDE connector.

Master and Slave Configuration

Each IDE connection supports two drives, and these are commonly identified as *master* and *slave* drives. The system will try to boot to the master drive, but it doesn't automatically know which drive to select. Instead, you have to manipulate jumpers on the drive to let the system know which drive is the master and which is the slave.

> **NOTE DEVICE 0 AND DEVICE 1**
>
> In later versions of ATA specifications, the master and slave drives were renamed to device 0 (master) and device 1 (slave). However, the master/slave names are commonly used and even mentioned in the CompTIA objectives. You can think of the master drive as simply the first drive for the IDE connector and the slave as the second drive.

Figure 4-4 shows the back of an EIDE drive. You can see that it has a 40-pin connector for the ribbon cable and a Molex connector for power. It also has a set of jumpers used to identify whether the drive is the master or the slave.

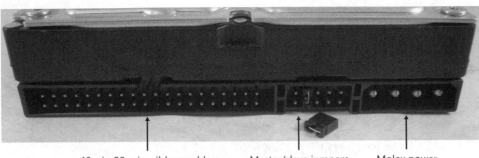

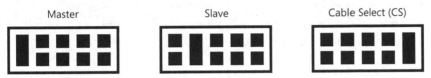

40-pin 80-wire ribbon cable   Master/slave jumpers   Molex power

FIGURE 4-4 Rear of EIDE drive showing jumpers.

If you're replacing or adding a drive, it's important to understand these jumpers. You'll often find a chart on the back of the drive, similar to the chart shown in Figure 4-5, that identifies exactly how the jumper should be configured for each drive.

Master   Slave   Cable Select (CS)

FIGURE 4-5 Example chart for jumpers on an EIDE drive.

EXAM TIP

The most common reason why drives aren't recognized after an installation is that the jumpers are not configured correctly. If you've replaced a drive but find it isn't recognized, double-check the jumpers.

Cable Select

Cable select allows the system to identify the drive based on which connector is used. In Figure 4-3, you can see that the end connector of the ribbon cable is labeled Master and the middle connector is labeled Slave. If you configure the jumpers for both drives to use cable select, they are identified based on which connector is used. If the drives are jumpered for master and slave, the connector does not identify the drive.

PATA Power

PATA hard drives use a standard four-pin Molex connector, as shown in Figure 4-4 earlier. A four-wire cable from the power supply uses the following colors:

- Yellow 12 V
- Black ground (two middle wires)
- Red 5 V

Chapter 1, "Introduction to Computers," included a picture of the power supply with a Molex connector coming from the power supply.

SATA

Serial ATA (SATA) drives have replaced PATA drives in almost all new systems. The newest version, SATA 6G, can transfer as much as 600 MBps. In contrast, PATA ATA-7 tops out at 133 MBps.

EXAM TIP

SATA drives are much faster and much more prevalent than PATA drives. You should know the speeds of each generation, in addition to details about the cables and connectors. Each new version is backward-compatible with earlier versions.

Serial to Parallel to Serial

Early data transmissions sent data between components one bit at a time, or serially. Engineers later improved this by sending multiple bits at a time to improve the speed. Therefore, data could be sent using multiple wires so that bits were next to each other or in parallel. The tradeoff was that the cable needed more wires to send all the data at the same time.

For example, a 40-pin EIDE ribbon cable includes 16 bits for data. If you send 16 bits at a time, you can send as much as 16 times more data than if you send just one bit at time at the same speed. The idea that parallel is faster than serial held for many years, until a breakthrough with *low voltage differential (LVD)* signaling occurred.

LVD signaling is a standard that transmits data as the difference in voltages between two wires in a pair. These differences can be rather small, and engineers discovered they could send data serially along an LVD cable quicker than they could with parallel. Many technologies use LVD signaling, including SATA drives, HyperTransport used by AMD processors, and FireWire.

SATA Generations

Three generations of SATA are currently in use. It's important to know the capabilities of each and also to recognize the different names that have been used. Table 4-2 outlines the different versions and their speeds.

TABLE 4-2 SATA Versions

Generation	Bit speed	Byte speed	Names
SATA 1	1.5 Gbits/s	150 MBps	SATA 1.5G, SATA 1.5Gb/s, SATA 1.5Gbit/s, SATA 150
SATA 2	3.0 Gbits/s	300 MBps	SATA 3G, SATA 3Gb/s, SATA 3Gbit/s, SATA 300
SATA 3	6.0 Gbits/s	600 MBps	SATA 6G, SATA 6Gb/s, SATA 6Gbit/s, SATA 600

PATA versions are commonly described using speeds rated in bytes per second (Bps), and SATA versions often use bits per second (bps or bits/s). For example, SATA 1.0 can transfer data at 150 MBps, but it is commonly listed as 1.5 Gbit/s.

> **NOTE BITS TO BYTES AND 8B/10B ENCODING**
>
> If you multiply 150 MB by 8 to convert bytes to bits, you get 1.2 gigabits, not 1.5 gigabits, yet 150 MBps and 1.5 Gbits/s are both valid figures for SATA 1.5G. SATA uses 8b/10b encoding, which transmits each group of 8 bits (each byte) as a 10-bit symbol or code. If you divide 1.5 Gbits (1,500 Mbits) by 10, you get 150 MB.

One of the things that has confused people about SATA is the similarity of the names SATA 3.x and SATA 3G. Some products are marketed as SATA 3G, and customers think they are getting a third-generation SATA product. However, as you can see from Table 4-2, SATA 3G refers to a transfer rate of 3 Gbits/s provided by the second generation of SATA.

SATA and SSD

Before SATA, hard drives were typically capable of sending data faster than the motherboard could accept it. The interface was the bottleneck. Even though each newer ATA version allowed faster data transfers, the drives were still faster than the interface.

It's different with SATA 6G. You won't be able to find a mechanical hard drive that can transfer as much as 6 Gbits/second (or 600 MBps). Some extremely fast (and extremely expensive) hard drives can transfer data as quickly as 157 MBps. That is, these drives benefit from using SATA 3G but they never exceed 300 MBps, so they don't benefit from SATA 6G. You just won't see any performance difference in these hard drives if you plug them into a SATA 3G or SATA 6G port.

With this in mind, you might be wondering why you'd want SATA 6G. It's a great question. The answer is for solid state drives (SSDs). SSDs are discussed later in this chapter, but in short, they don't have any moving parts and are much faster. SSDs are available that can read and transfer data as fast as 500 MB/s.

SATA Data Connectors and Cables

SATA cables are much smaller than the 80-wire ribbon cables used with PATA. They include only seven wires, and cables can be as long as 1 meter (about 3.3 feet). A distinctive characteristic of SATA cables is that they have an *L*-shaped connector, which works as a key. Each drive is connected to a single SATA connector on the motherboard, so you don't have to worry about master/slave jumpers on SATA drives.

Figure 4-6 shows part of a motherboard with five SATA ports. SATA 5 is on the left as a single unoccupied port. Ports 1 and 2 are stacked and ports 3 and 4 are stacked, allowing more ports in the same amount of space.

FIGURE 4-6 SATA connectors on a motherboard.

I removed the connector from the SATA 3 port so that you can see it, and I left SATA ports 1 and 2 connected. The other ends of these cables connect to similar *L*-shaped ports on the SATA drive.

The SATA ports on a motherboard are commonly color-coded, but there isn't a standard. For example, on this motherboard, SATA 1 and SATA 2 are both blue, and the other three connectors are black. The documentation for the motherboard states that the blue ports are 6 Gbit/s SATA 6G ports and that the black ports are 3 Gbit/s SATA 3G ports.

Also, you'll run across different-colored SATA cables, but the colors don't indicate a specific version. They do help you trace the cables. If you have five black SATA cables going to five different drives, it's difficult to tell which drive is connected to which port. However, when the cables are different colors, it's easier to trace them from the port to the drive.

SATA Power Connectors and Cables

SATA power connectors have 15 pins, but the cables have only five wires. The color coding for the wires is as follows:

- **Orange**—3.3 V to pins 1, 2, and 3.
- **Black**—Ground to pins 4, 5, and 6.
- **Red**—5 V to pins 7, 8, and 9.
- **Black**—Ground for pins 10, 11, and 12. Pin 11 can be used to delay the startup of the drive or to indicate drive activity.
- **Yellow**—12 V to pins 13, 14, and 15.

Figure 4-7 shows the back of a SATA drive, along with the power cable from the power supply. The SATA data connection is on the right, and you can see that both have the distinctive *L*-shaped key, although the power connector is larger. Also, the power connector has a square tip on one side.

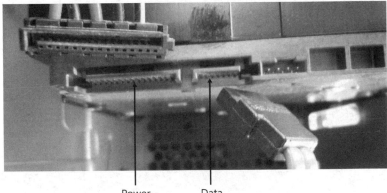

Power   Data

FIGURE 4-7 SATA power and data connectors.

EXAM TIP

In some cases, you can use an adapter to connect a 4-pin Molex power cable from the power supply to a SATA drive. The Molex cable does not provide 3.3 V, so the adapter includes electronics to convert power to 3.3 V for pins 1, 2, and 3.

Hot-Swappable

All versions of SATA drives are *hot-swappable*, which means that you can plug in or remove the drive while the system is powered on. Several ground pins on the power cable are longer than the pins carrying voltage so that the ground pins connect first. This prevents any damage when they are plugged in. In contrast, you must power down a system before replacing a PATA drive.

You're not likely to replace an internal SATA drive while the system is powered on. However, some systems have drive bays that allow you to plug in or remove a drive from the front panel or that are in an external enclosure. If a drive fails, you can swap it out without powering down the system.

> *NOTE* **HOT-SWAPPABLE**
>
> Hot-swappable refers only to the hardware ability. If you remove a device while a program is writing data to it, it can corrupt data. Ensure that the device is not being used before removing it.

> ✔ **Quick Check**
>
> 1. What are the speeds of SATA 2 and SATA 3?
> 2. What types of connectors are used with SATA?
>
> **Quick Check Answers**
>
> 1. *L*-shaped connectors.
> 2. SATA 2 is 3 Gbps, and SATA 3 is 6 Gbps.

SCSI

Small Computer System Interface (SCSI, pronounced *scuzzy)* is a drive interface standard that has been around as long as the earliest ATA standards. It has traditionally provided higher performance compared to the PATA drives, but it is more expensive and not widely used on desktop computers. With the popularity of SATA drives, SCSI drives are used even less on desktop computers.

The three primary standards used with standard SCSI are as follows:

- **SCSI-1 (also called narrow SCSI).** Uses a 50-pin cable with a maximum transfer rate of 5 MBps. Narrow SCSI uses an 8-bit bus and supports a maximum of 8 devices.
- **SCSI-2.** Uses a 25-pin, 50-pin, or 68-pin cable. This was first called fast SCSI because it could transfer data at 10 MBps, twice as fast as SCSI-1. It originally used an 8-bit bus.

Fast-Wide SCSI is an update that uses a 16-bit bus and supports 16 devices with transfer rates of 20 MBps.

- **SCSI-3.** Uses a 50-pin, 68-pin, or 80-pin cable. The most common cable is an 80-pin Single Connector Attachment (SCA). SCSI-3 is also called Ultra SCSI and includes several different versions.

Table 4-3 lists several recent versions of SCSI-3. Each of these use a 16-bit bus and can support as many as 16 devices.

TABLE 4-3 Ultra SCSI Types

Type	Speed: bytes per second	Speed: bits per second
Ultra-160	160 MBps	1.28 Gbit/s
Ultra-320	320 MBps	2.56 Gbit/s
Ultra-640	640 MBps	5.12 Gbit/s

SCSI Interfaces

SCSI cables and connectors come in several different versions. Some are ribbon cables similar to the cables used with PATA drives, and other cables are round. Some examples of SCSI connectors include:

- **25-pin.** This is a very old SCSI connector, also known as a DB25. It has one row of 13 pins and a second row of 12 pins.

- **50-pin.** Several types of 50-pin SCSI connectors have been used. Some have two rows, and some have three rows. A Centronics 50-pin connector has connectors lined up in slots.

- **68-pin.** This includes two rows of pins close together and is referred to as high-density. It is sometimes used for external SCSI connections.

- **80-pin.** This is known as a Single Connector Attachment (SCA) connection, and it is used as an alternative to 68-pin connections. It includes pins for both data and power and supports hot-swapping.

SCSI IDs

SCSI devices are controlled by a SCSI controller. Each device, including the controller, is assigned a *SCSI identifier (SCSI ID)* using numbers from 0 to 15. The controller is normally assigned the highest priority SCSI ID of 7. The priorities don't make sense unless you know a little SCSI history.

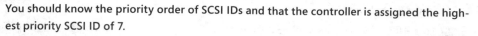

EXAM TIP

You should know the priority order of SCSI IDs and that the controller is assigned the highest priority SCSI ID of 7.

Early SCSI implementations supported eight devices and used SCSI IDs numbered 0 to 7, with SCSI ID 7 being the highest priority and SCSI ID 0 being the lowest. When SCSI began supporting 16 devices, they added 8 SCSI IDs (8 to 15). However, they did not modify the original priorities. Instead, the additional 8 device IDs (8 to 15) were given lower priorities than the first 8 IDs. In the second set of 8 IDs, 15 is the highest and 8 is the lowest. Therefore, the priority order from highest to lowest is as follows:

- 7, 6, 5, 4, 3, 2, 1, 0, 15, 14, 13, 12, 11, 10, 9, and 8.

When you need to assign an ID to a device with a jumper, you'll often see four jumpers, listed as 3, 2, 1, 0. These refer to four binary bits that can be used to count from 0 to 15. These bits have the values 8, 4, 2, and 1.

MORE INFO CHAPTER 1

Chapter 1 covered binary numbering systems. As a reminder, 2^3 is 8, 2^2 is 4, 2^1 is 2, and 2^0 is 1. Jumper 3 is used for 2^3, jumper 2 is for 2^2, jumper 1 is for 2^1, and jumper 0 is for 2^0.

For example, if you wanted to assign the number 7 to a controller, you would use the binary number 0111. The jumper for 3 would be removed to indicate a 0, and the jumpers for 2, 1, and 0 would be installed to indicate 1s. Table 4-4 shows the binary values for IDs 0 to 15.

TABLE 4-4 SCSI IDs Binary Values

ID	Binary	ID	Binary	ID	Binary	ID	Binary
0	0000	4	0100	8	1000	12	1100
1	0001	5	0101	9	1001	13	1101
2	0010	6	0110	10	1010	14	1110
3	0011	7	0111	11	1011	15	1111

In some cases, the SCSI ID can be assigned through the SCA adapter or with software. You might not need to assign it with jumpers.

Daisy-Chaining and Termination

SCSI devices are connected together in a *daisy chain* fashion, which indicates that devices are connected to each other like links in a chain rather than each device being connected directly to a central device.

Figure 4-8 shows how internal and external devices can connect to a SCSI controller. The SCSI controller is an expansion card plugged into the motherboard, and it has an internal connection for internal devices and an external connection for external devices.

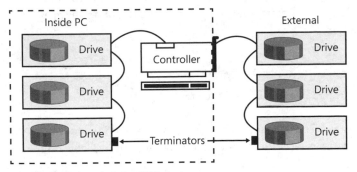

FIGURE 4-8 Daisy-chaining SCSI devices.

Each device has two connectors to support the daisy chain connection. Additionally, the last device in the chain must be terminated to let the controller know that there aren't any additional devices in the chain. The figure shows both an internal chain with three drives and an external chain with three drives. Each chain must be terminated.

The terminator can be a plug that plugs into the connector or a switch that indicates which is the last device. In most new systems, the terminator is automatically configured. The last device recognizes that there is nothing plugged into the second connector, so it automatically terminates the connection.

Serial Attached SCSI

Serial Attached SCSI (SAS) is a newer form of SCSI that uses a serial interface. It uses data and power cables similar to the SATA connections and supports transfer speeds of up to 6 Gbit/s. SAS is used in some high-end servers but is more expensive than SATA, so it is rarely used in desktop computers.

External Connections Types

If you don't have room inside your computer or you just want to have something portable, you can add an external drive. This includes adding an external hard disk, optical drive, tape drive, or a floppy drive. The following sections describe common ways you can add an external drive.

USB

Almost every computer has Universal Serial Bus (USB) ports, and many external devices use them. USB 2.0 supports speeds of up to 480 Mbits/s, and USB 3.0 supports speeds of up to 5 Gbits/s. USB cables can be as long as 5 meters (over 16 feet), and you can attach as many as 127 devices to any single USB hub.

> **MORE INFO** CHAPTER 5, "EXPLORING PERIPHERALS AND EXPANSION CARDS"
>
> **Both USB and FireWire are covered in more depth in Chapter 5.**

Figure 4-9 shows several ports accessible on the back of a computer, and the four ports on the top left are USB ports. Computers will often have additional USB ports available on the front panel.

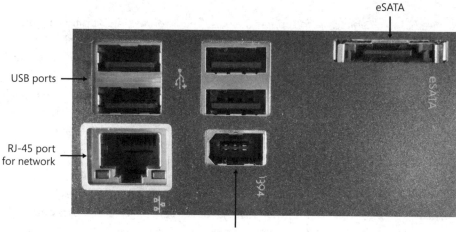

FIGURE 4-9 Ports on back of computer.

> **NOTE** USB LOGO WITH PLUS SIGN
>
> The USB logo starts with a circle on one end, then has a trident of a circle, an arrow, and a square on the other end. Some USB 2.0 ports are also labeled with a plus sign (as shown in Figure 4-9) to indicate that it is USB 2.0.

FireWire

Many computers also have a FireWire port. FireWire was created by Apple and then formalized as IEEE 1394, so you'll see it with both names. Figure 4-9 shows a single FireWire port labeled 1394. FireWire 400 (or 1394a) supports speeds of up to 400 Mbps, and FireWire 800 (or 1394b) supports speeds of up to 800 Mbps. FireWire cables can be as long as 4.5 meters (almost 15 feet), and you can daisy-chain as many as 63 devices to a single FireWire port.

FireWire ports can have 4, 6, or 9 pins. The port shown in Figure 4-9 is a 6-pin port, and it provides power to the device (as does a 9-pin FireWire port); 4-pin connectors do not provide power.

eSATA

SATA was originally designed for internal use only but is emerging as another alternative for external drives. There is no performance difference between SATA and *eSATA*, and most eSATA ports are based on SATA 3G providing transfer speeds of up to 3 Gbit/s.

Figure 4-9 includes an eSATA port, and you can see that it lacks the distinctive *L* shape of internal SATA connections. The eSATA cables have seven wires, just like internal SATA cables, but eSATA cables require shielding that isn't needed with internal SATA cables. The different connector ensures that an internal cable isn't used for an external connection.

The eSATA cable can be as long as 2 meters (about 6.6 feet), but unlike with USB and FireWire, you can connect only one device to the port.

EXAM TIP

If the eSATA drive is not recognized when you plug it in, there are two primary things to check. First, check the BIOS to ensure that the eSATA port is enabled. Second, ensure that you have drivers for the device. These will normally be available from the manufacturer.

eSATAp

Many laptop computers include a powered eSATA (*eSATAp*) port. It's also called an eSATA/ USB combo or eSATA USB Hybrid Port. It can be used for either an eSATA device or a USB 2.0 (or earlier) device. You simply plug in the device, and the system automatically recognizes whether it is eSATA or USB and uses the correct interface.

> **NOTE SATA VS. USB**
>
> SATA and USB are competing standards, and the eSATAp port that supports both USB and eSATA devices is not a formal standard. However, it is very common on laptop computers.

Figure 4-10 shows the side view of a laptop computer. It includes an eSATAp port, a standard USB port, and a 4-pin FireWire port.

FIGURE 4-10 Connectors on side of laptop.

The eSATAp port includes the 7 pins used by eSATA and 4 pins used by USB. If you plug in a USB device, it uses the 4 USB pins. If you plug in an externally-powered eSATA device with a standard eSATA cable, it uses the 7 pins for data, just like the eSATA port described previously.

Some smaller devices, such as solid state drives or 2.5 inch drives, can be powered by the 5 V available on the USB pins. A special eSATAp cable carries both the data and 5 V to the device.

Larger devices, such as 3.5-inch drives and optical drives, require 12 V power. Some eSATAp ports on desktop computers include two optional pins (located at the white arrows in Figure 4-10) that provide 12 V. If 12 V is provided via the eSATAp port, you can use a 12-V eSATAp cable that will deliver data, 5 V, and 12 V to the device.

> **IMPORTANT   ALL ESATAP CABLES AREN'T THE SAME**
>
> Some eSATAp cables carry both 5 V and 12 V, but most carry only 5 V. If an eSATAp device isn't working, check to see whether 12 V is required. If it is, verify that the eSATAp port has the additional pins for 12 V and that the eSATAp cable includes 12-V support. You can always use a standard eSATA data cable and provide external power to the device.

Ethernet

Another way you can add external data storage is with a network drive. You don't connect the network drive directly to the computer. Instead, you connect the network drive to a device such as a router or a switch. This is commonly called network attached storage (NAS).

For example, many people have home networks using wireless routers. It's relatively easy and inexpensive to add a NAS device to the network. Users with network access can then share the drive.

Figure 4-9 includes an RJ-45 port used to connect a computer to a network. You would typically connect this to a switch with a twisted-pair cable. Similarly, network drives commonly have an RJ-45 port used to connect them to a network. However, you would not connect the NAS device directly to a computer by using this RJ-45 port.

External Enclosures

As a technician, you'll find that an external hard drive enclosure is a handy tool. Instead of installing a drive inside a computer, you can install it in the enclosure and use it as an external drive.

You can find enclosures that will accept IDE/PATA drives and others that accept SATA drives. Also, some are designed to accept the 2.5-inch drives from laptop computers and others will work with 3.5-inch drives common in desktop computers. After installing the drive, you connect the enclosure to a computer with a USB connection.

For example, if a laptop fails, you might want to access the data on the hard drive. You can remove the hard drive from the laptop, install it in the enclosure, and plug the enclosure into a working computer. It will now work just like any other external drive.

✔ **Quick Check**

1. What is the most common connector used for peripherals?

2. What can you plug into an eSATAp port?

Quick Check Answers

1. USB.

2. USB or eSATA devices.

Solid State Drives

Solid state drives (SSDs) don't have any moving components but instead use only electronics to store and retrieve data. You can think of an SSD as a huge bank of random access memory (RAM). Most SSDs are nonvolatile, meaning that they won't lose data when power is removed. The most common type of memory used with SSDs is flash-based RAM, the same type of nonvolatile RAM used in USB flash drives.

SSD drives are lightning-fast when compared with mechanical hard drives. Additionally, they don't require motors to spin the platters and move the actuator, so they are lighter and draw less power. Mobile devices such as tablets commonly use SSDs, and many hobbyists replace laptop hard drives with SSDs.

With the price of memory continuing to fall, SSD drives have become very affordable. For example, you can purchase a 128-GB SSD drive for about the same price as a 2-TB mechanical drive. Some people use an SSD drive for the operating system and applications and use a mechanical drive for data. Most SSD drives use SATA and will install just like any other SATA drive.

In addition to SSD drives and USB flash drives, several types of flash memory are used in digital cameras and recorders, including the following:

- **CompactFlash (CF).** *CompactFlash* devices are manufactured by SanDisk and are very popular. The outer dimensions are 43 × 36 mm. Type 1 CF devices are 3.3 mm thick, and Type II devices (known as CF2) are 5 mm thick. They can hold up to 128 GB of data.

- **SD (Secure Digital).** *SD* is developed by the SD Card Association and used with many types of portable devices. It supersedes MultiMediaCard (MMC), which is the same size. Figure 4-11 shows a Compact Flash stick next to a standard SD stick. The dimensions of SD are 24 × 32 mm. They can hold up to 2 GB of data. Newer versions include SD High Capacity (SDHC) and extended Capacity (SDXC). SDHC can hold up to 32 GB, and SDXC can hold up to 2 TB of data.

FIGURE 4-11 CompactFlash and SD memory sticks.

- **Mini-SD.** This is a smaller version of the SD card. The dimensions of *mini-SD* devices are 21.5 × 20 mm.

- **Micro-SD.** This is the smallest of the three SD sizes. The dimensions of *micro-SD* devices are 15 × 11 mm.

- **xD.** The *xD* Picture card is an older flash memory card used in some digital cameras. It was developed by Olympus and Fujifilm, but Olympus cameras are now using SD cards.

Many computers have connectors on the front panel that will accept these memory sticks. This enables you to remove the memory from your camera and plug it directly into the computer to access the pictures.

Optical Discs and Drives

If you've used a computer or watched a movie at home, you've probably seen and handled an optical disc. However, you might not be aware of the different types of *compact discs (CDs)*, *digital versatile discs (DVDs)*, and *Blu-Ray discs (BDs)* currently available.

> **NOTE   DISK VS. DISC**
>
> When referring to hard disk drives, the correct spelling is *disk,* with a *k*. When referring to optical disc drives and optical discs, the correct spelling is *disc*, with a *c*.

Table 4-5 lists the different types of optical discs and their capacities. In this context, ROM indicates that it is read-only media (ROM), but it is possible to write to discs.

TABLE 4-5 Media Capacity

Type	Capacity	Comments
CD-ROM	700 MB (80 minutes of audio)	The standard size is 12 cm (4.7 inches).
Mini CD-ROM	194 MB (24 minutes of audio)	These are 6 to 8 cm. Vendors sometimes release software or audio using this size.
DVD-ROM	4.7 GB	Dual-sided DVD-ROMS hold 4.7 GB on each side.
Dual-Layer DVD-ROM	8.5 GB	Dual-sided dual-layer DVD-ROMS hold 8.5 GB on each side.
Blu-Ray Single-layer	25 GB	Blu-Ray discs use a blue laser, and CD and DVDs use a red laser.
Blu-Ray Dual-layer	50 GB	This is the common size used for movies. Triple-layer holds 100 GB, and quad-layer holds 128 GB.

EXAM TIP

Know the capacity of the different discs as shown in the table.

Combo Drives and Burners

Most optical drives support multiple types of optical discs. It's common to have a single optical disc drive that can read and write CDs and DVDs. For just a little more money, you can get a combo drive that can also read and write Blu-Ray discs.

Optical discs use lasers to read and write data. The process of writing data to a disc is commonly called *burning a disc*. However, you can't burn just any disc. For example, CD-ROMs and DVD-ROMs are read-only media. You can't overwrite the data on these discs. However, you can burn data to R, RW, and RE discs.

- **R (Recordable).** A recordable disc can have data written to it once. It is sometimes referred to as *write once read many (WORM)* and is used for backups and archives. It is possible to write the data in multiple sessions, but after an area is written on the disc, it cannot be rewritten. The R applies to CDs (as in *CD-R*), DVDs (as in *DVD-R*), and Blu-Ray discs (as in *BD-R*).

- **RW (Rewritable).** A rewritable disc can be rewritten many times. The RW applies to CDs (as in *CD-RW*) and DVDs (as in *DVD-RW*).

- **RE (Recordable Erasable).** Blu-Ray discs use RE (as in *BD-RE*) to indicate that the disc is rewritable.

> **NOTE** +R, +RW, -R, AND -RW
>
> CDs and DVDs come in + and – versions, such as DVD-R and DVD+R. These are competing versions of discs, but most combo drives and burners will be able to read and write data using both types of discs. However, if you plan on making a DVD that you want to play on a DVD player, you might have problems—many players support only one disc type or the other.

If you insert an optical disc that is not recognized by the drive, applications will often just ignore it. For example, you might decide to copy a DVD disc from DVD drive 1 in your system to DVD drive 2. If you put a CD disc instead of a DVD in drive 2, you won't receive an error saying that you've installed a CD. Instead, you'll be prompted to insert a DVD.

Speeds

The speeds of optical disc drives are stated as multipliers using a base speed. The base speeds are as follows:

- **CD:** 150 KBps
- **DVD:** 1.39 MBps
- **Blu-Ray:** 4.5 MBps

For example, you might see a DVD drive listed as 24x for R and 8x for RW. This indicates that it can write to a recordable disc at a speed of 24 × 1.39 MBps and that it can write to a rewritable disc at a speed of 8 × 1.39 MBps.

Installing Optical Drives

Here's some good news: if you understand how to install PATA and SATA drives, you know how to install an optical drive. Optical drives come in both PATA and SATA versions, and you install them the same way you install those drives.

If it's a PATA optical drive, you need to ensure that the master/slave jumpers are configured correctly to recognize the drive. If it's a SATA drive, just plug the cables in and ensure that the SATA port is enabled in BIOS. If it's a SATA optical drive, it uses a SATA power connector. Older PATA drives use the standard PATA Molex power connector.

The only other consideration is that older CD-ROM drives need an audio cable connected from the drive to either the motherboard or the sound card. Figure 4-12 shows the back of an IDE-based drive that includes audio connections. Newer drives can send the audio through the IDE or SATA cable, so this extra cable is not needed.

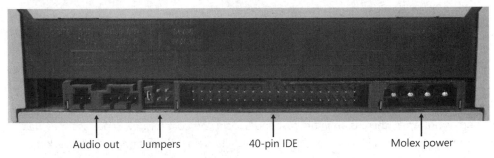

Audio out   Jumpers   40-pin IDE   Molex power

FIGURE 4-12 Connectors on back of optical drive.

Removing Discs Without Power

There might be a time when you need to remove a disc from a drive but don't have any power. It could be that the drive has failed and won't power up, or it could be you are disposing of an old computer and want to ensure that there isn't a disc left in the system. You can open the drive with a paperclip.

All disc drives have a small pinhole in the front. Unbend a paperclip and poke it into the hole to manually open the drive.

> ✔ **Quick Check**
>
>   **1.** How much data can you store on a single-layer Blu-Ray disc?
>
>   **2.** What does RE indicate with an optical disc?
>
> **Quick Check Answers**
>
>   **1.** 25 GB.
>
>   **2.** Recordable Erasable.

Tape Drives

Tape drives are often used to back up large amounts of data. A tape drive can read and write data by using reusable magnetic tapes, and the tapes are contained within tape cartridges. Tape cartridges that hold 320 GB of data are widely available.

In many organizations, backups are scheduled to occur in the middle of the night. A technician ensures that a tape is in the drive before leaving. The next day, the technician checks the backup for errors, stores the backup tape, and inserts another tape. If data is ever lost or corrupted, it can be retrieved from these tapes. In larger organizations, tape libraries house multiple tapes in holding slots, which are automatically inserted into drives as needed.

Two common tape cartridge types are as follows:

- **Digital Linear Tape (DLT).** These are self-contained tape cartridges that come in different capacities and qualities. *DLT* can transfer data as fast as 60 MB/s, and cartridges as large as 800 GB are available.

- **Linear Tape-Open (LTO).** *LTO* is a newer, faster standard. The cartridges are about the same size but can hold more data and transfer it faster. LTO-5, released in 2010, can transfer data at 140 MB/s and can hold as much as 1.5 TB.

When using tapes, there is an initial cost and a recurring cost for new tapes as tapes wear out. For example, imagine that an organization has a large database and wants to back it up daily and retain backups for a year. A common backup strategy requires about 20 tapes to hold different backups—daily, weekly, monthly, quarterly, annually, and for off-site storage.

Backup tape drives commonly use SCSI interfaces. Internal drives will use one of the Ultra SCSI versions, and external SCSI drives often use SAS.

It's very rare for a regular user to use a tape drive for backups. It's often cheaper and easier to back up data to an external hard drive or even to an optical disc.

Floppy Drives

For many years, floppy disks were the primary way many people copied files from one system to another. USB flash drives have replaced them and made them all but obsolete. You might not even see a system with a *floppy disk drive (FDD)* today, but they are specifically mentioned in the objectives.

Older disks were 5.25 inches and were bendable, giving them their "floppy" name, but the most recent version is 3.5 inches and not very floppy or bendable. In the original IBM PC computers, users booted their system up with this disk. It was identified as the A drive. Dual floppy disk systems had a second one, identified as the B drive.

> **NOTE A AND B DRIVE NAMES**
>
> Even though you might never see or a use a floppy, the letter names A and B are still reserved for floppies. The first hard drive starts with the letter C.

Floppy drives can hold 1.44 MB of data. It's relatively easy to create a bootable floppy disk, and for years, technicians kept bootable floppies that included software troubleshooting tools. When a system failed, they booted the system to the floppy and ran tests from there. Today it's more common to use a bootable CD or DVD or a bootable USB flash drive for this purpose.

Recovering Data

There was a time when 1.44 MB of data was considered a lot, and many users copied data onto a floppy for long-term storage. The primary reason why a system might have a floppy drive today is to recover this archived data.

Floppy Connections

Floppy disk drives are usually mounted inside the computer, with the slot for the floppy disk accessible from the front panel. They have two primary connectors:

- **Power.** A 4-pin mini-Molex connector provides power. Chapter 1 shows a picture of a common power supply including this connector.

- **Data.** The data cable is a 34-pin ribbon cable similar to the 40-pin ribbon cable used with PATA drives. Connectors aren't always keyed, but the red stripe on the ribbon cable should go to pin 1 on the motherboard and pin 1 on the floppy drive.

EXAM TIP

A common problem with floppy disk installations was connecting the ribbon cable backwards on one of the connectors. Typically, the floppy LED stays lit and drives aren't recognized. In some cases, data on the floppy is corrupted.

Many floppy drives have a jumper to identify the first and second drive (drive A and drive B). It was common to leave them both set to drive A and use a ribbon cable with three connectors and a twist before the last connector. You'd connect the last connector to drive A and the middle connector to drive B. It's also possible to manipulate the BIOS to designate which drive is which.

If you come across a floppy drive that isn't working, check the BIOS to see whether it's disabled. They are rarely used in day-to-day work, so it could be disabled without anyone noticing.

RAID

A *redundant array of independent (or inexpensive) disks (RAID)* uses multiple disks to provide increased performance and fault tolerance. In general, fault tolerance refers to any system that can suffer a fault but can still tolerate the error and continue to operate. With RAID, a disk can fail but the system will continue to operate.

Fault tolerance is achieved by using extra disks in specific configurations. When extra components are added for fault tolerance, they are commonly referred to as *redundant components*.

Both software-based RAID and hardware-based RAID are available. In software-based RAID, the operating system manages the RAID configuration. For example, in Windows-based systems, you can use dynamic disks and create software-based RAID arrays. One big benefit is that it doesn't cost anything.

> **MORE INFO** **CHAPTER 16**
>
> Chapter 16 covers RAID configurations supported within Windows. Windows 7 uses dynamic disks, which can be used to create RAID-0 and RAID-1 disk arrays.

Hardware-based RAID is supported on some motherboards, and you can also purchase external hardware-based arrays. Hardware-based RAID arrays outperform software-based arrays, so if you can afford it, it's a better option. The operating system views a hardware-based array simply as another disk.

There are multiple types of RAID, but the exam focuses on only four: RAID-0, RAID-1, RAID-5, and RAID-10.

RAID-0

RAID-0 uses two or more disks and is commonly called *striping* or a *striped volume*. It does not provide fault tolerance. However, because the data is spread across multiple disks, the system can read and write to the array more quickly than it can read or write to a single disk.

Imagine that you had a file named Study Notes and that it took exactly 100 milliseconds (ms) to save it to a single disk. The majority of this time is taken by physical components in the hard disk, so if you could save parts of the file to two disks at the same time, you could cut the time almost in half, as shown in Figure 4-13. There is some overhead from other components, such as the disk controller, so it's not exactly half. When it needs to read the file, the array reads it from each disk at the same time, so reads are quicker, too.

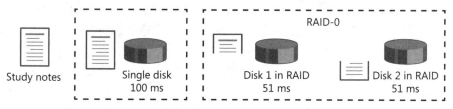

FIGURE 4-13 Comparing a single disk with RAID-0.

What if one of the disks fails? The system can't interpret half-files, so all the data is lost. At this point, you'd better hope you have a backup.

You can use more disks in a RAID-0 configuration for better read and write performance. For example, if you have four drives, it takes about 25 percent of the time for a read or write compared to a single disk. However, each additional disk adds risk. For example, if you have four disks in a RAID-0, you're four times more likely to experience a failure, and if one drive fails, all the data is lost.

RAID-1

RAID-1 uses two disks only and is commonly called *mirroring* or a *mirrored volume*. Everything that is written to one physical disk in the RAID-1 is also written to the second disk. The biggest benefit is fault tolerance. If one drive fails, you still have a copy of the data on the second drive.

Figure 4-14 compares this to a single disk. Because you're writing the entire file to a single disk, you don't get any write performance gains. However, many RAID-1 controllers recognize that the other disk has the same file and can read from both disks simultaneously. Therefore, RAID-1 often provides increased read performance.

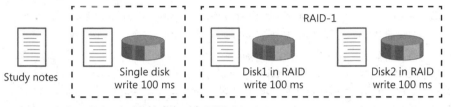

FIGURE 4-14 Comparing a single disk with RAID-1.

The primary drawback of a RAID-1 is that you have less usable disk space. If you create it with two 500 GB disks, you have only 500 GB of usable disk space.

Some RAID-1 configurations can automatically switch over to the other disk if one disk fails. You'll see some type of error or notification, but the system will continue to run.

In other RAID-1 configurations, you might have to manually intervene. For example, if Disk 1 from Figure 4-14 failed, you might have to reconfigure the system to use Disk 2 in place of Disk 1. If the RAID-1 is being used as the boot disk, you might have to reconfigure a system file to boot from Disk 2. Or, you might need to reconfigure the drives so that Disk 2 is recognized as Disk 1.

> **NOTE** **DUPLEXING**
>
> As an additional measure, some RAID-1 configurations include an additional disk control-ler. Each drive uses a dedicated controller. This is called *duplexing*, or *RAID-1 duplexing*, and ensures that the system continues to operate even if one controller fails.

RAID-5

RAID-5 uses at least three disks and is commonly called *striping with parity*. It uses the equiva-lent of one drive as parity to provide fault tolerance. Chapter 3, "Understanding RAM and CPUs," describes parity as a method of error detection used with memory. RAID-5 uses it as a method of fault tolerance.

As an example of how parity works with RAID-5, consider Table 46. It includes the decimal numbers 0 through 3. Each of these numbers can be represented with two binary bits. For example, the decimal number 1 is represented as 01 and the decimal number 2 is 10.

TABLE 4-6 Calculating Odd Parity with RAID-5

Decimal Number	Data Bit 1 21 (2)	Data Bit 0 20 (1)	Number of 1's in Bits	Odd Parity
Zero (0)	0	0	Zero	1
One (1)	0	1	One	0
Two (2)	1	0	One	0
Three (3)	1	1	Two	1

On a RAID-5, a group of data bits are combined with parity in a stripe. For example the row for three includes three bits in the stripe: 1 and 1 for the data and 1 for parity.

The parity bit is set to a 0 or a 1 to ensure that the stripe has an odd number of 1 bits. For example, three is represented as 11. The system calculates the number of 1 bits in 11 as two. The number two is even, so the parity bit is set to 1 so that the total number of 1 bits in the stripe is three (an odd number). Similarly, two is represented as 10, which is one 1 bit. One is odd, so the parity bit for the stripe is set to 0.

In a RAID-5, you will always have at least three drives, and the equivalent of one drive is used for parity. When a RAID-5 array writes data to a drive, it calculates the parity bit and writes it along with the data.

For example, Table 4-7 shows how you can think of these two data bits and the parity bit as three drives. In the table, Drive 2 has failed and the data isn't available. However, if you can count the number of 1 bits in a stripe and identify even numbers from odd numbers, you can tell what the bits in Drive 2 should be.

TABLE 4-7 Calculating Odd Parity with RAID-5

Drive 1 Data Bit 1 [21 (2)]	Drive 2 Data Bit 0 [20 (1)]	Drive 3 Odd Parity
0	Fail	1
0	Fail	0
1	Fail	0
1	**Fail**	**1**

The last stripe is in bold. You can see that it has two 1s, which is an even number. The missing bit in Drive 2 must be a 1 to give the stripe an odd number of 1s. Can you fill in the bits for Drive 2 without looking back at Table 4-6?

When a drive fails in a RAID-5, the array can calculate the missing bit on the fly. That is, an entire drive can fail and the array will continue to work. It will be slower, but it will still work. However, if two drives fail, it can no longer operate.

RAID-5 doesn't write data one bit at a time. Instead, it writes the data and parity in 64-KB stripes. Also, even though it uses the equivalent of one drive for parity, parity is not contained on just one drive. A RAID-5 alternates which drive is holding the parity bits in different stripes, as shown in Figure 4-15.

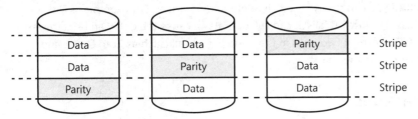

FIGURE 4-15 Raid-5 array with three drives.

A RAID-5 array can have more drives, such as five or six, but it still devotes the equivalent of one drive for parity. If it had a total of five drives, four drives would be for data and one drive would be for parity.

RAID 10

RAID-10 is a combination RAID-1 (mirror) and RAID-0 (striped). It's often referred to as a *stripe of mirrors* and includes at least four disks. It's the best of the four RAID options but is more expensive. RAID-10 is often used on servers with databases.

Figure 4-16 shows an example of how this is configured. Disks 1 and 2 are a RAID-1 (mirror), and they each hold a copy of the same data. Disks 3 and 4 create another RAID-1, and they each hold a copy of the same data. Combined Array A and Array B are configured as a RAID-0 (stripe).

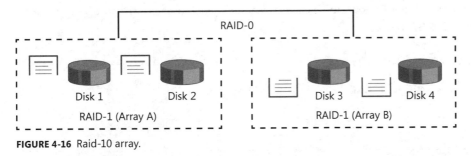

FIGURE 4-16 Raid-10 array.

NOTE **ADDITIONAL MIRRORS POSSIBLE**

You can create a RAID-0 array with more than just two disks. Similarly, you can create a RAID-10 with more than just two mirrors. A RAID-10 will always have an even number of disks.

Disks in the mirror labeled Array A hold half the data, and disks in the array labeled Array B hold the other half of the data. This is similar to how a two-disk RAID-0 would hold half the data on each of two disks. The RAID-10 has superior read and write performance, similar to a RAID-0, and also has fault tolerance similar to a RAID1.

Additionally, a RAID-10 can survive the failure of multiple drives. For example, if Disk 1 in Array A fails and Disk 3 in Array B fails, it can still operate because the data can be retrieved from Disks 2 and 4. However, if two disks in the same mirror fail (such as both Disk 1 and Disk 2), it's time to look for your backups.

RAID and Backups

An important point you should understand about RAID is that it is not a replacement for backups. RAID provides fault tolerance, and backups ensure that you can restore data if the original data is lost.

For example, consider a system with a RAID-5. If one of the drives fails, the RAID-5 provides fault tolerance allowing the system to continue to operate. What if the system suffers a catastrophic failure from a power spike or fire, or what if it is stolen? Without a backup, the data is lost forever.

Calculating Usable Storage Space in RAID

In some versions of RAID, some of the space is used for redundancy, so it isn't available for data. For example, if you have two 1-TB drives used in a mirror, you can store only 1 TB of data. The mirror holds a complete copy, so even though you have 2 TB of drive space, only 1 TB of drive space is available for data.

You should be able to identify how much usable drive space you have with different RAID configurations. Table 4-8 shows some examples of how much usable disk space you'll have if each disk is 500 GB in size.

TABLE 4-8 Calculating Storage Space

RAID	Number of Disks	Usable Disk Space
RAID-0	Two	1 TB
RAID-0	Three	1.5 TB
RAID-1	Two	500 GB (500 GB is mirrored)
RAID-5	Three	1 TB (500 GB is used for parity)
RAID-5	Five	2 TB (500 GB is used for parity)
RAID-10	Four	1 TB (1 TB is mirrored)
RAID-10	Six	1.5 TB (1.5 TB is mirrored)

RAID Summary

Table 4-9 compares key points for each of the RAID configurations. The Read/Write Benefits column compares the benefits of reading and writing data to the array instead of to a single disk drive.

TABLE 4-9 RAID Array Summary

RAID	Fault Tolerance	Read/Write Benefits	Min # of Disks	Comments
RAID-0	No	Improved Read/ Write	2	Use for performance only
RAID-1	Yes	Improved Read	2	Duplexing adds a second controller
RAID-5	Yes	Improved Read/ Write	3	Writes are slower than RAID-0 due to parity calculations
RAID-10	Yes	Improved Read/ Write	4	Best and most expensive

✔ **Quick Check**

1. Name three RAID configurations that provide fault tolerance.

2. How many disks are used in RAID-5?

Quick Check Answers

1. RAID-1, RAID-5, and RAID-10.

2. Three or more.

Common Symptoms

Some of the common problem symptoms of hard disk drives and RAID arrays are described in the following sections. The only hardware tool you'll need when working on hard drives is a screwdriver.

Loud Clicking Noise

This is never a good noise to hear from a hard drive. It indicates that as the platter is spinning, it's hitting something it shouldn't. The heads are riding on an extremely thin pocket of air, and if they are jarred just the slightest bit, they can crash onto the spinning platter. This is why, when hard drives fail, technicians often refer to it as a hard drive crash.

If you hear a clicking noise coming from a hard drive, back up the data as quickly as possible and replace it. It's just a matter of time before it fails.

REAL WORLD   AS A LAST RESORT, TRY THE FREEZER TRICK

I once had a drive that started giving some random errors and then started making all sorts of clicks that you just don't want to hear out of a hard drive. I powered it down to let it rest and then came back the next day to back up the data. The symptoms returned almost immediately. I needed to try something different.

I powered down the system, removed the hard drive, sealed it in a plastic bag, and stored it in a freezer overnight. It's an old trick I'd heard about but never tried before. I put it back into the system the next day and powered it up. Thankfully, it worked long enough for me to get my data back. Cold causes objects to contract, and while the drive was cool, it was running without problems. As soon as it started heating up, the problems returned, but by then I had my data. You don't want to try the freezer technique as the first step, but it might be useful as a last-ditch effort.

Read/Write Failure

When clusters on a hard drive fail, a hard drive is unable to read or write data to the cluster. Whenever you see errors related to hard disk reads and writes, it's safe to assume that there are problems with clusters on the drive. These are relatively easy to overcome on Windows-based systems, using simple tools such as chkdsk and Check Disk. Both of these tools are presented in Chapter 16.

EXAM TIP

Chapter 16 also covers formatting a disk. You usually have the option of doing a full format or a quick format. A full format checks disk clusters and marks faulty clusters as bad so that they won't be used. A quick format does not check the clusters. It's always a good idea to do a full format when putting a new disk into service.

Slow Performance

The most common reason for a hard drive's performance to slow down is fragmentation. Ideally, files are written in contiguous clusters, but as the drive is heavily used or fills up, there aren't as many contiguous clusters available. Instead, a file is divided into multiple fragments on clusters scattered throughout the disk.

When too many files are fragmented, the drive appears slower because it's having to work harder and harder to retrieve all the file fragments. Again, the solution is simple if you know what tools to use. Chapter 16 covers the defrag and Disk Defragmenter tools that can check a disk for excessive fragmentation and that can defragment drives when they need it.

> **NOTE DISK THRASHING**
>
> *Disk thrashing* indicates that the hard drive is constantly working. You can often hear the constant movement of the actuator arm and see that the disk LED is constantly blinking. This is often an indication that the disk is fragmented. Alternatively, it might indicate that the system doesn't have enough memory, but you should check for fragmentation first.

Failure to Boot or Operating System Not Found

If the system won't boot at all or gives an error indicating that it can't find the operating system, it could be that the bootable drive failed. If so, you'll need to replace it and rebuild the system. However, you should check the basics first.

The most common reason is that the system is trying to boot to a device that does not have a bootable operating system. If the system has floppy or optical drives, remove any disks/discs and then try to reboot. You might also need to check the BIOS to ensure that the system is configured to boot from the hard drive.

If you see this problem after a system was recently worked on or a drive was replaced, double-check the cabling and jumpers. It's very likely you'll find the problem.

If the system is using a RAID-1 and the first drive in the array fails, you might need to reconfigure the system to use the second drive. Some RAIDs will automatically boot to the alternate drive, but occasionally you'll need to manually reconfigure the disks. For example, you might need to swap the wiring or jumpers for the two disks in the array so that the good drive is recognized as the first drive.

RAID Not Found

Hardware RAID systems often come as external RAID enclosures, and when you first hook them up to a system, they might not be recognized. The most common reason is that the operating system doesn't have the drivers needed to use it.

In this case, the solution is simple. Locate the drivers and install them. For new RAID systems, the manufacturer will include drivers. Follow the instructions that came with the device to install them. If it's not a new system, you can usually download the correct drivers from the manufacturer's website.

> **MORE INFO CHAPTER 15, "CONFIGURING WINDOWS OPERATING SYSTEMS"**
>
> Chapter 15 covers device drivers in more depth, including the use of tools such as Device Manager to install new drivers.

RAID Stops Working

If a RAID-0 has a failure in any single drive, it will stop working completely. You'll need to replace the drive, rebuild the array, and restore the data from a backup.

However, other RAID arrays have built-in redundancy, so you usually won't see this symptom unless more than one drive fails. For example, if you have a RAID-5 array with five disks and two disks fail, the RAID-5 will stop working completely. In this case, the solution is the same as with a RAID-0. Replace the drives, rebuild the array, and restore the data from a backup.

This brings up an important point. When you see errors starting to appear in a RAID array, fix them immediately. A technician who sees a failed drive in a RAID-5 array might say, "I'll fix that tomorrow." However, if a second drive fails, it's too late.

BSOD

It isn't common to have a stop error or blue screen of death (BSOD) from a hard drive or RAID problem. If it occurs, the most common reason is because the operating system doesn't have the correct driver for the drive. The most common solution is to boot into Safe Mode and install the correct driver.

> **MORE INFO** **CHAPTER 17, "TROUBLESHOOTING WINDOWS OPERATING SYSTEMS"**
>
> Chapter 17 covers Safe Mode, including how to access it and the tools that are available.

✔ **Quick Check**

1. What tool can you use if a drive gives read/write failure errors?
2. What tool can you use to check a disk if it is slow?

Quick Check Answers

1. Check Disk or chkdsk.
2. Disk Defragmenter or defrag.

Chapter Summary

- Hard disk drives include platters, read/write heads, and actuator arms. Data is written onto ferromagnetic material on the platters. Platters spin at rates such as 5400, 7200, 10,000, and 15,000 revolutions per minute (rpm).

- IDE (or PATA) interfaces are being replaced by SATA interfaces. Most motherboards include two IDE connectors, and each connector supports two drives. You need to configure jumpers, selecting master, slave, or cable select.

- PATA drives use 80-wire, 40 pin ribbon cables for data. 4-pin Molex power connectors provide 5 V and 12 V. ATA-7 (UDMA/133) can transfer data at a rate of 133 MBps.

- Motherboards have a single connector for each SATA drive. SATA connectors have a distinctive L shape. Data cables include seven wires. Power cables have five wires, providing 3.3 V, 5 V, and 12 V, but the power connector has 15 pins.

- SATA speeds are as follows: SATA 1.5G 150 MBps (1.5 Gbit/s), SATA 3G 300 MBps (3 Gbit/s), and SATA 6G 600 MBps (6 Gbit/s).

- SATA data connectors use a 7-pin L-shaped connector, and power connectors use a 15-pin L-shaped connector.

- External drives can be connected to a computer with USB, FireWire, and eSATA connections. Many eSATA connectors on laptops use combo eSATA and USB ports.

- Some common SCSI speeds are as follows: Ultra-160 160 MBps (1.28 Gbit/s), Ultra-320 320 MBps (2.56 Gbit/s), and Ultra-640 640 MBps (5.12 Gbit/s). SCSI devices use 25-pin, 50-pin, 68-pin, or 80-pin ribbon cables.

- A single SCSI controller supports as many as 15 devices identified with a device ID. The controller is normally assigned ID 7, which has the highest priority.

- SSDs have no moving parts but instead are nonvolatile RAM used as a drive. They are much quicker than hard disk drives but also more expensive.

- Digital cameras and recorders use a similar type of portable memory. Common brands are CompactFlash, Secure Digital, mini-SD, and micro-SD.

- Optical disk capacities are as follows: CD 700 MB, mini-CD 194 MB, DVD 4.7 GB, dual-layer DVD 8.5 GB, single-layer Blu-Ray 25 GB, and dual-layer Blu-Ray 50 GB.

- Optical discs designated with R are recordable, indicating data can be written to them once. RW indicates rewritable, and data can be written to the disc many times. Blu-Ray RE discs are recordable and erasable.

- Combo drives can read and write data to multiple types of optical discs, including CDs, DVDs, and Blu-Ray discs.

- Tape drives can be used for backups but are rarely used on desktop computers. Floppy drives support 3.5-inch 1.44-MB drives but are rarely included with computers today.

- RAID configurations provide different benefits by combining multiple disks. RAID-0 does not provide fault tolerance, but RAID-1, RAID-5, and RAID-10 do provide fault tolerance.
- Hardware RAID is more efficient than software RAID. Ensure that you have the correct drivers for a hardware RAID enclosure.
- Clicking noises from a hard drive indicate a hard drive crash. Back up data as soon as possible.
- Use tools such as chkdsk, Check Disk, defrag, and Disk Defragmenter to maintain drives.

Chapter Review

Use the following questions to test your knowledge of the information in this chapter. The answers to these questions, and the explanations of why each answer choice is correct or incorrect, are located in the "Answers" section at the end of this chapter.

1. You are adding an internal SATA drive to an existing system. How many drives can you connect to a SATA connector?

   A. One

   B. Two

   C. Three

   D. Four

2. What type of data connector is used for a SATA 3G drive?

   A. 40-pin, 40-wire ribbon cable

   B. 40-pin, 80-wire ribbon cable

   C. 7 pins with an *L*-shaped connector

   D. 15 pins with an *L*-shaped connector

3. Which of the following is not a valid external connector for a hard drive?

   A. USB

   B. FireWire

   C. eSATA

   D. 1934b

4. How much data can you store on a DL DVD disc?

   A. 700 MB

   B. 4.7 GB

   C. 8.5 GB

   D. 17.1 GB

5. What is the minimum number of drives in a RAID-1?

   A. One

   B. Two

   C. Three

   D. Four

6. You hear a hard drive making loud clicking noises. What does this indicate?

   A. Failing hard drive

   B. Normal operation

   C. Disk thrashing

   D. Bad clusters

Answers

1. **Correct Answer:** A

   A. **Correct:** SATA connectors support only one drive.

   B. **Incorrect:** IDE connectors support two drives.

   C. **Incorrect:** None of the interfaces support three drives.

   D. **Incorrect:** A single motherboard includes two IDE drives and can support four SATA drives.

2. **Correct Answer:** C

   A. **Incorrect:** Older PATA drives use 40-pin, 40-wire cables.

   B. **Incorrect:** Newer PATA drives use 40-pin, 80-wire cables.

   C. **Correct:** SATA data connectors use a 7-pin *L*-shaped connector.

   D. **Incorrect:** SATA power uses a 15-pin *L*-shaped connector.

3. **Correct Answer:** D

   A. **Incorrect:** USB connectors can be used to connect drives.

   B. **Incorrect:** FireWire connectors can be used to connect drives.

   C. **Incorrect:** Hard disk drives can be connected with eSATA.

   D. **Correct:** 1394a and 1394B are FireWire 400 and FireWire 800, but an external connector named 1934b doesn't exist.

4. **Correct Answer:** C

   A. **Incorrect:** A standard CD holds 700 MB.

   B. **Incorrect:** A single-layer DVD holds 4.7 GB.

   C. **Correct:** A dual-layer DVD holds 8.5 GB.

   D. **Incorrect:** A dual-layer double-sided DVD holds 17.1 GB.

5. **Correct Answer:** B

   A. **Incorrect:** None of the RAID configurations use one drive.

   B. **Correct:** RAID-1 (mirror) uses only two drives.

   C. **Incorrect:** RAID-5 requires a minimum of three drives.

   D. **Incorrect:** RAID-10 requires a minimum of four drives.

6. **Correct Answer: A**

   A. **Correct:** This indicates a failing hard disk drive.

   B. **Incorrect:** Clicking noises from a hard disk drive are not normal.

   C. **Incorrect:** Disk thrashing is when you can hear the actuator busily working and see the LED constantly blinking.

   D. **Incorrect:** Bad clusters will give read and write errors.

CHAPTER 5

Exploring Peripherals and Expansion Cards

In this chapter, you'll learn about different components that you can add to a computer and how you can do so. The most common way of connecting external devices is with Universal Serial Bus (USB) connections, but there are other methods such as FireWire, and a variety of miscellaneous connections are available at the rear of a computer. In addition to using available connections to add components, you can add expansion cards to give your computer additional capabilities.

Exam 220-801 objectives in this chapter:

- 1.4 Install and configure expansion cards.
  - Sound cards
  - Video cards
  - Network cards
  - Serial and parallel cards
  - USB cards
  - FireWire cards
  - Storage cards
  - Modem cards
  - Wireless/cellular cards
  - TV tuner cards
  - Video capture cards
  - Riser cards
- 1.7 Compare and contrast various connection interfaces and explain their purpose.
  - Physical connections
    - USB 1.1 vs. 2.0 vs. 3.0 speed and distance characteristics
      - Connector types: A, B, mini, micro
    - FireWire 400 vs. FireWire 800 speed and distance characteristics

- Other connector types
  - Serial
  - Parallel
  - Audio
- 1.11 Identify connector types and associated cables.
  - Display connector types
    - miniDIN-6
  - Device connectors and pin arrangements
    - USB
    - IEEE1394
    - PS/2
    - Parallel
    - Serial
    - Audio
  - Device cable types
    - USB
    - IEEE1394
    - Parallel
    - Serial
- 1.12 Install and configure various peripheral devices.
  - Input devices
    - Mouse
    - Keyboard
    - Scanner
    - Barcode reader
    - KVM
    - Microphone
    - Biometric devices
    - Game pads
    - Joysticks
    - Digitizer
  - Multimedia devices
    - Digital cameras
    - Microphone
    - Webcam

- Camcorder
- MIDI enabled devices
- Output devices
  - Speakers

Peripherals and Device Drivers

A *peripheral* is any device that you connect to a computer. This term includes critical components such as keyboards, mice, and display monitors. It also includes additional components such as speakers, scanners, printers, external hard drives, and flash drives.

Chapter 2, "Understanding Motherboards and BIOS," describes how the Basic Input/Output System (BIOS) is used when a computer is first turned on. The processor runs this program to access basic hardware such as the keyboard, display, and hard drives. It locates an operating system (such as Windows) on a disk drive and loads it. The operating system then loads additional software, including device drivers, used to access other peripheral devices.

Device Drivers

When manufacturers create hardware devices, they also create a *device driver* for different operating systems. The device drivers give the operating system the information it needs to communicate with the device. Without the correct device driver, the device doesn't work.

Windows and other operating systems include many drivers, so you can often just connect a device and it'll work. Windows does some work behind the scenes that isn't apparent. When you insert a device, Windows recognizes it, looks for a suitable driver, and associates it with the device. In most cases, this happens automatically without requiring you to do anything else.

However, sometimes Windows doesn't have the driver for the device. In these cases, you need to install it.

> *MORE INFO*   **CHAPTER 15, "CONFIGURING WINDOWS OPERATING SYSTEMS"**
>
> **When you need to manipulate device drivers manually, you use Device Manager in Windows-based systems. Device Manager is discussed in Chapter 15.**

Install Device Drivers before Installing Device

New devices often include a CD with a device installation program. You insert the CD and follow the directions to install the drivers. In some cases, the instructions are very specific about installing the drivers *before* installing the device.

The following situation doesn't occur often, but when it does, it can take a lot of time to resolve. Specifically, it is possible for Windows to misidentify a device and install a similar but incompatible driver. The device might work partially or not at all. If you try to install the correct driver with the installation CD later, Windows might continue to use the first driver it installed.

When manufacturers are aware of this problem, they provide clear instructions to install the driver first. If you see a note saying to install the driver first, it's best to do so.

Plug and Play

Windows includes a great feature called *Plug and Play (PnP)* that automates the installation and configuration of many device drivers. Many people recognize that it is automatically installing the correct driver, but they're unaware that it is also configuring resources for the driver. Two important resources that are automatically assigned are a specific range of memory addresses used by the device and an *interrupt request (IRQ)* number.

When devices want to get the attention of the CPU, they raise an IRQ, just as you might raise your hand to get someone's attention. The CPU identifies the device based on the IRQ number and answers the request by addressing the device with the memory address.

Years ago, in addition to finding and installing the correct driver, you also had to configure the memory and IRQ settings manually, which could be quite tedious. I'm happy to say that I haven't had to configure these settings manually with Windows XP, Windows Vista, or Windows 7.

> **REAL WORLD** **FOLLOWING THE DIRECTIONS AVOIDS PROBLEMS**
>
> I know it's tempting to install first and follow directions later—I've been guilty of it a few times in the past. Manufacturers know this too and will often use special, highly visible labels saying something like, "Install software before attaching device."
>
> I remember helping a friend with a new digital camera he had purchased. The directions clearly said to install the drivers first, but like a kid at Christmas, he just ripped the packaging open and plugged it in after taking some pictures. Unfortunately, the operating system didn't recognize it, so he went back to the directions to install the correct driver, but the operating system still used the original.
>
> We had to go through several steps to get it working. We went into Device Manager to uninstall the driver, shut the system down, and disconnected the camera. We then rebooted and went through the process of installing the software provided with the drive. When we reconnected it, it worked.
>
> While this ended up being a success story, it was avoidable. If the directions say to install the driver first, it's best to do so. If you're not sure, installing the driver first is always safe.

USB

The most common method of connecting peripherals to a computer is by using *Universal Serial Bus (USB)*, and a popular USB device is a USB flash drive (also called a USB thumb drive). Figure 5-1 shows a picture of a 16-GB flash drive that you can use to store all your A+ notes plus several thousand songs, pictures, and other files.

> **NOTE   FLASH MEMORY**
>
> The memory used in USB flash drives is flash memory. This is the same type of memory commonly used to store the BIOS program on a motherboard. It is nonvolatile, meaning that it retains data without power and it is hot-swappable.

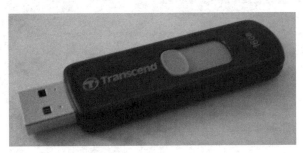

FIGURE 5-1 USB flash drive.

You've probably seen USB flash drives before, so I'm betting this is familiar to you. However, as an A+ technician, you should be aware of some important details about USB. Table 5-1 outlines some details about the three versions of USB.

TABLE 5-1 USB Versions

Version	Common Name	Speed
USB 1.1	Low Speed Full Speed	1.5 Mbps (low speed) or 12 Mbps (full speed)
USB 2.0	High Speed	480 Mbps (60 MBps)
USB 3.0	Super Speed	5 Gbps (625 MBps)

Most computers support USB 1.1 and USB 2.0, but USB 3.0 is relatively new and not as common.

> **EXAM TIP**
>
> Know the speeds of each of the USB versions when preparing for the exam.

USB 1.1 and 2.0 Connections

The most common USB port is the Standard Type A port. You find at least one Standard Type A port on almost every PC and laptop computer, and many devices also use the Standard Type A port. Other connection types are the Standard Type B, Mini-B, Micro-A, and Micro-B connections.

> **NOTE PORTS VS. CONNECTORS**
>
> In general, a port is the connection on a device and a connector is the connection on a cable that plugs into a port. For example, when you connect an external USB hard disk drive, you use a cable with two connectors. One connector plugs into the port on the computer, and the other connector plugs into the port on the external USB hard disk drive. However, don't be surprised if you see these terms interchanged.

Figure 5-2 shows a picture of the three most common USB connectors (Standard Type A, Standard Type B, and Micro-B) along with a diagram of all the connectors.

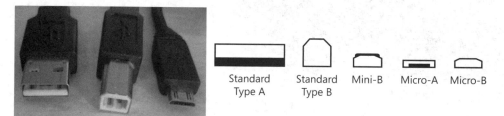

Standard Type A Standard Type B Mini-B Micro-A Micro-B

FIGURE 5-2 Common USB connectors.

Some larger devices, such as printers and video recorders, use the Standard Type B port. One end of the cable is a Standard Type A connector that plugs into the computer, and the other end of the cable is a Standard Type B connector that plugs into the device. Smaller devices, such as smartphones, digital cameras, and global positioning system (GPS) devices, need smaller connections and use the mini and micro connections. The Mini-A connector is no longer used.

Both the Standard Type A and the Standard Type B connectors have four pins and provide 5-V power to the device via pin 1. Each of the mini and micro connectors has five pins and also provides 5-V power to the device on pin 1. The extra pin is used to distinguish the host from the device.

USB 3.0 Connections

While USB 1.1 and 2.0 connectors are identical, USB 3.0 connectors have some significant differences. Despite these differences, USB 3.0 ports still accept connections from older USB devices.

Table 5-2 shows the wiring of the Standard A and B connectors for each of the versions. They are physically the same size, but USB 3.0 ports and connectors are blue to make them easily distinguishable.

TABLE 5-2 USB Standard A and Standard B wiring

Pin	1.1 and 2.0 A and B	USB 3.0 Standard A	USB 3.0 Standard B
1	VBUS (5 V)	VBUS (5 V)	VBUS (5 V)
2	Data -	Data -	Data -
3	Data +	Data +	Data +
4	Ground	Ground	Ground
5	N/A	Receive -	Transmit +
6	N/A	Receive +	Transmit -
7	N/A	Ground	Ground
8	N/A	Transmit +	Receive -
9	N/A	Transmit -	Receive +

USB 3.0 includes two additional sets of pins used to send and receive data at the same time. The A port sends data on pins 8 and 9 and receives data on pins 5 and 6. The device using the B port sends data on pins 5 and 6 and receives data on pins 8 and 9. Only newer USB 3.0 devices take advantage of the new pins. Older devices don't have the pins, so they simply aren't used.

The table also shows that pins 1 through 4 are identical for each version. You can plug any USB device into any of these ports and it will work, but you only can get 3.0 speeds when you plug a USB 3.0 device into a 3.0 port. Possible combinations include the following:

- **USB 1.1 or 2.0 device in USB 3.0 port.** This will work at the device's speed. For example, a 2.0 device will run at 480 Mbps.
- **USB 3.0 device in USB 2.0 port.** This will work at the USB 2.0 speed of 480 Mbps.
- **USB 3.0 device in USB 3.0 port.** This is the only combination that allows the full 5-Gbps speed.

In addition to the USB Standard A and Standard B connectors, USB 3.0 also has a USB Micro-B connection. It includes the exact same connector as the USB 2.0 Micro-B connection and adds an extension with five more pins, as shown in Figure 5-3.

USB 2.0 Micro-B   USB 3.0 Micro-B

FIGURE 5-3 USB Micro-B connectors.

USB Controller

Computers have one or more USB controllers used to control USB devices, and the controller is a part of the chipset on the motherboard. Each version of USB supports a total of 128 devices, including the controller. Therefore, the USB controller can support as many as 127 devices.

It's common for a desktop computer to have USB ports available at the front and in the back. These ports can be controlled by the same controller or, in some cases, by separate controllers.

The ports provide power to the devices that need it, but it's important to realize that there is a limited amount of power shared by the ports. If you plug in too many devices, one or more of the devices will stop working. For example, if you plug a camcorder (video recorder) into a USB port, your keyboard or mouse might stop working. This is rarely a problem, unless you plug in a device that draws a lot of power, such as a camcorder.

There are two solutions to this problem. The first is to provide power to the device with its own power cord. You can also connect an externally powered USB hub (like the one shown in Figure 5-4) to the computer. It plugs into a USB port and provides additional powered ports to external devices without drawing power from the computer.

FIGURE 5-4 USB hub.

In addition to sharing power, each of the devices connected to a controller shares the same bandwidth. For example, if you have a USB 2.0 controller with five USB devices connected, each device does not have 480 Mbps of bandwidth available. Instead, the devices share the 480 Mbps bandwidth.

USB Cable Lengths

When connecting devices by using a USB cable, the cable can be as long as 5 meters (about 16 feet). This is useful for devices such as printers. It's very rare to find a device with a 5-meter USB cable, but USB extension cords are available. The maximum recommended cable length for USB 3.0 is 3 meters (almost 10 feet).

EXAM TIP

Know the maximum cable lengths when preparing for the exam.

Dirty Bit

USB devices are hot-swappable, meaning that you can insert and remove them without powering a system down. However, you shouldn't remove a USB device if it has an open file. When you open and modify a file in Windows, a bit is set indicating that the disk has an unsaved file. This bit is commonly called a *dirty bit*. When all the files have been saved, the dirty bit is cleared.

If you insert a flash drive that has the dirty bit set, you'll see a message similar to this: "Do you want to scan and fix Removable Disk? There might be a problem with some files on this device or disc. This can happen if you remove the device or disc before all files have been written to it." If you choose to scan and fix it, the system will run a program called chkdsk on the drive and resolve the problem.

> **MORE INFO** **CHAPTER 16, "UNDERSTANDING DISKS AND FILE SYSTEMS"**
>
> Chkdsk can also be used to manually check disks for problems and repair them. Chapter 16 explores chkdsk in more depth.

You can avoid this completely by ensuring that all files are closed before removing a flash drive. Additionally, ensure that the computer is not writing to the flash drive before you remove it. If you remove a drive while a file is being modified, the system might corrupt the file.

 Quick Check

　　1. How many devices are supported by a USB hub?

　　2. What is the speed of USB 3.0?

Quick Check Answers

　　1. 127.

　　2. 5 Gbps.

FireWire

FireWire was originally created by Apple and later standardized as IEEE 1394. It is a high-speed serial bus similar to USB and is often used for audio and video editing. It can transfer data between a computer and digital video cameras or external hard drives at the high speeds needed for effective editing.

When it was updated, versions became known as FireWire 400, or *IEEE 1394a,* and FireWire 800, or *IEEE 1394b*. In addition to being used as a high-speed serial bus with a computer, FireWire 800 can also be used to network computers together with common Category 5e twisted-pair cable, although this isn't common. Table 5-3 compares the two versions.

TABLE 5-3 FireWire Versions

Version	IEEE Name	Speed	Max Cable Length
FireWire 400	1394a	400 Mbps	4.5 meters (about 15 feet)
FireWire 800	1394b	800 Mbps	100 meters (about 330 feet)

> **NOTE   I.LINK AND LYNX**
>
> FireWire is also called i.LINK by Sony, and Lynx by Texas Instruments.

FireWire Cables and Connections

When connecting FireWire 400 devices, the cable can be as long as 4.5 meters (about 15 feet). It's common to daisy-chain FireWire devices by plugging devices into each other. This way, a single FireWire port supports multiple devices, so FireWire can support as many as 63 devices.

You can use FireWire hubs to connect multiple FireWire devices. They work the same way as USB hubs, where you plug the hub into a FireWire port and the hub has multiple FireWire ports. You can also daisy-chain FireWire devices by connecting them to each other. You can have as many as 16 cables for a maximum cable length from the FireWire 400 port of 72 meters (about 236 feet).

There are three types of FireWire connections:

- **4-pin.** This port does not provide power. It's found on smaller devices that don't need power and on laptop computers, instead of the full-size 6-pin port.
- **6-pin alpha connector.** This port includes pins for data and power. It is the port that is most closely associated with FireWire.
- **9-pin beta connector.** This port includes the same connections as a 6-pin port but adds pins for a grounded shield. The shield prevents interference from nearby devices or cables and is required for FireWire 800.

Figure 5-5 shows the 4-pin and 6-pin FireWire 400 connectors. It also includes a diagram of all three connections, including the less common FireWire 800 9-pin connection.

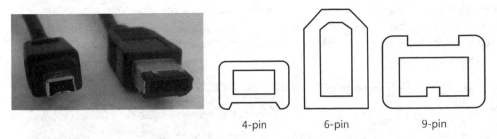

4-pin   6-pin   9-pin

FIGURE 5-5 FireWire connectors (4-pin and 6-pin, with added diagram of 9-pin).

EXAM TIP

Know the speeds of each FireWire type and the details of each connection. The 4-pin port does not provide power, but the 6-pin port does. The 9-pin port is required for FireWire 800.

FireWire S1600 and S3200

IEEE 1394b also included specifications for S1600 and S3200, although devices aren't as readily available for them. S1600 supports speeds up to 1.6 Gbps, and S3200 supports speeds up to 3.2 Gbps. These devices use the 9-pin beta connection.

FireWire S1600 and S3200 devices have been slow to appear for desktops. However, as more USB 3.0 devices with 5 Gbps speeds come to market, it's very likely that you'll see FireWire devices using these faster speeds.

✔ **Quick Check**

    1. How many devices are supported by FireWire?

    2. What is the speed of IEEE 1394b?

Quick Check Answers

    1. 63.

    2. 800 Mbps.

Miscellaneous Connections

Although they are rarely used with typical computers today, some older connections are specifically mentioned in the A+ objectives, so you should be aware of them. Figure 5-6 shows the back of an older computer with these ports, and the following list provides a brief description of each port.

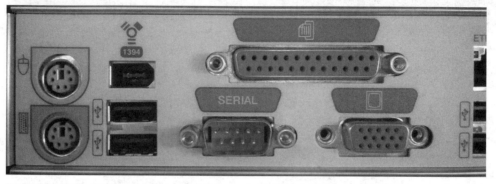

FIGURE 5-6 Back of older computer.

- **PS/2.** At the far left of Figure 5-6 are the older PS/2 ports. The top port is for a mouse, and the bottom port is for a keyboard.
- **Mini-DIN.** The two PS/2 ports are 6-pin mini-DIN ports, but you might run across other mini-DIN ports. *DIN* is short for *Deutsche Industrie Norm*, the German national standards organization that created the standard.
- **1394/USB.** This computer includes one FireWire port and two USB ports.
- **Parallel.** The long, 25-pin female port on the top to the right of center in Figure 5-6 is the parallel port. It is a *DB-25* port.
- **Serial.** The 9-pin male serial port is shown at the bottom center of Figure 5-6. It is a *DB-9* port.
- **VGA.** The 15-pin, three-row port on the bottom right of Figure 5-6 is an old Video Graphics Array (VGA) port. It is a *DB-15* port.

Devices that previously used the PS/2, mini-DIN, parallel, and serial ports commonly use USB ports today. The VGA connection might be present, but other video ports are usually available and used instead. Chapter 6, "Exploring Video and Display Devices," covers video in more depth.

NOTE **D CONNECTORS**

The parallel, serial, and VGA connectors are all loosely shaped like the letter *D*. Each has an official letter designation, but they are commonly called *DB connections*. The 25-pin parallel connection is called a DB-25 (officially DB-25), the 9-pin serial connection is called a DB-9 (officially DA-15), and the 15-pin VGA connection is called a DB-15 (officially DE-15).

PS/2

The *PS/2* name comes from the original IBM personal system/2 computers that used these ports. It is a 6-pin mini-DIN connection. It wasn't originally color-coded, but later implementations used a standard of green for the mouse and purple for the keyboard. Both the connectors on the cable and the ports on the computer are color-coded.

A challenge with these ports is that they are not hot-swappable. It's possible to cause damage by plugging in a device with the power on, although most ports are configured today to help prevent damage. More often, devices that are plugged in with power just aren't recognized. If a mouse or keyboard cable comes loose, you often have to turn off the system to plug it back in.

EXAM TIP

Know the connection colors when preparing for A+ exams. The keyboard is purple, and the mouse is green. (One way to remember this is that "mouse" has five letters and "green" also has five letters.) Also, you should be able to recognize any connection by its shape.

Mini-DIN

Several different types of *mini-DIN* connections are available. Versions come with three, four, five, six, seven, eight, and nine pins. In addition to its use for the PS/2 connections, the 6-pin DIN can also be used for video and audio connections. Another common mini-DIN connection is the Separate Video (S-Video) connection, which is a 4-pin DIN used for video.

Parallel

The *parallel* port was the primary port used for printers before USB became so prevalent, and it was often called the printer port. Data was sent out by the port eight bits (a byte) at a time. Compared to the serial port, which could send data only one bit at a time, the parallel port could send data eight times faster. A ribbon cable connected the printer to the parallel port.

Parallel ports were designated as LPT (short for *line printer*). Most computers had only one parallel port, so it was identified as LPT1.

New printers use USB, FireWire, and/or network connections, and these connections are far superior to the older parallel interface. It's rare to see the parallel port on a new computer.

Serial

The *serial* port was used for devices that could handle data being sent one bit at a time. Figure 5-6 shows a 9-pin male serial port on the back of the computer.

Some computers included both a 9-pin male serial port and a 25-pin male serial port. Combined with the DB-25 parallel port, the DB-25 serial port sometimes confused techs. The primary way to tell the difference is that the serial ports always have pins and the parallel ports always have pinholes.

There is a significant difference between serial data sent via the serial port and serial data sent through USB or FireWire ports. USB and FireWire use low voltage differential (LVD) signaling, which is described in Chapter 4, "Comparing Storage Devices." As a reminder, LVD sends data as differences in voltages between two wires in a pair and can achieve lightning-fast speeds. It's used for USB, FireWire, SATA, AMD HyperTransport busses, and more.

In contrast, the serial ports use *RS-232*. RS is short for *recommended standard,* and RS-232 is the common standard used to send serial data. RS-232 is still used in specialized equipment, but it's rare to see a serial RS-232 port in modern computers.

Serial ports are referred to as *COM* ports. Each COM port has a number, such as COM1, COM2, and so on.

> ✔ **Quick Check**
>
> 1. What color is the keyboard PS/2 connector?
> 2. What is the purpose of a DB-9 connector?
>
> **Quick Check Answers**
>
> 1. Purple.
> 2. Serial communications.

Sound

One of the computer outputs that many people enjoy is audio. Sound can be provided by a simple speaker, by a set of headphones, or with an elaborate 7.1 surround sound system.

> **MORE INFO** **CHAPTER 6 AND CHAPTER 7**
>
> Other output devices include video, covered in Chapter 6, and printers, covered in Chapter 7, "Exploring Printers."

Common Sound Systems

An important piece of knowledge that you need for the A+ exam is how sound systems can be connected. A basic mono sound system has a single channel. No matter how many speakers you connect, the same sound comes out of each one. However, many sound systems include multiple channels. For example, stereo is a two-channel sound system and plays different sounds from the left and right speakers. Some other common sound systems include the following:

- **2.1.** The *2* indicates that it is stereo, and the *.1* represents a subwoofer. The subwoofer provides deep bass sounds.

- **5.1.** A 5.1 sound system is also known as a surround sound system and has five speakers and a subwoofer. It has left and right speakers in the front, left and right speakers in the rear, and a central speaker, often used for voice or dialog.

- **7.1.** A 7.1 sound system includes the same five speakers and subwoofer found in a 5.1 surround sound system and adds two speakers: one on the right side and one on the left side.

Many games and other programs use 3D sound and positional audio to play audio so that it seems as if the sound is in a specific location. For example, you might hear a dog bark from behind you, a bird singing in a tree on your right, or an explosion in front of you. Combined with the deep bass of the subwoofer, you're often able to feel many of the sounds, creating a realistic experience.

Connecting Sound Systems

Most motherboards have built-in sound capabilities as part of the chipset. They provide connections at the back of the system and sometimes at the front. These connections are color-coded and have icons that give you an idea of what they do.

For example, Figure 5-7 shows the back of a system with several ports for a 7.1 sound system, and Table 5-4 describes these ports.

FIGURE 5-7 Sound connectors for 7.1 system.

TABLE 5-4 Sound Connections

Purpose	Color	Comments
Microphone	Pink	Top left. Microphone icon.
Front speakers or headphones	Lime green	Top middle. When on front panel, it often has a headphone icon.
Line in	Light blue	Top right. This accepts sound from sources other than a microphone.
Middle speakers	Brown	Bottom left. Used only for 7.1 systems.
Subwoofer and center speaker	Orange	Bottom middle. Center speaker used for 5.1/7.1 systems and subwoofer used for any x.1 system.
Rear speakers	Black	Bottom right.

> **NOTE COLORS NOT ALWAYS FOLLOWED**
>
> While there are standard colors followed by most vendors, you'll very likely encounter some sound ports that differ from the standard. For example, sometimes gray is used instead of brown for the middle speakers.

Some sound cards also include a Musical Instrument Digital Interface (MIDI) connector. This is a DB-15 connector. Musicians can connect musical instruments and other electronics here to play music. Older joysticks can also plug into this connector.

Most audio connections use a *tip ring sleeve (TRS)* connector. As shown in Figure 5-8, a TRS connector has three contacts, one on the tip, one on a ring around the pin, and one on a sleeve.

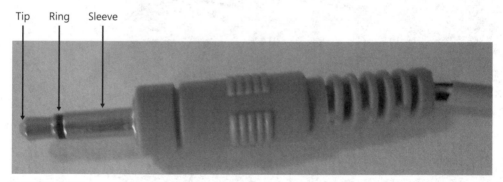

Tip   Ring   Sleeve

FIGURE 5-8 TRS connector.

Some sound systems use a specialized connection called *Sony/Philips Digital Interconnect Format (S/PDIF)*. It is a single connection, and the digital signal includes all the channels.

Figure 5-9 shows the S/PDIF port on a motherboard. It is next to the blue line-in jack, the green front-speaker jack, and the pink microphone jack (from top to bottom).

FIGURE 5-9 S/PDIF connector next to three other sound connectors.

If you come across a system that isn't playing sound, there are a few things to check. First, check the sound controls in the operating system. The Control Panel has a Sound applet, and a sound control is usually available in the notification area on the right side of the taskbar. You can use these controls to mute/unmute the sound and adjust the volume. Next, ensure that the speakers are plugged into the correct jack. Last, ensure that the correct device drivers are installed.

> ✔ **Quick Check**
>
> 1. What does .1 indicate in a 7.1 surround sound system?
>
> 2. What is the standard color for the front speaker jack?
>
> **Quick Check Answers**
>
> 1. Subwoofer.
>
> 2. Lime green.

Input Devices

The basic flow of information through a computer is input, processing, and output. Chapters 2 and 3 spend a lot of time on the motherboard and CPUs that handle much of the processing, but it's also important to be aware of the different types of input devices and how they are installed.

Keyboard

A keyboard is a primary input device used on desktop computers, but there are several variations. For example, Figure 5-10 shows an ergonomically shaped keyboard with some extra keys. The keyboard is specially shaped to encourage a more natural hand and wrist posture.

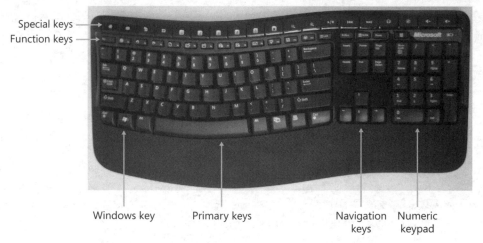

FIGURE 5-10 Ergonomic keyboard.

The special keys along the top are programmed for specific tasks, such as opening the web browser, starting the email client, or controlling audio or video playing on the system. The function keys (F1 through F12) perform specific functions in different programs. For example, F1 will usually start the Help screen, and F5 will usually refresh the display. Windows-based systems make special use of the Windows key with a variety of shortcuts. For example, you can press Windows+E to start Windows Explorer.

Navigation keys are used to move the cursor, and a numeric keypad includes numbers and basic math keys. The numeric keypad includes a Num Lock key, and by toggling it, the numeric keypad can be used for navigation.

Keyboards are very easy to install, and most are Plug and Play. You simply plug them into the purple PS/2 port or a USB port and they work. Some keyboards are wireless and come with an installation CD to install device drivers. After installing the drivers, you plug in a USB transceiver that resembles a small USB flash drive. The keyboard has batteries and can often be used from up to 30 feet away.

Mice

Older mice used mechanical components, such as a rolling ball and wheels, to track the movement. These components often got dirty, resulting in a jerky mouse movement. An improvement to the mechanical mouse is an optical mouse that uses a light emitting diode (LED) and photodiodes. The LED shines light on a surface, and the photodiodes detect movement based on the reflections. They work well on most flat surfaces but don't work on glossy surfaces such as glass.

Many newer mice include lasers and photo sensors that can track the movement of the mouse with greater accuracy and on more surfaces. For example, Microsoft's BlueTrack Technology allows you to use a mouse on a carpet or the arm of a chair.

A mouse is as easy to install as a keyboard. Most newer mice use a USB port. Wireless keyboards often come with a wireless mouse, and after you install the keyboard, the mouse works too.

NOTE **SOLITAIRE TRAINING**

The card game Solitaire, often included with Windows-based systems, is used by many trainers to get new users accustomed to how a mouse works. After just a few games, using the mouse becomes second nature. (Be careful, though. It tracks how many games you've played and when you get past a hundred or so games, it's no longer considered training.)

Microphone

Microphones are used as input devices to capture audio. They are sometimes used for real-time interaction, and at other times they are used to record audio for later playback. One of the challenges with a microphone is that it can pick up other noise or sound artifacts that aren't desired. This is especially important when using the recording function. Higher-quality microphones eliminate the artifacts, resulting in better voice recordings.

Figure 5-11 shows three common types of microphones. The headphones include a microphone and are often used by gamers in multiplayer games. Players can be in different physical locations but still interact with each other. A headset microphone is often inexpensive but usually not suitable for recordings.

The middle microphone in Figure 5-11 is a desktop version that users can speak into, and the one on the right can be clipped onto a collar or shirt similarly to the microphones that some television reporters use. Both of these are of higher quality than the headset microphone on the left. You can also find very high-quality microphones similar to those that musicians use.

Typically, microphones will either plug into the pink microphone jack of the sound system using a TRS jack or use a USB connector. Microphones are so common that you usually won't have to install additional drivers.

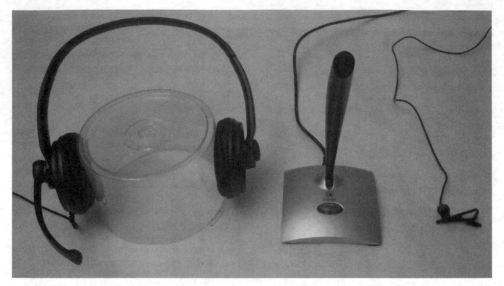

FIGURE 5-11 Microphones.

Scanners and Digitizers

Scanners and *digitizers* are used to scan documents and photos and are similar to office copiers in the way they work. You can purchase a stand-alone scanner, but it's much more common to use a multifunction printer that can print, scan, fax, and copy documents. Figure 5-12 shows an HP multifunction printer that includes a document feeder and a flatbed scanner.

Document feeder

Paper tray   Control panel   Moving light source

FIGURE 5-12 Multifunction printer with scanner.

You can place documents in the document feeder, or you can open the printer and place the item on the glass. This printer includes a touchscreen control panel that you can use to make a copy by simply selecting Copy. Alternatively, you can use software provided by HP to capture the image and save it as a file.

This software supports saving the file as a Portable Document Format (PDF or .pdf) file, a Joint Photographic Experts Group (JPEG or .jpg) graphics file, and several other common graphics formats. Scanners and digitizers commonly include optical character recognition (OCR) software that allows you to scan a text document and save it as editable text. Some also include intelligent character recognition (ICR) software that can read handwriting, although ICR is more commonly used on tablet devices.

Most scanners include software with drivers that you should install before connecting the device. The printer/scanner shown in the figure includes a USB connection, but you might also see scanners or multifunction printers that include FireWire connections. Additionally, printers often include a network connection, allowing you to connect a printer/scanner in a network and share it with multiple users.

> **MORE INFO** **CHAPTER 7 AND CHAPTER 21**
>
> Chapter 7 covers printers in more depth, and Chapter 21, "Comparing IPv4 and IPv6," covers networking in more depth, including how to reserve a specific IP address for a printer.

Barcode Reader

If you've been to a store in the last 30 years or so, you've seen a Universal Product Code (UPC) barcode and barcode readers. Handheld barcode readers are available for personal computers. They use the same scanning technology as a scanner and are often used with hardware inventory systems.

For example, a barcode inventory system includes rolls of preprinted barcode stickers, a handheld barcode reader, and a database application. When a valuable piece of hardware, such as a computer, is purchased, technicians put a barcode sticker on the hardware and record its details in the inventory. Details include information such as the model, the serial number, and the location where it will be used. Periodically, technicians use the barcode reader to scan barcodes on the equipment so they can complete an inventory rather quickly.

Barcode scanners are typically connected with a USB cable, although some are available using the PS/2 connection.

KVM

A *keyboard video mouse (KVM)* switch allows you to use a single keyboard, video monitor, and mouse with multiple computers. It is most commonly used in server rooms, allowing you to have one KVM for multiple servers in a single equipment bay, but it can be used anywhere that you have more than one computer and you need to save desktop space.

In some cases, the KVM has physical switches or buttons that you use to select a specific computer. However, in other cases, you can just press a special key combination on the keyboard called a keyboard shortcut. Some keyboard shortcuts that allow you to toggle between computers connected to a KVM are the following:

- **Ctrl, Ctrl.** Tap the Ctrl key twice.
- **Scroll Lock, Scroll Lock.** Tap the Scroll Lock key twice.
- **Alt+Ctrl+Shift+number.** The number refers to a port number on the switch. For example, if you wanted to connect to the computer by using port three, you'd press Alt+Ctrl+Shift+3.

The KVM switch has ports for a single keyboard, a display monitor, and a mouse. It also has cables for each computer. You connect the devices to the KVM instead of to a computer and then connect the computers to the KVM, as shown in Figure 5-13.

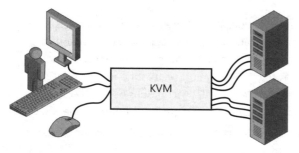

FIGURE 5-13 KVM connections.

Biometric Devices

Biometric devices identify individuals based on their physical characteristics. The most common type of biometrics in use is fingerprinting. Other types include retinal scans, which scan the retina of an eye, and iris scans, which scan the iris.

Biometrics is often used for authentication. Authentication occurs when someone claims an identity and then proves the identity with something else. For example, you can log on to a computer with a user name and password. You are claiming an identity with your user name and proving the identity with a password. Similarly, you can log on with the same user name and prove it's you by using a fingerprint. Biometrics is much more secure than passwords, but it is more expensive.

Many laptops have built-in fingerprint readers. You can also find external biometric devices that commonly connect to a USB port. It's rare for the driver to be included with the operating system, so you'll need to install it using the installation software from the manufacturer.

Joysticks

Joysticks have been used in aviation for more than a century. A joystick is connected to a base, and the pilot can pivot it to control the direction of the plane. Joysticks often include buttons. For example, fighter planes and jets require buttons to fire bullets or missiles.

Similar joysticks have been used in computer games. Users can pivot the joystick around the base to control the movement within the game. A joystick can have multiple buttons used for different purposes in games, including firing bullets and missiles.

Joysticks originally connected to the DB-15 sound card port, which is the same port used by MIDI devices. Joysticks are available with USB connectors, although they have largely been replaced by game pads.

Game Pads

For some gamers, the keyboard and mouse—or even the joystick—just aren't enough to get the gaming performance they desire. Instead, the gamers add a *game pad* to their system. A game pad is a handheld device that includes multiple controls used within games.

Popular game pads can be held with both hands and include multiple buttons and at least one analog stick. The analog stick mimics the functionality of a joystick but isn't as big and bulky. As users hold the game pad, they can manipulate the analog stick with a thumb. Figure 5-14 shows a game pad. The buttons and analog sticks are used differently, depending on the game being played.

FIGURE 5-14 Game pad.

Game pads often connect with a USB connection or with a wireless connection. Wireless connections typically use a wireless USB dongle, similar to those used with wireless keyboards and mice.

✔ **Quick Check**

1. What type of device can create a digital file from a paper document?
2. What is used to control multiple computers with a single keyboard and monitor?

Quick Check Answers

1. Scanner.
2. KVM switch.

Multimedia Devices

Multimedia devices include cameras, webcams, camcorders, and MIDI devices. Most multimedia devices are connected to a computer with a USB cable, but some camcorders use FireWire.

Digital Cameras

Digital cameras are easy to use and very affordable, and they provide a rich set of features. They store the pictures on flash memory sticks, and it's relatively easy to transfer the pictures to your computer or to get them printed.

Figure 5-15 shows a digital camera with a few highlights. The cover on the left is open, showing where the battery and flash memory are installed. In the middle is a Micro-B USB port. When you attach the cable from the camera to the computer, it appears as another disk drive that you can access by using Windows Explorer.

Many computers and printers include CompactFlash (CF) and Secure Digital (SD) slots. To access the photos, you can remove the memory stick from the camera and plug it into the slot instead of connecting the camera directly to the computer. Similarly, you can take the memory stick to a photo shop to get your photos printed.

> **MORE INFO** **CHAPTER 4**
>
> Chapter 4 covers the different types of flash memory used in cameras within the context of solid state drives.

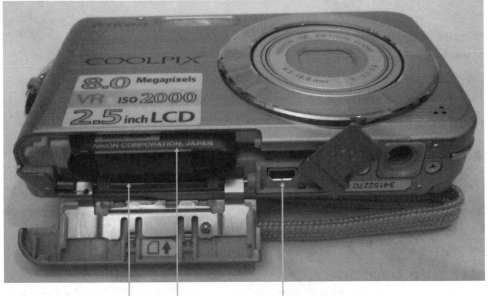

Flash   Battery   USB connection
memory

FIGURE 5-15 Digital camera.

Camcorder

A camcorder is a camera that can capture live recordings of both *audio and video (A/V)*. It has been known as a video recorder but is more commonly called a camcorder. Many digital cameras can capture A/V recordings in addition to still pictures. The difference is that a camcorder is a dedicated device that is optimized for these recordings.

One of the challenges with camcorders has been storage space because video quickly consumes a lot of space. Camcorders have been available using tapes and built-in hard drives, but many current versions use high-capacity memory sticks.

You typically have the same connectivity options with a camcorder that you have with a digital camera. You can usually connect a camcorder to a PC by using a USB cable, or you can remove the memory stick and insert it into a memory card reader on the computer. Some camcorders also have FireWire connections.

Webcam

A *webcam* is a camera attached to a computer, and it's often attached to the top of the monitor. One of the popular uses of webcams is for Skype to make real-time phone calls that include both voice and video, and they're also used with some instant messaging systems. When both parties are using a webcam, they can each look at their monitor and see the other person in real time.

Many laptops include a built-in webcam centered at the top of the display, but you can also purchase external webcams. External webcams commonly connect using USB cables.

MIDI-Enabled Devices

Musical Instrument Digital Interface (MIDI) devices can play synthesized music from a MIDI file. MIDI files include instructions about what notes to play and how to play them. In contrast, many sound files are actual recordings of music. A benefit is that a MIDI file can be much smaller than a music recording. MIDI devices can simulate just about any type of musical instrument, including pianos, drums, violins, trumpets, and oboes.

Older sound cards included a DB-15 MIDI connector used for either a MIDI device or a joystick. Most current MIDI devices use a USB interface instead.

Expansion Cards

Motherboards include expansion slots, and it's very common to add or replace an *expansion card* in desktop computers. The primary type of expansion card with which you'll be working is Peripheral Component Interconnect Express (PCIe), although you might occasionally use a traditional PCI card.

MORE INFO **CHAPTER 2**

Chapter 2 covers motherboards and expansion slots, including PCI and PCIe.

The three reasons to add or replace an expansion card are as follows:

- **To replace a failed component.** The chipset on the motherboard includes an expected feature, but if something fails, you can add an expansion card to provide the same feature.

- **To improve a capability.** If the chipset includes a feature but you want something better, you can often add a card. This is commonly done with graphics cards.

- **To add a capability.** If your system doesn't include a feature that you want, you can add a card.

For example, imagine that you wanted to use a computer to watch and record TV shows. This is certainly possible, but you need a *TV tuner* expansion card similar to the one shown in Figure 5-16. You could purchase the card, install it in the system, and be ready to go. However, if you're using one of the Media Center editions of Windows, you can use Media Center to manage the recordings.

NOTE **TV TUNERS**

The card shown in Figure 5-16 includes two tuners. This allows the computer to record one TV program while another one is being watched. It also includes connections for the TV signal.

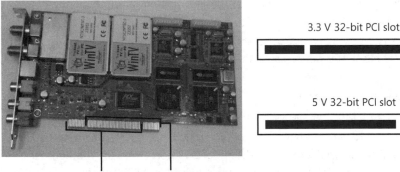

3.3 V 32-bit PCI slot

5 V 32-bit PCI slot

3.3 V connection   5 V connection

FIGURE 5-16 TV tuner expansion card.

It's extremely important that you consider your system's current motherboard configuration before purchasing a card. Chapter 2 covers the different types of slots available on a motherboard, and you want to get a board that can fit in an available slot. The card shown in the figure is a 32-bit PCI card that can plug into either a 3.3 V or a 5 V 32-bit PCI slot. That's good if you have either one of these slots open and available, but it's not so good if you don't have any available slots.

You probably have some empty PCIe slots, but it's important to remember the differences. Figure 5-17 shows some common-sized PCIe slots. You can plug a smaller PCIe card into a larger PCIe slot. For example, if you have an empty PCIe x16 slot, you can plug a PCIe x1, x4, or x8 card into it. However, you cannot plug a larger card into a smaller slot.

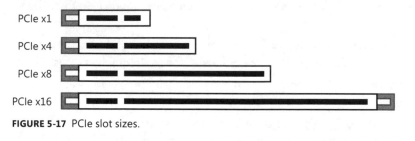

FIGURE 5-17 PCIe slot sizes.

EXAM TIP

You will need to know how to mix and match PCIe slots and PCIe expansion cards.

Expansion Card Types

Some of the different types of expansion cards that you can add include the following:

- **Video cards.** Users sometimes want a video card that includes more onboard RAM or better capabilities. You can find a wide assortment of video cards.

- **Sound cards.** Sound cards are available that provide anything from basic sound to elaborate 7.1 surround sound.

- **Network cards.** Network cards can be added to increase the throughput. You can install one that has better performance than the original or as an additional network connection.

- **Serial and parallel cards.** Many systems do not include the DB-9 serial port or the DB-25 parallel port, but they can be added with an expansion card if needed.

- **USB cards.** USB cards are available to provide additional ports using a separate hub. These ports will not share the same bandwidth of USB ports from the motherboard. USB 3.0 is not on many systems, but it is possible to add a USB 3.0 card.

- **FireWire cards.** Multiport FireWire cards can add FireWire capabilities to a system or provide it with additional ports.

- **Storage cards.** Storage cards allow you add additional disks beyond the capabilities of the original system. For example, you can add a Serial ATA (SATA) card to support additional internal or external SATA drives. Many SATA storage cards have built-in support for a redundant array of independent disks (such as RAID-0, RAID-1, or RAID-5). While less common for a desktop, you can also add Parallel ATA (PATA) or Small Computer System Interface (SCSI) cards.

- **Modem cards.** Many computers no longer include a modem, but if there is a need, you can add an internal modem. Modem cards include two RJ-11 ports so that the phone line can be shared. An RJ-11 port is the same type of port a typical phone line uses. One port connects the phone line to the computer, and the second connects to a standard phone. It's also possible to add external modems that plug into a USB port.

- **Wireless cards.** Wireless capabilities are included with most laptop computers. People often want to add wireless capabilities to desktop computers so that wires aren't needed. These are available as expansion cards. They're also available as a USB dongle that plugs into a USB port.

- **Cellular cards.** Cellular cards allow a computer to connect to a cellular network. This is the same network used by mobile smartphone users for Internet access with a subscription. While expansion cards are available, it is more common to use a USB port and connect a cellular card externally.

- **TV tuner cards.** These allow you to watch and record television. They include an F-type connector used to connect an RG-6 coaxial cable, similar to what is used with a TV.

- **Video capture cards.** A video capture card has the ability to capture all video going to a computer. A TV tuner is a type of video capture card that captures the television signal. Other cards can capture video from other sources, such as VCR or DVD players or gaming consoles.

- **Riser cards.** A riser card plugs into a slot and includes an identical slot configured at a right angle. You can then plug an expansion card into the riser card. The end result is that the expansion card is positioned horizontally to the motherboard. This is useful in some small-sized computer cases where the expansion card wouldn't otherwise fit.

Checklist

If you plan on adding an expansion card, you need to take several steps. You can use the following list of steps as a guide:

- **Identify an open slot.** Before purchasing an expansion card, you need to verify that the computer has space. If you purchase a PCIe x16 card but then find you don't have an open PCIe x16 slot, you might be out of some of your money.

- **Purchase the right card.** Buy a card that meets your needs and will fit in an available slot.

- **Power down and unplug the computer.** You can damage the computer or yourself if you try to replace an expansion card while the system is powered on.

- **Use electrostatic discharge (ESD) protection.** When you're ready to install the card, use ESD protection, such as an ESD wrist strap and an ESD mat.

- **Open the computer and remove components.** If you're replacing a card, you need to remove the old card. If you're adding a new card to an empty slot, you need to remove the slot cover at the back of the computer. The card's external connections will be available here.

- **Install the new card.** Follow the manufacturer's directions. Different types of cards have different connections, so you might need to connect additional cables either internally or after the card is installed. Ensure that you screw it down so that the card remains in place.

- **Consider the BIOS.** If you're replacing a feature that is built into the chipset, you might need to disable the feature in BIOS. For example, if you're adding a new sound card, you might need to disable the sound capabilities in the BIOS.

- **Install the drivers.** The manufacturer will normally provide a CD that you can use to install the drivers. If recommended, you should install the drivers prior to the installation.

✓ **Quick Check**

1. What is the most common type of expansion card used in desktop computers?

2. Is it possible to plug a PCI x4 card into a PCI x2 slot?

Quick Check Answers

1. PCIe.

2. No.

Chapter Summary

- Peripherals are devices that are connected to a computer, and device drivers provide the operating system with the instructions on how to access these devices.

- USB is the most commonly used connection port. USB 1.1 can transfer data at 1.1 Mbps (low speed) or 12 Mbps (full speed). USB 2.0 supports speeds of up to 480 Mbps, and USB 3.0 supports speeds of up to 5 Gbps.

- Ports on the computer and on most devices use Standard Type A connections. Larger devices such as printers and video recorders can use the Standard Type B port. Smaller devices such as digital cameras and smartphones use the Mini-B, Micro-A, or Micro-B ports. USB 3.0 ports are blue.

- A single USB controller can support up to 127 devices, and the USB cables can be as long as 5 meters (about 16 feet).

- FireWire 400 (1394a) supports speeds of up to 400 Mbps, and the cable can be as long as 4.5 meters (about 15 feet). FireWire 800 (1394b) supports speeds of up to 800 Mbps,

- and the cable can be as long as 100 meters (about 15 feet). FireWire supports up to 63 devices on a system.

- The 4-pin FireWire connector does not provide power. The 6-pin connector does provide power to devices. The 9-pin connector uses additional pins to prevent interference and is required for FireWire 800.

- The green PS/2 port is for a mouse, and the purple PS/2 port is for a keyboard. A parallel port is a DB-25 female port, and a serial port is either a DB-9 or a DB-25 male port.

- Surround sound systems include as many as seven speakers and a subwoofer (designated as 7.1). Sound connections include the following: front speakers or headphones (lime green), rear speakers (black), center speaker and subwoofer (orange), side speakers (brown), microphone (pink), and line in (light blue).

- Input devices are used to provide an input to the computer. Most use USB connections.

- Multimedia devices include cameras, camcorders, webcams, and MIDI devices. These commonly connect to USB ports.

- Expansion cards are added to a motherboard to provide an additional capability. Before purchasing an expansion card, ensure that you have an open slot to accept it.

- Most desktop computers include PCIe expansion slots. It's possible to install a smaller PCIe card (such as PCIe x2) in a larger slot (such as PCIe x8), but you cannot install a larger card in a smaller slot.

- When adding an expansion card to upgrade a computer's capabilities, you might need to access the BIOS to disable the original feature. For example, if you add a sound card, you might need to disable the sound provided from the chipset.

Chapter Review

Use the following questions to test your knowledge of the information in this chapter. The answers to these questions, and the explanations of why each answer choice is correct or incorrect, are located in the "Answers" section at the end of this chapter.

1. How many USB devices can a USB controller support?

    A. 2

    B. 4

    C. 63

    D. 127

2. You want to plug in a USB 3.0 device. What port should you use?

    A. A blue rectangular port

    B. A rectangular port with a curved top

C. A pink TRS connector

D. A green PS/2 connector

3. What is the maximum length of a FireWire 400 cable?

   A. 3 meters

   B. 5 meters

   C. 4.5 meters

   D. 100 meters

4. You want to control two computers with a single keyboard, mouse, and monitor. What should you use?

   A. PCIe expansion card

   B. KVM switch

   C. MIDI device

   D. 7.1 system

5. You need to identify a device that can create files from printed documents. Of the following choices, what would you select?

   A. Multifunction printer

   B. Biometric device

   C. Barcode reader

   D. MIDI-enabled device

6. You want to watch and record TV shows on a desktop computer. What is needed?

   A. KVM switch

   B. Webcam

   C. TV tuner card

   D. Camcorder

Answers

1. **Correct Answer:** D

    A. **Incorrect:** A controller supports more than 2 devices.

    B. **Incorrect:** A controller supports more than 4 devices.

    C. **Incorrect:** FireWire supports as many as 63 devices.

    D. **Correct:** A USB controller supports as many as 127 devices.

2. **Correct Answer:** A

    A. **Correct:** USB 3.0 ports are blue and the same rectangular size as USB 1.1 and USB 2.0 ports.

    B. **Incorrect:** A FireWire port is rectangular with a curved top.

    C. **Incorrect:** Microphones have tip ring sleeve (TRS) connectors and plug into a pink port.

    D. **Incorrect:** The green PS/2 connector is for the mouse.

3. **Correct Answer:** C

    A. **Incorrect:** The maximum recommended length of a USB 3.0 cable is 3 meters.

    B. **Incorrect:** The maximum length of a USB cable is 5 meters.

    C. **Correct:** The maximum length of a FireWire 400 cable is 4.5 meters.

    D. **Incorrect:** The maximum length of a FireWire 800 cable using a Category 5e twisted-pair cable is 100 meters.

4. **Correct Answer:** B

    A. **Incorrect:** An expansion expands the capabilities of a single computer.

    B. **Correct:** A keyboard video mouse (KVM) switch is used to manage more than one computer with a single keyboard, mouse, and monitor.

    C. **Incorrect:** A Musical Instrument Digital Interface (MIDI) device is used to play MIDI music files.

    D. **Incorrect:** A 7.1 system is a surround sound system with seven speakers and a subwoofer.

5. **Correct Answer: A**

   A. **Correct:** Multifunction printers commonly include scanners or digitizers that can scan documents.

   B. **Incorrect:** A biometric device reads information about a person, such as a fingerprint or eye retina.

   C. **Incorrect:** A barcode reader includes a scanner, but it can read only barcodes.

   D. **Incorrect:** A MIDI-enabled device can play synthesized music from MIDI files.

6. **Correct Answer: C**

   A. **Incorrect:** A KVM switch allows multiple computers to share a single keyboard, video monitor, and mouse.

   B. **Incorrect:** A webcam is a camera attached to the computer and is used for live interactions, such as a phone call.

   C. **Correct:** A TV tuner card is required to watch and record TV shows on a desktop computer.

   D. **Incorrect:** A camcorder provides video recordings.

CHAPTER 6

Exploring Video and Display Devices

I n this chapter, you'll learn about different types of display devices used to provide video for monitors. Most monitors are flat-panel displays, but there are other types you should know about. There are several different interfaces used by monitors, and these interfaces have different connectors that you should be able to recognize. If you come across any of the older monitors, you need to understand some important safety concerns. Last, this chapter includes many of the common symptoms of problems with video and how you can resolve them.

Exam 220-801 objectives in this chapter:

- 1.4 Install and configure expansion cards.
    - Video cards
- 1.7 Compare and contrast various connection interfaces and explain their purpose.
    - Physical connections
        - Other connector types: VGA, HDMI, DVI
        - Analog vs. digital transmission : VGA vs. HDMI
- 1.10 Given a scenario, evaluate types and features of display devices.
    - Types
        - CRT
        - LCD
        - LED
        - Plasma
        - Projector
        - OLED
    - Refresh rates
    - Resolution
    - Native resolution

- Brightness/lumens
- Analog vs. digital
- Privacy/antiglare filters
- Multiple displays
- 1.11 Identify connector types and associated cables.
  - Display connector types
    - DVI-D
    - DVI-I
    - DVI-A
    - Displayport
    - RCA
    - miniHDMI
  - Display cable types
    - HDMI
    - DVI
    - VGA
    - Component
    - Composite
    - S-video
    - RGB
- 1.12 Install and configure various peripheral devices.
  - Input devices
    - Touch screen
  - Output devices
    - Display devices
- 5.1 Given a scenario, use appropriate safety procedures.
  - Personal safety
    - CRT safety – proper disposal

Exam 220-802 objectives in this chapter:

- 1.5 Given a scenario, use Control Panel utilities (the items are organized by "classic view/large icons" in Windows).
  - Common to all Microsoft Operating Systems
    - Display: Resolution

- 4.4 Given a scenario, troubleshoot common video and display issues.
  - Common symptoms
    - VGA mode
    - No image on screen
    - Overheat shutdown
    - Dead pixels
    - Artifacts
    - Color patterns incorrect
    - Dim image
    - Flickering image
    - Distorted image
    - Discoloration (degaussing)
    - BSOD

Display Devices

One of the most important output devices of a computer is the display device or monitor. As an A+ technician, you need to be aware of some common terms related to display devices and the different types commonly in use today.

Common Terms

The following are some common terms used when describing display devices:

- **Pixels.** On monitors, a pixel (short for *pixel element*) includes three colored dots (red, green, and blue). A pixel can be any color, illuminating the dots with varying intensity.
- **Resolution.** The resolution of a monitor describes the width and height of a display in pixels. For example, the resolution of VGA is 640 × 480, meaning that it can display 640 pixels across the screen (width) on 480 separate lines (height). A higher number of pixels results in a higher resolution and an overall better display.
- **Native resolution.** Most new monitors are designed to use a specific resolution, referred to as the native resolution. If a different resolution is used, it distorts the display.
- **Refresh rates.** This is the frequency with which the screen is redrawn. For example, a refresh rate of 60 Hz indicates that the screen is redrawn 60 times per second.
- **Brightness/lumens.** Monitors have controls that allow you to control the brightness of the display. On some displays, the intensity of the light is measured in lumens.

CRT

CRT (cathode ray tube) monitors are the oldest type of analog monitor. They are heavy, take up a lot of desk space, and consume a significant amount of power compared with modern displays. You probably won't see anyone purchase a new CRT monitor, but some older ones are still in use.

> **NOTE** **CRTS REPLACED TO SAVE MONEY**
>
> Most organizations recognize the amount of power that CRTs draw and have replaced them with new flat-panel displays. The flat-panel displays consume very little power in comparison, and companies save a noticeable amount of money on their power bills.

Besides drawing a significant amount of power, the refresh rate can also be a problem on these monitors. If the refresh rate is less than 72 Hz, many people notice a flicker that causes eyestrain and headaches.

These monitors include a large vacuum tube and an electron gun that shoots electrons from the back onto a fluorescent screen. Compared to a typical flat-screen monitor, the CRT monitor is massive, as you can see in Figure 6-1. CRT monitors often extend a foot or more behind the front of the viewable screen.

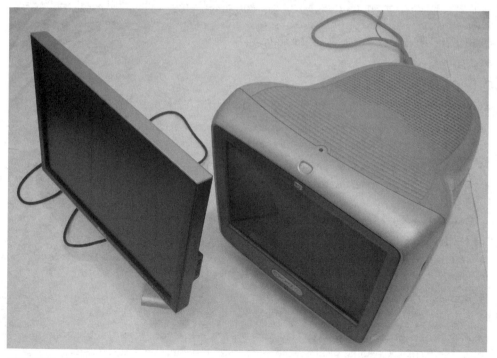

FIGURE 6-1 Flat panel display and CRT monitor.

LCD

 LCD *(liquid crystal display)* monitors are flat-panel displays that have largely replaced CRT monitors. They are thinner and lighter, and they consume significantly less power than CRTs.

LCD Backlights

A *backlight* is used to shine light through liquid crystals in an LCD monitor to create the display. By changing the way the crystals are oriented, they refract the light differently and display different colors.

This is similar to how you can see different colors by turning a prism. Light is refracted through the prism, and as you turn it, you see different colors. However, if you took a prism into a dark closet and turned it in your hand, you wouldn't see anything because a prism doesn't produce light.

Similarly, liquid crystals don't produce light. Instead, LCD displays depend on light shining through the crystals. Most LCD monitors include a *cold cathode fluorescent lamp (CCFL)* that shines from the back through the liquid crystals. If the CCFL fails, you probably won't see any display at all. In some cases, the display picks up some ambient light and you can see a very dim display, but most often, you won't see anything at all.

> **EXAM TIP**
>
> **If an LCD monitor doesn't have any display, ensure that it is plugged in and turned on. If it is connected and turned on but you still have no display, the problem is likely the backlight.**

CCFLs on most LCD monitors shine from the back to the front, and these monitors are called backlit-LCD monitors. Some use a refractor and can have the light shining from an edge.

LCD Refresh Rate and Native Resolution

Another benefit of LCD monitors over CRT monitors is that they don't flicker at all. The refresh rate for LCD monitors is normally set at 60 Hz.

LCD monitors are designed to use a *native resolution*. If you change the resolution to something different, it distorts the display. Many video cards can automatically sense the native resolution of a monitor and will show this as the recommended resolution.

LED

A LED (light emitting diode) monitor is an LCD monitor that uses LEDs for the backlight instead of a CCFL. This provides several benefits, including a brighter display, better contrast, and lower power consumption. The difference in the display is often dramatic. I recently bought a new LED monitor and hooked it up next to a CCFL backlight display, and I was quite surprised at the differences.

✔ **Quick Check**

1. What type of monitor consumes the most power?

2. What provides illumination in an LCD monitor?

Quick Check Answers

1. CRT.

2. Backlight.

Plasma

A plasma display device is another type of flat-panel display. They can produce some vivid colors but are more susceptible to screen burn-in. Additionally, they draw more electricity than LCD monitors.

Plasma displays use a concept similar to fluorescent lights. A fluorescent light is a gas-filled tube, and when electricity is applied to the gas, it emits a light. A plasma display includes millions of small cells filled with a gas, and when voltage is applied to these cells, they can emit different-colored lights.

Projector

People often use projectors for giving presentations. This includes trainers or instructors teaching different topics, and also people giving presentations in a variety of different business situations. The projector is often mounted to the ceiling and projected onto a blank screen or sometimes a blank wall. Sometimes presenters carry a portable projector with them.

Two primary characteristics to look for with projectors are lumens and throw ratio.

- **Lumens.** This identifies the brightness of the display. In classroom or small business settings, a 2,000 lumen projector provides adequate brightness even when competing with other lights within a room. Projects used in large conference hall settings can have as many as 15,000 lumens.

- **Throw ratio.** The size of the display from the projector is affected by where the projector is positioned. For example, if you want the display to be six feet wide and the throw ratio is 2:1, the projector is mounted 12 feet from the screen.

OLED

An *organic light-emitting diode (OLED)* is a newer type of display device that is used in some smaller mobile devices. Unlike an LCD device, it can emit light without a backlight. OLED devices are thinner and lighter, and they provide better pictures and wider viewing angles than LCD devices.

With all these benefits, you can expect to see more of them, but maybe not for a few years. I recently checked prices, and a 17" OLED monitor from Sony was available for $4,100 and a 25" model was available for $6,100. I didn't buy one.

Using Multiple Displays

Many people use more than one display device when working on computers. For example, I've occasionally created training videos for the web with Camtasia. Having two monitors has made the process of editing the video much easier.

Windows will normally recognize the second display as soon as you plug it in. However, you need to know how to configure it. On Windows 7, you can right-click the desktop and select Screen Resolution. You'll see a display similar to Figure 6-2.

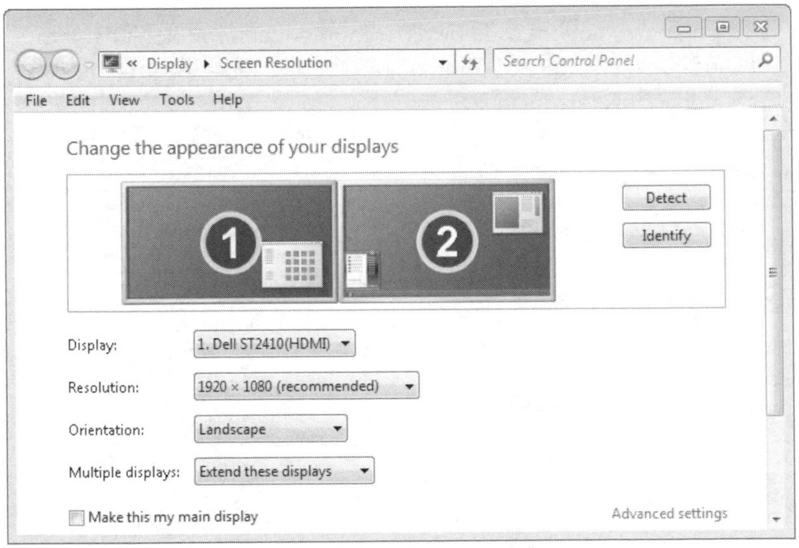

FIGURE 6-2 Configuring multiple displays.

If the monitor isn't recognized, ensure that it is connected and turned on and then click the Detect button. In Figure 6-2, the two monitors are labeled as 1 and 2. If you click Identify, it will display a large number on each of the monitors corresponding to the number shown on the Screen Resolution page.

In the figure, the number 1 monitor is selected and the number 2 monitor is the main display. Items like the Windows Start menu and taskbar appear on the main display.

The Multiple Displays drop-down box gives you two primary choices:

- **Duplicate These Displays.** The same information is displayed on both. This is useful when giving presentations. The presenter can manipulate the monitor in front of them, and the same thing is shown to anyone watching the presentation.

- **Extend These Displays.** This allows you to drag windows between the displays. For example, you can have Internet Explorer open in one display while you're taking A+ notes in Microsoft Word in the other display.

A key requirement for using multiple displays is that your computer must support more than one display. That is, your computer needs to have active interface connections for more than one monitor. Video cards commonly have more than one active connection.

> **EXAM TIP**
>
> Dual monitors are used by many people doing any type of editing. This includes audio and video editing and even editing of books or articles.

Common Resolutions

There are more than 20 different resolutions used by different monitors. You don't need to memorize them all, but you should be aware of common resolutions. Table 6-1 lists the resolutions that CompTIA included in their acronym list.

TABLE 6-1 Display Resolutions

Name	Resolution
VGA (Video Graphics Array)	640 × 480
SVGA (Super VGA)	800 × 600
XGA (Extended GA)	1024 × 768
EVGA (Extended VGA)	1024 × 768
SXGA (Super XGA)	1280 × 1024
UXGA (Ultra XGA)	1600 × 1200
WUXGA (Wide UXGA)	1920 × 1200
HDMI (High-Definition Multimedia Interface) 1080	1920 × 1080
HDMI 780	1280 × 720

Configuring the Resolution

As an A+ technician, you need to be able to adjust the resolution for a computer. The following steps show you how to adjust it on computers running Windows 7, Windows Vista, and Windows XP.

Windows 7:

1. Click Start and select Control Panel.

2. Select Large Icons in the View By selection.

3. Double-click Display.

4. Select Adjust Resolution from the menu on the left.

5. Select the resolution from the Resolution drop-down box. If a native resolution is needed, it will often be listed as "Recommended," as shown in the following graphic.

Change the appearance of your display

Display: 1. VX2450 SERIES

Resolution: 1920 × 1080 (recommended)

Orientation: Landscape

EXAM TIP

There are other ways of getting to the Screen Resolution page. For example, on Windows 7, you can right-click the desktop and select Screen Resolution. However, the exam objectives specifically identify the Control Panel by using the Classic View/large icons. On the job, use whatever method you desire. For the exam, know these steps.

Windows Vista:

1. Click Start and select Control Panel.

2. Select Classic View.

3. Double-click Personalization.

4. Select Display Settings.

5. Use the slider to adjust the screen resolution as desired.

Windows XP:

1. Click Start and select Control Panel.

2. Select Classic View from the menu on the left.

3. Double-click Display.

4. Click the Settings tab.

5. Use the slider to adjust the screen resolution as desired.

Touch Screens

Touch screens are becoming more and more common. Instead of using a mouse to point and click, you can use different touch gestures with your fingers to manipulate the computer.

> **MORE INFO** CHAPTER 9, "UNDERSTANDING MOBILE DEVICES"
>
> Chapter 9 covers many of the common touch gestures used with touch screens on mobile devices. These same gestures are used with touch screens for desktop computers.

Touch screens are widely available on tablet devices, such as Apple's iPad, and on smartphones. They've also been available with regular monitors for a long time and are most commonly used in kiosks. For example, many airlines have these available for customers to check in and print their tickets.

Windows 7 supports touch screens, and you're likely to run across Windows 8 notebooks with touch screens instead of traditional display devices.

Privacy and Anti-Glare Filters

Some monitors have a glare that bothers people and causes eye strain. Filters are available that act like sunglasses, but instead of the user wearing them, they fit over the screen. Many filters are designed with plastic tabs that lay on top of the monitor with the filter covering the screen. Others use Velcro attached to the monitor. Either way, the filter covers the screen to remove the glare.

In addition to stopping glare, filters are also available to limit the viewing angle of the display. "Shoulder surfers" sometimes try to look at displays to get some private information. With a filter over the monitor, the only person who can see the contents of the monitor is the person sitting right in front of it.

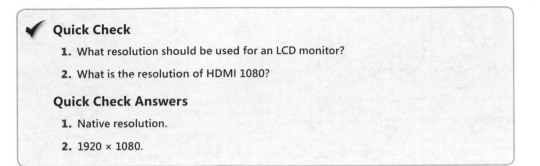

Interfaces, Connections, and Cables

As a PC technician, you need to be able to identify the different types of connections used for video displays and know which interface is being used. Because monitors can use different types of interfaces, video card manufacturers commonly include more than one port on the video cards. For example, Figure 6-3 shows a circuit card with three different ports. These ports are described in the following sections.

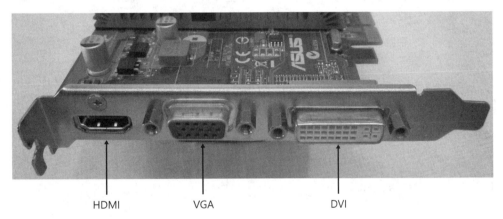

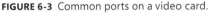
HDMI   VGA   DVI

FIGURE 6-3 Common ports on a video card.

Analog vs. Digital

Video displays have evolved quite a bit over time, and one of the primary changes is related to analog and digital data. Computers work with *digital* data sent as 1s and 0s. However, older monitors such as CRTs can display data only when it is sent as *analog* data. Analog data is created as modulation on an alternating current sine wave.

For example, Figure 6-4 shows how data is sent to an analog monitor. The PC creates digital data, sends it to the video card, which formats it as analog data, and then sends it to the monitor.

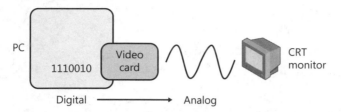

FIGURE 6-4 Sending analog data to an analog monitor.

This works fine for analog monitors. However, many newer display devices, such as LCD monitors, use digital data. When they receive the analog data, they need to convert it back to digital data, as shown in Figure 6-5. Because of this, many LCD monitors have extra electronics to do this conversion.

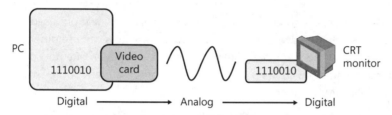

FIGURE 6-5 Converting analog data back to digital data for a digital monitor.

Do you see a problem here?

If the computer creates digital data and the monitor needs digital data, why not just send digital data to the monitor instead of using time and resources to convert it twice? Actually, that's exactly what is occurring with many interfaces today, as shown in Figure 6-6.

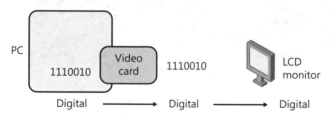

FIGURE 6-6 Sending digital data to a digital monitor.

Ten years from now, this will be ancient history for IT technicians, but right now there is still a mixture of analog and digital devices in use. Therefore, you need to be aware of the differences and know which devices and interfaces are analog and which are digital.

EXAM TIP

When studying the devices and interfaces, pay attention to which ones are analog and which ones are digital. In some cases, you can use a simple adapter to match dissimilar connections. However, simple adapters cannot change the signal from analog to digital or from digital to analog.

VGA

Video Graphics Array (VGA) has been the standard analog video interface used for many years. New display devices use improved interfaces, but it's still common to see VGA connectors. Figure 6-7 shows a connector on a standard VGA cable. It is a DB-15 connector with three rows of pins.

FIGURE 6-7 VGA cable.

VGA also indicates a very basic resolution of 640 × 480. However, the VGA interface can transmit data using higher resolutions.

DVI

The *Digital Visual Interface (DVI)* connector is rectangle-shaped and is commonly found on many PCs and monitors today. It was primarily created to provide a digital interface but also supports analog. The three primary versions are as follows:

- DVI-A connectors supply only analog data.
- DVI-D connectors supply only digital data.
- DVI-I connectors are integrated and supply both analog and digital data.

Additionally, DVI comes in both single-link and dual-link versions. Single-link DVI supports resolutions up to 1920 × 1200. Dual-link DVI uses more pins and wires and is used for higher resolutions up to 2560 × 1600.

> **NOTE** **SINGLE-LINK DVI MORE COMMON**
>
> The single-link DVI cables are cheaper than dual-link cables and are more readily available. You can plug a single-link DVI cable into dual-link ports without any problem as long as the resolution isn't higher than 1920 × 1200.

Figure 6-8 shows the different types of connections you'll see with DVI. The DVI-A connector includes pins that can transmit the same data as a standard VGA cable. The DVI-D connector includes pins that are required to transmit the video signal digitally. The DVI-I connector includes the pins needed for both.

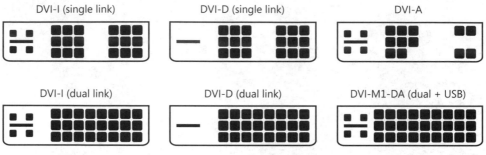

FIGURE 6-8 DVI connector versions.

The dual-link connectors include six extra pins in the middle, which are used to carry additional signals for higher bandwidths. The DVI-M1-DA connector adds three extra pins for a USB connection. Monitors supporting this will also have USB ports that connect with a USB controller in the computer via the DVI connection.

> **NOTE USB PORTS ON MONITORS**
>
> Many monitors include a built-in USB hub. You can connect the monitor to the PC with a USB cable and then use the USB ports on the monitor. If the monitor and video interface support the DVI-M1-DA connection, the USB cable isn't needed.

HDMI

High-Definition Multimedia Interface (HDMI) uses a single cable that can transfer both audio and video in a digital format. The audio signal supports eight channels used by 7.1 sound systems. It's used on many flat-panel displays and also on a wide variety of high-definition televisions and DVD/Blu-Ray players.

HDMI is backward-compatible with DVI-D and DVI-I and is believed by many to be the successor to DVI. There are some other digital video standards, but, currently, HDMI is more popular.

Figure 6-9 shows the end of a typical Type A HDMI cable used with display devices. Most cables have Type A connections on both ends.

FIGURE 6-9 Type A HDMI cable.

EXAM TIP

HDMI includes digital video and 8-channel digital audio. It is backward-compatible with DVI-D and DVI-I but not with VGA or DVI-A. It is definitely a requirement for anyone who is building a home theater PC.

The Type A connector is the most common, but you might also run across the Type C (or mini-HDMI) connector. The Type A connector is 13.9 mm × 4.45 mm, and the Type C connector is 10.42 mm × 2.42 mm.

You might remember from Chapter 5, "Exploring Peripherals and Expansion Cards," that some USB cables have a Standard Type A connector on one end to connect with the computer and a mini or micro connector on the other end to connect with smaller devices such as cameras. Similarly, HDMI cables are available with the Type A connector on one end for the computer and a mini-HDMI connector on the other end.

HTMI resolutions are commonly identified as 1080 and 720.

- HDMI 1080 uses a resolution of 1920 × 1080.
- HDMI 720 uses a resolution of 1280 × 720.

Comparing VGA and HDMI

The previous sections show the progression of video interfaces from VGA to DVI and then to HDMI. In brief, the key differences between VGA and HDMI include the following:

- VGA provides analog video.
- HDMI provides digital video plus 8-channel digital audio.

Adapters

Passive adapters are available that allow you to plug a cable of one type into a different type of port. These reroute the connections from one connector to the specific pins on the other connector. For example, DVI and HDMI both use the same type of signals, and adapters are available to convert one connector to another.

Imagine that you have an HDMI cable coming from a display but have only a DVI-D port on the computer. You can use an HDMI-to-DVI adapter like the one shown in Figure 6-10. The HDMI cable plugs into the adapter, and the DVI-D side plugs into the DVI port on the computer. DVI-A-to-VGA adapters are also available.

FIGURE 6-10 HDMI-to-DVI adapter.

EXAM TIP

You cannot use a passive converter to convert a digital HDMI signal to an analog VGA signal—it just won't work. You might be able to find an active converter to convert the signals, but they are expensive. A better choice is to get a new monitor or a new video card.

✔ **Quick Check**

   1. What types of signals are supported by DVI?

   2. What are the primary differences between VGA and HDMI?

Quick Check Answers

   1. Analog and digital.

   2. VGA is analog video only, and HDMI is digital video and audio.

Other Connections

While the primary connections used for display devices are VGA, DVI, and HDMI, you might come across other connections. This section covers the other connections mentioned in the CompTIA objectives.

DisplayPort

DisplayPort is an interface developed by the Video Electronics Standards Association (VESA), an organization that has developed many standards used for displays and video peripherals. It can transmit video, audio, and USB signals for monitors that have USB connectors.

Figure 6-11 shows the outline of the DisplayPort next to an HDMI connection. The shape is distinctive when you're looking at the line drawing, but when you're looking at the back of a computer without adequate light, it's easy to confuse the two. (Figure 6-15 includes a picture with both connectors.) The DisplayPort port is recessed in the case, so the shape isn't as clear.

DisplayPort   HDMI

FIGURE 6-11 DisplayPort and HDMI port.

Composite and RCA

Composite cables use an RCA jack and carry only video. They are most commonly used with TVs and are combined with two additional jacks that carry stereo audio. *RCA* is a type of connector created by the Radio Corporation of America in the 1940s. RCA isn't an acronym, but the cables are commonly known as RCA connectors.

Figure 6-12 shows both ends of a combined composite and audio cable. The jacks are color-coded, with the yellow connector used for the composite video and the white and red connectors used for audio.

FIGURE 6-12 RCA jacks used for composite video and audio.

RGB

Red Green Blue (RGB) cables also use three RCA jacks: one for red, one for green, and one for blue analog signals. The cable includes three connectors, with each connector carrying one of the primary colors as an analog signal. These are more commonly used with televisions and disc players, but they have been used with some monitors. Using three cables instead of the single cable used with a composite signal provides a higher-quality display. RGB cables are commonly color-coded with red, green, and blue.

> **NOTE** **VGA COMMONLY CALLED RGB**
> VGA uses a 3-row, 15-pin DB connector, and it is often referred to as RGB because it transmits the red, green, and blue video signals.

Component

Component video is similar to RGB in that it uses a cable with three jacks and provides an analog signal. It is often referenced as YP_BP_R, and these three signals are derived from an RGB signal.

Cables and connections are commonly color-coded. Green is used for Y, blue is used for P_B, and red is used for P_R. However, the signals aren't the same as RGB. That is, the red cable carrying the P_R signal is not the same signal as Red in an RGB cable.

S-Video

A Separate Video (S-Video) connector is a 4-pin DIN used for analog video. It transmits the video over two channels and provides a higher-quality display than a single-channel composite video signal, but not as good as 3-channel RGB and component video.

Figure 6-13 shows two ends of an S-Video cable. It has been used on some monitors but has been more common on TVs and DVD players.

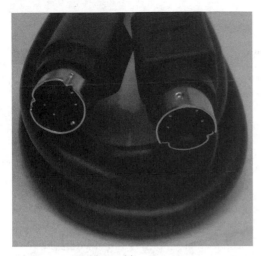

FIGURE 6-13 S-Video cable.

Video Interface Summary

Table 6-2 provides a summary of the key video interfaces.

TABLE 6-2 Video Interface Summary

Interface	Analog/Digital	Comments
HDMI	Digital	Includes video and 8-channel audio. Compatible with DVI-D and DVI-I.
DVI-D	Digital	Compatible with HDMI but doesn't include audio.
DVI-A	Analog	Compatible with VGA.
DVI-I	Analog and Digital	Compatible with VGA and HDMI. Doesn't include audio.
VGA	Analog	This commonly refers to the 15-pin, 3-row DB-15 connector.
Composite	Analog	Uses a single RCA jack. Often used with two RCA jacks for audio.
Component and RGB	Analog	Use three RCA jacks each carrying a separate analog signal.
DisplayPort	Digital	Not compatible with DVI or HDMI. Includes audio, video, and USB.
S-Video	Analog	Uses round 4-pin DIN connection

Quick Check

1. What type of connection includes USB?

2. What type of connector does S-Video use?

Quick Check Answers

1. DisplayPort.

2. A 4-pin DIN.

Video Cards and Drivers

The chipset on most motherboards includes video capabilities, and different chipsets provide different types of video. There might be times when the video provided by the chipset doesn't meet the user's needs and doesn't provide the quality of graphics expected. Users can purchase an additional video card, also called a graphics device interface (GDI), and use the video from the GDI instead.

Figure 6-14 shows two different video cards. Both have *graphics processing units (GPUs)* and onboard RAM. The GPUs can generate a lot of heat, just like a central processing unit (CPU), so it's common to see heat sinks (highlighted by the white boxes), as shown in Figure 6-14.

FIGURE 6-14 Video cards with GPUs.

 EXAM TIP

If a video card is added to a system, the video provided by the onboard features of the chipset should be disabled in the BIOS. This prevents any conflicts between the two.

Some manufacturers have used two or more video cards that work together to provide a faster high-quality single output. For example, NVIDIA created Scalable Link Interface (SLI) to link multiple GPUs on separate video cards.

Video Memory

Video cards include onboard RAM, which provides two important benefits. Without onboard RAM, the video card shares the system memory. For example, imagine your display needs 500 MB of RAM and your system has 3 GB of usable RAM. The display reserves the 500 MB of RAM, leaving your system with only 2.5 GB of usable RAM. The second benefit is that the RAM is closer to the GPU, making it quicker.

The type of RAM used in video cards is often different than RAM used in the computer. Past graphics cards have used video RAM (VRAM) and synchronous graphics RAM (SGRAM), which were quicker than the RAM used in the systems at the time.

Many current video cards use Graphics Double Data Rate version 5 (GDDR5), which is similar to the Double Data Rate version 3 (DDR3) memory described in Chapter 3, "Understanding RAM and CPUs." GDDR5 uses additional buffers that aren't included with DDR3.

Drivers

Just as with other hardware devices, the operating system needs a device driver to use a video card. One big difference with graphics cards is that these drivers tend to be updated more often.

The video graphics card market is very competitive. Gamers spend a lot of money on games and want quality graphics that often just aren't available from a motherboard's chipset. They're willing to pay more for the cards and are more vocal when things aren't perfect.

Manufacturers release the driver with the video card, typically on a CD, and then provide updates through their site. For example, AMD provides drivers from Support.amd.com. You just need to select your video card and identify your operating system.

> *NOTE* **VIDEO CARD APPLICATIONS**
>
> **Many video card manufacturers also provide applications you can use to view and manipulate the properties of the display. For example, AMD includes the Catalyst Control Center, which includes tools to adjust the color, rotate displays, view properties, and even configure settings to overclock the video card.**

Video Card Ports

When installed, the video card will have ports available at the back of the computer. A typical video card will include multiple ports designed to support various interfaces.

For example, Figure 6-15 shows the video card outputs available on the back of a computer. These are provided by a single video card installed in the system, and this video card supports multiple monitors using any or all of these ports. For example, it's possible to hook up two monitors using DVI, or one DVI and one HDMI, or even four monitors using all the ports.

FIGURE 6-15 Multiple ports on back of computer.

NOTE **GRAPHICS CARDS AND HEAT**

Figure 6-15 shows the output ports of a single graphics card. This card includes a temperature-controlled fan installed on the card and a special vent to help air flow over the graphics card and keep it cool.

Safety Concerns

When working with monitors, there are some specific safety concerns technicians need to know about. When working with CRTs, the primary concerns are your safety and the environment. With flat-panel displays, you want to use the proper cleaning materials.

Working with CRTs

CRT monitors require very high voltages to power the vacuum tube and the electron gun. If the monitor is opened and you touch the wrong component, these voltages can very easily kill you. Even after you turn the CRT monitor off, these components retain the voltage. Most organizations have safety policies in place directing technicians not to open a CRT monitor. If the monitor fails, replace it.

IMPORTANT **ELECTROCUTION DANGER**

Deadly voltages are contained within a CRT monitor even after it has been turned off. You should not open a CRT monitor unless you have been specially trained to do so.

Disposal of CRTs

CRTs contain a significant amount of toxic substances, including cadmium and lead. Therefore, they should be treated as hazardous waste. They should not be discarded in the trash, taken to landfills, or incinerated.

In the United States, the Environmental Protection Agency (EPA) has created specific rules for the disposal of CRTs. A company can be fined for discarding CRTs in landfills instead of taking them to recycling centers. In Europe, disposal is governed by the Waste Electrical and Electronic Equipment (WEEE) Directive.

Cleaning Supplies

If you ever saw *My Big Fat Greek Wedding*, you might remember the father's response to most problems was to use Windex. No matter what the problem was, the solution was, "Put some Windex on it." They were memorable lines, but Windex is not a good solution for many computer components, especially LCD and plasma screens.

The ammonia and alcohol contained within many common household cleaners can easily scratch, smudge, or cloud the display. The recommended method for cleaning these displays is to wipe them down with a dry lint-free cloth and then use a cleaner specially designed for the screen. You should not spray the screen directly. Instead, put the cleaner on the cloth, and clean the screen with the cloth.

CRT monitors are an exception. These monitors have glass screens, and it is OK to use glass cleaners such as Windex on them.

Troubleshooting Video and Display Issues

If you understand the basics about how displays operate and how they're connected, you'll be able to resolve most of the problems without any difficulty. The following section describes a Windows Diagnostic tool and some common display problems you might see.

Dxdiag

Windows-based systems use a suite of multimedia technologies for video and audio known as DirectX. Windows also includes the *DirectX Diagnostic Tool (dxdiag)*, which you can use to run a quick check on DirectX. You can start this on Windows 7 by clicking Start, typing **dxdiag** in the Search Programs And Files text box, and selecting dxdiag. If you are prompted to check whether your drivers are digitally signed, select Yes. You'll see a display similar to Figure 6-16.

You can either click Next Page to view the output in order, or you can select any of the tabs. In addition to giving you information about your system and the current version of DirectX, it also provides information about the display and sound drivers. For example, if you suspect your driver isn't up to date, you can use DirectX to identify your version and compare it to available versions.

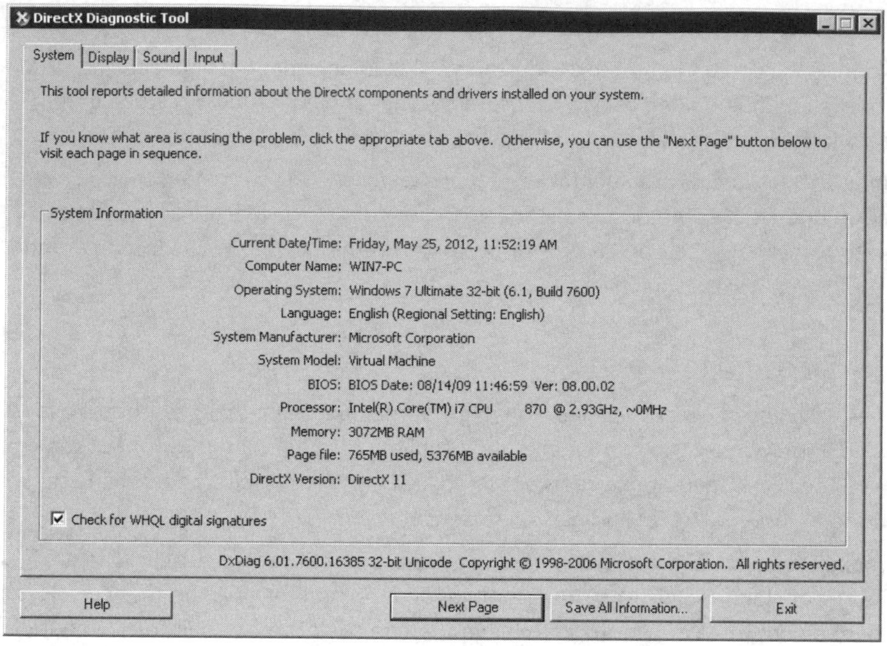

FIGURE 6-16 Dxdiag.

VGA Mode

In some cases, your display can default to VGA mode with a basic resolution of 640 × 480. You'll normally be using a much higher resolution, but with VGA mode, you'll see fewer items and items on the screen will be larger. It will be apparent that something is wrong.

The most common reason that a system defaults to VGA mode is due to a faulty or incorrect driver used with the video card. The solution is to get the correct video driver.

> **MORE INFO   CHAPTER 15, "CONFIGURING WINDOWS OPERATING SYSTEMS"**
>
> Chapter 15 covers device drivers in more depth, including how to use the Device Manager to update and modify drivers.

No Image on Screen

If a display has no image at all, check the basics first. Ensure that it is plugged in and turned on. Any monitor should have some indication that it has power, such as a power LED. If the display is working, it will either display normal video from the computer or display a message indicating that it's not connected.

The most common reason for no image on LCD-based monitors is a failed backlight. The liquid crystals do not emit light, and without the backlight, the screen is dark. In many cases, the cost to replace the backlight is high. Therefore, instead of trying to replace it, most organizations replace the monitor.

> **NOTE** **BACKLIGHTS AND LAPTOPS**
>
> An exception is when a backlight fails on a laptop. Instead of replacing the entire laptop, many organizations choose to replace the backlight.

A common problem that many people make when plugging in a new monitor is using the wrong port. For example, Figure 6-17 shows the back of a PC with two standard ports provided from the motherboard and three additional ports provided from a video card.

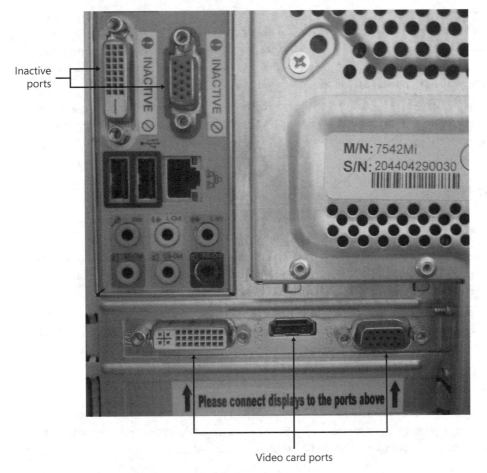

FIGURE 6-17 Inactive and active ports on PC.

The two top ports are labeled "Inactive" with yellow stickers and have been disabled in BIOS. Additionally, there's a note in bright yellow below the video card ports saying, "Please connect displays to the ports above." If either of the top ports is used, you will typically see a default message indicating that the monitor isn't connected. Some monitors won't display anything.

Dim Image

If the image is dim, first check the brightness controls on the monitor. In some cases, you can simply turn up the brightness to get the image back.

A dim image is often the result of a failed backlight on LCD-based monitors. Some monitors can pick up some light from the room or possibly from the sun if they are by a window. In this case, you'll see a dim image, but it will be barely perceptible.

CRT monitors gradually dim as they age. There's no solution other than sending them to the recycling center and getting an LCD monitor that will be gentler on your power bill. Similarly, some bulbs with projectors will dim with age. The solution is to replace the bulb.

Flickering Image

Flickering images are common with CRT monitors when the resolution is set too low. It's irritating and often causes eye strain. In general, you can eliminate the flicker by setting the resolution to 72 Hz or higher. This isn't a problem for LCD-based monitors.

Discoloration (Degaussing)

Discoloration of the image is most commonly seen on CRT monitors. One of the causes is placing magnetic materials too close to the monitor. Moving external hard drives and any other electronic devices away from the monitor often solves the problem.

In some cases, the monitor has electromagnetic buildup that needs to be removed. Most CRT monitors have a button labeled Degauss that sends a magnetic pulse through the monitor to release this buildup. When you press the button, you'll often hear a loud "thunk" that sounds a little ominous the first time you hear it, but it is normal. This often clears up the display.

Overheat Shutdown

Video cards generate a lot of heat, and by now you probably realize that heat is a computer's enemy. Video cards commonly have heat sinks on the GPU to keep them cool, and many also have thermal-controlled fans. These fans automatically speed up as the temperature rises.

If the video card overheats, it can cause the system to shut down. In some cases, sensors recognize that it is getting too hot and they shut down the system. In other cases, the heat causes a hardware failure, shutting down the system. If you suspect a heat problem related to the video card, check all the cooling methods.

Dead Pixels

A dead pixel is an area on the screen that is always black on an LCD monitor. These are relatively common on LCD monitors, but you usually won't see many. If a new monitor has too many dead pixels or too many in a certain area of the screen, the warranty might allow you to replace it. However, different manufacturers have different policies about how many pixels can fail before the warranty covers it.

> **NOTE   DEAD PIXELS AND WARRANTIES**
>
> Manufacturers do not always guarantee that 100 percent of the pixels are operational. That is, a monitor with some dead pixels is still considered a good monitor. You won't be able to return it for warranty repair just because of a few dead pixels. About the best you can do is what one of my students did: he had a T-shirt made that said, "I see dead pixels."

A stuck pixel is stuck in a specific color such as white or red. Some people have had success with videos from YouTube or software developers to unstick them. These tools quickly flash the screen with different colors and, in some cases, can unstick the pixels.

Artifacts and Distorted Images

Visual artifacts are simply drawing errors where the screen is displaying something that it shouldn't. Some examples include the following:

- Horizontal or vertical lines through the display. These can be thin black lines or wide bars with distorted colors.
- A repeating pattern of small bars or rectangles over the entire screen.

- Wobbly vertical lines equally spaced across the screen.
- A small number of random dots in one area, or a huge number of random dots distorting the entire image.

The most likely cause of artifacts is an overheating video card. Check to ensure that all the cooling components within the system are working correctly.

Wobbly vertical lines are specifically related to the DVI interface. Ensure that the cable is seated firmly on the interface and the monitor. If you have two DVI connectors, try the other one. The problem might affect only one DVI port.

In some cases, these problems can be due to an incorrect video card driver. Update the driver, or if these symptoms appeared after updating the driver, roll it back to the previous version.

Color Patterns Incorrect

In some cases, the colors displayed on the monitor are not completely accurate. This isn't noticeable to many people. However, it is noticeable and important to some people. For example, graphics artists often manipulate photos and other graphics that they'll print. They want to ensure that what they see on the screen is what they'll see when it is printed. Calibration is the answer.

For very basic calibration, you can display a test image on your screen and adjust the contrast, brightness, tone, and hue. However, this is very difficult and tedious to do manually. A more efficient method is using a calibration tool that plugs into the USB port. It includes optical sensors that can "view" the colors displayed on the monitor and modify the display electronically.

BSOD

In some cases, a faulty driver can result in a serious stop error in Windows—also known as the Blue Screen of Death (BSOD). That sounds much more ominous than it really is; you simply need to replace the driver. You first restart your machine and go into safe mode, and then use Device Manager to install the correct driver.

> **MORE INFO** **CHAPTER 17, "TROUBLESHOOTING WINDOWS OPERATING SYSTEMS"**
>
> Chapter 17 covers different methods used to troubleshoot Windows, including how to start safe mode. As mentioned previously, Chapter 15 covers Device Manager.

Chapter Summary

- CRT monitors are heavy, large, power-hungry, analog-based monitors. They are frequently replaced with flat-panel displays to save money on power.

- LCD monitors are light, thin, digital-based monitors that consume significantly less power than CRTs.

- Backlights illuminate crystals in LCD monitors. If the backlight fails, the LCD will be dim or completely dark. LED monitors are LCD monitors that use LEDs for backlights.

- Plasma monitors are flat-panel displays. They include gas-filled cells that emit colors but are susceptible to screen burn-in. LCD monitors aren't susceptible to burn-in.

- VGA mode uses a resolution of 640 × 480. Resolutions have been regularly improved, and WUXGA uses 1920 × 1200.

- Operating systems allow you to modify the resolution of monitors, but you should always use the native resolution required by LCD monitors.

- Multiple displays allow you to display the same information on multiple monitors or to extend the display.

- The primary interfaces used by video devices are VGA, DVI, and HDMI. VGA is analog, DVI supports both analog and digital, and HDMI is digital. HDMI also supports audio.

- Adapters are available to convert VGA to DVI-A, DVI-D to HDMI, and DVI-I to HDMI. However, you cannot convert analog VGA data to digital HDMI data with an adapter.

- Video cards include a GPU and additional RAM. It's important to update drivers when installing new cards.

- CRT monitors include deadly voltages and should not be opened. They should be disposed of as hazardous waste.

- Dxdiag provides information on a system, DirectX, the display, and sound capabilities. It can be used to diagnose some problems related to the display.

- Many display problems can be attributed to the incorrect driver, an overheated video card, or the connection. Ensure that the driver is up to date, the cooling system is working, and that cables are plugged into the correct ports.

Chapter Review

Use the following questions to test your knowledge of the information in this chapter. The answers to these questions, and the explanations of why each answer choice is correct or incorrect, are located in the "Answers" section at the end of this chapter.

1. Of the following display interfaces, what uses an analog signal? (Choose all that apply.)

   A. HDMI

   B. DVI-D

    C. DVI-A

    D. VGA

2. Which of the following display interfaces include both audio and video signals?

    A. HDMI

    B. DVI-D

    C. DVI-A

    D. VGA

3. You have a computer with a DVI port and an HDMI port. One monitor is connected to the DVI port, and you want to add a second monitor. The second monitor has a single VGA port. How can you accomplish this?

    A. Plug the VGA cable into the HDMI port.

    B. Use a passive VGA-to-HDMI adapter.

    C. Plug the VGA cable into the DVI port, and plug the DVI cable into the HDMI port.

    D. None of the above.

4. Your company is replacing all the CRT monitors with flat panel displays. What should be done with the old monitors?

    A. Take them directly to a landfill.

    B. Throw them in the dumpster.

    C. Take them to an incinerator.

    D. Dispose of them as hazardous waste in compliance with local regulations.

5. You have recently installed a new video card with a DVI interface. The display always defaults to VGA mode and can't be changed. What is the most likely problem?

    A. Nothing; this is normal for DVI.

    B. Incorrect driver.

    C. Faulty monitor.

    D. Faulty video card.

6. You are troubleshooting a problem with a blank LCD display. You have verified that it is connected to the computer and has power. What's the most likely problem?

    A. Incorrect driver

    B. Faulty CRT tube

    C. Failed backlight

    D. Dead pixels

Answers

1. **Correct Answers:** C, D

   A. **Incorrect:** High-Definition Multimedia Interface (HDMI) uses digital transmissions.

   B. **Incorrect:** Digital Visual Interface—Digital (DVI-D) uses digital transmissions.

   C. **Correct:** Digital Visual Interface—Analog (DVI-A) uses analog transmissions.

   D. **Correct:** Video Graphics Array (VGA) uses analog transmissions.

2. **Correct Answer:** A

   A. **Correct:** High-Definition Multimedia Interface (HDMI) includes both 8-channel audio and video.

   B. **Incorrect:** Digital Visual Interface—Digital (DVI-D) includes video in only a digital format.

   C. **Incorrect:** Digital Visual Interface—Analog (DVI-A) includes video in only an analog format.

   D. **Incorrect:** Video Graphics Array (VGA) uses only analog video.

3. **Correct Answer:** D

   A. **Incorrect:** A VGA cable with a DB-15 connector will not plug into an HDMI port.

   B. **Incorrect:** A passive adapter cannot convert analog VGA signals to digital HDMI signals.

   C. **Incorrect:** The VGA cable cannot plug into a DVI port, and the DVI cable can't plug into the HDMI port.

   D. **Correct:** HDMI is digital, and VGA is analog, and none of these solutions can convert the signals.

4. **Correct Answer:** D

   A. **Incorrect:** Monitors should not be taken to a landfill.

   B. **Incorrect:** Monitors thrown in the dumpster go to a landfill.

   C. **Incorrect:** Monitors should not be incinerated.

   D. **Correct:** CRT monitors include toxic substances and should be disposed of as hazardous waste.

5. **Correct Answer:** B

   A.   Incorrect: VGA mode (640 × 480) is not common for DVI.

   B.   Correct: The most common reason for a new video card defaulting to VGA mode is an incorrect driver.

   C.   Incorrect: Problems with the monitor can affect the display quality but wouldn't change the resolution.

   D.   Incorrect: A faulty video card can default to VGA mode, but it is much more likely that the driver isn't installed for the new video card.

6. **Correct Answer:** C

   A.   Incorrect: An incorrect driver would give some other symptoms.

   B.   Incorrect: An LCD monitor does not have a CRT tube.

   C.   Correct: LCD crystals do not emit light, so the most likely problem is that the backlight failed.

   D.   Incorrect: LCDs might have a few dead pixels, but if the screen is completely blank, all the pixels would be dead.

CHAPTER 7

Exploring Printers

In this chapter, you'll learn about laser, inkjet, impact, and thermal printers. These are the four common types of printers you run across as an A+ technician. It's important to have a basic understanding of how they work so that you're better prepared to maintain and troubleshoot them. You'll also learn how printers are connected and the basic steps for installing and configuring printers.

Exam 220-801 objectives in this chapter:

- 1.12 Install and configure various peripheral devices.
  - Output devices
    - Printers
- 4.1 Explain the differences between the various printer types and summarize the associated imaging process.
  - Laser
    - Imaging drum, fuser assembly, transfer belt, transfer roller, pickup rollers, separate pads, duplexing assembly
    - Imaging process: processing, charging, exposing, developing, transferring, fusing and cleaning
  - Inkjet
    - Ink cartridge, print head, roller, feeder, duplexing assembly, carriage and belt
    - Calibration
  - Thermal
    - Feed assembly, heating element
    - Special thermal paper
  - Impact
    - Print head, ribbon, tractor feed
    - Impact paper
- 4.2 Given a scenario, install, and configure printers.
  - Use appropriate printer drivers for a given operating system
  - Print device sharing

- Wired
  - USB
  - Parallel
  - Serial
  - Ethernet
- Wireless
  - Bluetooth
  - 802.11x
  - Infrared (IR)
- Printer hardware print server
- Printer sharing
  - Sharing local/networked printer via Operating System settings
- 4.3 Given a scenario, perform printer maintenance.
  - Laser
    - Replacing toner, applying maintenance kit, calibration, cleaning
  - Thermal
    - Replace paper, clean heating element, remove debris
  - Impact
    - Replace ribbon, replace print head, replace paper

Exam 220-802 objectives in this chapter:

- 1.4 Given a scenario, use appropriate operating system features and tools.
  - Administrative
    - Print management
- 4.9 Given a scenario, troubleshoot printers with appropriate tools
  - Common symptoms
    - Streaks
    - Faded prints
    - Ghost images
    - Toner not fused to the paper
    - Creased paper
    - Paper not feeding
    - Paper jam
    - No connectivity

- Garbled characters on paper
- Vertical lines on page
- Backed up print queue
- Low memory errors
- Access denied
- Printer will not print
- Color prints in wrong print color
- Unable to install printer
- Error codes
- Tools
  - Maintenance kit
  - Toner vacuum
  - Compressed air
  - Printer spooler

Printing Basics

A printer is a peripheral device that provides you with a hard copy of your data. I'm betting that you've seen a printer in action, so that shouldn't be any surprise. However, you might not be aware of the different printer types. The following sections describe these in more depth, but briefly, here are basic descriptions of the various printer types:

- *Laser printers* use lasers to paint an electronic image onto a rotating drum. The drum then transfers the image to a piece of paper by using toner, which is then melted onto the paper. They are fast and produce a high-quality output but are the most expensive. Larger organizations commonly use them.

- *Inkjet printers* send little streams or jets of ink from the print head onto the paper. They are inexpensive and can produce vibrant color printouts, but the ink is expensive. Inkjet printers are very popular among home users and small offices.

- *Impact printers* create a printout using little pins that work like hammers to force ink from a ribbon onto paper. They are slow and noisy but are the only type of printer that can print the multipart forms used by some businesses.

- *Thermal printers* heat up the paper to print the output. They are used to print cash register receipts, ATM receipts, and lottery tickets.

EXAM TIP

You'll need to understand the basics of each of these printers. However, you'll find that the CompTIA exams focus heavily on laser printers.

Terminology

Printers use some common terminology and acronyms that are important to understand. These terms are used to describe the characteristics of the printer and help you determine their quality. Some of the common terms include the following:

- **PPM (pages per minute).** *PPM* identifies how quickly the printer can print. For example, laser printers can print between 10 and 100 PPM. Impact printers are much slower and are sometimes measured in characters per second (CPS) instead.

- **dpi (dots per inch).** The resolution or clarity of a printer is determined by *dpi*, or how many dots it can print per inch. This is often the same number vertically and horizontally. For example, a 600-dpi printer can print 600 dots in a 1-inch horizontal line and 600 dots in a 1-inch vertical line. 600 dpi is referred to as letter quality.

> **NOTE** DPI RESOLUTION VALUE EXPRESSION
>
> Some printer specifications use two numbers, such as 600 × 600, to describe the resolution, but when the numbers are the same, you'll often see it as one number. That is, a 600-dpi printer implies a 600 × 600 dpi resolution. Some printers have a different horizontal and vertical resolution, and when they are different, you will always see them as two numbers. For example, some photo printers have a resolution of 2880 × 1440.

- **Duplexing assembly.** Printers with a *duplexing assembly* can print double-sided print jobs. They flip the page so that the printer can print on the other side. Figure 7-1 shows an example of a duplexing assembly from an HP OfficeJet printer. It normally plugs into the back of the printer, but it's removed and turned over so that you can see the rollers. Printer settings often include a setting to enable or disable duplexing when two-sided printing is supported.

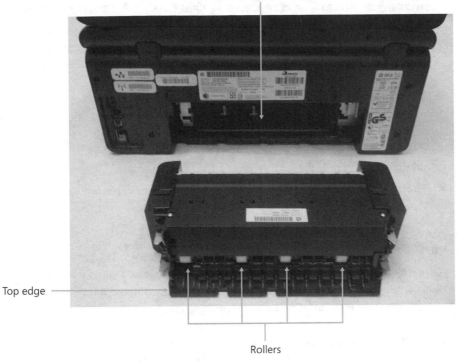

Top edge plugs in here

Top edge

Rollers

FIGURE 7-1 Duplexer on back of inkjet printer.

EXAM TIP

A duplexing assembly is required for printing two-sided print jobs. It is commonly found on laser printers and inkjet printers.

Paper

Paper comes in different types and forms, and printers covered in this chapter use the following types of paper:

- **Single-sheet paper.** Laser jet and inkjet printers use single-sheet paper fed into the printer from a *feeder* or a *paper tray*. Some general-purpose paper can be used in both laser jet and inkjet printers, but there are many higher-quality papers used to print better-quality color pages. Low-quality paper can cause printing problems such as paper jams or poor printouts. Printers commonly include sensors to indicate when the paper runs out.

- **Continuous-feed paper.** This is also known as fan-fold or sprocket paper, or even paper with holes. The sheets are connected and include sprocket holes on each side of the paper. A *tractor feed* mechanism feeds the paper using these sprocket holes. Each sheet includes perforations so that you can separate the pages and the edges after printing. Continuous-feed paper is used by impact printers.
- **Thermal paper.** This is used by thermal printers. It is covered with a chemical that changes color when it is heated.

One of the biggest problems with paper occurs when it is exposed to high humidity. The paper won't actually be wet, but it can absorb the humidity from the air, making it more difficult for the printer to move it through the paper path. The result is more paper jams. Paper should be stored in locations that aren't subjected to high humidity and not opened until it's needed.

Common Maintenance Tools

One of the basic maintenance tasks with any type of printer is cleaning it, and there are several common tools you'll use, such as the following:

- **Compressed air.** You can use compressed air in a can or compressed air from a compressor. It's best to take the printer outside before blowing out the paper dust. This is the same type of compressed air discussed in Chapter 1, "Introduction to Computers."
- **Computer vacuum.** When you're working inside a building, it's not always a good idea to blow the dirt and dust out of a printer into the workspaces. Instead, you can use a vacuum. Regular vacuum cleaners can cause electrostatic discharge (ESD) damage, so only ESD-safe vacuums should be used.
- **Isopropyl alcohol.** Many of the rollers within a printer will get dirty, and isopropyl alcohol is an ideal choice to clean them. For example, Figure 7-2 shows the pickup roller in a laser printer used to pick up paper from a paper tray. When the pickup roller gets dirty, it can have problems picking up the paper. A benefit of isopropyl alcohol is that it evaporates quickly and doesn't leave any residue. You apply it to a cotton swab or lint-free cloth and then clean the roller.

FIGURE 7-2 Pickup roller in an empty paper tray.

Laser Printers

Laser printers provide a very high-quality output and are most commonly used in medium-to-large organizations that require fast, high-quality printers. They have become more affordable and are also used in small offices/home offices (SOHOs) and even by some individual users.

Laser Components

A laser printer includes several key components. The next section covers the laser imaging process in more detail, but the following are brief descriptions of these components:

- *Pickup rollers* are used to pick up a sheet of paper and begin feeding it through the printer.

- *Separator pads* work with the pickup rollers to ensure that only one piece of paper is picked up at a time.

- *Imaging drums* are round, rotating cylinders that are covered with a *photosensitive surface,* meaning it is sensitive to light. A laser uses light to write an image onto the drum.

- *Toner* is an extremely fine powder that includes carbon and plastic. It is electrically charged during the imaging process, causing it to stick to the drum where the laser wrote the image. Later in the process, it is transferred to the paper.

- *Transfer rollers* charge the paper. The image is transferred to the paper because the charged paper attracts the toner.

- *Fuser assemblies* heat the toner and melt into the paper.

- *Transfer belts* are used only on some high-end color laser printers. Colors are first applied to the transfer belt and then applied to the paper.

- A high-voltage power supply provides voltages as high as -1,000 VDC. This is used only in laser printers.

Chapter 1 described an uninterruptible power supply (UPS) used as a battery backup for systems. While an UPS is useful for computers, laser printers should not be plugged into an UPS. The high-voltage power supply draws a significant amount of power in a very short time and can damage an UPS.

Where should you plug in the laser printer? The best choice is to use a dedicated surge protector that does not have any additional equipment plugged into it. The next best choice is to plug it into a grounded wall outlet. It should not be plugged into a power strip shared by other devices.

Laser Imaging Process

As an A+ technician, you will very likely work with laser printers, so it's important to understand how they work so that you'll be better prepared to maintain and troubleshoot them. The laser imaging process includes seven stages or steps, and these steps work in a specific sequence as the imaging drum is rotating.

EXAM TIP

CompTIA A+ printing topics focus heavily on laser printers. When preparing for the exams, make sure you understand the seven steps of the laser printing process and how the different components are used within the printer. This will also help you with troubleshooting.

Figure 7-3 shows an overview of these stages, labeled as Processing, Charging, Exposing, Developing, Transferring, Fusing, and Cleaning. The following sections describe these steps in more depth.

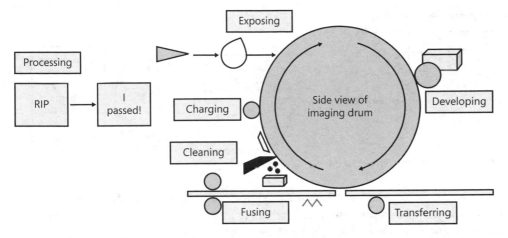

FIGURE 7-3 Laser imaging process.

Processing

The *processing* stage is also known as the raster image processing stage. A raster is a single line of dots, and a *raster image* is the combination of all the raster lines for a page. As you read this page, you perceive it as words and maybe a graphic. A laser printer identifies the page as a raster image of dots.

Consider a 600 × 600 dpi laser printer. For any given square inch of a sheet of paper, the raster image includes details about each of these 360,000 dots. These details include whether or not it should be printed, how light or how dark the dot should be, and, if it's a color printer, what color the dot should be.

Most laser printers include a *raster image processor (RIP)* that creates the raster image. The computer sends the print job to the printer in a format the RIP understands, and the RIP then creates the raster image.

Raster images can take up a lot of space. If you print pages using 600-dpi graphics, it takes about 4 MB of RAM per page to hold the raster image. If it's a color page, it takes about 16 MB of RAM per page. If the printer doesn't have enough space to hold the print job, it will often give a "low memory" or "out of memory" error message.

Charging

In the *charging* step, a primary charge roller applies a high-voltage negative charge to the imaging drum, as shown in Figure 7-4. In older laser printers, this was applied with a corona wire that was easily broken during maintenance, but most new laser printers use a primary charge roller. This voltage is typically between -500 and -600 VDC but can be as high as -1,000 VDC.

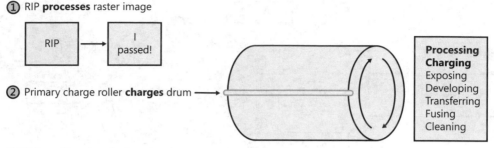

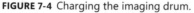

FIGURE 7-4 Charging the imaging drum.

This has two purposes. First, if there is any residual charge from a previous print job, it removes it. Second, it prepares the imaging drum to accept the image from the laser. Notice that even though the raster image is created, we aren't using it yet.

Exposing

After the drum has a uniform charge, the laser exposes the imaging drum with the raster image in the *exposing* stage. It does this by sending a highly focused laser beam through one or more mirrors and lenses, and when the beam hits the photosensitive drum, it neutralizes the charge applied in the previous step. However, it neutralizes the charge only where the laser beam hits the drum, as shown in Figure 7-5.

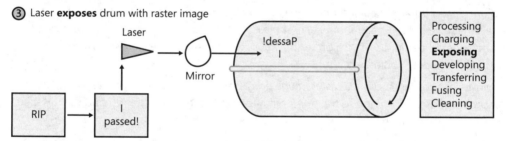

FIGURE 7-5 Exposing the imaging drum.

> ***NOTE*** **EXPOSING IS WRITING**
>
> Some books refer to *exposing* as *writing*. You can think of it as the laser writing the image onto the drum. However, the CompTIA objectives specifically list it as exposing.

At this point, the drum has a high-voltage negative charge everywhere except for where the drum has been exposed by the light beam. Anywhere the drum has been exposed, it has a neutral charge.

Developing

The toner is applied to the imaging drum in the *developing* stage. First the toner is given a negative charge. At this point, the imaging drum has a negative charge except for where the image has been exposed, and the toner also has a negative charge.

When dealing with electricity, like charges repel and opposites attract. Therefore, if you have two components with similar charges, they pull apart from each other, while two components with opposite charges are attracted to each other. In this case, the negatively charged toner is attracted to the exposed areas of the drum that have a neutral charge.

Figure 7-6 shows a side view of the imaging drum. Toner is in the toner cartridge, and the developer roller makes the toner accessible to the drum. As the drum rotates, the toner sticks to the drum where the image has been written to the drum.

④ Image is **developed** by applying toner to imaging drum

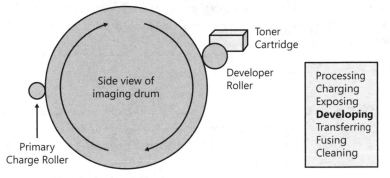

FIGURE 7-6 Developing the image.

There are many different types of toner and toner cartridges. For example, some manufacturers include the developer roller (sometimes called just the *developer*) in the toner cartridge.

Transferring

The toner is applied to the paper in the *transferring* stage. First, pickup rollers roll over the top of the paper in the paper tray to pick up a page. Separator pads roll the opposite way from underneath to ensure that only one sheet of paper is picked up. Next, a transfer roller (sometimes called a *transfer corona*) charges the paper, giving it an opposite charge from the toner. Just as the toner was attracted to the drum in the developing stage due to opposite charges, it will be attracted to the paper in this stage due to opposite charges. After the paper is charged, it's passed to the drum and the toner jumps to the paper, as shown in Figure 7-7.

Laser printers have a static charge eliminator that removes the static charge from the paper immediately after the image is transferred. You've probably noticed how socks stick together after you remove them from the clothes dryer. Similarly, the paper can stick to the drum if the static charge isn't removed.

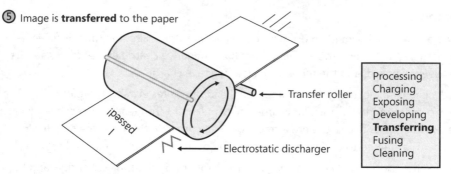

⑤ Image is **transferred** to the paper

Transfer roller

Electrostatic discharger

Processing
Charging
Exposing
Developing
Transferring
Fusing
Cleaning

FIGURE 7-7 Transferring the image.

EXAM TIP

When preparing for the exam, it's important to know the steps in the laser imaging process and the order. For example, developing can occur only after exposing, and fusing can occur only after transferring.

Fusing

The toner isn't attached to the paper in the transferring stage. If you could pick it up and shake it, the toner would just fall off. The toner is fused to the paper in the *fusing* step. Toner is composed of carbon and plastic particles, and if you heat plastic, it melts. The fuser assembly heats the toner so that it melts into the paper.

Figure 7-8 shows how the paper is passed between two fuser rollers. One of the fuser rollers is heated, and the other fuser provides friction to press the toner into the paper as it is melted.

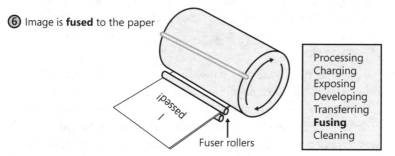

⑥ Image is **fused** to the paper

Fuser rollers

Processing
Charging
Exposing
Developing
Transferring
Fusing
Cleaning

FIGURE 7-8 Fusing the image.

If you've ever taken a sheet of paper off a laser printer immediately after it printed, you've probably noticed that it's warm. That's not from the laser; it's from the melted toner.

Cleaning

In the *cleaning* stage, excess toner is scraped off the drum and collected for disposal. The scraper is a small plastic or rubber blade that scrapes the toner off without damaging the drum. Next, an erase lamp neutralizes the charge on the drum, as shown in Figure 7-9.

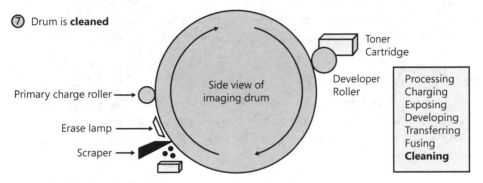

FIGURE 7-9 Cleaning the drum.

Notice that when the drum rotates clockwise, the primary charge roller is located after the scraper and the erase lamp. At this point the whole process can start again. Another image could be processed, charged, exposed, developed, transferred, and fused, and the drum can be cleaned to do it again.

What Comes First?

You might come across technical manuals that say that cleaning is the first step in the laser printer imaging process. This raises a logical question: What comes first?

A laser printer will typically start processing the next image before the current image is completed, so this is actually the first step. For example, after one image has been sent to the laser, the RIP can start processing the next image. Depending on how much memory a printer has, the RIP might be able to process several images in advance. However, if it first erased the image, it couldn't start until the current image had completed the printing cycle.

The drum must be cleaned before writing another image, and as long as this is done at the end of the last cycle, the process works. However, there are some special situations, such as a power loss, that can result in the last cycle not completing. Printers commonly include a fail-safe process of cleaning the drum when a printer is first turned on or before doing a print job after the printer has been idle.

EXAM TIP

If you see a question that asks what the first stage in the laser printer imaging process is, look for "processing." Processing takes the longest and is often started before the previous image has completed. If "processing" is not an available answer, look for "cleaning."

Color Laser Printers

Most laser printers print only in black and white. Color laser printers are available but at a much higher cost. They can produce some vibrant images, but the imaging process is more complex than a typical laser printer. Laser printers use the CMYK color model of cyan (a blue-green or aqua color), magenta (a purplish-pink color), yellow, and black.

NOTE CMYK AND RGB

Primary colors are red, green, and blue. When you mix magenta and yellow, you get red. When you mix cyan and yellow, you get green. When you mix cyan and magenta, you get blue. When you mix cyan, magenta, and yellow, you get black. In contrast, when you mix red, green, and blue, you get white.

A color laser printer applies each of the four CMYK colors with varying intensity to create images. In some laser printers, these colors are applied to the paper in four separate passes. However, if the paper is slightly misaligned during any of these passes, it results in blurring and other color problems.

High-end color laser printers use a transfer belt to prevent these types of problems. They apply the four colors to the transfer belt in four passes and then transfer the image from the transfer belt to the paper in a single pass. The transfer belt is stronger than a piece of paper and less susceptible to misalignment issues.

✔ **Quick Check**

    1. What are the seven stages of the laser printing process?

    2. In what laser printing process stage is the image written onto the drum?

Quick Check Answers

    1. Processing, charging, exposing, developing, transferring, fusing, and cleaning.

    2. Exposing.

Laser Printer Maintenance

Even though there are many different models of laser printers, you'll find that they share common maintenance tasks. This section covers these tasks and includes some important safety considerations.

Safety

One of the most important things to realize is that a laser printer includes a high-voltage power supply. Voltages are as high as -1,000 VDC and can be deadly. Stay safe and unplug the laser printer before performing any maintenance. Also, capacitors within a power supply can still hold a charge after a device is unplugged. Even after you unplug the printer, be careful of what you touch.

The fuser assembly melts the toner onto the paper and reaches a temperature of about 180 degrees Centigrade (about 356 degrees Fahrenheit). Even after you turn the printer off and unplug it, this will still be hot.

If the imaging drum is exposed during maintenance, you should be careful not to touch it. You can easily scratch it or leave a mark that won't be cleaned during a print cycle. These scratches or marks will appear on every printout until the drum is replaced.

> **IMPORTANT** **DANGER OF INJURY OR WORSE**
>
> A laser printer has potentially deadly voltages and extremely hot components within. You should turn it off and unplug it before servicing it.

Replacing Toner

As the toner runs low, the print quality of your printouts degrades. Also, most laser printers give software alerts letting you know that the toner is running low. The solution is simple: replace the toner.

> **NOTE** **TONER CARTRIDGES**
>
> In some laser printers, the toner cartridge includes the imaging drum, the developer, and/or a cleaning blade used to clean toner during the cleaning process. Therefore, when you replace the toner cartridge, you might also be replacing other components.

Different models have different procedures for replacing the toner, and it's important to follow the manufacturer's directions. The following are some general guidelines that apply to most toner cartridges:

- Instructions will usually direct you to shake the cartridge up and down and from side to side. This loosens the toner and helps ensure that you get full usage out the cartridge.

- Most toner cartridges include some type of seal to prevent the toner from leaking out. It's often a piece of tape or plastic that you remove prior to installing the new cartridge. If you don't remove it, your printouts will be blank.

- Be careful when handling the new toner cartridge. Ideally, you should the remove the new cartridge from the packaging and insert it immediately in the printer. This means that you have already removed the old cartridge.

- If the toner spills on you or someone else, consult the instructions or Material Safety Data Sheet (MSDS) to determine what to do. In general, you can wash it off with cold water. It's designed to melt, so you should not rinse it off with warm or hot water. If it spills on a desk, you can remove it with paper or cloth towels soaked with cold water.

- If you need to vacuum a toner spill, you should use a special vacuum with a high-efficiency particulate arresting (HEPA) filter. Without a HEPA filter, the toner particles might just blow right back into the air.

- Recycle the old cartridge. Many companies will purchase these. Companies refurbish them, fill them with toner, and sell them at a discounted cost.

Most laser toner cartridges include replacement filters and instructions about what should be cleaned. The high-voltage power supply creates a small amount of ozone, which is a gas that can be harmful in large amounts. Laser printers include an ozone filter to limit the danger from ozone, and it's common to replace this filter when replacing the toner cartridge. Other filters can usually be cleaned.

REAL WORLD   GETTING EXTRA PAGES FROM AN EMPTY TONER CARTRIDGE

When the laser printer runs out of toner, it's usually not completely out. If you come across a printer that appears to have run out and you don't have a replacement toner cartridge available, you can usually use the following technique to get some printouts while you wait for the replacement to arrive.

Turn off the printer and remove the toner cartridge. Gently shake the cartridge from side to side and up and down. The toner is a very fine powder, and these actions release toner that has become stuck to the sides. After replacing the toner cartridge, you can usually print 20 or more pages without any problems

Be careful, though. Some toner cartridges have openings that stay exposed when you remove them. If you start shaking them, you might end up shaking toner all over yourself and the room.

Applying Maintenance Kit

When maintenance is required, many laser printers provide messages such as "Service Required" or "Perform Printer Maintenance." This message is normally timed to appear after the printer has printed a specific number of pages. Maintenance kits are available that include items such as pickup and separator rollers, transfer rollers, and fuser assemblies.

Sometimes you might notice that more than one sheet of paper is being pulled through at a time or that the paper is coming out crumpled. You might be able to clean the pickup and separator rollers to resolve the problem, or you might need to replace them with a maintenance kit.

Cleaning

It's often recommended to clean certain pickup rollers when replacing the toner. Isopropyl alcohol with a lint-free cloth or cotton swabs works best.

If the laser printer has a lot of paper dust buildup, you should use an ESD-safe vacuum to clean it. You should not use compressed air within a laser printer because you can potentially blow the dust into the imaging drum.

Calibration

Color laser printers have the potential to produce misaligned colors or lines. Many printers use a transfer belt to minimize this problem, but the problem can still occur. The solution is to run a calibration routine provided by the printer vendor. This will ensure that the printer heads are aligned.

Laser Component Replacement

Besides the toner cartridge and filters, many laser printer components can be replaced if they fail. You'll need to dig into the technical manual for the procedures, but it is possible. Figure 7-10 shows ace A+ technician José Vargas with a fuser assembly and a laser assembly that he has removed from a laser printer. The customer asked José to send him an update via text as soon as José had more information, and that's exactly what he's doing.

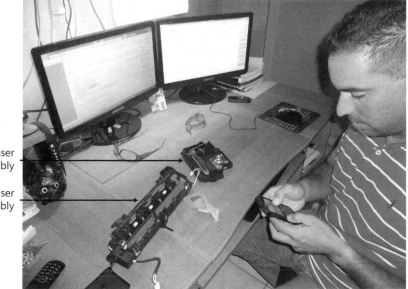

FIGURE 7-10 José texting a customer with information about a laser printer.

Inkjet Printers

Inkjet printers can produce very high-quality color printouts and are very affordable. These two benefits make them very popular among home users and some SOHOs. They don't have as many serviceable parts within them, so you don't need to have a deep understanding of how they work to maintain them.

Figure 7-11 shows the basic components of an inkjet printer. One or more print heads are attached to a carriage and belt assembly, and this assembly moves the heads from side to side as the paper is fed through the printer. Ink cartridges can be attached to the print head or located elsewhere.

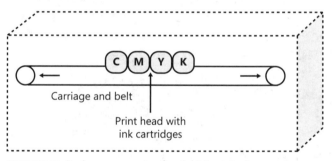

FIGURE 7-11 Basic components of an inkjet printer.

The carriage and belt assembly is controlled with a stepper motor and a pulley and usually includes a plastic guide and sensors. The sensors detect the position of the print head and paper. The assembly also includes a data cable connected from a printed circuit board to the print head.

While they are not shown in the figure, the printer will also have a paper feeder or paper tray where you insert the paper, and one or more rollers that pull the paper through the printer.

Many inkjet printers support duplexing assemblies so that they can print on both sides of the paper. The duplexing assembly shown in Figure 7-1 is from an inkjet printer.

The print speed of inkjet printers is relatively low when compared to a laser printer, but it is usually quick enough for most users. The primary drawback is the high cost of the ink.

Inkjet Ink Cartridges

Inkjet printers use the same CMYK model used by color laser printers. Some models use only two ink cartridges—one for all three CMY colors and another one for black ink. Other models use four cartridges, with separate cartridges for each CMYK color.

For example, Figure 7-12 shows the ink cartridges for an HP OfficeJet inkjet printer (on the left). They are accessible from the front panel to the left of the paper tray, and I've removed the black cartridge. Most people print black ink more than color, so the color ink cartridges are normally smaller than the black cartridge in any inkjet printer.

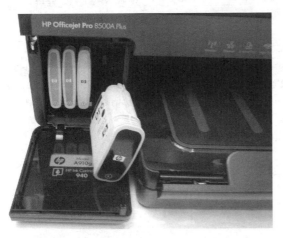 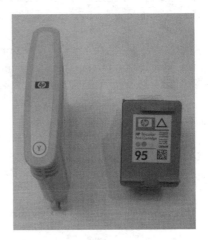

FIGURE 7-12 Ink cartridges.

For comparison, on the right in Figure 7-12, you can see a tri-color ink cartridge for another inkjet printer next to the Y inkjet cartridge from the printer shown on the left side of the figure. The tri-color cartridge includes the CMY colors. Even though these are both HP inks, they are for different printers and have a completely different shape and size.

> **NOTE   INK CARTRIDGE LOCATION**
> The location of the ink cartridge varies from one printer to another. In many printers, the cartridges are close to the print head or even include the print head. In others, the cartridges are located farther away. Either way, ink cartridges are easy to replace.

The ink for inkjet printers often represents the highest cost for inkjet printers. In some cases, you can get a free printer with the purchase of a computer. Printer manufacturers realize that if you have the printer, you'll buy the ink, so they're willing to lose some money on the initial sale.

Refilling Inkjet Cartridges

Due to the cost of the ink, many people look for alternatives. You can buy do-it-yourself refill kits, but in general, these are not recommended. Most ink cartridges are vacuum-sealed, and it's difficult to replace the ink and keep the seal. Without the vacuum seal, the cartridge can leak and damage the printer.

> **NOTE   REFILLING DOESN'T VOID WARRANTY**
>
> By law, manufacturers can't void the warranty simply because you're not purchasing new ink from them. However, if the cartridge is filled incorrectly, it can damage the printer, and you're unlikely to get it fixed under warranty. Similarly, when you buy a car, you can change the oil yourself. However, if you don't secure the oil filter and the oil leaks out, don't expect the car company to cover the engine damage under the car's warranty.

Another option is to have a professional service refill your cartridges. These services use high-quality ink and have the equipment necessary to keep a vacuum seal. For example, I was recently at a Costco store and learned that they do this in the photo department for many cartridges. You can bring in empty cartridges, and they'll refill them within an hour at a significantly lower cost than new ones.

Inkjet Printing Process

Inkjet printers work by ejecting ink onto the paper through microscopic nozzles in the print head. There are two primary methods used in the printing process: thermal (or bubble) and piezoelectric.

> **NOTE   PAPER AND OTHER MEDIA**
>
> General purpose paper will work for inkjet printers, laser printers, and copiers. However, if you want to get a higher-quality color printout, especially when printing photographs, you need to use paper created specifically for inkjet printers. A cool feature of inkjet printers is that they can print to a wide source of media. For example, you can buy transfer paper that allows you to print a photo and transfer it to something else, like a coffee mug or clothing.

Thermal (or Bubble Jet) Printing

The print head in thermal or bubble jet printing uses small heaters to heat up the ink. As the ink heats, it creates a small bubble that is then ejected onto the paper.

Figure 7-13 shows the front of a print head for an inkjet printer. It has hundreds of microscopic nozzles, and each of these nozzles has the ability to eject ink bubbles onto the paper.

Microscopic nozzles

FIGURE 7-13 Inkjet printer print head.

This process was first discovered by Canon. Canon creates Bubble Jet printers. Many other manufacturers use a similar process, but they are generically referred to as thermal inkjet printers.

> **NOTE** **THERMAL INKJET PRINTERS VS. THERMAL PRINTERS**
>
> Thermal inkjet printers are not the same as thermal printers. Thermal printers (discussed later in this chapter) use a special type of paper, and the print head heats the paper.

Piezoelectric Printing

The *piezoelectric printing* process uses a crystal that vibrates when a voltage is applied. The printer sends a stream of ink to the print head and applies voltage to the crystal. The vibrations of the crystal cause the ink to break up into thousands of minute droplets. These droplets are given an electric charge as they form. Based on the charge, the droplets either stick to the paper or drop into a reservoir. Ink droplets sent to the reservoir are recycled.

There is a significant difference between thermal printing and piezoelectric printing. In a thermal inkjet printer, ink is sent through the head only when it's needed. In a piezoelectric inkjet printer, ink is sent through the head in a continuous stream whenever the printer is printing. The result is that the piezoelectric print heads rarely clog up. In contrast, the thermal inkjet print heads will often clog up, especially if they aren't used for a while.

Inkjet Print Heads

Inkjet print heads can be either fixed or disposable.

- **Fixed.** These are intended to last the lifetime of the printer. The cost to replace these is high compared with the cost of the printer. If they fail, you usually replace the printer.

- **Disposable.** Some disposable print heads are built into the ink cartridge. When you replace the ink, you're also replacing the print head. Other disposable print heads are separate from the ink, but they are usually very easy to replace.

A primary problem with inkjet print heads is that they can become clogged with dried ink. Manufacturers know this and include software tools you can use to clean them. It sends ink through the print head to clean it, so each time you clean it, you are using ink. Some printers have automatic cleaning cycles and will clean themselves periodically.

Inkjet Calibration

Inkjet print heads can develop minor alignment issues over time, resulting in a blurry output or lines that aren't straight. Printer manufacturers are aware of this and commonly include software tools you can use to check your printer and recalibrate if necessary.

For example, I have an inkjet printer that includes a print quality diagnostic tool. It prints out a page of different test patterns, including directions about what to look for and what actions to take.

- If lines aren't straight on one test pattern, the diagnostic tool recommends aligning the print heads by clicking a button.

- If it prints out thin white lines in another test pattern, it recommends cleaning the print heads by clicking a button.

Inkjet Printer Maintenance

Inkjet printers don't require a lot of maintenance. The primary issues are related to the paper path, the ink, and the print heads.

- **Paper path.** Paper jams sometimes just happen, but if they're happening often, the two things to check are the rollers and the paper. You can clean the rollers with iso-propyl alcohol and a lint-free cloth or cotton swab. Ensure that you're using the right paper and that it isn't exposed to high humidity. You can clean the path with compressed air or an ESD-safe vacuum.

- **Ink.** When the ink runs out, you need to replace the cartridge. These are vacuum-sealed cartridges so it's very rare to see ink leak. Most printers include software tools you can use to check the current levels of the ink.

- **Print heads.** The print heads can become clogged with dried ink or can become mis-aligned with each other. Use the software tools to clean the heads or align the heads. Disposable heads can be replaced, and software will usually indicate when the heads are at the end of their lifetime.

✔ **Quick Check**

1. What is the most expensive element of an inkjet printer?
2. What should be done if an inkjet printer includes misaligned colors?

Quick Check Answers

1. Ink.
2. Calibrate it.

Impact Printers

Impact printers are one of the first types of printers used with computers. Even though the technology for impact printers is very old, they are still used in businesses where multipart forms are printed. I was recently at a car dealership, and they were using impact printers for contracts and other forms. Other places where you might see them include finance departments or billing services companies.

NOTE Multipart forms

A multi-part form has multiple sheets of paper separated with carbon paper. The impact of the print head also prints the other copies with the carbon paper. In contrast, other types of printers will print only the top sheet of paper in the multipart form.

The primary components of an impact printer are the platen, the ink ribbon, and the print head, shown as items 1, 2, and 3 in Figure 7-14. Impact printers commonly use a tractor feed and use continuous-feed paper. The paper has holes on the edges (item 4) that fit into sprockets in a tractor feed mechanism in the printer. The tractor feeder moves a continuous fan-fold roll of paper through the printer.

The platen is a hard, rubber-like material that provides a back for the print head. The ink ribbon is a long strip of cloth saturated with ink. It's connected to two rollers that steadily wind the ribbon from one roller to the other, and when it reaches the end, it switches directions. The print head has little hammer-like pins that hit the ribbon and press the ink from the ribbon onto the paper. A motor-and-carriage assembly moves the print head from side to side as it prints. When the printer finishes a line, the tractor feed advances the paper to the next line.

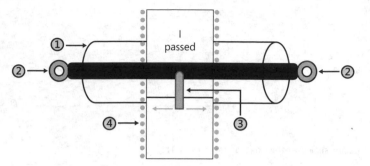

FIGURE 7-14 Elements of an impact printer.

Continuous-feed paper is perforated on the sides and between each individual sheet. After printing, you can tear it off the printer and remove the sides.

Some impact printers use regular sheets of paper instead of tractor-fed paper. The paper is moved through the printer with friction instead of with the tractor.

It's also worth pointing out that an impact printer can be very noisy. The pins have to strike the ribbon with force, and with more pins, it's more noise. In contrast, other printers are very quiet.

Creating Characters with a Dot Matrix

An impact printer print head includes multiple wires or pins that punch the ink ribbon onto the paper, leaving little dots. All the possible dots in a certain area represent a dot matrix, and dots within the matrix are printed to create characters or graphics.

Figure 7-15 shows how characters can be created with a simple 9-pin print head. The first part of Figure 7-15 represents the 9 pins in the print head. Each of these pins can be hammered onto the ink ribbon to create a dot. The middle part of the figure shows a sample dot matrix composed of six vertical lines of nine dots. The figure shows what you'd see if the 9-pin print head printed all nine dots in a 6 × 9 dot matrix.

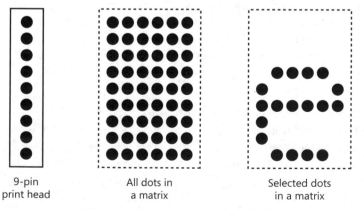

9-pin print head   All dots in a matrix   Selected dots in a matrix

FIGURE 7-15 Forming a letter *e* with a dot matrix printer.

In the last part of the figure, you can see how the printer forms the letter *e* by selectively printing certain dots. Similarly, it can form any character or even simple graphics by printing dots.

Near-Letter Quality

Print heads with only 9 pins produce very basic outputs. For example, the letter *e* in Figure 7-15 clearly has many gaps between the dots. Today, most print heads include 24 pins or 48 pins and can produce near-letter quality (NLQ) output. The extra pins fill in the gaps between the dots.

The resolution from an NLQ printer is much better than what you'd see from a basic 9-pin print head. However, it isn't comparable at all to the resolution you can get from inkjet or laser printers.

Impact Printer Maintenance

Impact printers are relatively easy to work with, and you don't have many problems. The primary maintenance issues include the following:

- **Paper dust.** It's very common for these printers to build up a lot of paper dust within them, especially with tractor feed paper. You should clean them out regularly with compressed air or an ESD-safe vacuum cleaner.
- **Paper path.** As with other printers, the paper path can get jammed. You can normally see the entire path of an impact printer, so it's usually fairly easy to clear a paper jam.
- **Ink ribbon.** As the ink ribbon is used, the ink runs out and the printout fades. The solution is easy: replace the ribbon.
- **Print head.** The pins on the print head can jam so that they no longer fire. The most common cause is paper dust, so when you clean out the printer, you should also clean the print head. Compressed air works well. When a pin stops firing in a print head, the only option is to replace the head.
- **Platen.** The platen can develop dents over time, but you can often rejuvenate it by rubbing it with isopropyl alcohol.

Thermal Printers

Thermal printers are used to print cash register receipts, ATM transaction slips, and even lottery tickets. Older fax machines used thermal printers too, but most fax machines now capture the incoming fax as a file that can be printed with a laser or inkjet printer.

Thermal printers use a special type of thermal paper that is covered with a chemical. When the chemical is heated, it changes color. Most thermal printers can print only a single color, but some can print two colors. The paper is normally on a roll with a center sprocket, and cashiers can usually replace an empty roll in less than a minute.

Other components of a thermal printer are as follows:

- A feed assembly that feeds the thermal paper through the printer. The feed assembly uses the sprocket in the center of the roll to advance the paper.
- A print head that includes a heating element to heat the paper.

Thermal printers are relatively slow, with their speed measured in inches per second (ips). However, they don't need to print much.

As with most printers, thermal printers need to be cleaned periodically with compressed air or an ESD-safe vacuum to remove debris. You can clean the print head with isopropyl alcohol and a lint-free cloth or a cotton swab. Cleaning the print head extends its life, but you can replace it if it fails.

EXAM TIP

Know where each type of printer is most commonly used. Laser printers are used in larger organizations. Inkjet printers are used by home users and SOHOs. Impact printers are used in businesses that need multipart forms. Thermal printers are used for receipts.

✔ **Quick Check**

1. Which type of paper does an impact printer typically use?
2. What do thermal printers commonly print?

Quick Check Answers

1. Tractor-fed continuous paper.
2. Receipts and lottery tickets.

Installing and Configuring Printers

Printers must be installed before you can use them, but this is usually very easy. The majority of printers use a USB interface, and Windows will configure the printer automatically as soon as you plug it in. However, you should know about some other possibilities when installing and configuring printers.

Device Drivers

When printer manufacturers create printers, they also write device drivers for different operating systems. These drivers provide the operating system with the details it needs to communicate with the device. When you buy a new printer, the manufacturer includes a CD with software that you can use to install it.

MORE INFO **CHAPTER 5, "EXPLORING PERIPHERALS AND EXPANSION CARDS"**

Chapter 5 discusses drivers related to any peripherals and how it is sometimes necessary to install the driver before connecting the device. If the instructions say you should install the driver first, you'll save yourself a lot of problems by doing so.

Most manufacturers also submit drivers to Microsoft. If the drivers meet certain quality assurance requirements, Microsoft makes them available via Windows Update. Chapter 15, "Configuring Windows Operating Systems," covers drivers and Windows Update in more depth, but you can also watch a short video that goes through the process here: *http://windows.microsoft.com/en-us/windows7/Find-and-install-printer-drivers*.

If none of these methods work, you can go to the manufacturer's website to locate the correct driver. If you can't find a suitable driver, the printer will typically produce a garbled output.

NOTE **DRIVER AVAILABILITY**

When a new operating system comes out, it often takes time before drivers are written and made publicly available. For example, when Windows Vista first came out, many printers had drivers for Windows XP but not for Windows Vista. The good news is that any printer driver that works for Windows Vista will for Windows 7.

Required Permissions

On Windows Vista and Windows 7, regular users can install the printer without any special permissions as long as the print driver is available. If the print driver isn't available, the user will need administrative permission to install a different print driver. Also, administrative permissions are required to install applications, so regular users will not be able to install software applications that come with a printer.

On Windows XP, users need to be in the Power Users group to install a printer or add a different driver.

MORE INFO **CHAPTER 25, "UNDERSTANDING IT SECURITY"**

The Power Users group is included in Windows Vista and Windows 7 for backward compatibility only. Chapter 25 discusses groups in more depth.

Wired Connections

The most common way a printer is connected is by using a USB connection. Printers commonly have a USB Type B port, and you use a cable with a USB Type A connector on one end for the computer and a USB Type B connector on the other end for the printer.

Before USB became so popular, printers were connected to a printer via the parallel DB-25 port mentioned in Chapter 5. While rare, it was also possible to connect some printers to the serial DB-9 port. USB is much faster than either parallel or serial, so you're unlikely to see these connections unless you're working with an old printer.

Another option is connecting a printer to a network by using Ethernet. Chapters 18 through 24 cover networking in much more detail, but for a quick preview, take a look at Figure 7-16. You can see two networked printers on the left and one locally connected printer on the right. One is connected to a server that functions as a print server, and the other is connected directly into the network through a switch. The first printer can be connected to the server with a USB connection, and the second printer will typically be connected with a twisted-pair cable and an RJ-45 connection.

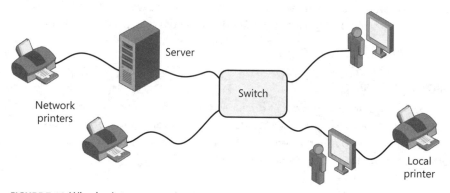

FIGURE 7-16 Wired printer connections.

> **NOTE LOCAL PRINTER**
>
> When you connect a printer directly to a computer, it's referred to as a *local printer*. When a printer is accessed over a network, it's called a *networked printer*.

The benefit of having printers on the network is that multiple users can access them. When they are connected with a print server, the server manages the print jobs and can also store and distribute printer drivers. The print server makes it easier to manage the printers but has additional costs for the server.

When printers are connected directly to the network, they have more management requirements. For example, you typically need to manually assign a specific Internet Protocol (IP) address to the printer or configure Dynamic Host Configuration Protocol (DHCP) to reserve a specific IP address for it. Don't worry if this sounds unfamiliar right now; networking will become clearer later in this book.

Wireless Connections

Many printers include wireless capabilities that allow wireless systems to connect to them without a wired connection. The common types of wireless connections include the following:

- **802.11.** Wireless networks use one of the 802.11 protocols, such as 802.11a, 802.11b, 802.11g, or 802.11n. Chapter 23, "Exploring Wireless Networking," covers wireless technologies in more detail.

- **Bluetooth.** Bluetooth is commonly used to create personal area networks (PANs), such as with a mobile phone and a headset. Some printers support Bluetooth, and with Class 2 Bluetooth, the printer can be as far as 10 meters (33 feet) away.

- **Infrared.** Television remotes use infrared, and it has been used with printers. A drawback is that it requires a clear line of sight between the printer and the computer.

> **MORE INFO** **CHAPTER 9 AND CHAPTER 23**
>
> Chapter 9, "Understanding Mobile Devices," mentions both Bluetooth and Infrared. The 802.11 protocols are covered in more depth in Chapter 23.

Printer Sharing

In addition to sharing printers by placing them on the network, you can also share local printers. If you share a printer on a networked computer, other users on the network will be able to send their print jobs through this computer. For example, if you have a wireless network, you can connect a local printer to one computer and share it. Other users on the network can then print to the printer.

The following steps show how to share a printer on Windows 7:

1. Click Start and select Devices And Printers.

2. Locate the printer in the Printers And Faxes section. Right-click the printer and select Printer Properties.

3. Click the Sharing tab.

4. Select the Share This Printer check box, as shown in the following graphic.

5. If desired, you can change the share name. Click OK.

> **NOTE** **RENDERING PRINT JOBS**
>
> It's best to select Render Print Jobs On Client Computers, as shown in the graphic. The computer that is sending the print job will use its processing power to format the print job.

At this point, users can use the Universal Naming Convention (UNC) to connect and install the printer. The format is *computerName**shareName*. For example, if the computer is named Win7 and the printer is named OfficePrinter, users can connect by using \\Win7\OfficePrinter.

Adding a Network Printer

USB printers are automatically installed when you plug them in. However, you have to take some additional steps to add a networked printer to a computer. You can use the following steps to add a networked printer on a Windows 7–based computer.

1. Click Start and select Devices And Printers.

2. Click Add A Printer.

3. Click Add A Network, Wireless Or Bluetooth Printer.

4. Windows 7 will search the network looking for the printer. When you see the printer, select it and click Next.

5. Windows will attempt to automatically locate the driver. If it can't locate it, you'll be prompted to select it by first selecting the manufacturer and then selecting the printer model.

6. Select the printer, click Next, and then click Finish.

Print Management

Print Management is available in Windows Vista and Windows 7 (and in Windows Server products), and you can use it to manage multiple shared printers. It's not common to manage multiple printers on a desktop system such as Windows 7, so you're unlikely to use Print Management on these systems. However, it is useful on print servers.

One big benefit is that you can update the drivers for printers in the Print Management console. When a system connects to the computer sharing the printer, it automatically receives the updated driver.

You can access the Print Management Console on Windows 7 by clicking Start, typing **Print Management** in the Search Programs And Files text box, and pressing Enter. Alternatively, you can access it via the Control Panel by clicking Systems And Security, Administrative Tools, and Print Management.

Printer Webpages

Many network-compatible printers include software that allows them to serve webpages. If you know the IP address of the printer, you can type it into a web browser to access these pages. If you don't know the IP address, print a local test page. It's usually included on the printout. Figure 7-17 shows a sample webpage.

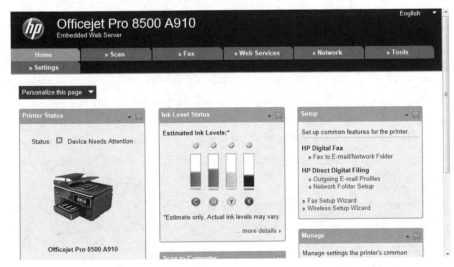

FIGURE 7-17 Printer webpage.

In Figure 7-17, you can see that the printer has a problem and needs attention. This printer includes multiple tools that can be used to troubleshoot and resolve the problem. These tools are available on the Tools tab for this printer. It also includes settings that can be configured for the printer.

Print Spooler

When you send a print job to a printer, it isn't sent to the printer right away. Instead, your computer sends the print job to a file called a spooler. The printer has a limited amount of memory and can print only so fast, so the spooler coordinates with the printer to get the print job to it in chunks.

You can think of the print job as a thread that is collected and wound onto a spool when you print it, and it's unwound when it's sent to the printer. After the spooler captures the print job, you can go on to other things. It works in the background to spool the print job out to the printer.

If you send multiple print jobs to a printer, the print spooler will queue each of these jobs. When one print job finishes, it starts sending the next print job.

The print spooler runs as a service, and services start up automatically when the computer starts. In contrast, applications such as Internet Explorer start only when a user starts them. Therefore, you don't need to start the print spooler service. However, you might need to *restart* it.

A common problem with the print spooler is that it can occasionally lock up and stop sending print jobs to the printer. If you try to print more print jobs, they just back up in the queue. The solution is to restart the print spooler service.

EXAM TIP

If print jobs back up in the queue, restart the spooler service. Each computer includes a printer spooler and a print queue so that it is possible for one user to print without any problems while the print queue on another computer is backed up.

Chapter 13, "Using Windows Operating Systems," covers the Services applet in more detail, but in brief, you can use it to manipulate any services. You can stop, start, pause, resume, or restart a service. You can also disable a service or configure how it will start.

✔ **Quick Check**
1. How are printers commonly connected to a PC?
2. What is the print spooler?

Troubleshooting Printers

If you understand the basics about how different printers operate, you can often identify printer problems and resolve them without too much difficulty. Still, it's good to have a little cheat sheet listing common symptoms, causes, and solutions, similar to the following:

- **Printer will not print.** Check the basics. Ensure that it is plugged in, turned on, and properly connected. Some printers have an online/offline selection, and when it is offline, Windows treats it as though it is turned off. Setting it back to online allows everything to work normally.

- **No connectivity—local printer.** The computer might give an error indicating the printer can't be contacted. Ensure that the data cables are connected. Sometimes reseating the cables by disconnecting and reconnecting them will resolve the problem.

- **No connectivity—network printer.** If all users are having the same problem, ensure that the printer is on, connected, and configured. If only one user is having the problem, ensure that the user is sending the print job to the correct printer. You might need to reinstall the printer for that user's computer.

EXAM TIP

A common problem with a network printer occurs if it is getting an IP address from DHCP instead of having a static IP address. When it is turned off and back on, it will receive a different IP address and users won't be able to connect to it anymore. Refer to Chapter 21, "Comparing IPv4 and IPv6," for a discussion about assigning a static IP address or reserving a specific IP address.

- **Paper not feeding.** Check the rollers or tractor feed to ensure that they are working. In some cases, rollers can become dirty and work inconsistently. Cleaning them resolves the problem.

- **Creased paper.** Printers often crease the paper as it is fed through the paper path, but it should not be noticeable unless you're using a heavier bond paper. A solution is to send the paper through the feeder rather than through the paper tray.

- **Paper jam.** The first solution is to clear the jam, but you should also check the paper path to ensure that it is free of debris. Repeating paper jams can be due to using low-quality paper or paper that has been exposed to high humidity. It's also possible that the pickup and separator rollers are worn and more than one sheet of paper is being picked up. Some printers report a paper jam when the rollers are unable to pick up the paper. Replacing the rollers with a maintenance kit might resolve the problem.

- **Garbled characters on paper.** The most likely reason for this is using the wrong print driver. Double-check to ensure that the correct driver is installed, and if necessary, update the driver. This might also be due to a cable issue. For example, the maximum distance of a USB 2.0 cable is 5 meters (about 16 feet), and using a longer cable can result in a garbled output. Reseating the cable will ensure that you don't have a loose connection.

- **Backed-up print queue.** If the printer or the print spooler service has been paused, print jobs won't print. Instead, they stay in the queue. Resume the print spooler service. In some cases, the print spooler service just locks up, and the only way to resolve the problem is to restart it.

- **Access denied.** By default, the Everyone group is assigned Allow Print permission so that anyone can print. However, administrators can modify this. If you're seeing this error, it indicates that the user isn't authorized to use the printer.

- **Unable to install printer.** In Windows XP, a user needs to be in the Power Users or Administrators group to install a printer, and if not, they will be unable to install a printer. Regular users can install printers on Windows 7.

- **Blank pages.** If you see this on a laser printer, it could indicate that the toner is empty, although users would normally complain as the toner gets low. You can also see this after replacing a toner cartridge without removing the sealing tape. Last, it's possible that the charging process isn't occurring due to a problem with the high-voltage power supply, the primary charge roller, or the corona wire.

- **Faded print.** This indicates that you're low on toner or ink. Replacing the toner, ink cartridge, or ink ribbon should eliminate this problem. On impact printers, this problem occurs if the ink ribbon stops moving.

- **Streaks on a laser printer.** Streaks on a laser printer are most likely the result of scratches on the imaging drum, especially if they are occurring in the same location on the printed page. The only solution is to replace the drum.

- **Streaks on an inkjet printer.** On inkjet printers, this can be caused by dirty or misaligned print heads. Use the software tools to clean and align them.

- **Ghost images due to image problem.** Ghosting can occur on laser printers after printing a dark image. Try printing a blank page between images. Also, you can reduce the resolution or darkness of the first page to eliminate the problem.

- **Ghost images due to hardware problem.** If the drum isn't adequately cleaned or adequately charged, it can cause ghosting. You might need to replace the cleaning scraper or the primary charge roller.

- **Vertical lines on page.** You can see this on laser printers if the toner gets clogged. The solution is to remove the cartridge and shake it or to replace the cartridge. It can also occur if the drum is scratched or dirty. On inkjet printers, this can occur if the print heads are dirty or misaligned. Clean and align them.

- **Color prints in wrong print color.** If the ink cartridges or color toner cartridges are inserted in the wrong location, you'll see some psychedelic results. The solution is to put them into the correct locations, but it might take time for the colors to return to normal. Some inkjet printers recycle the ink, so you'll still have a mixture of the wrong ink.

- **Low memory errors.** When the RIP creates the raster image, it stores it in memory. If the image is larger than the available memory, you'll receive a memory error. The best solution is to add memory to the printer if it supports additional memory. An alternative is to simplify the image by using a lower resolution or fewer graphics.

- **Error codes.** Many printers give error codes. They can be cryptic numbers you need to look up in a printer manual, or they can be plain words, such as "Out of paper." Many inkjet printers have a color LCD panel that displays the error, and if you touch it for information, it shows graphics demonstrating how to resolve the problem.

- **Toner not fused to the paper.** The fuser assembly fuses the toner to the paper. Replace the fuser to resolve the problem.

✔ **Quick Check**

1. What is the most likely cause of a garbled output?

2. What should be done to resolve a backed-up print queue problem?

Quick Check Answers

1. Incorrect driver.

2. Restart the print spooler service.

Chapter Summary

- Duplexing assemblies are required to print two sides.

- Common maintenance tools used with printers include compressed air, ESD-safe vacuum cleaners (with HEPA filters for laser printers), isopropyl alcohol, and lint-free cloths or cotton swabs.

- Common printers are laser, inkjet, impact, and thermal.

  - Laser printers are fast and provide a high-quality output. They are more expensive than other printers and are commonly used in larger organizations.

  - Inkjet printers are inexpensive and provide high-quality color output but are slower than laser printers. They are very popular among home users and small businesses. Ink is very expensive.

  - Impact printers are slow, noisy, and generate a lot of paper dust. They are used most often by businesses that need to print multipart forms.

  - Thermal printers are special-purpose printers used to create receipts or print lottery tickets.

- Laser printers use the following seven-step imaging process: processing, charging, exposing, developing, transferring, fusing, and cleaning.

- The RIP processes the image and stores it in memory during the processing stage. Complex images require more memory.

- A high-voltage charge is applied to the drum from a primary charge roller during the charging stage. A laser then writes the image onto the drum during the exposing stage.

- Toner is a fine powder of carbon and plastic. It is charged during the developing stage and applied to the drum.

- A transfer roller electrically charges paper, and the image is transferred to the paper during the transferring stage.

- Toner is melted onto the paper by a fusing assembly in the fusing stage. The drum is then cleaned to prepare for the next image in the cleaning stage.

- Laser printers include dangerously high voltages and hot components. They should be unplugged prior to servicing.

- You typically apply a maintenance kit when replacing the toner, which often includes a replacement ozone filter.

- Inkjet printers have print heads with microscopic holes that inject ink onto the paper. They can create high-quality color output and are very popular with home users.

- Inkjet print heads can become clogged or misaligned. Cleaning or aligning them will resolve most problems.

- Impact printers hammer pins against an ink ribbon to print dots on paper. They are used to print multipart forms.
- Thermal printers use a special thermal paper that changes color when heated by the print head.
- USB printers will install automatically without any user intervention. Network printers must be installed.
- The print spooler service coordinates sending print jobs to a printer. If the print queue backs up, restart it.
- Many printer problems have clear symptoms, causes, and solutions. You'll often find that taking steps to clean a printer resolves many problems. Additionally, replacing a toner cartridge on a laser printer resolves many problems.

Chapter Review

Use the following questions to test your knowledge of the information in this chapter. The answers to these questions, and the explanations of why each answer choice is correct or incorrect, are located in the "Answers" section at the end of this chapter.

1. What is a duplexing assembly used for in a printer?

   A. To print on both sides of the paper

   B. To improve RAID-1

   C. To allow two-way communication

   D. To double the speed of the printer

2. A customer wants to buy a printer for home use that can print color. She asks you for your advice. What would you recommend?

   A. Dot matrix printer

   B. Color laser printer

   C. Inkjet printer

   D. Laser printer

3. You are preparing to replace a toner cartridge on a laser printer. Which of the following steps should you take first?

   A. Restart the print spooler.

   B. Turn off the printer.

   C. Remove the new toner from the package.

   D. Print a test page.

4. Of the following choices, what is *not* used to connect a wired printer?

   A. USB

   B. Parallel

   C. 802.11

   D. Ethernet

5. What should you do if an inkjet printer is printing random streaks?

   A. Replace the toner cartridge.

   B. Clean the fusing assembly.

   C. Update the drivers.

   D. Clean the print heads.

6. You are troubleshooting a problem with an HP6L laser printer. One LED is steady red, and another is blinking orange. The customer complains that it prints streaks in the same place on every page. What is the most likely problem?

   A. The imaging drum

   B. The fuser

   C. An incorrect print driver

   D. Impossible to tell without the manual

Answers

1. **Correct Answer:** A

    A. **Correct:** Duplexing assemblies can automatically flip paper in a printer to print both sides.

    B. **Incorrect:** Duplexing improves RAID-1 by adding a second disk controller, but this is not related to printers.

    C. **Incorrect:** In networking, duplex indicates a device has two-way communication, but that is unrelated to printers.

    D. **Incorrect:** They do not increase the speed.

2. **Correct Answer:** C

    A. **Incorrect:** A dot matrix printer would be appropriate if she wanted to print multipart forms.

    B. **Incorrect:** A color laser printer is much more expensive than an inkjet printer.

    C. **Correct:** Inkjet printers print color and are very popular for home users.

    D. **Incorrect:** Regular laser printers do not print color.

3. **Correct Answer:** B

    A. **Incorrect:** Restart the spooler if the queue is backed up.

    B. **Correct:** You should turn off the printer as a safety precaution before servicing a laser printer.

    C. **Incorrect:** You should unpack the new toner only when you're ready to install it.

    D. **Incorrect:** You could print a test page as a final step to confirm proper operation of the printer.

4. **Correct Answer:** A

    A. **Incorrect:** USB is the most common method.

    B. **Incorrect:** Parallel is not a common method, but it has been used to connect a wired printer.

    C. **Correct:** 802.11 refers to wireless technologies.

    D. **Incorrect:** Ethernet is used to connect printers over a wired network.

5. **Correct Answer:** D

    A. **Incorrect:** Inkjet printers do not have toner cartridges.

    B. **Incorrect:** Inkjet printers do not have fusing assemblies.

    C. **Incorrect:** A driver would not cause random streaks.

    D. **Correct:** Cleaning and aligning the print heads will likely resolve this problem.

6. **Correct Answer: A**

   A. **Correct:** Streaks are very likely caused by scratches on the imaging drum for any type of laser printer.

   B. **Incorrect:** If toner wasn't sticking to the paper, the fuser is the likely problem.

   C. **Incorrect:** The wrong driver results in garbled output.

   D. **Incorrect:** The manual will help you interpret the lights, but the streaks indicate a scratched drum.

CHAPTER 8

Working with Laptops

I n this chapter, you'll learn about many of the common features of laptops. Laptops often have special keys on the keyboard that are used to enable and disable hardware. Their displays are similar to regular monitors, but some have additional hardware not included in other monitors. Some hardware is relatively easy to install and replace, but other components can be quite challenging, especially if you don't follow some basic processes for disassembling the laptops. You'll also learn about methods used to conserve power on these systems and some key things to look for when troubleshooting them.

Exam 220-801 objectives in this chapter:

- 3.1 Install and configure laptop hardware and components.
  - Expansion options
    - Express card /34
    - Express card /54
    - PCMCIA
    - SODIMM
    - Flash
  - Hardware/device replacement
    - Keyboard
    - Hard Drive (2.5 vs. 3.5)
    - Memory
    - Optical drive
    - Wireless card
    - Mini-PCIe
    - Screen
    - DC jack
    - Battery
    - Touchpad
    - Plastics

- Speaker
- System board
- CPU

- 3.2 Compare and contrast the components within the display of a laptop.
  - Types
    - LCD
    - LED
    - OLED
    - Plasma
  - Wi-Fi antenna connector/placement
  - Inverter and its function
  - Backlight
- 3.3 Compare and contrast laptop features.
  - Special function keys
    - Dual displays
    - Wireless (on/off)
    - Volume settings
    - Screen brightness
    - Bluetooth (on/off)
    - Keyboard backlight
  - Docking station vs. port replicator
  - Physical laptop lock and cable lock

Exam 220-802 objectives in this chapter:

- 1.5 Given a scenario, use Control Panel utilities (the items are organized by "classic view/large icons" in Windows).
  - Common to all Microsoft Operating Systems
    - System
      - Hardware Profiles
    - Power options
      - Hibernate
      - Power plans
      - Sleep/suspend
      - Standby

- 4.8 Given a scenario, troubleshoot, and repair common laptop issues while adhering to the appropriate procedures.
  - Common symptoms
    - No display
    - Dim display
    - Flickering display
    - Sticking keys
    - Intermittent wireless
    - Battery not charging
    - Ghost cursor
    - No power
    - Num lock indicator lights
    - No wireless connectivity
    - No Bluetooth connectivity
    - Cannot display to external monitor
  - Disassembling processes for proper re-assembly
    - Document and label cable and screw locations
    - Organize parts
    - Refer to manufacturer documentation
    - Use appropriate hand tools

Common Laptop Features

 Laptops are mobile computers, and there are many different types. You can find high-performance laptops with screens of over 17 inches and as much power as a desktop computer. Stripped-down netbooks have screens of about 10 inches and are used to surf the Internet and check email but can't do much more. And of course, there are a multitude of laptop types between these two. Despite their differences in size and performance characteristics, laptops have many common features.

> **MORE INFO** **CHAPTER 9, "UNDERSTANDING MOBILE DEVICES"**
>
> Tablets are in a different category and are covered in Chapter 9.

Special Function Keys

Keyboards commonly have *function keys,* labeled F1 to F12, that you can use when working with any computer. For example, you can press the F1 key to open help. Similarly, you can press the F5 key in just about any application to refresh the display.

On laptop computers, you'll often find that the function keys have more than one purpose, which you can access by pressing the *Fn key* at the same time that you press the given function key. This is similar to how regular letter keys have two purposes. You can press the *A* key to get a lowercase *a,* or you can press the Shift key with the *A* key to get an uppercase *A.*

Figure 8-1 shows part of a laptop keyboard with some keys highlighted. The function keys are across the top, and the special Fn key is on the bottom. The following sections describe the purpose of special function keys found on many laptops.

FIGURE 8-1 Laptop keyboard with Fn and function keys.

> **NOTE SPECIAL KEYS AREN'T ALWAYS THE SAME**
>
> Figure 8-1 shows how one laptop manufacturer is using the function keys, but there isn't a standard. Another laptop manufacturer might be using these keys for different purposes.

Dual Displays

The dual-display key is useful when you have a second monitor connected to the laptop or when the laptop is connected to a projector during a presentation. In Figure 8-1, the F1 key has an icon of two monitors and is used for dual displays. If you press this key, you'll usually see four choices, with one selected. Press it again and the next choice is selected. The four choices are as follows:

- **Computer Only.** The video is displayed on the laptop's monitor but not on external devices.

- **Duplicate.** The same data is displayed on the computer and on an external monitor. Speakers use this so that they can see the same display on the laptop as the audience sees.
- **Extend.** This selection allows you to extend the desktop and move windows between the displays.
- **Projector Only.** The laptop display is disabled, and only the projector display is used.

Wireless (On/Off)

Most systems also have a key that can be used to enable or disable the wireless card. In Figure 8-1, the F2 key has an icon of a radio transmitting tower and is used for wireless. By toggling this key, wireless can be turned on or off.

You might see the wireless control in different locations. Some HP laptops have a touch panel above the keyboard that can control some features. One LED looks like a transmitting antenna, and it is blue when wireless is enabled. If you touch it, it changes to orange and disables wireless. Some laptops have a switch on the side.

REAL WORLD   **SOME PROBLEMS CAN BE SOLVED BY PRESSING A KEY**

Sometimes problems have amazingly simple solutions. Not too long ago, I was out at a coffee shop and noticed another customer working with his laptop. Well, actually, he was banging his mouse on the table out of frustration because his laptop wasn't working with him. I mentioned I knew a little about computers and offered to help.

He said he was answering an email when the wireless connection from the coffee shop stopped working, but we could see that it was still working for others in the coffee shop. I pointed to a key on his keyboard and said, "Press that once." He did, and a moment later, his connection was restored. Everything is simple when you know how things work.

Volume Settings

Some function keys can be used for volume controls. The keyboard in Figure 8-1 uses F7 to mute the sound, F8 to decrease the volume, and F9 to increase it. Volume settings commonly use a speaker icon with another indicator. The mute icon often shows a speaker with an X. A speaker with a single sound wave is used to indicate it will decrease the volume, and multiple sound waves increase the volume.

Screen Brightness

Keyboards will often have keys to increase or decrease the brightness. The keyboard in Figure 8-1 uses F4 to decrease the brightness and F5 to increase it. The brightness controls commonly use a circular icon resembling the sun, with a down arrow to decrease the brightness and an up arrow to increase the brightness.

> **NOTE SCREENS ARE DIM WHEN USING BATTERIES**
> Laptops often switch to a low power plan when on battery power. When using a low power plan, the screen brightness keys might be disabled. Pressing them won't change the display.

Bluetooth (On/Off)

Some systems with Bluetooth capability include a key to enable or disable Bluetooth. It is usually indicated by an icon resembling an uppercase *B*. It works similarly to the wireless switch.

Keyboard Backlight

Some keyboards have backlights illuminating the keys so that they can easily be viewed at night. The keys are often laser-etched, and white, red, yellow, or blue light-emitting diodes (LEDs) shine through them so that they can be easily identified.

These are sometimes popular with gamers, but there isn't much use for the backlight when the sun comes up. A key with an icon of a light is usually available to toggle the backlight on or off.

Lock and F-Lock Keys

Many keyboards also have Lock and F-Lock keys that are important to understand. They sound the same, but the usage is different.

The Lock key often has a lock icon, and it locks the operating system when you press it. This is similar to pressing the Ctrl+Alt+Del keys on Windows Vista and Windows 7 and selecting Lock This Computer.

When an F-Lock key is present, it often has the *F* in a box and the word *Lock*. Toggling this key locks the function keys to be used as F1 to F12, using the alternate purpose of the key.

Using the F-Lock key is similar to using the Caps Lock key to force letters to always be typed as lowercase or uppercase.

Num Lock Indicator

The number pad on a computer usually has a dual purpose of typing numbers or moving the cursor around. You can press the Num Lock key to use the numbers and press it again to use the navigation keys.

Most desktop keyboards include an LED that turns on or off when you press the Num Lock key. However, many laptops don't include an LED. Instead, when you press the Num Lock key, you'll see an indication on the screen that the Num Lock is on or off. Similarly, you'll see the same type of display for the Caps Lock and the F-Lock keys. Figure 8-2 shows how these appear on one computer.

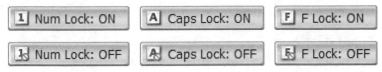

FIGURE 8-2 Lock indicator examples.

Default Usage of Fn Key

The default usage of the Fn key isn't the same on all laptops. For example, think of the F1 key used to open help, which can also be used to enable or disable wireless.

- On one computer, pressing only the F1 key will start help. If you want to toggle wireless, you need to press the Fn and F1 keys at the same time.

- On a different computer, pressing only the F1 key will toggle wireless, turning it on or off. If you want to start help, you need to press the Fn and F1 keys at the same time.

Troubleshooting Keyboard Issues

When you understand how the keys work, most problems with keyboards are relatively easy to resolve. They usually require just a little effort on your part to educate the user, or in some cases you can break out your trusted can of compressed air.

Num Lock Indicator Lights

If you've been using a computer for a while, you probably understand how the Num Lock and Caps Lock keys work. However, this is often misunderstood by many new users. They might complain that numbers no longer type from the number pad.

In this case, there probably isn't anything wrong with the user's computer—the user just doesn't understand how it's displayed or how to change it. Take a minute to demonstrate.

Sticking Keys

This is often a food issue. People often eat or snack at their desks, and food and liquid can drop into the keyboard. The solution is to clean the keyboard with compressed air. In extreme cases, you can remove all the keys and clean them individually with alcohol.

Educating the user about the source of the problem can help, or at least reduce how often the keyboard needs to be cleaned. Another option is to use a plastic keyboard cover. Users can type normally through the cover, and it protects the keyboard from collecting food.

> ### ✔ Quick Check
>
> 1. How can a user easily get a laptop to send the display to an external monitor?
> 2. What should you check if wireless suddenly stops working on a laptop?
>
> ### Quick Check Answers
>
> 1. Toggle the function key for the display.
> 2. Press the function key to enable or disable wireless.

Docking Station vs. Port Replicator

Laptops are very useful when users are traveling. However, compared to the full features available with a desktop computer, laptops look and feel rather small, and users often want more capabilities when they're back at the office.

Docking stations and port replicators are often used with laptops to extend their capabilities. Figure 8-3 compares the two.

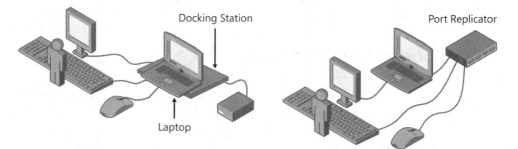

FIGURE 8-3 Docking station and port replicator.

A *docking station* is a case or a cabinet that the laptop plugs into to give the laptop additional capabilities. When you plug the laptop into the docking station, the laptop is connected to other peripherals, such as a standard-sized monitor, keyboard, and mouse. It has additional ports you can use to hook up other devices, such as external drives, and sometimes has expansion slots you can use. It's common for a docking station to be directly connected to a network.

Port replicators are simpler devices. You can usually plug a port replicator into a single USB port on the laptop, and it provides additional ports. Port replicators often include additional USB ports, sound ports, and network connections. If you want to use a full-sized monitor, you would plug it directly into the laptop.

A docking station must be specifically designed for the laptop because the laptop plugs directly into it. Because of this, docking stations are more expensive than port replicators.

EXAM TIP

Docking stations usually provide power to the laptop. If the laptop is on battery power while it's in the docking station, it indicates that it isn't connected. You can usually just remove the laptop and plug it back in to reseat it.

Hardware Profiles

Hardware profiles are used in Windows XP but not in Windows Vista or Windows 7. They allow a user to select the set of hardware to which the laptop is hooked up when the system boots.

For example, the user might want to use the wireless network interface card (NIC) while traveling or at home but prefer to use the wired NIC in the office. You can set up two hardware profiles and name them Office and Traveling.

You could disable the wireless NIC in the Office profile and enable the wired NIC. Similarly, you can disable the wired NIC in the Traveling profile and enable the wireless NIC.

In Figure 8-4, in the screen shot on the left, you can see the Hardware Profiles page of a Windows XP system with these two profiles. The system is currently booted into the Office profile, and the hardware has been configured in this profile to use a docking station. The traveling profile has been configured with only the laptop's hardware.

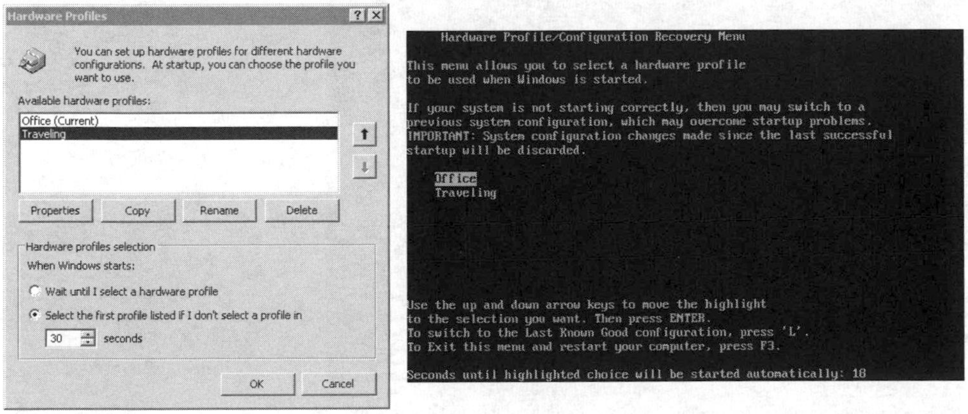

FIGURE 8-4 Setting up hardware profiles.

When you reboot the system, you will see a menu choice similar to the screen shown on the right in Figure 8-4. This is configured to give the user 30 seconds to choose a different hardware profile or boot into the Microsoft Office profile.

To access the Hardware Profiles page, use the following steps:

1. Click Start, Control Panel. If necessary, change the display to Classic View.

2. Double-click System to open the System applet.

3. Click the Hardware tab.

4. Click the Hardware Profiles button. You can select any profile and use the Copy, Rename, and Delete buttons to copy, rename, or delete the profile.

Locks

Laptops disappear quite easily. It's very easy for someone to simply put a laptop under their arm and walk away. I've heard many stories of people returning to a conference after lunch to find their laptops missing. I know of one conference speaker who returned from a 15-minute break to find that the laptop he was using for his presentation had disappeared.

Simple physical security measures can prevent these thefts. For example, Figure 8-5 shows an example of a *cable lock* connected to a laptop computer. It's similar to a cable lock used to secure a bicycle to a bike stand.

FIGURE 8-5 Cable lock for a laptop.

The cable has a combination lock. When set at the correct combination, you can plug it into a port on the laptop. You first wrap it around something stable such as a desk, and then plug the cable into the laptop. Spin the combination and the laptop is secure.

This isn't perfect, but it is enough to deter most thefts. A thief might be able to hammer the lock off, but that risks damage to the laptop. A thief could use large bolt cutters to cut the cable, but someone carrying around bolt cutters looks suspicious.

✔ **Quick Check**

    1. What provides additional features for a laptop while working in an office?

    2. What provides physical security for a laptop?

Quick Check Answers

    1. Docking station or, to a lesser degree, a port replicator.

    2. Cable lock.

Laptop Displays

As with any computer, laptops have a display. The primary difference is that the display is attached to laptops whereas it's a separate piece of hardware in desktop computers. The section covers the different types of displays you'll run across with laptops, along with some specific concerns.

Display Types

The primary display types you'll find in laptop computers are liquid crystal display (LCD) and light emitting diode (LED) monitors. Organic light emitting diode (OLED) and plasma are available but less common. Chapter 6, "Exploring Video and Display Devices," provides information about these types of monitors, and the underlying technology is the same whether it's on the laptop or as a stand-alone monitor.

> *NOTE* **CLEANING THE DISPLAY**
>
> Use the same method of cleaning a laptop display as you do with other LCD monitors. A dry lint-free cloth works for most situations. You can also use a cleaner that is specially designed for the screen. Spray the cleaner on the cloth and then wipe the display.

Backlight

Backlights are used in LCD and LED display monitors because the crystals in these monitors do not emit light. The backlight shines light from the back of the display to the front, going through these crystals. You can see different colors based on how the crystals are oriented.

Traditional LCD monitors use a cold cathode fluorescent lamp (CCFL) as a backlight, and the CCFL requires alternating current (AC) voltage. This isn't a problem for stand-alone monitors because the monitor is plugged into an AC outlet.

In laptops, the display is attached to the computer and the computer runs on direct current (DC) voltage. When you plug a laptop computer into an AC outlet, you use a power adapter that converts the AC voltage to DC voltage. If it's running on battery power, it's also using DC voltage. This DC voltage must be converted to AC voltage to power the CCFL. Laptops use an inverter for this purpose.

Inverter

Laptops that include a CCFL use an *inverter* to convert the DC voltage provided from the motherboard to the AC voltage needed by the CCFL. An inverter is a small circuit board connected with just a couple of screws and two plug-in connectors. One receives the DC voltage from the motherboard, and the other sends the AC voltage to the CCFL.

Unfortunately, inverters often fail. They sometimes include a fuse you can replace, but typically, you have to replace the entire circuit board when it fails. Figure 8-6 shows a picture of an inverter held by technician José Vargas to give you an idea of its size.

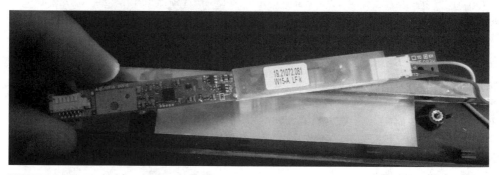

FIGURE 8-6 Inverter inside a laptop computer.

> *IMPORTANT* **RISK OF SERIOUS ELECTRICAL SHOCK**
>
> Dangerous voltages exist on the inverter when the system is turned on. You should not open a laptop or handle the inverter when the system is turned on, and you should remove the battery before opening a laptop. When handling any printed circuit cards, you should also use an Electrostatic Discharge (ESD) wrist strap.

LCD

LCD displays used with laptop computers work like any regular LCD display. The biggest difference is that they require an inverter to power the CCFL backlight, while stand-alone monitors don't need an inverter. If either the inverter or the CCFL fails, the display will go dark and you'll need to replace the failed component.

EXAM TIP

When an inverter fails, the CCFL backlight doesn't work. The result is that the display will be dim or, possibly, completely dark.

LED

LED monitors are LCD monitors that use LEDs as backlights. Because the LEDs do not require AC voltages, the LED monitors do not require an inverter. Most laptops are now shipping with LED display monitors instead of the LCD monitors.

This provides two important benefits. First, the manufacturer saves money by not requiring the inverter. Second, technicians have one less component to worry about checking for failure. Inverters often fail, but this isn't a concern for LED monitors.

EXAM TIP

LED monitors (LCD monitors using LED backlights) do not use CCFLs. When used on laptop computers, LED monitors do not require inverters.

OLED

OLED devices do not require a backlight at all. They are thinner and lighter, and they provide exceptional graphics. Unfortunately, they are still quite expensive when compared to LED or LCD monitors. You might see them in small mobile devices such as smartphones, but they are rarely used in laptops.

Plasma

Plasma displays also don't require a backlight. They use very small gas-filled tubes that can emit lights. Each pixel includes a red, green, and blue tube that are used to produce different colors.

While a plasma display can provide vibrant images, it has two problems. Most important for a laptop computer is that a plasma display requires more power than an LCD or LED monitor. The result is that a laptop with a plasma display won't stay powered on as long when using a battery. Second, a plasma display is susceptible to burn-in if the same image is left on the monitor for a long period of time.

Wi-Fi Antenna

Most laptops have built-in wireless (often called Wi-Fi) capabilities. To connect with the wireless access point, they need to have an antenna. The antenna is commonly located inside the display, either at the top, when the display is opened, or on one or more edges. Wires run from the antenna to a wireless card inside the laptop.

Troubleshooting Display Issues

You might need to troubleshoot problems with a monitor's display. The following sections identify some common problems.

No Display

If your monitor has no display at all, the LCD screen has likely failed. However, always check the easy fixes first:

- Ensure that the laptop is on. You'll usually have some type of power indicator that verifies power is on.
- Ensure that the monitor hasn't been disabled by using a function key. An easy check is to toggle the function key and look for a change.

Another check is to plug in a second monitor and view the display. You might need to toggle the display function key to enable output to this second monitor. If you can't see a display on either monitor, the video card or the motherboard's video capability has likely failed. If you can view the display on the second monitor but not the laptop's display, it's very likely the LCD screen has failed.

You'll need to replace the LCD screen if it's failed, but before replacing the entire display, you should check to verify that it is not displaying anything at all. It's possible that it's just a dim display.

Dim Display

A dim display indicates a failed backlight. On traditional LCD displays, the problem might be due to a failed inverter. The solution is to replace the backlight and/or inverter. Sometimes a dim display looks dark, but if you shine a flashlight into the monitor you can see data displayed. This is also a clear indication that the problem is the backlight or the inverter.

LED displays don't use inverters, but the backlight can fail, resulting in a dim display. The solution is to replace the backlight.

Flickering Display

One of the symptoms you might see with laptop displays is a flickering display. It could be due to a problem with the backlight, the inverter powering the CCFL, or the LCD panel itself.

More often than not, this is caused by a loose connection within the laptop. Laptops are moved, jostled, and tossed around a lot more than desktop computers. All this activity can jiggle something loose. If you can reproduce the symptom by moving the display, it is most likely due to a loose connector. The solution is to take it apart and reseat the display's connectors.

If this doesn't resolve the issue, the next best choice is the CCFL. Just as a fluorescent light can flicker when it ages, the CCFL can flicker. Similarly, the inverter can become more sensitive to heat as it ages. When the computer first turns it on, it will work fine. As the computer is used and heats up, the inverter can start failing, causing the flicker. Less common is flickering due to a problem with the LCD display itself, but it is possible.

Cannot Display to External Monitor

The most common reason a laptop cannot send the output to the display monitor is that the function key is set to send it to the primary display only. This should be your first check.

Another item to check is the dual-monitor display settings from within the operating system. Chapter 6 includes information about using multiple displays and how to configure them.

Ghost Cursor

Occasionally users complain of a ghost cursor. This means different things based on the symptoms. The three things to consider are the touchpad, the pointing stick, and settings for the mouse.

Figure 8-7 shows a laptop with a touchpad and the common location for a pointing stick. Instead of using a mouse, users can use gestures on the *touchpad* to mimic mouse movements. The pointing stick is a small pointing device that can be manipulated with your finger to move the mouse.

Pointing stick

Touchpad

FIGURE 8-7 Laptop keyboard with touchpad.

When the touchpad or pointing stick is enabled, users sometimes inadvertently touch it, causing the cursor to jump around. If users are using an external mouse and not using these controls, the easiest solution is to just disable them.

The other option is to manipulate their sensitivity. Manufacturers often modify the Control Panel's Mouse applet so that it includes properties for these devices. You can use these settings to reduce the sensitivity of the touchpad or pointing stick.

EXAM TIP

If users are not using the touchpad, it's best to disable the touchpad. This will prevent the user from accidentally causing the mouse pointer to jump around the screen.

Apple users sometimes complain about this, and Apple has published a support article to address it (*http://support.apple.com/kb/TS2302*). On Apple systems, the solution is to enable the Trackpad setting to Ignore Accidental Trackpad Input.

Another possibility that might cause users to complain of a ghost cursor is a setting in the Windows Mouse applet. The Pointer Options tab in the Mouse applet includes a setting labeled Display Pointer Trails. When it is enabled, the mouse pointer includes ghost images or trails of the mouse as it's moved.

Installing and Configuring Laptop Hardware

When you work as a PC technician, there will likely be times when you need to install or swap out hardware. Some items can be incredibly easy to replace, while others will take a significant amount of time.

Disassembling Processes

Laptops are made by different manufacturers, and you'll find that there are multiple differences in how they are assembled. With that in mind, there isn't a specific set of hardware replacement steps you can follow that will work for any laptop. However, there are some basic disassembling processes you can follow.

Turn System Off

Ensure the laptop is turned off and that the battery is removed before starting. Some components, such as the inverter, have dangerous voltages that can harm you. Other components can be damaged if the system is opened with the power on.

Document and Label Cable and Screw Locations

A lot can happen between the time that you disassemble a laptop and when you put it back together. It's worth your time to document and label everything as you go along. One method of labeling wires is with small pieces of tape and a pen. Put the tape on the wire and mark it so that you'll know where it goes. If you have a camera phone, you can also take some pictures to help you remember.

Organize Parts

As you're removing screws and parts, it's best to organize them as you're proceeding. For example, put the screws holding the case in one container and put screws holding specific components within the laptop in separate containers.

Some screws are close in size but can be just a little longer or larger, and if you put a screw into the wrong location, you can damage the laptop. Organizing the screws in separate containers helps avoid this problem.

> **NOTE CONTAINERS**
>
> Blank CDs and DVDs come on spindles covered with a plastic case. I have several of these that I use as containers when I'm working on a system. It makes it easy to keep the screws and other parts separate. I often include notes (such as "external screws" or "hard drive screws") that I add to the container to help me remember.

Refer to Manufacturer Documentation

This is extremely important. The disassembling steps are usually different from one laptop to another, but the manufacturer's documentation shows the specific steps for your laptop. Without this documentation, it's very easy to destroy the laptop, especially when you start removing items such as the keyboard or display screen.

You can often find documentation for systems on the web. For example, I used an HP Pavilion dv7 laptop for many of the pictures in this chapter. I used Bing to search for "dv7 manual" and quickly found and downloaded the manual.

Use Appropriate Hand Tools

You'll find that a few different size screw drivers (flat-blade and Phillips) are the primary tools that you'll need when taking a laptop apart. Another valuable tool is a plastic wedge or plastic shim, which you can use to pry open the case. This can be any piece of plastic strong enough to give a little leverage but thin enough to fit into tight spots. You can use something as simple as a guitar pick.

If you'll be handling the circuit boards, it's also very important to prevent electrostatic discharge (ESD) damage. At the very least, ensure that you're using an ESD wrist strap. Connecting the wrist strap to yourself and a metal part of the laptop ensures that you have the same electrical potential as the laptop and thus prevents ESD damage.

Hardware and Device Replacement

The majority of hardware that you'll replace is accessible from the rear panel. You usually have only a few screws that you need to remove to access removable components. Some laptops have multiple panels, and others have a single panel.

> **IMPORTANT AVOID SERIOUS ELECTRICAL SHOCK**
>
> Always disconnect power and remove the battery before adding or replacing any hardware in a laptop computer. The exceptions are hot-swappable devices, such as USB flash drives.

Figure 8-8 shows the rear of a laptop with the case closed and opened. The case on the left has arrows pointing to the screws. When these screws are removed, you can remove the panel and access the internal components as shown on the right.

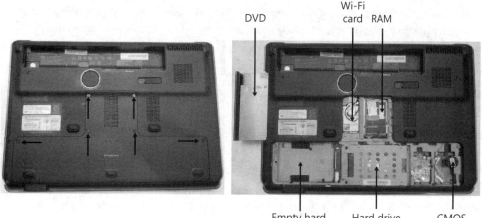

FIGURE 8-8 Rear of laptop with access panel on (left) and removed (right).

Plastics

Laptop computers commonly have plastic cases and covers that you need to remove to gain access to internal components. They are normally secured with screws and often with clips or latches. Even after removing the screws, you often need to pry the plastic cover off with a wedge.

The size and location of these covers varies widely from computer to computer. This chapter has pictures of cases from one computer, but there is no standard, so you'll see different covers.

EXAM TIP

A plastic wedge is useful when removing plastic covers or opening cases. If you use a metal screwdriver you might scratch the case, but a plastic wedge will not cause damage.

Battery

A core component of a laptop is the battery. It allows the system to run even when it's discon-nected from an AC power source. Most batteries are very easy to remove and replace.

Figure 8-9 shows a battery removed from the underside of a laptop computer. Batteries are typically held in place with a latch that you can slide to one side to release it. These often fit snugly in the laptop, but gravity can help you remove it. Turn the laptop over and release the latch, and the battery will fall into your hand.

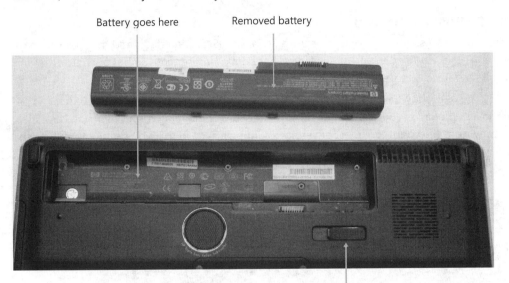

FIGURE 8-9 Removing a battery.

All laptop batteries aren't the same. You'll see them in many different shapes, sizes, and even types.

The most common type of battery used in laptop computers is the *lithium-ion (Li-ion)* battery. It will typically last between one to three years or between 300 and 800 charge and recharge cycles, depending on the quality of the battery. As it ages, it will gradually lose its ability to hold a charge.

> **NOTE TWO-WEEK RULE FOR PROLONGING BATTERY LIFE**
>
> Batteries age quicker if they stay fully charged or if they're allowed to remain discharged. If the laptop will not be used for two weeks or more or if it will remain plugged into an AC outlet for two weeks or more, remove the battery. It doesn't need to be stored in a refrig-erator, but if you do store it there, you need to let it warm up to room temperature before using it.

Li-ion batteries are environmentally friendly, but you should observe local regulations when disposing of them or recycling them. They should not be incinerated because they can explode.

Older batteries such as *nickel cadmium (NiCd)* and *nickel metal hydride (NiMH)* were common but are used much less in laptops today. NiCd batteries include cadmium, which is toxic to the environment. NiMH batteries are environmentally friendly but cannot be recharged as many times as a Li-ion battery.

Hard Drive (2.5 vs. 3.5)

Most hard drives in laptop computers use a Serial ATA (SATA) interface, and they are very easy to replace. If you need to purchase a laptop hard drive, ensure that you get one 2.5 inches in size. Standard disk drives are 3.5 inches in size.

Figure 8-10 shows a laptop with two drive bays and with one drive removed. When you're removing the drive, you first need to remove the screws holding it in, and then you can slide it away from the connector. Most drives have a little plastic tab that you can use to pull them away and then out.

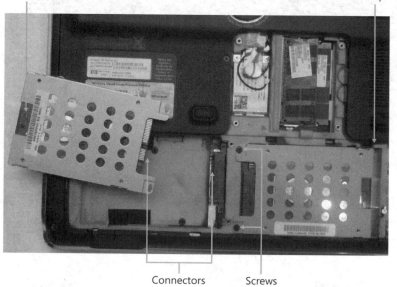

FIGURE 8-10 Removing a hard drive.

The hard drives fit into the drive bay with a little gap, as you can see on the drive shown on the right in Figure 8-10. When you're putting a drive in, this gap allows you to place it flat in the bay and then push it into the connector. Replace the screws, and you're done.

Flash

A popular trend with many hobbyists is to replace the primary hard drive with a solid state drive (SSD) in laptop computers. These use flash memory and are available in 2.5-inch SATA versions. They don't have any moving parts, consume less power, and are extremely fast when compared with a standard hard drive.

In systems with two hard drive bays, you can use something like a 256-GB flash drive for the operating system to get super-fast boot times. If the user needs more space for data, the other hard drive can be a 1-TB traditional hard drive to provide ample space for storage. Of course, you can also use two flash drives.

Memory

Memory is another item that is usually easy to replace on laptop computers. If you have an open slot, you can add additional memory to increase the system's performance, or you can replace the existing memory with higher-capacity RAM. For example, if a system has two 1-GB memory sticks, you might be able to replace them with two 2-GB sticks to double the capacity.

Two primary concerns when replacing memory is ensuring that you use compatible memory and that you follow ESD practices. Laptop computers use small outline dual in-line memory modules (SODIMMs), which are smaller than dual in-line memory modules (DIMMs) that are used in desktops.

> **MORE INFO**   **CHAPTER 3, "UNDERSTANDING RAM AND CPUS"**
>
> Chapter 3 covers different types of DIMM and SODIMMs.

Figure 8-11 shows a laptop with one SODIMM installed and one removed. They are held in place with latches that fit into the round slot on each side of the SODIMM. When secured, the SODIMM lays flat, but when you release the latches, it rises to about a 30-degree angle and you can easily remove it.

To replace the SODIMM, push it into the slot. When it is plugged in, press it down so that it lays flat. The two latches will snap into place, which will secure it. Put all the covers back into place, plug the computer in, and turn the computer on. The system should recognize the new RAM. If not, you might need to double-check your work and ensure that the SODIMM is seated properly in the slot.

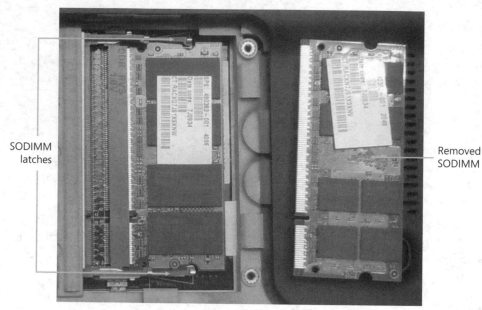

SODIMM latches

Removed SODIMM

FIGURE 8-11 Replacing a SODIMM.

Optical Drive

When a laptop computer includes an optical drive such as a CD, DVD, or Blu-Ray drive, you'll find that they are very easy to replace. Most are held in place with a single screw.

Figure 8-12 shows the location of the screw and an optical drive partially removed from a laptop computer. After removing the screw, you can pry the drive away from the case with a plastic wedge.

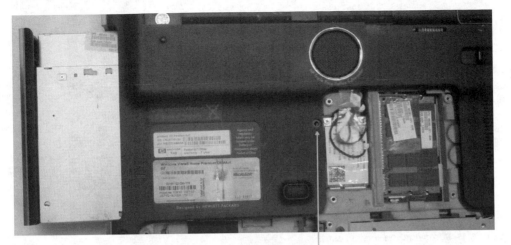

Single screw

FIGURE 8-12 Removing an optical drive.

Mini-PCIe

Laptop computers commonly include Mini Peripheral Component Interconnect Express (Mini-PCIe) slots for expansion. For example, the wireless card shown in the next section is a Mini-PCIe card.

Mini-PCIe is an upgrade to MiniPCI slots, similar to how PCIe is an upgrade to PCI. Mini-PCIe circuit cards are smaller than typical PCIe cards used in desktop computers.

Wireless Card

The wireless card is another easy component to replace. It's easy to identify because it will have two or three wires attached to it, depending on the type of wireless it supports.

Figure 8-13 shows a wireless card partially removed from a laptop computer. In this system, the wireless card is next to the RAM and is annotated with a wireless icon, shown at the bottom of the figure.

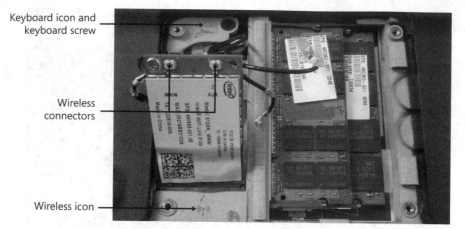

Keyboard icon and keyboard screw

Wireless connectors

Wireless icon

FIGURE 8-13 Removing the wireless card.

This wireless card has two connectors, but the laptop computer has three wires. This provides an excellent example of the importance of labeling wires when you're taking a system apart. One wire must connect to pin 1 (MAIN), and the other wire must connect to pin 2 (AUX). If the wires are not labeled, you should label them. They were already labeled in this system, and the third cable is labeled MIMO, indicating that it is used if the wireless card supports 802.11n.

> **MORE INFO** **CHAPTER 23, "EXPLORING WIRELESS NETWORKING"**
>
> Chapter 23 covers wireless technologies in more depth, including 802.11n. Multiple input multiple output (MIMO) is used with 802.11n but not with other wireless standards such as 802.11a, 802.11b, and 802.11g.

The cables from the wireless card run to an antenna transceiver normally located on the top of the laptop display. In some cases, the transceiver is located on the sides of the display.

It might not show up in Figure 8-13 very well, but there is also a rectangular keyboard icon next to a screw. This lets you know that this is one of the screws holding the keyboard in place.

Keyboard

You'll often have to remove the keyboard to access the motherboard and some other internal components. There are different methods for different motherboards, so your best bet is to check the manual.

NOTE **GIVE YOURSELF *PLENTY* OF TIME**

When you start removing components from the front of the laptop (such as the keyboard, touchpad, and screen), you'll find that the process becomes much more difficult. It's often tedious and time-consuming. Even when you have the manual with detailed directions, it can take you quite a while, so ensure that you have plenty of time before starting.

On some models, you'll first need to remove components from the bottom of the laptop, such as the battery, RAM, DVD player, and the wireless card. With these removed, you'll have access to the screws holding in the keyboard. These often have a small icon of a keyboard.

After removing the screws, you can flip the laptop back over and remove the laptop case or cover. In some cases, you might need to remove additional screws after removing the laptop case, and you'll usually have to pry the case loose with a plastic wedge. When the case is removed, you'll be able to pull the keyboard out. Before removing it completely, carefully remove the connectors.

Touchpad

If you need to remove the touchpad, you can usually access it after removing the keyboard. It is usually held in place with a clip and connected to the motherboard with a cable. Carefully remove the clip and the connector, and you'll be able to remove it.

Speaker

You can usually access the speaker after removing the keyboard. It is often held in place with one or more screws and has a connection to the motherboard. Remove the screws and the connector, and you'll be able to remove the speaker.

Screen

The display typically cannot be removed until you've removed components from the bottom of the laptop to gain access to the screws holding in the keyboard. After removing the keyboard, you'll usually have sufficient access to the display screen.

It's important to remember that the wireless card includes connections to the antenna transceivers and that these transceivers are in the display screen. Therefore, don't try to remove the display screen without first disconnecting these cables from the wireless card. Additionally, many displays include other components, such as a webcam, and you'll need to remove these connections.

With the keyboard removed and the cables removed, you can then locate the screws holding the display to the case. These are normally part of the hinged assembly used to open and close the laptop.

Some manufacturers sell replacements of the entire display assembly. In other models, you'll need to take the display apart to access the LCD display panel. This can be relatively simple or extremely complex, depending on the model and the additional components included in the display screen.

DC Jack

Laptop computers run on DC power. They use a power adapter that plugs into an AC outlet and converts the AC voltage to DC voltage. The other side of this adapter plugs into the DC jack.

Occasionally, the DC jack connection becomes loose and needs to be replaced. This is rarely an easy endeavor because you often need to remove the system board to gain access to the DC jack. As with other components, follow the procedures in the manual.

System

If you need to remove the system board (often called the motherboard), you usually have to remove all the other components in the system. This includes removing all the components accessible from the bottom of the laptop and then removing the keyboard and other components from the top.

One important step you'll need to add is to remove the clock battery. In laptops, this might be called the RTC (real-time clock) battery or the complementary metal oxide semiconductor (CMOS) battery. It is providing power to the system board to keep the clock running and should be removed before removing the system board.

Unless you do this regularly, expect it to take you quite a while to remove all the components from the laptop computer and then remove the system board. Instead of reinstalling the board the same day, you might postpone the job for another day. With that in mind, it becomes especially important to document the screw and cable locations.

CPU

The CPU is often soldered into the motherboard so you will rarely replace it individually. However, if the CPU can be replaced on a laptop, refer to the manufacturer's manual for detailed instructions.

Expansion Options

In addition to allowing you to add or replace hardware internally, many laptops also include expansion slots that you can use without taking them apart. Laptops commonly have USB ports, just as regular desktop computers do, but they will often have extra slots found only on laptops.

MORE INFO CHAPTER 5, "EXPLORING PERIPHERALS AND EXPANSION CARDS"

Chapter 5 covers USB connections, which you'll find on almost every laptop computer. Chapter 4, "Comparing Storage Devices," covers external Serial ATA powered (eSATAp) ports, which are also found on many laptop computers. An eSATAp port can be used as an external SATA (eSATA) port or as a USB port.

PCMCIA

PC Cards were often used with laptop computers before the release of the ExpressCard, but they are very rare today. They were created by the *Personal Computer Memory Card International Association (PCMCIA)* and were previously called PCMCIA cards. They came in three types with three different thicknesses, as follows:

- Type I cards are the thinnest at 3.3 mm. A Type I card can plug into a Type II, Type II, or Type III slot.
- Type II cards are a little thicker at 5.0 mm. A Type II card can plug into a Type II or Type III slot.
- Type III cards are 10.5 mm and are often used for hard drives. A Type III card can plug into a Type III slot only.

ExpressCards

Most laptops manufactured since 2007 include *ExpressCard* slots, and there are a wide variety of ExpressCards available. They are available as adapters to add additional USB, eSATA, network, or FireWire ports. Some provide you with additional memory card slots, including SecureDigital (SD) or CompactFlash memory slots. They are also available as wireless network cards, sound cards, and much more.

ExpressCards come in the following two versions:

- **ExpressCard/34.** This card is 34 mm wide and has 26 pins.
- **ExpressCard/54.** This card is 54 mm wide and has 26 pins.

Figure 8-14 compares the size of these cards with the legacy PC Card. Notice that /34 and /54 refer to the overall width of the cards but that each ExpressCard has 26 pins and fits into the same type of slot. That is, there are two types of ExpressCards but only one type of ExpressCard slot. Both ExpressCard versions are 5.0 mm thick, the same thickness as a Type II PC Card.

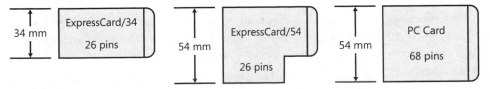

FIGURE 8-14 Comparing an ExpressCard/34, an ExpressCard/54, and a PC Card.

A logical question is, "Why are there two versions of ExpressCard?" There are two reasons:

- **More space.** The ExpressCard/54 provides manufacturers with more space to house the components. For example, a hard drive with a 1.8-inch platter can fit on an ExpressCard/54 but not on the smaller ExpressCard/34.

- **Better heat dissipation.** Some cards include components that tend to get hotter than others. By using a larger card, it has more surface space to dissipate the heat.

NOTE **NO PERFORMANCE DIFFERENCES BETWEEN EXPRESSCARD VERSIONS**

There are no performance differences between ExpressCard/34 and ExpressCard/54. They both fit into the same slot and use the same technology.

Conserving Power

One of the great benefits of a laptop computer is that you can still run it even if you're disconnected from a primary power source. Laptops have batteries that will continue to power the system, but these batteries don't last forever.

Most users don't want to lug around a 50-pound battery with their laptop, but they also want the laptop to stay powered as long as possible. Manufacturers try to strike a balance between how long a battery will last and how heavy it is. You can also take steps to conserve power and keep systems running longer.

EXAM TIP

Conserving power isn't limited only to laptop computers. Most of the concepts in this section apply both to desktop computers and to laptops.

ACPI

An open standard supported by Windows operating systems and most hardware devices is *advanced configuration power interface (ACPI)*. This is an update to an earlier standard called *advanced power management (APM)*.

Systems that support ACPI allow the operating system to send signals to devices to change their power state. For example, ACPI can be used to turn off a display monitor after 10 minutes of inactivity.

ACPI defines many power states for systems and hardware, such as global power states that apply to the entire computer, device power states that apply to individual devices, and processor states that apply to the central processing unit (CPU).

The following four global states identify the level of computer operation for the system:

- **G0.** The system has full power and is working normally.
- **G1.** The system is in one of four low-power states.
- **G2.** The system is off but still has power available.
- **G3.** The system is completely disconnected from power.

EXAM TIP

If you are going to perform hardware maintenance on a computer, it should be in the G3 power state. The G2 state supports soft power. It can be turned on from the front panel power switch or from signals sent over a network. For example, administrators can send Wake-on-LAN "magic packets" to a system in the G2 state to wake it up.

G1 is divided into four separate sleep or low-power states. The S1 and S2 states define levels of sleep for the processor, but for a PC technician, the most important states are S3 and S4:

- **S3.** This is commonly called *sleep, suspend,* or *standby*.
- **S4.** This is known as *hibernation* or sometimes *suspend to disk*.

Sleep/Suspend/Standby (G1 S3)

Sleep mode is a low-power state that allows the computer to quickly return to full power. It's also known as *suspend* mode or *standby* mode and is defined in the S3 sleeping state within the G1 global state.

It provides trickle power to maintain the contents of the RAM and low power to the CPU. The CPU periodically checks to see whether you've taken any action indicating that it should wake the system. Other components, such as the disk drive and display, are powered off.

When a user takes an action, such as pressing a key, the system wakes up and returns power to normal for all the components. A system can return to normal from sleep mode very quickly.

Hibernate (G1 S4)

Hibernate mode saves the most power. It's also known as *suspend to disk* and is defined in the S4 sleeping state within the G1 global state.

The computer takes a snapshot of the entire contents of random access memory (RAM) and stores it on the hard drive. It then completely shuts down the computer. When you turn the computer back on, it copies the snapshot from the hard drive and restores it into RAM. Many laptops are configured to go into hibernation mode when you close the lid.

For example, if you were taking notes on a laptop computer and then realized you needed to leave for an appointment, you could close the lid of your laptop. The system would copy the contents of RAM to the hard drive and turn itself off. When you open the lid and turn the system back on, your session will be restored just as it was when you closed the lid.

EXAM TIP

Hibernate saves the most power because the computer is turned completely off, but it takes longer for the system to turn back on. Standby or sleep modes still use power and will consume battery power, but the system can return to full operation much quicker.

Hybrid Sleep

Many systems support a hybrid sleep mode. It copies the contents of RAM to the disk as if it were hibernating. However, instead of shutting down, it goes into a low-power sleep mode. It can wake up quickly when it's needed. Additionally, if the system loses power, it can return to operation from the hibernation mode.

Power Options

Windows XP, Windows Vista, and Windows 7 all include an applet called Power Options in the Control Panel. You can use this to configure different power plans for a system.

You can access the Power Options applet by clicking Start, Control Panel. On Windows XP and Windows Vista, change the view to Classic View. On Windows 7, change the view to Large Icons. You can then double-click the Power Options applet to start it.

It looks a little different in Windows XP than it does in Windows Vista and Windows 7. Windows XP uses power schemes, but Windows Vista and Windows 7 use power plans providing you with more control.

Power Plans

When you open the Power Options applet in Windows 7, you'll see the following available *power plans*:

- **Balanced (recommended).** This plan attempts to balance the performance of the system with how much power is used. It's recommended for most uses, including on desktop computers.

- **Power saver.** This reduces energy consumption and can help a system stay on battery power longer. Laptops often switch to this automatically when they are on battery power.

- **High performance.** This favors performance over saving energy. It is hidden by default.

If you click one of the plans, you can configure some basic settings, and if you click Change Advanced Power Settings, you can view the advanced settings. Figure 8-15 shows the advanced settings page for the Balanced (Active) plan that is active on this system. Notice that the display is set to turn off after 10 minutes of inactivity and that the hard drive will turn off after 20 minutes. Also, you can see that Allow Wake Timers is enabled for Sleep. This allows the system to wake up to perform a scheduled task.

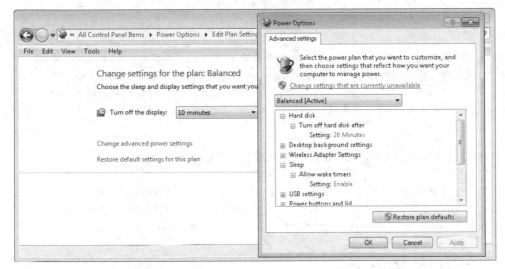

FIGURE 8-15 Viewing the balanced plan settings.

Troubleshooting Power Issues

Power issues on laptop computers are normally limited to either the power adapter or the battery. The following sections describe the two common symptoms that you'll likely encounter.

No Power

If the system has no power, there could be several reasons. The obvious reason is that it isn't plugged in. Laptops use special power adapters that convert AC power to DC. The adapter plugs into an AC outlet, and the other end plugs into the laptop's DC jack.

You can usually check two indicators to determine whether the adapter is providing power to the system. First, most adapters have a small LED as a power indicator that illuminates when it is plugged in. Second, most laptops have an LED at the DC jack that illuminates when it is receiving power from the adapter.

If an LED isn't lit, double-check the connections. You might need to reseat the cables into the different jacks. After reseating the connections, check the LEDs again. If the adapter LED isn't lit, you might need to replace it. If the LED at the DC jack isn't lit but the adapter is working, you might need to replace the DC jack.

Battery Not Charging

If the battery is not charging, check to ensure that the system is receiving power. Without power, it won't charge. In some cases, the battery will fail and just won't be able to accept a charge anymore. The system will work with AC power without any problem but won't work while on battery power. The solution is to replace the battery.

Stay Cool

Heat is the enemy of any type of electronics, and this includes laptops and batteries. Many laptops don't include any internal fans, so they have a tendency to get hot. Laptop pads are available that include fans. These often plug into a USB port, and the fans spin to keep the system cool when it's turned on.

Troubleshooting Connectivity Issues

This chapter covered many troubleshooting issues, but you might also experience some issues with connectivity for wireless or Bluetooth connections. The primary user complaints you'll hear are related to intermittent connections or no connection at all.

Intermittent Wireless

An intermittent wireless connection often indicates that there is interference with the signal. You can either identify the source of the interference to eliminate it or find a way avoid it. Chapter 23 includes information about common types of interference and how to change wireless channels to avoid it.

Intermittent connection can also occur when the laptop computer is too far away from the wireless access point (WAP). The simple solution is to move the laptop closer to the WAP. If this isn't possible, you might be able to boost the power output of the wireless access point, adjust the antenna position, or move the WAP.

Last, if the system has been worked on recently, it's possible that the connections to the wireless card are loose. You can open the system to verify that the wires are secured to the wireless card.

No Wireless Connectivity

A good question to ask when a user complains about wireless connectivity is something like, "Did it stop working recently?" If a system had wireless but it just stopped, check the function key or wireless switch on the keyboard. It's very possible that the user accidentally turned the wireless off. This is almost always the case if other users can connect but one user cannot.

If it hasn't worked at all, you might need to configure the wireless connection from scratch. Check out Chapter 23 for steps to take. It's also possible that the wireless card has failed. If so, you'll need to replace it by using procedures mentioned earlier in the chapter. Alternatively, you can purchase a USB wireless dongle. These plug into a USB port and can be used to connect to a wireless network.

No Bluetooth Connectivity

If a user doesn't have any Bluetooth connectivity, you can follow the same procedures you used for no wireless connectivity. Find out if it recently stopped, and if so, look for the function key to enable or disable it. If it hasn't worked at all, you might need to pair Bluetooth devices and configure them to work together. Chapter 9 covers details about Bluetooth.

Chapter Summary

- Laptop keyboards typically have special function keys that can control hardware. This includes keys used for dual displays, to enable or disable wireless and Bluetooth, control the volume, and control the screen brightness.

- A docking station extends the capabilities of a laptop when the laptop is plugged into it. A port replicator provides additional ports for a laptop computer.

- Windows XP uses hardware profiles with docking stations, but they are not available in Windows Vista and Windows 7.

- Most laptops include a port used for a physical cable lock.

- Laptops primarily use LCD or LED displays. LCD displays include an inverter to convert DC to AC for the CCFL. The Wi-Fi antenna is normally in the display, and a cable runs to a wireless Mini-PCIe card in the system.

- If the LCD inverter or CCFL fails, the display will be dim or dark. If the display is flickering, it might be due to a loose cable. If you can't see a display on the laptop monitor or an external monitor, the video card might have failed.

- Use specific steps when replacing components on a laptop, starting with removing all power sources including the battery. Locate and use manufacturer documentation. Document and label cable and screw locations as you're taking the laptop apart, and organize the parts. Last, make sure that you have the right tools, including a plastic wedge.

- ExpressCard/34 and ExpressCard/54 slots provide expansion capabilities for laptops. They replace older PCMCIA cards. The /34 and /54 specifications refer to the overall width but not the number of pins.

- Sleep modes consume very little power and can return to operation very quickly. Hibernate mode stores the data in RAM onto the disk and turns off the laptop. Hibernate mode does not consume any power but takes longer to start up than sleep mode does.

- Windows-based systems use power plans to conserve energy. Laptops will commonly switch to a power-saving plan when they are switched from AC power to battery power.

- Connectivity issues can be resolved by manipulating the wireless switch on the keyboard. If necessary, you can replace the Wi-Fi card.

Chapter Review

Use the following questions to test your knowledge of the information in this chapter. The answers to these questions, and the explanations of why each answer choice is correct or incorrect, are located in the "Answers" section at the end of this chapter.

1. Which key can often be used with a function key to disable wireless on a laptop computer?

   A. F1 key

   B. Num Lock key

   C. Fn key

   D. Caps Lock key

2. Which of the following best describes a docking station?

   A. A device designed to enhance the capabilities of a laptop and allow it to function as a desktop computer

   B. A device that has one connection and provides additional ports for the laptop

   C. A component that provides AC power to an LED display

   D. A component used for laptop physical security

3. A laptop display is dark, but you can see information on the screen when you shine a flashlight into it. Of the following choices, what is the problem? (Choose two.)

   A. Backlight

   B. Inverter

   C. LCD display

   D. Video card

4. You are preparing to replace the keyboard in a laptop computer. Of the following choices, what should you include in the process? (Choose all that apply.)

   A. Toggle the Fn key before starting.

   B. Obtain the manufacturer's documentation for the laptop.

   C. Remove the LCD display first.

   D. Remove all power including the battery.

5. A user wants to conserve power on his system when he's not using it. Which of the following saves the most power?

   A. Turning off the display after inactivity

   B. Turning off disks after inactivity

   C. Sleep

   D. Hibernate

6. Wireless has failed on a laptop computer. Which of the following options would restore the capability? (Choose two.)

   A. Install a Mini-PCIe card.

   B. Install a USB wireless adapter.

   C. Install a PCI wireless card.

   D. Install an AGP wireless adapter.

Answers

1. **Correct Answer:** C

    A. **Incorrect:** The F1 key by itself is used to open Help.

    B. **Incorrect:** The Num Lock key configures the numeric keypad to use numbers or as navigation keys.

    C. **Correct:** The Fn key is often used with a function key to disable wireless.

    D. **Incorrect:** The Caps Lock key configures letters to be always uppercase or lowercase.

2. **Correct Answer:** A

    A. **Correct:** Docking stations provide additional capabilities to laptops when used in an office.

    B. **Incorrect:** Port replicators provide additional ports.

    C. **Incorrect:** An inverter provides AC power to LED displays.

    D. **Incorrect:** Cable locks are used for physical security.

3. **Correct Answers:** A, B

    A. **Correct:** If the backlight fails, the display will be dark or dim.

    B. **Correct:** The inverter powers the backlight on LCD laptop displays, so it can exhibit these symptoms.

    C. **Incorrect:** Data can be viewed when the flashlight is shined into the panel, so the LCD display has not failed.

    D. **Incorrect:** If the video card failed, you wouldn't see any display.

4. **Correct Answers:** B, D

    A. **Incorrect:** It is not necessary to toggle any keys before starting.

    B. **Correct:** The documentation provides the steps you'll use.

    C. **Incorrect:** The display usually isn't replaced before the keyboard, but the manual provides the specific steps.

    D. **Correct:** All power should be removed before starting.

5. **Correct Answer: D**

    A. **Incorrect:** Turning off just the display is useful, but other components are still consuming power.

    B. **Incorrect:** Turning off just the disks is useful, but other components are still consuming power.

    C. **Incorrect:** Sleep mode reduces power consumption but not as much as hibernate.

    D. **Correct:** A system turns off in Hibernate mode, so this saves the most power.

6. **Correct Answers: A, B**

    A. **Correct:** A Mini-PCIe card can add wireless to a laptop.

    B. **Correct:** A USB wireless adapter can add wireless to a laptop.

    C. **Incorrect:** PCI cards won't fit in a laptop.

    D. **Incorrect:** AGP is a video technology bus.

CHAPTER 9

Understanding Mobile Devices

In this chapter, you'll learn about the different types of mobile devices, with an emphasis on tablets such as Apple's iPad. These devices have enjoyed great popularity in recent years, and it's clear that they are here to stay. This chapter compares tablets to laptops, compares different operating systems on the devices, and covers methods used to connect them. You'll also learn some basics about using these mobile devices and important information about how you can secure them.

Exam 220-801 objectives in this chapter:

- 1.7 Compare and contrast various connection interfaces and explain their purpose.
    - Speeds, distances and frequencies of wireless device connections
        - Bluetooth
        - IR
        - RF
- 2.7 Compare and contrast Internet connection types and features.
    - Cellular (mobile hot spot)

Exam 220-802 objectives in this chapter:

- 3.1 Explain the basic features of mobile operating systems.
    - Android vs. iOS
        - Open source vs. closed source/vendor specific
        - App source (app store and market)
        - Screen orientation (accelerometer/gyroscope)
        - Screen calibration
        - GPS and geotracking
- 3.2 Establish basic network connectivity and configure email.
    - Wireless / cellular data network (enable/disable)

- Bluetooth
  - Enable Bluetooth
  - Enable pairing
  - Find device for pairing
  - Enter appropriate pin code
  - Test connectivity
- Email configuration
  - Server address
    - POP3
    - IMAP
    - Port and SSL settings
  - Exchange
  - Gmail
- 3.3 Compare and contrast methods for securing mobile devices.
  - Passcode locks
  - Remote wipes
  - Locator applications
  - Remote backup applications
  - Failed login attempts restrictions
  - Antivirus
  - Patching/OS updates
- 3.4 Compare and contrast hardware differences in regards to tablets and laptops.
  - No field serviceable parts
  - Typically not upgradeable
  - Touch interface
    - Touch flow
    - Multitouch
  - Solid state drives
- 3.5 Execute and configure mobile device synchronization.
  - Types of data to synchronize
    - Contacts
    - Programs
    - Email
    - Pictures

- Music
- Videos
- Software requirements to install the application on the PC
- Connection types to enable synchronization

REAL WORLD **LOCATING YOUR LOST iPAD**

Not too long ago, a friend of mine lost his iPad. He used it all the time and was sure that someone had stolen it. When he mentioned it to me a few days later, I asked if he had enabled Location Services. His puzzled look indicated that he didn't know what I was talking about, but he did say that when he bought it, his brother-in-law helped him set it up. It was possible that Location Services was enabled and that we could find it.

We ended up downloading a location app, and he signed in using his information. Within a couple of minutes, we pinpointed the exact location of his iPad. Interestingly, it was at my house. I assured him I didn't have it but suggested it might be in his car, which was in my driveway. After a few minutes of searching, he found it beneath some papers under a car seat.

This location feature is common on most mobile devices, not just iPads. Not only can the device be located but you can also send signals to erase all the data or lock the device. Knowing what features are available will help you be a better technician, even if you don't have a mobile device of your own.

Tablets vs. Laptops

Tablets are handheld devices such as the Apple iPad, the Samsung Galaxy Tab, or the HP Touchpad. They have a touchscreens allowing you to operate them without a keyboard or mouse. Instead you use gestures (described later in this chapter) to operate them.

These devices use solid state storage drives and flash memory, providing excellent speed when being rebooted and while running applications. Solid state drives (covered in Chapter 4, "Comparing Storage Devices") are lighter and consume less power. This allows the rechargeable battery to be smaller, and the overall weight of a tablet is less than that of a typical laptop.

Tablets commonly include Wi-Fi capability, allowing them to connect to a wireless network. Some tablets also include the ability to access a cellular network for Internet access. When using the cellular network, the user needs to sign up with a wireless provider such as Verizon or AT&T. The cellular network used by tablets is the same cellular network used by smartphones.

Hardware for tablets is rarely upgradable or serviceable. If you buy a 16-GB iPad and later decide you want a 64-GB iPad, you need to buy a new one. If it breaks, you might be able to send it back to the company to get it serviced, but this can be quite expensive if it isn't under warranty.

In contrast, laptops are bigger, include more hardware, and are upgradable and serviceable. Laptops include keyboards along with the display screens, but tablets use a display keyboard that allows you to touch the keys on the touchscreen. You can purchase laptops with display screens as big as 17.3 inches, which are much bigger than the 9.7-inch diagonal display of an iPad or the 10.1-inch diagonal display of the Galaxy Tab.

> **NOTE TABLET SIZES**
>
> Tablet display sizes are commonly quoted as the diagonal display size. This is the length of the screen from an upper corner to the opposite lower corner and includes only the viewable area.

Table 9-1 summarizes some of the important differences between tablets and laptops related to the A+ exams.

TABLE 9-1 Comparing Tablets and Laptops

	Tablet	Laptop
Upgrades	Rarely upgradable	Memory and hard drives easily upgradable.
Repairs	No field-serviceable parts	Technicians can open and replace components.
Hard drives	Solid state drives	Most use traditional hard drives. Some can use solid state drives but these are not as common.
Interface	Touch interface	Keyboard and mouse.

> **EXAM TIP**
>
> Tablets do not have field-serviceable parts and are rarely upgradable. They include solid state drives, contributing to their high performance and lighter weight.

Tablets have many common features that aren't always in laptops. The following sections cover these features.

Accelerometers and Gyroscopes

Many devices include an *accelerometer* and a Micro-Electro-Mechanical System (MEMS) *gyroscope* to measure the orientation of the device. In many devices, a single chip includes both. The output of the accelerometer and gyroscope indicates the orientation of the device, and the device can use this information to change the display.

The most basic use of accelerometers and gyroscopes is to determine whether the device is positioned horizontally or vertically in front of a user. If the user changes the orientation of the device, the software can automatically switch the screen orientation to landscape or portrait mode.

A more sophisticated use is to sense the exact orientation of the device and change the display to match. For example, Star Walk (shown in Figure 9-1) is an application that shows information about satellites, planets, stars, constellations, and more.

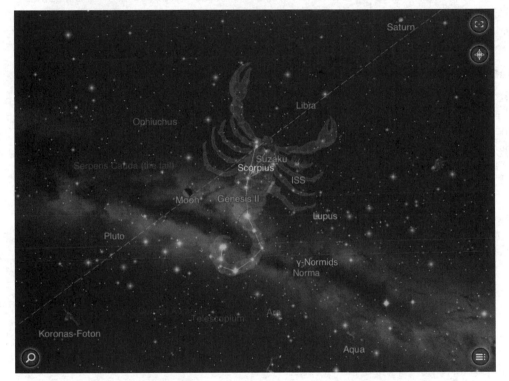

FIGURE 9-1 Star Walk application screen.

If you hold the tablet up with the back pointing toward the sky, the display shows the names of everything in that direction. Move the device in any direction, and the display automatically changes to show you what's in the new direction. If you were looking for Saturn, you could scan the sky with the back of the tablet until Saturn was displayed. You could then look at the sky in that direction. Similarly, many games use this feature. For example, in some racing games, you can hold the tablet like a steering wheel to make turns within the game.

GPS

Most tablets and smartphones include access to a *Global Positioning System (GPS)*, which can be used to determine the exact location of the device. The location is used by many apps on tablets to provide location-specific data. For example, if you use Google Earth, this feature allows GPS to zoom in on your location. Similarly, weather service apps use the GPS to provide local weather reports.

Geotracking

Geotracking is the practice of recording the location of a mobile device and using it to track the movements of the device. The location is identified based on cell towers accessed by the device and can provide specific information including latitude, longitude, the azimuth or compass heading from the tower, and the time and date. It can also record information if users connect to geographically tagged Wi-Fi hot spots.

NOTE APPLE'S USE OF GEOTRACKING

Apple has stated this data is used for apps that need location-based information. They mention that calculating a phone's location by using only GPS satellite data can take several minutes, but the time can be reduced to a few seconds by using the logged location data.

Mobile devices store this data in a file on the device, and if someone knows how to retrieve it, they can track the location of the device over a period of time. Some forensics classes teach specifically how to retrieve this information from a device. Similarly, some applications can retrieve the data from a device.

There are also apps that you can install on devices to track their movement and location. Parents sometimes use them to keep track of their children, and employers have used them to keep track of employer-supplied devices.

Screen Calibration

In some cases, the touchscreen can become uncalibrated. You might find that instead of touching directly on an item, you have to touch somewhere else close to the item. For example, if you touch a button on the screen, it doesn't respond, but if you touch to the right of the button, it works. This isn't common with many current tablets but has been an issue with tablets and devices using touchscreens in the past.

If the device needs to be calibrated, you need to follow the directions for the device to start the calibration program. For example, on one version of an Android Samsung tablet, you start the screen calibration program by holding the menu button down for 10 seconds.

After the calibration program starts, you see a circle or prompt displayed somewhere on the screen that you need to touch. Touch it, and another circle appears with a prompt to touch it. It's common for the calibration program to display this circle in each of the four corners and at the center of the screen. Each time you touch the circle, the device records this as the correct calibrated location. After touching the last circle, the screen is calibrated.

✔ **Quick Check**

1. What's the difference in upgradability between a laptop and a tablet?

2. What is used to identify the location of a device?

Quick Check Answers

1. Tablets are not upgradable.

2. GPS. Geotracking can track the movement of a device.

Comparing Operating Systems

The primary operating systems used on mobile devices are from Apple, Google, and Microsoft. Apple uses iOS, Google uses Android, and Microsoft uses Windows-based operating systems.

These operating systems are used on tablets and smartphones. A smartphone is a mobile device that includes additional features beyond making phone calls. Some of the common features of smartphones today include surfing the Internet, sending and receiving email, taking pictures with built-in digital cameras, and playing music as an MP3 player does. Smartphones often include other *personal digital assistant (PDA)* features, such as contact lists and/or an address book, calendar and appointment lists, and note-taking capabilities.

The following sections describe the basics of the operating systems and some key differences between them.

Open Source vs. Closed Source

When talking about mobile operating systems, it's important to understand the basic differences between *open source* and *closed source* software. Closed source software is sometimes referred to as *vendor-specific*, although this term isn't as common.

The primary differences are the availability of the code to the public and the cost to use the code.

- **Open source.** Open source software is code that is freely available to anyone. Developers have access to the code and can modify, improve, and at times, freely redistribute it. The Android operating system is open source software, and it was derived from the open source Linux operating system.

- **Closed source/vendor-specific.** Closed source software is code that is not freely available to the public but is instead protected by the company that developed it. It is often viewed and protected as a trade secret or intellectual property, and any usage of the software is subject to restrictions. Both the Apple iOS and Microsoft Windows operating systems are closed source operating systems, although the licenses are different.

EXAM TIP

While you can also find open source and closed source applications, the A+ 220-801 exam is focused only on understanding the differences between open source and closed source operating systems. More specifically, you should know that Android is open source and the Apple iOS is closed source.

---

iOS

The *iOS* is the operating system used on Apple products including iPhones, iPads, iPod Touch, and Apple TV. A unique characteristic of the iOS is that Apple does not let anyone but Apple use it. This is the same philosophy they've employed since their early Apple and Macintosh computers. If you want to use the Mac OS X operating system, buy a Mac from Apple. If you want to use iOS, buy an Apple product.

Additionally, Apple controls all software sales through the Apple App Store. Therefore, if you want to buy an app, you purchase it through their store.

The benefit to users is that they are less likely to download malicious software from the App Store. The benefit to Apple is that they receive about 30 percent from every sale. With enough 99-cent apps, this starts to add up. Based on a recent query, Apple's stock market value of over 500 billion dollars (yes, that's a *B* as in *billion*), this strategy seems to be working for them, at least for now.

NOTE iPHONE OS TO iOS

Apple's iOS was previously called iPhone OS. Apple began using the lowercase *i* on its products in 1998 with the iMac. Cisco uses the Cisco IOS (shortened from *Internetwork Operating System* with an uppercase *I*) for networking devices. However, iOS and IOS are two completely different operating systems.

Android

The *Android* operating system is a Linux-based operating system, but it's not owned by a single company. Google purchased Android, Inc., in 2005 and ultimately came out with the Android operating system in 2007. Google leads the Open Handset Alliance (OHA), a consortium of 84 companies that work together to develop open standards for mobile devices, and the Android operating system is a major product developed by OHA. Currently, the Android Open Source Project (AOSP) maintains and develops improvements for Android.

As mentioned previously, Android is an open source operating system, and any hardware developer can use it to create a device with Android as the base operating system. There is no obligation to pay Google, the OHA, or AOSP for Android. This has resulted in an explosion of devices running the Android operating system, including smartphones (such as Droids), tablet computers (such as the Kindle Fire or the Samsung Galaxy Tab), and many more.

As of February 2012, the Android operating system was reportedly running on over 300 million smartphones and tablets worldwide. Some experts expect Android-based tablets to exceed sales of the iPad by 2015.

Windows

The Windows Phone operating system is used on smartphones such as Windows Phone 7. Additionally, most Windows desktop operating systems can run on tablets. For example, all versions of Vista and Windows 7 can run on tablets, except for the Starter editions. Similarly, Windows 8 can run both on tablets and on PCs. Windows XP had a dedicated version called Windows XP Tablet PC Edition that ran on tablets.

Microsoft licenses the operating system to hardware developers. These hardware developers can then design the hardware around the operating system, and they include the operating system license as part of the price.

Windows 8 is in a different category. It can run on desktops, and Microsoft has developed its own tablets known as the Surface and the Surface Pro. However, CompTIA had already released the objectives for the A+ exam before Windows 8 was released, and it stated that Windows 8 will not be on these exams. CompTIA can change its mind later and decide to add Windows 8. If it does, I'll blog about it at *blogs.getcertifiedgetahead.com*.

EXAM TIP

As a comparison between the three mobile operating systems, Apple does not license iOS to anyone, the Android operating system is free for everyone, and Microsoft licenses the operating system to hardware vendors.

Application Sources

Applications are what make these devices useful, and some apps really help people be more productive. Some, like Angry Birds, are just fun. There have been over 500 million downloads of Angry Birds (including the Angry Bird spinoffs), indicating that many people are using mobile devices for some fun. A logical question is, "Where can you get these apps?"

Apps for mobile devices are available almost exclusively online. The user connects to the store with the device and makes a purchase, and the app is immediately downloaded and installed. For the iOS, Android, and Windows operating systems, the primary application sources are:

- **Apple App Store**. Links directly to Apple's App Store are included in Apple mobile devices. Users can click the link, connect, shop, and buy. Apple-based apps are not easily available through other sources. Figure 9-2 shows the App Store on an iPad.

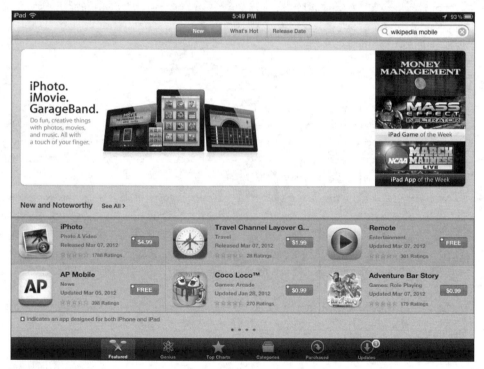

FIGURE 9-2 App Store as seen on an iPad.

- **Google Play.** Android-based apps are available through Google Play: *https://play .google.com/store*, and other sources. Google Play was previously called Android Marketplace. Other sources for Android apps include Amazon.com in the Appstore for Android section, Mobihand.com, and Handango.com.

- **Windows Store and Windows Phone Marketplace**. Windows apps are available through the Windows Store and the Windows Phone marketplace: *http://www .windowsstore.com/* and *http://www.windowsphone.com/marketplace*. As with other mobile stores, users can connect to them from within a mobile device. Users can also use a regular browser to connect to the marketplace and purchase applications. These applications are then synchronized to their devices.

Application developers who create an app for one device must rewrite the code for other devices. For example, an app that runs on an iOS-based device will not run an on Android-based device until the developers modify the code to match the Android operating system. However, when developers recode the app, you often can't tell the difference between the functionality on the different devices.

✔ **Quick Check**

1. What operating system is used on Apple devices?

2. What is the major difference between the Android operating system and the operating system used on Apple devices?

Quick Check Answers

1. iOS.

2. Android is open source, while the iOS is closed source and vendor-specific.

Connectivity

Mobile devices have the ability to connect wirelessly to an outside network by using one or more different technologies. As mentioned previously, many mobile devices include either Wi-Fi capability or cellular access. Two other connectivity methods are Bluetooth and infrared.

RF (Wireless)

Radio frequency (RF) connections on mobile devices enable the devices to connect to a wireless network. If your mobile device supports wireless connections and a wireless network is in range, you can configure the device to connect to the wireless network. Almost all mobile devices include this ability.

When connected, it will have access to the same resources as other devices on the wireless network. For example, you can connect smartphones and tablets to wireless networks and then use the network to surf the Internet or answer email. Wireless networks are covered in more depth in Chapter 23, "Exploring Wireless Networking." That chapter includes the information you need to connect any device to a wireless network.

Cellular

Many mobile devices can tap into the same cellular network used by smartphones. The cellular network has been steadily improving and currently provides speeds up to 1 Gbps in some areas. Cellular has gone through the following generations, with each generation providing an improvement over the previous one:

- **1G (first generation).** These were analog phones that had no digital capabilities.
- **2G (second generation).** These were the first generation of digital phones, and 2G is still used in some rural areas.
- **3G (third generation).** A large portion of cellular devices connect with 3G today, and the 3G networks are widely available in both urban and rural areas. Telecommunications companies are regularly updating the capabilities of the cellular towers and steadily improving the service.
- **LTE (Long Term Evolution).** LTE is a standard that is an improvement over 3G but doesn't necessarily meet the requirements of 4G. Some LTE networks are marketed as 4G LTE but don't fully meet the specifications of a 4G network.
- **4G (fourth generation).** 4G networks are available in many major cities and major metropolitan areas but not in rural areas. 4G is sometimes called WiMax.

A subscription is required to use these cellular data services. If you have a smartphone or a tablet that includes cellular access, you can pay additional money for these data services. They give you Internet access anywhere that you have cellular access. Plans often limit how much data you can download in a month, with limits such as 3 GB or 5 GB. If you exceed the limit, you're charged more.

> **EXAM TIP**
>
> It takes power to periodically communicate with cellular towers and wireless networks. You can conserve the battery by disabling these connections when you're not using them. This is very effective with tablets, and it increases the amount of time you can use the tablet before recharging it. You can also limit bandwidth usage by disabling the connection.

In contrast, if you have a wireless capability, you don't have to pay a monthly subscription fee. Anywhere there's a wireless network and you have the means to connect you can do so without paying a subscription fee.

Mobile Hotspot

Many wireless providers also sell portable wireless devices that act as hot spots. They're commonly called MiFi (pronounced My Fye, similar to Wi-Fi). They can connect to the Internet by using the cellular network, and they provide access to up to five other wireless users.

Bluetooth

Bluetooth is a type of wireless protocol used with many mobile devices. Devices that support Bluetooth are called *Bluetooth-capable* or *Bluetooth-enabled* devices, and it is common to use Bluetooth to create personal area networks (PANs).

> **MORE INFO   CHAPTER 18**
>
> Chapter 18, "Introducing Networking Components," covers other types of networks, including local area networks (LANs), wireless local area networks (WLANs), wide area networks (WANs), and metropolitan area networks (MANs). A WAN connects two or more LANs that are in separate geographic locations. A MAN covers a large metropolitan area, such as a city.

For example, you can have a Bluetooth-enabled phone and a Bluetooth-enabled headset like the one shown in Figure 9-3. These types of headsets have an earpiece and microphone and are worn on the ear.

FIGURE 9-3 Bluetooth headset.

However, the headset won't work with the phone until you pair the two devices together. Pairing is the process of configuring the devices so that they can communicate with each other. After pairing the devices, you can keep the phone in your pocket or purse and use the headset to carry on conversations.

You need to follow the directions for the devices you're pairing, but the basic steps for pairing are:

- Enable Bluetooth if required
- Enable pairing if required

- Enter a personal identification number (PIN) if required
- Test connectivity

EXAM TIP

The same PIN needs to be entered on both devices, but sometimes one of the devices won't have a way to enter a PIN. For example, it's not possible to enter a PIN on most Bluetooth headsets. In this situation, you can enter the PIN only on the other device. What PIN should you use? Normally, you'd use either 0000 or the last four digits of the headset's serial number.

Depending on the version of Bluetooth that the devices are using, you might not need to take these steps. For example, Bluetooth version 2.1 uses Secure Simple Pairing (SSP), and one type of SSP is called Just Works. As the name implies, it just works without requiring the user to go through these steps. As a security precaution, the devices might require the user to approve the pairing process.

While Bluetooth is normally used for PANs, it can support distances farther away than someone's personal space. Table 9-2 shows the three classes of Bluetooth and their ranges.

TABLE 9-2 Bluetooth Classes and Ranges

Bluetooth Class	Approximate Range
Class 1	100 meters (about 328 feet)
Class 2	10 meters (about 33 feet)
Class 3	5 meters (about 16 feet)

Many wireless mouse and keyboard combos use Bluetooth. They include a USB transceiver (commonly called a *USB dongle*) that you plug into any USB port. Most are Class 2 devices so that you can use the mouse and keyboard from up to 33 feet away. Additionally, most use the Just Works version of SSP, so they don't require any user interaction.

Infrared

Infrared (IR) is a line-of-sight wireless technology used with many computing devices. The IR standards are developed by the *Infrared Data Association (IrDA)*. IR devices use light-emitting diodes (LEDs) to send IR signals that can be picked up by IR sensors.

You can use IR to connect and transfer information between two mobile devices or between a mobile device and a PC. For example, if someone has a ringtone you want, you can often transfer it between the devices with IR. Of course, both devices must have IR capabilities.

This is the same technology used with television remotes. You point the remote at the TV, select a button, and it does your bidding. However, it has a primary weakness that you probably know: if there is anything between the remote and the TV, the signal doesn't make it to the TV. A single piece of paper can block the signal. Similarly, if there is anything between the two devices, the IR signal is blocked.

> **NOTE** **INFRARED NEEDS TO BE ENABLED**
>
> Infrared is usually not enabled by default on devices. You need to go into the device settings to enable it.

There was a time when infrared was common on desktop PCs and laptops and used with some printers. However, the line-of-sight restriction has caused a lot of problems. All you have to do is put a book in the wrong location on your desk, and you lose the connection. Because of this, IR connections aren't very common except on some smartphones.

> ✔ **Quick Check**
>
> 1. What PIN is used when a PIN can't be entered with a Bluetooth device?
> 2. What is the range of Class 2 Bluetooth?
>
> **Quick Check Answers**
>
> 1. 0000, or the last four digits of the serial number.
> 2. 10 meters, or about 33 feet.

Email Configuration

One of the great benefits of mobile devices is the ability to access email while you're on the go. As long as you have connectivity to the Internet via either a wireless network or a cellular subscription service, you can usually access your email.

You'll learn more about protocols in Chapter 20, "Understanding Protocols," but as a short introduction, the following protocols are used for email:

- **Simple Mail Transport Protocol (SMTP).** This is the primary protocol used to send email.
- **Post Office Protocol version 3 (POP3).** This is the primary protocol used to receive email.
- **Internet Message Access Protocol (IMAP).** This protocol allows users to access and manage email stored on a mail server.

Configuring Settings

Internet Service Providers (ISPs) manage mail servers for their customers. Similarly, many organizations manage mail servers for their employees. To use these servers, you need to have an account on the server and know the full server name. After entering the correct information on the mobile device, you can use it to send and receive email.

As an example, Figure 9-4 shows the settings page to add a new email account on an iPad. The incoming mail server (using POP3) is named mail.GetCertifiedGetAhead.com, and the outgoing mail server using SMTP is named smtp.GetCertifiedGetAhead.com. This account (as with most accounts) requires a user name and password, so they are both added. After saving this information, I can send and receive email with this account on the iPad.

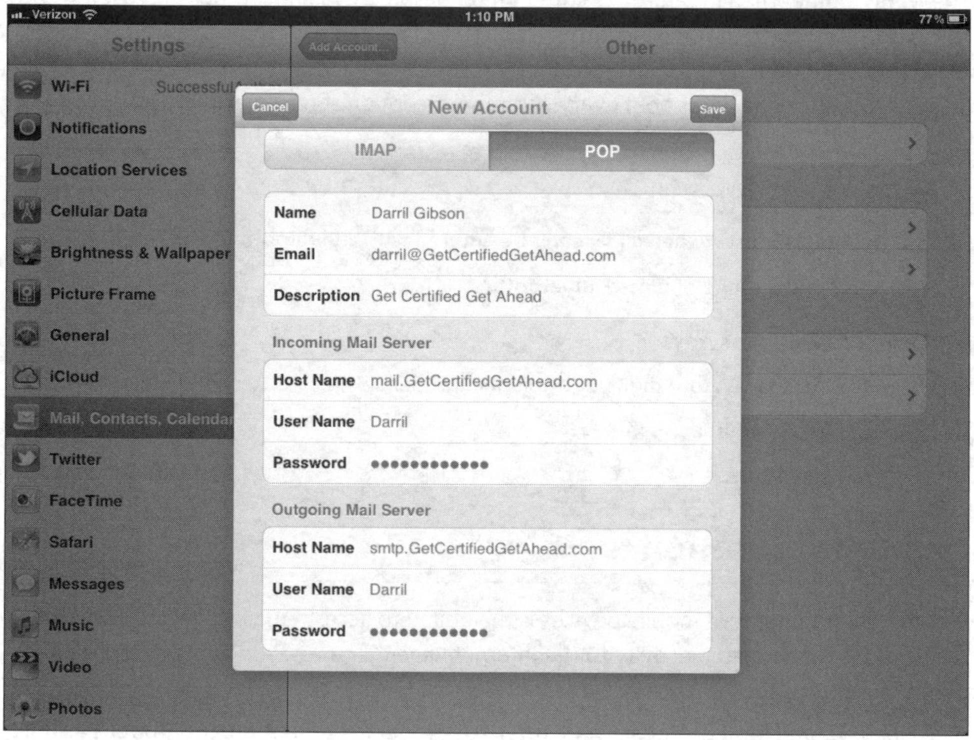

FIGURE 9-4 Configuring email on an iPad.

You need to enter the *fully-qualified domain name (FQDN)* of the mail server. The first part is known as the host or computer name, and everything following the first period is known as the domain name. For example, a computer named mail in the domain getcertifiedgetahead.com has an FQDN of mail.GetCertifiedGetAhead.com.

While the example in Figure 9-4 shows the settings, you probably don't have an account with GetCertifiedGetAhead.com. However, you might have a Microsoft Exchange email account with your company or a Gmail account through Google.

Microsoft Exchange is a server application that many organizations use for email. If your company is using Microsoft Exchange and it has been configured so that it is accessible via the Internet, you'll need the following information to connect:

- Email address of your account
- User name and password of the account
- Name of the Microsoft Exchange server

If you want to connect to a Gmail account, you can usually simply enter the email address and password to connect. Most email apps have the name of the Gmail server, but if you're prompted to add it, use smtp.gmail.com.

Email Port Settings

Occasionally, you're required to enter port data when configuring email settings. Chapter 20 provides more information about ports, but as an introduction, protocols are mapped to numbers called ports. These numbers indicate the type of data contained in traffic being sent over a network.

For example, when SMTP data is sent over the network, instead of including the words "Simple Mail Transport Protocol" within the data packet, it uses the port number of 25. Port numbers 0 through 1023 are known as well-known ports and are used for specific protocols. The well-known ports for the basic mail protocols are as follows:

- SMTP—port 25
- POP3—port 110
- IMAP—port 143

Many email servers require secure connections, and they use Secure Sockets Layer (SSL) or Transport Layer Security (TLS) to create secure connections. For example, SSL is used with Hypertext Transfer Protocol (HTTP) as HTTPS to create secure connections in web browsers. It's also used to create secure connections for many other protocols, including SMTP, POP3, and IMAP. If you're prompted to enter the SSL port number or the secure port number, use the following:

- SMTPS (SMTP over SSL)—port 465
- POP3S (POP3 over SSL)—port 995
- IMAPS (IMAP over SSL)—port 993

NOTE **PORTS**

Ports 993 and 995 are formally assigned to POPs and IMAPs, respectively. Port 465 is not formally assigned for SMTPS but is commonly used.

Using Mobile Devices

Mobile devices have touchscreens that allow you to control the actions by touch using specific gestures. If you've never used the devices, the gestures might take a moment to get used to. However, when you understand the basic motions, most mobile devices are remarkably easy to use. The common gestures are:

- **Tap.** You can select items with a single tap with any finger. You simply touch the screen by using a quick up-and-down motion with a finger. It is similar to clicking an item with a mouse.

- **Double-Tap.** Double-tapping is done with two quick taps and is similar to double-clicking an item with a mouse. It will often allow you to zoom in or zoom out on an item.

- **Flick.** You can flick the screen to scroll up or down or to pan from side to side. This is done by placing your finger on the screen and quickly swiping it in the desired direction. This is sometimes called *fling*.

- **Touch and Hold.** In this action, you touch a selection but don't remove your finger. Different items react differently to this action. For example, if you do this on the iPad's main screen, the items will shake and you can move them or press the X to delete them. This is sometimes called *press* or *long press*.

- **Drag.** Some items can be moved with a drag action. You select an item with your finger and then drag your finger across the screen to move the selected item. This is sometimes called *pan* or *scroll*.

- **Pinch.** This is commonly done by touching the screen with your finger and thumb at the same time and dragging them closer together, as if you were pinching the screen. It will often zoom in closer. For example, if you do this with a picture or a map, you can zoom in. You can also do this with two fingers instead of a finger and a thumb. Pinch is sometimes called *pinch close*.

- **Spread.** This is similar to the finger pinch but is done in the opposite direction. You touch the screen with your finger and thumb (or with two fingers) at the same place and spread them apart. It will often zoom out. Spread is sometimes called *pinch open*.

These capabilities are available on touch-based devices using two important technologies: multitouch and touch flow.

Multitouch refers to a device's ability to sense a user touching the surface at two or more places at a time. This is important when a user is doing pinch and spread gestures.

Touch flow refers to the ability of the screen to recognize users moving their finger across the screen. This is important when a user is doing flick gestures and when doing pinch and spread gestures.

EXAM TIP

Touch flow and multitouch are two primary capabilities supported by the touch interface on mobile phones and tablets.

Synchronizing Data

Synchronization is the process of storing the same data in two separate locations and ensuring it's the same in both places. For example, if you add music, pictures, or contacts to an iPad, you can synchronize it with a PC so that the same music, pictures, and contacts are on the PC.

Synchronizing also provides you with a backup. If you lose the data on the device (or lose the device), you still have a copy of the data. You can restore the data onto the original device or another device from the synchronized data.

Most mobile devices give you the ability to synchronize just about any type of data. This includes music, videos, pictures, contacts, programs, and email.

NOTE AUTHORIZING A COMPUTER

As a security precaution, you are often required to authorize a computer with a mobile device. This usually requires you to enter a user name and password associated only with you. This helps prevent someone from accessing your data through a synchronization program on their computer.

Installing Synchronization Applications

Mobile devices commonly have specific applications you use for synchronization. For example, you can use the iTunes application to synchronize most iOS-based devices. iTunes is available as a free download from the Apple website.

EXAM TIP

You need administrative rights to install an application on most systems. This is granted to users differently, but if the user does not have administrative rights, the installation will fail.

Connection Types for Synchronization

The connection type you use when synchronizing mobile devices is dependent on the device. However, the most common method is by using a USB cable from the device to a PC. After you connect the device, you can initiate the synchronization process with the application.

Many devices use USB cables such as the ones discussed in Chapter 5, "Exploring Peripherals and Expansion Cards." The cables have a Standard-A connector on one end to connect to a computer and a Mini-B, Micro-A, or Micro-B connector that connects to the device. Some devices have special one-of-a-kind connections. They require a cable with a unique connection on the device and a Standard-A USB connector on the other end.

Instead of connecting using a cable, you might be able to connect using one of the following methods:

- **Wireless or cellular to the Internet.** Using the cloud for synchronization is becoming more common. You'll need to first connect to the Internet via either a wireless network or a cellular connection. When connected, you can synchronize. You can also set up many devices to automatically synchronize at different times without any interaction.

- **Bluetooth.** You need to ensure that the devices are paired before the synchronization will work.

- **IR.** Some devices can use IR to connect to a PC and synchronize. Of course this requires the PC to have an IR interface and also requires a clear line of sight between the two.

✔ **Quick Check**

1. What technology allows a tablet to sense a user touching the screen in two places at the same time?

2. What types of connections are commonly used to synchronize mobile devices?

Quick Check Answers

1. Multitouch.

2. USB, wireless, cellular, Bluetooth, and IR.

Securing Mobile Devices

If lost or stolen, mobile devices have tools that you can use to help protect them or the data stored on them. These tools are available on many smartphones and tablets.

> **NOTE DEFENSE IN DEPTH**
>
> Thieves have many tools at their disposal to circumvent or override many security settings. None of the security methods described here are completely reliable, but by using a variety of tools, you can increase the security. Using multiple layers of security is referred to as *defense in depth*.

Passcode Locks

A passcode is a simple password or set of digits that you must enter to start using the device. On some devices, it's called a *screen lock,* and it works like a password-protected screensaver. On other devices, it is a four-digit PIN. When the device is idle for a period of time, it locks. The user must then enter the passcode to use the device.

If you lose the device or it's stolen, another person won't be able to easily access the device because the person won't know the passcode. Of course, when a user writes the passcode on the device or attaches a sticky note with the passcode to the device, it defeats the purpose. You may laugh, but more than a few users have done this.

Failed Logon Attempts Restrictions

In addition to using a passcode lock, many devices include failed logon restrictions. For example, Figure 9-5 shows the screen for an iPad Passcode Lock. The Erase Data section can be turned on so that all data on the iPad is erased when the user enters the wrong passcode too many times. This prevents a thief from accessing data on a device by entering all the possible combinations.

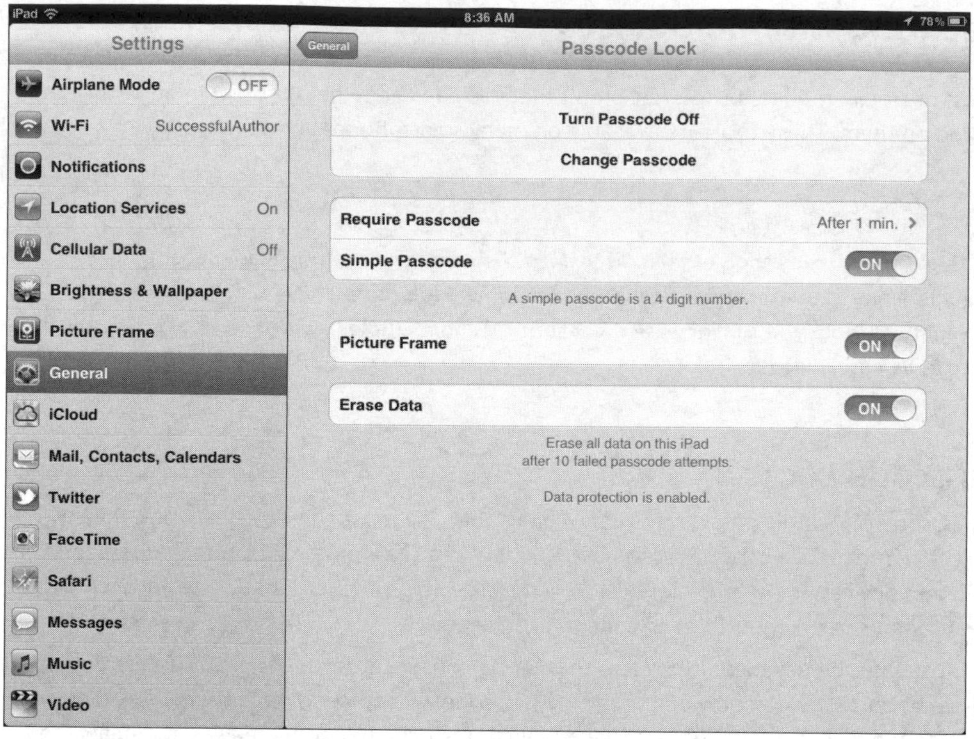

FIGURE 9-5 Enabling the Passcode Lock and Erase Data as a failed logon restriction.

Remote Wipe

A remote wipe is a signal that, when sent to a lost device, removes all data on the system. If you lose the device or it's stolen, you can send the remote wipe signal to the device and it will wipe it clean. While it won't get the device back to you, it will ensure that any sensitive data on the device cannot be used by someone else.

> **EXAM TIP**
>
> The remote wipe capability must be enabled before the device is lost. If it is lost, you can then send the remote wipe signal to the device. Many mobile devices send a confirmation email when the remote wipe signal has been received and has erased the data on the device.

Locator Applications

Many applications are available to identify the location of a lost device. They use the GPS capability of the device and can pinpoint its location. These are useful if you've recently lost the device, and especially useful if it has been stolen.

Figure 9-6 shows an example of a locator application on an iPad. The application allows you to zoom in on the exact street address or zoom out. In the figure, I've zoomed it out to show a general location on the East Coast of the United States.

FIGURE 9-6 Locating an iPad.

This application also includes the following capabilities:

- **Play Sound.** This sends a signal to play a sound on the device. It's useful if you've lost it between the cushions of a couch or somewhere else within earshot. The sound continues to play until it's dismissed on the device.

- **Send Message.** It's possible that a Good Samaritan has found your device and would love to return it if only she knew who you were. You can send a message to the device with your contact information to let the person know that you lost it, you miss it, and you'd love to have it back.

- **Remote Lock.** Remote Lock works similarly to a passcode lock except that you can send the signal remotely. After it's set, users can't access the device unless they know the passcode.

- **Remote Wipe.** This sends the remote wipe signal to remove all data from the device.

- **Email When Found.** If you send any signal to the device, you can have an email sent to you when the signal has been received by the device. This provides verification that it has been completed.

Remote Backup Applications

Many devices support storing backup data in the cloud. For example, Android-based systems support Android backup, which allows you to back up all data to the cloud (the Internet). Windows 8 has a backup ability using Windows Azure–based technologies. Windows Azure is a group of cloud-based technologies used in several different Microsoft applications.

Apple's iOS-based systems allow users to back up their data and settings with iTunes, an application running on a PC. Recently, Apple launched iCloud Backup, which can automatically back up photos, accounts, documents, and settings. It senses when the unit is plugged in and receiving a charge, locked (indicating it isn't in use), or connected to a wireless network. Apple provides 5 GB of free storage, and you can purchase additional storage if you need it.

If the device is lost or destroyed, or you've sent a remote wipe signal to it, you can use the cloud-based backup to restore the data.

Antivirus Software

Sadly, malicious software (malware) is making its way onto mobile devices. Chapter 26, "Recognizing Malware and Other Threats," covers malware in much more depth, but as an introduction, malware includes viruses, worms, Trojans, rootkits, spyware, and more.

In January 2011 there were a reported 80 infected Android apps. This grew to more than 400 infected apps by June 2011. Compared with the millions of viruses that can infect PC-based systems, this number is small. However, they have started and they're on the rise.

The Apple iOS has had relatively few problems with malware. One of the things that Apple does is vigorously screen apps before they are offered for sale in the Apple App Store. It is difficult for an attacker to create an infected app and get it into the store.

Google Play requires developers to create an account before they can upload apps. The app is made available almost immediately, and Google doesn't follow the same vigorous screening process used for apps in the Apple App Store. However, if an infected app is discovered, it is quickly removed from the store, and Google has information about the developer who uploaded it. If users download apps from other sources, there is a higher level of risk.

EXAM TIP

One of the safest steps you can take to protect mobile devices against malware infection is to purchase apps only from the official stores. This includes Apple's App Store, Google Play, and Microsoft's Marketplace. Other sources aren't policed as vigorously, making it easier for attackers to upload malware.

At this writing, very few antivirus programs are available for mobile devices. However, as the malware for these devices increases, you can expect antivirus programs to become available.

Patching/Operating System Updates

Bugs and security issues are detected with any operating system after it is released. As issues are detected, the vendor updates and releases patches and operating system updates. As a best practice, you should always ensure that your system is up to date. This includes the operating systems on mobile devices and the operating systems on any desktop PC.

The method of patching the system varies by device. Windows-based systems can be configured to automatically download and install patches and updates without any user intervention. Apple iOS-based systems require you to connect your device to a PC with a USB cable and use iTunes to update it. Android-based systems often prompt you when an update is available.

EXAM TIP

Before applying a patch or doing an update, it's always a good idea to synchronize the device. This will save all your applications, data, and settings, and if something goes wrong during the update, you can fully restore the device.

✔ **Quick Check**

1. What can be enabled to prevent a thief from easily using a stolen mobile device?

2. What is used to remotely erase data on a lost device?

Quick Check Answers

1. Passcode lock.

2. Remote wipe.

Chapter Summary

- Tablets are not upgradable or serviceable by technicians in the field. In contrast, technicians can upgrade and service laptops.

- The orientation of a tablet's screen is automatically sensed by an accelerometer and/or gyroscope. Applications use this data to change the display for the user, such as switching between landscape mode and portrait mode.

- GPS identifies the exact location of the device. It can be used to locate a lost device and is also used by geotracking. Geotracking records the location of a device and stores the data in a log on the device.

- Apple devices use iOS, a closed source operating system that is not licensed to any other company. Applications can be purchased only via Apple's App Store.

- Android is an open source operating system developed by a consortium of companies led by Google. It is used on mobile devices created by many different companies. Users primarily buy applications from the Google Play website, but applications can be purchased through other sources.

- Mobile devices commonly connect to the Internet through wireless or cellular connections. Disabling these connections reduces battery consumption. Other connections are Bluetooth and infrared.

- Bluetooth devices need to be paired before they can be used. In some cases, a PIN is needed. If you are unable to enter a PIN on a device (such as on a headset), the common PIN code is either 0000 or the last four digits of the device's serial number.

- Class 2 Bluetooth connections have a range of 10 meters (about 33 feet). Class 1 and Class 3 Bluetooth connections have a range of 100 meters (about 328 feet) and 5 meters (about 16 feet), respectively. IR connections are limited by line of sight.

- When configuring email, you'll need to know the full name of the SMTP, POP3, and/or IMAP servers, depending on what the email server is using. You might also need to know the basic and secure ports used for the connections.

- The basic and secure port numbers are SMTP port 25, SMTPS port 465, POP3 port 110, POP3S port 995, IMAP port 143, and IMAPS port 993.

- Tablets have a touch interface using touch flow and multitouch capabilities to sense different gestures.

- Synchronization allows you to keep a backup of all the data and settings for a device. Many devices allow you to synchronize with a PC through a USB cable, and some devices allow you to synchronize through a cloud-based service on the Internet.

- Security for mobile devices is enhanced through several features, including passcode locks, remote wipe, and GPS locator applications.

- When updates and patches are available, they often include security enhancements and should be installed as soon as possible. Data and settings should be backed up before doing an update.

Chapter Review

Use the following questions to test your knowledge of the information in this chapter. The answers to these questions, and the explanations of why each answer choice is correct or incorrect, are located in the "Answers" section at the end of this chapter.

1. Of the following choices, what would cause a device to change from portrait mode to landscape mode when the device is moved?

    A. Touch flow

    B. Accelerometer

    C. Gyro

    D. Geotracking

2. Of the following choices, what represents a benefit to users of purchasing apps only through Apple's App Store?

    A. Cheaper than purchasing at a store

    B. Automatically includes source code

    C. Upgrades are automatic

    D. Less chance of downloading malicious software

3. What is required before using two Bluetooth devices together?

    A. Subscribe to a cellular plan

    B. Connect to a Wi-Fi network

    C. Enable POP3

    D. Pair them

4. You are helping a user configure email on a tablet. It is prompting you for the port used for secure POP3. What is the most likely port number you should enter?

    A. 25

    B. 110

    C. 993

    D. 995

5. A business owner wants to ensure that her tablet is as secure as possible. Of the following choices, what should she enable? (Choose all that apply.)

    A. Remote wipe

    B. GPS location services

    C. Passcode lock

    D. Bluetooth pairing

6. What should you do before updating the operating system of a mobile device?

    A. Flash the BIOS

    B. Back up the device

    C. Enable remote wipe

    D. Disable Wi-Fi and cellular connections

Answers

This section contains the answers to the questions for the Lesson Review in this chapter.

1. **Correct Answer:** B

    A. **Incorrect:** Touch flow is used to sense when a user moves a finger across a touch screen.

    B. **Correct:** Devices commonly include accelerometers (and electronic gyroscopes) to sense the orientation of the device and change the display.

    C. **Incorrect:** A gyro is type of sandwich sold in many Greek restaurants, wrapped in a flatbread or pita.

    D. **Incorrect:** Geotracking uses recorded GPS information to track the past locations of a device.

2. **Correct Answer:** D

    A. **Incorrect:** You can't purchase Apple Apps at a store, so there is no cost benefit.

    B. **Incorrect:** Purchased software is typically closed source, so it does not include the source code.

    C. **Incorrect:** While software can often be upgraded, upgrades are not automatic with Apple App Store apps.

    D. **Correct:** Apple screens all software in their App Store, so software purchased through their site is less likely to be infected with a virus or other malicious software.

3. **Correct Answer:** D

    A. **Incorrect:** Cellular plans are used with smartphones and some mobile devices, but they are unrelated to Bluetooth.

    B. **Incorrect:** Connecting to a wireless network is not required to pair two Bluetooth devices.

    C. **Incorrect:** Post Office Protocol v3 (POP3) is configured for email but not for Bluetooth.

    D. **Correct:** Bluetooth devices must be paired before they can be used together. This can be automatic or can require entering a PIN on one or both devices.

4. **Correct Answer:** D

   A. **Incorrect:** Port 25 is the well-known port for Simple Mail Transport Protocol (SMTP).

   B. **Incorrect:** Port 110 is the well-known port for Post Office Protocol3 (POP3).

   C. **Incorrect:** Port 993 is the well-known port for IMAP over Secure Sockets Layer (IMAPS).

   D. **Correct:** Port 995 is the well-known port for POP3 over Secure Sockets Layer (POP3S).

5. **Correct Answers:** A, B, C

   A. **Correct:** Remote wipe allows her to send a remote signal to a lost device to delete all information on the device.

   B. **Correct:** Global Positioning System (GPS) location services allow a lost device to be located.

   C. **Correct:** Passcode locks require a user to enter a passcode before using a device.

   D. **Incorrect:** Bluetooth pairing is done to match two Bluetooth devices. However, you don't enable Bluetooth pairing. Instead, you pair devices after enabling Bluetooth.

6. **Correct Answer:** B

   A. **Incorrect:** Flashing the BIOS is commonly done for a motherboard BIOS to update it. It can be done on a mobile device, but it is not necessary before an update.

   B. **Correct:** It's possible to lose data, applications, and settings during an update, so all data should be backed up before an update whenever possible.

   C. **Incorrect:** Remote wipe is a security feature that allows you to remove data on a lost device.

   D. **Incorrect:** It is not necessary to disable connectivity during an update, and sometimes the connectivity is required.

CHAPTER 10

Working with Customers

You can be the best technician in the world, but if you aren't able to work with customers, you might end up with more opportunities to update your résumé than you'll care to have. The most successful technicians have a good mix of technical knowledge, communication skills, and troubleshooting ability. This chapter covers some core skills related to communicating with customers and troubleshooting problems effectively. Additionally, it ties some of the concepts from previous chapters together so that you can help customers identify the right components to meet their needs.

Exam 220-801 objectives in this chapter:

- 1.9 Evaluate and select appropriate components for a custom configuration, to meet customer specifications or needs.
    - Graphic / CAD / CAM design workstation
        - Powerful processor
        - High-end video
        - Maximum RAM
    - Audio/Video editing workstation
        - Specialized audio and video card
        - Large fast hard drive
        - Dual monitors
    - Virtualization workstation
        - Maximum RAM and CPU cores
    - Gaming PC
        - Powerful processor
        - High-end video/specialized GPU
        - Better sound card
        - High-end cooling
    - Home Theater PC
        - Surround sound audio
        - HDMI output

- HTPC compact form factor
- TV tuner
- Standard thick client
  - Desktop applications
  - Meets recommended requirements for running Windows
- Thin client
  - Basic applications
  - Meets minimum requirements for running Windows
- Home Server PC
  - Media streaming
  - File sharing
  - Print sharing
  - Gigabit NIC
  - RAID array
- 5.2 Explain environmental impacts and the purpose of environmental controls.
  - Temperature, humidity level awareness and proper ventilation
  - Protection from airborne particles
    - Enclosures
    - Air filters
- 5.3 Given a scenario, demonstrate proper communication and professionalism.
  - Use proper language – avoid jargon, acronyms, slang when applicable
  - Maintain a positive attitude
  - Listen and do not interrupt the customer
  - Be culturally sensitive
  - Be on time (if late contact the customer)
  - Avoid distractions
    - Personal calls
    - Talking to co-workers while interacting with customers
    - Personal interruptions
  - Dealing with difficult customer or situation
    - Avoid arguing with customers and/or being defensive
    - Do not minimize customer's problems
    - Avoid being judgmental
    - Clarify customer statements (ask open ended questions to narrow the scope of the problem, restate the issue or question to verify understanding)

- Set and meet expectations/timeline and communicate status with the customer
  - Offer different repair/replacement options if applicable
  - Provide proper documentation on the services provided
  - Follow up with customer/user at a later date to verify satisfaction
- Deal appropriately with customers confidential materials
  - Located on a computer, desktop, printer, etc
- 5.4 Explain the fundamentals of dealing with prohibited content/activity.
  - First response
    - Identify
    - Report through proper channels
    - Data/device preservation
  - Use of documentation/documentation changes
  - Chain of custody
    - Tracking of evidence/documenting process

220-802 Exam objectives in this chapter:

- 1.9 Explain the basics of client-side virtualization.
  - Purpose of virtual machines
  - Resource requirements
  - Emulator requirements
  - Security requirements
  - Network requirements
  - Hypervisor
- 4.1 Given a scenario, explain the troubleshooting theory.
  - Identify the problem
    - Question the user and identify user changes to computer and perform backups before making changes
  - Establish a theory of probable cause (question the obvious)
  - Test the theory to determine cause
    - Once theory is confirmed determine next steps to resolve problem
    - If theory is not confirmed re-establish new theory or escalate
  - Establish a plan of action to resolve the problem and implement the solution
  - Verify full system functionality and if applicable implement preventive measures
  - Document findings, actions and outcomes

Interacting with Customers

Being a good personal computer (PC) technician requires more than just knowing about the hardware and software and how to fix the systems. An extremely important element is the ability to interact with customers. You might be the best technician in the world, but if you can't maintain a professional attitude when working with customers, you'll either be unemployed or find yourself working alone in an isolated room, with no room for advancement.

An important principle to remember is that you and the customer need to have a collaborative relationship. If you think about a customer as an adversary, you'll end up with an adversarial relationship. If you think about customers as collaborators, you're much more likely to have rewarding experiences. Remember, they need you to fix the problem. You need them for a job.

Communication and Professionalism

Effective communication skills combined with a professional attitude are easily the most important skills you'll need when interacting with customers. They'll help you collect information about the problem, diffuse difficult situations, and get the customer working with you instead of against you.

> **EXAM TIP**
>
> CompTIA took out customer service objectives in an earlier version of their A+ exams. However, they received a lot of feedback from companies about the importance of communication skills when working with customers and have since added these objectives back in. You can often answer the questions if you simply apply the golden rule—treat customers as you want to be treated when you are a customer.

Use Proper Language

Whenever possible, you should avoid jargon, acronyms, and slang. I sometimes watch "Through the Wormhole," hosted by Morgan Freeman, which covers some pretty complex topics. I have great respect for the scientists on the show who can explain complex scientific theories in easy terms. They use terms and analogies that just about anyone can understand, and it's clear that they are really trying to help viewers understand.

If you want to ensure that customers understand what you're talking about, you need to use language they can understand. Imagine that a system was having problems due to dust buildup within the case and around the CPU fan. After cleaning it out, you could tell the customer, "The BIOS was reporting a thermal problem from the CPU causing intermittent reboots. The internal cooling devices weren't able to regulate the temperature due to foreign debris, so I used an ESD-safe device to remove the excess particles."

Or, you could say, "It had a lot of dust built up, so I cleaned it out."

If you give the first explanation, the customer might not understand and might think that you're just full of yourself. Hearing the second explanation, the customer will understand and might even ask what to do to prevent it from getting so dirty.

EXAM TIP

Avoid jargon and acronyms when talking with customers. Jargon is often used when talking with other technicians, but when talking to customers, you should use language that anyone can understand.

Maintain a Positive Attitude

Maintaining a positive attitude is an important part of troubleshooting and working with others. You will run into problems—that's unavoidable. However, how you respond when you run into these problems is entirely your choice.

From the customer's point of view, they are coming to you because they have a problem they can't solve. They might be frustrated and even angry. However, they are not angry at you; they are angry at the situation. As long as you remain positive, you have a much better chance at getting them to remember that you're there to help.

Listen and Don't Interrupt Customers

When you're working with customers, it's important to take the time to listen to what they're saying and not interrupt them. Give them time to explain the problem. The customer might not know what is important and what isn't important. However, giving the customer time to talk and listening to what they have to say will help you get a better idea of the problem.

After listening, it's useful to restate the issue or symptoms. This lets the customer know that you have been listening and that you understand the problem. Sometimes, you might need to restate the issue a little differently to clarify it, or you might need to ask questions to get more information.

When asking questions, it's often useful to ask open-ended questions. An open-ended question is any question that can't be answered with a one-word response such as yes or no. For example, "Can you explain the problem?" or "What type of symptoms are you seeing?" are open-ended questions.

Communicate Status

After you have an understanding of a problem, you'll have a good idea of how long it'll take to resolve it. Some problems are relatively easy to fix and can be resolved in minutes. Other problems can take much longer. For example, if you need to order new hardware and wait for it to arrive, it could take days or weeks to complete the repair.

Most people are reasonable, and by communicating the status, you can help set their expectations. If you tell them it will take a week or longer because a part needs to be ordered, most people will understand. They might not be happy with the situation, but they'll understand. However, if you don't tell them anything, they might expect it to be fixed within minutes and will get more and more frustrated as the days drag by.

In addition to communicating the status, consider providing additional information, including the following:

- **Options.** Based on the problem, there might be different repair or replacement options available. If there are options, let the customer know so that the customer can decide based on his or her needs.
- **Documentation on services.** If your company has specific documentation for services, ensure that you provide it to the customer.
- **Follow-up.** A simple call to the customer at a later date can help you verify that the customer is satisfied. If they aren't, you'll have an opportunity to fix the problem. If they are satisfied, this follow-up helps build rapport, showing that you care.

REAL WORLD **DEFUSE SITUATIONS WITH A SOFT VOICE**

I remember dealing with a customer once who was extremely frustrated and angry. Another technician was successful only at getting the customer angrier, and the customer was passed to me. I was able to ask a couple of open-ended questions to get the customer to explain the situation, and during this time, I was well aware how loud the customer was.

However, I didn't respond with the same volume. Instead, I used a normal voice and when the customer became louder, I became quieter. At some point, the customer recognized the huge disparity in our volumes and recognized that I wasn't angry but truly trying to help. He became embarrassed and apologetic.

At that point, we began making much better progress at solving his problem. I could just as easily have matched this customer's volume and anger, but it's unlikely that we would have solved his problem. Instead, I recognized the customer wasn't angry with me, and I did my best to calmly focus on the problem. You'll likely come across an angry customer at some point, and it's best to have different methods you can use to defuse the situation and help the customer.

Dealing with Difficult Customers or Situations

Not all customers calm down; this is sad but true. How you respond to these customers can make the difference between the customer becoming angrier and an adversary, or calmer and a collaborator.

There are a few things you can do in these situations, including the following:

- **Avoid arguing or being defensive.** Under no circumstances should you argue with a customer. That will only make the situation worse.
- **Do not minimize a customer's problems.** Customers don't come for help for problems that they know how to solve. It might be a simple problem for you because

you're knowledgeable and experienced, but it's best not to minimize the impact on the customer. A little empathy goes a long way.

- **Avoid being judgmental.** If you take a judgmental attitude toward customers in general, this is likely to come across in your dealings with customers. You'll often end up with an adversarial relationship with customers without understanding why. For example, some technicians use cutesy phrases camouflaging their dislike of customers. I've heard technicians refer to a problem as an ST1 problem (pronounced as *S T one*), or an ID 10 T problem (pronounced as *I D ten T*). What they mean is that the customer is as dumb as a stone (S T one) or is an idiot (I D 10 T). You can feel when someone is talking down to you or acting in a condescending manner. Other people can feel it when you're doing it to them.

It's valuable to remember that customers do not start out being angry with you. They might be frustrated or angry with the situation, but not with you as a person. However, if you respond to the customer's emotions instead of to the problem, the customer can end up becoming angry with you.

EXAM TIP

It's never acceptable to yell or argue with a customer. If a situation is escalating and you find yourself getting angry or losing your control, find a way to defuse the situation. If that's not possible, seek assistance based on your company policies.

It's possible that you are doing all the right things but the customer is not calming down and is not giving you the information you need to solve the problem. In that case, most organizations have a method of passing the customer off to someone else. In some cases, this is done by referring the customer to a manager or, sometimes, passing the customer to another technician who might be able to get the customer to calm down. Managers will often have training for how to deal with these customers and will use forceful, assertive language to get unreasonable customers to calm down.

Be Culturally Sensitive

A culture has a set of attitudes, values, and practices that are shared among people within that culture. Some language and communication techniques can be completely acceptable in one culture but quite offensive in another culture.

For example, if you flick your hand from under your chin outward, it means very little to many people living in the United States. However, do this to someone from Italy and you might have a fight on your hands. Being culturally sensitive means that you recognize that there are differences among cultures and that you respect those differences.

Respect Customer Materials

When you assist customers at their work area, they'll often have work materials open and accessible. This could include open files or emails, and papers on their desk or printer. You should respect the privacy of the individual and not read through the material.

If material is in your way, you might want to hand it to the customer. For example, if you're called to work on a printer and it has printouts marked as confidential, hand these to the customer as you begin your work.

Rebooting systems often solves many problems, so you might choose that course of action. Let customers know that you plan on rebooting a system so that they have a chance to save and close any files they're working on. Rebooting without saving files could result in the loss of the customer's data or recent work.

Be Professional

Successful technicians regularly demonstrate common professional behaviors. These are many of the same behaviors that you would want professionals to demonstrate when you are the customer. Some of these include the following:

- **Be on time.** If you tell customers that you'll be there at a certain time, they'll be waiting. If something is holding you up, contact the customer and let them know.
- **Avoid distractions and interruptions.** This includes not taking personal phone calls. If a coworker contacts you for help or assistance, offer to help them when you're done with the customer.

Responding to Prohibited Content/Activity

In the course of your job, you might occasionally run across content or activity that is prohibited. Prohibited content and activity is anything that is against the law and anything that is counter to an organization's policy.

It could be an action on the part of an external attacker or by an employee. Within the realm of information technology (IT), this is often referred to as a security incident. Some examples include the following:

- **Unauthorized applications.** Many organizations prohibit users from installing applications on their systems, but you might find an unauthorized application running on a user's system.
- **Unauthorized drives.** Some organizations restrict the use of USB flash drives as a security precaution. Other times, any types of external drives are prohibited.
- **Unauthorized access.** This includes unauthorized individuals in secured areas of a building or the unauthorized access of sensitive data.
- **Any types of attacks.** Attacks commonly come from external sources but can also come from a malicious insider.

- **Online activities.** Some online activities might be illegal and/or counter to the organization's policy. For example, gambling during company time is very likely prohibited.
- **Illegal pictures or video.** Offensive pictures and video might be more than just inappropriate in a workplace; they could be illegal, depending on the content.

> **NOTE   NSFW**
>
> NSFW is an acronym for *not safe for work*, or *not suitable for work*. There might be activities that people are comfortable with at home but should not engage in at work. It includes going to some forums and blogs, viewing pictures of people in various stages of undress, and forwarding pictures or jokes that can offend others. Many employees have been reprimanded and even fired for engaging in NSFW activities because they fall into the category of prohibited content and activity.

First Response

Within IT security, the first IT professionals on the scene of an incident are referred to first responders and they provide the *first response* to an incident. You can compare them to first responders in the medical community.

Medical first responders are dedicated, trained individuals, such as emergency medical treatment (EMT) personnel, who respond to auto accidents. Their goal is to treat and stabilize injured people and get them to a medical facility if needed. They aren't doctors, and they aren't expected to do surgery. However, they can identify life-threatening injuries, know when to call for help, and know what to do to preserve life until help arrives or until they get a patient to a hospital.

Similarly, you might be the first responder for a security incident. You aren't expected to know how to perform in-depth computer forensics. However, you'll be expected to identify an incident, know how to report it, and know how to preserve evidence.

If you do come across any prohibited content or activity, you'll need to take the following three basic actions:

- **Identify.** This is where you recognize that the content or activity is either not authorized or illegal. Understanding your organization's security policies will help you identify incidents. If it's prohibited by a company security policy, it's an incident.
- **Report through proper channels.** If you run across content or activity that is clearly illegal, you're obligated to report it. If you don't report it, you might inadvertently become an accessory to the crime. Organizations commonly have procedures to follow in these situations, and your first step is often to report it to your supervisor.
- **Preserve data or devices.** Any data or devices involved in the incident need to be protected as evidence. Often, the best thing you can do is not touch it and not allow anyone else to touch it until help arrives. Turning a system off or manipulating the keyboard or mouse can destroy or modify evidence.

Many organizations include specific procedures to isolate or contain an incident in certain situations. For example, if a system is infected with a virus or worm, procedures often state that the network cable should be disconnected from the system. This isolates the system and prevents the infection from spreading to other systems.

Protecting Evidence and Chain of Custody

If there is any possibility that evidence needs to be collected and analyzed for an incident, the first step is to protect it.

For example, if a computer is running, don't turn it off or reboot it. Data within the system's random access memory (RAM) can be retrieved with forensic tools, but if you turn it off, it is lost. Similarly, you should not access any files. Files have attributes that identify when they were last accessed or modified. If you access or modify the files, these attributes will be changed and the original evidence is lost.

> **EXAM TIP**
>
> Data in a computer's RAM is lost when the power is removed. This RAM is commonly referred to as *volatile RAM*. Computer forensics tools are available to retrieve data from volatile RAM, but they cannot retrieve the data after the system has been turned off.

Occasionally, you might be required to collect evidence. If so, you should ensure that it is controlled at all times. This means that someone has it in their physical possession or that it is secured, such as in a locked cabinet. You shouldn't just leave it on a desk where anyone can access and manipulate it.

Additionally, you should establish a *chain of custody* log to verify that the evidence has been controlled. A chain of custody log verifies that evidence presented in court is the same evidence that was collected. For example, if you must collect an external hard drive or USB flash drive, you should establish a chain of custody log to document how the drive was protected after it was collected.

✔ Quick Check

1. You are due to arrive at a customer's location in 10 minutes, but you'll be late. What should you do?
2. You have come across a security incident. What three things should you do?

Quick Check Answers

1. Inform the customer that you'll be late.
2. Identify, report, and preserve data or devices.

Troubleshooting Theory

An important part of working as a PC technician is troubleshooting. Troubleshooting is more than just fixing a system. Successful technicians employ several steps in the troubleshooting process to ensure that they can identify and resolve problems as efficiently as possible and not cause additional problems.

CompTIA has specifically stated six steps in troubleshooting theory, and you'll need to know each of these and in the following order:

1. Identify the problem.

2. Establish a theory of probable cause.

3. Test the theory to determine cause.

4. Establish a plan of action to resolve the problem, and implement the solution.

5. Verify full system functionality, and if applicable, implement preventive measures.

6. Document findings, actions, and outcomes.

EXAM TIP

The preceding steps are not the only troubleshooting steps that you're likely to see in your career. However, know them exactly when preparing for the A+ exam. CompTIA is known to ask questions specifically related to the troubleshooting theory, which they include with the A+ objectives.

Identify the Problem

In this step, you'll gather information about the problem. Many problems occur because of a recent action, so it's important to ask the user whether anything has recently changed. Users often make changes to their system and don't recognize the impact that the change can have.

When questioning users, it's very easy for them to get defensive and stop giving you helpful answers, especially if a technician asks questions in a threatening manner. For example, ask someone, "What did you do?" and the answer is very often, "Nothing."

However, if you think of the user as a partner in your quest to resolve the problem, you can start a conversation and get them to help you. For example, asking something like, "When did it last work?" and "Do you know whether anything has changed since then?" doesn't attack the user and is likely to get you more information.

Also, if a user is working in an environment with other users, it's worthwhile to ask them whether they're having the same problem. This is especially true when troubleshooting network problems. If it's affecting one user, the problem is likely with that user's system. If it's affecting all users, the problem is likely a network problem.

Establish a Theory of Probable Cause

In the next step, you'll make an educated guess to identify the source of the problem. During this step, it's important to question the obvious. A useful troubleshooting practice is to check the easy things first. If a computer display is dark, an obvious theory is that the monitor isn't plugged in and turned on or that the computer isn't plugged in and turned on.

Test the Theory to Determine Cause

Next, you'll test your theory by looking at the system. If it's a simple problem, such as a blank display, it can be as easy as checking all the plugs and power connections. Some problems aren't so simple and obvious, so you might need to take a few steps to test the theory. You'll probably be using different hardware or operating system tools described throughout this book to help identify the problem.

It's very possible that your educated guess about the cause wasn't correct. If so, look for a new theory of the probable cause.

Establishing and testing are listed as separate steps, but experienced technicians go through the steps very quickly. For example, if you have a blank display, you might go through the following steps.

- **Theory:** Computer not on.
    - **Test theory:** Check to see whether it's on.
- **Theory:** Monitor not plugged in or turned on.
    - **Test theory:** Check for power indicator on monitor.
- **Theory:** Monitor not plugged into correct graphics port.
    - **Test theory**: Verify cable plugged into extension card port instead of into motherboard onboard connector.

If you run out of ideas, you might need to escalate the problem by calling in some help. Many organizations have several levels of technicians. If a technician on one level can't solve the problem, the technician escalates it to the next level, and a technician from that level will try to resolve it.

Establish a Plan of Action and Implement It

After you've confirmed your theory, you'll need to establish a plan of action to resolve the problem and implement the solution. Ideally, this will solve the problem. If not, you'll need to go back to step 2 to establish a different theory.

It's important to take your time with this. Experienced technicians sometimes use the term *shotgunning*, referring to a process of just trying everything without taking the time to think things through or analyze the problem.

Consider the following problem. You turn a computer on, and the fans are spinning but nothing else is working. This could be a faulty power supply, faulty CPU, faulty motherboard, faulty RAM, or faulty expansion card. You could just start replacing everything one by one. You might get lucky and fix the problem, but if you take the time to test your theories and implement fixes individually, you'll end up with better results.

- **Theory:** Faulty power supply.
    - **Test theory:** Measure voltages supplied via the primary motherboard connector and CPU power connector with the system turned on.
    - **Plan of action:** If these are out of tolerance, replace the power supply. If you replace the power supply without checking the voltages, you might be replacing a good component and inadvertently cause another problem in the process.
- **Theory:** Faulty expansion card. In some cases, a faulty expansion card can load down a system and prevent anything from working.
    - **Test theory:** About the only way to test this theory is to remove all the cards to see whether the problem disappears. You can then reinstall the cards one by one to see if the problem comes back when you install a card.
    - **Plan of action:** This will be time-consuming and very risky. It's very possible for a card to be damaged while a technician is removing it. Additionally, it's very possible cables and connectors might not get returned to their original locations when the cards are reinstalled. This theory should not be tested before doing simpler checks, such as checking the power supply voltages.

When you're faced with a challenging problem, it's important to document your steps. Each time you test a theory, take some notes so that you can easily recall what you did, and list the results of your actions. If you end up working for several hours on a problem, you might find that your actions from a couple hours ago aren't crystal clear.

One more thing: if you implement a change and it doesn't resolve the problem, you should undo your change. This is especially important when making configuration changes. I've witnessed several problems that started as a simple configuration issue that could be resolved by making one change. However, technicians made multiple changes in an attempt to resolve the problem but never undid them. Eventually, the original problem is resolved, but unfortunately these other changes have caused a host of other problems.

Verify Full System Functionality

After implementing a solution, it's important to check out the entire system to ensure that it is operating as expected. For example, imagine that you're troubleshooting a printer with two paper trays. You could fix a problem with one paper tray, test it, and verify that it works. However, you should also check the second paper tray to ensure that you can print using this tray, too.

In some situations, preventive measures are needed when you implement a fix. For example, if you're troubleshooting a system and notice that the fans and the inside of the system are clogged with an excessive amount of dust, you should use the proper tools and vacuum it out.

Document Findings, Actions, and Outcomes

In the last step, you document what you did to resolve the problem. Many organizations have dedicated applications used to track all troubleshooting activity in trouble tickets. These trouble tickets track the progress until it's resolved. This information is searchable to allow technicians to easily share their knowledge or to research the solution to a previously solved problem.

For example, Microsoft uses a Knowledge Base (KB) system. Problems that have been troubleshot and resolved are documented as KB articles. If you're troubleshooting a software problem that is giving you a specific error, you can type the error in as a search phrase on Bing. This will often take you directly to a KB article that describes the problem and the solution.

Trouble ticket databases are also useful in other situations, such as tracking trends. Some systems fail more than others, and when the trend is identified, it's possible to take proactive steps to reduce the problems. Also, management often uses information in the database as justification for hiring additional workers and sometimes to identify the most productive workers.

✔ **Quick Check**
   1. What's the first step in the CompTIA troubleshooting model?
   2. What should you do after establishing a plan of action and implementing it?

Quick Check Answers
   1. Identify the problem.
   2. Verify full system functionality.

Identifying Customer Needs

Customers are often confused by the dizzying array of options available when buying a computer and simply don't know which options are best for them. They often look to experts like you to help them buy the computer that will meet their needs.

One of the core questions you'll need to ask is, "What do you plan on doing with the computer?" If you have an idea of what they'll use it for, you'll be better prepared to help them.

While there are many different options available for computers, most can be summarized in five specific components. If you understand these components, you can then match their importance to different workstation roles. The following sections describe these components and the common workstation roles.

- **CPU/Processor.** Some systems require powerful processors to meet the demands of the applications that they'll run. These include processors with multiple cores and faster speeds.

> **NOTE NEWEST CPUS ARE THE MOST EXPENSIVE**
>
> When shopping for CPUs, the newest and fastest are the most expensive. However, when new CPUs are released, older versions are almost always reduced in price. Some people want only the newest and fastest, and that might be what they need. However, you can often save a significant amount of money with an earlier CPU version. The earlier version might have a little less power, but this is rarely noticeable to the average user.

- **RAM.** The amount of memory a system has is the second most important resource behind the processor. You want to make sure that you get at least the minimum recommended amount of RAM for the operating system. Based on the role, you might want to add more.
- **Disk.** The three basic options related to disks are size, speed, and redundancy. Some roles require large drives to store more data, some require faster hard drives for better performance, and some require fault tolerance with a redundant array of inexpensive disks (RAID).
- **Graphics/Video.** Many applications require high-end graphics. This includes a high-end graphics card with onboard memory and monitors that provide the best display.
- **Audio.** Sophisticated audio systems provide realistic sound, and they are important for gamers and home theaters.
- **Network Interface.** If the computer will be used to transfer a large amount of data over a network, it might require a fast network interface card (NIC) to provide the best performance on the network.

Standard Thick Client

A standard *thick client* is a computer that has an operating system and basic applications. It isn't used for any dedicated role but instead is for day-to-day use.

> **NOTE** THICK VS. THIN CLIENTS
>
> The term *thick* isn't referring to size. It is commonly used in larger organizations that deploy computer images that include both the operating system and user applications. When applying it to individual user systems, it simply means that the computer has applications installed. In contrast, thin clients access applications that are installed and running on remote systems.

For example, a student might use a computer to do research on the Internet and write papers. Similarly, many people commonly have a computer for Internet access, email, and social networking, but for little else. Within an organization, employees doing day-to-day work could be using standard thick clients.

If you ask for what purpose a customer plans on using the computer but the customer really isn't sure, a standard thick client will often meet the customer's needs. When shopping for a thick client, consider the following points:

- **Minimum recommended for operating system.** Start by ensuring that the system has at least the minimum amount of processing power and RAM recommended by the vendor. You'll often see two minimums. One is the absolute minimum to run the operating system. However, the *recommended minimum* refers to what is needed for a satisfying user experience.

- **Desktop applications.** Customers might need assistance in identifying applications to do basic tasks. For example, Microsoft's Office suite includes several basic applications that can be useful to users. It includes Microsoft Word to write papers, résumés, newsletters, and more; Microsoft Excel to work with finances; Microsoft OneNote to create digital notebooks; and Microsoft Outlook to manage contacts, track appointments, and exchange email.

Thin Client

A *thin client* is one that has only minimal resources and applications running on it. The thin client computer is used to boot into the operating system and connect to a remote server, but little is actually done on the thin client.

For example, personnel at my doctor's office use netbooks as thin clients. They are running Windows 7 with very basic hardware installed, and everyone has connectivity to a server hosting a specialized application and data. Nurses and doctors walk from room to room with wireless netbooks, but they access the application and data on the server. Because the application is actually running on the server, the individual netbooks don't require much processing power. Also, the netbooks are very small and light, which is something the nurses and doctors appreciate.

If you are helping someone identify the resources needed for a thin client, ensure that it meets minimum recommended requirements for the operating system and the application used to connect to the remote systems.

Gaming PC

The PC gaming industry is big business and grosses billions of dollars annually. Gamers expect top-notch graphics and audio, and the game developers deliver. Some of the most popular games are first-person shooter and online role-playing games, and many of the games are available on separate consoles, such as the Xbox 360.

You'll often find that gamers are very knowledgeable about PCs, so you might not need to educate them. However, if you need to provide some assistance to a gamer, ensure that the system includes the following items:

- **Powerful processor.** Games often consume a significant amount of processing power, so a fast processor with multiple cores is a must.

- **High-end video.** A top-notch video card with onboard memory and a specialized Graphics Processing Unit (GPU) is needed for many of the games. It ensures that the graphics are quickly displayed without any lag or latency.

- **High-end audio.** Games often have three dimensional (3D) sound, and a 5.1 surround sound system provides a realistic experience. It includes right and left front speakers, right and left rear speakers, a central speaker (often used for dialog), and a subwoofer for deep bass sounds, including realistic explosions. A 7.1 system adds speakers to the right and left of the user in addition to the right and left front speakers and the right and left rear speakers.

- **High-end cooling.** Gamers often run their systems close to full capacity, and some even overclock their processors to get the highest performance possible. High-end cooling systems protect these systems from overheating. These can include high-quality variable speed fans that spin faster when the system is hotter. They can also include liquid-cooled systems that circulate water to keep it cool without the noise generated by fans.

EXAM TIP

Gaming PCs are the primary type of end-user PC where you'll see liquid-cooling systems. Other PCs can use high-quality variable speed fans without liquid cooling.

Virtualization Workstation

Virtualization has become quite popular in recent years. Don't be surprised if someone asks you for help picking out a computer that they plan to use as a virtualization workstation. This section will give you some details on virtualization and the basic hardware requirements.

Understanding Virtualization

A *virtualization* workstation is used to run one or more virtual computers within a single workstation. The workstation is commonly called the host, and virtual systems are commonly called *virtual machines (VMs)* or guests.

Figure 10-1 shows an example of how a Windows 7 system can be used to host a virtual network with four VMs. The network includes Windows 7–based, Linux-based, and Windows 8–based systems running as desktop VMs, and one Server 2008 VM.

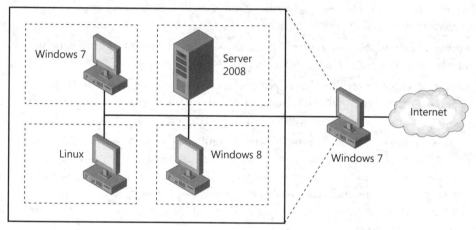

FIGURE 10-1 One physical host running four VMs.

Each VM runs as if it is a separate physical PC. You can run separate applications within them, shut them down, and reboot them, all without affecting the other VMs.

It's possible to configure each VM to be completely isolated from any other, but in Figure 10-1, they are connected via a virtual network. Additionally, each VM can access the Internet through the host NIC.

Hypervisor

The software running on the physical host is called the *hypervisor* and acts as the virtual machine manager. It provides access to the host hardware and ensures that the VM runs in its own space without affecting other VMs or the host system.

The following are some popular VM software products used on workstations for virtualization:

- **Windows Virtual PC.** This is available as a free download from Microsoft at *http://www.microsoft.com/windows/virtual-pc*. You can also access Windows XP Mode from here. Windows XP Mode is a fully functioning version of Windows XP that can run as a virtual system on Windows 7. You can run 32-bit guest operating systems but not 64-bit operating systems in Windows Virtual PC.

- **VMware Player.** VMware has several products, but the VMware Player is free. You can get it from *http://www.vmware.com/products/player/overview.html*. It supports running both 32-bit and 64-bit guest operating systems.

- **VirtualBox.** Oracle has published VirtualBox as an open source virtualization tool. It is available as a free download at *https://www.virtualbox.org/wiki/Downloads*. It allows you to run both 32-bit and 64-bit guest operating systems.

NOTE **VIRTUALIZATION ON YOUR OWN**

Installing and using each of these products is beyond the scope of this A+ book, but they are worth your time. If you want to dig a little deeper, the following blog article includes detailed steps to install Windows 8 and Windows Server 2012 using Virtual Box on a Windows 7–based system: *http://blogs.getcertifiedgetahead.com/windows-server-8-virtual/*.

These hypervisor applications allow you to adjust the resources dedicated to each VM. You can adjust how much RAM is assigned to the VM and control access to other resources such as the network.

Figure 10-2 shows the settings page for a Windows Virtual PC VM that I'm using to run Windows 7. In the figure, I've selected the memory, and you can see that I've dedicated 2,048 MB of RAM for this system. I've also attached several virtual hard disks and configured one network adapter for the VM.

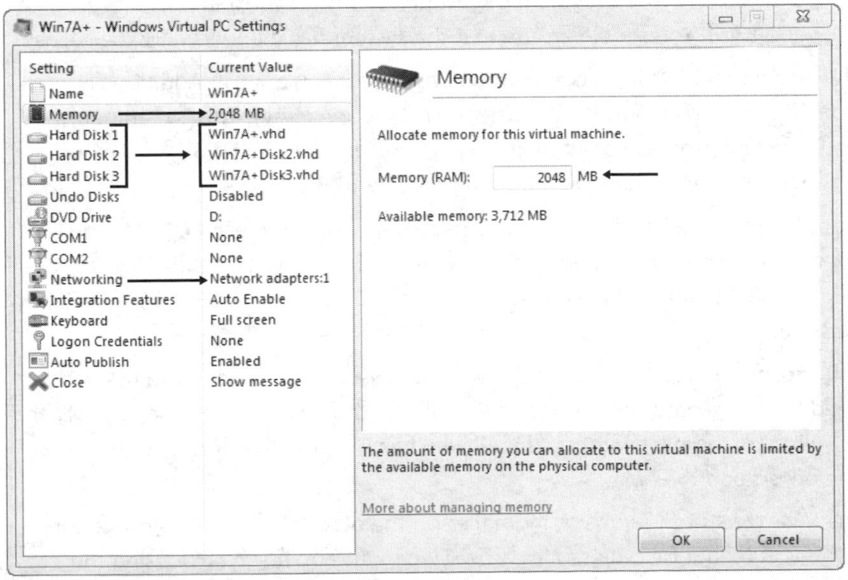

FIGURE 10-2 Virtual PC settings showing RAM.

Purpose

There are several reasons why people use virtualization on workstations, including the following:

- **Learning.** When learning new operating systems and applications, you can install them as VMs. You're free to experiment without fear of causing any real damage. The worst that can happen is that the VM no longer works and you get to install it again.

- **Testing.** New operating systems and new applications can be installed on a virtual system, even when they're in the beta stage. If the software is buggy, causing random problems, only the VM is affected. The host machine remains unaffected.

- **Legacy applications.** If an application won't run in a newer operating system, you can install it on a VM within an older operating system. For example, Windows XP Mode lets you run legacy applications that aren't compatible with Windows 7.

- **Security.** Many security professionals use VMs for security testing. For example, when a new virus is discovered, it can be released in an isolated VM without fear of it infecting the host system.

EXAM TIP

It's always important to keep operating systems up to date with current patches and updates. This is true for the host system and for each VM. However, updating the host does not update any VMs. You need to update each VM separately.

Hardware Requirements

Each VM will consume some of the host system's resources, but the most important resources are the processor and RAM. You should ensure that the system has the following:

- **Powerful processor.** A fast processor with multiple cores is a must. Additionally, the processor should support *hardware assisted virtualization (HAV)*. This is commonly available in current processors but might need to be enabled in the BIOS, as mentioned in Chapter 2, "Understanding Motherboards and BIOS."

- **Maximum RAM.** The amount of RAM you need depends on how many VMs you'll run and their requirements. For example, if you want to run four VMs with 2 GB each, you'll need at least 8 GB beyond what you'll use in the host. A system with 12–16 GB will meet most needs.

- **Network requirements.** If you want the VMs to have access to a physical network, you'll need to have a network interface card (NIC) in the host system. Also, all VMs and the host will share the bandwidth of this NIC, so heavy network usage by one VM will affect the others and the host.

- **Disk.** The VMs are stored as one or more files on the disk. As you install applications on the VM or add data to it, these files grow. Depending on how you're using the VMs, these files can become quite large, so you need to ensure that the disk drive is big enough to hold them.

Home Theater PC

A *home theater PC (HTPC)* is a personal computer that has been configured to work as a digital video recorder (DVR) for television, audio player for music, and video player for movies.

Using software such as Windows Media Center, which is included with Windows 7 Home Premium, you can use just about any computer as an HTPC. However, there is a special case called the HTPC compact form factor that looks a little nicer than a bulky computer when placed on a shelf by a TV. Some of the components that you'll need to ensure are included are as follows:

- **TV tuner within the computer.** You plug in the TV signal source, such as from cable TV into the tuner. If you want to be able record one station while watching another or record two at a time, you'll need two TV tuners.

- **High-Definition Multimedia Interface (HDMI) output.** High-quality TVs support HDMI, so you'll want to ensure that the theater has an HDMI output.

- **Surround sound audio.** You'll want a sound system that is at least as a good as the 5.1 surround sound system described in the Gaming PC section. Movie makers do some exceptional magic with 3D positional sound. For example, you'll be able to hear a jet approach from behind, roar over your head, and disappear in the distance in front of you.

- **Disk space.** If you plan on recording TV shows, you'll need to ensure that you have plenty of disk space to hold them.

Home Server PC

Many people manage networks at home with multiple users connected on a network, and it's common to share resources among these users. A home server can be an effective way of sharing resources among multiple users. Some common uses of a home server include the following:

- **File sharing.** Users can share files via the home server. Additionally, users can back up their data to the home server.

- **Media streaming.** Audio and video files can be stored on the server and streamed to user systems.

- **Print sharing.** You can configure the server as a print server. This allows you to easily share a single printer for all users. Print jobs are sent to the print server and spooled to printers from there.

When using a home server, the two primary resources to which you'll need to pay attention are the NIC and the disk subsystem. All users will be sharing the same NIC, so you'll want the maximum bandwidth supported by your network. It's common to have a least a gigabit NIC.

The disk system needs to be both large and quick. Additionally, you'll often want to add some fault tolerance with the disks. A RAID-5 array gives you all three. For example, you can use four 1-TB disk drives for a total of 3 TB of disk space. Reading and writing is spread across all four drives, improving performance over a single system. And with a RAID-5, a single disk can fail and you'll still be able to continue operating.

EXAM TIP

RAID-5 was described in more depth in Chapter 4, "Comparing Storage Devices." It includes at least three disks, and the equivalent of one disk is dedicated to storing parity bits. When it has a fault, such as one drive failing, RAID-5 can tolerate the fault and will continue to operate.

Graphic/CAD/CAM Design Workstation

A graphics design workstation is used for high-end graphics and video processing. It includes computer-aided design (CAD) and computer-aided manufacturing (CAM) uses.

CAD applications are used to create two-dimensional (2D) and three-dimensional (3D) drawings for tools, machinery, and buildings. These types of drawings take a lot of processing power to render and display. Resources on which you should focus for this type of workstation include the following:

- **Powerful processor.** This includes fast speeds and multiple cores.
- **Maximum RAM.** You should start with at least 8 GB of RAM, but having as much as 16 GB might be needed, depending on the drawings. Ensure that the motherboard will support more RAM if needed.
- **High-end video.** To render and display the graphics as fast as possible, a high-end graphics card with onboard memory is needed.

Audio/Video Editing Workstation

PCs can also be used to edit audio and video as the final stage of processing. For example, many companies create their own videos and post them on YouTube as advertisements. Similarly, many companies create professional videos used for courseware and other types of training.

Some of the hardware that you'll need to consider for this system includes the following:

- **Specialized audio and video card.** This will often have a dedicated processor to take some of the load off the computer's CPU.
- **Large, fast hard drive.** Audio and video files become very large. You'll want to ensure that you have enough storage space on the drives to store them.
- **Dual monitors.** Professionals editing audio and video files often need multiple views of the data that they are editing. Instead of moving the windows around a single monitor, dual monitors allow them to make a modification on one monitor and view the results on the other monitor.

Environmental Impacts

In some cases, you might need to consider the impact of the working environment on the systems. More specifically, you need to consider the temperature, humidity level, and ventilation:

- **Temperature.** Heat is an enemy of any electronic device. If a system gets too hot, it can often damage components or cause intermittent symptoms such as random reboots. If the work area is hotter than normal, you can use advanced methods of cooling, such as a liquid-cooling system.

- **Humidity level.** The ideal humidity level is about 50 percent. When the humidity level is too low, static can build up and result in electrostatic discharge (ESD) damage. When the humidity level is too high, it results in condensation and water damage. You wouldn't want to pour a glass of water into your system. Similarly, you don't want a high humidity level to build up condensation.

- **Ventilation.** Free airflow through the system helps to keep it cool. If there is an excessive amount of airborne particles, the particles can build up within the system and clog up the vents. As they build up, it becomes harder to keep the system cool.

You might run across these environmental conditions in busy work areas. However, you can also run across some of these conditions in a home. For example, if a user is putting a home server into a closet or a basement, the location might not have the same temperature or humidity controls. When advising the customer, you can point this out to help him or her prevent a problem.

Also, a user might have pets that shed, resulting in a quick buildup of pet fur on the vents. Cleaning the vents more often is one way to prevent problems. In some extreme situations, you can use air filters on the computer vents or place the computer within an enclosure to filter out airborne particles.

✔ **Quick Check**

1. What are the primary hardware resources needed for a virtualization workstation?

2. What are the primary environmental factors that can affect a PC's performance?

Quick Check Answers

1. Processor, RAM, NIC, and disk.

2. Temperature, humidity, and ventilation.

Chapter Summary

- Effective communication skills include using proper language, listening, maintaining a positive attitude, avoiding distractions, and giving the customer status information.

- When dealing with difficult customers or situations, you should avoid arguing, being defensive, or being judgmental.

- Asking open-ended questions helps you get more information about a problem. You can clarify customer statements and verify that you understand the problem by restating the issue to the customer.

- When responding to prohibited content or activity, you should identify the issue, report it based on existing laws or your organization's policies, and preserve evidence. A chain of custody form is used to document how evidence has been protected after it was originally collected.

- The CompTIA troubleshooting model includes the following six steps:
  - Identify the problem.
  - Establish a theory of probable cause.
  - Test the theory to determine cause.
  - Establish a plan of action to resolve the problem, and implement the solution.
  - Verify full system functionality, and if applicable, implement preventive measures.
  - Document findings, actions, and outcomes.

- Workstations are used for different purposes, and some have differing needs. The processor and RAM are often the most important, especially for graphics workstations, virtualization workstations, and gaming PCs.

- Virtualization within a workstation is often used for testing, learning, and security purposes. A hypervisor is the application that runs the virtual machines. It requires the maximum amount of RAM and CPU power and often requires a large amount of disk space.

- Specialized graphics cards with powerful graphics processing units (GPUs) and onboard RAM are needed for some workstations, such as graphics workstations, audio and video editing workstations, and gaming PCs.

- You sometimes need hard drives that are large, fast, and that provide fault tolerance with RAID. Audio and video editing workstations need large, fast hard drives. Home servers need disks protected with a RAID array.

- Environmental controls help ensure that the temperature is not too hot and that humidity is close to 50 percent. If the humidity is too high, it can cause water damage from condensation. If it is too low, it can cause ESD damage.

- If the area has a high amount of dust or other airborne particles, you can use enclosures and/or air filters to protect PCs.

Chapter Review

Use the following questions to test your knowledge of the information in this chapter. The answers to these questions, and the explanations of why each answer choice is correct or incorrect, are located in the "Answers" section at the end of this chapter.

1. You are working with a customer to resolve a problem with his laptop, and your personal cell phone rings. What should you do?

   A. Ignore it.

   B. Switch the cell phone to vibrate.

   C. Excuse yourself and answer the phone.

   D. Explain that it is an emergency and that you have to answer the phone.

2. You are a technician helping an executive resolve a problem with her computer. While helping her, you see some confidential company papers on her printer. Of the following choices, what is acceptable?

   A. Look at the papers only if she leaves.

   B. Throw them away.

   C. Ignore them.

   D. Tell her she shouldn't print them.

3. A network printer with multiple paper trays was no longer printing due to a network problem. A technician reconfigured the printer and verified that it was connected. Later, customers complained that the printer could print to one tray but not the other. What troubleshooting step did the technician miss?

   A. Identify the problem.

   B. Verify full system functionality.

   C. Establish a plan of action to resolve the problem.

   D. Documentation.

4. Sally wants to purchase a computer that she'll use as a basic computer at home. She plans on doing research on the Internet, accessing email, and writing some documents. Which of the following choices best meets her needs?

   A. Thick client.

   B. Thin client.

   C. HTPC.

   D. Virtualization workstation.

5. Of the following types of workstations, which would most likely use a high-end liquid-cooling system?

   A. Thick client.

   B. Gaming PC.

   C. Home server.

   D. Home theater PC.

6. A user is planning to add a home server PC that will be used by five users in his home for data sharing. He asks you what type of disk storage would be best. What would you recommend?

   A. Solid state disk.

   B. Blu-ray.

   C. RAID array.

   D. HDMI-compatible.

Answers

This section contains the answers to the chapter review questions in this chapter.

1. **Correct Answer: B**

   A. **Incorrect:** A ringing phone that can be heard by you and the customer is disruptive, so it should not be ignored.

   B. **Correct:** The best choice is switch the phone to vibrate and return your attention to the customer.

   C. **Incorrect:** Your attention should stay with the customer.

   D. **Incorrect:** You have no idea whether it's an emergency or not, and lying about it will easily be recognized by the customer.

2. **Correct Answer: C**

   A. **Incorrect:** It is not acceptable to snoop through someone's papers even if they leave the room.

   B. **Incorrect:** You should not throw away someone else's property.

   C. **Correct:** You should respect customers' confidential property, so the best solution of those given is to ignore them.

   D. **Incorrect:** There is no indication that she should not use her printer for printing confidential papers.

3. **Correct Answer: B**

   A. **Incorrect:** The first step is to identify the problem, and the technician did so for the original problem.

   B. **Correct:** The fifth step in the CompTIA troubleshooting model is to verify full system functionality after resolving a problem. In this case, the technician likely bumped or opened the second tray, preventing it from printing.

   C. **Incorrect:** The technician did establish a plan of action and did resolve the original problem.

   D. **Incorrect:** Documentation is the last step, and it could be that the technician was documenting that the problem was resolved at the same time that the customers identified the second problem.

4. **Correct Answer: A**

   A. **Correct:** A standard thick client includes an operating system and application needed by typical users.

   B. **Incorrect:** A thin client has minimal software and connects to a remote system for most applications.

   C. **Incorrect:** A home theatre PC (HTPC) is used for TV, movies, and music.

   D. **Incorrect:** A virtualization workstation is used to run one or more multiple VMs within the host but isn't needed here.

5. **Correct Answer: B**

   A. **Incorrect:** A thick client is a standard PC and doesn't require any high-end components.

   B. **Correct:** Gaming PCs often use high-end cooling, such as a liquid-cooling system to keep the systems from overheating.

   C. **Incorrect:** Home servers require high-end disk subsystems and fast network interface cards but would not require high-end cooling.

   D. **Incorrect:** A home theater PC requires high-quality graphics, sound, and a TV tuner, but not high-end cooling.

6. **Correct Answer: C**

   A. **Incorrect:** A solid state disk (SSD) is quick but is often very expensive and not the best choice for a home server that will be storing a high volume of data.

   B. **Incorrect:** A Blu-ray player would be needed in a home theater PC but is not used for shared disk storage.

   C. **Correct:** A redundant array of inexpensive disks (RAID) array is a good choice for a home server. A RAID-5 can be configured to store a high volume of data, have better performance than typical drives, and provides fault tolerance.

   D. **Incorrect:** A High-Definition Multimedia Interface (HDMI) is used for graphics, not disks.

CHAPTER 11

Introducing Windows Operating Systems

Windows operating systems are used more than any other operating systems in the world. It's important for an A+ technician to know the basic differences between the different versions of Windows and the differences between editions of specific versions. This chapter introduces the different versions of Windows and compares their features.

Exam 220-802 objectives in this chapter:

- 1.1 Compare and contrast the features and requirements of various Microsoft Operating Systems.
    - Windows XP Home, Windows XP Professional, Windows XP Media Center, Windows XP 64-bit Professional
    - Windows Vista Home Basic, Windows Vista Home Premium, Windows Vista Business, Windows Vista Ultimate, Windows Vista Enterprise
    - Windows 7 Starter, Windows 7 Home Premium, Windows 7 Professional, Windows 7 Ultimate, Windows 7 Enterprise
    - Features:
        - 32-bit vs. 64-bit
        - Aero, gadgets, user account control, bit-locker, shadow copy, system restore, ready boost, sidebar, compatibility mode, XP mode, easy transfer, administrative tools, defender, Windows firewall, security center, event viewer, file structure and paths, category view vs. classic view

An Overview of Windows Operating Systems

Three elements that make a computer useful are the hardware, the operating system, and applications. Earlier chapters focused heavily on the hardware and its capabilities. This section of the book focuses on operating systems.

An *operating system* interacts with the hardware and allows you to run programs or applications. Years ago, operating systems were all text-based. That is, every time you wanted to run a program, you had to type in a command. Today, the majority of operating systems are *graphical user interface (GUI)*-based. In a GUI operating system, you point and click with a mouse to interact with the computer.

Microsoft desktop operating systems are commonly used in enterprises around the world. Certainly, there are other desktop operating systems, but Microsoft systems make up more than 90 percent of the systems in use.

A survey in 2012 by Net Market Share, an information technology (IT) research group, indicated that more than 92 percent of desktop computers use Windows operating systems.

In April 2012, about 46 percent were Windows XP, 39 percent were Windows 7, and 7 percent were Windows Vista. Windows 7 usage continues to climb as Windows XP and Windows Vista systems are upgraded or replaced with Windows 7.

With this in mind, any A+ technician can fully expect to run across Windows-based systems and needs to know about their features. The three primary Windows operating systems are as follows:

- Windows XP—Oldest of the three
- Windows Vista—Released between Windows XP and Windows 7
- Windows 7—Newest of the three

Windows 7 is the newest of the three, and new desktop systems that include Windows have Windows 7 installed. Windows XP is the oldest of the three, and it has become a well-established operating system since it was released in 2001. Windows Vista was released between Windows XP and Windows 7. However, systems that are being upgraded today from Windows XP are typically skipping Windows Vista and going straight to Windows 7.

Each of these operating systems has multiple editions, and some of the editions support 32-bit and 64-bit computers.

Comparing 32-Bit and 64-Bit Capabilities

Current operating systems are available in both 32-bit and 64-bit versions. If the hardware is 64-bit hardware, you can install either the 32-bit or 64-bit operating system versions. However, if the system has 32-bit hardware, you can install only 32-bit versions.

The central processing unit (CPU) is the primary hardware component that determines whether a system is a 32-bit or 64-bit system. If you install a 32-bit operating system on 64-bit hardware, it can work in 32-bit mode. However, it can't take advantage of extra benefits of the 64-bit hardware.

> **NOTE** 64-BIT OPERATING SYSTEMS
>
> As a general recommendation today, 64-bit operating systems are the best choice if the hardware supports it. They offer better speed and enable you to use more memory. If you install a 32-bit operating system on 64-bit hardware, it is slower than it would be if it used the full 64-bit capabilities.

x86 vs. x64

The operating systems are referred to as 32-bit and 64-bit operating systems. However, the hardware is named a little differently: as x86 and x64.

 32-bit processers are commonly called *x86* processors referring to the x86 family of processors. The first x86 processor was the Intel 8086 processor released in 1978, and it went through multiple improvements over the years.

64-bit processors are commonly called *x64*. In some cases, you might see the term AMD64 instead of x64, indicating that the processor is an AMD processor instead of an Intel processor. Similarly, some Intel processors are designated as Intel 64.

EXAM TIP

The hardware on 32-bit systems is identified as x86, and only 32-bit operating systems can be installed. The hardware on 64-bit systems is identified as x64 (sometimes AMD 64), and they support 64-bit and 32-bit operating systems. You can't install a 64-bit operating system on 32-bit hardware.

Increased Memory

One of the biggest benefits of using a 64-bit operating system is access to more random access memory (RAM). A 32-bit operating system can address only 4 GB of RAM, whereas a 64-bit operating system can theoretically address as much as 16 exabytes of RAM.

EXAM TIP

For reference, the order of byte names is as follows: kilobyte (KB), megabyte (MB), gigabyte (GB), terabyte (TB), petabyte (PB), and exabyte (EB). Even though the processors can address as much as 16 exabytes of RAM, you won't see desktop systems with this much RAM in the near future. The maximum RAM for Windows XP and Windows Vista is 128 GB. Windows 7 supports as much as 192 GB.

Users who only surf the Internet or answer email don't need much memory, so the extra RAM that is supported by 64-bit systems isn't necessary. On the other hand, many power users have applications that require more RAM. This is especially true when users have multiple applications open at the same time.

Missing RAM

If you install 4 GB of RAM on a 32-bit operating system, you'll find that some of it appears to be missing. For example, Figure 11-1 shows the System Properties of a Windows XP system. If this system had 4 GB installed, it would instead indicate that only about 3.25 GB was installed. In the figure, you can see that the system is reporting 512 MB of RAM, and that's exactly how much RAM is installed.

EXAM TIP

Even though a 32-bit operating system can address 4 GB of RAM, it can't use it all. It commonly can use only about 3.2 GB to 3.5 GB of RAM installed on a system. 64-bit operating systems do not have this limitation.

Where's the missing RAM? It's still in the computer, but it is unusable. A 32-bit operating system can address only 4 GB of RAM, but it needs to reserve some of the addressable space for hardware devices such as graphics cards and other peripherals. On this Windows XP system, it's reserving about 760 MB of addressable space. If you install 4 GB of RAM or more into a 64-bit system, it will all be available to the operating system.

If you're running Windows XP, you can view the page shown in Figure 11-1 by clicking Start, right-clicking My Computer, and selecting Properties. You can use the same steps on Windows Vista and Windows 7, although the display is different. Figure 11-2 shows the display on a Windows 7 system with the RAM highlighted.

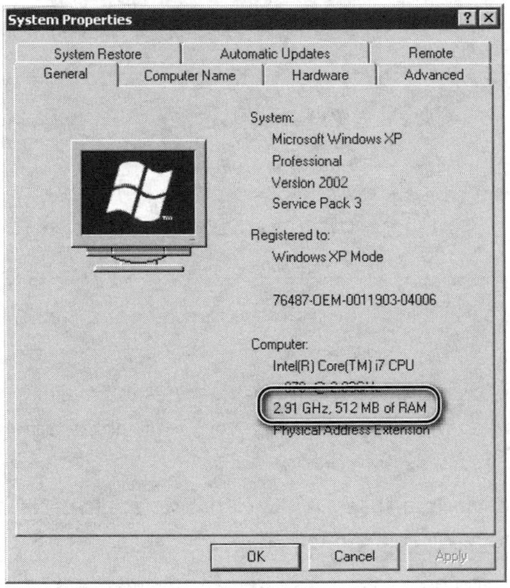

FIGURE 11-1 Windows XP System Properties dialog box.

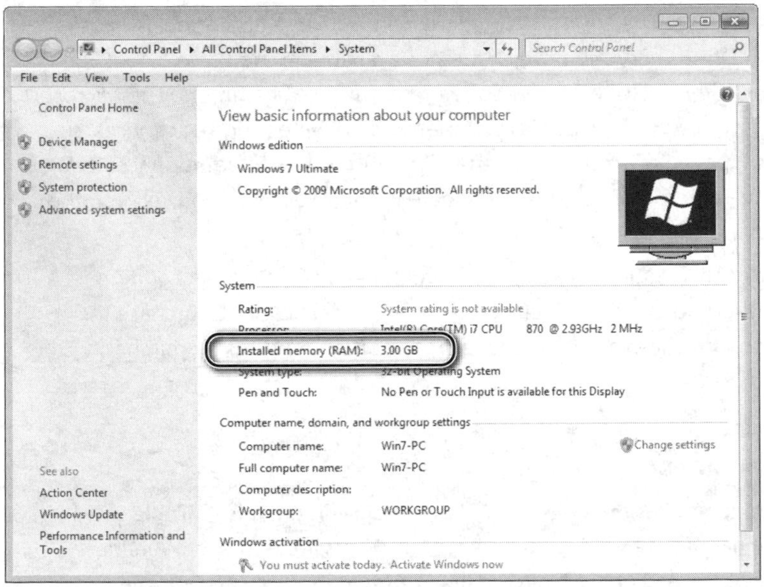

FIGURE 11-2 Windows 7 system properties.

Windows 7 Editions

Microsoft has released several editions of Windows 7, following a progression of good, better, best. The Windows 7 editions are as follows:

- **Starter Edition.** This edition is the most basic and has the fewest features. It's available only to manufacturers, and it's installed on some netbooks (very small lightweight laptops). The Starter edition is available only in 32-bit editions.

- **Home Premium Edition.** This is targeted at home users and includes several features, such as Aero, homegroups, and the Windows Media Center.

- **Professional Edition.** A step above the Home Premium Edition is the Professional edition. A major difference compared to the Home Premium Edition is that computers can join a domain within a network.

- **Windows 7 Enterprise.** The Enterprise edition includes some additional features, such as BitLocker Drive Encryption, which are not available in the Professional Edition. Enterprise is available only to Microsoft Software Assurance customers. The Microsoft Software Assurance program provides customers with a wide range of services, such as 24/7 phone support, reduced costs for training, and access to additional software. Many medium-to-large organizations participate in this program and likely run the Enterprise edition.

- **Ultimate Edition.** This edition includes all the features available in any edition of Windows 7, including Windows 7 Enterprise. Home users cannot purchase the Enterprise edition, but they can get the Enterprise edition features by purchasing this edition.

NOTE **WINDOWS 7 HOME BASIC EDITION**

Another edition of Windows 7 is the Windows 7 Home Basic Edition. It is available only in regions that are designated as emerging markets. This includes areas in South America, Africa, and the Middle East, and only a limited number of features are enabled. The CompTIA A+ objectives do not reference this edition.

Windows 7 System Requirements

One of the primary decisions when deciding which edition to use on a system is identifying the hardware requirements. If the hardware doesn't meet the minimum system requirements, you won't be able to run the operating system.

Most editions are available in both 32-bit and 64-bit versions. The exception is Windows 7 Starter, which is available only for 32-bit systems. The minimum system requirements for Windows 7 are as follows:

- Processor—At least 1 GHz or faster
- Minimum RAM
    - 1 GB required for 32-bit systems
    - 2 GB required for 64-bit systems
- Available hard drive space
    - At least 16 GB of free hard drive space required for 32-bit systems
    - At least 20 GB of free hard drive space required for 64-bit systems
- Graphics hardware supporting DirectX 9 with a Windows Display Driver Model (WDDM) 1.0 or higher driver

EXAM TIP

CompTIA A+ exams often focus on the minimum requirements for different operating systems. It's valuable to know what the minimum requirements are.

Even though you can run Windows 7 Ultimate with a 1-GHz processor and 1 GB of RAM, that doesn't mean you should. If you do, it might not be a very satisfying experience. In short, any operating system that uses only the minimum amount of resources won't perform as well as a system that has more resources. Purchasing faster processors and more RAM than the minimum provides much better performance.

Many technicians talk about the "sweet spot" for RAM, or the amount of RAM that provides the best user experience for most users. A figure often recommended is 3 GB for 32-bit systems and 4 GB for 64-bit systems. Power users running multiple resource-intensive applications need more. On the other hand, a user who is only browsing the web and using email might need fewer resources.

Windows 7 System Limits

When deciding on an operating system, it's also important to understand its limits related to hardware support. Table 11-1 shows a comparison of hardware limitations related to memory and processors with the different Windows 7 editions.

TABLE 11-1 Windows 7 System Limits

	Max RAM 32-bit	Max RAM 64-bit	Max processors
Starter	2 GB	n/a	1
Home Premium	4 GB	16 GB	1
Professional	4 GB	192 GB	2
Enterprise	4 GB	192 GB	2
Ultimate	4 GB	192 GB	2

If you install Windows 7 Home Premium on a system with two processors, it will still work. However, it will use only one of the processors.

The limitation on physical processors does not include processor cores. For example, Windows 7 Professional supports two physical processors. However, each of these processors can have multiple cores. All cores on the processor are supported.

Windows 7 32-bit systems include support for processors with up to 32 cores, and 64-bit systems can support up to 256 cores in any single processor. At this writing, some 12-core processors are emerging, but you probably won't see 32-core or 256-core processors for a while.

EXAM TIP

It's valuable to know the limitations of different operating systems. For example, users might complain that they have two processors but their Windows 7 Home Premium operating system recognizes only one. You can let them know that Windows 7 Home Premium supports only one processor and recommend that they upgrade to Windows 7 Professional or Ultimate to access the additional processor.

✔ **Quick Check**

1. What is the difference between Windows 7 Enterprise and Windows 7 Ultimate?

2. What is the maximum amount of RAM supported by Windows 7 Enterprise?

Quick Check Answers

1. Enterprise is available only to Microsoft Software Assurance customers, but anyone can buy Windows 7 Ultimate.

2. 192 GB.

Windows XP Editions

Windows XP operating systems have been around since 2001, and they are well-established. The relevant editions of Windows XP are as follows:

- **Windows XP Home**. The Home edition was targeted for home users. It provided basic capabilities.

- **Windows XP Professional**. The Professional edition was targeted for business users and included many more capabilities. For example, users can join a domain, encrypt files, and use remote desktop capabilities.

- **Windows XP Media Center**. Media Center is an enhanced edition of Windows XP Home and gives users additional multimedia capabilities. For example, users can watch and record TV shows, view DVD movies, and listen to music.

- **Windows XP 64-bit Professional**. This edition was for users who wanted more memory and power and is also known as Windows XP Professional x64 Edition. It runs on Advanced Micro Devices (AMD) processors designated with "AMD64" and on Intel processors designated with "Intel 64."

> **NOTE** **RETAIL SALES OF WINDOWS XP DISCONTINUED IN 2008**
>
> Microsoft stopped retail sales of Windows XP in June 2008, and sales of PCs with Windows XP preinstalled stopped in October 2010. However, Microsoft continued to provide mainstream support for Windows XP systems until April 2009, and they will continue to provide extended support until April 2014.

Mainstream vs. Extended Support

Microsoft provides support for operating systems long after they stop selling them. Customers can continue to use the product and will continue to get updates, so you're likely to see these products even if you can't purchase them anymore. Microsoft refers to two types of support: *mainstream support* and *extended support*.

In general, you can think of mainstream support as normal support. Customers receive security updates and other non-security hotfixes and can also receive support for bugs or problems.

The extended support phase ends sometime after the mainstream support phase. Customers will still continue to receive security updates. However, other updates and support are available only to customers who purchase an extended hotfix support agreement. You can read more about it here: *http://support.microsoft.com/gp/lifepolicy*.

Windows XP 64-Bit

Windows XP Professional included two 64-bit editions. In contrast, the Home and Media Center editions are available only in 32-bit editions. The two editions of 64-bit Windows XP systems are as follows:

- **Windows XP 64-Bit Edition.** Windows XP 64-bit systems ran on the Intel Itanium family of processors. Hewlett Packard sold Windows XP 64-bit systems for a while but stopped selling them in 2005.

- **Windows XP Professional x64 Edition.** This edition ran on x86-64 compatible processors sold by both Intel and AMD.

Each 64-bit edition supports as much as 128 GB of RAM, compared to the 4 GB limit of 32-bit systems.

The 64-bit editions of Windows XP weren't as popular as the 32-bit editions. One of the challenges was that many drivers were available only in 32-bit versions and weren't compatible with the 64-bit operating systems. In contrast, most vendors created both 32-bit and 64-bit versions of their drivers for Windows 7 systems, making the 64-bit versions of Windows 7 very popular.

Windows XP System Requirements

System requirements for Windows XP are very light compared to the power that most computers have today. However, when Windows XP first came out, many computers didn't have the hardware to support the recommended minimums.

The minimum system requirements for each edition of Windows XP are as follows:

- Processor
  - Pentium 233 MHz minimum
  - Pentium 300 MHz recommended
- RAM
  - 64 MB minimum
  - 128 MB recommended
- 1.5 GB minimum free hard drive space

Windows XP System Limits

Windows XP editions also have limitations on the maximum amount of RAM and the maximum number of processors they support. Table 11-2 shows a comparison of these limitations with the different Windows XP editions.

TABLE 11-2 Windows XP System Limits

	Max RAM	Max processors
Home	4 GB	1
Professional	4 GB	2
Media Center	4 GB	2
XP 64-bit	128 GB	2
Professional x64	128 GB	2

Windows Vista Editions

Windows Vista operating systems were released in 2007. The goal of Windows Vista was to replace Windows XP, but it wasn't widely embraced. Windows 7 was released in 2009 and is much more popular than Windows Vista. However, there are still many Windows Vista systems out there, and they are covered on the A+ exams.

The relevant editions of Windows Vista are as follows:

- **Windows Vista Home Basic.** This is a basic edition of Windows Vista for home users. It doesn't include many of the features of Windows Vista, such as Windows Aero.

- **Windows Vista Home Premium.** This edition provides many more capabilities for home users and is comparable to the Windows XP Media Center Edition.

- **Windows Vista Business.** The Business edition is targeted for businesses and enterprises. Some additional features include the ability to join a domain, use encrypted files, and use offline files.

- **Windows Vista Enterprise.** Similar to the Windows 7 Enterprise edition, Enterprise is available only to Microsoft Software Assurance customers. It includes additional features, such as BitLocker Drive Encryption.

- **Windows Vista Ultimate.** The Ultimate edition includes all the features available in any edition of Windows Vista. In Windows 7, the Enterprise and Ultimate editions have the same features. In Windows Vista, the Ultimate edition has some additional features that aren't in any other edition. The "Ultimate Extras" included more features, such as games and active backgrounds using Windows DreamScene.

NOTE **RETAIL SALES OF VISTA DISCONTINUED IN 2010**

Microsoft stopped retail sales of Windows Vista in October 2010, and sales of PCs with Windows XP preinstalled stopped in October 2011. However, Microsoft has indicated that it will continue to provide mainstream support for Windows Vista systems until April 2012 and extended support until April 2017.

Windows Vista System Requirements

Windows Vista took advantage of improved hardware available at the time it was released. Compared to Windows XP, it required quite a bit more processing power and RAM and often required hardware upgrades.

The minimum system requirements for Windows Vista are as follows:

- Processor
    - 800-MHz processor minimum
    - 1-GHz processor recommended
- RAM
    - 512 MB minimum
    - 1 GB recommended
- Available hard drive space
    - 20-GB hard drive with at least 15 GB free space
    - 40-GB hard drive with at least 15 GB free recommended
- Graphics hardware supporting DirectX 9 with WDDM
    - 32 MB video RAM for the Home Basic edition
    - 128 MB video RAM for other editions

Windows Vista System Limits

Windows Vista editions have limitations on what hardware they support, just as other operating systems do. Table 11-3 lists the hardware limitations with Windows Vista Editions.

TABLE 11-3 Windows Vista System Limits

	Max RAM 32-bit	Max RAM 64-bit	Max processors
Home Basic	4 GB	8 GB	1
Home Premium	4 GB	16 GB	1
Business	4 GB	128 GB	2
Enterprise	4 GB	128 GB	2
Ultimate	4 GB	128 GB	2

Windows Features

Some features are common to all three versions of Windows (Windows 7, Windows XP, and Windows Vista), whereas some features are available only in specific versions. Table 11-4 identifies features available in the different versions of Windows and identifies the chapter in this book where each topic is covered.

TABLE 11-4 Comparison of Windows Features

Feature	Windows XP	Windows Vista	Windows 7	Chapter
Action Center	--	Yes	Yes	13
Aero	--	Yes	Yes	11
BitLocker	--	Yes	Yes	25
Gadgets	--	Yes	Yes	11
Easy transfer	--	Yes	Yes	12
Homegroups	--	--	Yes	24
Ready boost	--	Yes	Yes	15
Sidebar	--	Yes	--	11
Shadow copy	--	Yes	Yes	15
Security Center	Yes	--	--	13
UAC	--	Yes	Yes	11
Windows Libraries	--	--	Yes	13
Windows XP Mode	--	--	Yes	11

> **NOTE FEATURES VARY BY EDITIONS**
>
> Some features are not available in every edition of an operating system. For example, BitLocker is available in Windows 7, but it's not available in the Starter, Home Premium, or Professional editions of Windows. It is available in the Ultimate edition. Other tables in this chapter focus on the differences between editions of each of these operating systems.

Common Features

Many of the features that are common in Windows XP, Windows Vista, and Windows 7 are described in the following list.

- **Administrative Tools.** Administrators and advanced users access these tools to configure and troubleshoot a system. The available tools are slightly different between operating systems, but each version includes an Administrative Tools group via the Control Panel. Chapter 13, "Using Windows Operating Systems," covers Administrative Tools.

- **Backup.** Backup tools allow you to back up data so that you can restore it if it becomes corrupted. Backup capabilities are discussed in Chapter 15, "Configuring Windows Operating Systems."

- **Compatibility Mode.** If an application doesn't work in the current operating system, you can use Compatibility Mode to run it with settings from a previous operating system. Methods are presented later in this chapter.

- **Event Viewer.** Each operating system logs events in one of several logs as they occur, and you can view these events in the Event Viewer. Chapter 17 covers the Event Viewer.

- **Join Domain.** Many organizations use domains with central domain controllers for centralized management. If a computer has joined the domain and a user has a user account in the domain, users can log on to the domain with the computer. Steps to join a domain or a workgroup are included in Chapter 18.

- **Offline Files.** Users often access files that are stored on a server when connected in a network. However, mobile computers don't have connectivity to these servers when they are disconnected from the network. Offline Files stores a copy of the files on the user's computer and synchronizes the files when the user reconnects to the network. Chapter 16 covers Offline Files.

- **System Restore.** If a system update or change causes a problem, you can use System Restore to revert the system to a previous state. It allows you to undo system changes without modifying any of the user's files, such as email, documents, and photos. Chapter 15, "Configuring Windows Operating Systems," covers System Restore.

- **Windows Defender.** This is a free download that you can use to protect your systems from viruses and other malicious software (malware). Chapter 26, "Recognizing Malware and Other Threats," covers different types of malware and Windows Defender.

- **Windows Firewall.** Firewalls provide a layer of security protection for systems by filtering network traffic. In many cases, this can reduce a system's vulnerability to attacks. Windows Firewall is covered in Chapter 22, "Network Security Devices."

Windows 7 Features

Table 11-5 shows some of the features that you'll find only in specific editions of Windows 7, along with the chapter where you can read more about the feature.

TABLE 11-5 Windows 7 Features

Feature	Starter	Home Premium	Professional	Ultimate Enterprise	Chapter
64-bit support	--	Yes	Yes	Yes	11
Aero	--	Yes	Yes	Yes	11
Back up and Restore	Yes	Yes	Yes	Yes	15
Back up to network	--	--	Yes	Yes	15
BitLocker Drive Encryption	--	--	--	Yes	25
Encrypting File System (EFS)	--	--	Yes	Yes	16
Join a domain	--	--	Yes	Yes	18
Join homegroup	Yes	Yes	Yes	Yes	24
Offline Files	--	--	Yes	Yes	16
Windows XP Mode	--	--	Yes	Yes	11
UAC	Yes	Yes	Yes	Yes	11

EXAM TIP

CompTIA A+ exams often focus on the different features available in different systems. For example, it's valuable to know that Windows XP Mode is supported in the Professional and Ultimate Editions of Windows 7 and that you can back up to network locations in the Professional and Ultimate Editions, but that these features are not supported in the Starter and Home Premium editions.

Windows Vista Features

Table 11-6 shows some of the features that you'll find only in specific editions of Windows Vista, along with the chapter(s) in which you can read more about each feature.

TABLE 11-6 Windows Vista Features

Feature	Home Basic	Home Premium	Business	Ultimate Enterprise	Chapter
Aero	--	Yes	Yes	Yes	11
Automatic Backups	--	Yes	Yes	Yes	11
BitLocker	--	--	--	Yes	25
Share documents	--	Yes	Yes	Yes	22, 25
Sidebar	Yes	Yes	Yes	Yes	11
Windows Complete PC Backup	--	--	Yes	Yes	11

> ✔ **Quick Check**
>
> **1.** Which operating systems use libraries?
>
> **2.** Which Windows 7 operating system(s) can back up data to a network location?
>
> **Quick Check Answers**
>
> **1.** Only Windows 7.
>
> **2.** Windows 7 Professional, Ultimate, and Enterprise.

Windows Aero

Windows *Aero* is a new feature that became available in Windows Vista and was improved on in Windows 7 with additional features such as Peek, Shake, and Snap. It uses a variety of graphics features, such as translucent effects and animations that enhance the user interface. It also includes some great features that enhance the usability of the system.

Figure 11-3 shows an example of Aero Peek. You can hover the mouse over any item on the taskbar, and Aero displays the item. In the figure, Task Manager is running, and the cursor hovering over the Task Manager icon on the taskbar displays a thumbnail view of the application.

> *TIP* **WINDOWS+TAB**
>
> An easy way to access different applications on your system is by using the Windows+Tab keys. By holding down the Windows key and tapping the Tab key, the screen will scroll through open applications. If you don't have the Windows key on your keyboard, you can use the Alt key instead, although the display isn't the same.

FIGURE 11-3 Windows Aero showing Task Manager from the taskbar.

Peek also allows you to view the desktop, even with multiple windows open. If you hover over the end of the taskbar on the far right (just to the right of the time and date display), all the windows become transparent. If you click this area, all the windows minimize, giving you easy access to your desktop.

Shake allows you to minimize all the windows on the system except for the one you're shaking. Click and hold the title bar of a window, and shake the mouse. All the other windows will be minimized. If you shake the window again, all the other windows will be restored as they were before they were minimized.

Snap is an easy way to resize windows by dragging them to the edge of the screen. Click and hold the title bar, and drag the window to the right, left, or top of your screen. If you drag it to the top, it maximizes the window. If you drag it to the right or left, the window will be resized to half of the screen. You can drag one window to the right, another to the left, and easily compare the two windows side by side.

User Account Control

User Account Control (UAC) is a security feature that first appeared in Windows Vista. It helps prevent malicious software from taking action on a user's computer without the user's knowledge. To understand the benefit, it's worthwhile to understand the problem that it is addressing.

Understanding the Risk Without UAC

If a user is logged on with administrative privileges and the system is infected with a virus, the virus has full administrator access. Because of this, users are strongly encouraged not to use an administrator account for regular work.

> **NOTE PRIVILEGES**
>
> Privileges are rights and permissions. Rights indicate what a user can do on a system, such as change the system time or install a driver. Permissions indicate the access that users have to resources such as files or printers. For example, you can grant users permissions to read and modify files or to print to a printer.

The administrator account is required to do some tasks, such as change a system configuration or install drivers. If a user isn't logged on with an administrator account, the user needs to access a second administrator account to complete these tasks.

Whereas IT professionals commonly use two accounts in this way, it isn't reasonable to expect regular users to use two accounts. Instead, many end users are always logged on with an administrator account, making them more susceptible to virus infections.

Account Separation with UAC

Windows Vista and Windows 7 have two types of accounts: a standard user account and an administrator account. A standard user can do regular work and configure settings that do not affect other users. An administrator account has complete control over the computer.

However, if a user with an administrator account is logged on, UAC works as if the user actually has two accounts (a standard user account and an administrator account) by using two access tokens. One token provides the user with regular user access. When necessary, the second token provides the user with administrative access.

If a user takes action that requires elevated administrator rights, UAC prompts the user to approve the action with a pop-up window similar to Figure 11-4.

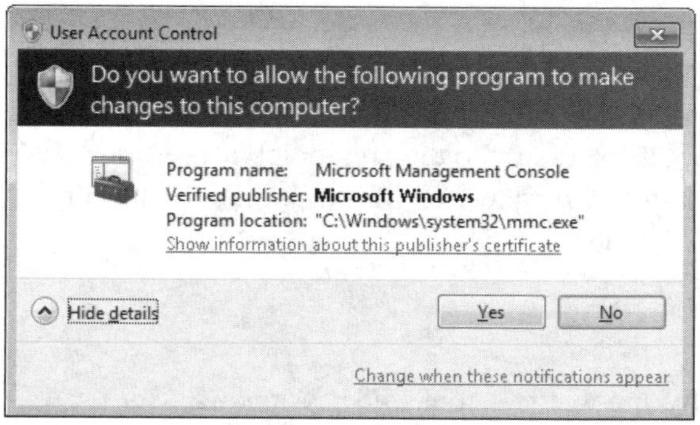

FIGURE 11-4 User Account Control prompt.

NOTE   SHIELD ICON

Any actions requiring administrator rights have a small icon of a shield to provide a visual cue to the user. The icon is the same as the UAC shield icon shown in Figure 11-4.

You can click Show Details to get the location of the program that caused the UAC dialog box to appear, or click Hide Details to hide this information. Figure 11-4 shows the result after clicking Show Details and indicates that the Microsoft Management Console (Mmc.exe) is being started.

An important piece of information in the UAC dialog box is the Publisher, which identifies who created the application that is being started. If the publisher can be verified, the publisher appears as a Verified Publisher. However, if the publisher cannot be verified, the publisher appears as Unknown, as shown in Figure 11-5.

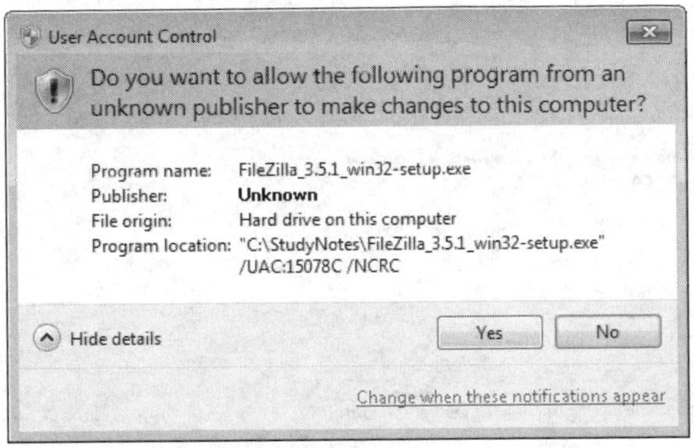

FIGURE 11-5 User Account Control prompt with Unknown publisher.

Legitimate companies can usually be verified. However, attackers trying to install malicious software on your systems will always appear as Unknown. If you see a UAC dialog box with Unknown, you should be suspicious, especially if you didn't take action to modify your system. UAC is trying to protect your system, but you can override the warning by clicking Yes.

By default, UAC dims the desktop and disables all other interaction with the system. The dimmed desktop is also called the secure desktop, and it prevents any other programs, including malicious software, from running. In other words, the action can be approved only with user interaction. The user must either click Yes to approve the action or click No to block it.

If a user does not have administrator permissions with the current account, UAC will prompt the user to enter the user name and password for an account that does have appropriate permissions.

You can manipulate the settings for UAC on Windows 7 with the following steps:

1. Click Start, Control Panel. If necessary, change the display from Category to Large Icons.

2. Select Action Center.

3. Select Change User Account Control Settings.

EXAM TIP

There are multiple methods of finding applets in Control Panel. However, the objectives specifically list using Classic View or the Large Icons view. It's worth your time to explore the Control Panel by using these views.

---

4. Your display will look similar to the following graphic. You can accept the settings by clicking OK, or you can click Cancel.

User Account Control Settings

Choose when to be notified about changes to your computer

User Account Control helps prevent potentially harmful programs from making changes to your computer.
Tell me more about User Account Control settings

Always notify

Default - Notify me only when programs try to make changes to my computer

- Don't notify me when I make changes to Windows settings

Recommended if you use familiar programs and visit familiar websites.

Never notify

OK   Cancel

Table 11-7 explains the actions associated with the different UAC settings on a Windows 7 system.

TABLE 11-7 UAC Settings

UAC Setting	UAC Action	Comments
Always Notify.	You'll be notified before programs make changes to your computer or to Windows settings that require administrator permissions.	The most secure setting. Uses secure desktop. (Desktop is dimmed.)
Notify Me Only When Programs Try To Make Changes To My Computer.	You'll be notified before programs make changes to your computer that require administrator permissions, or if a program outside of Windows tries to make changes to a Windows setting. You won't be notified if you try to make changes to Windows settings that require administrator permissions.	This is the default setting and is shown as selected in the graphic from the previous steps. Uses secure desktop. (Desktop is dimmed.)
Notify Me Only When Programs Try To Make Changes To My Computer. (Do Not Dim My Desktop.)	Same as Notify me only when programs try to make changes to my computer, but without using secure desktop.	Desktop is not dimmed. Applications can make changes.

Never Notify.	You won't be notified before any changes are made to your computer. If you're logged on as an administrator, programs can make changes to your computer without you knowing about it. If you're logged on as a standard user, any changes that require the permissions of an administrator will automatically be denied.	Least secure setting and not recommended. Desktop is not dimmed.

Windows Vista did not have the preceding options with UAC. Instead, users could only turn UAC on or off. You can use the following steps to disable or enable UAC on a Windows Vista system:

1. Click Start, Control Panel. If necessary, change the display from Category to Classic View.

2. Select User Accounts.

3. Select Turn User Account Control on or off. If prompted by UAC, click Continue.

4. Your display will resemble the following graphic. You can select or deselect the check box to enable or disable UAC.

IMPORTANT   **DISABLING UAC IS NOT RECOMMENDED**

UAC protects against unauthorized changes, and with it disabled, malicious software can make changes without the user's knowledge.

Windows XP Mode

 Windows XP Mode is a cool feature available in Windows 7 that allows you to run Windows XP applications on Windows 7 in a virtual Windows XP environment. It is very valuable if an application is incompatible with Windows 7 but will run on Windows XP. This allows users to migrate to Windows 7 even if they need to run legacy applications.

EXAM TIP

Windows XP Mode is available on the Windows 7 Professional and Ultimate editions, but it is not available on Windows Vista.

XP Mode is not installed on Windows 7 systems by default, but it is available as a free download. If you are interested, you can find the instructions and download it from here: *http://www.microsoft.com/windows/virtual-pc/download.aspx.*

This also installs Windows Virtual PC, which allows you to run other virtual operating systems from within your Windows 7 system.

Windows XP Mode includes a fully functional version of Windows XP. You can start XP Mode just as you can start any other application on your Windows 7 system. Additionally, after it's started, you can install and run any applications from within this virtual system. Figure 11-6 shows Windows XP Mode running within Windows Virtual PC.

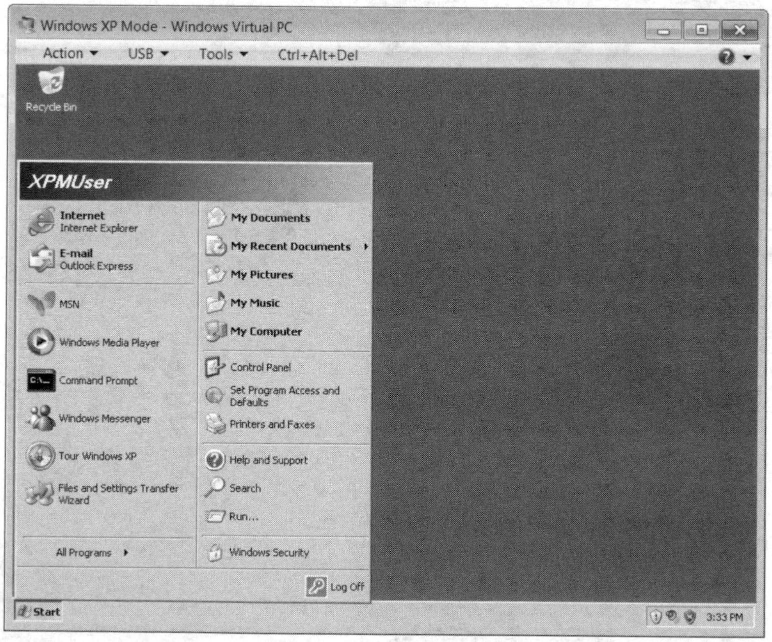

FIGURE 11-6 Windows XP Mode.

Even better, after you've installed applications in the Windows XP Mode virtual system, you can shut down the Windows XP Mode Virtual PC and start the application from the Windows 7 All Programs menu. Users don't have to start Windows XP Mode to start the program. This makes it seamless for the end users.

Chapter 15, "Configuring Windows Operating Systems," talks about the importance of keeping Windows systems up to date with patches. This also applies to Windows XP Mode if it's being used.

Start Bar Layout

Often, the first step in starting an application is clicking the Start button. That sounds simple enough. However, the Start button has changed somewhat between operating systems. Figure 11-6 shows how the Start button looks in Windows XP. Figures 11-7 and 11-8 show the Start button in Windows Vista and Windows 7. (Also, the figures show you some of the changes in the interfaces between the operating systems.)

FIGURE 11-7 Windows Vista Start button.

NOTE **EASY SEARCH**

Windows Vista and Windows 7 include a text box right above the Start button, labeled Start Search in Windows Vista and Search Programs And Files in Windows 7. You can often type in the name of the program here and a link to the program will appear. For example, if you type in **Backup**, several links appear related to the Backup And Restore program.

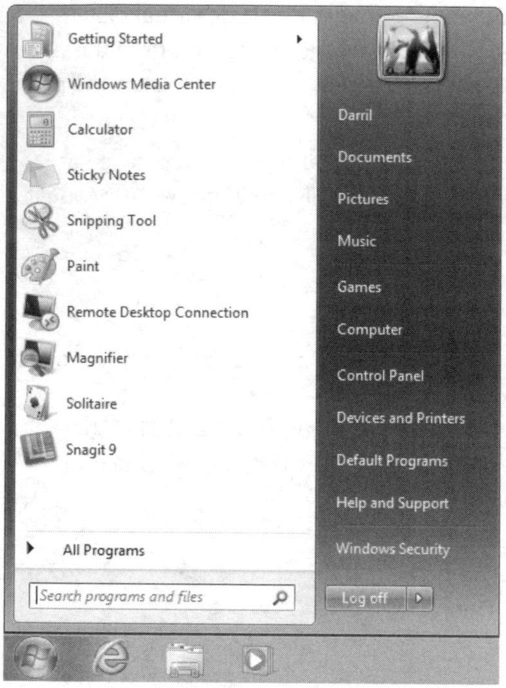

FIGURE 11-8 Windows 7 Start button.

Notice that in Windows XP the button is actually labeled Start, but it's not labeled on Windows Vista and Windows 7. However, if you hover over the button on these operating systems, a tooltip will appear indicating that it is the Start button.

In Windows XP, items were labeled as My Documents, My Computer, and so on, but this terminology isn't used on the main menu anymore. It caused a few humorous problems with help desk professionals talking to users over the phone. If the professional asked the user to "open my computer" or "open my documents," the user sometimes became a little flustered, responding with, "I'm not at your computer."

You can see many commonalities between the operating systems. Each Start menu provides access to All Programs, Control Panel, the user's documents, Help and Support, Windows Security, and more.

> **NOTE** **CONTEXT MENUS**
>
> Many of these menu items provide additional capabilities by right-clicking (sometimes called alt-clicking) the menu item. This often brings up a context menu. For example, you can start Computer Management by right-clicking Computer (or My Computer in Windows XP) and selecting Manage.

Windows Sidebar and Gadgets

The Windows *Sidebar* hosts *gadgets* that users can add to their system in Windows Vista. Gadgets are mini-programs that have a specific functionality. For example, a weather gadget will show the weather for a specific location. Windows Sidebar isn't available in Windows 7, but users can still add gadgets to their desktop.

The sidebar is normally on the right side of the screen with the gadgets docked in the sidebar. However, you can manipulate the settings and the gadgets. You can also add more gadgets by right-clicking the sidebar and selecting Add Gadgets. Your display will be similar to Figure 11-9.

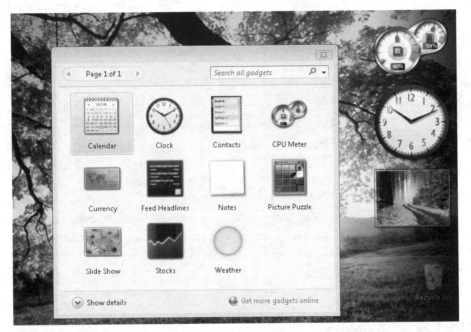

FIGURE 11-9 Adding gadgets to the Windows Vista Sidebar.

You can also add gadgets to the Windows 7 desktop, even though it doesn't have a Sidebar. If you right-click anywhere on the desktop and select Gadgets, you'll see what gadgets are available. You can then double-click any of them to add them to your desktop and even move them wherever you like on the desktop.

Figure 11-10 shows the gadgets available on a Windows 7 system, with two gadgets added to the desktop.

Several gadgets are available by default, but many more are available online. By clicking the link Get More Gadgets Online (shown at the bottom of the Gadgets window in Figures 11-9 and 11-10), users can browse through available gadgets on Microsoft's website.

FIGURE 11-10 Viewing gadgets on Windows 7.

IMPORTANT **DOWNLOAD ONLY FROM TRUSTED DEVELOPERS**

Malicious attackers can write gadgets, so it's important to download gadgets only from trusted developers. Some of the gadgets posted to Microsoft's site are unverified submissions. They can potentially access system files, show objectionable content, or change the behavior of your system.

Sidebar vs. SideShow

Windows Sidebar and SideShow are not the same thing. The sidebar is on the Vista desktop and displays different types of gadgets after a user logs on.

Windows SideShow allows a user to connect a device (such as a Bluetooth or USB device) to the computer. For example, a user could connect a digital photo frame to a computer that has a weather SideShow gadget. The SideShow gadget displays the information on the photo frame. In contrast, the Sidebar gadget is displayed only on the desktop.

Compatibility Mode

You can often manipulate the settings for a legacy application to get it to work without using XP Mode. You can use the Program Compatibility program wizard, or you can manually configure compatibility settings.

The following steps show how to start and run the Program Compatibility program wizard on Windows 7:

1. Click Start and select Control Panel.

2. Select Programs.

3. Select Run Programs Made For Previous Versions Of Windows.

4. On the Program Compatibility screen, click Next. The wizard will identify applications installed on your computer.

5. Select the application that is having problems and click Next.

6. If the program is not listed, select Not Listed (the first item in the list) and click Next. You'll then be able to browse and select the application.

7. You'll be asked to answer some questions related to the problem, and the wizard will configure the settings for you.

Alternatively, you can use Windows Explorer to browse to the application, right-click it, and select Properties. Select the Compatibility tab, and you'll see a display similar to Figure 11-11.

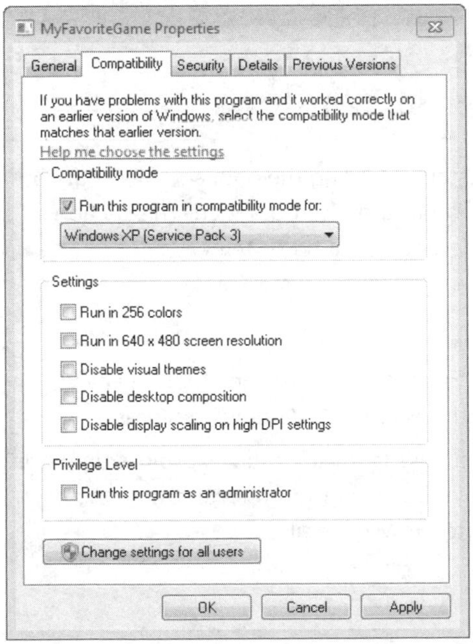

FIGURE 11-11 Manually configuring compatibility settings.

The Compatibility mode section allows you to select a previous operating system. The figure shows the check box that enables the program to run using compatible settings for Windows XP (Service Pack 3). You can select other operating systems all the way back to Windows 95.

Some applications have problems with the advanced graphics features of Windows Vista and Windows 7, and the Settings area allows you to disable some of the graphics features or to use the most basic settings. For example, if the Themes feature is causing problems for the legacy application, select the box to Disable Visual Themes.

Additionally, UAC sometimes causes problems for applications that require administrator privileges to run. You can select Run This Program As An Administrator to overcome this problem.

✔ **Quick Check**

1. What Windows security feature helps prevent malicious software from taking action on a user's computer without the user's knowledge?

2. What can you use to run an application using settings that mimic a previous operating system?

Quick Check Answers

1. User Account Control (UAC).

2. Compatibility Mode.

Examining Directory Structures in Windows

One of the challenges when using any operating system is finding the data and files that you need. As operating systems are improved, these locations are often changed. This section identifies many of the common file locations on different operating systems.

Windows Explorer

The primary tool you use to access files is Windows Explorer. As with many tools in any version of Windows, you can choose from multiple methods to start Windows Explorer.

The following steps outline some methods you can use to start Windows Explorer in different operating systems. Certainly, there are other ways, but the most important thing here is that you should be able to open Windows Explorer to browse the files.

To start Windows Explorer on Windows XP, click Start, right-click My Computer and select Explore.

To start Windows Explorer on Windows Vista, click Start, All Programs, Accessories, and select Windows Explorer.

To start Windows Explorer on Windows 7, right-click Start and select Open Windows Explorer.

Common File Locations

There are many common files and folders among all of the Windows versions. Some of these files are in common locations in each version of Windows, and some are in different locations. Table 11-8 shows the location of common files and folders in each of the Windows editions covered in this chapter.

TABLE 11-8 Common File Locations

	Default location	Comments
Root drive	C:\	Also called system partition
Program files	C:\Program Files	Includes application files
Windows files	C:\Windows	Also called boot partition
System files	C:\Windows\System32	Includes Windows system files
Temporary files	C:\Windows\Temp	Operating system for temporary file storage
Offline Files	C:\Windows\CSC	Also called Client Side Cache
Fonts	C:\Windows\Fonts	Numbers, symbols, and characters with different typefaces

Windows 64-bit operating systems can run both 32-bit and 64-bit applications. In some cases, an application will have both 32-bit and 64-bit versions, giving the user the option of which one to run. However, many potential conflicts are possible if both 32-bit and 64-bit versions of the files are stored in the same location. To avoid problems, these different versions are stored in different locations.

On 64-bit systems, you'll see two Program Files folders. One holds 32-bit application files, and the other folder holds 64-bit application files. They are shown in Table 11-9.

TABLE 11-9 Locations of 32-Bit and 64-Bit Application Files

	32-bit Windows	64-bit Windows
C:\Program Files	32-bit application files	64-bit application files
C:\Program Files (x86)	Not used	32-bit application files

You might remember from earlier in this chapter that x86 indicates a 32-bit system. The folder with (x86) holds all of the 32-bit application files, and the folder without (x86) holds the 64-bit application files on 64-bit systems. Because 32-bit systems don't support 64-bit applications, they have only the C:\Program Files folder.

> **NOTE** **X86 FOLDERS ON 64-BIT SYSTEMS**
>
> Both the C:\Program Files and C:\Program Files (x86) folders are needed on 64-bit systems. Occasionally, users think that because they're running a 64-bit operating system they can delete the (x86) folder. This will break many applications and, most often, requires a complete reinstallation of the operating system to restore functionality.

Boot vs. System Partition

You're likely to hear the terms boot partition and system partition as you work with operating systems. The functions of these are fairly straightforward, but the names can be confusing.

The *system partition* is the location where files necessary to boot the computer are found. It is usually the root of the C drive. The *boot partition* is the location where operating system files are found. On Windows-based systems, the boot partition is usually C:\Windows.

This sounds backward to many people (me included), but it's accurate. The system partition holds the boot files. The boot partition holds the system files. When preparing for the A+ exams, it's valuable to know the difference.

Profile Locations

Any system can support multiple users who can log on to the same computer at different times. These users can personalize the system by changing different settings based on their preferences. For example, users can change the background, modify themes, and save different Favorites in Internet Explorer.

Windows keeps these personal settings for each user in the user's profile. When any user logs on, the user's profile is loaded, giving the user the same settings from the last time the user logged on. Table 11-10 shows the locations of the profiles for different operating systems.

TABLE 11-10 Profile Locations

	Default Profile Location
Windows XP	C:\Documents and Settings
Windows Vista	C:\Users
Windows 7	C:\Users

Figure 11-12 shows Windows Explorer opened to the profile of a user named Darril on a Windows 7 system. You can view these folders with Windows Explorer, but most settings are manipulated through the operating system. For example, when a user creates a Favorite in Internet Explorer, the information is stored in a folder in the profile but the user manipulates only Internet Explorer.

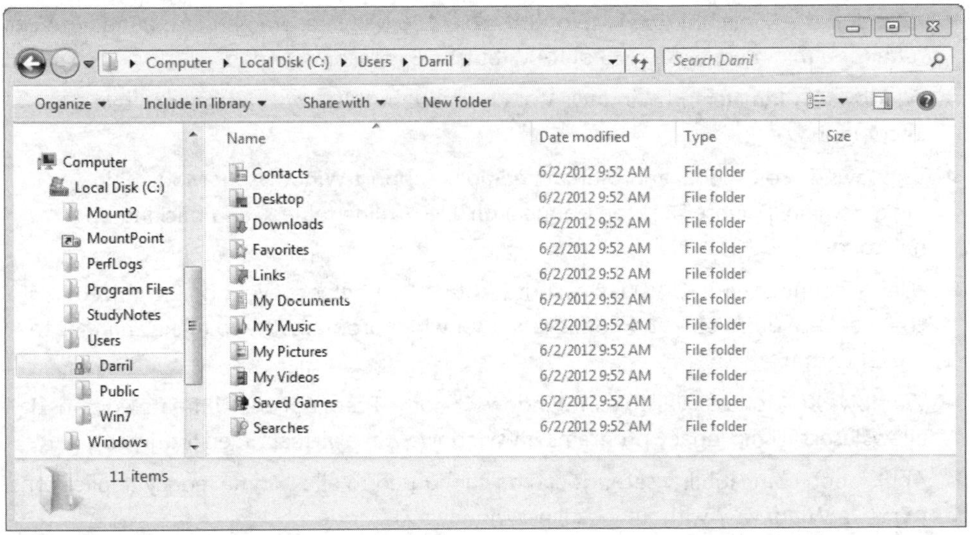

FIGURE 11-12 User profile location on Windows 7.

Chapter Summary

- 32-bit operating systems are based on x86 processors, and 64-bit systems are based on x64 processors. 32-bit systems can address up to 4 GB of RAM but will utilize only about 3.2 to 3.5 GB of RAM if 4 GB of RAM is installed.

- XP and Vista 64-bit systems can use as much as 128 GB of RAM, and Windows 7 64-bit systems can use as much as 192 GB of RAM. Windows 7 Starter is not available in 64-bit versions.

- Windows 7 requires at least 1 GB of RAM and 16 GB of hard drive space for 32-bit systems and at least 2 GB and 20 GB of hard drive space for 64-bit systems.

- Windows 7 Starter and Home Premium use only one processor, whereas Professional and Ultimate use as many as two processors.

- XP requires a minimum of 64 MB of RAM, but 128 MB is recommended. Windows Vista requires a minimum of 512 MB of RAM, but 1 GB is recommended.

- Windows 7 Ultimate and Windows Vista Ultimate both support BitLocker Drive Encryption.

- Windows 7 Professional and Ultimate editions support Windows XP Mode, joining a domain, Remote Desktop Connection, EFS, offline folders, and backing up to a network.

- User Account Control (UAC) is a security feature that helps prevent unauthorized changes. The default setting notifies the user when programs try to make changes to the computer.

- Windows XP Mode is available in Windows 7 Home Premium and Ultimate editions. It allows users to run legacy programs on Windows 7 in a virtual XP environment.

- Application compatibility settings can be configured to allow some legacy applications to run in Windows 7 without installing Windows XP Mode.

- Vista Home Premium, Business, and Ultimate editions support backing up to a network, but full image backups using Windows Complete PC Backup cannot be used to back up data to a network.

- Windows Explorer is the primary tool used to browse files. The system partition is the location where the boot files are located (C:\ by default). The boot partition is the location where the operating system files are located (C:\Windows by default).
- On a 64-bit system, 64-bit application files are in the C:\Program Files folder, and 32-bit application files are in the C:\Program Files (x86) folder.

Chapter Review

Use the following questions to test your knowledge of the information in this chapter. The answers to these questions, and the explanations of why each answer choice is correct or incorrect, are located in the "Answers" section at the end of this chapter.

1. Which of the following Windows 7 editions include both 32-bit and 64-bit versions? (Choose all that apply.)

    A. Starter

    B. Home Premium

    C. Professional

    D. Ultimate

2. A user is running a 32-bit version of Windows 7 Home Premium with 6 GB of RAM installed. However, the system is recognizing only 3.2 GB of RAM. What is the problem?

    A. Home Premium does not support more than 3.2 GB of RAM.

    B. A 32-bit Windows operating system can recognize only about 3.2 GB of RAM.

    C. The processor is not configured in x64 mode.

    D. The processor is an x86 processor.

3. A user is shopping for a computer and sees some computers labeled as x86 and some as x64. What does x86 mean?

    A. The processor supports 32 bits for addressing RAM.

    B. The processor supports 64 bits for addressing RAM.

    C. The processor supports 86 bits for addressing RAM.

    D. The processor includes eight cores but defaults to two 6 cores.

4. What's the minimum amount of RAM required for Windows 7 on a 32-bit system?

    A. 512 MB

    B. 1 MB

    C. 1 GB

    D. 2 GB

5. What's the maximum number of processors that a Windows 7 Home Premium system can recognize?

   A. 1

   B. 2

   C. 32

   D. 256

6. Which of the following editions of Windows 7 support Windows XP Mode? (Choose all that apply.)

   A. Starter

   B. Home Premium

   C. Professional

   D. Ultimate

7. A user is trying to enable BitLocker on a 32-bit edition of Windows 7 Professional with 2 GB of RAM but is having problems. What is the likely reason?

   A. BitLocker is not supported on 32-bit editions of Windows 7.

   B. BitLocker has not been enabled in the Control Panel.

   C. BitLocker is not supported on systems with less than 3 GB of RAM.

   D. BitLocker is not supported on Windows 7 Professional.

8. A user was able to run a program in Windows XP but cannot get it to run in Windows 7 Home Premium. What's the best solution?

   A. Enable Windows XP Mode

   B. Use the Program Compatibility wizard

   C. Enable UAC

   D. Reinstall Windows XP

9. A user was able to run a program in Windows XP but cannot get it to run in a 64-bit edition of Windows 7 Professional. What's a possible solution?

   A. Use Windows XP Mode

   B. Upgrade to Windows 7 Ultimate and use Windows XP Mode

   C. Enable BitLocker

   D. Reinstall Windows 7 using a 32-bit edition

10. Which of the following Windows 7 editions support backing up to a network location? (Choose all that apply.)

   A. Starter

   B. Home Premium

   C. Professional

   D. Ultimate

11. Where are 32-bit application files stored in a Windows 7 64-bit system?

   A. C:\Windows

   B. C:\Program Files

   C. C:\Program Files (x32)

   D. C:\Program Files (x86)

Answers

1. **Correct Answers:** B, C, D

   A. **Incorrect:** Windows 7 Starter edition comes only in 32-bit versions.

   B. **Correct:** Windows 7 Home Premium edition comes in both 32-bit and 64-bit versions.

   C. **Correct:** Windows 7 Professional edition comes in both 32-bit and 64-bit versions.

   D. **Correct:** Windows 7 Ultimate edition comes in both 32-bit and 64-bit versions.

2. **Correct Answer:** B

   A. **Incorrect:** Windows 7 Home Premium 64-bit versions support up to 16 GB of RAM.

   B. **Correct:** Any 32-bit operating system can address only 4 GB of RAM, and it also reserves some of this space to address other hardware in the system.

   C. **Incorrect:** Processors don't have an x64 mode, but even if a system had a 64-bit processor, a 32-bit operating system could still access only about 3.2 GB of RAM.

   D. **Incorrect:** Because the operating system is a 32-bit edition, it's likely the processor is an x86-based processor, but the reason it can't address more RAM is directly related to the operating system, not the processor.

3. **Correct Answer:** A

   A. **Correct:** The x86 label indicates that the processor is a 32-bit processor and can address only 4 GB of RAM.

   B. **Incorrect:** An x64-based processor supports 64-bits for addressing RAM.

   C. **Incorrect:** There aren't any processors that use 86 bits for addressing RAM.

   D. **Incorrect:** The 8 and 6 in x86 do not have anything to do with the number of cores in the processor.

4. **Correct Answer:** C

   A. **Incorrect:** All editions of Windows 7 require more than 512 MB.

   B. **Incorrect:** All editions of Windows 7 require more than 1 MB.

   C. **Correct:** Windows 7 32-bit versions require a minimum of 1 GB of RAM.

   D. **Incorrect:** Windows 7 64-bit versions require a minimum of 2 GB of RAM.

5. **Correct Answer:** A

   A. **Correct:** Windows 7 Home Premium can recognize and use a maximum of one processor.

   B. **Incorrect:** Windows 7 Professional and Ultimate editions can recognize and use a maximum of two processors.

C. **Incorrect:** Windows 7 32-bit systems can recognize and use as many as 32-cores within any processor.

D. **Incorrect:** Windows 7 64-bit systems can recognize and use as many as 256-cores within any processor.

6. **Correct Answers:** C, D

   A. **Incorrect:** The Windows 7 Starter edition does not support Windows XP Mode.

   B. **Incorrect:** The Windows 7 Home Premium edition does not support Windows XP Mode.

   C. **Correct:** The Windows 7 Professional edition does support Windows XP Mode.

   D. **Correct:** The Windows 7 Ultimate edition does support Windows XP Mode.

7. **Correct Answer:** D

   A. **Incorrect:** BitLocker is supported on 32-bit editions of Windows 7 Ultimate edition.

   B. **Incorrect:** BitLocker needs to be enabled in the Control Panel, but it is not supported in Windows 7 Professional, so it can't be enabled on this system.

   C. **Incorrect:** BitLocker does not have any restrictions related to memory.

   D. **Correct:** BitLocker is not supported on Windows 7 Professional, but it is supported on Windows 7 Ultimate.

8. **Correct Answer:** B

   A. **Incorrect:** Windows XP Mode is not available in Windows 7 Home Premium, but it is available in the Professional and Ultimate Editions.

   B. **Correct:** The Program Compatibility Wizard can be used to run an application using settings from previous operating systems.

   C. **Incorrect:** User Account Control (UAC) is a security feature that is normally enabled, but enabling it if it was disabled will not help the compatibility of older applications.

   D. **Incorrect:** Many programs can run using older compatibility settings without reinstalling Windows XP, so a reinstallation is not the best solution.

9. **Correct Answer:** A

   A. **Correct:** Windows XP Mode is a feature available in Windows Professional and Ultimate editions.

   B. **Incorrect:** Windows XP Mode is supported in Professional, so it is not necessary to upgrade to Ultimate.

C. **Incorrect:** BitLocker provides full disk encryption but does not assist with compatibility issues, and it is not available in Windows 7 Professional.

D. **Incorrect:** It is not necessary to reinstall Windows 7, and there is no indication that the application will run in a 32-bit edition.

10. **Correct Answer:** C, D

A. **Incorrect:** Windows 7 Starter does not support backing up to a network location.

B. **Incorrect:** Windows 7 Home Premium does not support backing up to a network location.

C. **Correct:** Windows 7 Professional supports backing up to a network location.

D. **Correct:** Windows 7 Professional supports backing up to a network location.

11. **Correct Answer:** D

A. **Incorrect:** Operating system files are stored in C:\Windows.

B. **Incorrect:** The C:\Program Files folder stores 64-bit application files on a 64-bit system.

C. **Incorrect:** There is no such folder as C:\Program Files (x32).

D. **Correct:** The C:\Program Files (x86) folder stores 32-bit application files on a 64-bit system.

CHAPTER 12

Installing and Updating Windows Operating Systems

A common task that any A+ technician needs to know is how to install or upgrade Windows. Chapter 11, "Introducing Windows Operating Systems," mentions some of the basic requirements for different versions of Windows. In this chapter, you'll learn about different methods of installing Windows, and supported upgrade paths.

Exam 220-802 objectives in this chapter:

- 1.1 Compare and contrast the features and requirements of various Microsoft Operating Systems.
  - Upgrade paths – differences between in place upgrades, compatibility tools, Windows upgrade OS advisor
- 1.2 Given a scenario, install, and configure the operating system using the most appropriate method.
- Boot methods
  - USB
  - CD-ROM
  - DVD
  - PXE
- Type of installations
  - Creating image
  - Unattended installation
  - Upgrade
  - Clean install
  - Repair installation
  - Multiboot
  - Remote network installation
  - Image deployment

- Load alternate third party drivers when necessary
- Workgroup vs. Domain setup
- Time/date/region/language settings

- 1.4 Given a scenario, use appropriate operating system features and tools.
  - Other
    - User State Migration tool (USMT), File and Settings Transfer Wizard, Windows Easy Transfer

- 4.6 Given a scenario, troubleshoot operating system problems with appropriate tools.
  - Common symptoms
    - RAID not detected during installation

REAL WORLD **HAVE YOU EVER INSTALLED AN OPERATING SYSTEM?**

Teaching IT classes over the years, I've been a little surprised at how many students have never installed an operating system from scratch. I realize it seems daunting if you've never done it before, but it's not a difficult task.

Also, after you install one operating system, you'll find that it is relatively easy to install any operating system. For example, after you've installed Windows 7, you'll find it's easy to install Server 2008 R2 when it comes time to expand your knowledge.

I strongly encourage you to actually go through the steps of an installation to experience it. If you don't have a spare system, install one of the free virtualization products such as Microsoft Virtual PC or Windows Virtual PC and install a 32-bit version of Windows in a virtual environment. There's no substitute for experience.

Installing and Upgrading Windows

When a new operating system is released, it's common to upgrade existing systems to take advantage of the new capabilities. In some cases, organizations perform clean installations of the new operating system. Before starting, it's important to ensure that the hardware is compatible. Chapter 11, "Introducing Windows Operating Systems," listed the system requirements for different operating systems. For example, Windows 7 requires at least 1 GB of RAM for 32-bit systems and at least 2 GB of RAM for 64-bit systems.

It's important to know the difference between a clean install and an upgrade. The following sections go a little deeper, but briefly, the primary differences are as follows:

- **Clean install.** Windows is installed as a fresh installation. It does not include any applications or settings from previous installations. Windows 7 calls this a Custom installation.

- **Upgrade.** This is an installation on a system with an existing operating system. Supported programs and settings in the previous operating system will be included in the new installation.

> **NOTE** **PROGRAMS AND APPLICATIONS**
>
> The terms *programs* and *applications* mean same thing. For example, Internet Explorer is a program that is also called an application. End users commonly refer to them as programs, but IT professionals often call them applications. You'll see the term applications used in the A+ objectives most often.

Clean Install

An installation is often referred to as a clean installation. This helps emphasize the point that the installation starts fresh.

Applications and settings from any previous installation are not included in the new installation. For example, if a user had the game "Age of Empires" installed on Windows and then did a new installation, the game would not be included in the custom installation.

There are two types of new installations:

- **Bare metal installation.** This is an installation on a system with no software or operating system on it. For example, if a system's hard drive failed and had to be replaced, you could do a bare metal installation after replacing the hard drive.

- **Install on existing system.** If the system already has an operating system installed, you can perform a clean install over it. None of the applications that worked in the previous operating system will work in this new installation. In some instances, it is possible to preserve the previous operating system and create a dual-boot system.

Dual-Boot System

A *dual-boot* system is one that can boot to multiple operating systems. For example, you can have a system running Windows XP and then do a custom install of Windows 7 on the same computer. When you're done, the system can boot to either Windows XP or Windows 7.

> **NOTE** **MULTIBOOT SYSTEM**
>
> It is possible to add multiple operating systems to a computer, making it a multiboot system. However, you'll often hear technicians refer to systems as dual-boot systems even if they can boot to three or more operating systems.

After creating the dual-boot system, users will see a screen similar to Figure 12-1 when they boot. They can use the Tab key to choose which operating system to start. If they choose Earlier Version Of Windows, it will boot to that version of Windows. If they choose Windows 7, it will boot to Windows 7.

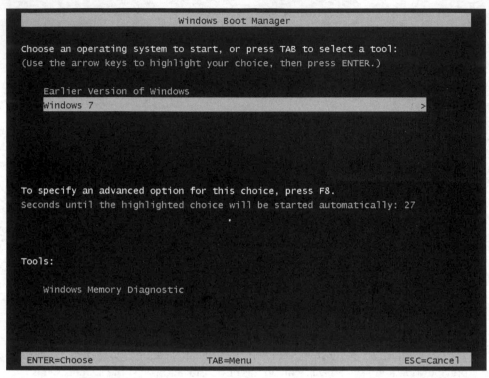

FIGURE 12-1 Dual-boot menu.

The menu gives users some time (typically 30 seconds) and will automatically boot to the default operating system. In Figure 12-1, the default operating system is Windows 7, and it will boot to Windows 7 in 27 seconds. The user can press the Tab key or use the Up and Down Arrows to select different choices, and then press Enter to start it.

There are two important rules you need to follow when using any dual-boot system:

- Always install operating systems on different partitions.
- Always install the newer operating system last.

EXAM TIP

Dual-boot systems should always be installed on different partitions, and newer operating systems must be installed after earlier operating systems. If these rules aren't followed, one or both of the operating systems will stop working.

If you install two operating systems on the same partition, they will corrupt files on the other operating system when they are booted. For example, if Windows 2000 is running on the C partition and you installed Windows XP on the same partition, Windows XP would corrupt Windows 2000 after you booted into it once or twice. If you were able to boot into Windows 2000, it would corrupt Windows XP.

If you install Windows 7 on the same partition as in previous installation, it will detect the previous installation and move data and settings to a folder named Windows.old. You won't be able to boot to the previous operating system anymore. If you're running Windows XP on the C partition, you can install Windows 7 on the D or E partition as long as it exists.

The second point to remember when creating a dual-boot system is to install the newer operating system first. A newer operating system is aware of the older operating system and preserves critical files. However, an older operating system isn't aware of newer operating systems and often corrupts critical files.

For example, if you install Windows XP first and Windows 7 last, Windows 7 recognizes Windows XP and preserves critical files needed by Windows XP. However, if you install Windows XP after Windows 7, it doesn't recognize files needed by Windows 7 and deletes or overwrites them. In many cases, Windows 7 will no longer be bootable. There are advanced methods to fix Windows 7 after installing Windows XP, but they can be avoided by installing Windows 7 last.

Upgrade

An upgrade will include files, settings, and applications from the previous installation. For example, if you have Microsoft Office on a Windows Vista Ultimate installation and you upgrade to Windows 7 Ultimate, Windows 7 would also include Microsoft Office. You wouldn't have to reinstall Microsoft Office.

An upgrade is often the easiest path for many users. The system retains most of the functionality of the previous operating system but gains the additional features of the newer operating system. However, there are limitations on what systems can be upgraded. The "Upgrade Paths to Windows 7" section later in this chapter provides more information.

When upgrading an earlier operating system to Windows 7 on the same partition, Windows 7 retains data from the previous installation in a folder named Windows.old. You can copy data from the Windows.old folder to anywhere else on your system.

> **EXAM TIP**
> The Windows.old folder holds data from a previous installation of Windows. It includes the Windows folder, the Program Files folder, and user profiles. The user profiles include data that a user might have stored, such as documents, music files, and more. If the previous installation was Windows XP, profiles are in the Windows.old\Documents and Settings folder. If the previous installation was Vista or Windows 7, the profiles are in the Windows.old\Users folder.

When you're satisfied that you no longer need the data in the Windows.old folder, you can delete the folder by using Disk Cleanup. Click Start, type in **Disk Cleanup**, and press Enter to start this program. Select Previous Windows Installation(s) and click OK to delete the folder.

File Systems

Chapter 16, "Understanding Disks and File Systems," covers file systems in more depth, but in short, there are two file systems you should understand when installing an operating system. Both of the following file systems provide access to files and folders stored on disks:

- **FAT32.** The File Allocation Table (FAT) 32-bit file system is a basic file system. It does not include security features such as the ability to assign permissions to files and folders. Technicians sometimes refer to FAT32 as simply FAT. However, FAT refers to an older 16-bit version of FAT, and FAT32 refers to the 32-bit version. Most USB flash drives and USB external drives use FAT32.

- **NTFS.** The New Technology File System (NTFS) is the preferred file system for Windows. It provides increased security and reliability compared to FAT32. You can assign permissions to files and folders, and it has additional features that improve its performance.

All versions of Windows support both FAT32 and NTFS for reading and writing files. However, some versions of Windows cannot be installed on FAT32 drives, as shown in Table 12-1.

TABLE 12-1 Installing Windows on FAT32 or NTFS

	Install on FAT32	Install on NTFS
Windows XP	Yes	Yes
Windows Vista	No	Yes
Windows 7	No	Yes

✔ **Quick Check**

1. What is not included in a new installation of Windows that is included in an upgrade?

2. What is a computer that can boot to two different operating systems called?

3. On which file system(s) can you install Windows 7?

Methods of Installation

There are several methods you can use to install a copy of Windows. The three primary types of installations are as follows:

- With installation media such as a CD or DVD
- Over the network
- Using images

Each of the preceding methods allows you to install Windows on a computer with an existing operating system or on a new computer. However, even if you're installing it on a system with an existing operating system, it doesn't mean that it's an upgrade. Applications needed by the user will still need to be installed.

EXAM TIP

When preparing for the A+ certification, you should understand the basic methods of installing Windows. This includes installing Windows with installation media, performing an installation over the network, and using images.

Installation Media—CD or DVD

If you purchase a retail copy of Windows, it comes on a bootable CD or DVD with all the files you need. You can place the CD or DVD into your system, turn it on, and start the installation.

EXAM TIP

If your system doesn't boot to the DVD by default, you'll need to configure your BIOS to boot to the DVD first.

The "Installing Windows 7" section later in this chapter includes steps you can follow to install Windows 7 from scratch. During the installation, you can configure your hard drives by partitioning or formatting them as desired.

Remote Network Installation

In some cases, it's more convenient to install Windows over the network. You first copy all of the installation files to a folder on a server and then share the folder. Users can then connect to the network share and start the installation.

For example, you can copy the entire contents of the Windows 7 installation DVD onto a network share and install systems from there. Figure 12-2 shows a Windows XP system connected to a network share named Win7Install on a computer named power-PC. After connecting, users can double-click Setup to start the installation.

FIGURE 12-2 Connecting to a share over the network.

> **NOTE** **UNIVERSAL NAMING CONVENTION**
>
> The path to a network share is *serverName**shareName*, also known as the Universal Naming Convention (UNC). If the server is named power-pc and the share name is Win7Install, the path is \\power-pc\Win7Install.

Each system still needs a valid license key to activate it. However, the contents of the DVD are not tied to the license key, so a single DVD can be used with multiple license keys.

A drawback to this installation method is that it can consume a lot of network bandwidth. If the network is already busy, this added network traffic can slow network performance down for all users.

Image Deployment

A very common method of installing Windows today is with imaging. It saves a lot of time and reduces the cost of deploying systems. An *image* is a snapshot of a system, and after this snapshot is captured, it can be deployed to multiple systems.

For example, an administrator might need to install Windows 7 on 30 new computers. The administrator could do all 30 computers individually or could use imaging to speed up the process. Figure 12-3 shows an overview of this process.

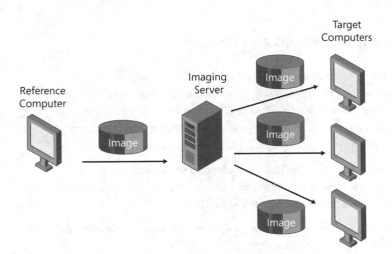

FIGURE 12-3 Installing Windows with imaging.

The administrator first installs Windows 7 onto a reference computer and then installs applications, such as Microsoft Office, based on the needs of the users. The administrator configures security and desktop settings and then tests the system to ensure that it works. After preparing the system, the administrator captures the image and stores it either on a server or on an external drive. After this image is captured, the administrator can deploy it to multiple computers.

> *NOTE* **IMAGING TOOLS**
>
> There are many tools you can purchase to create images, such as Symantec's Ghost. However, you can also use free tools provided by Microsoft, such as the Windows Automated Installation Kit (WAIK) or Windows Deployment Services (WDS). The WAIK includes the imagex and dism command-line tools that you can use to capture, manipulate, and deploy images. WDS is installed on a server.

It is common to store the image on an imaging server, but it's also possible to store the image on an external USB drive or even a DVD if the image is small enough. The administrator can then deploy these images to multiple systems.

After deploying the images, some setup is still required. For example, you can't have 100 computers all named Computer1, so each system needs to have a unique computer name. However, it is possible to automate this process.

EXAM TIP

Imaging is a valuable tool to deploy Windows to multiple systems. It reduces the time needed to configure and deploy systems, reducing overall costs.

All Windows 7 Installations Use Images

It's worthwhile pointing out that all Windows 7 installations actually use images. If you have a Windows 7 installation DVD, you can look in the sources folder and find the Install.wim file. This is a Windows Image file, and it includes all the files needed for different Windows 7 editions. For example, the Install.wim file normally includes images for Windows 7 Home Premium, Professional, and Ultimate.

There are separate Install.wim files for 32-bit versions and 64-bit versions of Windows 7. However, an installation DVD will be either a 32-bit version or a 64-bit version, so you won't have both versions on the same DVD.

Image files in the Install.wim file are the same types of images that can be created by using Microsoft tools such as WAIK or WDS.

PXE Clients

Many desktop systems include *preboot execution environment* (*PXE,* pronounced as *pixie*) components that are used during the imaging process. These systems include a network interface card (NIC) and Basic Input/Output System (BIOS) that can be configured to boot the system by using the NIC. That is, the system boots without any operating system on the disk drive. Instead, it connects to an imaging server over the network and downloads an image.

The overall steps of a PXE boot are as follows:

1. The system is turned on. Sometimes the user needs to press F12 to start the PXE boot process after it is turned on.

2. The system queries a Dynamic Host Configuration Protocol (DHCP) server for an IP address and other network configuration data.

3. The system contacts an imaging server.

4. An image is downloaded and installed onto the client. In some cases, this can be a predetermined image for the computer. In other cases, the user is prompted to log on and choose from a selection of images.

EXAM TIP

The two requirements for a PXE client are the PXE-aware NIC and BIOS that can be configured to boot via the NIC.

Installing from a USB

It's also possible to create a bootable USB flash drive and then copy the image onto the USB. A DVD holds 4.7 GB of data, so an 8-GB or larger USB flash drive will easily hold the data needed to boot from the USB and the image.

Sysprep

One of the potential problems with imaging is that you can have multiple computers with identical settings that should be unique. For example, the operating system identifies computers with a security identifier (SID), and the SID must be unique. If you have two or more computers with the same SID, you'll have problems. Similarly, computers need different computer names, although it's much easier to change the name of a computer than it is to change a computer's SID.

The *system preparation (Sysprep)* tool helps you avoid these problems by preparing a system for imaging. After you install Windows 7 on a reference computer, install appropriate applications, and configure it, you run Sysprep. Sysprep sanitizes the computer by removing the SID along with other unique settings.

You can find the Sysprep program in the C:\Windows\System32\Sysprep folder by default. Figure 12-4 shows the Sysprep tool with the recommended settings to prepare a system for imaging.

```
System Preparation Tool 3.14                        [ x ]

System Preparation Tool (Sysprep) prepares the machine for
hardware independence and cleanup.

System Cleanup Action
  Enter System Out-of-Box Experience (OOBE)    ▼
      ☑ Generalize

Shutdown Options
  Shutdown                                     ▼

              [   OK   ]    [  Cancel  ]
```

FIGURE 12-4 Running the system preparation (Sysprep) tool.

EXAM TIP

Sysprep must be run on Windows-based systems before capturing the image. It can be run from the GUI or from the command line. The typical command from the command line is **Sysprep /oobe /generalize /shutdown.**

The System Out-Of-Box Experience (OOBE) option, with the Generalize check box selected, resets the required settings to prepare the system for imaging. After running this, the system is shut down and the image is ready to be captured.

When you deploy this image to a system and boot it up, many of the settings will be automatically re-created for the new system. The installation program prompts the user to answer questions for other settings, such as the primary user name and the name of the computer.

Unattended Installation with Answer Files

You can use answer files to perform unattended installations. When an *answer file* is used, the installation program looks for the information it needs from it instead of prompting the user for the answer. If the answer isn't there, the installation program prompts the user for the answer.

The answer file can include all the answers so that the entire installation is automated. It's also possible to include the answers for part of the installation and prompt the user for other information. For example, an answer file could include information needed to format the hard drive as a single formatted partition but not include other information. The user won't be prompted to configure the drive but will be prompted to provide other answers.

You can use answer files when installing the operating system with installation media or over the network. You can also create an answer file to be used with images so that after an image is deployed, these settings are automatically answered without any user action.

The WAIK includes the System Image Manager (SIM), and the SIM is used to create answer files. The SIM has a lot of functionality. It can be used to add drivers and applications to an answer file, and administrators can configure many more details of Windows 7 installations by using this feature. For example, if administrators want to ensure that games are not included in an installation of Windows 7 Ultimate, they can specify this in the answer file. Many of the choices made available by using an answer file are not available when manually installing Windows 7.

Recovery Disc or Factory Recovery Partition

Many computer vendors provide a method for users to return their system to the way it was when it left the factory. This is very useful if the operating system becomes corrupted and can no longer boot. Sometimes the vendor provides a recovery CD or DVD, and other times the vendor installs a recovery partition.

Both methods allow the user to recover the system if Windows is no longer bootable. The differences are as follows:

- **Recovery Disc.** This is a bootable CD or DVD. It includes an image that can be reapplied to the computer to return it to its original configuration.
- **Recovery Partition.** The recovery partition is a partition on the hard drive. It holds all the files needed to recover the system if the system fails. This partition is often hidden, but instructions from the vendor show how to use it to recover the system.

✔ **Quick Check**

1. What are the three primary methods of installing Windows?
2. What do you run to prepare a Windows-based system before capturing an image of it?

Quick Check Answers

1. With installation media, over the network, or with images.
2. Run Sysprep.

Upgrade Paths to Windows 7

When considering upgrading a Windows operating system today, the primary system to which you'll upgrade is Windows 7. You can't buy retail versions of Windows XP or Windows Vista systems anymore, but Windows 7 is available. With that in mind, it's important to understand which operating systems can be upgraded to Windows 7 and which can't.

Two key points to remember are as follows:

- You can upgrade Windows Vista to Windows 7.
- You cannot upgrade Windows XP directly to Windows 7.

If desired, you can upgrade Windows XP to Windows Vista and then upgrade Windows Vista to Windows 7. However, most IT professionals recommend performing a clean install. You'll have to reinstall applications after the install, but you can migrate user data and settings from Windows XP to Windows 7.

NOTE **DATA MIGRATION TOOLS**

The two tools used to migrate user data and settings are the Windows Easy Transfer tool and the User State Migration Tool. Both are discussed later in this chapter.

Table 12-2 lists the available upgrade paths from earlier versions of Windows. If an upgrade path is not available, you must do a clean installation of Windows 7.

TABLE 12-2 Windows 7 Upgrade Paths

	Upgrade to Home Premium	Upgrade to Professional	Upgrade to Ultimate
From Windows XP	No	No	No
From Windows Vista Home Premium	Yes	Yes	Yes
From Windows Vista Business	No	Yes	Yes
From Windows Vista Ultimate	No	No	Yes
From 32-bit to 64-bit	No	No	No
From 64-bit to 32-bit	No	No	No

Note that when you're doing an upgrade from Windows Vista to Windows 7, you can upgrade only to a comparable edition or higher. For example, you can upgrade Vista Home Premium to Windows 7 Professional or Ultimate. You cannot upgrade Vista Ultimate to Windows 7 Home Premium because Home Premium is a step down from Ultimate. Likewise, you can't upgrade a consumer version of Windows 7 to a business version (that is, from Windows 7 Ultimate to Windows 7 Enterprise).

Upgrade vs. Upgrade

Upgrade means two different things depending on the context. One is related to the purchase price, and the other is related to how Windows can be installed.

Operating systems can be purchased at full retail price or at a reduced upgrade price if a user is running a qualified earlier version. For example, if users are running Windows 2000, XP, or Vista, they can purchase and install the upgrade version of Windows 7 at a reduced cost. The only difference between this version and the full retail version is that this version checks to ensure that users have an earlier version of Windows. If they don't have a qualifying version of Windows, they need to purchase the retail version at full price.

However, when doing the installation, they can do an upgrade only from Windows Vista to Windows 7. If they are running Windows 2000 or XP, the actual installation will be a clean install, not an upgrade.

Windows Anytime Upgrade

You can use *Windows Anytime Upgrade* to upgrade some editions of Windows 7 to a higher edition. This is primarily targeted at home users who decide that they want to increase the capabilities of Windows 7 installed on their systems. For example, if users are running

Windows 7 Home Premium edition and want to upgrade to the Ultimate edition, they can use Anytime Upgrade to do so.

> **NOTE** **ANYTIME UPGRADE AVAILABILITY**
>
> Anytime Upgrade is available only for Windows 7 at this time. It was available for Windows Vista when Vista was being sold. However, Anytime Upgrade is no longer available for Windows Vista.

Table 12-3 shows the available paths for Anytime Upgrades.

TABLE 12-3 Anytime Upgrade Paths

	Upgrade to Premium	Upgrade to Professional	Upgrade to Ultimate
From Windows 7 Starter	Yes	Yes	Yes
From Windows 7 Home Premium	No	Yes	Yes
From Windows 7 Professional	No	Yes	Yes

EXAM TIP

Windows Anytime Upgrade allows users to upgrade to a higher edition of Windows 7. Users purchase a license key, and the upgrade is completed without the installation DVD or downloading files.

The upgrade process usually only takes about 10 minutes, and it doesn't require any additional installation media. Users can complete the process online by purchasing a new license key, or they can purchase a retail key at a store and enter it on their computers.

Any installation of Windows 7 includes all the appropriate files to enable all the features. However, some features are enabled or disabled based on the Windows 7 edition. When a computer is upgraded with Windows Anytime Upgrade, the additional features are enabled.

If you want to get more information about the Windows Anytime Upgrade, you can watch this short video: *http://windows.microsoft.com/en-US/windows7/help/videos/getting-more -out-of-your-pc-with-windows-anytime-upgrade.*

Repair Installation

In some extreme cases, Windows will no longer boot. One way to fix it is to complete a repair installation, sometimes called a *repair-in-place* upgrade. This reinstalls Windows and repairs any corrupted files. During the process, it is possible to upgrade the operating system from an earlier edition to a new edition. This will work only if the upgrade path is supported, as shown in Table 12-2.

A repair installation should be completed only when all other methods have been exhausted. Chapter 17, "Troubleshooting Windows Operating Systems," covers some tools you can use to troubleshoot and repair a system before trying this.

> **NOTE** **LICENSE KEY NEEDED**
>
> A repair-in-place upgrade is also called a repair installation. You'll need the installation CD or DVD as well as the license key to complete the installation.

When performing a repair installation on Windows 7, the upgrade process will attempt to save existing data in the Windows.old folder. You can often retrieve data from this folder after the repair, but don't count on it. You should first attempt to back up any data before attempting the repair.

> ✔ **Quick Check**
>
> 1. Can you upgrade Windows XP to Windows 7?
> 2. Can you upgrade a 32-bit edition of Vista to a 64-bit edition of Windows 7?
>
> **Quick Check Answers**
>
> 1. No; this upgrade path is not supported.
> 2. No; you cannot upgrade 32-bit editions to 64-bit editions.

Windows 7 Upgrade Advisor

 If you're considering an upgrade to Windows 7 on an existing system, you might want to verify that your system doesn't have any compatibility issues. The *Windows 7 Upgrade Advisor* is a free tool that you can use to check a system. You can access the site to download it by clicking the Check Compatibility Online link from the initial Windows 7 installation screen. You can also download it from here: *http://windows.microsoft.com/en-us/windows/downloads /upgrade-advisor.*

> **NOTE** **ONLINE UPGRADE ADVISOR**
>
> You can also find the upgrade advisor from Microsoft's download site (*http://www .microsoft.com/download/*) by searching on Windows Upgrade Advisor. You can use this same method to find many free downloads provided by Microsoft.

If you're running the Upgrade Advisor on Windows XP, the installation wizard will ensure that .NET Framework 2.0 is installed. If it isn't installed, the installation wizard will prompt you for approval and will then download and install it.

After installing the Upgrade Advisor, you can run on it the system from the Start, All Programs menu. The advisor will check all devices that are connected to your system and turned on, so it's important to ensure that you have connected them and turned them on before starting the check.

Compatibility Tools

The following two websites are useful when checking compatibility for a Windows-based system:

- **Windows Compatibility Center.** This site lists hardware and software that is compatible with Windows. You can access it here: *http://www.microsoft.com/windows/compatibility.*

- **Windows Logo'd Products list (LPL)**. This site lists hardware devices that have been verified to work with different versions of Windows. It was previously known as the hardware compatibility list (HCL). You can access it here: *https://sysdev.microsoft.com/.*

If you want to get more information on software and hardware compatibility, check out this video: *http://windows.microsoft.com/en-US/windows7/help/videos/software-and-hardware-compatibility-in-Windows-7.*

Installing Windows 7

A simple job interview question might be, "Have you ever installed Windows 7?" You want to be able to reply, "Yes." It's not difficult, but you should be aware of what you'll see during the installation. This section describes the process.

Selecting Time/Date/Region/Language Settings

The first screen you'll see when installing Windows 7 is shown in Figure 12-5. You are prompted to choose settings based on where you're installing Windows 7.

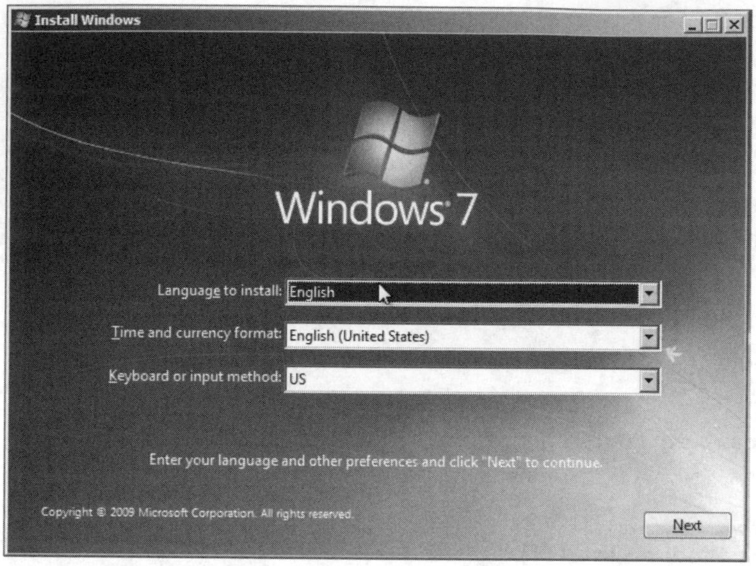

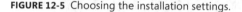

FIGURE 12-5 Choosing the installation settings.

You'll normally have only one choice for the Language To Install field. However, the Time And Currency Format and the Keyboard Or Input Method fields will have multiple choices.

The time and currency format affects how the time, date, and currency are displayed. For example, July 4, 2013, using English (United States), is displayed as 7/4/2013. The same date, using English (Australia), is displayed as 4/07/2013. Keyboards have alternate keys to support different languages, and there are also several alternate layouts available. These settings can also be manipulated by using the Region And Language applet in the Control Panel after the installation completes.

During the installation, you'll also be prompted to verify the correct time and date and to set the time zone. If you want to modify this later, you can use the Date And Time applet in the Control Panel.

Choosing the Install Method

When installing Windows 7 from the installation DVD, you'll have two options, Upgrade or Custom (Advanced), as shown in Figure 12-6. You'll choose Upgrade if you're upgrading from an operating system that is included in the upgrade path. Custom (Advanced) is used for new installations.

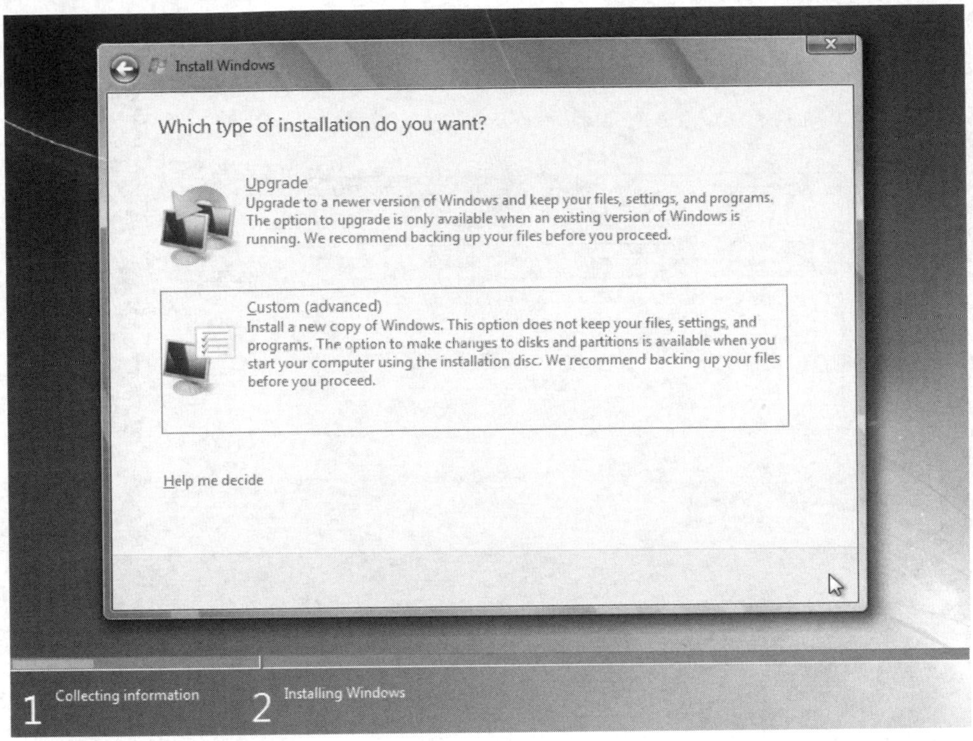

FIGURE 12-6 Choosing the type of installation.

You can also choose where to install the operating system. Most of the time, you'll have only a single disk, but sometimes you will want to create additional partitions. For example, if you plan on creating a dual-boot system, you'll need at least two partitions. Additionally, some people like to have one partition for the operating system and another partition for data. The installation program gives you several options for configuring the hard drive.

Drive Options

When installing Windows 7, you are prompted to identify where you want to install Windows. If you have a single drive with a single partition, the choice is clear; select it and move on. However, if you have multiple drives or multiple partitions on a drive, you'll have more choices. Additionally, you might want to manipulate existing drives and partitions during the installation.

Figure 12-7 shows the options that will appear if you click Drive Options (Advanced) on the Where Do You Want To Install Windows? screen.

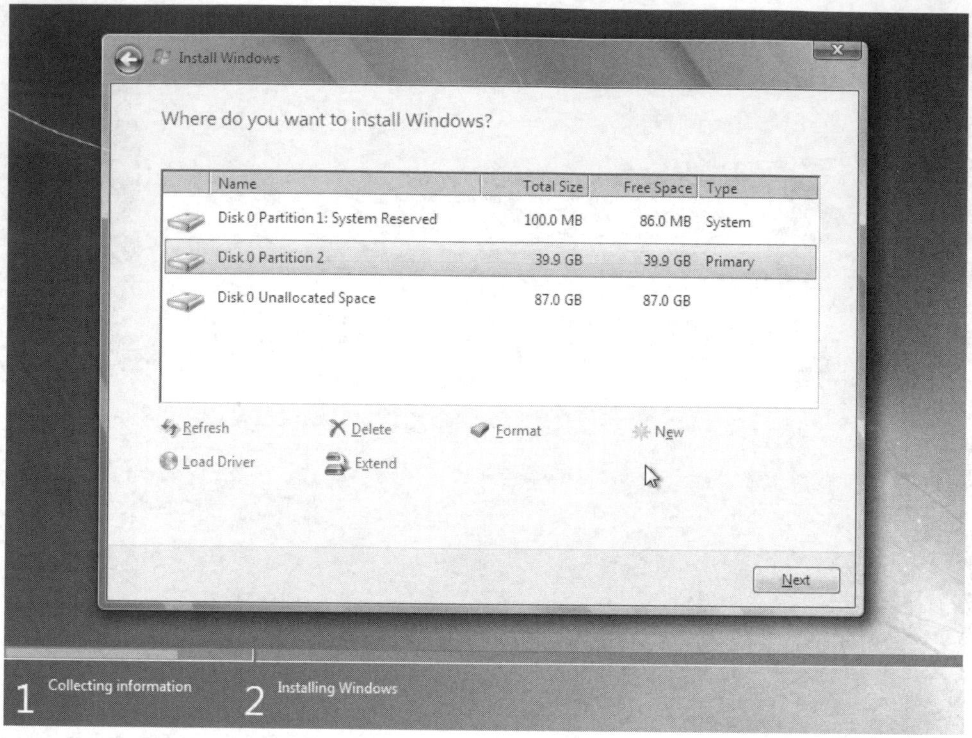

FIGURE 12-7 Manipulating partitions.

> **EXAM TIP**
>
> If your disk drive is not recognized by the installation program, you can load the required drivers by clicking Load Driver. This is often required if your system is using a hardware-based redundant array of independent disks (RAID) subsystem and the RAID is not detected during installation. Chapter 16 covers RAID configurations in more detail.

Figure 12-6 shows two partitions and 87 GB of unallocated space on the drive. The hard drive shown in the figure started as a single 127-GB disk listed as Disk 0 Unallocated Space. I clicked New and entered 40960 to create a partition of about 40 GB in size. The installation program also created the 100-MB system partition (described in the next section).

You have multiple options available to manipulate the hard drive, including the following:

- **Load Driver.** If your hard drive is not recognized, it might be that Windows 7 doesn't have a driver for it. For example, if your system is using a hardware-based RAID system, it might not be recognized until you load the driver. Drivers can be loaded from a floppy disk, CD, DVD, or USB flash drive.

- **Delete.** Choose this to delete an existing partition. All data and files on the partition will be lost, so be careful when choosing this option. The space from the deleted partition will be reported as unallocated space.

- **Extend.** You can extend an existing partition onto unallocated space. For example, in Figure 12-7, partition 2 is about 40 GB. You can extend this to include any amount of the 87 GB of unallocated space.

- **Format.** This option will format the partition with NTFS, and doesn't give you any options. All data on this partition will be lost.

- **New.** If your drive has unallocated space, you can click the unallocated space, select New, and create a partition. This gives you the option of choosing the size of the partition.

- **Refresh.** After making a modification to a drive, you might need to click Refresh to show the changes.

You can use the following steps to manipulate partitions. These steps assume that your hard drive is a single hard drive without any allocated space.

1. Click Drive Options (Advanced).

2. Click New.

3. In the Size text box, enter the desired size of the partition. For example, in the following graphic, I entered 40960 for a size of about 40 GB.

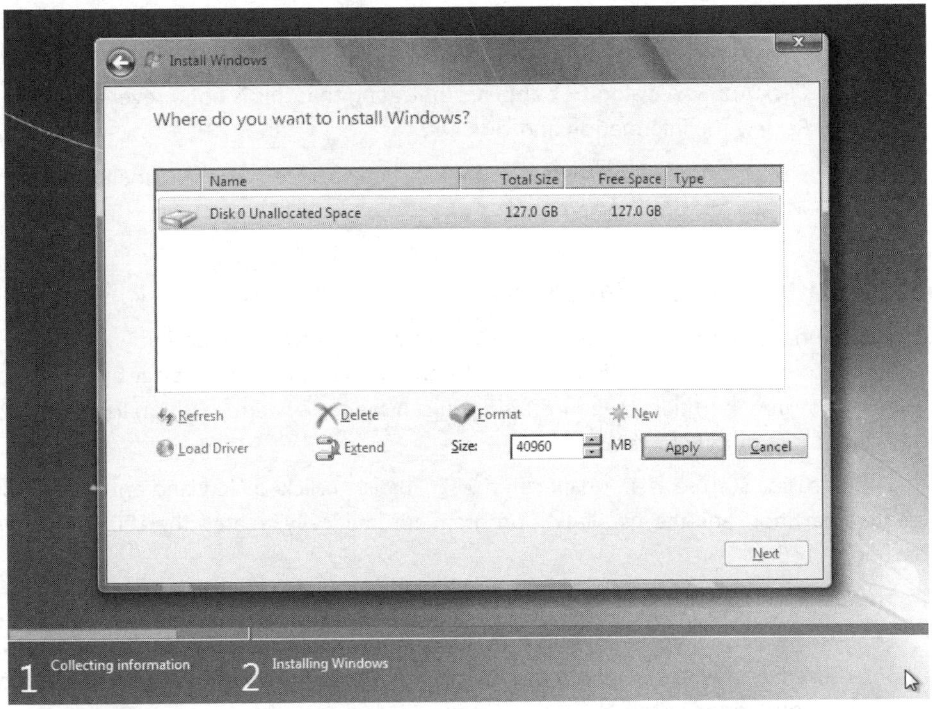

4. Click Apply.

5. If you want to delete a partition, do the following:

   A. Select the partition and click Delete.

   B. Review the warning and click OK. All the data on the partition will be deleted, and space from this partition will be added to the unallocated space.

> **IMPORTANT** DELETING OR FORMATTING A PARTITION DELETES ALL THE DATA ON THE PARTITION.
>
> **You will not be able to recover data after deleting or formatting the partition.**

6. If you want to format a partition, do the following:

   A. Select a partition and click Format.

   B. A warning appears indicating that any data stored on the partition will be lost. Review the warning and click OK. The partition is formatted with NTFS.

7. If you want to extend a partition to included unallocated space, do the following:

   A. Select a partition and click Extend.

   B. Enter the size that you want the partition to be after it is extended in the Size text box. The text box defaults to the maximum size. If you want to include all the unallocated space, leave this text box unchanged.

   C. Click Apply. A dialog box appears indicating that this is not a reversible action. Review the information and click OK.

   D. The partition will be resized to the size you specified, and the unallocated space will decrease by that amount.

System Reserved Partition

If there is unallocated space on a drive, Windows 7 often creates an additional 100-MB partition during the installation. This system partition doesn't have a drive letter but instead is listed as a system partition. In Figure 12-7, you can see the system partition listed first as Disk 0 Partition 1: System Reserved.

This partition started as an unallocated 127-GB disk. I clicked New and entered 39960 to create a partition, and the installation program automatically created the 100-MB system partition.

This partition is reserved for the following:

- **System boot files.** The partition includes bootmgr, bootsect.bak, and the boot folder. These files are used during the boot of the system. If the system partition is not created during the install, Windows 7 stores these files in the system partition.

- **BitLocker drive encryption.** This reserved space ensures that BitLocker can later be enabled on the system.

- **Windows Recovery Environment (WinRE).** The WinRE can be used to recover from many system errors after a failure.

The system partition isn't always created. For example, if you are installing Windows 7 on a system with another operating system as a dual-boot system, the installation program does not create the system partition. Similarly, if the drive does not have any unallocated space available, the install program does not create the system partition.

If the system partition was created during the installation of Windows 7, it should not be deleted. If a user does manage to delete it, you can recover the system by using Windows 7 recovery procedures and the installation DVD. If you want to ensure that the system partition isn't created, you can format your drive using 100 percent of the space before starting the installation of Windows 7.

> *NOTE* **ACCESSING COMMAND PROMPT DURING INSTALL**
>
> An advanced method that you can use to prevent the system partition from being created is to have diskpart available at the command prompt. You can access the command prompt from within the installation program by pressing Shift+F10. Chapter 14, "Using the Command Prompt," covers the command prompt in more detail.

Performing a Clean Install

You can complete a clean installation of Windows 7 Ultimate with the following steps:

1. Place the installation DVD into the DVD drive and start the system. If the system is not configured to boot to the DVD, you might need to change the BIOS settings as described in Chapter 2, "Understanding Motherboards and BIOS."

    A. If you're running another Windows-based system, you can also start the installation from within the operating system. Place the DVD into the DVD drive.

    B. Browse to the DVD and double-click the setup program.

2. An installation screen will appear, similar to Figure 12-5. Select the appropriate language, time and currency format, and keyboard or input method based on your location. Click Next.

3. Click Install Now.

4. The Microsoft Software License Terms screen appears. Review the license terms and select I Accept The License Terms. Click Next.

5. When prompted to select an Upgrade or a Custom (Advanced) installation, click Custom (Advanced).

6. You'll be prompted to choose where to install Windows. You can manipulate the drive partitions by clicking Drive Options (Advanced) as mentioned in the "Drive Options"

section earlier in this chapter. Select the drive and partition where you want to install Windows 7 and click Next.

Windows 7 will begin the installation. It copies files to your system, starts installing them, and restarts on its own. This process can take some time, but it does not require any interaction until the Set Up Windows screen appears.

7. When the Set Up Windows screen appears, enter a user name. The name of the computer will be created automatically by appending the user name with -PC as shown in the following graphic. However, you can enter a different computer name if desired.

8. Click Next.

9. On the Password page, enter a password in the Type A Password (Recommended) text box and in the Retype Your Password text box.

> **NOTE PASSWORDS PROVIDE SECURITY**
>
> You can skip the password, but as a security precaution, it's recommended to use a password to protect your user account from other users.

10. Type a word or phrase in the Type A Password Hint text box. If you forget your password, Windows will show you your hint.

11. On the Windows Product Key page, enter your product key. Click Next.

12. On the Update page, you can select Use Recommended Settings, Install Important Updates Only, or Ask Me Later. The recommended settings will automatically install updates and are the easiest settings for many uses. Select the option you want.

13. On the time and date page, select your time zone and click Next.

14. If your computer is connected to a network, you'll be prompted to choose your computer's location, as shown in the following graphic. Click on your location.

15. If you're connected to a home network that has a homegroup, you'll be prompted to enter the homegroup password. If you know it, you can enter the password here and click Next. If you don't want to join the homegroup, you can click Skip.

> **MORE INFO**   **CHAPTER 24, "CONNECTING AND TROUBLESHOOTING A NETWORK"**
>
> Homegroups are explained further in Chapter 24, and networking concepts are presented in the Chapters 18 through 24. Also, your system will be automatically configured in a workgroup named WORKGROUP, but this can be changed. Chapter 18, "Introducing Networking Components," includes information about workgroups and domains, including steps to join a workgroup or a domain.

16. Windows 7 will complete the setup, and your desktop will appear. If you chose the recommended settings for updates, updates will automatically be downloaded. If prompted to restart the computer, click Restart Now.

Activation

Microsoft operating systems use an activation program. This helps verify to users that their copy of Windows is genuine. It also ensures that Windows has not been used on more computers than the Microsoft Software License Terms allow.

Windows 7 needs to be activated within 30 days after installation and can be activated over the Internet or by phone. Most installations are configured to automatically activate Windows when the users are online. Automatic activation begins trying to activate Windows three days after the user logs on for the first time.

The activation program pairs the activation key with details on the computer hardware. If you need to reinstall Windows 7 on the same computer, you can use the same key. However, if you try to install it on a different computer, the activation key will not work.

> *NOTE* **HARDWARE REPLACEMENT MAY REQUIRE REACTIVATION**
>
> If a hardware failure requires you to make a significant hardware change, you might need to reactivate the system. This can usually be completed over the Internet, but in some cases, users must call Microsoft to reactivate the system after replacing hardware.

✔ **Quick Check**

1. How can you add drivers for a disk drive during an installation of Windows 7?

2. What does the 100-MB partition created during some installations of Windows contain?

Quick Check Answers

1. Select Load Driver from the Drive Options screen.

2. System boot files, space for BitLocker, and the Windows Recovery Environment (WinRE).

Upgrading Windows Vista

If you are upgrading Vista to Windows 7, you can start the installation program after booting into Windows Vista. Place the installation DVD into the drive, and if it doesn't start automatically, browse to the DVD and double-click the setup program.

This works very much like the clean installation of Windows 7 but with a couple of differences. First, instead of choosing Custom (Advanced) on the installation screen, you'll choose Upgrade. Second, the upgrade will try to keep all of the applications, settings, and data intact.

You should ensure that the current service pack is applied to Windows Vista before upgrading. Windows Service Pack 2 was released in April 2009, and it's unlikely that another service pack will be released for Windows Vista. Therefore, apply Service Pack 2 to Vista before upgrading.

> **NOTE** **BACK UP DATA BEFORE AN UPGRADE**
>
> An upgrade is considered a risky operation. Everything will usually work fine, but things can go wrong. It's important to back up all important data before starting an upgrade.

Migrating User Data

When you install a new operating system for a user who had a previous computer, the user often wants to keep data and settings from the previous installation. There are two valuable tools you can use to capture this information from the older version of Windows and reapply it the new version of Windows: Windows Easy Transfer and User State Migration Tool.

Each of these tools can capture a wide variety of data and settings, including the following:

- Files and folders
- User accounts and profiles
- Multimedia files such as photos, music, and videos
- Email files such as Outlook data files, including email, contacts, and calendar events
- Settings for Windows, applications such as Internet Explorer, and other programs

Each of these tools is described in the following sections.

> **NOTE** **MIGRATION NOT NEEDED FOR UPGRADE**
>
> If you're doing an upgrade, there is no need to migrate the user data and settings. This information will be migrated to the newer version as part of the upgrade process.

One of the tasks that these programs perform is to move the files and folders to locations that Windows 7 understands. For example, in Windows XP, the user profiles are stored in C:\Documents and Settings by default. In Windows 7, they are stored in C:\Users. If you migrate user accounts and profiles from Windows XP to Windows 7, the migration tool moves them to the C:\Users folder on Windows 7.

Windows Easy Transfer

You can use *Windows Easy Transfer* to transfer files and settings from one computer to another. For example, you can transfer files and settings from Windows XP to Windows 7, from Windows Vista to Windows 7, or even from one computer running Windows 7 to another computer running Windows 7.

Windows Easy Transfer enables you to migrate information by using one of the following methods:

- **An Easy Transfer cable.** This is a special cable that plugs into the USB port of the two computers. You can purchase it on the web or in an electronics store. It allows you to transfer files directly between the old computer and the new computer.

- **A network.** If the computers are connected to each other in a network, you can transfer the files over the network.

- **An external hard disk or USB flash drive.** You can transfer the files to an external disk or a flash drive connected to the old computer. You can later connect the drive to new computer and transfer the files from the drive.

Windows Easy Transfer is included in Windows 7. However, if you are migrating data from Windows XP or Windows Vista, you'll first need to download and install the appropriate Windows Easy Transfer tool onto that system.

For example, if you want to capture data from Windows XP, you can download Windows Easy Transfer for XP and install it on the Windows XP–based computer. Free versions are available for 32-bit and 64-bit Windows XP and for 32-bit and 64-bit Windows Vista. Go to the Windows download site (*http://www.microsoft.com/download*) and search for *Windows Easy Transfer for Windows XP* or *Windows Easy Transfer for Windows Vista,* based on your needs.

EXAM TIP

Windows Easy Transfer can capture data from Windows XP, Windows Vista, and Windows 7. It replaces the Files And Settings Transfer (FAST) wizard used with Windows XP.

You can start the Windows Easy Transfer tool on Windows 7 by clicking Start, All Programs, Accessories, System Tools, and selecting Windows Easy Transfer. Because this tool can access files and folders for all users on the system, you must have administrative access to run it.

This tool automatically selects files in the Documents, Music, and Pictures folder, and also gives you the option of selecting additional files and folders. Figure 12-8 shows the screen you can use to select or deselect categories such as Documents or Music. If you click Advanced on this page, you can select individual files and folders to migrate.

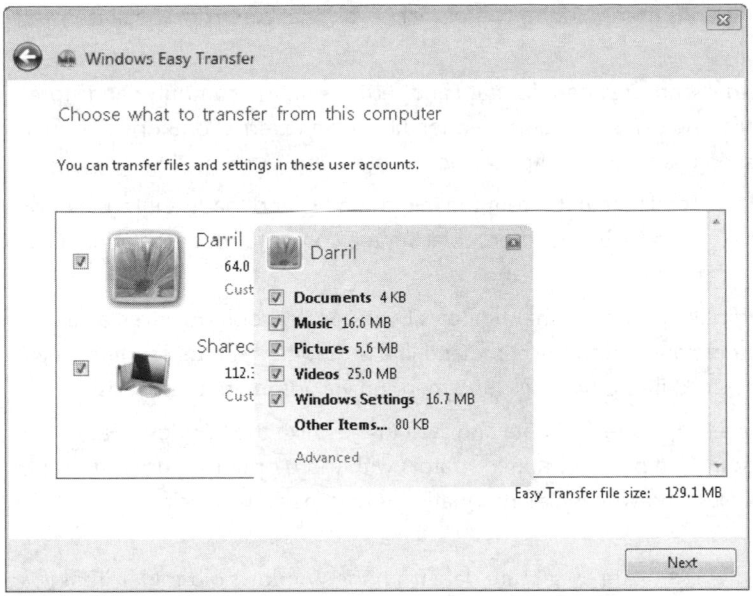

FIGURE 12-8 Windows Easy Transfer.

After you've run this program, you can view any reports it has created by running the Windows Easy Transfer Reports. The report identifies any files or settings that weren't transferred.

The Windows Easy Transfer tool doesn't transfer applications. However, if the application is installed on both the old and the new operating systems, it can transfer settings for the application. For example, if a user had specific settings for Microsoft Word, these settings would be migrated.

EXAM TIP

Windows Easy Transfer is used to transfer files and settings from earlier editions of Windows to Windows 7. It is easy to use when migrating a single user's computer, such as in a home or small office environment. You must be logged on with an administrative account to run it.

You can view a video of the Windows Easy Transfer tool in action here: *http://windows .microsoft.com/en-US/windows7/help/videos/transferring-files-and-settings-from-another-pc.*

User State Migration Tool

The *User State Migration Tool (USMT)* is a tool you can use to save user data and settings in larger environments. It includes the following two primary tools that run from the command line:

- **Scanstate.** *Scanstate* scans a system for data and settings on the computer and stores it in a migration file. You can store this migration file on an external USB drive or on a network share, as long as the computer can access the share.

- **Loadstate.** *Loadstate* reads the data from the migration file and loads it into the new operating system. You run loadstate after replacing the computer or completing a new installation.

The USMT is more difficult to run than the Windows Easy Transfer tool. However, a valuable benefit of running commands from the command line is that they can be scripted. That is, the command can be placed into a batch file and then run via automated methods.

Scanstate can capture a wide variety of data and settings, just like the Windows Easy Transfer tool. However, scanstate provides administrators with more options. Administrators can configure additional files to restrict what information is migrated or to include additional data.

Additionally, you can use scanstate to capture data from the Windows.old folder. That is, if Windows.old was created during the installation, you can use scanstate and loadstate to migrate data after you've installed Windows 7 over the older operating system.

EXAM TIP

The USMT is used to migrate data and settings in a business or enterprise environment. Scanstate captures information, and loadstate restores it. You need to use a version that is compatible with the newer operating system.

The USMT is included in the WAIK, available as a free download from the Windows download site (*http://www.microsoft.com/download*). Search for *Windows Automated Installation Kit Windows 7.*

File And Settings Transfer Wizard

The File And Settings Transfer (FAST) wizard is included in Windows XP. It was designed to migrate user files to Windows XP from another Windows XP system or from older operating systems such as Windows 2000 or Windows ME. You cannot use this to transfer files to Windows Vista or Windows 7. Instead, you need to use Windows Easy Transfer or the USMT.

You can access FAST by clicking Start, All Programs, Accessories, System Tools, and selecting Files And Settings Transfer Wizard.

Chapter Summary

- A clean install does not include any applications or settings from a previous installation.

- An upgrade will include compatible applications and settings from a previous installation.

- Installation methods include using installation media, installing over the network, and using images.

- Before capturing an image, you must run Sysprep to remove any settings that need to be unique, such as the SID.

- You can upgrade Windows Vista to a comparable edition or higher of Windows 7.

- You cannot upgrade Windows XP to Windows 7. You cannot upgrade 32-bit versions to 64-bit versions.

- Windows Anytime Upgrade allows users to upgrade Windows 7 editions to editions with additional features.

- You can manipulate installed drives during an installation. This includes creating, extending, formatting, and deleting partitions.

- If the Windows 7 installation program doesn't recognize the drive, you can click Load Driver to load a driver. Drivers can be loaded from a floppy disk, CD, DVD, or USB flash drive.

- The Windows 7 installation often creates a 100-MB hidden system partition during the installation. This partition includes system boot files, space for BitLocker, and the WinRE, and it should not be deleted.

- Windows Easy Transfer allows you to migrate user data and settings from previous installations of Windows to Windows 7. Data can be transferred by using an Easy Transfer cable, over the network, or via an external hard disk or USB flash drive.

- USMT includes two tools used to migrate user data and settings in larger environments. Scanstate captures the user's data and settings from a previous installation. Loadstate will load this information onto Windows 7.

Chapter Review

Use the following questions to test your knowledge of the information in this chapter. The answers to these questions, and the explanations of why each answer choice is correct or incorrect, are located in the "Answers" section at the end of this chapter.

1. A user wants to create a dual-boot system running Windows XP and Windows 7. What is important to remember? (Choose two.)

    A. Install Windows XP first.

    B. Install Windows 7 first.

    C. Install both operating systems on different partitions.

    D. Install both operating systems on the same partition.

2. What is the difference between a clean installation and an upgrade?

    A. A clean install includes applications and settings from previous installations.

    B. An upgrade includes applications and settings from previous installations.

    C. A clean installation starts by formatting the hard drive.

    D. There is no difference; they are the same.

3. A user is running Windows XP and wants to upgrade to Windows 7. Is this possible?

    A. Yes; the user can do an upgrade directly to Windows 7.

    B. Yes, as long as the file system is formatted with NTFS.

    C. Yes, as long as both versions are 32-bit versions.

    D. No; XP cannot be directly upgraded to Windows 7.

4. A user has completed a clean installation on a single-partition system running Windows XP. The user wants to access data files that were stored in the user's My Documents folder. Is this possible?

    A. No; existing files are deleted during a clean installation.

    B. Yes; these file locations were not modified at all.

    C. Yes; these files are in the Windows.old folder.

    D. Yes; the user can reinstall Windows XP to access the older data files.

5. You are tasked with installing Windows 7 onto several systems within a network. How can you do this without carrying the installation media to each computer?

   A. Create an image of the installation media and copy it to a bootable DVD.

   B. Copy the contents of the installation DVD to a USB flash drive and install Windows 7 from this drive.

   C. Copy the contents of the installation DVD to a USB external drive and install Windows 7 from this drive.

   D. Copy the contents of the installation DVD to a network location and install Windows 7 from this drive.

6. You want to install Windows 7 with several applications onto 25 existing computers in your network. What can make this job easier?

   A. Installation using the installation DVD.

   B. Installation over the network.

   C. Installation using images.

   D. Installation using the USMT.

7. You are installing Windows 7 on a system, but the hard drive is not recognized. What should be done?

   A. Replace the hard drive.

   B. Install drivers for the hard drive from the Drive Options page of the installation program.

   C. Reformat the hard drive from the Drive Options page of the installation program.

   D. Repartition the hard drive from the Drive Options page of the installation program.

8. You are upgrading a home user's computer from Windows XP to Windows 7. What tool can you use to capture the user's data and settings?

   A. File and Settings Transfer (FAST)

   B. Windows Easy Transfer

   C. USTM

   D. Windows backup

Answers

1. **Correct Answer:** A, C

   A. **Correct:** Windows XP should be installed first, and Windows 7 second.

   B. **Incorrect:** If Windows 7 is installed first, Windows XP will overwrite key files needed by Windows 7 and Windows 7 won't be bootable.

   C. **Correct:** Both operating systems should be installed on different partitions to prevent each from interfering with the other.

   D. **Incorrect:** If they are installed on the same partition, they will modify and corrupt files in the other operating system.

2. **Correct Answer:** B

   A. **Incorrect:** In a clean installation, the user must reinstall all the applications.

   B. **Correct:** An upgrade includes compatible applications and settings from the previous operating system.

   C. **Incorrect:** A clean installation can start with a freshly formatted operating system, but it can also be installed on an existing partition without the partition being formatted.

   D. **Incorrect:** There are significant differences between a clean install and an upgrade.

3. **Correct Answer:** D

   A. **Incorrect:** It is not possible to upgrade Windows XP directly to Windows 7, but it can be upgraded to Windows Vista and then to Windows 7.

   B. **Incorrect:** Windows 7 requires NTFS for an installation, but XP still can't be upgraded to Windows 7.

   C. **Incorrect:** You can upgrade 32-bit versions only to 32-bit versions, but XP cannot be upgraded to Windows 7.

   D. **Correct:** You cannot upgrade Windows XP directly to Windows 7.

4. **Correct Answer:** C

   A. **Incorrect:** Existing files are not deleted during a clean installation unless the drive is reformatted.

   B. **Incorrect:** The files are moved to the Windows.old folder.

   C. **Correct:** The Windows.old folder holds files from the previous installation, including files in the user's profile, such as the My Documents folder.

   D. **Incorrect:** Reinstalling Windows XP won't provide access to older data files.

5. **Correct Answer: D**

   A. **Incorrect:** The installation DVD already includes an image of Windows 7 on a bootable DVD. If you create an image of this DVD, you'll still need to carry it to each computer.

   B. **Incorrect:** While it is possible to copy the contents to a bootable USB flash drive and install from there, you'll still need to carry the flash drive to each computer.

   C. **Incorrect:** While it is possible to copy the contents to a USB external drive and install from there, you'll still need to carry the USB drive to each computer.

   D. **Correct:** This step allows you to install Windows 7 from a network location.

6. **Correct Answer: C**

   A. **Incorrect:** Installing it using the DVD takes longer and doesn't address the installation of the applications.

   B. **Incorrect:** Installing it over the network takes longer and doesn't address the installation of the applications.

   C. **Correct:** If you create one image with all the required applications, you can then deploy this image to multiple computers.

   D. **Incorrect:** The User State Migration Tool helps migrate user data and settings, but it won't install Windows 7.

7. **Correct Answer: B**

   A. **Incorrect:** You should replace the hard drive only if it is faulty.

   B. **Correct:** If the hard drive is not recognized, you can install drivers for the hard drive from the Drive Options page of the installation program.

   C. **Incorrect:** You can reformat the hard drive from the Drive Options page, but not if it is not recognized.

   D. **Incorrect:** You can repartition the hard drive from the Drive Options page, but only if it is recognized.

8. **Correct Answer: B**

   A. **Incorrect:** The Files and Settings Transfer (FAST) wizard was used to transfer files to Window XP from earlier operating systems but is replaced with Windows Easy Transfer in Windows Vista and Windows 7.

   B. **Correct:** The Windows Easy Transfer tool can be used to capture and transfer user's data and settings.

   C. **Incorrect:** The User State Migration Tool (USMT, not USTM) can also be used to transfer files and settings, although it is harder to use than Windows Easy Transfer.

   D. **Incorrect:** Windows Backup utilities can be used to back up data, but it will not capture settings.

CHAPTER 13

Using Windows Operating Systems

It's important for any PC technician to be able to navigate through the Windows operating systems and access the different tools. You should have a clear understanding of how to use tools like the Task Manager, applets within the Control Panel, and the tools within the Administrative Tools group. You'll learn about all of these tools in this chapter, including some basics about navigating Windows.

Exam 220-802 objectives in this chapter:

- 1.4 Given a scenario, use appropriate operating system features and tools.
    - Administrative
        - Computer management
        - Performance monitor
        - Services
        - Task scheduler
        - Component services
        - Data sources
    - Task Manager
        - Applications
        - Processes
        - Performance
        - Networking
        - Users
    - Run line utilities
        - MMC

- 1.5 Given a scenario, use Control Panel utilities (the items are organized by "classic view/large icons" in Windows).
  - Common to all Microsoft Operating Systems
    - Internet options
      - Connections
      - Security
      - General
      - Privacy
      - Programs
      - Advanced
  - Folder options
    - Sharing
    - View hidden files
    - Hide extensions
    - Layout
  - Unique to Windows XP
    - Add/remove programs
    - Network connections
    - Printers and faxes
    - Automatic updates
    - Network setup wizard
  - Unique to Vista
    - Tablet PC settings
    - Pen and input devices
    - Offline files
    - Problem reports and solutions
    - Printers
  - Unique to Windows 7
    - HomeGroup
    - Action center
    - Remote applications and desktop applications
    - Troubleshooting

Windows Basics

Most people understand how to use and get around within an operating system but don't always understand the terminology. As a PC technician, you should be familiar with common terms and actions.

Mouse Actions

Some common actions used with a mouse include the following:

- **Single click.** This indicates a single click with the left button on the mouse. It selects an item.
- **Double-click.** This is done with two quick clicks of the left button. It normally opens an item.
- **Right-click.** Many items include a mini-menu of items that you can view by right-clicking an item. This is also known as a context menu.

NOTE **RIGHT-CLICK AND ALT-CLICK**

Left-handed people often reconfigure their mouse so that the buttons are reversed. In this case, a right-click is actually accomplished by clicking the left button. You might see right-click referred to as alt-click so that it applies in both situations. The mouse button can be changed by using the Mouse applet within the Control Panel.

- **Dragging.** Use this to move items. Press and hold the button to select the item, and then move the mouse. When you've reached the new location, release the mouse button.

- **Hover.** If you move your mouse over an item but do not click, it is called hovering. Many applications include tooltips that appear when you hover over an item.

Windows Actions

Windows applications are displayed in a window, and you can manipulate these windows with common methods. Figure 13-1 shows the Windows Calculator open on top of Windows Explorer, with several common elements labeled.

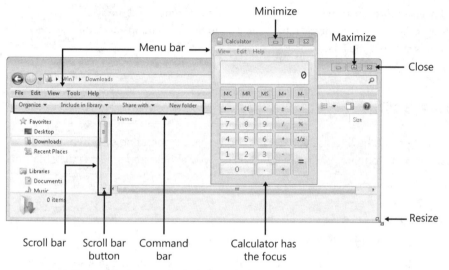

FIGURE 13-1 Windows Explorer and Windows Calculator.

- **Minimize.** Click this button and the window is minimized to the taskbar. If you select it on the taskbar, it returns to the previous size.

- **Maximize.** This button resizes the window to full screen.

- **Close.** Clicking the X closes the application. If you have unsaved work, many applications will prompt you to save it before it closes.

- **Menu bar.** Most windows include drop-down menus. Select any menu item, and you'll see a list of choices.

- **Command bar.** Some applications include a dynamic command bar. When you select an item, you'll see common commands associated with that item that you can select.

- **Scroll bar.** When there are additional items for a screen, a scroll bar appears. You can drag the scroll bar, or you can click within the empty space of the scroll bar to move it.

- **Scroll bar button.** You can click the small arrow to move the scroll bar down just a little.
- **Resize window.** Many windows allow you to resize them by hovering over an edge or corner. When the arrows appear, click and hold the mouse button, and then move the mouse to resize the window. Release the mouse to set the change.
- **Focus.** You can open multiple windows at the same time. The top window has the focus and responds to commands, but the bottom window is still open and running. You can select the bottom window to change the focus to that window. In Figure 13-1, the calculator is the top window and has the focus.

Libraries

Windows 7 includes libraries, which provide a method of organizing files and folders stored in different locations. The default libraries are Documents, Music, Pictures, and Videos. Libraries don't hold any data but instead are pointers to the actual location.

For example, you might have MP3 files stored in C:\Rock and C:\Pop folders on your system. You could add these folders to the Music library so that you can access them. A library can include pointers to multiple folders on a local hard drive, an external hard drive, and folders on a network drive. When the user clicks on a library folder, it shows all the folders, no matter where they are located.

EXAM TIP

Libraries are included in Windows 7 but not in Windows XP or Windows Vista.

Task Manager

A common tool that you should master early as a PC technician is the *Task Manager*. You can use it to easily view activity on the computer and close misbehaving programs.

Starting Task Manager

You can start Task Manager using one of the following methods:

- Press Ctrl+Shift+Esc.
- Press Ctrl+Alt+Delete and select Start Task Manager.
- Right-click on the Windows taskbar (at the bottom of the screen), and select Task Manager in Windows XP and Windows Vista, or select Start Task Manager in Windows 7.

After starting it, you'll see a display similar to Figure 13-2. Notice that it has multiple tabs that you can select to get different views. In the figure, it's open to the Applications tab.

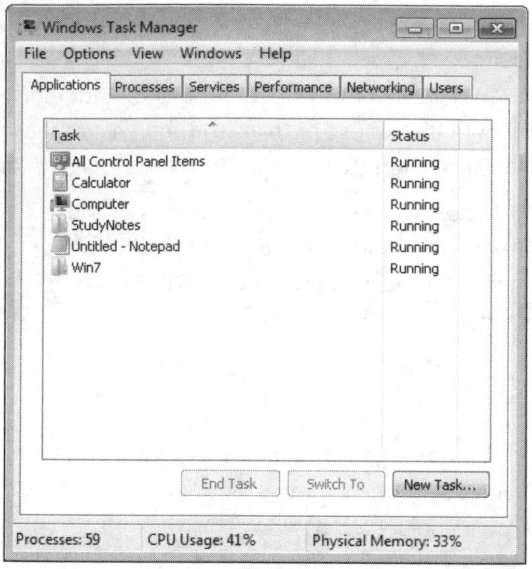

FIGURE 13-2 Task Manager with the Applications tab selected.

Applications

The Applications tab shows all the applications that are running, along with their current status. Occasionally, you might run across an application that is not responding to any key presses or mouse clicks. If you look here, the status might be "Not Responding."

A simple way to kill the application is to select it and click End Task. If the application doesn't respond normally, Task Manager will display a dialog box and ask if you want to proceed.

You don't need it very often, but you can click the New Task button and enter a command to start another application. This is similar to entering a command from the command prompt. For example, if you want to start the System Configuration tool, you can click New Task, type in **msconfig**, and click OK. Try it.

> **EXAM TIP**
>
> If an application locks up, use Task Manager to terminate it. If the application is interfering with the operating system, start Task Manager by pressing Ctrl+Shift+Esc.

Processes

The Processes tab identifies all of the running processes within a system and shows the resources currently being used. The most common use of this tab is to determine what process is consuming the most CPU processing time, or the most memory.

Figure 13-3 shows the Task Manager open with the Processes tab selected. Normally, you can see only processes associated with your account, but if you select Show Processes From All Users, it shows all the processes on the system.

Click on any title to reorder display

Right-click for context menu

Shows how much free time the system has

Clicking here kills a process

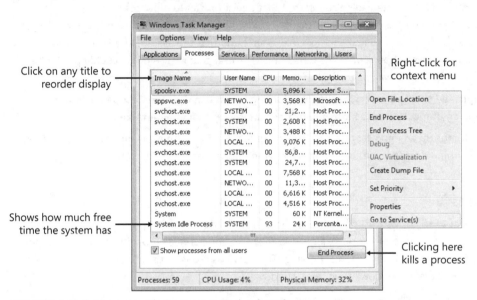

FIGURE 13-3 Task Manager with the Processes tab selected.

You can change the display order by clicking the title of any of the columns. Currently, it's showing the processes in ascending order based on their name. If you want to see which one is using the most CPU time, click the CPU column title.

The System Idle Process gives you an indication of how much time the CPU is not doing anything other than waiting for a command. In Figure 13-3, it's currently idle 93 percent of the time. In contrast, if a process has stopped responding, it might be consuming all of the CPU's time. You can select it and then click End Process.

If you right-click over any process, you'll see the context menu. A useful tool here is to select Go To Service(s). Occasionally, a process is running and you're not sure what it is. Sometimes looking at the related service helps you identify it.

You can also change the priority of a service from this menu. For example, if you have a process running in the background and you want to minimize the impact it can have on work you're doing, you can change the priority to Below Normal or Low.

> **REAL WORLD** **YOU CANNOT END THE SYSTEM IDLE PROCESS**
>
> You can't kill the System Idle Process, but that doesn't mean that people won't try. I remember helping a user who was convinced that the System Idle Process was causing problems. The user said that the system was slow and that the System Idle Process was consuming over 90 percent of the CPU's time. The user told me, "If only I could end this process, my system will be faster, but it won't let me."
>
> I explained that this process is simply recording how much time the CPU is idle, or not doing anything. When it's high, it indicates that the CPU isn't being tasked.
>
> This brings up an important point. Often, your job as a PC technician won't require you to fix anything. Instead, you can simply share your knowledge.

Services

The Services tab shows a list of all the services in the system, a description, and the current state such as Stopped or Running. Figure 13-4 shows the Services tab with the print spooler selected and the right-click menu showing. The Services tab is not available in Windows XP, but it is available in Windows Vista and Windows 7.

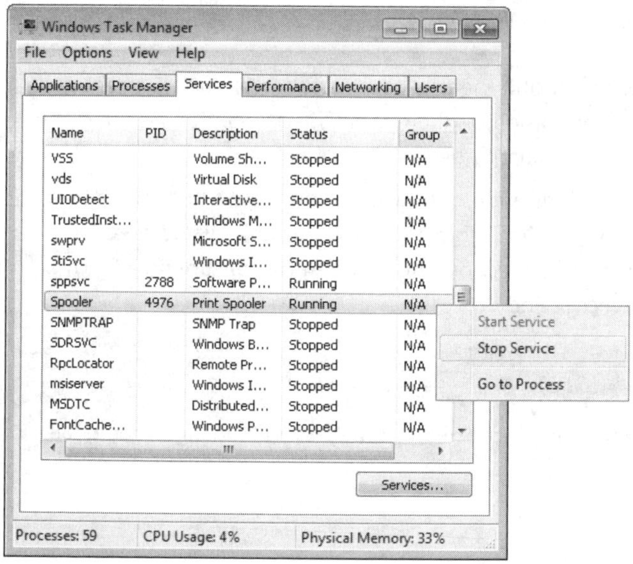

FIGURE 13-4 Task Manager with the Services tab selected.

EXAM TIP

Chapter 7, "Exploring Printers," covers printers and the spooler service. If the print queue backs up, it might be because the spooler service has failed. You can stop and restart any service by using Task Manager, or you can use the Services applet to manipulate the services.

Performance

The Performance tab gives you a quick visual indication of the computer's performance. Figure 13-5 shows the display on a Windows 7 system, and this tab includes the following listed items.

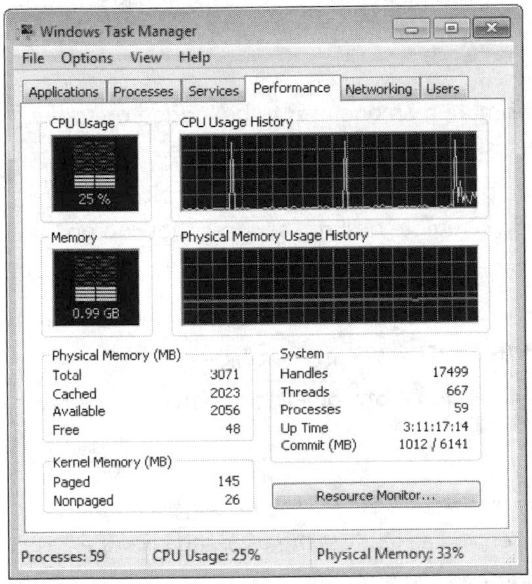

FIGURE 13-5 Task Manager with the Performance tab selected.

- **CPU Usage and CPU Usage History.** This shows the current usage as a percentage and the usage over the last 60 seconds.
- **Physical Memory and Physical Memory History.** This identifies how much memory is being used now and recently.
- **Physical Memory.** This shows the total RAM (3,071 MB), and the available RAM (2,056 MB). When the Available memory is close to zero, it indicates that the system needs more RAM.
- **Kernel Memory.** This shows how much RAM the operating system is using.

- **System.** A key piece of information here is the uptime reported in days, hours, minutes, and seconds.
- **Resource Monitor.** If you click this button, it starts another tool that you can use to get more information. The Resource Monitor is not available in Windows XP.

Networking

If your computer is connected to a network, you can use the Networking tab to show how much bandwidth your network interface card (NIC) is using. It includes a graph to show how much data is being transferred and indicates the Network Utilization as a percentage.

Users

The last tab on the Task Manager is the Users tab. This identifies all the users who are logged on to the system. Normally, you'll see only your account listed on this tab, but there are two ways that other users show up:

- **Fast User Switching.** This feature allows more than one user to be logged on to the system. If another user is logged on, the user shows up on the Users tab.
- **Remote Desktop Connections.** Remote desktop services allow users to connect into a system remotely. Users connected via remote desktop services show up on the Users tab.

> **MORE INFO**   **CHAPTER 20, "UNDERSTANDING PROTOCOLS"**
>
> Remote Desktop Connections and the Remote Desktop Protocol (RDP) are covered in more detail in Chapter 20.

If additional users show up, you can use this tab to send the user a message by right-clicking the user and selecting Send Message. You can also select the user and click the Disconnect or Logoff buttons to disconnect or log off the user.

✔ Quick Check

1. What tool can you use to end an application that won't respond?
2. What would you use to identify what is consuming a processor's time?

Quick Check Answers

1. Task Manager.
2. Task Manager, Processes tab.

Microsoft Management Console

The *Microsoft Management Console (MMC)* is a blank console used by many configuration tools. Some tools come preconfigured within an MMC, but you can also add snap-ins to an MMC to create your own tool.

For example, you can use the following steps on a Windows 7 computer to create an MMC for your own use:

1. Click Start, and type **MMC** in the Search Programs And Files text box.

2. Select MMC. If prompted by User Account Control, click Yes to continue. You'll have a blank MMC open at this point.

3. Click the File menu, and select Add/Remove Snap-In.

4. Select Services and click Add. Your Local Computer will be selected. You can also add Services from other computers in your network by selecting another Computer and entering its name. Click Finish.

> **NOTE** **ADMINISTRATIVE PRIVILEGES**
>
> You can add the snap-in for other computers, but you will not be able to use it if you do not have administrative privileges on the remote computer.

5. Select Component Services and click Add. Click OK. If you expand the Component Services and select COM+ Applications, your display will look similar to the following graphic.

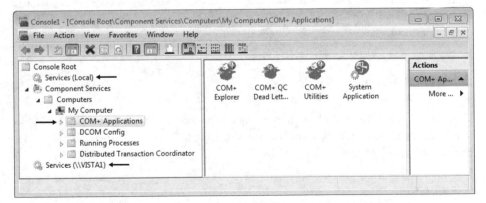

The first Services snap-in is labeled Local, indicating that it is the local computer. The second Services snap-in is labeled Vista1, indicating that it is a remote computer named Vista1. The center pane shows some component services that are running on this system.

6. Click File, Save As. Select Desktop.

7. Type in **MyConsole** as the name, and click Save. You can now start this console from the desktop without reconfiguring it.

EXAM TIP

You can use multiple methods to access any of these tools. For example, many are accessible via the Control Panel in the Administrative Tools category.

Many snap-ins can be started directly without having to be added as snap-ins in an MMC. On Windows XP, you can click Start, Run, and type in the command. On Windows Vista and Windows 7, you can click Start and type the command into the text box. Table 13-1 shows the command for some common snap-ins. With few exceptions, you need to include the .msc extension when using these commands.

TABLE 13-1 Commands to Start Common Snap-Ins

Command	Snap-in name	Description
taskschd.msc	Task Scheduler	Use to schedule tasks. This command does not work on Windows XP.
eventvwr.msc	Event Viewer	Use to view logs.
perfmon.msc	Performance	Use to monitor system performance.
services.msc	Services	View, start, stop, and manipulate services.
secpol.msc	Local Security Policy	View and manipulate security settings for local system.
gpedit.msc	Group Policy Editor	View and manipulate local Group Policy settings.
wf.msc	Advanced Windows Firewall	Use to manipulate advanced settings for firewall.

Control Panel

The *Control Panel* is a central location for many common tools that you'll use to view and manipulate computer settings. Tools within the Control Panel are mini-programs and are commonly called applets.

EXAM TIP

As you go through this chapter, I strongly encourage you to start these applets and look at them. If there are steps, go through them more than once. You can follow the steps explicitly and then use them as a guide to explore the applets on your own. Anytime you want to get more information, press F1 while an applet is open and the Help page will open.

Views

You can start the Control Panel in any of the Windows Systems by clicking Start and selecting Control Panel. By default, Control Panel applets are displayed in a Category view. That is, the applets are grouped together in categories instead of listed individually. You can modify the view so that the applets are listed individually.

On Windows XP and Windows Vista, choose the Classic View to list the applets individually. On Windows 7, choose Large Icons or Small Icons to list them individually.

Figure 13-6 shows the Control Panel in Windows XP on the left and in Windows 7 on the right. On Windows XP, the view is set to Classic View. You can click Switch To Category View to switch back. On Windows 7, the view is set to Large Icons.

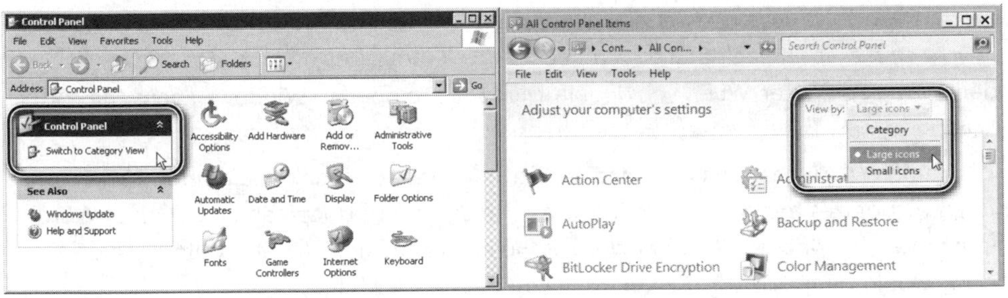

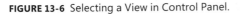

FIGURE 13-6 Selecting a View in Control Panel.

Windows Vista and Windows 7 Control Panels include a useful Search feature (in the upper-right corner in Figure 13-6). If you're looking for an applet, type its name or partial name in this box, and items that don't match the search disappear from the view.

For example, if you type only **admin** in the text box, everything disappears except for items that have "admin" in the title or description. If you type **administrative tools** in the text box, everything disappears except for the Administrative Tools group.

EXAM TIP

On the job, you'll probably use the Search feature to quickly find applets. When preparing for the CompTIA A+ exam, use the Large Icons view in Windows 7, and use the Classic View in Windows XP and Windows Vista.

Applets

The Control Panel has some differences between versions. For example, Windows XP has 29 applets, Windows Vista has 49 applets, and Windows 7 has 45 applets. Some of the applets have the same function between versions, some are modified, and others are new.

You don't need to know the functions of all the applets when preparing for the exam, but you should know the ones that are specifically mentioned in the objectives. The following sections introduce them and describe their purpose.

Common Applets

Several of the applets are common to each version of Windows, and some of these applets are described in this section.

Folder Options

A primary tool you'll use when working with files in Windows is Windows Explorer. Chapter 11, "Introducing Windows Operating Systems," showed steps you can use in different operating systems to open it. It's also important to know how to manipulate the *Folder Options* applet to control the views.

UNDERSTANDING EXTENSIONS

Files within Windows have two parts: the name and the extension. The name is something you give it so that it's meaningful to you, such as "A+ Study Notes," but the extension is needed by the computer. When you double-click a file to open it, Windows opens the correct application to view the file based on the extension.

For example, if you have a file named "A+ Study Notes.docx" and you double-click it, Windows recognizes the .docx extension as a Microsoft Word document. It will open Word and then open the document within Word. If the file was named "A+ Study Notes.xlsx," Windows would open Microsoft Excel when you double-clicked it.

SHOWING HIDDEN FILES AND FOLDERS AND EXTENSIONS

Many files and folders are hidden by default in different operating systems. Most users don't need to access these files. Hiding them avoids confusing users with files they don't need to access and prevents them from accidentally manipulating the files.

Similarly, the extensions often confuse the users, so extensions are hidden by default. Instead of a user seeing "A+ Study Notes.docx," only "A+ Study Notes" appears.

As a technician, you'll often need to see all the files and the extensions. You can use the steps listed in the following sections, on different operating systems, to make the changes.

SHOWING HIDDEN FILES AND EXTENSIONS ON WINDOWS VISTA AND WINDOWS 7

1. Select Start, Control Panel. If necessary, modify the view to Large Icons or Classic View.

2. Double-click Folder Options.

3. Select Display The Full Path In The Title Bar (Classic Theme Only).

> **NOTE** **FULL PATH IN TITLE BAR**
>
> Without this selected, the title bar shows a limited view of the path. As a technician, you might need to see the full path.

4. Select Show Hidden Files, Folders, And Drives.

5. Deselect Hide Extensions For Known File Types.

6. Deselect Hide Protected Operating System Files (Recommended). Review the warning, and click Yes to display the files. Your display will look similar to the following graphic.

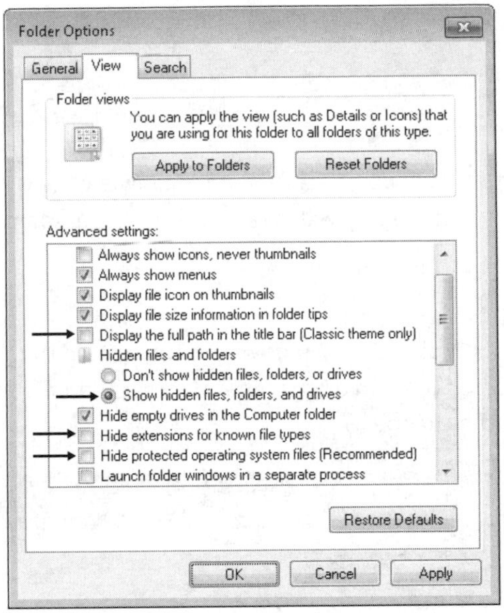

7. You can select either OK or Apply to make the change. OK will make the change and close the dialog box, but Apply keeps it open so that you can view or manipulate other settings.

Figure 13-7 shows two views of Windows Explorer opened to a user's profile on Windows 7. The one on the left is a normal view. The one on the right shows some of the hidden folders that appear after making the change. The full path shows in the title bar only with the Classic theme, so I changed the theme to show it.

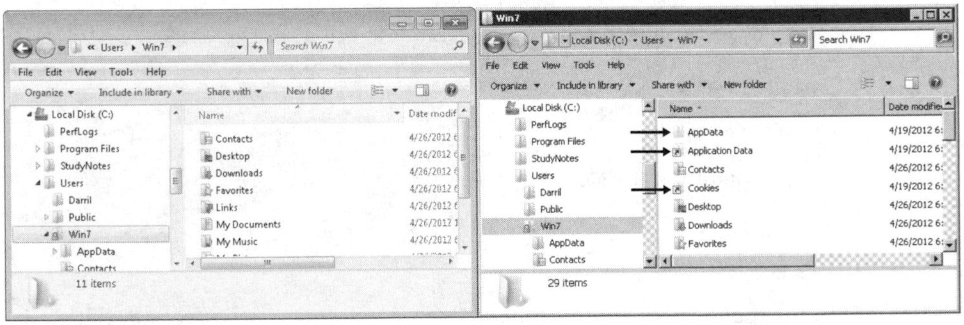

FIGURE 13-7 Windows Explorer with two views in Windows 7.

SHOWING HIDDEN FILES AND EXTENSIONS ON WINDOWS XP

1. Select Start, Control Panel. If necessary, modify the view to Classic View.

2. Select Folder Options. Click the View tab.

3. Select Display The Full Path In The Address Bar.

4. Select Show Hidden Files And Folders.

5. Deselect Hide Extensions For Known File Types.

6. Deselect Hide Protected Operating System Files (Recommended). Review the warning, and click Yes to approve the change. Your display will look similar to the graphic shown in the Windows 7 and Vista steps.

7. Click OK.

Figure 13-8 shows two views of Windows Explorer on Windows XP. The one on the left is a normal view. The one on the right shows some of the hidden files and folders and the extensions of the files that appear after making the change.

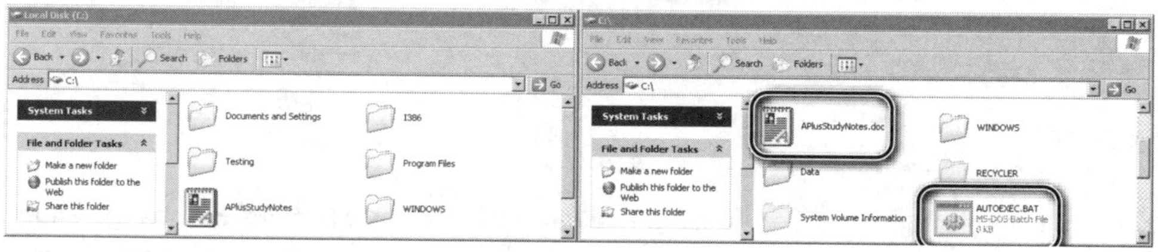

FIGURE 13-8 Windows Explorer with two views in Windows XP.

✔ **Quick Check**

1. You need to manipulate a hidden file, but you can't find it. What should you do?

2. What would you change to show file extensions in Windows Explorer?

Quick Check Answers

1. Change the view to show hidden files.

2. Change the view in Folder Options.

Internet Options

The Internet Options applet is used to manipulate the settings for Internet Explorer (IE). Even though you'll have different versions of IE on different operating systems, each version has Internet Options.

Figure 13-9 shows the Internet Options applet in Windows 7. As you can see, there are seven tabs, and the General tab is selected.

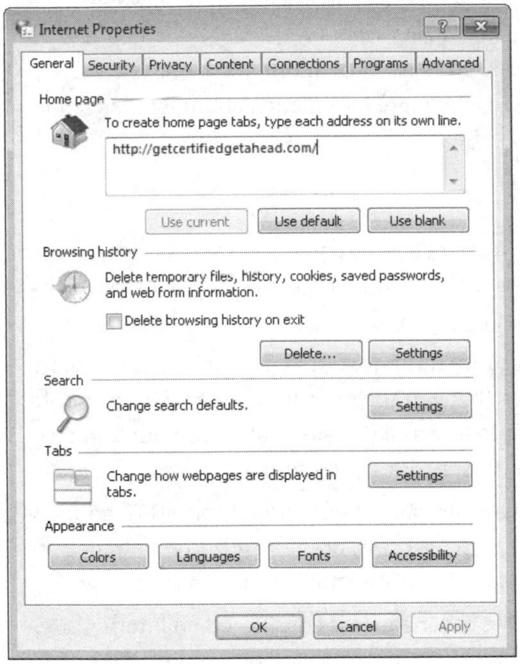

FIGURE 13-9 Internet Options in Windows 7.

GENERAL TAB

This page includes the following settings that you can manipulate:

- **Home page.** IE opens the URL listed here when it's started. You can use this section to change the home page or even add multiple home pages, which open in separate tabs.

- **Browsing History.** IE keeps a record of sites visited and keeps a temporary copy of files. You can delete the data or use the settings page to modify how much data is retained.

- **Search.** Use this to modify the default search engine used with the browser.

- **Tabs.** This provides some options to modify how tabs and pop-up windows are used.

- **Appearance.** You can change some elements on webpages by using the options available here.

SECURITY TAB

Unfortunately, many websites include malicious software (malware). For example, a drive-by download occurs when you visit a website and it runs active content that downloads and installs malware such as a virus on your system. To reduce risks, IE uses security zones with varying levels of security.

> **IMPORTANT** **KEEP YOUR ANTIVIRUS SOFTWARE CURRENT**
>
> Security zones provide a layer of protection, but it's important to always have up-to-date antivirus software running on your system. Criminals use a wide variety of methods to infect systems, take them over remotely, and steal personal information. Chapter 26, "Recognizing Malware and Other Threats," provides more information about malware and ways to protect systems.

The four security zones are as follows:

- **Restricted Sites.** This zone has the most restrictive settings. You can still visit a website in this zone, but the settings prevent the site from running active content that might damage your computer or steal your data.

- **Trusted Sites.** This zone has relaxed security settings so that a website can run more programs. You can add sites to this zone that you trust not to damage your computer or information. For example, if your employer has a website that has content that is blocked normally, you can add it to the Trusted Sites zone so that it runs.

- **Local intranet.** Sites that you access in an internal network using non-HTTP addresses, or HTTP addresses without periods (like http://success) are recognized as intranet sites. The security settings for this zone are relaxed to allow more content to run.

- **Internet.** Any site that is not in one of the other zones is considered an Internet site. This zone strikes a balance between security and usability. It allows some active content to run but also restricts some active content.

There aren't any sites in any of the zones by default. Administrators can use tools to automatically add sites to the zones, and you can manually add sites to the zones. To add a site to any zone, select the zone, click the Sites button, and enter the address.

PRIVACY TAB

The Privacy tab allows you to configure how cookies are used. Cookies are small text files that a website can store on your system when you visit them. When you return to the site, it reads the cookie to identify you or your behaviors. Websites commonly use information in cookies to enhance the user's experience on the website or to change the advertising based on the user's activities.

If you want to block cookies, you can use several settings on the Privacy tab, including the following:

- **Location.** You can prevent or allow a website from learning your location. Location is determined by your IP address.

- **Pop-up Blocker.** You can turn the pop-up blocker on or off. When turned on, you can configure the blocking level so that some pop-up windows are allowed or so that they are all blocked.

- **InPrivate.** InPrivate browsing is a feature in IE that prevents any data from a session from being stored. By default, this setting disables toolbars and add-ons, but you can use this setting to enable them.

CONTENT TAB

The Content tab includes the following settings that you can use to control what content is displayed and what data is saved after a session:

- **Parental Controls.** Parents can use this setting to set limits on Internet usage for specific accounts.

- **Content Advisor.** This section has ratings that can be used to restrict content based on different categories. When enabled, the administrator can enter a password to bypass the restriction and view the content.

- **Certificates.** Websites commonly use certificates to encrypt some sessions, such as when you use a credit card to buy something. Administrators use this section to view and manipulate the certificates.

- **AutoComplete.** AutoComplete remembers information you've typed in previously and can retrieve it to automatically fill in different forms or addresses for you. This can make browsing easier, but there might be times when you want to delete it. Figure 13-10 shows the different actions you can take. If you click Settings, you can disable AutoComplete for any of the options. If you want to delete data that has already been saved, click Delete AutoComplete History, select the items you want to delete, and click Delete.

- **Feeds and Web Slices.** You can use this to control the schedule for Really Simple Syndication (RSS) feeds or sites using Web Slices. Not all sites use these features.

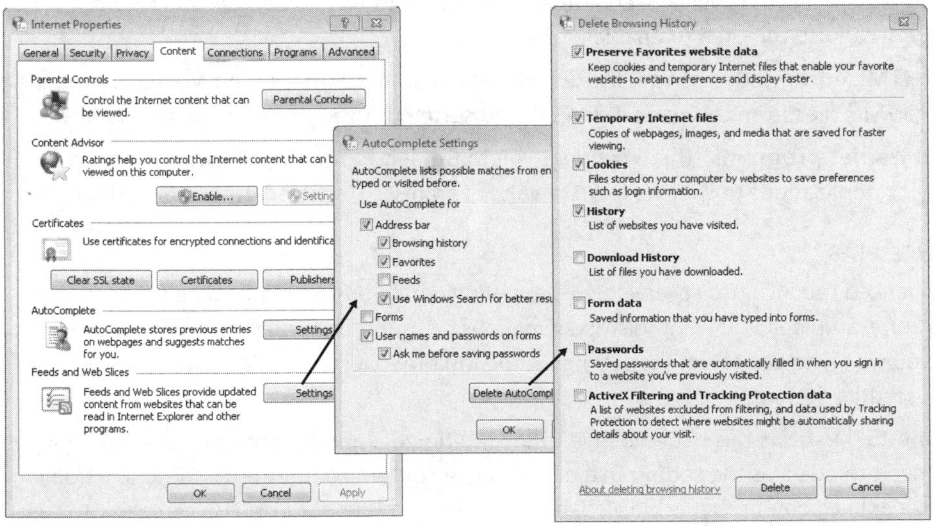

FIGURE 13-10 AutoComplete and deleting browsing history.

EXAM TIP

You should know how to manipulate all of the AutoComplete settings. They are valuable to know as a PC technician and as a regular user. Check the settings on your computer.

CONNECTIONS TAB

The Connections tab shows Dial-up and Virtual Private Network (VPN) Settings that exist on your computer, and you can configure when to use these connections. You can use the Local Area Network (LAN) settings to configure how IE connects to the Internet through your network.

> **MORE INFO** **CHAPTER 24, "CONNECTING AND TROUBLESHOOTING A NETWORK"**
>
> Chapter 24 includes steps to establish networking connections, including dial-up and VPN connections. Chapter 22, "Network Security Devices," covers how to configure the LAN settings to use a proxy server.

PROGRAMS TAB

The Programs tab includes the following sections:

- **Default web browser.** By default, IE checks to see whether it is the default browser when it starts. If not, it prompts you to set it as the default browser. You can change this behavior here. If you have installed another web browser but want to set IE as the default, you can set it here.

- **Manage add-ons.** An add-on is additional software that can work with IE. It includes toolbars, search providers, and other tools. Add-ons can sometimes slow IE down, and you can use this area to enable or disable them.

- **HTML editing.** You can set the default tool used to edit Hypertext Markup Language (HTML) files from this page if desired. This setting is used by webpage developers.

- **Internet programs.** This link brings you to Default Programs, which you can use to link applications to specific files. Default Programs is discussed in the next section.

ADVANCED TAB

The Advanced tab includes several low-level settings that you can manipulate for specific purposes. For example, if you want to stop animations or sound from playing within webpages when you visit, you can select the settings in the Multimedia section. This page also includes several security settings.

Figure 13-11 shows this page opened to the Multimedia and Security sections. An item you might need to adjust is the setting that allows active content to run from a CD. Many training CDs have active content that is blocked, but by clearing this check box, you can get it to run. You should do this only if you are confident the CD does not contain malicious software.

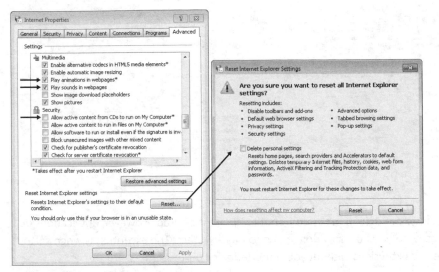

FIGURE 13-11 Resetting Internet Explorer settings.

If a user has made changes to the Advanced settings and you want to return to the original settings, you can click the Restore Advanced Settings button. If IE is having serious problems, you can use the Reset button. This restores all of the IE settings to their original settings. It also removes or disables any toolbars or add-ons. Notice that you can choose to save or delete your personal settings before resetting IE.

Default Programs

Extensions were mentioned earlier in this chapter, including what they're used for and how to hide them. You might want to look at what extensions are registered with your system, and you can do so from the Default Programs applet within the Control Panel. This is the same applet that starts from the Set Programs button in IE.

For example, the .docx extension starts Microsoft Word. If this is changed, you can use the Default Programs applet to restore the correct setting.

On Windows 7, you can access Default Programs with the following steps:

1. Click Start, and select Control Panel.

2. Select Default Programs from the Large Icons list.

3. Select Associate A File Type Or Protocol With A Program. It might take a moment for the list of extensions to display.

4. Select any extension in the list. You'll see a description and the current default program associated with the extension, as shown in the following graphic. In the graphic, .mp3 is selected and the Windows Media Player is the default program.

You can change the default program from this applet if desired. However, applications do this automatically, so you normally don't need to modify them. The exception is when software modifies the extensions without your knowledge or permission.

> **✔ Quick Check**
>
> 1. What view should you select to view all the Control Panel applets in Windows 7?
> 2. What would you manipulate to show file extensions?
>
> **Quick Check Answers**
>
> 1. Large Icons (or Small Icons).
> 2. Folder Options.

Applets Unique to Windows XP

You'll find the following applets only in Windows XP:

- **Add/Remove Programs.** Users can use this to add and remove programs or components on their computer. It is replaced with Programs And Features in Windows Vista and Windows 7. Many programs are installed with Microsoft Installer (.msi) files, so this isn't needed to install an application.

- **Automatic Updates.** You can enable, configure, or disable Automatic Updates. It is replaced with Windows Update in Windows Vista and Windows 7. Chapter 15, "Configuring Windows Operating Systems," covers updates.

- **Network Connections.** This applet is used to manipulate network interface cards or to set up new network connections. Windows Vista and Windows 7 include the Network And Sharing Center, which provides many tools to configure networking. Networking topics are covered in Chapters 18–24.

- **Network Setup Wizard.** This wizard is available from the Network Connections applet. If you click Set Up A Home Or Small Office Network, it starts the wizard. A similar wizard is available through the Network And Sharing Center in Windows Vista and Windows 7.
- **Printers And Faxes.** This applet is used to manually add printers or manipulate printers and their drivers. It is replaced with the Printers applet in Windows Vista and with the Devices And Printers applet in Windows 7.

Applets Unique to Windows Vista

The following applets are available only in Windows Vista:

- **Tablet PC Settings.** Use this to configure settings when Vista is running on a tablet. It can also be used to configure handwriting recognition. You can access a Tablet PC menu on Windows 7 by clicking Start, All Programs, Accessories, and selecting Tablet PC.
- **Pen And Input Devices.** This applet allows you to configure how different pen actions (such as a single tap or double-tap) are interpreted and whether the system provides visual feedback. It's used only on mobile devices, such as tablets.
- **Offline Files.** When enabled on a server hosting files and the user's computer, the user can keep a copy of shared files stored on the server locally. Users can access offline files even when they are disconnected from the network. The Offline Files feature is accessible via the Folder Options tool in Windows XP and via the Sync Center in Windows 7 (by clicking Start, All Programs, Accessories, Sync Center). Chapter 16, "Understanding Disks and File Systems," provides more information about offline files.
- **Problem Reports And Solutions.** When a system problem is detected, this feature checks with a Microsoft site to see whether the problem is known and whether a solution is available. Clicking on the solution provides steps that a user can take to resolve a problem. A similar feature is available in the Windows 7 Action Center.
- **Printers.** This is similar to the Printers and Faxes applet in Windows XP and the Devices and Printers applet in Windows 7.

Applets Unique to Windows 7

The following applets are available only in Windows 7:

- **HomeGroup.** Use this applet to create and join a homegroup. Homegroups are covered in Chapter 24.
- **Action Center.** The Action Center replaces the Security Center (mentioned in the next section) used in Windows XP and Windows Vista. It includes the same features but also includes additional alerts and notifications for other issues. When the Action Center has an alert, it adds a flag in the notification area of Windows (at the bottom right).

- **Remote Applications And Desktop Applications.** This feature provides users with a quick link to any remote programs or desktops if they are configured on their computer. These must first be published by a network administrator.

- **Troubleshooting.** This applet provides a central location for several other applets that you can use to troubleshoot problems. For example, it includes links for Program Compatibility, troubleshooting audio problems, and improving power usage.

Other Applets

If you've clicked through the Control Panel applets, you probably recognize they weren't all covered in this chapter. Many additional applets are covered in other chapters, including the following:

- **Device Manager.** Use this applet to manage devices and device drivers. It's available via the Control Panel in Windows Vista and Windows 7. It's available in Windows XP as part of Computer Management but not via the Control Panel. Device Manager is covered in Chapter 15.

- **Display.** You can use this applet to manipulate settings for the display, such as the resolution. Chapter 6, "Exploring Video and Display Devices," shows how to configure the resolution with this applet.

- **User Accounts.** You can add user accounts and manipulate their properties with this applet. It's available in each operating system via the Control Panel but works a little differently in each one. Chapter 25, "Understanding IT Security," covers User Accounts.

- **Security Center.** The Security Center monitors key security settings on a computer and provides notifications to users if a setting is making their computer less secure. For example, if a system doesn't have a firewall enabled, the user will be periodically reminded of the risks. It's available in Windows XP and Windows Vista. Windows 7 has the same features but includes them within the Action Center. Chapter 22 covers the Security Center.

- **Windows Firewall.** The Windows Firewall helps protect a system by filtering traffic going in or out of the system. It was introduced in Windows XP, and each of the operating systems includes it in the Control Panel. Chapter 22 covers the Windows Firewall in more depth.

- **Power Options.** This tool allows you to control power settings, such as the behavior of the power button or when a computer will sleep or hibernate. It's very valuable for laptops when they are on battery power but can be used for desktops too. Chapter 8, "Working with Laptops," covers the Power Options applet, which is in each of the operating systems.

EXAM TIP

This section has not covered all the applets in Windows 7, but I strongly recommend you simply go through each one and open it. If you're asked a question about one of these obscure applets, you'll at least know where it is. For example, if you've opened them all and someone asks you where they can find a list of fonts, you'll probably remember opening the Fonts applet in the Control Panel.

✔ **Quick Check**

1. What operating system(s) includes the HomeGroup applet?

2. What operating system(s) includes the Security Center?

Quick Check Answers

1. Windows 7.

2. Windows XP and Windows Vista. Windows 7 uses the Action Center.

Administrative Tools

Administrative Tools is a group of tools within Control Panel used by advanced users and administrators. The available tools are slightly different in different versions of Windows. For example, in Windows Vista, Component Services is not available in Administrative Tools but is still available on the computer. The following sections describe many of the common Administrative Tools.

To access Administrative Tools in any system, click Start, Control Panel, change the display to list applets individually, and select Administrative Tools.

EXAM TIP

Many of these tools require you to have administrative privileges on the system. On Windows Vista and Windows 7, you might be challenged by User Account Control for different applets, and if you don't have administrative privileges, you won't be able to use the tool.

Computer Management

The *Computer Management* tool is a valuable tool within the Administrative Tools folder that includes multiple snap-ins. Figure 13-12 shows Computer Management on a Windows 7–based computer.

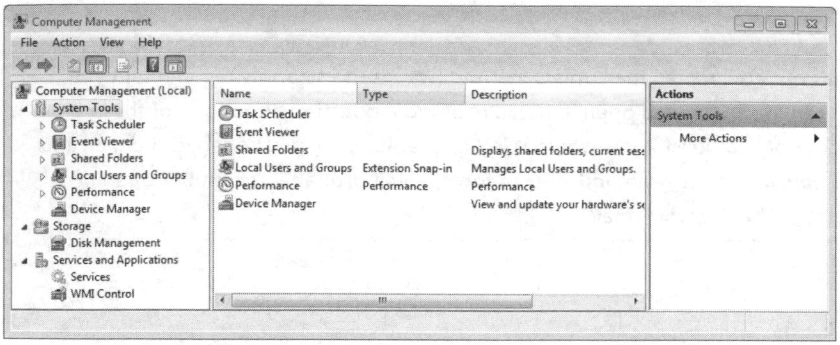

FIGURE 13-12 Computer Management.

In Figure 13-12, you can see that the tools are organized in three sections: System Tools, Storage, and Services And Applications. The following sections describe some of the tools. Other tools are covered individually in other chapters.

> **MORE INFO**   **WHERE TO FIND INFORMATION ABOUT OTHER ADMINISTRATIVE TOOLS**
>
> Shares and share permissions are covered in Chapters 16 and 25. Local Users and Groups is covered in Chapter 25. Device Manager is covered in Chapter 15. Disk Management is covered in Chapter 16.

Task Scheduler

You can use the *Task Scheduler* tool to schedule tasks to automatically run. Windows includes many preconfigured tasks.

> **EXAM TIP**
>
> Windows XP included Scheduled Tasks within the Control Panel, but not the Task Scheduler as part of Administrative Tools. Task Scheduler is available in both Windows Vista and Windows 7 from within Administrative Tools.

If you open Task Scheduler, you can view existing tasks or create your own. Figure 13-13 shows the Task Scheduler opened to the Defrag task, which is preconfigured to run at 1:00 AM every Wednesday.

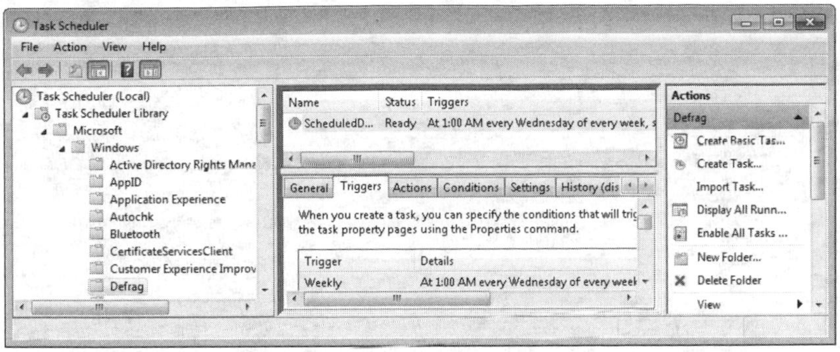

FIGURE 13-13 Task Scheduler.

Tasks have several configurable properties, including the following:

- **Triggers.** This identifies when the task runs and is normally based on a day and time.
- **Actions.** This identifies the task that will run.
- **Conditions.** You can set conditions, such as running only when the computer is using AC power (not on battery power).
- **Settings.** These settings allow you to fine-tune the behavior of the task. For example, you can select it to run as soon as possible if a schedule start is missed.
- **History.** This shows details about when the task has run.

Performance

Performance (also called *Performance Monitor*) is an extension of the Task Manager. The Task Manager gives you a snapshot of the performance of your system, but Performance provides many more details. Performance monitors four primary resources: processor, memory, disk, and network.

This tool was enhanced in Windows Vista and Windows 7 by adding Data Collector sets. You can quickly run a check on your system and view a comprehensive report by using the following steps on Windows 7.

1. Click Start and select Control Panel. If necessary, change the view to Large Icons.

2. Select Administrative Tools. Double-click Performance Monitor.

3. If necessary, double-click Data Collector Sets to expand it.

4. Double-click System.

5. Right-click System and select Start. It will run for one minute and then stop.

6. When it stops, expand Reports, System, and System Performance.

7. Select the report you just ran. Your display will resemble the following graphic.

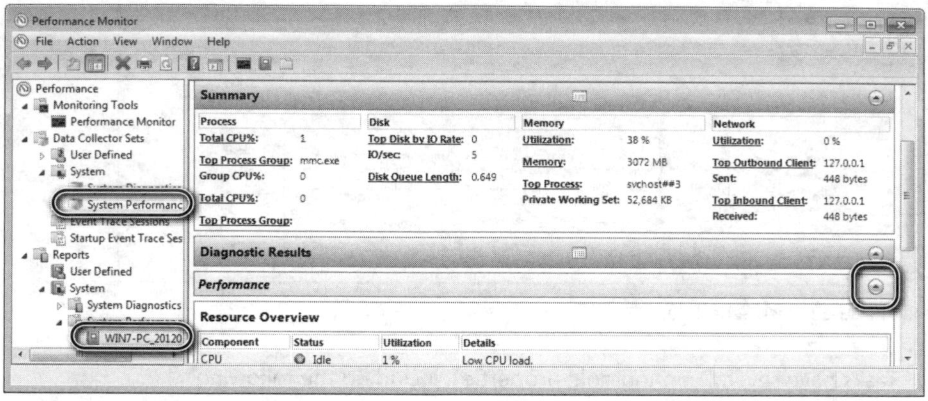

The left pane of the graphic highlights the System Performance Data Collector set and the System Performance report. The center pane shows a small portion of the report. You can scroll up and down to view more of the report, and you can click the arrows in the headers to expand or collapse different sections.

Key items to look for that can indicate problems are high CPU utilization and high memory utilization. If any items are high, you can expand the report to get more details.

Services

The *Services* applet is an important tool that you can use to stop, start, and configure services. As a reminder, a service starts without user intervention, and many services will start automatically when the system starts.

Chapter 7 covers printers and introduces a common reason why you might need to go into the Services applet. If the print spooler stops sending print jobs to your printer, print jobs will back up. A common solution is to restart the Print Spooler service.

Figure 13-14 shows the Services applet with the Windows Defender service selected and its property page opened. When you select any service, options appear on the left to stop, start, or restart the service, depending on its current state. Additionally, a short description appears. You can also right-click the service to manipulate it or to select Properties.

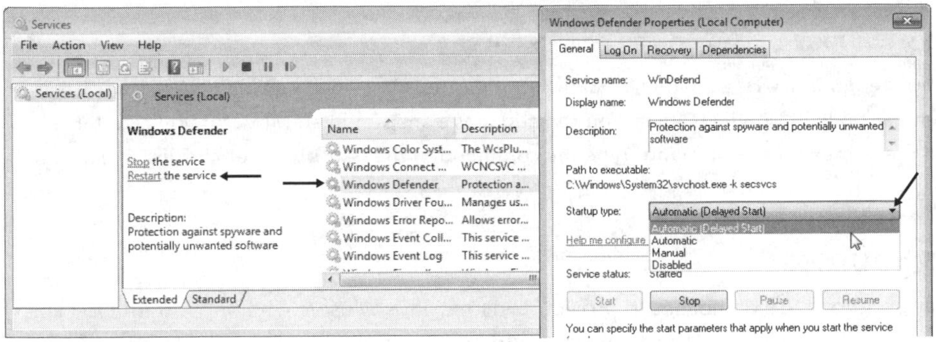

FIGURE 13-14 Services applet.

The Properties page allows you to configure how the service will start by using the following four options:

- **Automatic.** The service starts when Windows starts.

- **Automatic (Delayed Start).** The service starts a short time after Windows has started. The delay allows Windows to start more quickly. This option is available only in Windows Vista and Windows 7.

- **Manual.** The service starts when an application sends it a start signal or when a user manually starts it.

- **Disabled.** The service cannot start.

Some services will run only if another service is running. This is referred to as a *dependency*. If a service fails to start, it could be due to a problem with a dependent service. You can click the Dependencies tab to view a list of dependent services.

> **EXAM TIP**
>
> If you're seeing messages in Event Viewer logs indicating that a service cannot start, go into the Services applet and examine it. Verify that it is enabled and that the services it depends on are also enabled.

Component Services

Many developers use the Component Object Model (COM) as a standard for reusable code. That is, they code something once and reuse the code in other applications. For example, a developer could create code to determine the square root of a number. When it is created as a COM object, it can be used by multiple applications.

It isn't common, but in some cases components need to be manually added or configured. This is most common when an application is created by in-house developers. If required, developers will provide specific directions about how to add or configure the component.

Data Sources

Many applications use databases to provide dynamic data to users. The application typically allows users to choose what data they want, add additional data, and modify existing data. For the application to use the data, it must connect to the database.

Most applications using a database will automatically connect to it, but occasionally you might be required to manually add the connection. You would use the Data Sources (ODBC) applet and follow the directions provided by the application developer.

Other Administrative Tools

The following Administrative Tools are covered in other chapters:

- **Local Security Policy.** This provides several settings administrators commonly use to lock down security for a computer. Chapter 25 discusses the Local Security Policy.

- **Print Management.** Windows Vista, Windows 7, and Windows Server products include this tool, and it's used to manage multiple shared printers. Chapter 7 covers this tool.

- **System Configuration.** The System Configuration tool (commonly referred to as msconfig) is a valuable tool that you can use to help identify problems that can prevent Windows from starting correctly. Chapters 15 and 17, "Troubleshooting Windows Operating Systems," cover it.

- **Windows Firewall with Advanced Security.** The Windows Firewall helps protect a system from malicious traffic, and this tool provides additional capabilities to the Firewall. It's available in Windows Vista and Windows 7 but not Windows XP. Chapter 22 covers this tool in more depth.

- **Windows Memory Diagnostic.** If you suspect memory problems, you can use the Windows Memory Diagnostic to test it. Chapter 3, "Understanding RAM and CPUs," and Chapter 17 cover this tool, including steps to start it and how to view the results in the Event Viewer.

Chapter Summary

- The Task Manager includes several tabs. You can use the Applications tab to kill applications that are not responding. The Processes tab shows which processes are consuming the CPU's time, and the Services tab shows the status of all services. Use the Performance tab to see a snapshot of the system's performance displayed in graphs.

- A Microsoft Management Console (MMC) is an empty console, and you can add snap-ins based on your needs. Many tools are available with snap-ins already added to the MMC.

- The Control Panel includes several mini-programs called applets. Windows XP and Windows Vista list the applets individually, using the Classic View. Windows 7 lists the applets individually using Large Icons or Small Icons.

- Applets common to Windows XP, Windows Vista, and Windows 7 include Folder Options, Internet Options, Display, User Accounts, System, Windows Firewall, and Power Options.

- Folder Options is an applet used to control views in Windows Explorer. You can use it to show or hide hidden files and folders and to show or hide file extensions.

- Internet Options is an applet used to control many options in IE. It includes seven tabs: General, Security, Privacy, Content, Connections, Programs, and Advanced.

- Some applets are included only in Windows XP, such as Add/Remove Programs, Network Connections, Printers And Faxes, Automatic Updates, and the Network Setup Wizard.

- Some applets are unique to Windows Vista, such as Tablet PC Settings, Pen And Input Devices, Offline Files, Problem Reports And Solutions, and Printers.

- Windows 7 includes some unique applets, such as HomeGroup, Action Center, Remote Applications And Desktop Applications, and Troubleshooting.

- The Administrative Tools group is accessible from the Control Panel. It includes several tools, including Computer Management, Task Scheduler, Performance, and Services. You need administrative privileges to use these tools.

Chapter Review

Use the following questions to test your knowledge of the information in this chapter. The answers to these questions, and the explanations of why each answer choice is correct or incorrect, are located in the "Answers" section at the end of this chapter.

1. What would you use to end a program that is not responding?

   A. Application tab of Task Manager.

   B. Performance tab of Task Manager.

   C. Users tab of Task Manager.

   D. Services tab of Task Manager.

2. What can you use to identify what is consuming most of the CPU's processing power?

   A. The Services applet.

   B. The System applet.

   C. The Performance tab of the Task Manager.

   D. The Processes tab of the Task Manager.

3. A printer is no longer printing print jobs, and you suspect a problem with the print spooler. How can you restart it?

   A. Use the Applications tab of Task Manager.

   B. Use the Task Scheduler.

   C. Use the Services applet.

   D. Use the Programs tab of Internet Options.

4. You're working on a Windows 7–based system, and you need to access a folder in Windows Explorer. You can't find the folder, and you suspect it's hidden. What should you do?

   A. Use the Default Programs applet to modify the view.

   B. Change the View to Large Icons.

   C. Use Folder Options to show hidden files and folders.

   D. Use Folder Options to show extensions.

5. A user regularly accesses websites by using Internet Explorer. The user entered passwords in website forms and wants to remove them from the computer. How can this be accomplished?

   A. Use the Programs tab of Internet Options.

   B. Use the Content tab of Internet Options.

   C. Use the Security tab of Internet Options.

   D. Use the Privacy tab of Internet Options.

6. Which of the following tools is in the Administrative Tools group on Windows 7? (Choose all that apply.)

   A. Action Center.

   B. Computer Management.

   C. Event Viewer.

   D. HomeGroup.

Answers

1. **Correct Answer:** A

   A. **Correct:** You can select an application in this tab and click End Task.

   B. **Incorrect:** The Performance tab provides a graph to show current performance.

   C. **Incorrect:** The Users tab shows what users are logged on to a system but cannot be used to stop an application.

   D. **Incorrect:** The Services tab shows the status of services.

2. **Correct Answer:** D

   A. **Incorrect:** The Services applet is used to stop, start, and manipulate services.

   B. **Incorrect:** The System applet shows information about the system, such as its name and the hardware.

   C. **Incorrect:** The Performance tab of the Task Manager provides graphs to show the computer performance.

   D. **Correct:** The Processes tab includes a CPU column that shows the percentage of CPU time each process is taking.

3. **Correct Answer:** C

   A. **Incorrect:** The Print Spooler is not an application, so you can't manipulate it from the Applications tab.

   B. **Incorrect:** Task Scheduler is used to schedule tasks, not to end or restart services.

   C. **Correct:** You can restart the Print Spooler service from the Services applet.

   D. **Incorrect:** Internet Options is used to manipulate settings for Internet Explorer.

4. **Correct Answer:** C

   A. **Incorrect:** The Default Programs applet associates applications with file types.

   B. **Incorrect:** The Large Icons view is in Control Panel.

   C. **Correct:** The Folder Options applet includes settings to show hidden files and folders.

   D. **Incorrect:** Showing extensions will not show hidden files.

5. **Correct Answer:** B

    A. Incorrect: The Programs tab is used to configure default programs for web applications.

    B. Correct: Browsing history, including stored passwords, can be deleted from the AutoComplete Settings on the Content tab of Internet Options. This can also be done from the Browsing History settings on the General tab.

    C. Incorrect: The Security tab is used to configure security zones.

    D. Incorrect: The Privacy tab is primarily used to configure how cookies can be used.

6. **Correct Answer:** B, C

    A. Incorrect: The Action Center is in the Control Panel on Windows 7 but not in the Administrative Tools group.

    B. Correct: Computer Management is in this group.

    C. Correct: Event Viewer is in this group.

    D. Incorrect: HomeGroup is in the Control Panel on Windows 7 but not in the Administrative Tools group.

CHAPTER 14

Using the Command Prompt

The command prompt provides technicians with another way to accomplish tasks. Many end users can get by without ever using the command prompt. However, it provides a wealth of tools for technicians and administrators and is extremely valuable. When you're taking the live exams, don't be surprised if you come across a performance-based question that requires you to use the command prompt. Instead of an answer consisting of multiple choices, you might see a command prompt. You'll need to enter the appropriate commands to answer the question correctly.

220-802 Exam objectives in this chapter:

- 1.3 Given a scenario, use appropriate command line tools.
  - Networking
    - PING
    - TRACERT
    - NETSTAT
    - IPCONFIG
    - NET
    - NSLOOKUP
    - NBTSTAT
  - OS
    - KILL
    - BOOTREC
    - SHUTDOWN
    - TLIST
    - MD
    - RD
    - CD
    - DEL

- FDISK
- FORMAT
- DISKPART
- CHKDSK
- COPY
- XCOPY
- ROBOCOPY
- SFC
- [command name] /?

- 1.4 Given a scenario, use appropriate operating system features and tools.
  - Run line utilities
    - MSCONFIG
    - REGEDIT
    - CMD
    - SERVICES.MSC
    - MMC
    - MSTSC
    - NOTEPAD
    - EXPLORER
    - MSINFO32
    - DXDIAG

- 4.3 Given a scenario, troubleshoot hard drives and RAID arrays with appropriate tools.
  - Tools
    - CHKDSK
    - FORMAT
    - FDISK

- 4.6 Given a scenario, troubleshoot operating system problems with appropriate tools.
  - Tools
    - Sfc

Starting the Command Prompt

The *command prompt* originated from the older Microsoft Disk Operating System (MS-DOS). Before Windows, all commands were typed at the command line. Windows has come a long way since the old MS-DOS days, but much of the same functionality of MS-DOS is built into the command prompt.

NOTE   CLI

The command prompt is sometimes called the *command-line interface* (CLI).

Before you can start entering command prompt commands, you must first launch the command prompt. You can start it on Windows XP, Windows Vista, or Windows 7 by clicking Start, All Programs, Accessories, and selecting Command Prompt.

On Windows Vista and Windows 7, you can type **command** in the Search text box and select Command Prompt. On Windows XP, you can click Start, Run, type in **cmd**, and press Enter.

Figure 14-1 shows the basic Command Prompt window in Windows 7.

FIGURE 14-1 Command Prompt window on Windows 7.

After the Command Prompt window opens, you can start entering commands. You type in a command, press the Enter key, and the command is executed. For example, you can type **ipconfig** at the Command Prompt window and press Enter to view Internet Protocol (IP) configuration information for your system.

The text preceding the greater-than character (>) is called the command prompt, or sometimes just the prompt. You'll see a blinking cursor after the >, prompting you to enter a command.

EXAM TIP

CompTIA has indicated that the 220-801 and 220-802 A+ exams will have performance-based questions. That is, instead of just multiple choice questions, you might have a simulation where you have to perform a task. The command prompt environment is a good candidate for these types of questions. Take the time to start the command prompt and enter all of the commands in this chapter, and you'll have a better chance at getting these performance-based questions correct.

Access Denied Errors

Occasionally, you'll need to start the command prompt with administrative privileges. For example, you might enter a command and see one of the following errors:

- Access is denied
- The requested operation requires elevation

These errors indicate that the command needs to be executed with administrative privileges. If you start the command prompt with administrative privileges, the command will execute without the error.

> **NOTE ADMINISTRATIVE PRIVILEGES**
>
> If you start a command prompt with administrative privileges, all commands entered within the prompt have administrative privileges. However, permissions in other applications are not affected.

Starting with Administrative Privileges

On Windows Vista or Windows 7, right-click Command Prompt and select Run As Administrator as shown in Figure 14-2. If prompted by User Account Control (UAC), click Yes to continue. On Windows XP, right-click Command Prompt, select Run As, and enter the credentials for an administrator account.

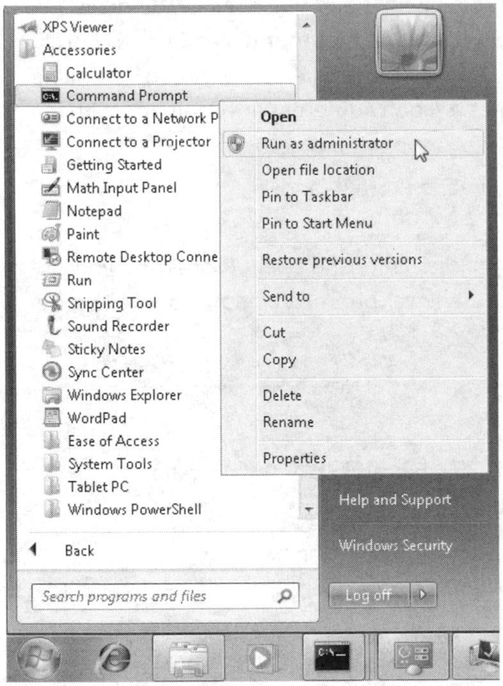

FIGURE 14-2 Launching the command prompt with administrative privileges.

Figure 14-3 shows the differences you'll see in the administrative Command Prompt window. You can see that the title bar is labeled Administrator: Command Prompt instead of just Command Prompt. The next section identifies some of the other differences.

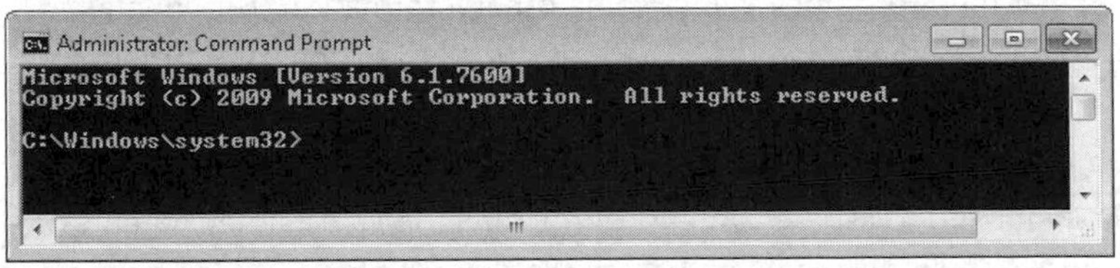

FIGURE 14-3 Command Prompt with administrative privileges.

Command Prompt vs. Cmd

The application that runs the command prompt is cmd.exe. Another way of starting the command prompt in Windows Vista and Windows 7 is by clicking Start, typing **cmd** in the search text box, and selecting cmd. In contrast, the previous instructions said to type in **command** and select Command Prompt. There are some subtle differences.

If you use **cmd**, it will start the cmd.exe program directly, and you'll see C:\Windows\system32\cmd.exe in the title bar of the window. If you use **command**, it creates a shortcut in your user profile that points to the C:\Windows\system32\cmd.exe application. The same cmd.exe application runs, but the shortcut creates a slightly different environment, with Command Prompt in the title bar.

Click Start, type in **command**, right-click Command Prompt, and select Properties. This shows all the properties of the shortcut.

In contrast, if you click Start, type in **cmd**, right-click cmd, and select Properties, you'll see the properties of the cmd.exe application. There are fewer property options for the application than for the shortcut.

✔ **Quick Check**

1. After running a command, you see an error indicating that the operation requires elevation. What should you do?

2. What is the name of the program that runs the command prompt?

Quick Check Answers

1. Start the command prompt with administrative privileges.

2. Cmd.exe.

Understanding Paths

You might have noticed that the > prompt includes some other information. This identifies the path, which is the current disk drive, and the current *directory*, or *folder*. For example, in Figure 14-1, the path is C:\Users\Darril.

The system will use this as the default path for any commands that you execute. For example, if you enter the **dir** command to list the contents of the directory, it lists the contents of the current path. Figure 14-4 shows this same path from Windows Explorer.

NOTE FOLDERS VS. DIRECTORIES

You'll commonly hear the term *folders* to refer to the folders in Windows Explorer. These folders are the exact same folders you see from the command prompt, but when using the command prompt, you'll often hear the term *directories*. In other words, folders and directories are the same thing.

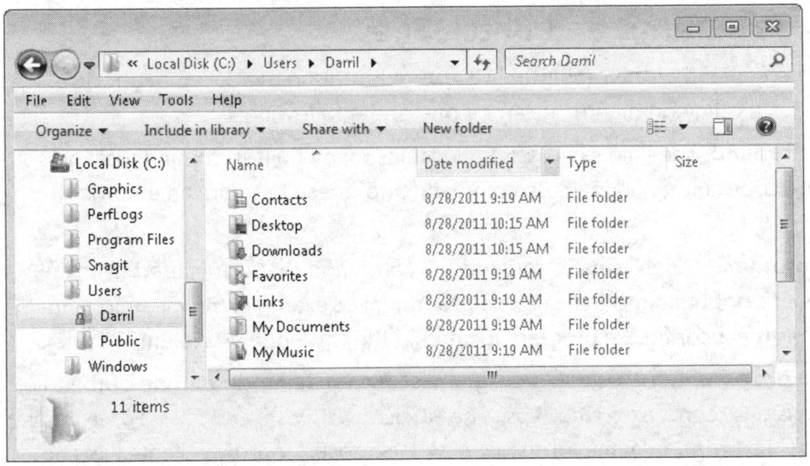

FIGURE 14-4 Windows Explorer folders.

Default Paths

In addition to the current path you see from the command prompt, the system also knows about other paths. If you run a command that is not included in the current directory, the system will search through these other paths for the command.

For example, if you enter the ipconfig command, the system will first look in the current path (such as C:\Users\Darril) for ipconfig. If it can't find the command, it searches through other known paths.

You can view the known paths for your system by typing

at the prompt and pressing Enter. You'll see something like this:

```
PATH=C:\Windows\system32;C:\Windows;C:\Windows\System32\Wbem;C:\Windows\System32\
WindowsPowerShell\v1.0\
```

Each path is separated by a semicolon, so this actually includes the following paths:

```
C:\Windows\system32

C:\Windows

C:\Windows\System32\Wbem

C:\Windows\System32\WindowsPowerShell\v1.0\
```

In this example, the ipconfig.exe program is located in C:\Windows\system32, so it will be run from that location. If the system can't locate the command in the current path or in any of the known paths, it will give an error. For example, if you incorrectly enter *ipconfig* as *ipnfig*, you'll see this:

```
'ipnfig' is not recognized as an internal or external command, operable program or batch
file.
```

Commands, Programs, and Batch Files

If you enter a valid command at the prompt, it will run. With this in mind, you might be asking yourself, "What is a valid command?" It can be one of the following:

- **Internal command**. The cmd.exe program includes many built-in commands. For example, the copy command is a core command and doesn't require an external application.

- **External command**. An external command is a command that is executed from an external file. It's not built into the cmd.exe program. For example, the ipconfig command will run the ipconfig.exe program located in the C:\Windows\system32 folder.

- **Executable program**. An executable program is any file that includes one of the following extensions: .com, .exe, .cmd, .vbs, .vbe, .js, .jse, .wsf, .wsh, and .msc. For example, dxdiag.exe is the program name for the DirectX Diagnostic Tool. If you enter dxdiag at the prompt, it will start the DirectX tool.

- **Batch file**. A batch file uses the .bat extension and is a grouping of one or more commands in a text file. When the batch file is executed, all of the commands are executed.

> **NOTE** **EXTERNAL COMMANDS AND EXECUTABLE PROGRAMS**
> An external command could also be considered an executable program because it usually has an extension of .exe. The major difference in this context is that external commands are considered those that have been around since the days of MS-DOS.

Understanding Extensions

In the early days of MS-DOS, all files were named with an eight-dot-three format. For example, ipconfig.exe includes eight letters (ipconfig), a dot, and a three-letter extension (.exe).

The extension is especially important. It tells the operating system what type of file it is, and the operating system associates many extensions with specific applications. For example, if someone emails you a file with .doc extension, you can double-click it and it will open Microsoft Word with the document showing. Similarly, if someone sends you a file with .xls extension, the file will open Microsoft Excel with the Excel spreadsheet showing.

When users were restricted to using only eight characters for the name, they often had to be creative when naming files. For example, an accountant might name a spreadsheet file stax1Q95.xls. It might not be apparent right away, but this is for state taxes for the first quarter of 1995.

Windows is no longer restricted to the eight-dot-three format. File names and extensions can now be longer, allowing you to name a file just about whatever you want. For example, the same accountant might name a file State Taxes First Quarter 2012.xlsx. If you double-click this file, it starts Microsoft Excel 2010 with the file showing.

Windows Vista and Windows 7 limit the full path, file name, and extension to 260 characters. For example, consider an Excel file stored in the C:\Data folder. The full name is C:\data \State Taxes First Quarter 2012.xlsx. This is 43 characters (C:\Data is 8 characters, and State Taxes First Quarter 2012.xlsx is 35 characters). Exceptionally long paths that cause the file to exceed the 260-character limit sometimes cause problems, especially when a user is trying to copy them.

✔ **Quick Check**

1. What is the difference between a folder and a directory?

2. How can you identify paths known to your system?

Quick Check Answers

1. Nothing; they are the same.

2. By entering the path command and the command prompt.

Command Prompt Basics

There are some basic rules and guidelines that are important to understand when using the command prompt. When you've grasped the basics, the more advanced topics are much easier to understand. The following sections cover basics from using uppercase and lowercase letters to using wildcards.

Case Sensitivity

For most commands entered within the command prompt, it doesn't matter what case you use when you enter them. You can use all uppercase, all lowercase, or a mixture. For example, the following three commands work exactly the same:

- **ipconfig**
- **IPCONFIG**
- **IPConfig**

There are some exceptions where you must enter the command using specific uppercase or lowercase letters, but they are rare. Where the case matters for any commands in this book, I'll stress its importance. Similarly, documentation usually provides emphasis if the case matters.

Understanding Switches

Most commands can be modified by using a switch. A switch is appended to the end of the command with a forward slash (/).

For example, the ipconfig command provides basic information on a computer's IP configuration. However, you can append it with the /all switch to get detailed information on the IP configuration. The command with the switch appended is ipconfig /all.

The switch should be preceded with a space. However, some commands will work without a switch. For example, ipconfig/all works the same as ipconfig /all. It's best to use a space before all switches because this will work consistently.

> **NOTE** **DASHES AND SLASHES**
>
> Many commands also support the use of the dash (-) as a switch, instead of the slash (/). That is, you can use **ipconfig -all** and it will work the same as **ipconfig /all**.

Different commands support different switches. Just because the /all switch works with ipconfig, you can't expect it to work with the xcopy command (as xcopy /all). If you don't know the valid switches for a command, the best thing to do is ask the system for help.

Getting Help

You can get help for almost all command prompt commands by appending the command with the help switch (/?). If you can't remember the exact syntax of the command, enter the command with /? to retrieve help on it.

Some commands also support the use of the help command. You can type in **help** followed by the command. The following two commands show how to get help on the chkdsk command:

```
chkdsk /?
```

```
help chkdsk
```

You can use these two commands for most commands by just substituting chkdsk with the name of the command. However, the help command isn't as universal as the /? switch. For example, if you enter **help ipconfig**, the system will instead prompt you to enter ipconfig /?.

Using Quotes with Spaces

The command prompt interprets spaces as the next part of a command. For example, consider the copy command. The syntax is as follows:

```
copy sourceFile destinationFile
```

You could enter the following command to create a copy of the study.txt file and name the file copy backup.txt:

```
copy study.txt backup.txt
```

The command is copy and it recognizes the name after the space (study.txt) as the source file. It also recognizes backup.txt as the destination file because there is a space between study.txt and backup.txt.

However, file names can have spaces. What if the study.txt file was named A Plus Study Notes.txt? If you tried the following command, it wouldn't work:

```
copy A Plus Study Notes.txt Study backup.txt
```

It would see "A" as the name of the source file. However, you probably won't have a file named A, so it will return an error indicating that it can't find the specified file. The following command is a little better, but it will still fail:

```
copy "A Plus Study Notes.txt" Study backup.txt
```

In this case, it interprets everything within the quotes as the name of source file (A Plus Study Notes.txt). However, it then sees Study and backup.txt as two separate elements. It's expecting only one destination file, so it gives an error indicating the syntax of the command is incorrect. The correct command is:

```
copy "A Plus Study Notes.txt" "Study backup.txt"
```

Notice that both the source file name and the destination file name include spaces, so they are both enclosed with quotes.

Beware of Typos

There might come a day when computers will do what we want them to do instead of what we ask them to do. However, that day isn't here yet. With this in mind, you must type in the commands with the correct spelling.

For example, if you mean to enter ipconfig but enter ipcnfig instead (with the "o" missing), the system will give you an error indicating that it can't locate the program ipcnfig.

Sometimes, you'll see an error like the following:

```
The syntax of the command is incorrect.
```

This indicates that your computer understands the command name, but it can't recognize the other parts of the command. It might be that you're using invalid switches, missing a space, or not using quotes correctly.

When you see an error, one of the first things you should do is double-check the spelling. Often, you can find the problem by looking at the command one character at a time.

Recalling Commands

The command prompt keeps a history of all the commands you've entered in the current session. This is very useful if you need to reenter a command. You don't need to type it in from scratch every time.

Table 14-1 shows keys you can use to recall information in the command prompt history.

TABLE 14-1 Recalling Commands in History

Key	Comments
Up Arrow	Retrieves the previous command in the history list
Down Arrow	Retrieves the next command in the history list
Page Up	Retrieves the first command in the history list
Page Down	Retrieves the last command in the history list
Esc	Clears the current command

I strongly encourage you to play around with this. Launch a command prompt, enter a few commands, and then use these keys to see how they work. It can be a huge timesaver.

You can also use a few other keys to move the cursor around after you've retrieved a command. Table 14-2 shows some of these keys.

TABLE 14-2 Using Keys to Move the Cursor

Key	Comments
Home	Moves the cursor to the beginning of the command
End	Moves the cursor to the end of the command
Left arrow	Moves the cursor to the left one space
Right arrow	Moves the cursor to the right one space

For example, imagine that you entered the following command and the system complained with a syntax error:

```
copy "a+ study notes.txt" study backup.txt"
```

After looking at it, you realize you forgot the quote (") before Study. You could type it in from scratch, but you might actually end up with another typo. Instead, you could do the following:

1. Press the up arrow. This retrieves the last command.

2. Press the left arrow until your cursor is before the *S* in Study.

3. Type in the quote (").

4. Press Enter. Note that you don't have to move your cursor to the end of the line to run the command.

> **NOTE   MOUSE DOES NOT CHANGE CURSOR POSITION**
>
> It's common to try to reposition the cursor with the mouse, but it won't work in the Command Prompt window. You need to use the arrows to move the cursor's position.

Copying and Pasting

You can also copy and paste data to and from the command prompt. It doesn't work with the typical Ctrl+C to copy or Ctrl+V to paste, but it is possible to copy and paste data into the command prompt. This can also save you some time.

Copying and pasting in the command prompt is easiest if you enable QuickEdit mode. Use the following steps to enable QuickEdit mode, and then copy and paste data to and from the Command Prompt window:

1. Launch the command prompt.

2. Right-click the title bar and select Properties.

3. Select the check box for QuickEdit mode. Your display will look similar to the following graphic. Click OK.

NOTE **PERSONAL PREFERENCES**

You can manipulate the appearance of the Command Prompt window by selecting the Font, Layout, and Colors tab. Many users like to manipulate the Colors tab for personal preferences.

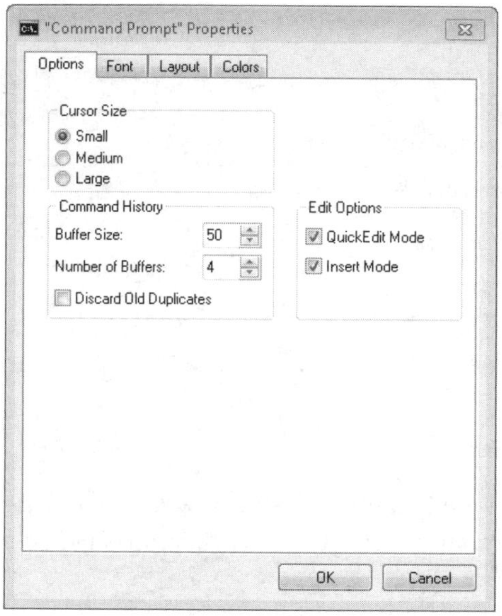

4. Type **notepad** and press Enter. This will open an instance of the Notepad editor.
5. Type **ipconfig** within Notepad, but don't press the Enter key.
6. Press Ctrl+A to select the text you typed, and press Ctrl+C to copy the text to the clipboard.
7. Select the Command Prompt window.
8. Right-click within the Command Prompt window. The text you copied from Notepad is pasted into the window.
9. Press Enter to run the command.
10. Use the mouse to select the text displayed in the Command Prompt window. Click in the upper left of the Command Prompt window and drag the mouse to the bottom right. Release the mouse when you've completed the selection.

11. After you've selected the text, press Enter. You can also right-click the mouse. Both actions copy the text to the Clipboard.

12. Return to Notepad. Press Ctrl+V to paste the text into the Notepad document.

At this point, you can save the Notepad document. For example, you could use method to save the IP configuration of a system in a file.

Saving the Output in a Text File

The previous section showed how you can copy text from the command prompt, but sometimes you might want to send the output directly to a text file. You can do so with the > symbol, which redirects the output to a file.

For example, instead of copying the output of ipconfig /all and then pasting it into a text file, you could use the following command:

```
ipconfig /all > MyConfig.txt
```

After entering the command, you could open it with the following command:

```
notepad myconfig.txt.
```

You can also view the contents of the text file with the following command:

```
type myconfig.txt.
```

As an alternative, you can copy the output of a command to the Windows Clipboard using | clip, as follows:

```
ipconfig /all | clip
```

You can then paste the contents from the clipboard into any file with Ctrl+V.

Understanding Variables

Windows uses variables to identify many system elements. For example, every computer has a name, but the name will be different on each computer. Windows uses the %computername% variable to identify the name of the local computer.

All variables start and end with a percent symbol (%). You can view the value of a variable with the echo command. For example, you can view the name of your computer with the following command:

```
echo %computername%
```

Table 14-3 shows some common variable names along with what they represent. I encourage you to look at each of these names by opening a command prompt and typing in **echo** followed by the variable (for example, **echo %computername%**). If you enter a typo, the system will output what you entered with the percent symbols. In other words, if you see an output with the percent symbols, double-check your spelling. Press the up arrow to retrieve the previous command and correct it.

TABLE 14-3 Command Variable Names

Variable	Comments
%systemdrive%	System drive (such as C:\)
%systemroot% %windir%	Location of Windows (such as C:\Windows)
%computername%	Name of local computer
%homepath%	Path to user's profile (such as C:\Documents and Settings\username on Windows XP or C:\Users\username on Windows Vista and Windows 7)
%path%	List of paths known to the system
%temp%	Path to temporary folder in users profile
%username%	User name for logged on user
%userdomain%	Name of domain if computer is joined to a domain, or name of computer if computer is not joined to a domain
%userprofile%	Location of the profile for the logged on user

You can view a list of all variables known by your system by entering the **set** command. The output shows each variable name (without the percent symbols) along with the value of the variable. If you want to view the value of one or more variables, you can use the set command followed by the first letters of the variable. For example, **set system** and **set sys** both show the value of the system drive and system root variables.

> *NOTE* **LOOKING AT VARIABLES IN THE GUI**
>
> You can look at variables in Windows Vista or Windows 7 by clicking Start, typing **Environment**, selecting Edit The System Environment Variables, and clicking Environment Variables. Alternatively, you can click Start, right-click Computer, and select Properties, select Advanced System Settings, and select Environment Variables from the Advanced tab.

Using Wildcards

You can also use the following wildcards when using the command prompt:

- ■ ***** The asterisk (*) can be used in place of zero or more characters.
- ■ **?** The question mark (?) can be used in place of a single character.

For example, the dir command can be used to provide a listing of files in a directory. Table 14-4 shows you can use the * wildcard to view different results.

TABLE 14-4 Using the * Wildcard

Command	Result
dir	List all files in the current directory
dir d*	List all files that start with a d
dir *g	List all files that end with an g
dir *.txt	List all files with a .txt extension

The ? symbol can be used only for a single character. For example, imagine that you have several study documents but that each one has different versions, such as StudyV1.doc, StudyV2.doc, and so on. You could use the following command to list them all:

```
dir studyv?.doc
```

✔ **Quick Check**

1. What are two methods of viewing help for the chkdsk command?
2. What can you press to retrieve the last command you entered at the command prompt?

Quick Check Answers

1. Chkdsk /? or help chkdsk.
2. The up arrow.

File Commands

There are several commands you can use from the prompt to view and manipulate files and folders. This section identifies the relevant commands for the A+ exam and shows how to use them. While you're going through this section, I strongly encourage you to open up a command prompt and try these commands out.

Attrib

The *attrib* command is short for attribute, and it is used to list and manipulate attributes assigned to files and folders. Table 14-5 lists the attributes that can be assigned.

TABLE 14-5 Common File Attributes

Attribute	Comments
A Archive	When cleared, it indicates a file has been archived (or backed up). When set, it indicates the file has not been archived or has been modified since the last archive.
H Hidden	The file is not normally displayed unless the user changes settings to view hidden files.
I Not Index	Indicates whether the file is included in the index. Indexed files can be more easily located by the system.
R Read-only	Users cannot modify a read-only file without changing the attribute.
S System	The operating system protects system files to prevent users and malicious software from causing damage.

If you enter the attrib command at the command prompt, it will list all the files in the current directory along with any attributes that are assigned. For example, the following code listing shows the output from the attrib command. You can see that some of the files have specific attributes assigned.

Output from attrib command

```
C:\Study\A+Study>attrib
            C:\Study\A+Study\Archived File.rtf
A    H      C:\Study\A+Study\Hidden File.txt
A    I      C:\Study\A+Study\Not Indexed File.rtf
A    R      C:\Study\A+Study\Readonly File.rtf
A    SH     C:\Study\A+Study\System and Hidden File.sys
```

The first file in the output doesn't have any attributes showing. But others show A for not archived, H for hidden, I for not indexed, and S for System.

You can set or clear any attributes with the + or - symbols. For example, if you want to make a file named study.txt read only use the following command:

```
attrib +r study.txt
```

If you want to clear the read-only attribute, use the following command:

```
attrib -r study.txt
```

> **EXAM TIP**
>
> Sometimes you might need to delete or copy over a hidden, system, read-only file. This is not possible when these attributes are set. However, you can change the attributes by using the attrib command, and then the system will let you copy over the file.

You can also see most of these attributes from Windows Explorer. Right-click any file and select Properties. You can see the Read-only and Hidden attributes on the General tab of this page. Click the Advanced button, and your display will look similar to Figure 14-5. It's not common to manipulate the system attribute of a file, so you can't do so from Windows Explorer.

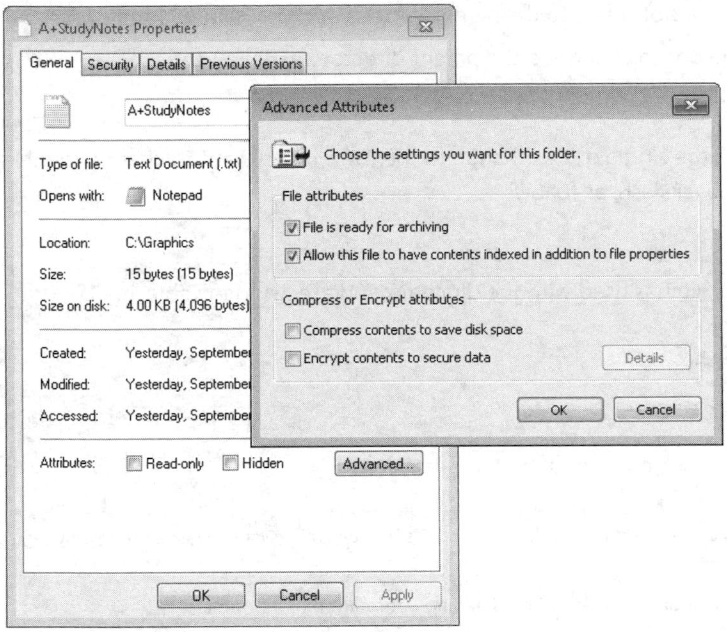

FIGURE 14-5 Attributes within Windows Explorer.

The compress and encryption attributes shown in Figure 14-5 can be manipulated with the compact and cipher commands, respectively. However, you're unlikely to come across these commands in the A+ exams.

Dir

The *dir* command is short for directory, and it is used to list files and directories. The "Using Wildcards" section earlier in the chapter showed some examples of how to use it. The following code listing shows the output you can expect from the dir command.

Using the dir command

```
C:\Study\A+Study>dir
 Volume in drive C has no label.
 Volume Serial Number is 78B1-B7A9
 Directory of C:\Study\A+Study
09/08/2012  02:16 PM    <DIR>          .
09/08/2012  02:16 PM    <DIR>          ..
09/08/2012  01:05 PM               198 A+Notes.rtf
09/08/2012  01:05 PM               198 Archived File.rtf
09/08/2012  02:12 PM                24 Hidden File.txt
```

```
09/08/2012  01:05 PM                198 Not Indexed File.rtf
09/08/2012  01:05 PM                198 Readonly File.rtf
              5 File(s)           816 bytes
              2 Dir(s)   119,378,903,040 bytes free
```

Notice that in addition to the files, the output also includes two other entries at the beginning: a single dot (.), and a double dot (..). The single dot refers to the root of the drive, which is C:\ in this case. The double dot refers to the parent folder, which is C:\Study in this case.

You can use the double dot to change to the parent directory as follows:

```
Cd ..
```

However, you can't use the single dot to change to the root. If you want to change to the root, you have to use the backslash, as follows:

```
Cd \
```

Some of the common switches used with the dir command are listed in Table 14-6.

TABLE 14-6 Common dir Switches

Switch	Comments
/w dir /w	Formats the output in a wide list with fewer details
/a dir /ah	Displays files that have specific attributes such as hidden (/ah), system (/as), or read only (ar)
/b dir /b	Displays files in a bare format without heading information or a summary
/q dir /q	Includes the name of the owner for each file
/s dir /s	Lists all files in the current directory, and all subdirectories

The dir command with the /s switch can be very useful when you're looking for a specific file. For example, imagine you're looking for a file that starts with study but you're not sure about the rest of the file's name. You can use the following command with wildcards:

```
dir study*.* /s
```

Or if you only know that the word study is somewhere in the name of the file, you can use the following command:

```
dir *study*.* /s
```

These commands will search subdirectories only within the current directory. If you want to search the entire drive from the root, you would need to either change the directory or include the path in the command. The following command would ensure that the search starts from the root of the drive by using the \ symbol to identify the root:

```
dir \*study*.* /s
```

Md

The *md* command is short for *make directory*, and it is used to create directories. Alternatively, you can use the mkdir command, which works exactly the same way. For example, if you wanted to create a directory named Study, you could use the following command:

```
md Study
```

You can use uppercase or lowercase for Study, and the directory will be created with the case you use. You can later access it by using either uppercase or lowercase.

You can also include the hard drive and the path, or just the path if you are creating the directory on the current drive. For example, if your current path is C:\Data and you want to create a directory at the root of the C: drive, you can use either of the following commands:

```
md C:\Study
```

```
md \Study
```

You can also create multiple directories with the same command. If your system didn't currently have a directory named Study but you wanted to create it along with a child directory named A+Study, you could use the following command:

```
md C:\Study\A+Study
```

The preceding command creates the Study directory and creates the A+Study directory as a child within C:\Study.

CD

The *cd* command is short for change directory, and it is used to change the current path. As an alternative, you can use the chdir command, which works exactly the same way.

As a reminder, all command prompt commands execute from the context of the current path. You can include the full path for commands or files in the command, but very often it's easier to change the directory.

For example, imagine that you are currently in the C:\Study\A+Study path, but you want to list the contents of the C:\Study folder. You could use the dir command with the path as follows:

```
dir C:\study
```

Or, you could first change the directory and then run the dir command as follows:

```
cd \study
dir
```

Notice that the backslash (\) is used in this command. The backslash refers to the root of the drive, so the command changes to the C:\Study directory.

Because you're only moving up one folder, you could also use the .. shortcut to change to the parent directory. If your current path is C:\Study\A+Study, the parent folder is C:\Study. The following commands can also work:

```
cd ..
dir
```

If you want to change to the root of the drive, you can use the following command:

```
cd \
```

Changing Drives

Often you'll want to view or manipulate files on different drives. For example, you might be in the C: drive but want to access files on the D: drive. To change drives, simply enter the drive letter followed by a colon, as follows:

```
C:\Windows\System32>d:
```

```
D:\>c:
```

```
C:\Windows\System32>
```

The first command (d:) changed to the D: drive, and the second command (c:) changed back to the C: drive.

Notice that when you change drives, the system uses a different path. The system remembers the path for each drive in the session, but if there isn't a path set, it uses the root. In the example, there wasn't a known path for D:, so it used the root of D:. However, it knew the path for C: was \Windows\System32, so it used this path when it returned to the C: drive.

Rd

The *rd* command is short for remove directory, and it is used to remove or delete directories. As an alternative, you can use the rmdir command which works exactly the same way.

Table 14-7 shows the two switches used with the rd command.

TABLE 14-7 Common rd Switches

Switch	Comments
/s Subdirectory	Used to remove a directory and all files and subdirectories within the subdirectory. This will prompt you with Are You Sure (Y/N). You can press Y to confirm the action or N to cancel it.
/q Quiet	Suppresses the Are You Sure question. This is useful if you include the command in a batch file.

For example, you can use the following command to delete all files and directories within a directory named test:

```
rd c:\test /s
```

EXAM TIP

If you try to remove a directory that has files or directories within it, you'll see an error unless you use the /s switch.

Del

If you want to delete individual files instead of full directories, you can use the *del* command. As an alternative, you can use the erase command, which works exactly the same way. The basic syntax is as follows:

```
del targetFile
```

You can use wildcards with the del command. For example, if you want to delete all the files in a directory, you can use the following:

```
del *.*
```

Table 14-8 shows some switches used with the del command along with examples.

TABLE 14-8 Common del Switches

Switch	Comments
/p Prompt	Prompts you for confirmation before deleting a file del study.txt /p
/f Force	Forces the deletion of read-only files del study.txt /f
/s Subdirectories	Deletes the file in all subdirectories del study.txt /s
/q Quiet	Suppresses confirmation prompt when using wildcards del *.* /q

Copy

As the name implies, the *copy* command can copy files and folders. The copy command was introduced in the "Using Quotes with Spaces" section earlier in this chapter. The basic syntax is as follows:

```
copy sourceFile DestinationFile
```

You can include the full path of the source file, the destination file, or both. It uses the current directory by default, so if either of the files are in different directories, you must include the directory for at least one.

For example, if your current path is C:\Study\A+ and you want to copy a file named A+Notes.txt to the C:\Study\Sec+ folder, you can use any of the following commands:

C:\Study\A+> **copy "StudyNotes.txt" "C:\Study\Sec+"**

C:\Study\A+> **copy "StudyNotes.txt" "C:\Study\Sec+\A+StudyNotes.txt"**

C:\Study\A+> **copy "C:\Study\A+\StudyNotes.txt" "C:\Study\Sec+"**

> **NOTE USING QUOTES**
>
> These commands are using quotes to identify the source file and destination file. You don't always need quotes. However, in this example, the command prompt gets confused by the + symbol, so the quotes are needed for any paths that include the + symbol.

In the first example, the source file *path* isn't included, so the copy command looks for the StudyNotes.txt file in the current path (C:\Study\A+). In the second example, the name of the destination file is given, so the copied file will be named A+StudyNotes.txt. If the name isn't given, the same file name is used. The third example includes both the source path and the destination path.

You can also use wildcards with the copy command. The following commands provide two examples:

C:\Study\A+> **copy *.* "C:\Study\Sec+"**

C:\Study\A+> **copy *.txt "C:\Study\Sec+"**

The first command will copy all files in the current folder to the C:\Study\Sec+ folder. In the second example, it copies only files with the .txt extension.

Table 14-9 shows three important switches you should know about with the copy command.

TABLE 14-9 Common copy Switches

Switch	Comments
/a ASCII	Indicates files are ASCII-based text files. The copy command uses the end-of-file character (Ctrl+Z) with these files. If omitted, it considers the files binary files and doesn't look for the end-of-file character.
/v Verify	This verifies that the files are written correctly when they are copied.
/y Suppress prompts	If the same destination file already exists, the copy command prompts the user to confirm the operation before overwriting the destination file. The /y switch suppresses this prompt. This is useful if you include the command in a batch file.

A neat trick you can do with the copy command is copy the contents of multiple text files together. For example, imagine you have three log files named log1.txt, log2.txt, and log3.txt. You can use the following command to combine them all into a single file named logall.txt:

```
copy log1.txt + log2.txt + log3.txt logall.txt
```

Xcopy

The *xcopy* command is an extension of the copy command. This is a very rich tool, and all of its capabilities are beyond the scope of the A+ exam. However, the most important things to remember about the xcopy command are as follows:

- It can do everything that the copy command can do.
- It can copy directories and subdirectories.

As an example, if you wanted to copy the entire contents of the C:\Study directory, including all subdirectories, to the C:\Data directory, you could use the following commands:

```
xcopy c:\Study c:\Data\ /s
```

```
xcopy c:\Study c:\Data\ /s /e
```

The first command copies files and subdirectories but does not include subdirectories that don't have any files or directories within them. The second command includes empty subdirectories.

EXAM TIP

The xcopy command includes all of the same functionality of the copy command but adds a lot more. For example, the xcopy command can copy entire directories and subdirectories.

Robocopy

The *robocopy* command name sounds like it's related to robots, but it's actually short for *robust copy*. In this context, *robust* means strong and vigorous. It is commonly used to copy entire directories and includes all the features of copy and xcopy. While copy and xcopy will copy the files, they can't copy the file's metadata.

NOTE **METADATA (DATA ABOUT DATA)**

Metadata is information about data, or often stated as "data about data." For example, you might have a file named Studynotes.docx, and the content of the file is the data—your notes. The file's metadata includes information about the file, such as when you created it, when you last saved it, and who has permissions to access it.

When you copy a file, it creates a second file but it isn't a true copy. The data within the file will be the same, but some of the metadata will be different. Robocopy allows you to copy the file and all the metadata. Information that you can copy with robocopy includes the following:

- **Data**. This is the core information in the file, which will also be copied using copy and xcopy.

- **Attributes**. Both basic and advanced attributes can be copied.

- **Timestamps**. Original timestamps, such as when the file was created, are included in the copy.

- **Security information**. This includes all the permissions, such as the ability to read or modify a file.

- **Owner information**. Instead of identifying the person that performed the copy as the owner, the original owner information can be retained.

- **Auditing information**. Audit settings allow the system to log when someone accessed a file. Robocopy allows you to copy audit settings from the original file.

Table 14-10 shows some key switches you can use with robocopy.

TABLE 14-10 Common robocopy Switches

Switch	Comments and Example
/copyall	Copies the data and all metadata for files robocopy c:\notes d:\copies /copyall
/e	Includes all empty subdirectories robocopy c:\notes d:\copies /e
/purge	Deletes destination files and directories that no longer exist in the source location robocopy c:\notes d:\copies /purge
/move	Moves files and directories and deletes them from the source after they are copied robocopy c:\notes d:\copies /move

Sfc

The *sfc* command starts the System File Checker. This is a valuable tool that you can use to check the integrity of protected system files. This can be useful if a system has been infected with a virus. You can use the sfc tool to detect whether the virus has tried to modify any system files.

Sfc can detect and repair problems with system files. Table 14-11 shows the common switches you can use with sfc.

TABLE 14-11 Common sfc Switches

Switch	Comments
/scannow	Scans all protected system files. It will attempt to repair files and will report on its success or failure. You can view a report from the scan by looking here: %windir% \logs\cbs\cbs.log. The command is: sfc /scannow
/verifyonly	This runs a scan, but it does not attempt to fix any problems. The command is: sfc /verifyonly
/scanfile	Instead of scanning all protected system files, it scans only the specified file. For example, you can use the following command to scan a specific file: sfc /scanfile=c:\windows\system32\kernel32.dll
/verifyfile	This runs a scan on the specified file, but it does not attempt to fix any problems. Here's an example: sfc /verifyfile=c:\windows\system32\kernel32.dll
/purgecache	This switch is available only in Windows XP. It removes the contents of a folder named %windir%\system32\dllcache and repopulates the folder with verified files.

Using Notepad to Create a Batch File

Notepad is a text editor accessible from the command prompt. You can use the following steps to open Notepad and create a batch file.

1. Launch the command prompt.

2. Type in **notepad** and press Enter. This will open the Notepad editor.

3. Within the editor, type in **ipconfig /all > c:\scripts\MyConfig.txt**. Note that if you entered this at the command prompt, it would send the output of the ipconfig /all command and save it into a file named myconfig.txt, in a folder named MyConfig.txt.

4. Press Alt+F. This allows you to access the File menu.

5. Use the down arrow to select Save As. Browse to the root of C:, and click New Folder.

6. Name the folder **Scripts**. Double-click the Scripts folder to open it.

7. Type in **ipc.bat** as the name of the file. Press Enter to select Save. At this point, you have created a batch file named ipc.bat in the c:\scripts folder, with the ipconfig /all command within it.

8. Press Alt+F to access the File menu again.

9. Use the down arrow to select Exit, and press Enter. You'll be returned to the command prompt.

10. Type in **c:\scripts\ipc.bat** to run the batch file you just created. This will run the ipconfig /all command and redirect the output to a text file named MyConfig.txt.

11. Type in **Notepad c:\scripts\MyConfig.txt**. This will open the text file you just created with the Notepad editor.

Operating System Commands

There are many commands that you can enter at the command prompt that open a Windows-based application. You can often get to the same application from within the Start menu. However, the name used to launch these applications has become well known by many technicians and provides an easy shortcut to them.

Table 14-12 lists some common tools that you can launch by entering the appropriate command at the command prompt, along with the chapter where the tool is covered in more depth. Many of the commands can also be launched from the search text box in Windows or Windows Vista, or from the Run line in Windows XP.

TABLE 14-12 Common Operating System Commands

Command	Tool Description	Chapter
dxdiag	DirectX Diagnostic Tool. Used to troubleshoot multimedia issues related to games or movies using DirectX.	6
explorer	Starts Windows Explorer. Note that Windows Explorer is used to view files on a system and is different from Internet Explorer, which is used to browse the Internet.	13
mmc	Opens a blank Microsoft Management Console. You can add snap-ins to an MMC.	13
msconfig	System Configuration tool. Used to configure the system, services, and startup applications.	15
msinfo32	System Information tool. Identifies hardware resources, components, and the software environment. This is useful for identifying the BIOS version, the amount of RAM installed on a system, and the processor type and speed.	2,3
mstsc	Opens the Remote Desktop Connection window, which can be used to connect to another system.	20
regedit regedt32	Opens the registry editor.	17
Services.msc	Opens the services applet. This can be used to stop, start, enable, and disable services.	13
sigverif	The File Signature Verification utility is used to identify digitally signed files and verify their integrity.	15

I strongly encourage you to start each of the programs listed in Table 14-12 and look at them. You don't need to master them at this point, but take a look around and see what information is available. If something interests you, look deeper. You'll be a step closer to mastering them for the A+ exams, and you'll have a better idea of what tool to use when you need to troubleshoot a computer.

On Windows Vista and Windows 7, click Start, type the name of the program in the Search text box, and press Enter.

On Windows XP, click Start, Run, type the command, and press Enter.

Table 14-13 lists some miscellaneous tools you can launch from the command prompt.

TABLE 14-13 Miscellaneous Operating System Commands

Command	Tool Description
date	View or set the date.
kill	Used on Unix-based operating systems to terminate a process.
shutdown	You can use this to force a shutdown (/s), restart (/r), or logoff (/l) from the Command Prompt.
time	View or set the time.
tlist tasklist	Shows a list of running processes. On Windows Vista and Windows 7, tlist has been renamed to tasklist.
type	Sends the output of a text file to the screen.
ver	Shows version information for the operating system.
winver	Opens the About Windows page, showing version information.

Disk Commands

Windows includes several commands that you can use to view, manipulate, and modify disks. These are described in detail in Chapter 16, "Understanding Disks and File Systems," but for an overview, they are listed in Table 14-14. These are entered at the Command Prompt, and each of them has help available by entering the command with the /? switch.

TABLE 14-14 Common Disk Commands

Command	Description
chkdsk	Checks and fixes disk errors.
convert	Converts a file system from FAT or FAT32 to NTFS. Data on the disk is retained.
format	Formats a partition with a file system. All data on the disk is lost.
diskpart	Tool used to manipulate hard disks. Diskpart replaces the older fdisk tool.
defrag	Defragments a volume for better performance.
fdisk	Legacy tool used to format and partition hard drives (replaced by diskpart).

EXAM TIP

It's best to run the disk commands in Table 14-14 and the networking commands listed in Table 14-15 at the command prompt. You should not run them from the Run line in Windows XP or the Start, Search text box in Windows Vista and Windows 7, because the Command Prompt window will open, run the command, and then close. You might not be able to see the results of the command. Try it with the ipconfig command.

Networking Commands

There are several common commands you can use to manipulate and troubleshoot a network. These commands are explored in greater depth in later chapters. However, as an introduction, they are listed in Table 14-15 with a short description and the chapter where they are covered.

TABLE 14-15 Common Networking Commands

Command	Description	Chapter
ipconfig	Displays IP configuration for network interface cards	24
ping	Checks connectivity with a device on a network	24
tracert	Checks connectivity with a device and shows the path through routers	24
nslookup	Used to query Domain Name System (DNS) Can verify records exist in DNS to resolve host names to IP addresses	24
arp	Shows mapping of IP addresses to media access control (MAC) addresses	24
nbtstat	Shows statistics for connections using NetBIOS over TCP/IP	24
netstat	Shows inbound and outbound connections	24

netsh	Advanced command used to manipulate and show network settings	22
net	Group of commands to view and manipulate network settings	24
telnet	Used to connect to remote system from the Command Prompt	20

EXAM TIP

When troubleshooting connectivity issues, ping and ipconfig are two of the most commonly used tools. Other commands are valuable, but you can often identify a problem by first checking the IP configuration with ipconfig and then checking connectivity with ping.

Chapter Summary

- The command prompt is a text-based window where you can enter MS-DOS–based commands.
- You can start the command prompt by entering **cmd** at the Run line in Windows XP. In Windows Vista or Windows 7, click Start, type **command** in the Search text box, and press Enter.
- If a command gives an access denied or command needs elevation error, start the command prompt with administrative privileges.
- You can get help on most commands by entering the command followed by the /? switch (such as **ipconfig /?**), or by entering **help** followed by the command (such as **help ipconfig**).
- The attrib command is used to view and manipulate attributes.
- Commands related to directories are dir to show the contents, md to make directories, cd to change directories, and rd to delete directories. The del command can delete individual files.
- Copy is used to copy files, and xcopy is an extended version of copy. Xcopy can do everything that copy can do and can copy subdirectories. Robocopy can do everything that copy and xcopy can do and can also copy metadata.
- Sfc (System File Checker) is used to verify the integrity of system files. The /purgecache switch included in Windows XP is not available in Windows Vista and Windows 7.
- Many applications can be launched from the command prompt, the Run line in Windows XP, or the Search text box in Windows Vista or Windows 7. You just need to know the command. Some common commands are:
  - Dxdiag starts the DirectX Diagnostic Tool.
  - Msconfig starts the System Configuration tool.
  - Msinfo32 starts the System Information tool.

- Mstsc opens the Remote Desktop Connection window.
- Regedit and Regedt32 open the registry editor.
- Sigverif starts the File Signature Verification tool.
- Shutdown can be used to shut down or log off of a system.
- Tlist or tasklist can be used to show running processes.

- Some of the common disk commands that you can execute from the command prompt are:
  - Chkdsk can check and fix disk errors.
  - Convert can change a FAT or FAT32 file system to NTFS.
  - Format is used to format a partition with a file system such as NTFS.
  - Diskpart can view and manipulate hard disks and partitions.
  - Defrag can defragment a volume for better performance.
  - Fdisk is an older tool used to format and partition hard drives, but it has been replaced by diskpart.

- Some of the common networking commands that you can execute from the command prompt are:
  - Ipconfig displays IP configuration for network interface cards.
  - Ping checks connectivity with a device on a network.
  - Tracert checks connectivity with a device and shows path through routers to the device.
  - Nslookup checks Domain Name System (DNS) for name resolution records.
  - Netstat shows inbound and outbound connections for a computer.
  - Netsh is an advanced command used to manipulate and show network settings.
  - Net is a group of commands used to view and manipulate network settings.
  - Telnet is used to connect to remote system from the Command Prompt.

Chapter Review

Use the following questions to test your knowledge of the information in this chapter. The answers to these questions, and the explanations of why each answer choice is correct or incorrect, are located in the "Answers" section at the end of this chapter.

1. You entered the chkdsk command at the command prompt but received a syntax error. What command can you enter to show you the proper format of the command? (Choose all that apply.)

   A. chkdsk /syntax

   B. chkdsk /?

- **C.** help chkdsk
- **D.** chkdsk /show

2. You need to copy over a system file in Windows XP. What command can you use to change the system attribute?

- **A.** msinfo32
- **B.** msconfig
- **C.** regedit
- **D.** attrib

3. Which of the following commands will change a file named Study.doc to a read-only file?

- **A.** attrib +r study.doc
- **B.** attrib +ro study.doc
- **C.** attrib +h study.doc
- **D.** attrib +s study.doc

4. What command can you use to delete a folder from the command prompt?

- **A.** md
- **B.** cd
- **C.** rd
- **D.** df

5. What can you do with the copy command that you can't do with the xcopy command?

- **A.** Nothing. The xcopy command can do everything that the copy command can do.
- **B.** You can copy entire subdirectories.
- **C.** You can suppress prompts.
- **D.** You can use wildcards.

6. A Windows 7 system was recently infected with a virus. After removing the virus, you want to verify the integrity of system files and repair any problems. What command would you use?

- **A.** sfc /purgecache
- **B.** sfc /scannow
- **C.** sfc /verifyonly
- **D.** msconfig

7. You suspect that the kernel32.dll file is corrupt. Which command can you use to verify the integrity of the file?

    A. chkdsk /verifyfile=c:\windows\system32\kernel32.dll

    B. sfc /verifyfile=c:\windows\system32\kernel32.dll

    C. attrib /verifyfile=c:\windows\system32\kernel32.dll

    D. cd /verifyfile=c:\windows\system32\kernel32.dll

Answers

1. **Correct Answer:** B, C

    A. Incorrect: The /syntax switch is not a valid switch.

    B. Correct: Almost every command supports the /? switch as a method to retrieve help.

    C. Correct: Most commands support the help command followed by the name of the command as a method to retrieve help.

    D. Incorrect: The /show switch is not a valid switch.

2. **Correct Answer:** D

    A. Incorrect: You can start the System Information tool with msinfo32 and view hardware resources, components, and the software environment.

    B. Incorrect: You can start the System Configuration tool with msconfig to configure the system, services, and startup applications.

    C. Incorrect: You can open the registry editor with regedit.

    D. Correct: The attrib command allows you to modify attributes of files.

3. **Correct Answer:** A

    A. Correct: The +r switch of the attrib commands set the read-only attribute of a file.

    B. Incorrect: The attrib +ro command is not valid.

    C. Incorrect: The attrib +h command sets the hidden attribute of the file.

    D. Incorrect: The attrib +s command sets the system attribute of the file.

4. **Correct Answer:** C

    A. Incorrect: The md command makes a directory.

    B. Incorrect: The cd command changes the path to a different directory.

    C. Correct: The rd command removes a directory (which is also known as a folder).

    D. Incorrect: The df command isn't valid and will fail.

5. **Correct Answer:** A

    A. Correct: The xcopy command can do everything that the copy command can do, plus a lot more.

    B. Incorrect: You can copy subdirectories with the xcopy command but not with the copy command.

    C. Incorrect: Both commands allow you to suppress the prompts.

    D. Incorrect: Both commands support the use of wildcards.

6. **Correct Answer: B**

   A. **Incorrect:** The /purgecache switch worked in Windows XP but does not work in Windows Vista and Windows 7.

   B. **Correct:** The sfc /scannow command will scan all protected system files and attempt to repair them.

   C. **Incorrect:** The sfc /verifyonly command will scan all protected system files, but it does not attempt any repairs.

   D. **Incorrect:** The msconfig command starts the System Configuration tool, which can be used to configure the systems, services, and startup applications.

7. **Correct Answer: B**

   A. **Incorrect:** The chkdsk command can check and fix a disk, but the given command will fail with a syntax error.

   B. **Correct:** This is a valid command to check the file.

   C. **Incorrect:** The attrib command shows attributes, but the given command will fail with a syntax error.

   D. **Incorrect:** The cd command changes the directory, but the given command will fail with a syntax error.

CHAPTER 15

Configuring Windows Operating Systems

Windows includes several configuration settings you can manipulate as a PC techni-cian. Many of these are configured by default, so you won't need to make changes to them. However, it's very possible that users will manipulate these settings, and you'll need to recognize what has been changed so that you can return the system to normal. Additionally, many of the tools you use to configure a system can also be valuable when troubleshooting Windows-based systems.

Exam 220-802 objectives in this chapter:

- 1.2 Given a scenario, install, and configure the operating system using the most appropriate method.
    - Driver installation, software and windows updates
- 1.4 Given a scenario, use appropriate operating system features and tools.
    - Administrative
        - Device manager
        - System configuration
    - MSCONFIG
        - General
        - Boot
        - Services
        - Startup
        - Tools
- 1.5 Given a scenario, use Control Panel utilities (the items are organized by "classic view/large icons" in Windows).
    - System
        - Performance (virtual memory)
        - Remote settings
        - System protection

- 1.7 Perform preventive maintenance procedures using appropriate tools.
  - Best practices
    - Schedules backups
    - Windows updates
    - Patch management
    - Driver/firmware updates
  - Tools
    - Backup
    - System Restore
- 4.6 Given a scenario, troubleshoot operating system problems with appropriate tools.
  - Tools
  - MSCONFIG

REAL WORLD **PREVIOUS VERSIONS CAN SAVE THE DAY**

I was recently helping a small business owner with her Windows 7–based computer, and she mentioned that she had accidentally deleted a file. To say that she was disappointed is a huge understatement. It had valuable data, and she didn't know how she was going to be able to re-create it.

Thinking of previous versions and shadow copy, I asked her whether she used restore points. She didn't know what I was talking about, which was good news. They're enabled by default on Windows 7, and they keep copies of previous versions of files.

We took a quick look, and with just a couple of clicks, we were able to retrieve her file. She had no idea that this feature was there and must have said "Thank you" more than a dozen times. Even though users don't know about this, A+ technicians should. You can use it to help users get their data back or to retrieve a lost file of your own.

Using System Configuration

The *System Configuration* tool is one of the tools you can use to view and manipulate the configuration of your system. It has changed a little between Windows XP and Windows Vista but is the same in Windows Vista and Windows 7.

You can start the System Configuration Tool by entering *msconfig* (short for Microsoft Configuration) at the command prompt or a run line and pressing Enter. It's also accessible via the Administrative Tools group from the Control Panel on Windows Vista and Windows 7.

General

Figure 15-1 shows the System Configuration Tool with the General tab selected on Windows 7 (on the left) and Windows XP. You can see that msconfig in Windows XP includes three additional tabs that allow you to easily configure three different initialization files: System.ini, Win.ini, and Boot.ini. Windows Vista and Windows 7 use different methods for these settings, so these files are not needed. However, the Boot tab on Windows 7 provides some of the same functionality as the Boot.ini tab in Windows XP.

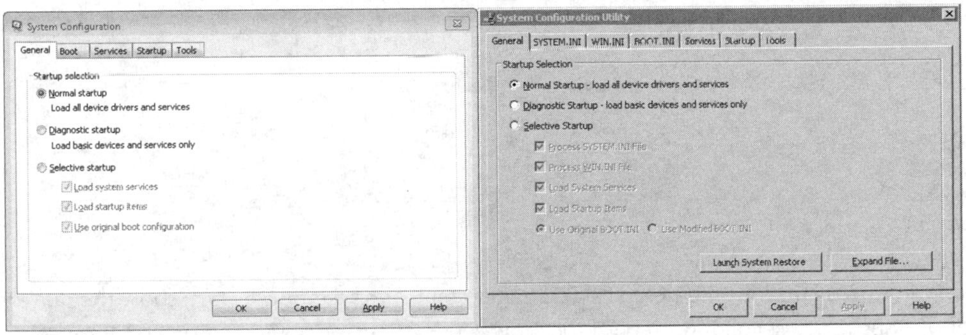

FIGURE 15-1 General tab of System Configuration tool.

The Startup Selection option is normally set to Normal Startup as shown. You can select Diagnostic Startup and restart the system, and it will start Windows using only basic services and drivers. If you modify any of the settings in the Services or Startup tab, it will automatically change to Selective Startup.

> **MORE INFO** **CHAPTER 17, "TROUBLESHOOTING WINDOWS OPERATING SYSTEMS"**
>
> Diagnostic startup is similar to starting the system in safe mode. Safe mode options are covered in Chapter 17.

Windows XP also includes a button to open System Restore, to create restore points, or to revert a system to a previously created restore point. The "System Protection" section later in this chapter covers restore points in greater depth.

Boot

The Boot tab allows you to control how a system starts. This can be useful if you want to change the behavior of a dual-boot system. For example, if you have a dual-boot system that currently starts Windows 7 by default but you want it to start Windows 8, you can use this tab to change it. Figure 15-2 shows the options for a dual-boot system configured with Windows 7 and Windows 8.

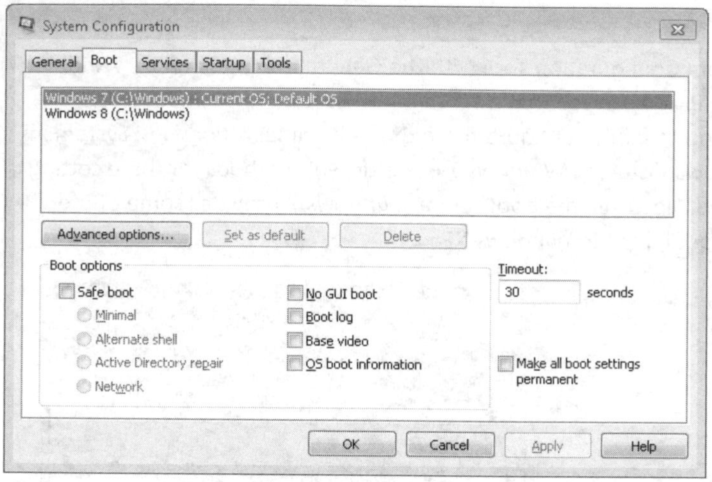

FIGURE 15-2 Boot tab of System Configuration.

Windows 7 is currently the default operating system. The system will start, show the dual-boot options for 30 seconds (based on the Time-Out setting), and start Windows 7 if the user doesn't take any action. You can select Windows 8 and click the Set As Default button to cause it to start Windows 8 by default instead. You can also change the Time-Out setting on this tab.

> **MORE INFO** **CHAPTER 17, "TROUBLESHOOTING WINDOWS OPERATING SYSTEMS"**
>
> Chapter 17 covers the Boot options available on this tab in the context of the different safe modes you can use while troubleshooting a system.

Services

The Services tab lists all the services that are available on the system and their current status, such as Running or Stopped. If the service has been disabled, it lists the date and time when it was disabled. Figure 15-3 shows this tab with the Windows Backup service disabled. You can deselect any check box to disable the service.

You can use this as a quick way to view the status or disable a service, but your choices are limited. The Services applet (covered in Chapter 13, "Using Windows Operating Systems," within the "Administrative Tools" section) provides you with many more options.

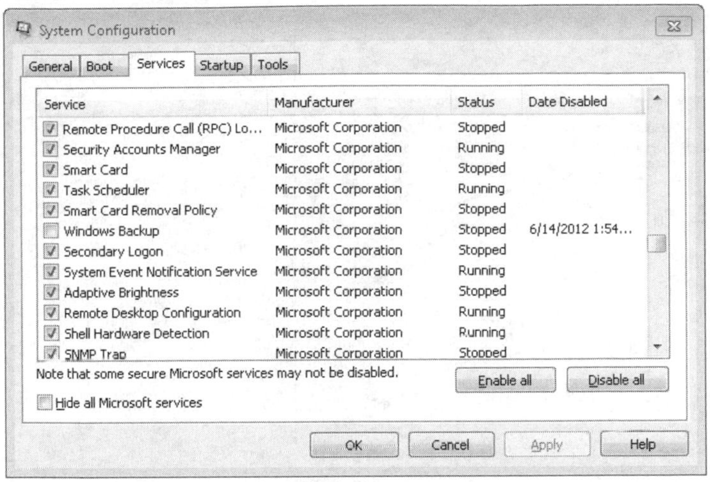

FIGURE 15-3 Services tab of System Configuration tool.

> **NOTE SYSTEM INFORMATION TOOL**
>
> System Information is another tool that allows you to view services. Chapters 2, "Understanding Motherboards and BIOS," and 3, "Understanding RAM and CPUs," introduced the System Information tool and showed how you can use it to get a quick overview of the system. Within the Software Environment group, you can select Services to view all the Services, their current state, the start mode, and more. You can start it by typing **msinfo32** from the command prompt or a run line.

Startup

The Startup tab shows all the applications that are configured to start when Windows starts. After using your computer for a couple of years, you'll have installed many different applications, and you might notice that the startup cycle is very slow. Many applications configure themselves to start automatically.

Figure 15-4 shows the Startup tab for a relatively new installation. The only two applications I've added are Virtual Machine User Services and Snagit. Compare this to your system. How many applications are configured to start automatically?

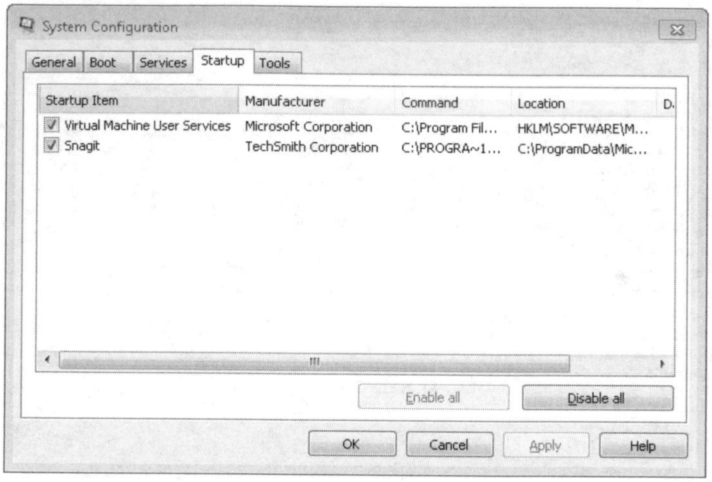

FIGURE 15-4 Startup tab of System Configuration tool.

You can deselect the check box for any of the items to prevent it from starting the next time Windows starts.

EXAM TIP

Manipulating the Startup applications is useful when troubleshooting infected computers or problem applications. You can use this to prevent an application from loading at startup.

The Windows Startup folder (available by clicking Start, All Programs, Startup) shows applications that are configured to start for the current user's profile. However, this does not show all the applications that will start when Windows starts. The Startup tab of the System Configuration applet shows all the applications.

Tools

The Tools tab provides a launching pad for many tools that are available on your system. These tools are covered in different areas of this book, but as an exercise, it's worth your time to open them. Select any of the tools and click Launch to start it.

> **✔ Quick Check**
>
> 1. What is the command used to open the System Configuration tool?
> 2. How can you change the default operating system in a dual-boot system?
>
> **Quick Check Answers**
>
> 1. Msconfig.
> 2. Modify the settings on the Boot tab of the System Configuration tool.

Using the System Applet

The *System* applet provides a quick snapshot of your system and includes some useful links to other tools. Figure 15-5 shows the System applet opened on a Windows 7–based system on the left and on Windows XP on the right. The Windows 7 version includes several active links in the left pane, and the middle pane provides some information about the system, such as the operating system version and the hardware.

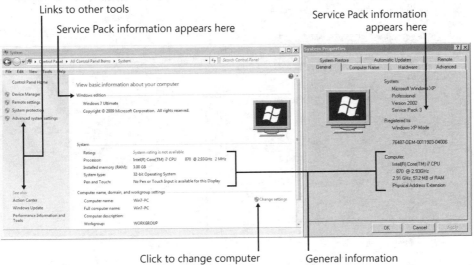

Links to other tools
Service Pack information appears here
Service Pack information appears here
Click to change computer name or join a domain
General information

FIGURE 15-5 System applet on Windows 7 (left) and System Properties on Windows XP (right).

Windows XP includes some of the same information. You can see that Windows XP has Service Pack 3 installed, but Windows 7 is blank in that area, indicating a service pack has not been installed. Instead of active links, Windows XP includes multiple tabs.

For example, you can click the Device Manager link in the Windows 7 version to open the Device Manager. On Windows XP, you can select the Hardware tab and click the Device Manager button. Device Manager is covered later in this chapter.

Remote Settings

The Remote Settings tab includes settings that allow or block remote connections for a system. Two types of remote connections are Remote Assistance and Remote Desktop.

- **Remote Assistance.** This is used to allow a remote helper to provide assistance to a user. For example, a friend of yours might be having computer problems and send you a remote assistance request. When you respond, you'll be able to see his desktop on your computer. If he approves, you can take control of his desktop to fix a problem. While you're fixing, he can observe all your actions and learn in the process.

■ **Remote Desktop.** Administrators use this to take full control of a remote system. With Remote Desktop, users do not see what the administrator is doing.

You can use the following steps to enable Remote Assistance and Remote Desktop on a Windows 7–based system.

1. Start the System applet from the Control Panel.

2. Click Remote Settings. The System Properties dialog opens with the Remote tab selected. You'll see something similar to the following graphic. Remote Assistance is enabled by default.

3. By default, the Windows Firewall blocks Remote Desktop connections. Use the following steps to configure the firewall:

   A. Click You Must Enable The Windows Firewall Exception For Remote Desktop. This starts Help.

   B. Select Click To Open Windows Firewall within the Help file.

   C. In the left pane, click Allow A Program Or Feature Through Windows Firewall.

   D. Click Change Settings. If you're prompted by User Account Control, click Yes to continue.

   E. Scroll down to Remote Desktop. Select the check box on the left to enable it. Ensure the check box for Home/Work (Private) is selected. This allows Remote Desktop to operate when it's connected in a home or work network. Your display will look similar to the following graphic.

F. Click OK to make the change.

> **MORE INFO** **CHAPTER 20, "UNDERSTANDING PROTOCOLS"**
>
> Chapter 20 shows how to use the Remote Desktop Connection (opened with the mstsc command) to connect with another computer. Chapter 22, "Network Security Devices," covers the Windows Firewall and exceptions in more depth.

System Protection and System Restore

System Protection includes System Restore and previous versions capabilities. System Restore is a Windows feature that allows you to restore your system to a previous state. For example, if you installed an application and find that it's causing problems with your system, you can use System Restore to undo the changes by applying a previously created *restore point*.

> **EXAM TIP**
>
> System Restore can uninstall applications, roll back drivers, and remove Windows Updates. You can also uninstall applications by using Add/Remove programs in Windows XP or Programs and Features in Windows Vista or Windows 7. Similarly, there are other tools to modify device drivers and updates. A restore point can modify all at the same time.

If you click the System Protection link from the System applet, it opens the System Properties page with the System Protection tab selected as shown in Figure 15-6. Click the System Restore button and click Next to access the System Restore dialog. Windows shows recent restore points that you can choose. If you want to view more options, select the Show More Restore Points check box.

On Windows XP, click Start, All Programs, Accessories, System Tools, and select System Restore to access restore points.

Windows automatically creates restore points every seven days and prior to certain events, such as a system update, an application installation, or a driver update. You can also manually create a restore point at any time by clicking the Create button.

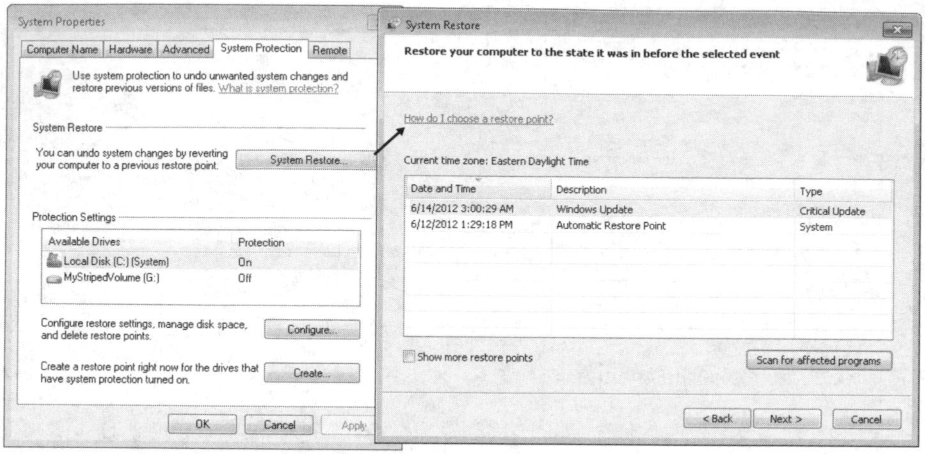

FIGURE 15-6 Accessing restore points on Windows Vista and Windows 7.

By default, System Restore will use up to 5 percent of the disk space to store restore points. You can click the Configure button to enable or disable System Protection or to modify how much disk space it will use. You can also delete the restore points to free up some disk space.

System Restore does not modify any user files, such as documents or pictures, when a restore point is applied. It restores only system files, applications, and drivers. However, when restore points are created, they do save previous versions of files that can be restored by using a feature called previous versions.

Shadow Copy (Previous Versions)

Previous versions are copies of files and folders that are automatically saved when a restore point is created. It's available in Windows Vista and Windows 7 and sometimes referred to as *shadow copy*, or shadow copies.

To use previous versions, your system must be configured to use restore points or have backups available. You can use Windows Explorer to right-click any file or folder, select Properties, and click the Previous Versions tab.

Figure 15-7 shows the properties of a file named A+ Study Notes with the Previous Versions tab selected. There is one previous version for this file, but it's possible for multiple versions to be available. When you select a previous version, you can select Open, Copy, or Restore.

- **Open.** This opens the file so that you can view the contents before actually restoring the file.

- **Copy.** You can create a copy of the file and store it in another location.

- **Restore.** Use this to overwrite the current version with the previous version.

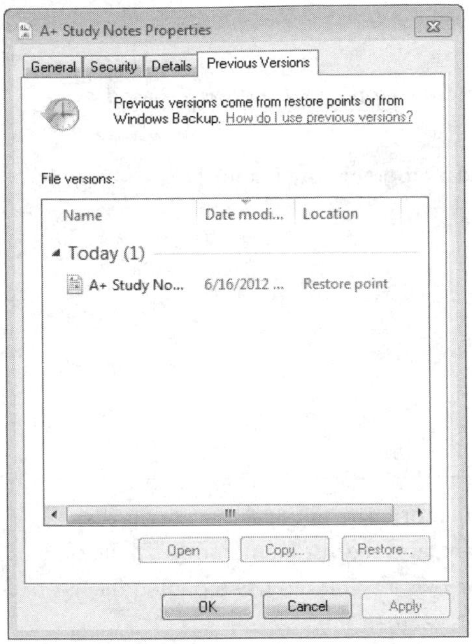

FIGURE 15-7 Using Previous Versions tab.

It's also possible to retrieve a previous version of a file that has been deleted, but the procedure is slightly different. If the file is deleted, you can't right-click it. Instead, use the following steps:

1. Open Windows Explorer by clicking Start, Computer.

2. Locate the folder where the file existed before it was deleted.

3. Right-click the folder and select Properties.

4. Click the Previous Versions tab.

5. Select a version of the folder that includes your file and click Open.

6. Double-click the file to open it. You can then save it.

Advanced System Settings

If you click on Advanced System Settings, it opens the System Properties page with the Advanced tab selected. There are three sections on this page: Performance, User Profiles, and Startup And Recovery.

The Performance section gives you options for viewing and configuring the paging file (covered in the next section). The User Profiles section is sometimes used by administrators to copy user profiles. Chapter 17 covers the Startup And Recovery options.

Understanding Paging

Computers use both physical memory and virtual memory. The physical memory is the random access memory (RAM) installed in the system, and the virtual memory is a file on the hard drive called a *paging file*. Virtual memory allows a system to use a paging file as an extension of RAM and operate as if it had more physical memory.

Paging Overview

Imagine that you're working on a computer and you have Internet Explorer (IE) and Microsoft Outlook running. The operating system takes up some RAM, and both IE and Microsoft Outlook take up the rest. For this scenario, imagine that the operating system and your two apps take up all the physical RAM.

Without virtual memory, you wouldn't be able to open up another application. If you tried to open up Microsoft Word, the operating system could refuse or, worse, crash. With virtual memory, the system swaps information between the physical RAM and a file on the hard drive. This allows you to work on more applications even if you've run out of physical RAM.

Figure 15-8 provides an overview of how this works. On the left, you can see that the operating system, IE, and Microsoft Outlook are in RAM. When you start Microsoft Word, the operating system looks to see what you haven't used recently and swaps it to the paging file on the hard disk. In the figure, it moved IE to the paging file on the hard disk to make room for Microsoft Word.

If you later go back to IE, the operating system looks for what hasn't been used recently. It could move Microsoft Outlook to the paging file and IE into physical RAM. You can then work with IE.

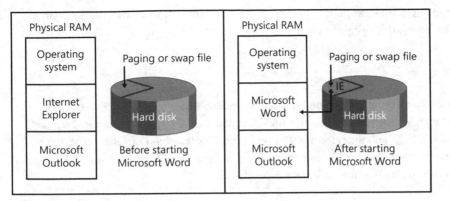

FIGURE 15-8 Using a paging file.

64-KB Pages

The preceding section provides a simplified explanation of paging, but it needs some clarification. RAM is organized in 64-KB pages, and the operating system works on these pages when swapping information back and forth between RAM and the hard disk. That is, when it needs to move something out of RAM, it looks for the 64-KB pages that haven't been used recently and swaps these page to the hard disk. If IE is consuming 500 MB of RAM and the operating system needs 128 KB of RAM, it swaps two 64-KB pages. It doesn't swap the entire 500 MB used by IE.

> **NOTE** **PAGING FILE OR SWAP FILE**
>
> This file has been called the swap file because it swaps information back and forth. It's called the paging file in Windows XP, Windows Vista, and Windows 7, referring to how it moves pages of memory. You're likely to hear both terms, but they are the same.

Excessive Paging

If a system doesn't have enough RAM for what a user is doing, it will experience excessive paging. Data will be constantly swapped back and forth between the hard disk and RAM, and the overall performance will slow to a crawl.

One solution is for the user to close some applications to free up some RAM. When the system has enough free RAM, there will be very little swapping. Another solution is to add more RAM. If a system has enough RAM, there will be very little paging.

How much is enough? That depends on what the user is doing. I'm currently working on a system that has 16 GB of RAM. I'm running three virtual PCs (one for Windows XP, one for Windows Vista, and one for Windows 7) and have several applications open for writing and to create graphics. Some paging is occurring, but my system isn't slow. Therefore, 16 GB is enough for me on this system. If I was only using IE to surf the Internet, 2 GB might be enough.

EXAM TIP

Disk thrashing is a symptom of a disk not having enough RAM. You'll be able to hear the disk constantly seeking as it reads and writes data, the disk LED on the front panel will be constantly blinking, and the system will be very slow. Disk thrashing can also occur if a drive is fragmented. Chapter 16, "Understanding Disks and File Systems," covers disk fragmentation, including how to check and resolve it.

Performance (Virtual Memory) Settings

You can configure the paging file from the System menu, but as a best practice, it's best to let Windows manage the size of the paging file on desktop systems. It sets the minimum and maximum size and grows the paging file as needed. If you do set the size of the paging file, you should ensure that the Maximum Size (MB) is at least 1.5 times the physical RAM.

One reason to modify the paging file settings is to move it. It is configured on the same drive as the operating system by default, but you can squeeze some performance gains out of the system by moving it to a different internal physical drive. This way, the operating system and paging file don't compete with each other for disk access.

You move the paging file location by creating a paging file on a different internal drive and then selecting No Paging File for the original drive.

NOTE **VIRTUAL MEMORY ADDRESSED AS DISK LOCATIONS**

One of the valuable features of virtual memory is that it is not tied to addressable memory space of the system. For example, a 32-bit system can address only 4 GB of physical RAM. The virtual memory is addressed as disk locations, so you can go beyond 4 GB.

The following steps show how you can view and modify the paging file settings on a Windows 7–based system.

1. Click Start, Control Panel. If necessary, change the view to Large icons.

2. Select System. Click Advanced System Settings. The System Properties page opens with the Advanced tab selected.

3. Click the Settings button in the Performance area.

4. Click the Advanced tab on the Performance Options page. You'll see a display similar to the following graphic. Automatically Manage Paging File Size For All Drives is selected by default.

Change button

If you deselect the check box, you can select Custom Size and enter the Initial Size and Maximum Size values for the file. If your system has multiple internal disks, you can select a different disk and configure the file for this disk. When moving the paging file, you need to configure it for a different disk and then select No Paging File for the current disk holding the paging file. When you are done, click the Set button.

EXAM TIP

If you have more than one internal hard drive, you can increase the performance by moving the paging file to a different internal hard drive. You cannot move the paging file to an external drive. Set the maximum size to at least 1.5 times the amount of physical RAM.

✓ **Quick Check**

   1. What allows Windows to use disk space as an extension of memory?

   2. If you manually configure the paging file, how large should it be?

Quick Check Answers

   1. Paging file.

   2. At least 1.5 times the amount of RAM.

Working with Device Manager

A common task for any A+ technician is installing and upgrading device drivers. The primary tool that you'll use is *Device Manager*. Chapter 5, "Exploring Peripherals and Expansion Cards," introduces device drivers in the context of installing peripheral devices. Devices will often work without any user intervention, but sometimes a technician needs to get involved.

Starting the Device Manager

Device Manager works similarly in Windows XP, Windows Vista, and Windows 7, but there are different methods of starting it.

To start Device Manager on Windows XP, click Start, Run. Type in **devmgmt.msc** and click OK.

To start Device Manager on Windows Vista or Windows 7, click Start, Control Panel. If necessary, change the view to Classic View on Windows Vista or to Large icons on Windows 7. Select Device Manager.

> **NOTE MANY PATHS**
>
> These methods show a couple of ways to start Device Manager, but as with many tasks, there are many methods you can use. For example, you can also click Start, right-click Computer (or My Computer on Windows XP), and select Properties to start System Properties and access it from there. You can also access it from Computer Management.

Viewing Device Manager

When you open Device Manager, it displays the devices by type in groups such as disk drives, network adapters, and so on. If all the devices in a group are working, the group is collapsed. If there's an issue with any device, the group is expanded.

For example, Figure 15-9 shows the Device Manager on Windows 7. Two groups (Floppy Disk Drive and Other Devices) are expanded, indicating a possible problem. If a device has an issue, you can right-click it and select Properties and the Device Status section provides information about the error. In this case, the error is clear. The device is disabled, and you can click the Enable Device button to enable it.

> **NOTE ERROR CODES**
>
> The errors aren't always so clear. The Microsoft knowledge base article at *http://support .microsoft.com/kb/310123* includes explanations for many error codes, in addition to steps you can take to resolve them. The article is geared towards Windows XP, but the same codes are used in Windows Vista and Windows 7.

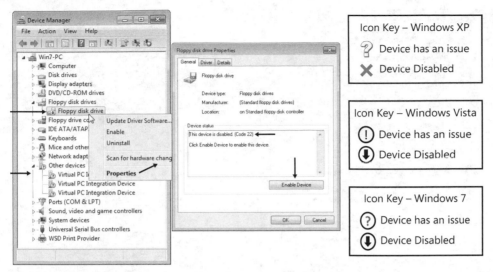

FIGURE 15-9 Device Manager.

The icons are slightly different on different operating systems, and Figure 15-9 has a partial key to show you some of the icons. The colors don't show up in the book, but for Windows XP, the question mark is yellow and the *X* is red. On Windows Vista, the exclamation mark is black on a yellow background. On Windows 7, the question mark is blue on a white background.

Additionally, the issues can be somewhat different. For example, a black exclamation mark on a yellow background usually indicates that the device driver for a device is missing. It could also indicate that the driver is corrupted or not the correct driver for the device.

EXAM TIP

A down arrow in Windows Vista and Windows 7 indicates that a device is disabled. A black exclamation mark on a yellow background often indicates that the device driver is missing.

Updating Drivers

You can replace the existing driver with a new one by updating it. This is required if the existing driver is missing or not working properly. At other times, you might realize that all the features of the device are not enabled. By installing a new driver, you'll enable all the features.

If you right-click the device, select Properties, and select the Driver tab, you'll see a display similar to Figure 15-10.

FIGURE 15-10 Driver tab.

> **NOTE ADVANCED TAB**
>
> If you compare Figure 15-9 to Figure 15-10, you can see that the Properties page for the Ethernet adapter in Figure 15-10 has more tabs than the Properties page for the floppy drive shown in Figure 15-9. It includes an Advanced tab and a Resources tab. The availability of additional tabs is primarily determined by the driver.

This tab has some basic information about the driver, such as the date it was released and its version. You can click the Driver Details button to get a listing of each of the files used by the driver and their location on the hard drive.

Clicking the Update Driver button shows a display similar to Figure 15-11. The easiest way to update the driver is to click Search Automatically For Updated Driver Software. If the driver is available, Device Manager will automatically locate and install it.

If a driver isn't functioning properly, all the features aren't working, or there is an updated driver you want to install, you can update it. The Update Driver Software is available from the right-click menu. You'll be prompted to allow Windows to search for the driver, or you can browse to the specific location.

Often the manufacturer will submit the driver to Microsoft, and it is available through this method. Sometimes you'll have to do a little more work. For example, if you've recently installed a new graphics card, the most up-to-date driver might not be available on Microsoft's site.

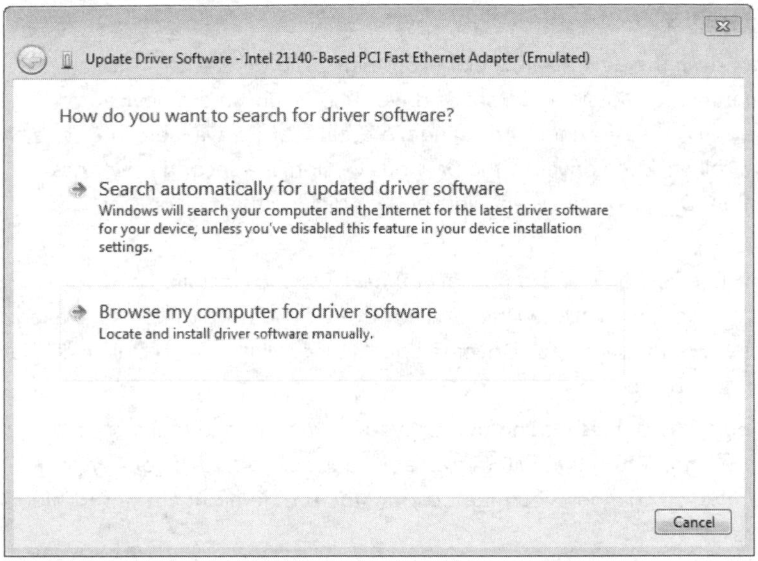

FIGURE 15-11 Updating a driver.

You can download a new driver from the manufacturer's website and select Browse My Computer For Driver Software. You can then browse to the location where you saved the driver. When you select the correct location, Device Manager will install it.

Disabling and Uninstalling

There can be times when you want to disable devices in the operating system. For example, if a computer includes hardware that a company doesn't want employees to use, disabling the unwanted device ensures that it won't be used. Chapter 2 shows how you can disable devices in the Basic Input/Output system (BIOS), but it's also possible to disable devices from within Device Manager.

You can right-click the device from within Device Manager and select Disable, or if you have the device properties page opened and the Driver tab selected, you can click the Disable button. Disabling the driver keeps it disabled even after it restarts.

The Driver tab also includes the Uninstall button, but this can be misleading. It uninstalls the driver, but only temporarily. The next time the system starts, plug and play will detect the device and will reinstall the driver automatically.

EXAM TIP

If you want to prevent users from using a built-in device, disable it from within Device Manager or from BIOS.

Rolling Back Drivers

Ideally, after updating a driver, the device will work better than it did before. Occasionally, that's not the case. Sometimes it's possible to install a driver that results in the device not working at all. However, you can easily undo the change. A great feature available in Device Manager is the ability to roll back the driver to the previous version. If a second driver has been installed, the Roll Back Driver button is enabled, and by clicking this button, you can revert the driver to the previous version.

You can roll back only one version. For example, if you have Driver A installed and you upgrade it to Driver B, you can roll it back to Driver A. However, if you have Driver A installed, and then you install Driver B, and then install Driver C, you cannot roll it back to Driver A. The best you can do is revert it to Driver B.

This brings up an important troubleshooting point: if you make a change to a system and it doesn't correct your problem, return the system to the previous condition. If your system has a problem and you make 10 changes, you might correct the problem but also insert nine additional problems.

Signed Drivers

Most drivers are digitally signed. This is a security feature that provides assurances about who published the driver and that the driver has not been modified since it was released.

With so many criminals looking for ways to infect computers and steal a user's data, a digitally signed driver is valuable. It prevents a criminal from modifying a driver with a virus that would be installed when the driver is installed.

Windows will alert you by default if you try to install an unsigned driver or install a driver that has been altered after it was originally signed. You'll see one of the following errors:

- Windows can't verify the publisher of this driver.
- This driver has been altered.
- Windows cannot install this driver.

Sigverif

If you suspect your system has unsigned drivers that could be causing problems, you can use the File Signature Verification Utility to check it. This tool examines the drivers and system files and verifies that they are digitally signed.

You can open it from the command prompt or a Run line by typing in **sigverif** and pressing Enter. After it opens, click Start. It might take a minute or so to complete, depending on how many files are on your system. When it completes, it a dialog box appears indicating that the files have been scanned.

Sigverif creates a file named Sigverif.txt and stores it in the Public Documents folder. You can easily view it by clicking the Advanced button and then clicking View Log.

Windows Update

Operating systems include millions of lines of code. In a perfect world, all this code would always work. The truth is that, despite extensive testing, problems do appear. Vendors regularly release patches to correct these problems. A *patch* is an update to an operating system or an application and is just a small piece of code that fixes a problem with existing software.

For example, criminals often look for vulnerabilities in software. When they find a vulnerability, they write malicious software (malware), such as viruses, to infect systems. When vendors become aware of vulnerabilities, they develop and release patches. Systems that are patched are not vulnerable to the viruses. The unpatched systems become infected, and often the user is unaware of the problem.

> *MORE INFO*   **CHAPTER 26, "RECOGNIZING MALWARE AND OTHER THREATS"**
>
> Chapter 26 presents information about different types of malware and common methods used to protect systems. One method is keeping systems up to date with current patches.

Microsoft uses *Windows Update* to help users keep their systems up-to-date. Additionally, it's very easy to configure a system to automatically check for and install updates when they're available.

Updates available through Windows Update can be related to security, performance, or stability issues. These are classified as important, recommended, and optional updates.

- Important updates improve security, privacy, and reliability of the system. They should be installed as soon as possible and can be installed automatically. These are called high-priority updates on Windows XP.

- Recommended updates target non-critical problems. They can be installed automatically.

- Optional updates provide updates to drivers or new software. They can be installed only through user interaction.

You can access Windows Update on Windows XP, Windows Vista, and Windows 7 by clicking Start, All Programs, and selecting Windows Update. The system checks with a Windows Update site and compares available updates with updates that are currently installed. If updates are available, you'll see a display similar to Figure 15-12. You can then click Install Updates to begin the installation.

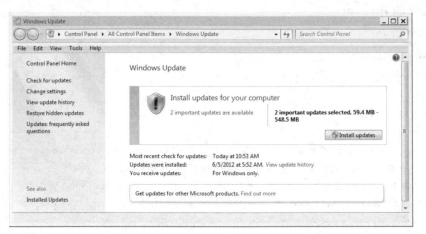

FIGURE 15-12 Windows Update.

EXAM TIP

Systems should be kept up-to-date with current patches and updates to keep them secure. Criminals use a variety of methods to prevent a system from receiving updates. If a system cannot contact Windows Update, it often indicates that the system is infected with malware.

Service Packs

A *service pack (SP)* is a cumulative group of patches and updates. For example, service pack 1 (SP1) for Windows 7 includes all the patches and updates that were released since Windows 7 came out. The next service pack is called SP2, then SP3, and so on. Service packs often include additional features and services.

Automatically Installing Updates

As a best practice, it's recommended that you use *Automatic Updates* to download and install updates automatically rather than manually. When configured this way, Windows periodically checks with Windows Update sites for new updates. When they're available, Windows automatically downloads and installs them.

Figure 15-13 shows the configuration page for Windows Update on a Windows 7–based system. You can get to this page by clicking the Change Settings link in the left column of Windows Update.

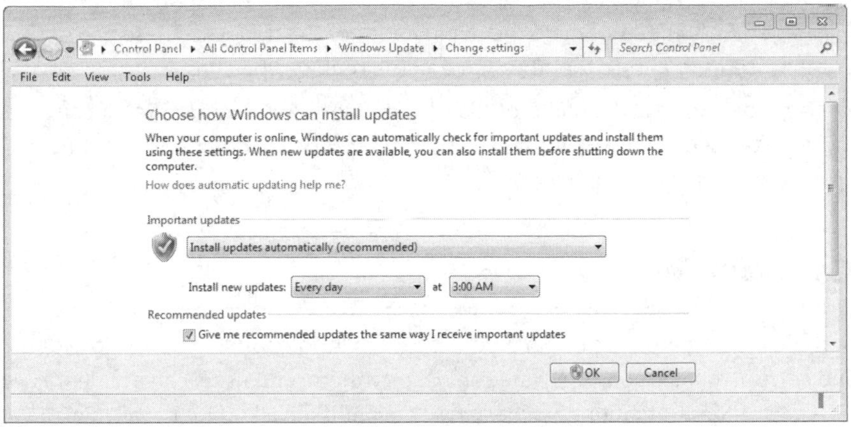

FIGURE 15-13 Windows Update Change Settings page.

NOTE **WINDOWS XP**

Windows XP has similar settings. You can access them on the Automatic Updates tab of the System Properties applet from the Control Panel.

Figure 15-13 shows recommended settings. The system will periodically check for updates and download them when they are available. Then, at 3:00 AM, the system will install the update. The drop-down box provides the following four options:

- **Install Updates Automatically (Recommended).** Most home users and SOHOs will use this.

- **Download Updates But Let Me Choose Whether To Install Them.** Some updates automatically restart the system, and users sometimes select this so that they can control when the update is applied and, therefore, the system is restarted.

- **Check For Updates But Let Me Choose Whether To Download And Install Them.** Users with slow Internet connections use this.

- **Never Check For Updates (Not Recommended).**

Patch Management

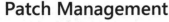
Patch management refers to the methods used to keep systems up-to-date. It includes evaluating, testing, and deploying patches, and it also includes periodic testing of systems to ensure that they are up-to-date.

Most home users and small organizations configure systems to automatically download and install updates when they are available. Many large organizations employ detailed change management practices to evaluate and test patches before deploying them. They commonly use tools such as Windows Server Update Services (WSUS) or System Center Configuration Manager (SCCM) to automate the deployment of the updates. These can periodically inspect the systems to ensure that they have all the required patches.

Another tool commonly used is the *Microsoft Baseline Security Analyzer (MBSA)*. It can check one or more systems in a network for many security settings in addition to ensuring that they are up-to-date with current patches.

Backup Capabilities

One of the sure things with computers is that if you use them long enough, you will lose data. Files can become corrupted, malicious software can destroy them, and users can accidentally delete their files. Each of these situations can be a major event if a backup isn't available.

Each Windows operating system supports backing up and restoring data, although there are significant differences among the versions of Windows. Windows Vista introduced a new program for backups, and this program was improved and enhanced in Windows 7.

Windows Vista and Windows 7 both support full image backups. A full image backup captures the entire hard drive contents, including the operating system, applications, and all the user's data. If the drive fails, the image backup can restore the system to its state when the image was captured.

Windows XP

Windows XP includes a backup program that you can use to back up and restore data on a computer. You can start the Back Up Or Restore Wizard with the following steps:

1.   Click Start, All Programs, Accessories, System Tools, Backup.

2.   Follow the directions in the wizard to back up or restore data.

This tool allows users to easily pick and choose what files they want to back up and restore. It includes the ability to back up everything on the computer to external devices and network locations.

Windows Vista

Windows Vista introduced the Backup And Restore Center, which is significantly different from the backup program included with previous editions of Windows. It allows you to back up and restore files, configure automatic backups, and perform a complete PC backup of the entire system. You can open the Backup And Restore center with the following steps:

1.   Click Start, Control Panel. If necessary, change the view to Classic View.

2. Double-click Backup And Restore Center. Your display will look similar to Figure 15-14.

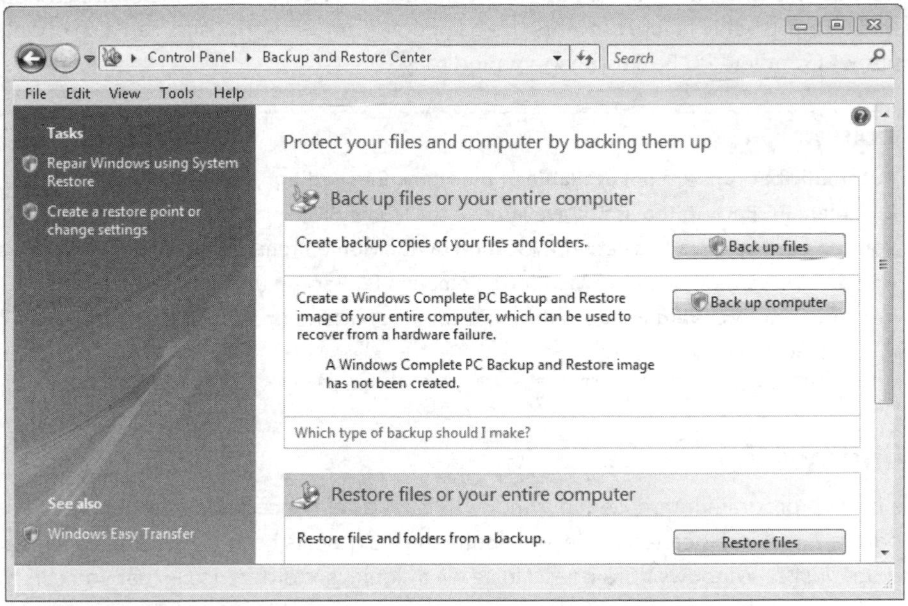

FIGURE 15-14 Windows Vista Backup And Restore Center on Vista Ultimate.

This tool gives you multiple capabilities for backing up and restoring files. You can choose what file types to back up based on categories. For example, you can choose to back up document files and music files. It will then locate all of the files in the category and back them up. You can also back up the entire computer.

The Backup And Restore Center allows you to back up data to multiple locations, including the following:

- **Internal hard drives.** You can't back up data to the same hard drive, but if your system has additional hard drives installed, you can back up data to one of these other drives.

- **External hard drives.** USB hard drives are relatively inexpensive and easy to plug into a system. When they are plugged in, the Backup And Restore program recognizes them and can be configured to back up to these drives.

- **Writable CDs or DVDs.** If your computer includes a CD or DVD burner, you can back up data to writable CDs or DVDs. It might take several CDs or DVDs to complete a backup, and you can't use automatic backups with these discs.

- **Network locations.** Windows Vista Home Premium, Business, and Ultimate editions support backing up to shared folders on network locations. Full image backups cannot be backed up to a network location.

The Windows Complete PC Backup And Restore tool creates an image of your computer. If users do this when they first set up their computer, they can recover the entire computer even if a catastrophic failure prevents the computer from starting. Users can also update the Windows Complete PC Backup image periodically.

EXAM TIP

Automatic backups are not available in the Home Basic edition, and the Windows Complete PC Backup tool is not available in the Home Basic or Home Premium editions. You can back up data to a network location on the Home Premium, Business, and Ultimate edition. You cannot perform a Windows Complete PC Backup (an image backup) to a network location. Windows Vista does not support backing up data to USB flash drives on any edition.

Windows 7

The backup program introduced in Windows Vista was enhanced and improved in Windows 7, making it easier to use and configure. It supports both file backups and image backups, just as Windows Vista does. However, a significant difference is that you can choose what files and folders you want to back up in Windows 7. In Windows Vista, you can choose only the file types to back up based on categories.

You can start the Backup And Restore tool with the following steps:

1. Click Start, Control Panel. If necessary, change the view to Large icons.

2. Double-click Backup And Restore.

You can back up data to multiple locations just as you can with Windows Vista. This includes internal hard drives, external hard drives, writable CDs and DVDs, and network locations.

There are two important differences between the capabilities of Windows Vista and Windows 7 backups. On Windows 7, you can create image backups to a network location, but this isn't possible in Windows Vista. Additionally, you can back up data to USB flash drives as long as they are at least 1 GB in size.

EXAM TIP

All editions of Windows 7 include backup and restore capabilities. However, the Starter and Home Premium editions do not support backing up data to network locations.

Quick Check

1. What is used to keep systems up to date without user intervention?
2. What version(s) of Windows 7 allow you to back up data to a network location?

Quick Check Answers

1. Automatic Updates.
2. All except Starter and Home Premium.

Program Compatibility

You might run across an application that works in a previous version of Windows but does not work in the version you're using now. You can use the Application Compatibility tool to configure the application to run by using specific settings from a previous operating system.

You can configure the settings manually by right-clicking the application file, selecting Properties, and clicking the Compatibility tab. You'll see something similar to Figure 15-15.

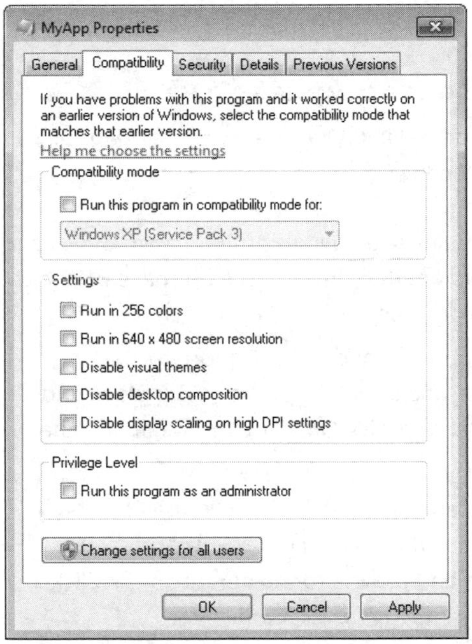

FIGURE 15-15 Manually configuring program compatibility.

You often need to experiment with different settings. For example, if you're having trouble running an application in Windows 7, you can try to run it using a compatibility mode for Windows XP SP3. If this doesn't work, you can try other settings.

An alternative is the Compatibility Wizard. It checks with a Microsoft site to determine whether there is a known setting that works for the application and, if so, will configure the settings. There are different methods of starting this wizard, including the following:

- On Windows XP, click Start, All Programs, Accessories, and select Program Compatibility Wizard.

- On Windows Vista, click Start, Control Panel. Use the Category View by clicking Control Panel Home. Select Programs and select Use An Older Program With This Version Of Windows.

- On Windows 7, Click Start Control Panel. Change the view to Category view if necessary and select Programs. Select Run Programs Made For Previous Versions Of Windows.

After starting the wizard, select the program and follow the wizard's steps.

Modifying Documents Location

User data is often stored in the Documents folder, which is part of a user's profile. In some cases, you might need to move the location of the Documents folder but still keep it as part of the user's profile.

MORE INFO CHAPTER 11, "INTRODUCING WINDOWS OPERATING SYSTEMS"

Chapter 11 covers profile locations. The profile is located in C:\Documents And Settings on Windows XP and C:\Users on Windows Vista and Windows 7.

For example, if a user has stored a significant amount of data in this folder, the C drive can become low on free space. You can move the data to another drive to free up space on the C drive. The following steps show how this is done on different operating systems:

- On Windows XP, click Start, right-click My Computer, and select Explore to start Windows Explorer. Right-click My Documents, and select Properties. Click Move and browse to the new location. Click Select Folder and click OK. Click Yes to confirm the move.

- On Windows Vista, click Start, Computer to start Windows Explorer. In the Folders area, expand your user profile (your user name). Right-click Documents and select Properties. Click the Location tab. Click Move and browse to the new location. Click Select Folder and click OK. Click Yes to confirm the move. Click OK.

- On Windows 7, click Start, Computer to start Windows Explorer. Expand the Documents folder within Libraries. Right-click My Documents and select Properties. Click Move and browse to the new location. Click Select Folder and click OK.

ReadyBoost

ReadyBoost is a feature available in Windows Vista and Windows 7 that can speed up a computer by using storage space on a USB flash drive. Your system can use this extra memory to cache disk content. There are a few basic requirements for this to work:

- Must be USB 2.0 or higher.
- It must have a minimum of 1 GB free space. For best performance, use a flash drive with twice as much RAM as your system has.
- ReadyBoost must be enabled on the drive.

You will usually be prompted if you want to use ReadyBoost when you plug a USB device into your system. You can also enable it manually with the following steps:

1. Start Windows Explorer by clicking Start, Computer.

2. Right-click the USB drive and select Properties.

3. Click the ReadyBoost tab.

4. Select Dedicate this device to ReadyBoost, and adjust the amount of space you want to use for ReadyBoost. Your display will look similar to the following graphic. Click OK.

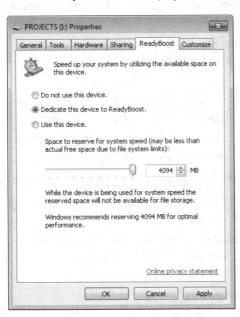

If you want to see a video and read more about ReadyBoost, check out this link: *http://windows.microsoft.com/en-us/windows7/Turn-ReadyBoost-on-or-off-for-a-storage-device*.

Chapter Summary

- The msconfig command opens the System Configuration tool. This tool has five tabs on Windows Vista and Windows 7: General, Boot, Services, Startup, and Tools.

- You can use msconfig to modify the boot configuration for a dual-boot system, disable services so that they cannot start, and disable applications configured to start when Windows starts.

- The System applet provides a quick snapshot of your system and includes links to change many settings.

- Remote settings are configured to allow remote connections to a computer. You need to configure an exception in the Windows Firewall to enable Remote Desktop.

- System Protection automatically creates restore points. You can apply a restore point to revert system, application, and driver files to a previous state. System Protection also creates copies of previous versions of user files.

- Users can use previous versions (sometimes called *shadow copy* or *shadow copies*) to restore previous versions of files and to restore a deleted file.

- The paging file is a file on the hard disk that is used as an extension of memory. Windows manages the paging file size by default and stores it on the same drive as Windows.

- You can move the paging file to another internal drive to improve performance. If configured manually, the maximum size should be set to 1.5 times the size of physical RAM.

- Device Manager is used to troubleshoot and maintain device drivers. You can use it to disable devices, update drivers, uninstall drivers, and roll back an updated driver.

- If a device or driver has an issue, it will automatically be expanded in Device Manager. Different versions of Device Manager use different icons to identify issues.

- You can locate unsigned drivers with the File Signature Verification utility (sigverif).

- Patches are small pieces of code applied to the operating system or applications and released as updates. They correct problems such as security vulnerabilities.

- Systems are kept up-to-date with Windows Update tools. Automatic updates can be configured to automatically download and install updates on to systems.

- Patch management practices ensure that patches are tested and deployed to all systems within an enterprise. Tools such as MBSA, WSUS, and SCCM help automate these tasks.

- All editions of Windows 7 include backup and restore capabilities. The Professional and Ultimate editions support backing up to network locations.

- Application Compatibility tools allow you to run incompatible applications by using settings that mimic previous versions of Windows.

Chapter Review

Use the following questions to test your knowledge of the information in this chapter. The answers to these questions, and the explanations of why each answer choice is correct or incorrect, are located in the "Answers" section at the end of this chapter.

1. You restarted a system and noticed an error message flash on the screen. You want to identify what applications are configured to start automatically. What can you use?

   A. Shadow copy

   B. Device Manager

   C. Services

   D. Msconfig

2. You are trying to optimize the performance of a computer with two internal hard drives and an external USB drive. Windows is on C, and D is used for data storage. You want to move the paging file. What is the best option?

   A. Move it to the external USB drive.

   B. Move it to the C drive.

   C. Move it to the D drive.

   D. Move it to the boot partition.

3. You are troubleshooting a system and decide to use a restore point from three days ago. You explain to the user that it will revert the system to the state it was in three days ago. The user is concerned that his data will be lost. How would you respond?

   A. Restore points will erase the data, so it should be backed up.

   B. Restore points won't modify user data.

   C. If the data is on the C drive, there is no problem.

   D. If the data is on the D drive, there is no problem.

4. You recently added a graphics card but realize that all the features are not working. What should you do?

   A. Enable System Protection.

   B. Update the driver.

   C. Configure Program Compatibility.

   D. Use Device Manager to disable the device.

5. Your company recently received some computers that include built-in modems, but users shouldn't use them. How can you prevent users from using these modems?

   A. Remove the modems.

   B. Disable them by using Device Manager.

   C. Disable them by using System Configuration.

   D. Enable ReadyBoost.

6. Which of the following tools can be used for patch management? (Choose all that apply.)

   A. WSUS

   B. SCCM

   C. Automatic Updates

   D. System Configuration

Answers

This section contains the answers to chapter review questions in this chapter.

1. **Correct Answer:** D

    A. **Incorrect:** Shadow copy helps restore previous versions of files but does not track startup applications.

    B. **Incorrect:** Device Manager is used to troubleshoot and maintain device drivers.

    C. **Incorrect:** The Services applet can be used to identify what services start automatically, but not applications.

    D. **Correct:** The Startup tab of the System Configuration tool (msconfig) shows what applications start automatically.

2. **Correct Answer:** C

    A. **Incorrect:** You can't move the paging file to an external drive.

    B. **Incorrect:** If you're trying to optimize performance, you should move the paging file to a drive other than the operating system drive. The C drive holds the operating system.

    C. **Correct:** For best performance, move the paging file to a drive different than the operating system, which is D.

    D. **Incorrect:** The operating system is on the boot partition.

3. **Correct Answer:** B

    A. **Incorrect:** A backup might be useful, but restore points will not erase the user data.

    B. **Correct:** Restore points won't modify user data.

    C. **Incorrect:** It doesn't matter where the user stored the data.

    D. **Incorrect:** It doesn't matter where the user stored the data.

4. **Correct Answer:** B

    A. **Incorrect:** System Protection is used for restore points.

    B. **Correct:** If all the features of a new device are not working, you should update the driver.

    C. **Incorrect:** Program Compatibility is for applications, not devices.

    D. **Incorrect:** If the device is disabled, it won't work at all.

5. **Correct Answer:** B

    A. **Incorrect:** If the modem is built-in, it cannot be removed.

    B. **Correct:** Devices can be disabled with Device Manager.

    C. **Incorrect:** System Configuration cannot disable devices.

    D. **Incorrect:** ReadyBoost cannot disable devices.

6. **Correct Answer:** A, B, C

    A. **Correct:** Windows Server Update Services (WSUS) is a free server tool used to automate deployment of patches.

    B. **Correct:** System Center Configuration Manager is a server tool used to automate deployment of patches.

    C. **Correct:** Automatic Updates can be configured to automatically install updates.

    D. **Incorrect:** System Configuration does not deploy updates.

CHAPTER 16

Understanding Disks and File Systems

When working with any operating system, it's important to understand how disks and file systems are used. Disks must be formatted using a specific file system, and the file system you choose can impact its performance and security. Windows operating systems include several different tools used to manage disks, and if you know how to use these tools, you can overcome most problems with any disk.

Exam 220-802 objectives in this chapter:

- 1.2 Given a scenario, install, and configure the operating system using the most appropriate method.
    - Partitioning
        - Dynamic
        - Basic
        - Primary
        - Extended
        - Logical
    - File system types/formatting
        - FAT
        - FAT32
        - NTFS
        - CDFS
        - Quick format vs. full format
    - Factory recovery partition
- 1.3 Given a scenario, use appropriate command line tools.
    - OS
        - FDISK
        - FORMAT

- DISKPART
- CHKDSK
- 1.4 Given a scenario, use appropriate operating system features and tools.
  - Disk management
    - Drive status
    - Mounting
    - Extending partitions
    - Splitting partitions
    - Assigning drive letters
    - Adding drives
    - Adding arrays
- 1.7 Perform preventive maintenance procedures using appropriate tools.
  - Best practices
    - Scheduled check disks
    - Scheduled defragmentation
  - Tools
    - Check disk
    - Defrag
- 1.8 Explain the differences among basic OS security settings.
  - Shared files and folders
    - Administrative shares vs. local shares
- 4.3 Given a scenario, troubleshoot hard drives and RAID arrays with appropriate tools.
  - Tools
    - CHKDSK
    - FORMAT
    - FDISK
- 4.6 Given a scenario, troubleshoot operating system problems with appropriate tools.
  - Tools
    - DEFRAG

Understanding Disks, Partitions and Volumes

 You probably remember from Chapter 4 that a hard disk drive is a physical piece of hardware with spinning platters and read/write heads. It's something you can touch. However, operating systems work with *partitions* or *volumes,* which are logical rather than physical.

You can divide, or partition, a physical disk into multiple volumes. Each volume is identified by a letter such as C, D, and so on. The operating system uses these letters as identifiers when accessing data on the different volumes.

> **NOTE PARTITIONS AND VOLUMES ARE THE SAME**
>
> Years ago, the terms *partitions* and *volumes* were used for different types of disks. However, these terms have merged and are interchangeable today. When you divide a disk, it's usually referred to as partitioning a disk, but when you use these partitions within the operating system, they are often called volumes. Don't be surprised if you see these terms mixed in different documentation, but the important thing to remember is that they are the same.

Figure 16-1 shows two ways you can partition a single hard drive, but there are more. In the first example, the disk is divided into four volumes. In the second example, a single disk is used to create a single volume.

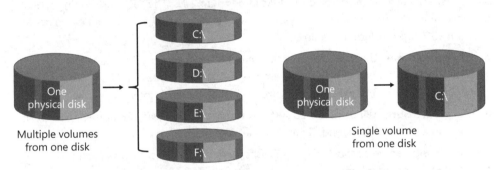

FIGURE 16-1 Partitioning a hard drive.

A logical question to ask is, "Why would you want multiple partitions?" It's not necessary, but some people like to have different partitions to organize their data. For example, the operating system is on the C drive, and they create a second partition to store their data. Then again, they could leave it as a single partition and create a folder named Data for their files. It's just a matter of preference.

MBR Partitions

The most common type of disk partitioning system in use is the *Master Boot Record (MBR)* partitioning scheme. You can divide an MBR disk into two types of partitions:

- **Primary partition.** A primary partition is used for a single volume, such as the C volume or D volume. One of the primary partitions is marked as active, indicating that it is bootable. During the startup process, the computer locates the active partition and attempts to boot from it. You can have as many as four primary partitions on a disk.

- **Extended partition.** An extended partition allows you to add multiple logical drives. For example, you can have one extended partition with three logical drives identified as G, H, and I. You can have only one extended partition on a disk. It isn't common to use extended partitions. The only reason you'd use one is to have more than four drive letters for a hard disk drive.

MBR disks have two limitations worth noting:

- The maximum size of a partition is 2 TB.

- You are limited to a total of four partitions for any disk. You can have four primary partitions, or you can have three primary partitions and one extended partition.

While these haven't been significant limitations in the past, larger hard drives are available, and a maximum disk size of 2 TB does pose problems for some users today.

GPT Partitions

The *Globally Unique Identifier (GUID) Partition Table (GPT)* overcomes the limitations of MBR disks and is specifically recommended for disks larger than 2 TB. The GPT partitioning scheme is supported in many current operating systems, such as Windows 7 and Linux. Key points to know about GPT disks include the following:

- **Larger volumes.** GPT has a theoretical limit of 9.4 zettabytes (ZB), and Windows-based systems support GPT disks as large as 256 TB. For context, a ZB is about a billion TB, but there aren't any disks of that size available—at least not yet.

- **More partitions.** Windows-based systems support as many as 128 primary GPT partitions on a single disk. Extended partitions are not needed or used with GPT disks.

Only fixed disks can be configured as GPT disks. Removable disks, such as flash drives, all use the MBR partitioning scheme.

Linux-based systems can use and boot from a GPT disk. Windows-based systems from Windows XP to Windows 7 can use a GPT disk. However, only 64-bit versions of Windows 7 can boot to a GPT disk and only if the computer is an Extensible Firmware Interface (EFI)-based system.

> **MORE INFO** **CHAPTER 2**
>
> Chapter 2 mentioned the UEFI, and as a reminder, UEFI is replacing or enhancing BIOS in many computers. Windows 7 can boot to GPT disks on UEFI-based systems but not on systems that only have a traditional BIOS.

Another benefit of GPT disks is that they are backward-compatible for applications that are expecting an MBR disk. A GPT disk includes a table called a *protective MBR* that simulates the MBR. Without this, older applications and disk utilities wouldn't be able to read the disk and might prompt the user to reformat it.

You can tell whether your system is using an MBR or GPT disk through the Disk Management tool by using the following steps on Windows 7:

1. Click Start, right-click Computer, and select Manage.

2. Select Disk Management.

3. Right-click a disk and select Properties. Select the Volumes tab and look at the Partition style as shown in the following graphic. The disk in the figure is an MBR disk.

You can convert an unpartitioned hard disk from MBR to GPT or from GPT to MBR from within the Disk Management console. For example, if it is an MBR disk, you can right-click the disk and select Convert To GPT. If it is a GPT disk, the option changes to Convert To MBR. These options are dimmed if the disk has any partitions on it.

Recovery Partition

Many computer manufacturers and resellers include a *recovery partition* with systems they sell. This is another partition on the hard drive that a user can access, often by pressing a specific key when the system starts.

If the primary partition develops a problem, the recovery partition can be used to restore the system to the exact state it was in when it was shipped. Users won't have access to any data or applications they added to their primary partition, but they will have a working system again.

EXAM TIP

A recovery partition is often invisible to the system. It isn't assigned a drive letter and usually isn't accessible with any applications other than the vendor's recovery application. If the primary partition is corrupted, such as from a virus, you can often use the recovery partition to restore the system to its original condition. Many vendors don't include media to restore a system, so if the recovery partition is modified or deleted, users won't be able to recover it.

Basic Disks vs. Dynamic Disks

 Windows-based systems since Windows 2000 have supported two types of disks: *basic disks* and *dynamic disks*. Basic disks are used most often and are the simplest to use, but dynamic disks provide some additional capabilities. Both basic and dynamic disks can use either the MBR or the GPT partitioning scheme.

> **IMPORTANT BEST PRACTICE IS TO LEAVE DISKS AS BASIC**
>
> If you convert one disk to dynamic in a computer, you will not be able to use the system as a dual-boot system.

Unless you have a specific reason to do so, you should leave disks as basic instead of dynamic. Of course, that prompts the question, "What's a reason to upgrade a disk to dynamic?"

Dynamic disks provide several benefits, such as the ability to create as many as 2,000 volumes on a single disk. This is useful for users who want to get beyond the four-partition limit of a basic MBR disk. You can also create striped, mirrored, and spanned volumes on dynamic disks, which are discussed in the following sections.

Dynamic Disks and RAID

One of the benefits of using dynamic disks is the ability to use a *redundant array of inexpensive disks* (*RAID*). Different RAID configurations provide different benefits. A primary benefit of RAID is fault tolerance. A drive can develop a fault and fail, but the system can tolerate it and continue to operate.

However, you'll find that dynamic disks do not support all the different RAID configurations on all operating systems. Common RAID configurations are presented in Chapter 4, and as a reminder, they are listed in Table 16-1.

TABLE 16-1 RAID Configurations

RAID	Number of Disks	Fault Tolerance	Dynamic Disk Support
RAID-0 Striped	At least two	No	Yes
RAID-1 Mirrored	Only two	Yes	Windows 7 (not Windows XP and Vista)
RAID-5	At least three	Yes	Only servers
RAID-10	At least four	Yes	No

If you convert the disk on any Windows-based system to dynamic disks, you can use RAID-0, but that is the only configuration that is universally supported. Only Windows 7 supports mirrored disks, and you can use RAID-5 (also called *striping with parity*) only on servers. Dynamic disks do not support RAID-10.

EXAM TIP

These limitations apply only to dynamic disks. Any system can support an external array of disks. For example, you can buy external disk enclosures configured as RAID-0, RAID-1, RAID-5, or RAID-10 and connect them with a USB, FireWire, or eSATA interface as described in Chapter 4. Windows views the external array as a single physical disk that can be partitioned as desired.

Striped Volumes (RAID-0)

You can create a striped volume (RAID-0) on any Windows-based system that supports dynamic disks. It includes space on more than one physical disk, but it appears to the operating system as a single physical volume. Dynamic disk striped volumes include at least two and up to 32 disks in the volume.

Each disk in the volume must be the same size, and data is stored in stripes on the different disks. For example, a two-disk striped volume would hold half of a file in one disk and the other half of the file in the other disk. The system can read both halves from the two disks at the same time, improving read performance. Additionally, the system can write both halves of a file to the two drives at the same time, improving write performance.

Mirrored Volumes (RAID-1)

Windows 7 supports mirrored volumes on dynamic disks. A mirrored volume includes two disks, and data written to one disk is also written to the other disk. If one of the disks fails, the system can continue to operate. Both disks must include partitions of exactly the same size.

EXAM TIP

You can create mirrored volumes (RAID-1) on Windows 7–based systems, but this configuration is not supported on Windows XP or Windows Vista. Windows XP and Windows Vista do support dynamic disks using RAID-0 and spanned volumes, but not RAID-1.

Spanned Volumes

A *spanned volume* includes space on more than one physical disk, but it appears to the operating system as a single physical volume. For example, if you have a D volume used for data but it's running out of space, you can add another physical disk and span the D volume to the new disk. The D volume will now have the additional space available.

You cannot span a boot or system volume, but you can span other volumes, such as one used for data. Chapter 11 describes the system and boot partitions in more depth. As a reminder, the system partition is where the system boot files are located (typically C:\), and the boot partition is the location where the Windows-based system files are located (typically C:\Windows).

Spanned volumes don't provide any performance gains or fault tolerance benefits. Worse, if any physical drive in the spanned volume fails, the entire volume fails and all the data is lost. A better option is to use a mounted volume (described later in this chapter), which can be created on a basic disk.

EXAM TIP

Spanned volumes can be created only on dynamic disks. You can create a spanned volume with the Disk Management graphical user interface (GUI) tool covered later in this chapter.

✔ **Quick Check**

1. What type of disk is limited to only four partitions?

2. What type of disk provides fault tolerance on Windows 7?

Quick Check Answers

1. Basic disk using MBR.

2. Dynamic disk using RAID-1.

File Systems

A file system is used to organize files and folders so that the operating system can access the files. Files are commonly organized in folders (sometimes called directories), and the file system allows users to browse through them to locate their files.

When you partition a hard drive, you are often prompted to choose a file system and format it. The *format* process organizes the partition based on which file system you choose. It also deletes existing data, so you don't want to reformat a disk unless you're willing to lose the data.

Several different file systems are available to format the hard drive with different characteristics. It's important to understand the differences between these file systems so that you can choose the best one.

NTFS is the recommended file system for most situations. However, there are other choices. The following sections describe the common file systems with a short discussion on disk clusters.

Understanding Clusters

You might recall that a hard drive has multiple platters and that each platter is divided using tracks, sectors, and clusters. These concepts are presented in Chapter 4, but as a reminder, the following bullets describe them and they're also shown in Figure 16-2.

- **Track.** A track is a complete circle around the hard drive. A drive will have many more tracks than the figure shows.

- **Sector.** The hard drive is logically divided into separate areas, similarly to how you'd cut a pie into separate slices, and a single portion of a track within a slice is a sector.

- **Cluster.** Multiple sectors are grouped together to form clusters. Clusters are also known as *allocation units*, and each cluster is identified with a unique number.

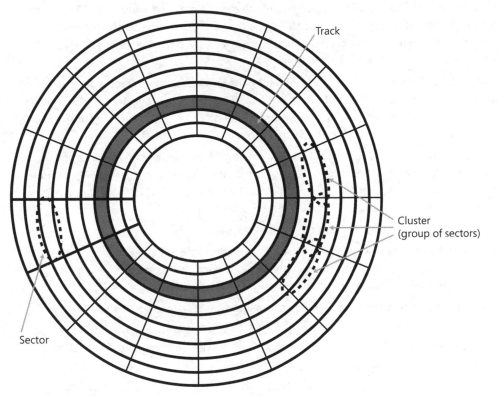

FIGURE 16-2 Tracks, sectors, and clusters.

File systems use a table to identify the location of files on a disk drive based on the clusters. For example, a file named A+Notes.docx stored on a hard drive might start in a cluster identified as 0x1357 and end at cluster 0x53A9. The operating system uses this information to locate and retrieve the file from the disk.

Cluster sizes vary between file systems, but the size of a cluster is commonly 4,096 bytes (or 4 KB). There aren't many files that are only 4 KB in size, so files are stored in multiple clusters.

Fragmentation

It's best if the files are stored in contiguous clusters so that the hard drive can start reading in one cluster and then continue reading until the entire file has been retrieved. For example, a 10-MB file would ideally start in one cluster on the hard drive and use each of the clusters after it until the entire file is stored on the drive. However, as a hard drive fills up, there isn't always enough space to store a file in contiguous clusters.

Instead, the file system divides or fragments a file and stores these fragments in different locations on a hard drive. A 10-MB file might have 5 MB written in one area, 3 MB in another area, and the last 2 MB in another area. When the file is read, the operating system retrieves each of these fragments and puts the file back together.

Some fragmentation is common on a disk. However, when a disk is used more and more often, fragmentation can become excessive. Instead of a file being divided into three fragments, it could be divided into dozens of fragments. The system has to work harder and harder to retrieve these fragments and put them back together.

Symptoms of a fragmented hard drive are as follows:

- **Disk thrashing.** The LED for the disk drive is constantly blinking, indicating heavy activity. Additionally, you can hear the drive working as the read/write head is constantly moving around the disk retrieving the different file fragments.

- **Slow performance.** The overall performance of the system slows down.

If you suspect a drive is highly fragmented, the best solution is to check it and defragment it. You can do so with the Disk Defragmenter GUI or the defrag command-line tool, both described later in this chapter.

EXAM TIP

If a system is slow and the hard drive LED shows constant activity, check for fragmentation. You can often optimize the overall performance of a computer and increase its efficiency by ensuring that disk drives are defragmented. You can use the defrag command or the Disk Defragmenter GUI to defrag a volume. If you have these symptoms but the drive is not defragmented, the system might need more physical memory.

Bad Sectors

Disk drives often have small areas that are faulty. As long as these areas are marked, they won't be used and they won't cause any problems. If you do a full format of a disk (described later in this chapter), it will check all the sectors on the disk and mark faulty areas as bad. You can also use the chkdsk command (also covered later in this chapter) to look for and mark bad sectors.

FAT16 and FAT32

The *File Allocation Table (FAT)* file system is native to Microsoft operating systems and widely supported by other operating systems, such as Linux. The two common versions of FAT are FAT16 and FAT32.

Each of the FAT versions uses a table to identify the location of files on a disk drive based on the clusters. FAT16 (commonly called just FAT) uses 16 bits, and FAT32 uses 32 bits to address these clusters. With more bits, the file system can address more clusters and support larger disks. Table 16-2 shows the different sizes of partitions and files supported by these FAT versions.

TABLE 16-2 FAT Versions

	FAT16	FAT32
Maximum partition size you can create	4 GB	32 GB
Maximum file size	2 GB	4 GB

If you ever try to copy or download a file larger than 4 GB to a FAT32 disk, you'll get an error that indicates you don't have enough space. You could have a brand new, empty 16-GB USB flash drive, but you'll still get this error. The reason isn't because you don't have enough space but because FAT32 can't handle files greater than 4 GB. Convert the drive to NTFS, and you won't have this problem.

EXAM TIP

When creating FAT32 partitions from within Windows, you are limited to a maximum size of 32 GB. It is possible to create larger FAT32 partitions by using other utilities or on other operating systems, and Windows-based systems can recognize and use them.

You can format disks as FAT, FAT32, or NTFS from Windows-based systems such as Windows 7. However, you can format disks as FAT only if they are smaller than 4 GB. If the disk size is larger than 4 GB, you can select only FAT32 or NTFS.

Windows-based systems support exFAT (or FAT64), but this format isn't widely supported on non-Windows-based systems. If you're formatting a disk larger than 32 GB, you'll also see exFAT as an option.

NTFS

New Technology File System (NTFS) is a secure file system, and when using Windows-based systems, it is by far the best choice compared to any of the FAT versions. Microsoft recommends the use of NTFS with Windows operating systems, and newer operating systems such as Windows 7 must be installed on NTFS. The install program won't allow you to install Windows 7 on a FAT volume.

NTFS provides better security, improved performance, and more features than any of the FAT versions. Some of the features and capabilities include the following:

- **File and folder permissions.** You can assign permissions to control access to any files and folders. Permissions are covered in more depth in Chapter 25.
- **Encryption.** Files and folders can be encrypted with the Encrypting File System (EFS) to prevent unauthorized users from viewing the file contents.
- **Compression.** Files can be compressed so that they take up less space on a disk drive.
- **Larger volumes.** NTFS volumes can be as large as 2 TB on MBR disks or as large as 256 TB on GPT disks.
- **Efficient.** NTFS uses clusters within a hard drive more efficiently than any of the FAT file systems.
- **Built-in fault tolerance.** NTFS can detect and recover from some disk-related errors without any user intervention.

CDFS

The *compact disc file system (CDFS)* is the standard used to access files on optical discs. It is formally defined in ISO 9660 and widely supported by different operating systems, including Windows, Linux and Unix systems, and the Mac OS.

✔ **Quick Check**

    1. What's the maximum size of a FAT32 partition you can create on Windows?

    2. What file system provides the best security?

Quick Check Answers

    1. 32 GB.

    2. NTFS.

Disk Management Tools

Windows provides several different tools that you can use to manage disks. Some of these tools, such as *Disk Management* and *Disk Defragmenter*, are available as GUI tools. Other tools, such as chkdsk and diskpart, are available from the command prompt.

Disk Management

Disk Management is a GUI available in all current Windows operating systems. It is included as a snap-in the Computer Management console, but you can also access it directly. You can start Disk Management by taking any of the following actions:

- Click Start, right-click Computer, and select Manage. Select Disk Management in the Computer Management console.

- On Windows Vista and Windows 7: Click Start, type **diskmgmt.msc** in the Search text box and press Enter.

- On Windows XP: Click Start and select Run. Type **diskmgmt.msc** in the text box and press Enter.

Figure 16-3 shows the Disk Management console within Windows 7. Following are descriptions of the three numbered areas in the figure:

1. This section lists the volumes and provides information about them, such as the type of disk, the file system, the volumes' health, how big they are, and how much free space they have.

2. Disk 0 is a basic disk, and this shows that it has a system-reserved partition, a C volume, and unallocated space. New partitions can be created from unallocated space.

3. Disk 1 is a dynamic disk, and it has one volume labeled as E and unallocated space that can be used to create new volumes.

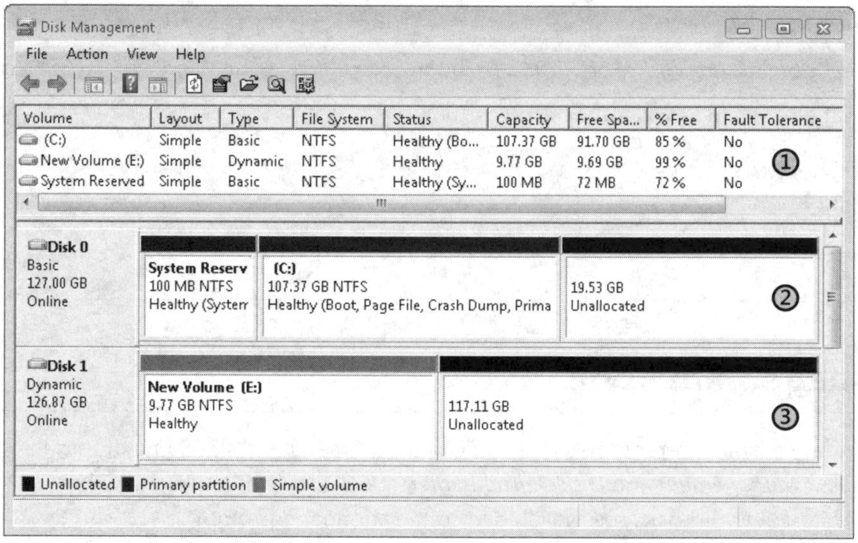

FIGURE 16-3 Disk Management.

> **NOTE IDENTIFY SYSTEM AND BOOT PARTITIONS**
>
> Notice that you can identify the system and boot partitions in the Disk Management console. This Windows 7–based system is using a special 100-MB System Reserved system partition on Disk 0. This is common on Windows Vista and Windows 7–based systems and is reserved so that users can enable BitLocker Drive Encryption if desired. It also holds some key boot files, so it should not be deleted.

Identifying Disk Status

The status column of the Disk Management console provides important information about the drive. Ideally, it will display Healthy, indicating that everything is fine. However, you also might see one of the following indicators:

- **Unreadable.** This often indicates a hardware failure.

- **Foreign.** When you move a dynamic disk from one system to another, the target system identifies it as a foreign disk. You can right-click the disk and select Import Foreign Disk so that the target system recognizes it.

- **Online.** Online disks are available for read/write access.

- **Online (Errors).** If input/output errors are detected on a dynamic volume, the status column will display this. You can right-click the disk and select Reactivate to return it to Online status. This error is a hint that the disk might be failing, so ensure that you have a good backup and then run some disk checks.

- **Offline.** The operating system might take a volume offline if it has detected a problem. The disk needs to be brought online to use it, and you can do so by right-clicking the disk and selecting Reactivate. If this doesn't work, there could be a hardware problem.

- **Missing.** This is displayed if one of the disks for a volume is not accessible. For example, this would appear if one of the disks in a mirrored or striped volume was not accessible. You might be able to reactivate the disk to get it to recognize the missing disk, but a missing disk often indicates a hardware problem.

- **Failed.** This indicates a hardware problem or that the file system is corrupted. You might be able to reformat it to still use the disk, or you can use chkdsk to repair the disk.

You have a variety of different commands from the context menus in these three areas. You can right-click a volume in the top pane or a volume within one of the disks to accomplish different tasks or view the volume's properties. The choices vary between different operating systems.

Disk Management on All Windows-Based Systems

Different operating systems provide different capabilities. The following list identifies what you can do on Windows XP, Windows Vista, and Windows 7.

- **Create partition/volume.** If the drive has unallocated space, you can right-click it and select New Partition (Windows XP) or New Simple Volume (Windows Vista and Windows 7).

- **Format.** You can right-click any volume and select Format. You'll be prompted to select the file system, such as NTFS or one of the FAT versions.

- **Delete.** Deleting a partition or volume changes the space to unallocated. If you delete an existing partition/volume, all data is lost.

- **Mount a volume.** You can mount a volume to an empty folder on a drive. Instead of the drive appearing as a separate letter, the space will be available in the mounted folder.

Disk Management on Windows Vista and Windows 7

You have some additional capabilities on Windows Vista-based and Windows 7–based computers from within the Disk Management console. These capabilities include:

- **Shrink a volume.** Shrinking a volume effectively allows you to repartition a hard disk without reformatting the entire disk. For example, if you have a single disk created as a single volume, you can shrink the volume to a smaller size, leaving unallocated space available. You can then create a new volume from the unallocated space.

- **Create a volume.** Use this to create and format a new volume from unallocated space.

- **Change drive letters.** If you want a drive, such as an optical drive, to use a specific drive letter, you can right-click the drive and select Change drive letters and paths. This causes the system to recognize the drive with the new letter.

- **Extend a volume.** This allows you to add space to a volume from unallocated space. For example, if you have a 10-GB volume and 5 GB of unallocated space, you can extend the volume to include the additional 5 GB of space, making it 15 GB in size.

> **NOTE EXTENDING A VOLUME VERSUS EXTENDED PARTITION**
>
> Extending a volume is not the same as creating an extended partition. Extending a volume is the opposite of shrinking a volume and essentially grows it from unallocated space. An extended partition is used with a primary partition and allows you to create multiple logical disks.

Initializing a Disk

When you add a new hard disk to a Windows-based system, it won't be recognized by the system until it is initialized. For example, if you start Windows Explorer, the disk won't appear. The solution is to open the Disk Management console and initialize the disk. This writes a signature onto the disk so that Windows recognizes it.

Initializing a disk doesn't affect any data on the drive. It also doesn't change any partitions or file systems.

If you start Disk Management, you'll be prompted to initialize new disks automatically. If you cancel this prompt, the status of the disk will be listed as Not Initialized.

Formatting a Volume or Array

Before an operating system can read and write data to a volume or disk array, it must be formatted. Windows-based systems will typically prompt you to format it as an NTFS volume, but you can also choose one of the FAT versions, as explained earlier.

If you format an existing volume, it removes access to any data on the volume. If the volume has data on it, back it up before formatting it.

When formatting a volume, you are often given two choices:

- **Full format.** In addition to preparing the drive, a full format scans a disk for bad sectors and marks them. A system will not write data to bad sectors.

- **Quick format.** A quick format does not scan a disk for bad sectors. It is quicker but not recommended for a regularly used system because the system might attempt to write data to bad sectors, resulting in corrupted files.

EXAM TIP

A full format checks for bad sectors and marks them. If you perform a quick format originally but later want to check the sectors on a disk, you can use the chkdsk /r command to check for and mark bad sectors.

You can format a disk from the command prompt with the format command or with the Disk Management GUI. The basic command from the command prompt is:

```
format volume /fs:file-system
```

For example, to format the P drive with NTFS, use the following command:

format p: /fs:ntfs

The following steps show how to create and format a volume in Disk Management on a Windows 7–based system:

1. Right-click the unallocated space and select New Simple Volume. Click Next.

2. The maximum size of the volume is automatically entered as the size of the new simple volume. You can change this size or accept the default. Click Next.

3. On the Assign Drive Letter or Path page, you can assign a specific drive letter or accept the default drive letter. Click Next.

4. On the Format Partition page, you can accept the default file system of NTFS or change it to one of the FAT versions based on the size of the volume. If you want to check the disk for bad sectors, deselect Perform A Quick Format. Your display will look similar to the following graphic. Click Next.

New Simple Volume Wizard

Format Partition
To store data on this partition, you must format it first.

Choose whether you want to format this volume, and if so, what settings you want to use.

○ Do not format this volume

● Format this volume with the following settings:

File system: NTFS

Allocation unit size: Default

Volume label: Data

☐ Perform a quick format

☐ Enable file and folder compression

< Back   Next >   Cancel

5. Click Finish. The operating system will format the drive.

Shrink a Volume

You can use these steps to shrink a volume in Windows Vista and Windows 7 by using Disk Management:

1. Right-click the C drive (or another drive if desired) and select Shrink Volume.

2. The system will identify the maximum amount of space in MB that you can shrink the drive to. You can accept the default or shrink it to a different size.

3. Click Shrink. When this is done, the amount of space you shrunk the drive by is identified as Unallocated space.

Extend a Volume

If you want to grow a disk by reclaiming unallocated space, you can do so by extending the volume. The following steps show how to extend a volume on Windows 7 by using Disk Management:

1. Right-click a volume and select Extend Volume. Click Next.

2. This will automatically select all of the unallocated space on the disk. You can change this to a smaller size and leave some unallocated space if desired. Click Next.

3. Click Finished. The volume you created in the previous step will be extended to take the additional space you specified.

Mount a Volume

An alternative to a spanned volume is a mounted volume. A mounted volume creates a mount-point folder path to a new disk rather than assigning a letter to the new disk. That is, it provides a logical pointer to the new disk.

Mounted volumes can be created on basic disks, eliminating the drawbacks of dynamic disks. The only requirements are that the existing disk must use NTFS and the mount-point folder must be empty.

EXAM TIP

Mounted volumes can be mounted only on empty NTFS folders.

You can use the following steps on a Windows 7 computer to create a mount point by using Disk Management:

1. Right-click the unallocated space of a disk and select New Simple Volume. Click Next.

2. This will automatically select all of the unallocated space on the disk. You can change this to a smaller size and leave some unallocated space if desired. Click Next.

3. Select Mount in the Following Empty NTFS Folder.

4. Click Browse. Browse to the location of an empty folder. You can also select an existing drive such as C and click New Folder and name your new folder. Click OK, and then click Next.

5. Select the formatting options you want and click Next. Click Finish.

Disk Management doesn't show that the new volume is a mount point. However, you can see it if you launch Windows Explorer. Click Start, select Computer, and select the C drive. Your display will look similar to Figure 16-4. In the figure, I named the mounted folder MountPoint. You can also see that instead of a folder icon it has a shortcut icon with an arrow.

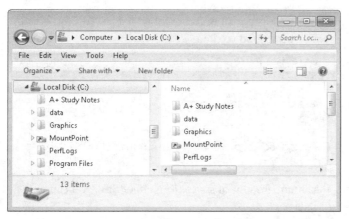

FIGURE 16-4 A mount point on a disk.

You can also identify mount points from the command prompt. If you enter the *dir* command, you'll see that the mounted folder appears as <JUNCTION> instead of as <DIR>.

Converting to Dynamic

You can use the following steps to convert a basic disk to a dynamic disk on a Windows 7–based system by using Disk Management. However, consider the following two important points before you do this:

- If any disk is dynamic, the system cannot be used as a dual-boot system.
- This is a one-way action. You shouldn't lose data converting to dynamic, but if you want to convert it back, you'll have to reformat the drive. All data will be lost if you convert a dynamic disk back to basic.

> **IMPORTANT** **CONVERTING A DISK TO A DYNAMIC DISK CAN BE RISKY**
>
> Ensure that you have backed up all data on the disk before continuing. Also, you cannot convert a dynamic disk back to a basic disk without first deleting all the volumes on the disk. When you delete the volumes, it deletes all the data on the volumes.

1. Right-click the disk in Disk Management, and select Convert to Dynamic Disk.
2. A dialog box will appear with the disk selected. Ensure that this is the disk you want to convert and click OK.
3. Click Convert on the Disks To Convert dialog box.
4. Review the warning from Disk Management indicating that you will no longer be able to use this system as a dual-boot system. Click Yes. After a moment, the disk will be listed as a dynamic disk.

Dynamic Disk Actions

If you created a dynamic disk, you have extra capabilities as described earlier. You can create a spanned volume, a mirrored volume, or a striped volume.

You can use the following steps to create a mirrored volume on Windows 7 by using Disk Management:

1. Right-click the unallocated space on a disk and select New Mirrored Volume. Click Next.
2. The disk you clicked will be selected. Select a second disk from the list of available disks and click Add.
3. The size will default to the maximum amount of space from either disk. You can change the size if desired. Click Next.
4. Click Next to accept the default drive letter.

5. Select the desired format options and click Next. Click Finish.

6. If the disks are basic disks, you will be prompted to convert them to dynamic. Click Yes. The system will create the mirrored volume.

You can use the following steps to create a striped volume on Windows 7 by using Disk Management:

1. Right-click the unallocated space on a disk and select New Striped Volume. Click Next.

2. The disk you clicked will be selected. Select a second disk from the list of available disks and click Add.

3. The size will default to the maximum amount of space from either disk. You can change the size if desired. Click Next.

4. Click Next to accept the default drive letter.

5. Select the desired format options and click Next. Click Finish.

Figure 16-5 shows Disk Management with three physical disks. Parts of disks 1 and 2 have been created as a mirrored volume, and other parts have been made into a striped volume. You would normally create either a single mirrored volume or a single striped volume using two physical disks. However, the figure shows what each looks like when they are created.

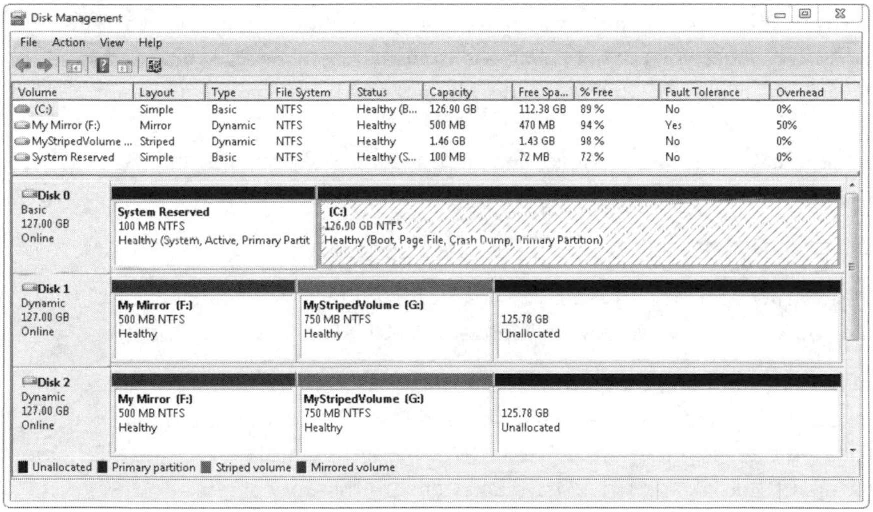

FIGURE 16-5 Mirrored and striped volumes in disk management.

You can see that only the mirrored volume (named My Mirror) provides fault tolerance. It shows 50% overhead because only half of the drive space is available. In contrast, the striped volume (named MyStripedVolume) includes two 750-MB disks and has about 1.43 GB of disk space available.

Diskpart

Diskpart is an advanced tool that you can use to manipulate a disk drive from the command prompt. You can do anything in diskpart that you can do in Disk Management. The benefit is that diskpart is available from the command prompt even when Disk Management is not available.

For example, when first installing Windows 7, you can press Shift+F10 to access the command prompt. You can then use diskpart to manipulate the disk before installing Windows 7.

You can start it from the command prompt by typing **diskpart** and pressing Enter. If you then type help and press Enter, you'll see a list of commands you can enter. Some of the common actions you can take are format, convert (between basic and dynamic, or between MBR and GPT disks), shrink, and expand.

When using diskpart, you must first select the object you want to work on. You can use the list command to list available objects, such as *list disk*, *list partition*, or *list volume*. You then select the object by using *select disk x*, *select partition x*, or *select volume x*, substituting *x* with the number shown from the list command. After the object is selected, you can run the desired command.

> **MORE INFO**   **CHAPTER 14**
>
> Chapter 14 covers the command prompt in more depth, including how to open it and how to get help. As a reminder, you can get help by using the help switch (/?) or by entering help followed by the command. This also works within the diskpart command prompt.

As a short exercise, you can use the following steps to start diskpart, list the disks, and list the partitions:

1.   Start the command prompt.

2.   Type in **diskpart**, and press Enter. If you are prompted by User Account Control to continue, click Yes. A new window will appear with DISKPART> as the prompt.

3.   Type in **list disk**, and press Enter. This lists all the disks in your system and will resemble the following graphic. Notice that Disk 1 and Disk have an asterisk in the Dyn column. This indicates that they are dynamic disks. All of these disks are of the MBR type. If they were GPT disks, they would have an asterisk in the Gpt column.

```
C:\Windows\system32\diskpart.exe                                    □ □ ▨

Microsoft DiskPart version 6.1.7600
Copyright (C) 1999-2008 Microsoft Corporation.
On computer: WIN7-PC

DISKPART> list disk

  Disk ###  Status      Size     Free     Dyn  Gpt
  --------  ----------  -------  -------   ---  ---
  Disk 0    Online      126 GB       0 B
  Disk 1    Online      126 GB   125 GB    *
  Disk 2    Online      126 GB   125 GB    *

DISKPART>
```

4. Type in **select disk 0**, and press Enter.

5. Type in **list partition**, and press Enter. This shows a listing of the partitions on disk 0.

6. Type in **exit**, and press Enter to exit diskpart.

Chkdsk and Check Disk

The *chkdsk* command is a valuable command that you can use to identify and resolve problems with disks and RAID arrays. If you run it without using any switches, it will run a check on the current disk and report the results back. However, it does not attempt any repairs unless one of the switches is used.

Two of the common switches used with the chkdsk command are listed in Table 16-3, along with the sample command.

TABLE 16-3 Common chkdsk Switches

Switch	Comments
/f chkdsk /f	Fixes errors on the disk.
/r chkdsk /r	Locates nd recovers readable information. This implies /f, so it also fixes errors on the disk.

EXAM TIP

If Windows Vista or Windows 7 detects a problem with a volume, it will often schedule chkdsk to run the next time the system reboots.

If you attempt to run chkdsk or Check Disk to check a volume that is in use (such as the C drive), Windows will indicate that it can't check it while it is in use. You'll be prompted to schedule the disk check the next time the computer is booted. If you select Schedule disk, the system will run the check when it reboots.

You can also check a disk from Windows Explorer with the following steps:

1. With Windows Explorer open, browse to the hard drive you want to check.

2. Right-click the drive, and select Properties.

3. Click the Tools tab, and click Check Now. You'll see a display similar to the following graphic.

4. The two options in the Check Disk Data dialog box work the same as the /f and /r switches do with chkdsk. The first option works like the /f switch to fix errors, and the second option recovers information like the /r switch.

EXAM TIP

Both the chkdsk command-line tool and the Check Disk GUI will verify the integrity of the physical disk and file system integrity. The chkdsk tool is also available from the command prompt in safe mode and via the System Recovery tool in Windows Vista and Windows 7.

Convert

Whenever possible, it's best to use NTFS instead of one of the versions of FAT. However, you're sure to come across some FAT volumes. If you want to convert a volume from FAT to NTFS, you can do so with the *convert* command. Converting a volume does not reformat it, so it doesn't result in the loss of data.

The basic syntax of the command is as follows:

```
convert volume /fs:ntfs
```

You specify the volume letter followed by a colon. For example, if you want to convert the E drive from FAT32 to NTFS, you could use the following command:

```
convert e: /fs:ntfs
```

EXAM TIP

The convert utility allows you to convert a FAT file system to NTFS without losing any data. However, if you want to revert an NTFS volume to FAT, you must reformat the volume, and you'll lose all the data on the drive.

Disk Defragmenter and Defrag

The *Disk Defragmenter* is a tool that allows you to easily determine whether a disk is fragmented. It is available within Computer Management in Windows XP and as a separate GUI in Windows Vista and Windows 7. Figure 16-6 shows the disk defragmenter tool within Windows XP. In the figure, the drive has been analyzed, but there is very little fragmentation on this drive.

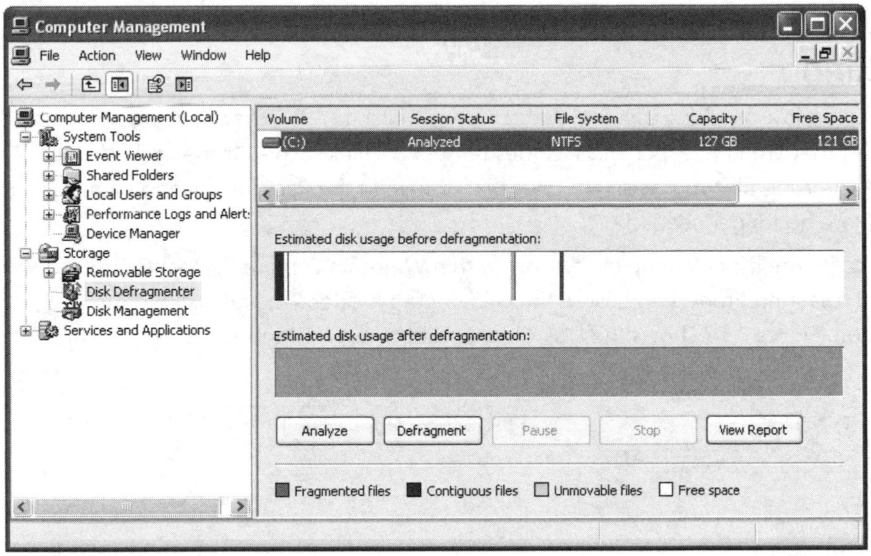

FIGURE 16-6 Using the Disk Defragmenter.

Windows Vista and Windows 7 both include schedules to automatically check a drive for fragmentation once a week. The schedule is included in the Windows Defrag menu within the Task Scheduler's Library of scheduled tasks. Unless these schedules have been disabled through Task Scheduler, you don't need to worry about defragmenting volumes on these systems.

Another way to defragment a hard drive is with the *defrag* command from the command prompt. The basic syntax is as follows:

```
defrag volume
```

For example, if you want to defrag the E drive, use the following command:

```
defrag e:
```

Table 16-4 shows two common switches you could use with the defrag command, along with sample usage.

TABLE 16-4 Common defrag Switches

Switch	Comments
/a defrag e: /a	Perform analysis of the drive. This provides a report but does not defrag the volume.
/c Defrag /c	Defragment all drives on the system.

Disk Cleanup

If you are running low on disk space on your system, you can use the *Disk Cleanup* utility to remove files that aren't needed. This includes temporary files such as those cached from browsing the Internet, files you've deleted but that remain in the Recycle Bin, and some system files that are no longer needed.

You can access the Disk Cleanup utility from within Windows Explorer by right-clicking any drive and selecting Properties. Ensure the General tab is selected, and click on the Disk Cleanup button. Figure 16-7 shows the Disk Cleanup utility within Windows 7.

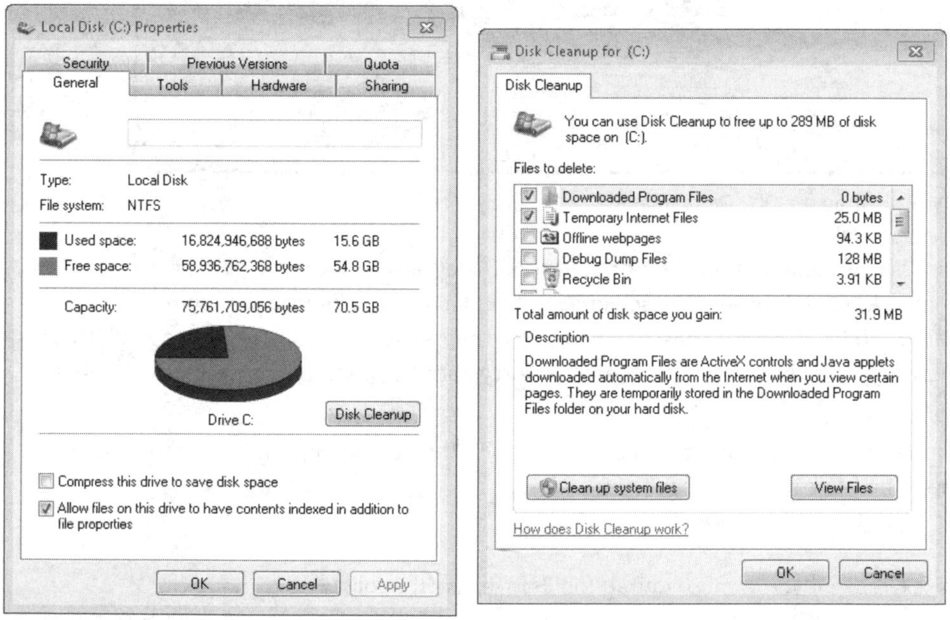

FIGURE 16-7 Using Disk Cleanup utility.

The system will calculate how much space can be saved by cleaning up the disk and allow you to choose which files to delete. If you click OK, it will delete the selected files. If you want to remove unneeded system files, you can click the Clean Up System Files button, and the system will calculate how much space you can save, including unneeded system files.

Fdisk

A very old command that you can use to partition a disk is called *fdisk*. It was required to partition a disk prior to installing an operating system. Technicians used bootable floppies with fdisk, and after booting, they used fdisk to partition the hard drive. However, most install programs now include built-in tools to partition a disk, so it is rarely needed.

✔ Quick Check

1. Name two common tools that you can use to partition a hard drive.
2. What tool can you use to discover and repair errors on a disk?

Quick Check Answers

1. Disk Management and diskpart. Fdisk is not common but can also be used.
2. Chkdsk or Check Disk.

Shares

One way that you can share data with other users is to create a share on a computer. A *share* is simply a folder that has been shared and is available to other users on a network. Organizations often have file servers with multiple shares available on each server.

Shares are accessed over a network by using the Universal Naming Convention (UNC). A UNC path is in the format of \\ServerName\ShareName. For example, if a folder named StudyNotes has been shared on a server named Server1, the UNC path is \\Server1\StudyNotes. UNC path names are not case-sensitive. You can use all uppercase, all lowercase, or a combination.

You can view a listing of all the shares available on a system by using the following command at the command prompt:

```
Net share
```

MORE INFO CHAPTERS 18–24 AND CHAPTER 25

Chapters 18 through 24 cover networking in more depth, and Chapter 25 covers security in more depth, including both NTFS and share permissions. If a computer is connected with a network, the UNC paths provide connectivity, and a user with appropriate permissions can access the data.

Administrative Shares

Operating systems automatically create several shares, known as *administrative shares*. These are available to administrators but often aren't known by other users.

Administrative shares end in a dollar sign ($), and any share that ends in a dollar sign is hidden. Anyone knowing the name of the share can access it. However, these shares are not visible to users browsing the network.

Table 16-5 lists some common administrative shares available on Windows-based systems.

TABLE 16-5 Administrative Shares

Share name	Resource
C$, D$, E$, and so on	This is created for each hard drive (C, D, E, and so on) on a system.
Print$	Location of printer drivers.
Admin$	Location of Windows folder.

The UNC path for administrative shares is the same as other systems. For example, if a computer is named after a user named Sally, the administrator can connect to Sally's C drive with the following UNC path: \\Sally\C$.

EXAM TIP

By default, administrative shares include a $ symbol to hide them. It's also possible to add a $ symbol to any share to hide it.

Local Shares

You can also share any folder on a disk by creating a share for it. The easiest way to do so is from within the Computer Management console.

Figure 16-8 shows the Computer Management console opened to the Shared Folders, Shares display on a Windows 7–based computer. It shows all the shares on this computer, including one named APlusStudy, which is sharing the C:\data\A+Study folder.

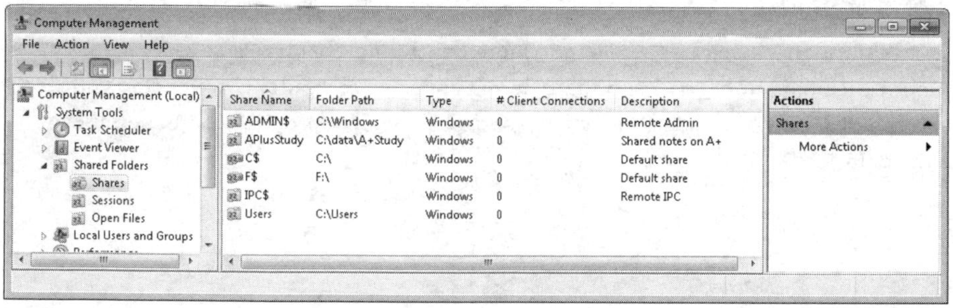

FIGURE 16-8 Viewing shares in Computer Management console.

You can create a share for any folder by right-clicking Shares and following the wizard to share it.

> **MORE INFO CHAPTER 24**
>
> Chapter 24 covers Windows 7 Homegroups used in small networks. Homegroups allow users to share files in their libraries. For example, users can share their Documents, Music, and Picture libraries. Shares can be used with Homegroups or without them.

Offline Files

Users can access shared files as long as they are connected to the network. However, if they aren't connected to the network, they can't access the computer sharing the files. Sometimes users want to have access to these files even when they are disconnected, and the *offline files* feature gives them this ability.

When the offline files feature is enabled, users can right-click a file on a share and select Make Available Online. Windows then stores a copy of the file on the user's system.

Users can access this copy of the file while they're disconnected from the network. When they reconnect, Windows will automatically sync the files to ensure that each location has the most up-to-date version.

On Windows Vista and Windows 7, you can access the offline files settings with the following steps:

1. Click Start, and type **offline files** in the text box.

2. Select Offline Files in Windows Vista or Manage Offline Files in Windows 7. The display resembles the following graphic.

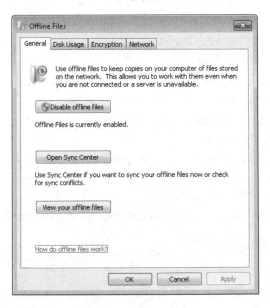

Users can disable offline files, force an immediate synchronization of the files, and view the offline files from here.

On Windows XP, you can access the Offline Files settings with the following steps:

1. Open Windows Explorer.

2. Select Tools | Folder Options.

3. Click the Offline Folders tab.

EXAM TIP

You can't use Offline Files and Fast User Switching on Windows XP. However, they will work together on Windows Vista and Windows 7.

> **✔ Quick Check**
>
> 1. What is used to allow access to folders on another system?
> 2. What allows users to access network-based files when users are disconnected from a network?
>
> **Quick Check Answers**
>
> 1. Shares.
> 2. Offline files.

Chapter Summary

- MBR disks support disks up to 2 TB and with as many as four partitions on a disk.

- Windows-based systems support GPT disks as large as 256 TB and with as many as 128 partitions per disk.

- Most disks are basic disks. Windows supports dynamic disks, which provide additional capabilities such as striped, mirrored, and spanned volumes.

- Windows 7 supports mirrored volumes (RAID-1) on dynamic disks, but RAID-1 is not supported on Windows XP or Windows Vista.

- FAT16 and FAT32 are the most common types of FAT file systems. Maximum partition sizes on Windows-based systems are 4 GB for FAT16 and 32 GB for FAT32. The maximum file sizes are 2 GB for FAT16 and 4 GB for FAT32.

- NTFS is the preferred file system for Windows. It provides better performance and security.

- Disk Management is the primary GUI used to manage disks. It can create, format, manipulate, and delete disks. Diskpart is the command-line equivalent of Disk Management.

- Dynamic disks are listed as foreign if moved from one system to another. A foreign disk can be imported by using Disk Management.

- Chkdsk is a command-line tool used to check the integrity of disks. The /f switch will fix errors, and the /r disk will identify bad sectors and recover readable information.

- Disks can be converted from FAT to NTFS by using the convert command. The file system is converted without losing data.

- Fragmented hard drives are slower, and their LEDs will show constant activity. They can be defragmented with the Disk Defragmenter GUI or the defrag command-line tool.

- The Disk Cleanup tool can identify and remove unneeded files.

- Shares provide access to folders over a network. Offline files store copies of shared files on the local system so that users can access the files, even when disconnected from the network.

Chapter Review

Use the following questions to test your knowledge of the information in this chapter. The answers to these questions, and the explanations of why each answer choice is correct or incorrect, are located in the "Answers" section at the end of this chapter.

1. You are adding a 1-TB hard drive to a Windows 7–based system. Which file system should you use for the best performance?

   A. FAT16

   B. FAT32

   C. FAT64

   D. NTFS

2. A user asks what tool he can use to create a mirrored volume on a Windows 7–based system. What would you tell him?

   A. You cannot create a mirrored volume on Windows 7.

   B. Use Disk Management.

   C. Use Windows Explorer.

   D. Use Convert.

3. You have added a new disk drive to a Windows 7–based system, but it is not recognized. What needs to be done?

    A. The disk needs to be converted to NTFS.

    B. The disk needs to be converted to dynamic.

    C. The disk needs to be imported.

    D. The disk needs to be initialized.

4. You want your DVD player to be assigned the letter M within the operating system. What tool would you use?

    A. Disk Defragmenter

    B. Device Manager

    C. Windows Explorer

    D. Disk Management

5. You suspect the D partition on a disk drive has a problem, and you want to check it for bad sectors, recover readable information, and fix errors. What command would you use?

    A. chkdsk d:

    B. chkdsk d: /f

    C. chkdsk d: /r

    D. Check Disk d:

6. A computer is slow, and the disk drive LED is constantly blinking. What can be done to improve the performance?

    A. Run chkdsk.

    B. Format the drive as NTFS.

    C. Shrink the volume.

    D. Run defrag.

Answers

1. **Correct Answer:** D

   A. **Incorrect:** FAT16 can't handle drives over 4 GB.

   B. **Incorrect:** You can create FAT32 volumes only as large as 32 GB.

   C. **Incorrect:** While FAT64 can handle a 1-TB drive, it isn't as efficient at handling clusters as NTFS.

   D. **Correct:** NTFS provides the best performance for large hard drives and also provides security.

2. **Correct Answer:** B

   A. **Incorrect:** You can create a mirrored volume on Windows 7 but not on Windows Vista or Windows XP.

   B. **Correct:** You can use Disk Management to create a mirrored volume on a Windows 7–based system.

   C. **Incorrect:** You can browse a mirrored volume with Windows Explorer, but you cannot create one.

   D. **Incorrect:** The convert command will convert a FAT-based system to NTFS.

3. **Correct Answer:** D

   A. **Incorrect:** Windows 7 can recognize FAT-based drives, so it isn't required to convert it to NTFS.

   B. **Incorrect:** Windows 7 can recognize basic disks, so it doesn't need to be converted to dynamic.

   C. **Incorrect:** If the disk is a dynamic disk, it will be recognized as foreign and must be imported.

   D. **Correct:** New disks need to be initialized within Disk Management if they aren't recognized.

4. **Correct Answer:** D

   A. **Incorrect:** The Disk Defragmenter can optimize a drive but cannot change the drive letter.

   B. **Incorrect:** The Device Manager is used to manage devices and drives but can't reassign drive letters.

   C. **Incorrect:** Windows Explorer accesses the drive but can't reassign drive letters.

   D. **Correct:** The Disk Management tool can change the drive letter of any disk drive.

5. **Correct Answer: C**

   A. Incorrect: Running chkdsk without a switch will check a drive, but it won't repair any errors.

   B. Incorrect: The /f switch will fix errors, but it does not recover readable information.

   C. Correct: The /r switch will locate bad sectors, recover readable information, and fix errors.

   D. Incorrect: Check Disk can be accessed from Windows Explorer, but it is not a command.

6. **Correct Answer: D**

   A. Incorrect: Chkdsk can detect and repair errors, but these symptoms indicate a fragmented hard drive.

   B. Incorrect: Formatting the drive will delete all the data.

   C. Incorrect: Shrinking a volume won't remove fragmentation.

   D. Correct: These symptoms indicate that the hard drive is fragmented, and defrag will defragment the hard drive.

CHAPTER 17

Troubleshooting Windows Operating Systems

One of the most valuable skills you'll need as a PC technician is the ability to troubleshoot Windows. You need to be able to look at the symptoms, identify the problem, and take steps to get Windows fully operational as quickly as possible. Some problems can be resolved quickly and easily by simply rebooting the system. Other problems can also be quickly resolved if you know what steps to take. This chapter includes many steps that you can use when troubleshooting a system and describes many of the common symptoms that require you to use those steps.

Exam 220-802 objectives in this chapter:

- 1.3 Given a scenario, use appropriate command line tools.
  - Recovery console
    - Fixboot
    - Fixmbr
- 1.4 Given a scenario, use appropriate operating system features and tools.
  - Administrative
    - Windows memory diagnostics
- 1.7 Perform preventive maintenance procedures using appropriate tools.
  - Common symptoms
    - Failure to boot
    - Drive not recognized
    - OS not found
  - Tools
    - Recovery image
- 4.3 Given a scenario, troubleshoot hard drives and RAID arrays with appropriate tools.
  - Tools
    - File recovery software

- 4.6 Given a scenario, troubleshoot operating system problems with appropriate tools.
  - Common symptoms
    - BSOD
    - Failure to boot
    - Improper shutdown
    - Spontaneous shutdown/restart
    - Device fails to start
    - Missing dll message
    - Services fails to start
    - Compatibility error
    - Slow system performance
    - Boots to safe mode
    - File fails to open
    - Missing NTLDR
    - Missing Boot.ini
    - Missing operating system
    - Missing Graphical Interface
    - Graphical Interface fails to load
    - Invalid boot disk
  - Tools
    - Fixboot
    - Recovery console
    - Fixmbr
    - Sfc
    - Repair disks
    - Pre-installation environments
    - MSCONFIG
    - DEFRAG
    - REGSVR32
    - REGEDIT
    - Event viewer
    - Safe mode
    - Command prompt
    - Emergency repair disk
    - Automated system recovery

- 4.7 Given a scenario, troubleshoot common security issues with appropriate tools and best practices.
  - Recovery console
  - Event Viewer

Understanding the Boot Process

When a computer starts, it goes through several stages before the Windows logon screen appears. If you understand these stages, you have a better chance of understanding the errors you'll see if any of these stages fail. The following sections describe these steps, including the differences between operating systems.

It's also worth repeating a common troubleshooting step mentioned in Chapter 10, "Working with Customers." Rebooting a system solves many ills, so it's common to try a reboot first. If the problem remains after rebooting, you need to take further steps to troubleshoot it.

Power On Self-Test (POST)

The computer loads information from Basic Input/Output System (BIOS) and completes basic hardware checks on the CPU, RAM, keyboard, and video. If this check fails, use the POST beep codes and displayed errors to identify the faulty hardware.

When POST completes successfully, it starts the bootstrap loader. Computers can boot from different devices, such as a hard drive, an optical disc, or a USB flash drive. The bootstrap loader is the last part of the BIOS programming that identifies where to look for a bootable operating system.

> **MORE INFO** **CHAPTER 2, "UNDERSTANDING MOTHERBOARDS AND BIOS"**
>
> Chapter 2 covers the BIOS and POST in more depth. The BIOS is a firmware program and allows you to configure the boot order of a computer.

Look For Master Boot Record and Boot Sector

The bootstrap loader looks for bootable media by using the boot order in the BIOS. When booting from a hard drive, it looks for a *master boot record (MBR)* and passes control to the MBR. Every MBR-based hard drive has a single MBR, and every partition on the hard drive has a single *boot sector*.

Figure 17-1 shows a single hard drive with three partitions. You might remember from Chapter 16, "Understanding Disks and File Systems," that a hard drive can have up to four primary partitions, with one partition marked as active. The active partition includes code within the boot sector that identifies the location of files used to start the operating system.

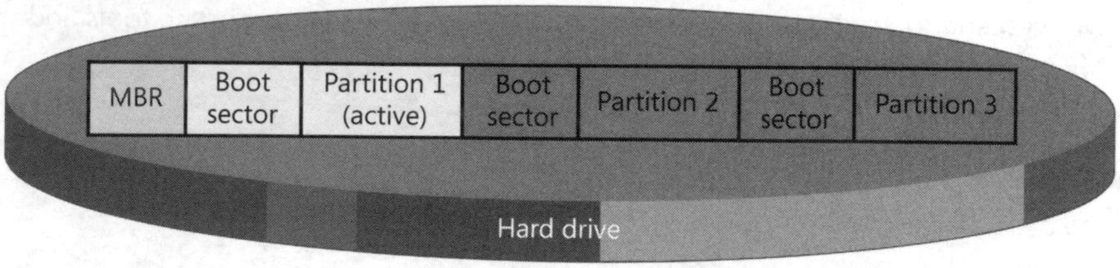

FIGURE 17-1 MBR and boot sectors on a hard disk.

The following steps show the boot process from a hard drive:

1. BIOS loads the master boot code from the MBR into memory.

2. The master boot code scans the partition table on the disk, looking for the active partition.

3. The contents of the active partition's boot sector are loaded into memory by the master boot code.

   A. On Windows XP, the NTLDR file is loaded.

   B. On Windows Vista and Windows 7, the boot manager (bootmgr) is loaded.

> **NOTE   ONLY HARD DISKS HAVE A MBR**
>
> Bootable media other than hard disks have a boot sector but do not have an MBR. For example, a floppy disk has only one partition, so it doesn't need an MBR to locate an active partition. Globally Unique Identifier (GUID) Partition Table (GPT)–based disks are supported on Windows Vista and Windows 7 for systems that use an Extensible Firmware Interface (EFI) instead of a traditional BIOS. The EFI includes an entry to start the bootmgr directly, without looking for an MBR.

Load System Boot Files on Windows XP

On Windows XP, the system boot files are located at the root of the active partition, which is typically C. They are hidden system files, so you won't see them by default. Following is a description of what each file does:

- **NTLDR.** This is a small program that loads the Windows operating system based on the contents of the Boot.ini file.

- **Boot.ini.** This text file identifies the disk, partition, and folder where Windows is located. On multiboot systems, it includes locations of different operating systems and specifies a default operating system.

- **Ntdetect.com.** NTLDR starts this to detect system hardware.

When NTLDR completes the initial load, it runs the ntoskrnl.exe program from the \Windows\System32 folder. This starts Windows XP.

Load Boot Manager on Windows Vista and Windows 7

You might remember from Chapter 12, "Installing and Updating Windows Operating Systems," that Windows Vista and Windows 7 usually create a 100-MB system partition when they are installed. This provides space for BitLocker to be enabled, includes the Windows Recovery Environment (RE), and is also used for system boot files.

The following system boot files are used on Windows Vista and Windows 7:

- **Boot manager (bootmgr) file.** This is a hidden system file located at the root of the system partition.

- **Boot configuration data (BCD).** The BCD is used instead of the Boot.ini file to identify the location of the operating system. On multiboot systems, it includes information for additional operating systems and a default operating system. It is located in the \boot folder of the system partition.

When the bootmgr completes the initial load, it runs Winload.exe from the \Windows \System32 folder. This starts Windows.

EXAM TIP

NTLDR, Ntdetect.com, Boot.ini, and Ntoskrnl.exe files are used only on Windows XP. On Windows Vista and Windows 7, bootmgr, BCD, and Winload.exe are used instead.

Understanding the Registry

The *registry* is a database used by Windows-based systems to store information about the computer's hardware, installed programs, system settings, and user profiles. When you make changes in Control Panel applets or through programs, these changes are often recorded in the registry and accessed by Windows.

Starting the Registry Editor

You can start the registry Editor with the *regedit* or *regedt32* command. In earlier operating systems, these two commands started different programs, but they both start the same registry editor in Windows XP, Windows Vista, and Windows 7.

On Windows XP, run the command from the command prompt or the Run line. On Windows Vista or Windows 7, run the command from the command prompt or from the Start, Search text box.

Hives, Keys, and Values

The registry is organized in five groups called *hives*. Each group includes settings called keys and values. The five hives are as follows:

- **HKEY_LOCAL_MACHINE (HKLM).** Settings that apply to the local computer are stored here.

- **HKEY_USERS (HKU).** These settings apply to all users.

- **HKEY_CURRENT_USER (HKCU).** These settings apply only to the user who is currently logged on.

- **HKEY_CURRENT_CONFIG (HKCC).** When the computer starts, it identifies and stores the current configuration here.

- **HKEY_CLASSES_ROOT (HKCR).** Data used by different software applications are stored here. For example, it includes file associations that associate specific file extensions with applications.

You can expand the hives to view the individual keys and subkeys. For example, Figure 17-2 shows the registry editor opened to a specific subkey. The five hives are in the left pane, with the HKEY_LOCAL_MACHINE hive expanded. You can double-click any value to open it, as shown with the SystemBIOSDate value and its data.

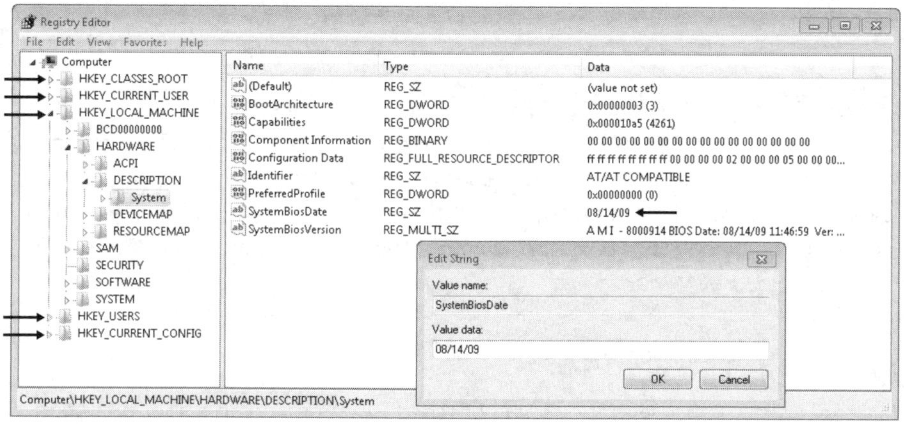

FIGURE 17-2 Viewing the registry editor.

This figure illustrates the differences between the hives, keys, and values, but you probably realize there are easier ways to identify the date of the BIOS. For example, using the msinfo32 command to start System Information shows this information in a more readable format.

If you want to look for a specific key or value, you can use the Find feature available in the Edit drop-down menu. First, select Computer to search the entire registry, or select a specific hive or key. Next, select Edit, Find, and enter your search term.

Back Up the Registry

You normally won't need to modify the registry directly, but as you advance in your IT career, you might encounter situations when it's necessary. It's important to realize that corruption in Windows can occur with an incorrect change, which can cause a system not to start. If you need to modify the registry back it up first and take your time when making the change.

You can use the following steps on Windows XP, Windows Vista, and Windows 7 to back up the registry:

1. Log on to the system by using an account with administrative privileges.

2. Start the registry editor with the regedit or regedt32 command from a command prompt or the Start, Search text box.

3. Right-click Computer and select Export.

4. Browse to the location where you want to store the backup, and type in a name for the backup. For example, you might choose to create a folder named RegBackup on the C drive and name the backup RegComputer. Click Save.

5. You can also back up any portion of the registry. For example, right-click HKEY_LOCAL_MACHINE and select Export.

6. Browse to the location where you want to store the backup, and type in a name for the backup. For example, you might choose to name the backup HKLM_Backup. Click Save.

Advanced Boot Options

Ideally, each time you start Windows, everything will work as planned and you'll be pointing and clicking in no time. Unfortunately, sometimes things go wrong. Windows has several troubleshooting tools available. Many of these tools are started from the Advanced Boot Options menu.

You can access the Advanced Boot Options page by pressing F8 during the boot process. Figure 17-3 shows what this looks like on a Windows 7–based system.

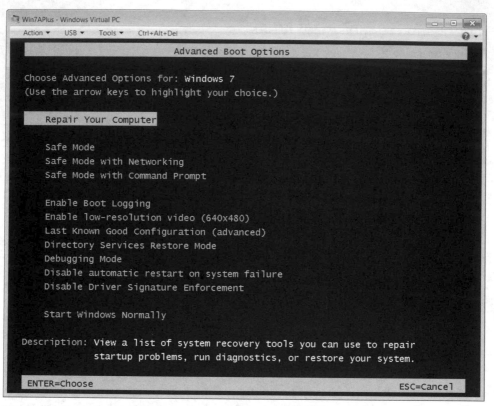

FIGURE 17-3 Access Advanced Boot Options page after pressing F8.

NOTE **TAP F8 REPEATEDLY**

Windows monitors the F8 key after BIOS finishes POST. If you aren't pressing the key, the system will boot into Windows and you'll have to restart to try again. There's nothing wrong with tapping the F8 key repeatedly as the computer starts. The worst that can happen is a Keyboard Error if POST interprets your tapping as a stuck key on the keyboard.

The following sections describe the options available from this menu. The options are the same on Windows Vista and Windows 7, but the following menu options do not appear on the Windows XP menu:

- Repair Your Computer
- Disable Automatic Restart On System Failure
- Disable Driver Signature Enforcement

Safe Modes

Occasionally, a change to Windows prevents it from starting normally. For example, after installing a hardware driver or updating software, the system might not be able to reboot successfully. You can use one of the safe modes to start Windows with only the basics and avoid loading the faulty driver or software.

There are three different versions of safe mode, as follows:

- **Safe mode.** This is the most basic version.
- **Safe mode with networking.** This mode includes network drivers and services needed to access network resources. Use it if you need to access the Internet from safe mode to download updates or other files.
- **Safe mode with command prompt.** Instead of the normal graphical user interface (GUI) used in Windows, it loads only the command prompt.

NOTE SAFE MODE HAS A BLACK DESKTOP

You'll know when you're booted into safe mode because the screen will be black and the words "safe mode" will be in white letters at the four corners of the display.

You can perform most recovery options within safe mode just like during normal operations. These functions include the following:

- Applying restore points by using System Restore.
- Rolling back drivers by using Device Manager.
- Restoring an image by using System Image Recovery, if a system image is available.

MORE INFO CHAPTER 15, "CONFIGURING WINDOWS OPERATING SYSTEMS"

Chapter 15 covers System Restore, restore points, Device Manager, and image backups.

Enable Boot Logging

If a system has a corrupted driver or service, it might prevent Windows from starting. You'll see Windows start, but before it finishes, it restarts. One method of identifying the problem is to enable boot logging from the Advanced Boot Options menu. When enabled, it logs activity from the startup process into a file named Ntbtlog.txt, located in the C:\Windows folder.

After enabling boot logging, try to start the system again. It will record the steps in the log, up to where Windows fails. After it fails, press F8 to access the Advanced Boot Options menu and select safe mode. It will append this log with the steps used to boot into safe mode, starting with a time stamp. You can view the log by using one of the following methods:

- Browse to C:\Windows and double-click the Ntbtlog.txt file.
- Open a command prompt and enter the following command:

```
notepad c:\windows\ntbtlog.txt
```

Sometimes the problem is related to something that loaded in the regular boot cycle but did not load in safe mode. Look for entries towards the end of the regular boot cycle starting with "Loaded driver" but listed as "Did not load driver" in the safe mode cycle. One of these drivers is likely the reason why Windows is failing.

Enable Low-Resolution Video

This can be useful if the current video driver is configured incorrectly. Imagine the following scenario. You just changed the display settings and clicked Keep Changes to confirm that you want to make the changes permanent. Suddenly, the video card blanks out because it can no longer display the video with these changes.

The solution is to reconfigure the Display settings, but you can't see the screen to access them. If you boot into safe mode, it uses the basic video driver and you wouldn't be able to modify the settings for the regular video driver, so safe mode won't help.

If you select Enable Low-Resolution Video and restart, it will use the current video driver but with the most basic settings. You can then modify the settings and restart the system.

> **NOTE** **ENABLE VGA MODE IN WINDOWS XP**
> The Enable Low-Resolution Video menu choice is named Enable VGA Mode in the Windows XP Advanced Boot Options menu but works the same as Enable Low-Resolution Video.

Last Known Good Configuration

The Last Known Good Configuration choice is a valuable option that allows you to easily revert changes from a previously logged on session. It's easier to understand how the last known good configuration can help you if you first understand how Windows records system settings.

Control Sets in the Registry

Windows considers a boot successful when a user logs on. Immediately after a user logs on, it copies the machine's system settings into an area of the registry known as a control set. Figure 17-4 shows the different control sets available in a Windows 7–based system.

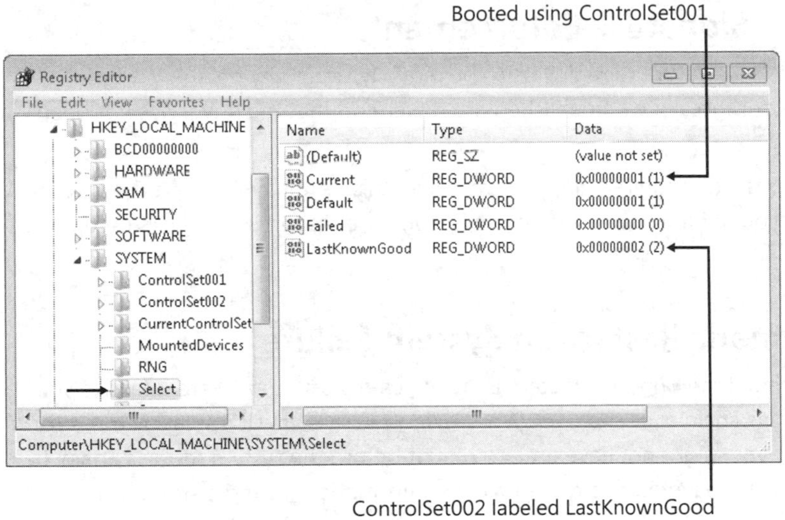

Booted using ControlSet001

ControlSet002 labeled LastKnownGood

FIGURE 17-4 Viewing control sets in the registry.

The system is started by using the settings from ControlSet001. Immediately after the user logs on, it copies these settings to ControlSet002 and labels ControlSet002 as LastKnownGood. While the user is logged on, system changes are applied to ControlSet001 but the known good settings in ControlSet002 are retained.

Using Last Known Good Configuration

Imagine that a user updated a graphics card driver and restarted the system. When the system starts, the graphics card driver is loaded and it crashes the system. Because the system can't start, the user hasn't logged on and the last known good settings are retained.

You can restart the system and press F8 to access the Advanced Boot Options menu. From this menu, select Last Known Good Configuration. This will restore the settings prior to the addition of the new graphics driver, and the system can now start.

EXAM TIP

The most important point to remember about using Last Known Good Configuration is that it can be used only before a user has logged on. If a user logs on again after making a change, the system creates a new last known good configuration that includes the change.

What if you were able to log on but you were having problems because of a recently updated driver? How could you resolve this problem? You can't use Last Known Good Configuration, but you can boot into safe mode and use Device Manager to roll back the driver. Chapter 15 covers the Device Manager and shows how to do this.

Disable Driver Signature Enforcement

Windows Vista and Windows 7 require drivers to be digitally signed by default. A digital signature provides assurances of who published the driver and that the driver has not been modified.

If you need to bypass this requirement, you can select this option and restart the system. A primary reason that you might choose this option is if you are testing new drivers before they have been finalized.

Disable Automatic Restart on System Failure

You can use this setting if the Windows system is stuck in a restart loop where it fails to start, tries to restart, and fails again over and over. When Windows fails, it will display a stop error on a blue screen, but you might not have time to read it before the system restarts again. If you use this setting, you'll have time to read the error information from the stop error.

Other Advanced Boot Options

The following options on the Advanced Boot Options page are rarely used:

- **Directory Services Restore Mode.** You use this only on Windows Servers that are configured as domain controllers. They run Active Directory Domain Services, but a Windows 7–based system cannot be a domain controller.
- **Debugging Mode.** This is an advanced troubleshooting mode used to troubleshoot advanced software problems.

Repair Your Computer

The Repair Your Computer option starts the *Windows Recovery Environment (Windows RE)* and provides you with a list of additional tools you can use to troubleshoot and repair problems. This is especially useful if you find that you can't boot into safe mode.

NOTE **WINDOWS RE FROM WINDOWS INSTALLATION DVD**

The Repair Your Computer option is available only if the tools were installed on your hard disk. By default, these are included in Windows 7 installations but not Windows Vista installations. You can access the same tools from many Windows installation DVDs: boot to the DVD, and select Repair Your Computer. You can also create a system repair disc by using steps later in this chapter to boot directly into the Windows RE from a CD or DVD.

When you select this option, you'll be prompted to select a keyboard language and then you'll need to log on with a local account. If you use an administrative account, the options will include the command prompt, as shown in Figure 17-5.

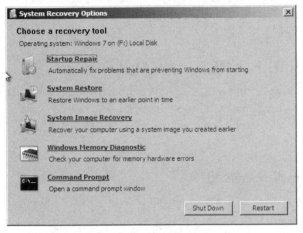

FIGURE 17-5 Using System Recovery Options.

- **Startup Repair.** This option runs a series of checks and attempts to repair problems automatically. If your system is a multiboot system, you'll need to select the operating system you want to repair. It will prompt you for confirmation before it tries to fix problems.

- **System Restore.** This option allows you to apply a restore point, similarly to how you can apply a restore point from within Windows or within safe mode.

- **System Image Recovery.** If you have created a system image, you can use this to restore it. This menu item is called Windows Complete PC Restore on Windows Vista-based systems.

- **Windows Memory Diagnostic.** Use this option to run thorough checks of the random access memory (RAM). It will open the same diagnostic tool that you can start from within Windows.

> **MORE INFO** **CHAPTER 3, "UNDERSTANDING RAM AND CPUS"**
>
> Chapter 3 covers the Windows Memory Diagnostic tool. The Event Viewer section in this chapter shows how to view the results of the Windows Memory Diagnostic in the System log.

- **Command Prompt.** This provides access to a Windows RE Command Prompt. It includes commands such as bootrec and bcdedit, but it doesn't include all normal command prompt commands.

The System Repair option will resolve the majority of problems on Windows Vista and Windows 7 with very little user interaction. Other problems affecting the MBR, boot sector, or BCD can be repaired by using the Windows RE Command Prompt.

Recovery Console and Windows RE Command Prompt

The *recovery console* is available in Windows XP and is used to run commands that can repair problems with the MBR, boot sector, and Boot.ini files. It's replaced by the Windows RE Command Prompt in Windows Vista and Windows 7. This section shows how to install and use the recovery console in Windows XP.

Install the Recovery Console in Windows XP

The recovery console is not available by default in Windows XP, but you can install it with the following steps:

1. Boot into Windows XP.

2. Insert the Windows XP installation CD into an optical drive, and identify the drive letter assigned to the drive.

3. Start a command prompt, and enter the following command using the drive letter assigned to the CD. The example assumes the letter D was assigned.

   d:\i386\winnt32.exe /cmdcons

4. You'll see a dialog box asking whether you want to install the recovery console. Click Yes.

5. When the installation completes, click OK.

When you restart the system, you'll see Microsoft Windows Recovery Console listed as another boot option. You can select it just as you'd select any operating system in a dual-boot system.

Using the Recovery Console on Windows XP

When you start a system with the Recovery Console installed, it shows a multiboot menu similar to the screen on the left in Figure 17-6. You can also start the recovery console from the installation CD. Boot to the CD and press R when the Welcome screen appears.

FIGURE 17-6 Starting the Recovery Console.

The system searches the computer, looking for operating systems, and will prompt you to select the operating system you want to repair. You'll then be prompted to enter the administrator's password for this operating system. You'll end up with a blinking cursor after C:\WINDOWS>, similar to the screen to the left in Figure 17-6, waiting for you to enter a command.

You should understand the following three important commands:

- **fixboot**—Writes a new boot sector on the system partition
- **fixmbr**—Repairs the master boot record (MBR)
- **bootcfg /rebuild**—Rebuilds the Boot.ini file

> **NOTE** **RECOVERY CONSOLE IS DIFFERENT FROM THE COMMAND PROMPT**
>
> The Recovery Console prompt looks similar to the command prompt window, but it's not the same. You can enter the **help** command to get a list of all supported commands, or you can use the *command* **/?** format to get help with individual commands.

Bootrec Commands on Windows Vista and Windows 7

The Windows XP Recovery Console and its commands are not available on Windows Vista or Windows 7. However, you can access similar commands from the System Recovery Options command prompt. The most important command for recovery is the *bootrec* (boot recovery) command.

You can execute bootrec with the following key switches:

- **bootrec /fixmbr.** This repairs the MBR.
- **bootrec /fixboot.** This writes a new boot sector onto the system partition. It is useful if an earlier version has been installed after installing Windows Vista or Windows 7. For example, if you install Windows XP after installing Windows 7, it corrupts the Windows 7 boot sector, but this command repairs it.
- **bootrec /rebuildbcd.** This rebuilds the BCD file on the computer. It forces a full scan of disks to locate bootable operating systems and re-creates the BCD file similarly to how bootcfg /rebuild re-creates the Boot.ini file on Windows XP.
- **bootrec /scanos**. This scans a system, looking for operating systems on the computer.

EXAM TIP

The fixboot and fixmbr commands are useful if a virus has damaged the MBR or boot sector on a Windows XP-based system. The bootrec /fixboot and bootrec/ fixmbr commands can repair similar problems on Windows Vista-based and Windows 7–based systems.

Msconfig and Advanced Boot Options

The System Configuration (covered in Chapter 15) is a valuable tool that you can use to iden-tify and troubleshoot problems. It is commonly started with the msconfig command and can also be accessed from the Administrative Tools menu in the Control Panel.

Figure 17-7 shows System Configuration open with the Boot tab selected. You can use this tab to force a system to boot into one of the safe modes without accessing the Advanced Boot Options menu.

![System Configuration dialog box showing the Boot tab with boot options including Safe boot, Minimal, Alternate shell, Active Directory repair, Network, No GUI boot, Boot log, Base video, OS boot information, and Timeout settings.]

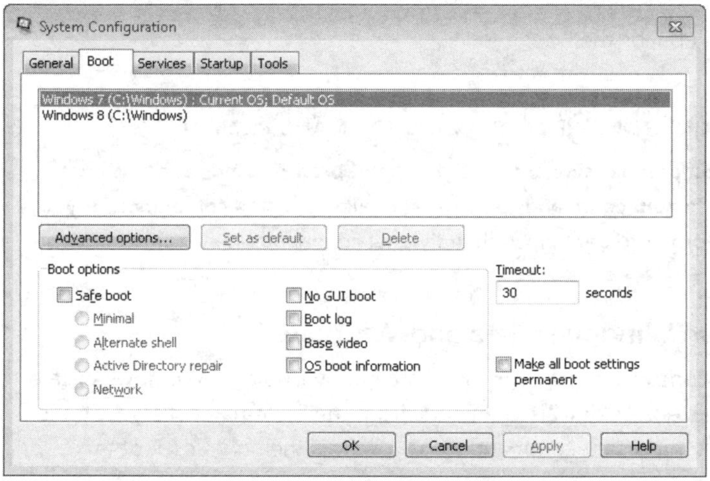

FIGURE 17-7 Accessing safe mode options from msconfig.

EXAM TIP

If you use msconfig to boot into one of the safe modes, the system will continue to boot into that safe mode until the setting is changed back. In contrast, if you use F8 and Advanced Boot Options to select a safe mode, it will start normally when you restart the system.

Most of the following selections in the Boot Options area of the Boot tab directly relate to menu items in the Advanced Boot Options menu:

- Safe Boot Minimal is the same as Safe Mode.
- Safe Boot Alternate Shell is the same as Safe Mode With Command Prompt.
- Safe Boot Active Directory Repair is the same as Directory Services Restore Mode.
- Safe Boot Network is the same as Safe Mode With Networking.
- No GUI Boot starts Windows without displaying the Windows Welcome screen. This option is not available from the Advanced Boot Options menu.
- Boot Log is the same as Enable Boot Logging.
- Base Video is the same as Enable Low-Resolution Video.

- OS Boot Information displays driver names as they are being loaded during the startup process. It shows the same information that is logged in the Ntbtlog.txt file if Boot Log or Enable Boot Logging is selected.

Startup and Recovery Options

You can manipulate some startup and recovery settings by using the advanced options available from the System applet. These settings allow you to manipulate how a system boots and to change the default behavior after a system failure.

Figure 17-8 shows the Startup And Recovery page on a Windows 7–based system. The page looks very similar on Windows XP and Windows Vista. Windows 7 is selected as the Default Operating System, and it will boot into Windows 7 after a delay of 30 seconds. If the computer is a multiboot system, you can click the down arrow to the right of Windows 7 and select a different operating system as the default.

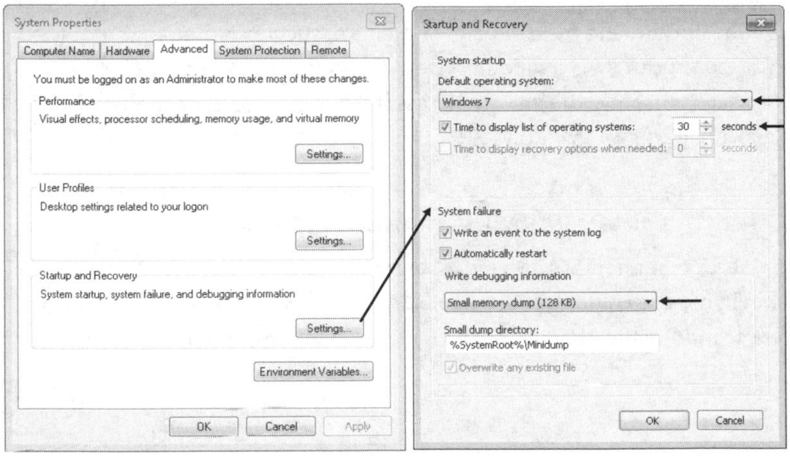

FIGURE 17-8 Startup And Recovery Options.

You can access this page by clicking Start, Control Panel, and selecting System. If necessary, change the view in the Control Panel to Classic View or Large icons, depending on the system you're using. On Windows XP, select the Advanced tab. On Windows Vista and Windows 7, select Advanced System Settings. You can then click the Settings button in the Startup And Recovery section.

The System Failure section identifies how Windows responds if Windows encounters a stop failure (also known as a blue screen). By default, it writes an event into the System log and will automatically restart after displaying the error.

It's also configured to write the contents of memory into a file that can be used for advanced troubleshooting. By default, this is set to Kernel Memory Dump, and it will create a large dump file named Memory.dmp. In Figure 17-8, it's changed to Small Memory Dump (256), and it will create a file named Minidump.

The benefit of the Minidump file is that you can read the contents with an advanced utility called Dumpchk.exe. Dumpchk.exe won't work with the large Kernel Memory Dump file, but more advanced forensics tools can read it.

> **MORE INFO** **DUMPCHK AVAILABLE ON MICROSOFT'S TECHNET SITE**
>
> The dumpchk utility is beyond the scope of A+, but if you want to dig into it, you can check out *http://technet.microsoft.com/library/ee424340* for more information.

Startup Options and the Boot.ini File

The Boot.ini text file provides the information needed to locate and start Windows XP. If you modify the Boot Options by using msconfig to force a system to go into safe mode, it modifies the Boot.ini file. Also, if you modify the System Startup settings from the Startup And Recovery page, it modifies the Boot.ini file.

You can also modify the Boot.ini file by using any text editor, such as Notepad, but it is a lot easier to use the GUI tools. Boot.ini is a hidden system file located at the root of the system partition, so you'll need to modify the view to access it. You can also click the Edit button on the Startup And Recovery page for Windows XP.

> **MORE INFO** **CHAPTER 13, "USING WINDOWS OPERATING SYSTEMS"**
>
> The "Folder Options" section in Chapter 13 includes steps you can use to change Windows Explorer views by modifying the Folder Options applet. Microsoft's knowledge base article 289022 includes steps to modify the Boot.ini file and is available at *http://support.microsoft.com/kb/289022*.

Startup Options and Boot Configuration Data

The boot configuration data (BCD) is used instead of the Boot.ini file on Windows Vista and Windows 7, and it is more than a simple text file. However, when you make modifications by using msconfig or the Startup And Recovery options, these changes are written to the BCD similar to how they are written to the Boot.ini file.

You can't access the BCD file with Notepad, but you can modify it with the bcdedit command. The details of the bcdedit command are beyond the scope of the A+ exam, but if you want to dig into it, check out the following page: *http://technet.microsoft.com/library/cc731662*.

The bootrec command and its switches are important for the A+ exam. You should know the key switches of the bootrec command described earlier.

Windows Troubleshooting Tools

The Advanced Boot Options and recovery console tools are effective when a system won't start. However, the system can often start while it still has other problems. The following sections describe some common troubleshooting tools you can use within Windows to resolve these problems.

Event Viewer

Windows regularly logs events into different logs, and you can use the Event Viewer to view them. Event Viewer was significantly enhanced in Windows Vista and Windows 7, but the core functionality available in the Windows XP Event Viewer is the same. For example, you'll find the following three Windows logs in each system:

- **System log.** Contains events logged by the Windows operating system. This includes events when a service is started or stopped or when a driver fails to load. These events are predetermined by the operating system.

- **Application log.** Contains events logged by applications or programs. For example, a third-party antivirus application can log when a virus is discovered or when a virus scan is started or stopped. Application developers choose which events to log.

- **Security log.** Contains security-related events. This includes when someone fails to log on due to an incorrect password or when someone accesses or deletes a file. Administrators choose which events to log.

EXAM TIP

Many errors are reported to users via a dialog box or a balloon type message in the bottom-right corner of the screen. If the user reports a message like this but doesn't remember what it says, you can go into the Event Viewer to open the message and get the details.

Starting Event Viewer

You can start the Event Viewer from the Administrative Tools group in the Control Panel or with the eventvwr.msc command. Figure 17-9 shows the Event Viewer in Windows 7 with a few items highlighted. You can see that the Windows Logs are expanded, showing the different logs.

The System log is selected, and the center pane shows the System log events with an error event selected. By default, the events are organized chronologically, but you can reorganize the display with a single click.

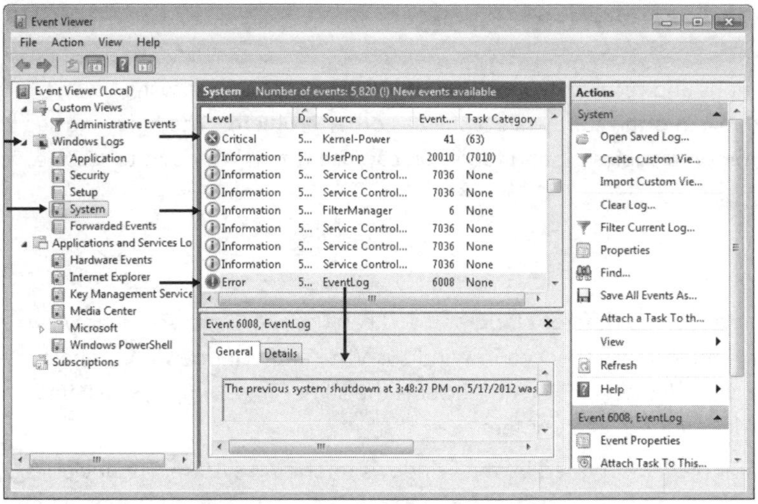

FIGURE 17-9 Event Viewer.

For example, if you click the Level heading, it will reorganize the display in alphabetical order, with Critical events first, then Error events, and so on. Click the Level heading again and it organizes them in reverse alphabetical order. Similarly, if you click the Event ID column, it will reorganize the events in Event ID order. This is valuable when you're looking for a specific event.

When you run Windows Memory Diagnostics from the System Recovery Options menu in Windows 7, it runs the diagnostics and then restarts. If you're not sitting in front of the computer when it ends, you won't see the results. However, it logs Event ID 1201 in the System log, with a source of MemoryDiagnostics-Results.

After the system reboots, you can open Event Viewer, select the System log, and find this event. If should be close to the top, but you can click the Event ID column to reorder the display and easily find Event ID 1201.

You can also search for a specific event. With the log selected, click Find on the Action drop-down menu. Enter **1201** or **MemoryDiagnostics-Results** in the text box, and click Find Next.

> **NOTE** **EVENT IDS HAVE CHANGED**
>
> Event IDs have the same number in different operating systems but have different meanings. For example, Event ID 1201 refers to a DNS server configuration issue on Windows Server 2008, but it is used for memory diagnostic results in Windows 7.

Viewing Events in Event Viewer

You can double-click any event to open and see all of the event information. Events are coded with the following error levels so that you can easily identify the serious events:

- **Information** events indicate a change or an activity on the system but do not indicate a problem. They are represented with a small blue *i* within a white circle.

- **Warning** events can impact the operation of the system or result in a more serious problem if action is not taken. They are identified with a black exclamation mark (!) in a yellow triangle.

- **Error** events indicate that a problem has occurred. The problem can impact the functionality of an application or the operating system. They are represented with a white *X* inside a red circle on Windows XP. On Windows Vista and Windows 7, they are represented with a white exclamation mark in a red circle.

- **Critical** events are the most serious and can be seen on Windows Vista-based and Windows 7–based systems. They record failures from an application or the operating system and indicate that the system can't automatically recover from the event. They often result in a stop error or a system reboot. They use a white *X* inside a red circle.

- **Audit** events are recorded in the security log. For example, if someone successfully logs on or fails to log on, the event is logged as a successful audit or a failure audit. These events are identified with a key icon.

Log Properties

Event logs are configured as circular logs by default. That is, they will write data into the log until they reach a maximum size. New events will overwrite older events. You can right-click over any log and select Properties to set the maximum size of the log and select one of the following settings:

- Overwrite Events As Needed (Oldest Events First)
- Archive The Log When Full, Do Not Overwrite Events
- Do Not Overwrite Events (Clear Logs Manually)

EXAM TIP

If the log is configured so that events are not overwritten, it will fill up if it isn't cleared. When full, it will regularly display errors indicating that it is full. You can right-click the log in Event Viewer and select Clear Log to clear it.

Recovery Images

Some Windows tools allow you to create full images of the operating system, all the applications, and the user's data. The following tools are available in Windows:

- Windows Complete PC Backup And Restore, available from the Backup And Restore center on Windows Vista.
- Create A System Image, available from the Backup And Restore applet on Windows 7.

Similarly, there are some third-party tools that provide this capability. If a system fails, you can restore the image and you'll have a fully functioning system with all the applications and the user data up to the moment of the last image save.

This is different than using images to deploy a new installation. A new installation does not include the user's data, but a recovery image from the operating system includes everything. Many computer manufacturers include a recovery partition with the computer. This does not include any data but can be used to restore the system to the state in which it was when the computer was new.

> **MORE INFO** **CHAPTER 15 AND CHAPTER 16**
>
> Chapter 15 shows how to start the backup tools in Windows Vista and Windows 7 and explains the differences between these tools. Chapter 16 discusses recovery partitions.

File Recovery Software

If a computer develops a problem, it's important to consider the user data. If possible, back up the user's data before performing a repair. There are times when you can't easily access the data, but there are some tools available just for this purpose.

For example, if a user accidentally deleted a file, you might be able to restore it from the Recycle Bin. Open the Recycle Bin from the desktop and locate the file. Right-click the file, select Restore, and the file will be restored to the original location.

If the Recycle Bin has been emptied or if the disk is damaged, you might be able to restore data by using third-party recovery tools. Some of these tools are dedicated specifically for file recovery. Other tools are designed for forensic analysis and can often recover more data than regular file recovery tools. Good tools have a cost, but when critical data needs to be recovered, the cost of the tool is minimal.

The best solution is to regularly maintain backups of data. Then, if critical data is lost, it's a simple matter to restore it.

Automated System Recovery

Automated System Recovery (ASR) is a recovery option available in Windows XP. It is intended as a last resort after trying Last Known Good Configuration, rolling back drivers, reverting to previous restore points, and troubleshooting in safe mode.

ASR includes two steps: ASR backup and ASR restore. ASR backup creates a copy of key files, and if you have an ASR backup, you can use ASR restore to recover from a catastrophic failure.

You can create an ASR backup from the Windows XP backup utility. Start Backup by clicking Start, Accessories, System Tools, and selecting Backup. When the Welcome screen appears, click Advanced Mode, and select Automated System Recovery Wizard.

When you create an ASR backup, it backs up operating system files on the system partition along with system information from other partitions that include operating system components. It does not back up user data. The primary backup is large, but ASR backup also creates an ASR floppy disk that holds a small file identifying information on the ASR backup.

If you need to use the backup, ensure that you have the original ASR backup file available, the ASR floppy, and the Windows XP installation CD. Insert the Windows XP installation CD, and reboot the system. When it starts the text mode section of startup, press F2. You'll be prompted to insert the ASR floppy disk, and a wizard will lead you through the process.

> **MORE INFO** **KB ARTICLE 818903 AND MICROSOFT TECHNET**
>
> You can read more about ASR in Microsoft Knowledge Base article 818903 (*http://support.microsoft.com/kb/818903*) and in the Microsoft TechNet article at *http://technet.microsoft.com/library/bb456980*. It isn't used very often on desktop systems due to the amount of work required to keep the backup up-to-date.

Emergency Repair Disk

The CompTIA objectives specifically mention the emergency repair disk (ERD) as an available tool. This was used with Windows 2000 and earlier operating systems for recovery, but Windows XP uses Automated System Recovery instead.

System Repair Disc

An important tool you'll use to repair Windows Vista-based and Windows 7–based systems is the Windows RE. Normally, you would access the Windows RE by selecting Repair Your Computer from the Advanced Boot Options on Windows 7 and Windows Vista, but what do you do if you can't access this menu?

One solution is to create a System Repair disk. This is a bootable CD or DVD that will boot you directly into the Windows RE.

If you have a working Windows 7–based system, you can create it from the Backup And Restore Center in the Control Panel. Insert a blank disc into a CD or DVD burner, and click Create A System Repair Disc. It's a short wizard, and you'll then have a system repair disc that you can use on both Windows Vista-based and Windows 7–based systems.

Another option is to boot using an installation DVD and select Repair Your Computer. This option is available on Windows Vista installation DVDs, but it is not available on all Windows 7 DVDs.

Troubleshooting Applet

The Troubleshooting applet is available in Windows 7–based systems from the Control Panel. You can access it by changing the Control Panel display to Large icons and selecting Troubleshooting.

This applet includes links to several different troubleshooters available in Windows 7, as shown in Figure 17-10. Each troubleshooter is a software wizard that checks for common issues and can often resolve them with little user interaction.

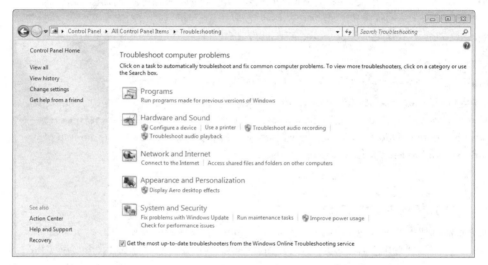

FIGURE 17-10 Troubleshooting applet in Control Panel.

Click any of the links to start the troubleshooter, read the information, and click Next to run it. After a moment, it will usually display a screen indicating that troubleshooting has completed. Occasionally, it will prompt you with information about a problem it has discovered and ask for confirmation to repair it.

The Troubleshooter completion screen includes a View Detailed Information link. If you click it, it opens a report showing all the items that were checked and the results of the check.

Common Symptoms and Their Solutions

This section lists many of the symptoms you might see when troubleshooting Windows. It also includes steps that you can take to resolve many of these common problems.

BSOD

BSOD is short for *blue screen of death*, but the name is much more dramatic than the reality. The computer is not dead. If Windows encounters a critical problem that it can't resolve, it stops and shows a blue screen with the error. If you read the error, you'll get some insight into the problem and be able to resolve it.

Stop errors start with 0x (read as hex or hexadecimal) followed by a string of zeros and a number. For example, the stop error of 0x0000007B (read as hex 7B) includes the text "inaccessible boot device" and indicates a problem with a hard drive.

There are many reasons why you'd get a 7B error, but the important point is that you now have information you can use to troubleshoot the system. An end user might say, "My system crashed," and never read the error. The problem could be due to just about anything.

A knowledgeable PC technician reads the error and investigates from there. For example, you could use Bing.com and search "0x0000007B" or "inaccessible boot device." You might find that a knowledge base article describes your problem perfectly and includes an easy-to-follow solution.

Failure to Boot

If you're unable to boot a system, you can use the following task list to help you repair it:

- **Restart.** Sometimes the failure is a fluke, and restarting resolves the problem.
- **Read the error.** If an error message is displayed, read it. It has some important clues.
- **Last Known Good Configuration.** If you recently changed hardware or hardware drivers and you haven't logged on since, try Last Known Good Configuration from the Advanced Boot Options menu.
- **Startup Repair.** On Windows Vista and Windows 7, try the Startup Repair option from the System Recovery Options.
- **Safe mode.** Boot into safe mode, and perform different repairs:
    - Run antivirus software from within safe mode.
    - Run System Restore to apply a previous restore point.
    - Verify system files with the sfc /scannow tool.
- **Fix the boot sector or MBR.** Use the appropriate Windows tools to repair potential boot sector or MBR problems.

- **Restore the system from an image.** If you have an image, restore the system with the image after recovering user data.

> **MORE INFO** **CHAPTER 26**
>
> Some problems are caused by viruses or other types of malware. A solution is to run up-to-date antivirus software on the system to remove it. You can do so while booted normally or in safe mode. Chapter 26 provides more details about how to detect and remove malware.

Fix Boot Sector and MBR on Windows XP

If you need to repair the boot sector and/or the MBR on a Windows XP-based system, use the following steps:

1. Start the recovery console.

2. Enter the following command to repair the boot sector:

   ```
   fixboot
   ```

3. Enter the following command to repair the MBR:

   ```
   fixmbr
   ```

Fix Boot Sector and MBR on Windows Vista and Windows 7

If you need to repair the boot sector and/or the MBR on a Windows Vista-based or Windows 7–based system, use the following steps:

1. Start the Windows RE Command Prompt.

   A. Start the computer, and press F8 to access the Advanced Boot Options.

   B. Select Repair Your Computer to access the System Recovery Options.

   C. Select Command Prompt to access the Windows RE Command Prompt.

2. Enter the following command to repair the boot sector:

   ```
   bootrec /fixboot
   ```

3. Enter the following command to repair the MBR:

   ```
   bootrec /fixmbr
   ```

Rebuild BCD in Windows Vista and Windows 7

If you need to rebuild the BCD on a Windows Vista-based or Windows 7–based system, you can use the following steps:

1. Start the Windows RE Command Prompt.

2. Enter the following commands to rebuild the BCD:

```
bcdedit /export C:\backup_bcd
c:
cd boot
attrib bcd -s -h -r
ren c:\boot\bcd bcd.old
bootrec /rebuildbcd
```

The Windows RE boots you into the hidden 100-MB system partition, and it is identified as C within Windows RE. The BCD file is in the boot folder of this partition. Following is a description of what each of the preceding commands does:

- bcdedit /export creates a backup of the current BCD. This is useful if you later need to import data from it.

- attrib removes the system, hidden, and read-only attributes of the BCD file so that it can be renamed.

- ren renames the file as Bcd.old. This is useful if you need the original file later.

- bootrec /rebuildbcd creates a new BCD for the system.

> **MORE INFO** **KB ARTICLE 927392 AND CHAPTER 14, "USING THE COMMAND PROMPT"**
>
> For more information about the bootrec tool, check out knowledge base article 927392 at *http://support.microsoft.com/kb/927392*. Chapter 14 covers command prompt commands such as cd, attrib, and ren.

Improper Shutdown

Ideally, Windows should be shut down logically by clicking Start, Turn Off Your Computer, or by clicking Start, Shut Down, depending on the operating system. This gives Windows time to logically close files and processes. However, if the system suddenly loses power, Windows doesn't have time to clean things up.

When the system is restarted from an improper shutdown, you'll see an error message. You can often ignore the error and continue to restart the system. However, if it won't restart, follow the procedures in the "Failure to Boot" section.

Spontaneous Shutdown or Restart

There are a few reasons why Windows might stop or restart without giving you any warning. If it happens once, you can ignore it. However, if it happens more than once, you need to do some troubleshooting. The following are possible causes and solutions:

- **Infected computer.** Run antivirus software to check it. You might need to run sfc /scannow to repair system files.

- **Faulty RAM.** Run memory diagnostics to check the RAM.

- **Faulty power supply.** Check the voltages on the power supply to ensure that they are within tolerance, as mentioned in Chapter 1, "Introduction to Computers."

Device Fails to Start

If a single device fails to start, it's almost always due to a problem with the device driver. You can check the System log in Event Viewer to see whether it provides you with any error messages and use the Device Manager to check or update the driver. Chapter 15 provides details about how to resolve problems with device drivers by using the Device Manager.

Missing DLL Message

Windows systems use *dynamic link libraries (DLLs)* as reusable code. A DLL includes code for multiple programming tasks and can be used in different applications. All DLLs have an extension of .dll.

For example, a programmer can create code to identify the square root of a number. The code accepts a number as an input and provides the square root of the number as an output. The programmer could use the code in 50 different applications, but instead of re-creating the code each time, it is placed in a DLL and referenced from there. Each of these 50 applications can reference the same DLL.

Windows includes a wealth of DLLs, and third-party applications also use them. If Windows or an application tries to access a DLL and it is corrupted or missing, you might see a missing DLL error. These errors include the phrase "A required .DLL file (name.dll) could not be found." If this is due to a missing system DLL, you can use the system file checker (sfc) tool to scan and repair the system.

> **MORE INFO**   **CHAPTER 14, "USING THE COMMAND PROMPT"**
>
> Chapter 14 includes information about sfc, including steps to run it. The sfc /scannow command will scan all protected system files, including system DLLs, and attempt to repair them. You can also use the sfc /scanfile command to repair a specific DLL.

If you see the error when you run an application, it's possible that the DLL is specific to the application. In this case, reinstall the application or use System Restore to revert your system to a restore point before the problem occurred.

Registering a DLL with Regsvr32

Sometimes you might need to register a DLL with the operating system so that it can use it. This is normally done automatically when an application is installed, but there are times when it is done manually. You can use the *regsvr32.exe* command to register and unregister DLLs manually. For example, if the DLL is named Success.dll, you can use the following commands to register or unregister it:

```
regsvr32 success.dll
```

```
regsvr32 /u success.dll
```

> **NOTE REGSVR32 IS NOT THE SAME AS REGSRV3**
>
> This command is frequently misspelled, so if you find the command isn't working, double-check the spelling. It is spelled as regsvr32.

Beware of Malware

A common response to a missing DLL error is to search on the Internet for a solution, but this can be dangerous. Many sites have infected files with the same or similar file name as a legitimate file. Criminals then use a variety of different methods to trick you into installing them. Users who download and install them might be giving up control of their computers or granting access to their bank accounts.

For example, users visiting a website could see an error pop up saying, "A required .DLL file (regsvr32.dll) could not be found." It could include a link to download the file and repair the problem. The truth is that there is no file named Regsvr32.dll (although there is a file named Regsvr32.exe). When users download and install this bogus file, they install malware and give a criminal access to their computers.

Similarly, the Kernel32.dll file is a legitimate Windows-based system file. Malware files named Kernel32.exe or Kernell32.exe (with an extra "L") are known malware, mimicking the legitimate file.

Some criminals host websites advertised as free DLL download sites where you can easily find missing DLLs. They actually host malware programs that look like legitimate DLLs. From a criminal's perspective, advertising a site as a free DLL download site is more successful than advertising it as a location hosting malware.

EXAM TIP

If you need to restore system DLLs, use the sfc /scannow command. Downloading and installing system DLLs from the Internet is not recommended.

Service Fails to Start

If a service fails to start, it will affect all the functions of the service. A good place to check is the System log in the Event Viewer. It will include log entries stating that the service failed to start and often includes hints about why.

Another good place to check is the Services applet covered in Chapter 13. Verify that the Startup Type is not set to Disabled, preventing the service from starting. Additionally, check the Dependencies tab of the service to identify any service dependencies. The service might not be starting due to a problem with another service.

Compatibility Error

Compatibility errors are most commonly associated with programs. If you're lucky, the program will fail and give an error saying directly that it's incompatible with the current operating system or with another application. More often, it will just fail to start.

You can check the Application log in the Event Viewer to see whether the error message gives you an indication of the problem. The best solution is to use the Compatibility tab of the application or to use the Compatibility Wizard as described in Chapter 11, "Introducing Windows Operating Systems," and in Chapter 15. You can use these tools to configure the application to run with settings that mimic a previous operating system.

Slow System Performance

If your system is running slowly, it could be because you're running more applications than it can manage, a process or application is causing a problem, or the system could be infected. Excessive paging is described in Chapter 16 and occurs if a system doesn't have enough memory. If that's the case, you can close some applications and it might return to normal.

Task Manager, described in Chapter 13, is a great tool to help you identify the source of the problem. You can open it by pressing Ctrl+Shift+Esc. If an application is hung up, it will be listed as Not Responding on the Application tab, and you can select it and click End Task to close it.

Check the Performance tab of Task Manager to see whether the CPU Usage is high. If it is, check the Processes tab to identify what process is consuming the CPU's time. It could be that antivirus software or some other application is running and consuming the system's resources.

One option is to right-click the offending application in the Processes tab and select Set Priority to set it to a lower priority, such as Below Normal. Don't do this with a system process; it could crash your system.

You might find that an unknown process is consuming your system resources. This could be malware, or it could be a legitimate process that you don't recognize. Sometimes a quick search on Bing.com will let you know the purpose of the processor.

Boots to Safe Mode

If a system consistently boots into safe mode, the most likely reason is that it is configured to do so. Normally, the only way you can access safe mode is by pressing F8 at startup and starting safe mode from the Advanced Boot Options menu. However, if the System Configuration (msconfig) tool is configured to boot into safe mode, it retains this configuration until you change it back.

The "Msconfig and Advanced Boot Options" section earlier in this chapter described the Boot tab of msconfig. If a system is rebooting into one of the safe modes, check the settings on this tab.

Another possibility is that the system is infected with malware. Malware can corrupt key system files, causing the system to go into safe mode automatically. The solution is to run up-to-date antivirus software from safe mode to clean the system.

File Fails to Open

Normally when you double-click a file, the associated application will start and the file will open within that application. For example, if you double-click a file named A+StudyNotes. docx, Microsoft Word 2010 will start and open the file. However, if the file has an unknown extension, such as .a+pass, the computer won't know what application to start and won't open the file.

On Windows XP, you can see and modify associations from the Folder Options applet by selecting the File Types tab. On Windows Vista and Windows 7, start the Default Programs applet in Control Panel and click Associate A File Type or Protocol With A Program. You can use the *assoc | more* command from the command prompt to see a list of extensions and the applications associated with each extension.

If you want to change an association from Windows Explorer, you can right-click the file and select Open With, Choose Default Program. Browse to the correct application, and select it.

Missing NTLDR and Missing Boot.ini

Windows XP-based systems use the NTLDR and Boot.ini files, and if they cannot be located, you might see one of the following errors:

- NTLDR is missing
- Invalid Boot.ini
- Windows could not start

These errors indicate that the system is trying to boot from a non-bootable disk. They indicate that there is a problem with either the NTLDR file or the Boot.ini file, or that the BIOS is not configured correctly. The following list identifies common fixes for these errors and steps for most of these fixes were provided earlier in this chapter. Chapter 2 includes information about working with BIOS.

- **Verify the boot order in BIOS.** Ensure that the system is not trying to boot to media without an operating system (such as a CD or DVD). You can also remove any CDs or DVDs from the drives.
- **Repair or replace the Boot.ini file.** It could be that the Boot.ini file is corrupt and pointing to the wrong location.
- **Fix the boot sector.** If the active partition has a corrupted boot sector, it might not be able to locate the NTLDR file.
- **Fix the MBR.** The MBR might be corrupted, causing this error.
- **Manually copy the file.** It's also possible that the NTLDR file is missing or corrupted, so you can manually copy it.

Manually Copy System Files in Windows XP

Some errors indicate that key files used in the Windows XP boot process have failed. One way to resolve the problem is to manually copy the files from the Windows XP installation CD. The two files you might need to copy are NTLDR and Ntdetect.com.

Both of these files are available in the i386 folder of the installation CD. They are normally in the root of the C drive, and you can copy them from the CD to the C drive with the following steps:

1. Start the Recovery Console.

2. Insert the installation CD and identify the drive letter. For these examples, assume it is assigned the letter D.

3. Use the following commands to copy the NTLDR and Ntdetect.com files from the installation CD to the C drive. If the system partition is something other than C, use that letter instead.

   ```
   copy d:\i386\ntldr c:\
   ```

   ```
   copy d:\i386\ntdetect.com c:
   ```

Rebuild Boot.ini File in Windows XP

The Boot.ini file is used only with Windows XP. There might be times when the Boot.ini file used in Windows XP needs to be modified or re-created. You can modify it with Notepad if you know the correct settings, or you can rebuild it with the following steps:

1. Start the Recovery Console.

2. Enter the following command to rebuild the Boot.ini file:

   ```
   bootcfg /rebuild
   ```

This command scans the system for bootable operating systems and automatically creates the Boot.ini file with the proper settings.

Boot Sector and MBR Errors

Many other errors are caused by problems with the boot sector or MBR. For example, if boot sector information is missing, a disk doesn't have an active partition, or there is a problem with the MBR, you might see one of the following errors:

- Missing operating system
- Error loading operating system
- Invalid partition table

Some errors indicate a problem with the boot sector (or that the system is trying to boot from the wrong disk). These include the following:

- Non-system disk or disk error
- Invalid boot disk
- Disk boot failure

On Windows Vista and Windows 7, a problem with the MBR can give you one of the following errors:

- Bootmgr not found
- Bootmgr is missing

The solution to all of these errors is summarized in the following three tasks:

- **Verify boot order in BIOS.** Check BIOS to ensure that you're booting from the correct media.
- **Repair or replace the BCD.** It could be that the BCD is corrupt and needs to repaired with the bootrec /rebuildbcd command.
- **Fix the boot sector.** Use fixboot on Windows XP and bootrec /fixboot on Windows Vista and Windows 7.
- **Fix the MBR.** Use fixmbr on Windows XP and bootrec /fixmbr on Windows Vista and Windows 7.

Chapter Summary

- The boot process starts with POST and loads code from the MBR. The MBR identifies the active partition and loads code from its boot sector. On Windows XP, it uses NTLDR, Boot.ini, Ntdetect.com, and Ntoskrnl.exe. On Windows Vista and Windows 7, it uses the bootmgr, BCD, and Winload.exe.

- Windows stores systems settings in the registry. You can use the registry editor (regedit or regedt32) to view, modify, and back up the registry.

- Press F8 on startup to access the Advanced Boot Options. It provides access to Repair Your Computer, safe modes, last known good configuration, and other troubleshooting tools.

- Safe modes load only basic drivers and services. Use safe mode with networking if you need to access the Internet. Last Known Good Configuration can be used to restore the settings from the last successful boot. It's useful only if the user hasn't logged on after making changes.

- Windows XP supports the recovery console and commands such as fixboot, fixmbr, and bootcfg /rebuild. Windows Vista and Windows 7 use the Windows RE and commands such as bootrec /fixboot, bootrec /fixmbr, and bootrec /rebuildbcd.

- The Event Viewer is used to view logs. System logs record system events, such as when a driver or service fails to load. Application logs record applications events, such as when a third-party virus application detects malware.

- You can create a system repair disc in Windows 7 and use it to boot directly into the Windows RE from a bootable CD.

- When troubleshooting problems, try a restart first. If the restart doesn't solve the problem, pay close attention to error messages for clues.

- Repair system DLLs with the sfc /scannow tool.

Chapter Review

Use the following questions to test your knowledge of the information in this chapter: The answers to these questions, and the explanations of why each answer choice is correct or incorrect, are located in the "Answers" section at the end of this chapter.

1. You need to start Windows 7 in safe mode. What should you do?

    A. Reconfigure the Boot.ini file.

    B. Restart it, and press F8 as it starts.

    C. Run bootrec /safemode.

    D. Select Safe Mode from Task Manager.

2. After installing a new driver, a user's system is caught in a reboot loop. Which of the following choices would be the easiest way to restore the system?

    A. Perform an image recovery.

    B. Start safe mode and roll back the driver.

    C. Start safe mode and revert to a previous restore point.

    D. Use Last Known Good Configuration.

3. A Windows 7–based system fails, showing a blue screen, but restarts before you can view the error. What should you do?

    A. Modify the Startup and Recovery boot options.

    B. Modify the options from the Advanced Boot Options menu.

    C. Boot into safe mode, and view the Ntbtlog.txt file.

    D. Reboot the system by using the System Repair disc.

4. A user complained that he saw an error message and then his system failed. He doesn't remember what the message said. How can you identify the contents of the error message?

    A. Use Task Manager.

    B. Use Performance Monitor.

    C. Use Event Viewer.

    D. Use Device Manager.

5. After booting a Windows XP-based system, you see an error indicating that NTLDR is missing. Of the following choices, which has the best possibility of resolving this problem?

   A. Run the fixmbr command from the recovery console.

   B. Run the System Repair utility.

   C. Format the disk with diskpart.

   D. Run the bootrec /fixmbr command from the Windows RE.

6. A Windows 7–based system fails to boot and gives a "Missing Operating System" message. Of the following choices, which has the best chance of resolving this problem?

   A. Run the fixboot command from Windows RE.

   B. Run the bootrec /fixboot command from Windows RE.

   C. Rebuild the Boot.ini file.

   D. Download a replacement Regsvr32.dll file.

Answers

This section contains the answers to the chapter review questions in this chapter.

1. **Correct Answer:** B

   A. **Incorrect:** Windows 7 does not use boot.ini.

   B. **Correct:** Safe mode is started from the Advanced Boot Options menu, which is shown by pressing F8 when a computer starts.

   C. **Incorrect:** Bootrec does not include a /safemode switch.

   D. **Incorrect:** Safe Mode cannot be started from Task Manager

2. **Correct Answer:** D

   A. **Incorrect:** Performing an image recovery would take the longest time of the given choices.

   B. **Incorrect:** Rolling back a driver from Safe Mode is possible, but it requires more steps than using Last Known Good Configuration.

   C. **Incorrect:** Reverting to a previous restore point is possible, but it requires more steps than Last Known Good Configuration.

   D. **Correct:** Last Known Good Configuration is possible because the user has not logged on yet. It is accessed after pressing F8 on boot to access the Advanced Boot Options menu.

3. **Correct Answer:** B

   A. **Incorrect:** If the system started, you could modify the Startup And Recovery boot options, but it won't start.

   B. **Correct:** You can select Disable Automatic Restart on System Failure from the Advanced Boot Options menu. This stops an automatic reboot so that you can view the error.

   C. **Incorrect:** Ntbtlog.txt isn't available unless Enable Boot Logging is enabled from the Advanced Boot Options menu.

   D. **Incorrect:** The System Repair Disc can be useful to help you repair the system but not to view the error.

4. **Correct Answer: C**

    A. **Incorrect:** The Task Manager is used to view current activity and end tasks that are not responding.

    B. **Incorrect:** Performance Monitor provides extended capabilities to monitor system resources.

    C. **Correct:** Event Viewer is used to view logs. Error messages are logged in the System or Application logs.

    D. **Incorrect:** The Device Manager is used to manage devices and their drivers.

5. **Correct Answer: A**

    A. **Correct:** The recovery console fixmbr command will repair many problems, including this error in some situations.

    B. **Incorrect:** The System Repair utility in Windows Vista and Windows 7 is not available on Windows XP.

    C. **Incorrect:** Formatting the disk causes you to start all over, but this problem can usually be repaired.

    D. **Incorrect:** The bootrec /fixmbr command is available in Windows Vista and Windows 7, but not in Windows XP.

6. **Correct Answer: B**

    A. **Incorrect:** The fixboot command is not available in the Windows Recovery Environment (Windows RE).

    B. **Correct:** The bootrec /fixboot command in the Windows RE will fix the boot sector and might resolve this problem.

    C. **Incorrect:** Windows 7 does not use boot.ini.

    D. **Incorrect:** Windows uses a regsvr32.exe file to register DLLs, but regsvr32.dll might be malware.

CHAPTER 18

Introducing Networking Components

Networks are an important part of computing today. Large businesses have used networks for decades, but today it's also common to find a network in small businesses and homes. They allow people to easily share resources with other users in the same room and even with other users anywhere in the world.

Exam 220-801 objectives in this chapter:

- 2.7 Compare and contrast Internet connection types and features.
  - Cable
  - DSL
  - Dial-up
  - Fiber
  - Satellite
  - ISDN
  - Cellular (mobile hotspot)
  - Line of sight wireless Internet service
  - WiMAX
- 2.8 Identify various types of networks.
  - LAN
  - WAN
  - PAN
  - MAN
- 2.9 Compare and contrast network devices and their functions and features.
  - Hub
  - Switch
  - Router

- Access point
- Bridge
- Modem
- NAS
- VoIP phones

Exam 220-802 objectives in this chapter:

- 1.2 Given a scenario, install and configure the operating system using the most appropriate method.
  - Workgroup vs. domain setup
- 1.6 Set up and configure Windows networking on a client/desktop.
  - Workgroup vs. domain setup

REAL WORLD   **NETWORKING KNOWLEDGE IS VALUABLE**

A+ technicians need to have a solid understanding of networks. You don't need to be an expert, but you should understand the basics. This chapter (along with Chapters 19 through 24) will help you create a foundation for networking.

You'll find that the A+ exams don't go very deep into networking, but don't underestimate its importance. The knowledge you gain about networking for A+ will help you with other career paths. Almost every computer is connected to a network, so this knowledge will help in many information technology jobs. You might also choose to follow your A+ certification with another certification on networking, such as Network+, and you'll be a step ahead in earning those certificates.

I have taught Microsoft classes where some students had a difficult time mastering the material in the class, often because they had to spend extra time trying to understand networking basics. They were certainly intelligent and able to learn the material, but it was like trying to learn algebra without learning multiplication and division. I helped them fill in the holes with basic networking, but the advanced topics often overwhelmed them.

In comparison, the students that came with a solid understanding of networking were able to advance their knowledge.

Types of Networks

Computers are connected together in networks. Some networks are small, such as two computers connected together in a small office. Other networks are huge, including thousands or even tens of thousands of computers spread over multiple cities or regions. However, the common theme of all networks is that they connect computers together.

The primary benefit of networks is that users can access and share resources over the network. For example, instead of requiring a printer for every user, you can have one printer on a network shared by multiple users. Users can also share data such as files over the network.

You probably use the Internet and email regularly. This is possible only because you're connected to a network. You might be connected directly to the Internet or connected through another network. Without network connectivity, you'd have no access to the Internet.

> **NOTE** **INTERNET IS A NETWORK OF NETWORKS**
>
> The Internet is also a network or, more specifically, a group of interconnected networks. It's often referred to as a network of networks. It is accessible by billions of users around the world.

Some networks are identified based on their connectivity. The following sections describe some common networks.

Local Area Network

A *local area network (LAN)* is a group of computers and other devices that are connected together. It can include just a few users or thousands of users, but the key is that the devices connected to the network are relatively close to each other.

> **NOTE** **NETWORK DEVICES**
>
> A network device is any device that can connect to a network. Typical examples are end user computers, servers, and printers. There are many more devices that can be connected to a network.

For example, a *small office/home office (SOHO)* refers to a business with between one and 10 users. Devices connected to a SOHO network are in the same office. In contrast, larger businesses can have LANs that take up multiple offices in a building or even an entire building.

Figure 18-1 shows an illustration of a local area network. In the figure, users have access to resources on the network. They can use the fax/copier, the scanner/printer, share data on the file server, send email through the email server, and access the Internet, all through the LAN. This figure also shows a router, which is explained in greater depth later in this chapter.

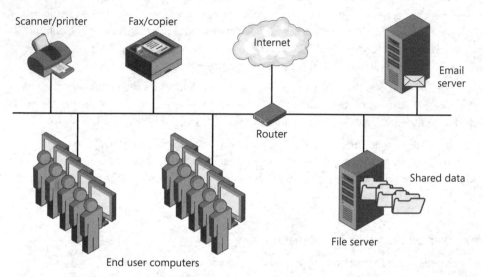

FIGURE 18-1 Local area network (LAN).

LANs can be smaller. For example, if you set up two computers in your home with a printer, this is a LAN. You don't need to have a router, servers, or Internet access.

One of the key characteristics of a LAN is that devices are relatively close to each other. In contrast, a wide area network (WAN) includes multiple LANs that aren't close to one another.

Wide Area Network

A *wide area network (WAN)* includes two or more LANs in separate geographic locations. Each LAN is local for users in the LAN, but other LANs are located elsewhere.

For example, Figure 18-2 shows a WAN for a company with its main offices in Virginia Beach, Virginia, and a small remote office in Raleigh, North Carolina. Connecting the two LANs creates a WAN.

EXAM TIP

Routers (described later in this chapter) are used to connect multiple networks together. This includes connecting networks in the same geographical location in a LAN, and connecting networks in separate locations as a WAN.

Most WAN connections are slower than the LAN connections. In the figure, you can see that the main office has a 1,000-Mbps (megabits per second) LAN, and the remote office has a 100-Mbps LAN. The WAN connection is considerably slower at 128 Kbps (kilobits per second).

Companies usually own all the hardware and cables within their company. However, instead of creating their own connections between two cities, they will often lease access to connections for WAN links. Telecommunications companies already have connection links in place, and they lease access to them. Fast connections are available, but faster connections are more expensive.

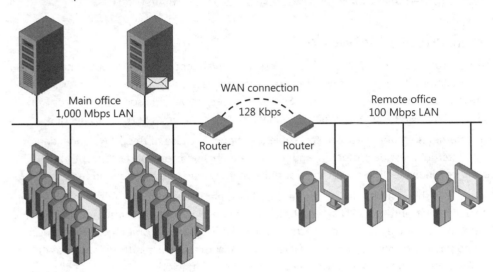

FIGURE 18-2 Wide area network (WAN).

Personal Area Network

A *personal area network (PAN)* is a network organized around a person. It includes mobile devices such as smartphones, earpieces for the smartphones, and personal digital assistants. It can also include handheld computers such as tablets and netbooks. A PAN will often use wireless technologies, so it is sometimes referred to as a *wireless PAN* (*WPAN*).

The range of a PAN is often identified as 10 meters or less (about 33 feet). This corresponds to the range of Class 2 Bluetooth devices, which also have a range of 10 meters. Chapter 9 discusses Bluetooth in the context of connecting mobile devices.

EXAM TIP

Bluetooth classes are related to their power output. Class 1 Bluetooth has the highest power output and has a range of about 100 meters. Class 3 Bluetooth has a range of about 5 meters (about 17 feet).

Metropolitan Area Network

A *metropolitan area network (MAN)* connects multiple LANs within a single metropolitan area. A MAN can be a large university campus or large organization with multiple buildings, or it can even encompass an entire city. Worldwide Interoperability for Microwave Access (WiMAX) is used for many MANs and is discussed later in this chapter.

Virtual Private Network

A *virtual private network (VPN)* provides access to a private network over a public network such as the Internet. Organizations often use VPNs to give employees access to internal network resources even when they're away. Some employees travel, and some employees work from home. With a VPN, they can easily connect to their company's network as needed.

The Internet is a public network accessible to anyone. Because of this, VPN connections over the Internet must be protected, and VPNs use tunneling protocols to encrypt traffic. If unauthorized individuals intercept the transmission, they won't be able to read the data.

Figure 18-3 shows a VPN. In this figure, Susan uses her laptop to connect to the Internet and then connects into the VPN server through a secure tunnel over the Internet. With some software, this is often as easy as connecting to a website. Susan is prompted to enter a user name and password, and her account is checked to ensure that she's authorized to use the VPN. When she's connected, she has access to the internal network.

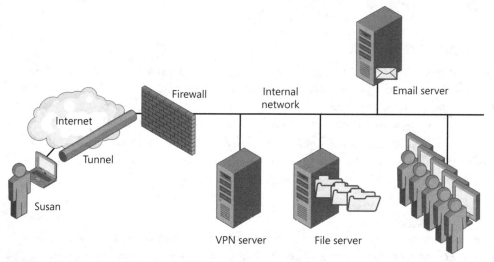

FIGURE 18-3 Virtual private network (VPN).

EXAM TIP

VPNs use tunneling protocols to protect VPN connections. These connections protect data transmitted over the Internet by using encryption.

In Figure 18-3, you can see that a firewall is separating the internal network from the Internet. Firewalls are explained in greater depth in Chapter 22, but in short, they provide a layer of protection for the internal network. They use access control lists (ACLs) to block or allow certain traffic.

When connected to a VPN, users have access to resources on the internal network. The figure shows an email server, a file server, and other users on the internal network. If users can access these resources while connected inside the company, they can usually access them through the VPN.

✓ **Quick Check**

1. What is a network called when it connects two networks from different locations?
2. What is used to protect VPN connections?

Quick Check Answers

1. Wide area network (WAN).
2. Tunneling protocols.

Identifying Basic Network Hardware

Any network has basic hardware used to connect devices to the network and to connect networks together. Network devices can be computers, printers, servers, network hard drives, or anything else you can connect to the network. This section describes network interface cards, hubs, switches, and routers, but it's important to remember the following points:

- Hubs and switches connect devices to a network.
- Routers connect networks together.

Network Interface Card

A *network interface card (NIC)* provides connectivity for a computer to a network. The most common connection you'll see in NICs is an RJ-45 connector. The RJ-45 connector is similar to an RJ-11 connector used in phones except that the RJ-11 connector is smaller.

> **MORE INFO** **CHAPTER 19**
>
> Connections and cables are described in more depth in Chapter 19. As an introduction, twisted-pair cable is commonly used in networks, and it uses RJ-45 connectors at each end of the cable. These RJ-45 connectors plug into RJ-45 ports. When connecting a computer to the network, one end of the cable plugs into the NIC on the computer, and the other end plugs into the RJ-45 port on a hub (or a switch, if used instead).

Most computers have built-in NICs on the motherboard, but you can also install an adapter card into an available expansion slot on the motherboard. You might want to add a NIC for the following reasons:

- The motherboard doesn't include a NIC.
- The built-in NIC developed a fault.
- You want to install a faster NIC.
- You want to add fault tolerance.

Other devices often have built-in NICs too. For example, many printers have NICs that allow you to connect them directly to the network.

Hub

A *hub* provides connectivity to several devices. For example, you can connect several computers and a printer to a hub, and all of these devices will be able to communicate with each other. Any computer can print to the printer. Users can share files such as pictures, music, and other documents from their computer, and other users can access them through the hub.

Most hubs have RJ-45 ports, and you can run twisted-pair cables from each of the network devices to the hub. For example, Figure 18-4 shows several computers configured in a LAN through a hub.

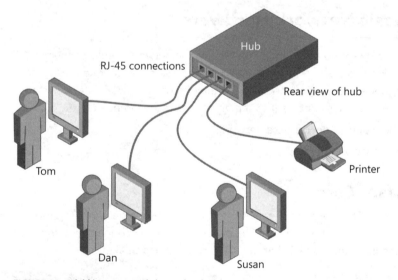

FIGURE 18-4 LAN connected through a hub.

A hub is not intelligent and has no ability to learn. If Tom is sending a print job to the printer, the same data is being sent to Dan's and Susan's computers. Dan's and Susan's computers won't process the data, but it does add traffic to their connection. If Dan was downloading pictures from Susan's computer, it would take longer than if Tom wasn't printing.

Similarly, Tom's print job will take longer than it would if Dan wasn't downloading pictures from Susan's computer.

The more traffic any connection has, the slower it becomes. You can think of this just like a road or highway. If you're the only person on the road, you can easily go the speed limit. If it's rush hour in a big city, traffic can slow to a crawl. If you have a lot of traffic going through a hub, network traffic can slow to a crawl.

> **NOTE MOST HUBS REPLACED BY SWITCHES**
>
> Hubs aren't common in network environments anymore. Many organizations replace them with switches to provide better performance. Also, the price of a basic switch is often the same as a hub, so you'll commonly see switches in smaller networks too.

Switch

 Switches connect computers and other network devices just as hubs do. The big difference is that switches have some intelligence and have the ability to learn. With just a little bit of time, they identify the devices connected to each port. They then send data addressed to a device only through the port associated with the device. In contrast, the hub sends traffic to all ports.

> **EXAM TIP**
>
> Switches connect network devices together on a network. Switches are more efficient than hubs because they direct traffic to specific ports instead of sending traffic to all ports.

For example, compare Figure 18-4 with Figure 18-5. If Tom sends a print job to the printer, the switch creates an internal connection between Tom's computer and the printer. This traffic doesn't reach Dan's or Susan's computers and doesn't impact the performance of their network connections. If Dan is downloading a file from Susan's computer, the print job traffic doesn't slow him down. Similarly, transferring files between Dan's and Susan's computers doesn't slow down Tom's print job.

The switch dynamically connects different devices depending on the traffic. For example, if Dan decides to print a picture he received from Susan's computer, the switch will make an internal connection from Dan's computer to the printer. Similarly, if Susan wants to download shared documents from Tom's computer, the switch connects the ports for these two computers.

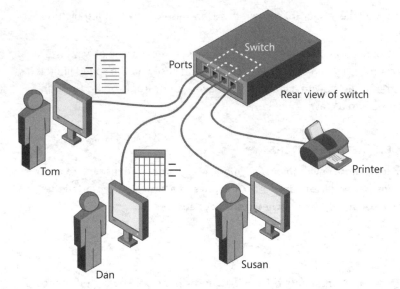

FIGURE 18-5 LAN connected through a switch.

Router

Routers connect networks together. In contrast, hubs and switches connect computers and other networking devices together. You can have multiple networks using switches to connect the devices together, and then connect these networks with a router.

> **MORE INFO** **CHAPTER 23**
>
> Chapter 23 covers wireless networks. In that chapter, you'll see how many wireless routers include a switch component. The switch component connects devices together in a network, and the router component connects networks together. Many SOHOs use wireless routers for connectivity within the office and for Internet access.

For example, WANs were described previously as two or more networks connected together over a large geographical distance. Each network would use a router to connect to other networks. You can also connect networks together within a single LAN using a router.

Consider Figure 18-6. It shows two separate networks (Network 1 and Network 2) connected together with the router. The router also provides access to all the users in both networks to the Internet.

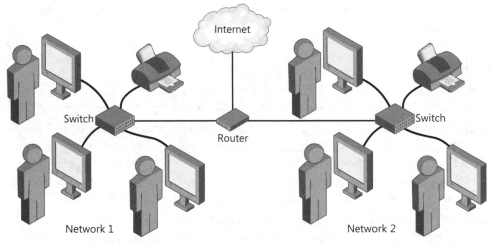

FIGURE 18-6 Connecting networks with a router.

Some advanced switches can function like a router. However, for the A+ exam, you won't see any questions on advanced capabilities of switches.

Bridge

A bridge performs like a switch with one basic difference: instead of having separate connections for each computer or device, it uses a single connection to connect two groups of devices.

For example, imagine that you had four computers connected with one hub and four computers connected with a second hub. It's possible to connect the hubs together simulating one larger hub. The problem with this is that each computer can now have up to twice the traffic. If you connect the two hubs with a bridge in the middle, the majority of the traffic in each hub is now passed to the other hub.

While bridges were used with hubs to reduce traffic, they are rarely used in this way today. Switches have replaced them, and many switches are referred to as *multiport bridges*. However, you might run across a wireless bridge.

A wireless bridge is often used to connect two separate networks that are separated by distance. For example, you might have a LAN in one area of a building and want to set up a temporary LAN in a different area of the building. Instead of running wires to the temporary

LAN, you can set up wireless access points in each LAN and use these to bridge the two networks together.

Modem

A *modulator-demodulator (modem)* is a device used to add digital data onto an analog signal through modulation. It can retrieve digital data from an analog signal through demodulation.

Analog data is transmitted as a sine wave similar to the alternating current (AC) sine wave described in Chapter 1. Modulation adds data to this sine wave in the form of variations, and the sine wave acts as the carrier signal for the data. Demodulation removes the carrier signal to read the data. The analog carrier wave can be transmitted over long distances more easily than digital data, especially with certain types of cable.

Users can connect to the Internet by using a standard telephone line and modem through an *Internet Service Provider (ISP)*. The speeds are very slow, so it isn't common to use telephone modems for Internet access except in rural areas where other methods aren't available.

Broadband Internet connections are discussed later in this chapter, and they also use a modem. Cable TV companies have cable running to homes and businesses to provide TV signals, and they use this same cable for an Internet connection. The Internet signal is modulated and demodulated with a cable modem.

Network Attached Storage (NAS)

Network attached storage (NAS) is a dedicated computer system used to provide disk storage on a network. It is often packaged as a small device or appliance that is very easy to connect and use.

For example, I have a Western Digital 1-TB NAS. I turned it on, plugged it into a port on my wireless access point, and with just a little configuration I soon had a 1-TB drive accessible to all the computers on the network. It's running Linux and includes a web-based management program for configuration. Figure 18-7 shows a screen shot from one of the setup pages. This device supports controlling access to specific users and groups with folder permissions.

FIGURE 18-7 Managing a NAS device with a web browser.

Larger organizations use NAS devices, but these devices are often more sophisticated. For example, a NAS device in an organization can include multiple drives configured as one or more RAID arrays. These drives are usually hot-swappable, allowing you to replace a failed drive without powering the system down. On a larger scale, organizations use *storage area networks (SANs)*, which are entire networks of storage devices.

EXAM TIP

One of the benefits of NAS is that it can be accessed by different operating systems. Users in the network could be running Windows, Linux, or Mac systems and still access the files.

VoIP Phones

Instead of traditional phone lines, a *Voice over Internet Protocol (VoIP) phone* uses an IP network to make telephone calls. Many people use these with an Internet connection to make phone calls instead of using a regular phone line.

VoIP phones look like typical phones, but instead of plugging into a telephone jack with an RJ-11 connector, they plug into a network port on a switch or a router with an RJ-45 connector. Some VoIP phones have wireless capabilities and can connect to a wireless network. You'll need a subscription with a VoIP provider such as Vonage to make phone calls.

EXAM TIP

You can use VoIP as an alternative to a traditional phone without a specialized VoIP phone. One way is with an analog telephone adapter that you connect between your computer and your traditional phone. You can also use a regular computer with a microphone, speakers, a sound card, and some software.

Link, Activity, and Speed Lights

NICs, hubs, routers, and switches have light emitting diode (LED) lights to show connectivity and provide information on the connection.

One LED might be labeled Link to indicate the status of the connection link. Another LED might be labeled *ACT* (for *activity*) to indicate whether any traffic is being transmitted or received on the link. It's common to have a combination Link/Act LED instead of two separate LEDs. These lights can have slightly different meanings for different vendors or models, but some common meanings are the following:

- **Solid green.** The link is connected.
- **Blinking green.** The link is connected, and data activity is occurring on the link.
- **Not lit.** Either nothing is connected or the device can't sense the connection. If you have a cable connected, this often means that the cable is faulty, the device on the other end of the cable is not connected, or the other device is faulty.

EXAM TIP

Many switches and routers allow you to disable a port. When it's disabled, it will not be lit even if you have a good connection. You need to use the device's documentation to enable the port.

Chapter 19 talks about speeds of different connections in more depth, but in short, network devices are rated for specific speeds. Many can also operate using multiple speeds.

For example, a switch might be able to communicate at either 100 Mbps or 1,000 Mbps. Devices that can communicate at different speeds will usually have autosense or auto-negotiation. That is, they automatically determine the fastest speed of the other connected devices and use that speed. A switch might be using 100 Mbps for an older, slower computer connected to one port and 1,000 Mbps for a newer computer connected to a different port. Autosense is built into most NICs and network devices today, and it's best to leave it enabled.

EXAM TIP

Some devices do not have autosense capabilities and might default to a slower speed. If the connection speeds are slower than they should be, you might need to manually configure the devices to use the faster speed.

Devices often include lights to indicate the speed of the link. Again, different vendors might have slightly different meanings for the lights, but some common meanings are as follows:

- **Solid green.** The connection is using the fastest speed (such as 1,000 Mbps).
- **Amber.** The connection is using the slowest speed (such as 100 Mbps).
- **Not lit.** Nothing is connected.

Switches and routers are similar to computers. Occasionally, things go wrong and they don't work as expected. A reboot on a computer is often a good step, as it cures many ills. If a switch or a router stops passing traffic, you can occasionally just power cycle the device and get it to work.

EXAM TIP

If all the activity light LEDs change to a solid green even though you know they should be blinking green to show activity, turn the switch off and then back on. If all the LED lights are off, check the power to ensure that it is on.

Comparing Workgroups and Domains

Most networks need both authentication and authorization to control who can access resources. The differences between these two are as follows:

- **Authentication.** Users prove who they are with credentials. A common method of authentication requires use of a user name and password.
- **Authorization.** Users are authorized access to resources based on their proven identity. For example, Dan might be granted authorization to files on a file server. However, just because he can log on and authenticate doesn't mean he has access to all resources in the network. Authorization is granted with permissions.

> **NOTE** **AUTHENTICATION REQUIRED FOR AUTHORIZATION**
>
> Just because someone can authenticate by logging on doesn't mean they are authorized to do anything and everything on the computer. However, you cannot restrict access to resources without users having different authentication credentials. If everyone logs on with the same account, everyone will have the same access.

There are two primary ways that users are authenticated in networks: workgroups and domains. The following sections describe them in more depth, but the distinguishing points between the two are as follows:

- Workgroups are typically for ten or fewer computers.
- In a workgroup, users need separate accounts to access different computers in a workgroup.
- In a domain, users have a single account that they can use to access different domain computers.

Workgroup

A *workgroup* is a group of computers configured in a network with separate account databases. For example, Windows-based computers have a security account manager (SAM) database. This database holds the user names and passwords for all users that can access the computer.

Figure 18-8 shows a workgroup with three users and a printer. Each computer includes a separate SAM. If Tom wants to log on to his computer, he authenticates with a user name and password contained in the SAM on his computer.

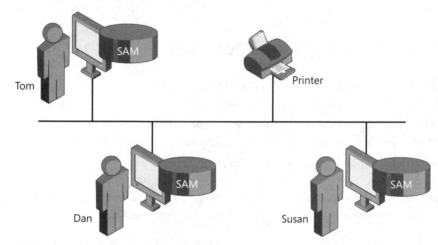

FIGURE 18-8 Computers connected in a workgroup.

> **NOTE HUBS AND SWITCHES NOT ALWAYS SHOWN ON DIAGRAMS**
>
> Hubs and switches often aren't shown on logical network diagrams. Instead, the computers are shown connected in a line diagram similar to Figure 18-8. This diagram implies connectivity with a hub or a switch. You can compare Figure 18-8 to Figures 18-4, 18-5, and 18-6, which specifically identify switches and hubs.

Tom's account on Tom's computer won't allow him to log on to Dan's or Susan's computers. If Tom wants to log on to Dan's computer, he needs another account stored on the SAM on Dan's computer. Tom would need three user names and three passwords to log on to each of the computers shown in Figure 18-8.

One reason to switch over to a domain is when users need to access multiple computers in the network. If they need multiple user accounts and passwords, they are more likely to write them down. They will have only a single account with a domain, and they'll be less likely to write them down.

Windows desktop–based systems limit how many users can connect at the same time. For example, if Susan is sharing pictures from her computer, there is a limit to how many other users can connect to her computer to access these pictures. This limit is technically known as the maximum number of concurrent connections allowed. Table 18-1 shows the maximum concurrent connections identified by the licensing terms of many common Windows-based systems.

TABLE 18-1 Windows Maximum Concurrent Connections

Operating System	Maximum Concurrent Connections
Windows XP Home	5
Windows XP Professional	10
Windows Vista Home Basic	5
Windows Vista Home Premium and Ultimate	10
Windows 7 Starter, Home Premium, Professional, and Ultimate	20

EXAM TIP

The maximum number of concurrent connections for Windows XP Professional is 10, but the maximum has been increased to 20 for all editions of Windows 7.

It is possible to add servers into a workgroup if you need to provide services to more than 10 or 20 users. However, after you add a server, it does not require much more to create a domain.

Domain

 A *domain* has a central server that holds accounts used for authentication. For example, a Microsoft domain includes a server configured as a domain controller, and this server hosts Active Directory. Active Directory is similar to the SAM in that it includes user accounts, but it also has many more capabilities. However, the most important point for the A+ exam is that the domain provides centralized authentication.

Figure 18-9 shows a domain controller configured in a domain. Users log on using one account, and they can use this account to access resources they're authorized to use. Therefore, users don't need a different account even if they log on to a different computer in the domain.

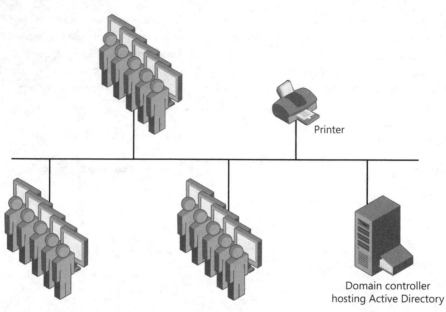

Printer

Domain controller
hosting Active Directory

FIGURE 18-9 Computers connected in a domain.

The domain controller can also be configured for other server roles. For example, a small company using a domain controller will often use it as a file server and a print server.

Joining a Workgroup or a Domain

You can use the following steps on a Windows 7–based system to join a computer to a workgroup or a domain. You need to know the name of the domain and have an account that is authorized to join the domain.

EXAM TIP

By default, any user with an account in the domain has permissions to join up to 10 computers to the domain. Administrative permissions are not needed.

1. Click Start, right-click Computer, and select Properties.

2. Select Advanced System Settings.

3. Click the Computer Name tab and click Change. Your display will resemble the following graphic.

4. If you want to join a different workgroup, enter the name of the workgroup and click OK.

   A. After a moment, you'll see a message welcoming you to the workgroup.

   B. Click OK, and you'll be prompted to restart the computer. After restarting, the computer will be a member of the workgroup.

5. If you want to join a domain, select Domain and enter the name of the domain. Click OK.

   A. You'll be prompted to enter the user name and password of an account that has permission to join the domain. Enter the name and password, and click OK.

   B. After a moment, you'll be prompted to restart the computer. Click OK. After restarting, the computer will be a member of the domain.

Connecting to the Internet

Most people who have a computer today want to access the Internet. They use it for email, research, news, sharing information with friends and family, and much more. However, everyone doesn't connect to the Internet in the same way. The following sections describe some common methods of connecting to the Internet.

Cable and Fiber Broadband Connections

In the context of an Internet connection, broadband connections refer to connections that have much greater bandwidth than connections using a phone line. More bandwidth means that you can download or upload data quicker than connections with less bandwidth. As a comparison, a dial-up connection (discussed later in this section) is much slower than a broadband connection.

For example, many people use Netflix to stream movies to their home computers. If you have a broadband connection, the movie is usually clear without distortion in the picture or sound. However, if you use dial-up, the movie will constantly stop and start and be highly distorted. You probably won't even be able to watch the movie over a dial-up connection.

Broadband cable service is usually offered by the same company that provides cable TV services. These companies have run cable to homes and business for TV connections in many city areas. One single cable can carry hundreds of TV channels, and users can simply change channels to watch whatever they want.

Telecommunications companies realized that they could also put a signal for the Internet onto the same cable. Just as a TV tuner can tune to the correct channel and block all other channels, cable modems can tune to the Internet connection and block the TV signals.

Figure 18-10 shows a basic connection path for a broadband cable connection for a home user. The telecommunications company provides both the TV signal and the connection to the Internet as an Internet Service Provider (ISP). The signal is split at the user's home with one cable going to the TV and the other cable going to a cable modem and then to the user's computer.

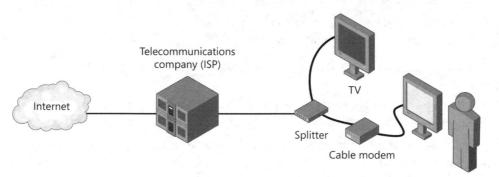

FIGURE 18-10 Cable broadband connection for a home user.

> **NOTE MODEMS**
>
> Cable providers often sell or rent cable modems, or you can buy one from an electronics store such as Best Buy.

The ISP provides the user with a public Internet Protocol (IP) address usable on the Internet. Of course, users can do more with their connection. It's a short leap to add a switch to connect multiple users in the home network and to add a router to provide Internet access to all the users in the home network.

Broadband cable has traditionally used coaxial cables. However, some telecommunications companies have been using fiber optic cables more and more. For example, where I live, Verizon provides FIOS service over fiber. It includes TV, Internet access, and telephone service.

Fiber optic cable provides the most available bandwidth, so users can often get faster speeds with fiber.

Phone Connections

Unfortunately, broadband connections aren't available everywhere. Many areas are too far from a city for telecommunications companies to run cable. Sometimes the cost of a broadband connection is just too high for a user, even when it is available. A cheaper alternative that is available almost anywhere is a phone connection.

Phone connections require modems, similar to how cable connections require cable modems. The signal going to a computer is digital and compatible with a computer. The signal from a phone line is often analog and compatible with phones. The modem ensures that the input and output signals are translated correctly.

> **EXAM TIP**
>
> **Phones and modems use cables with RJ-11 connections. The cables and RJ-11 connections are smaller than the RJ-45 connections used with NICS, hubs, switches, and modems.**

Most modems allow you to split the phone line. You can connect the phone line directly into the modem input jack. The modem then has another port that you can connect to your phone. With traditional phone lines, you can either talk on the phone or connect with the computer, but you can't do both at the same time.

Dial-up

The typical phone connection to the Internet is simply a dial-up connection. The *plain old telephone service (POTS)* provides voice-grade communications to users in most places in the world and can be used for Internet access. Users subscribe through an ISP for dial-up access, and when they want to connect, they connect through the modem.

Phones and phone lines are connected through a *public switched telephone network (PSTN)*. The PSTN includes all the connections throughout the world and allows us to easily make phone calls. Telecommunications companies have been steadily upgrading the PSTN, and it can often support digital signals instead of just analog.

A benefit of dial-up access is that it is available almost anywhere. If you have access to a phone line, you can connect. The drawback is the speed; dial-up connections are painfully slow.

The maximum speed you can get from a single phone line connection is 56 Kbps. In the United States, this maximum is limited by regulations to 53.3 Kbps. In comparison, I performed a speed test on my broadband cable connection and it showed a download speed of 33.02 Mbps.

ISDN

Integrated Services Digital Network (ISDN) is a special type of dial-up connection that uses a telephone network. Since the signals are digital, a traditional modem isn't used but instead ISDN lines use terminal adapters in the place of modems. There are two primary types of ISDN connections:

- **Basic Rate Interface (BRI).** A BRI uses two 64-Kbps channels providing a maximum speed of 128 Kbps. This is used by homes and small businesses. It also has a 16-Kbps signal control channel.

- **Primary Rate Interface (PRI).** A PRI uses 23 64-Kbps data channels and one 64-Kbps data channel. In North America, this is called a *T1* and provides a total of about 1.5 Mbps. In Europe, a PRI uses 30 data channels and one 64-Kbps signal control channel and is called an *E1*. T1 and E1 lines are typically used only by businesses, not home users.

You can make and receive phone calls while you're connected to most ISDN lines. However, ISDN will disconnect one of the channels, reducing the speed of the Internet connection.

DSL

Digital subscriber lines (DSLs) are another alternative that uses a PSTN. Similar to ISDN, DSLs send signals over the lines using digital signals instead of the analog connections used by traditional dial-up connections. There are several versions of DSL, and they are sometimes referred to as xDSL.

The two most common types of DSL are ADSL and SDSL:

- **ADSL.** Asymmetric DSL uses different speeds for uploads and downloads. Home users can often get ADSL lines with upload speeds of around 500 Kbps and download speeds of around 1 Mbps.

- **SDSL.** Symmetric DSL uses the same speed for uploads and downloads. It is often used for businesses, and they can lease lines at varying speeds, such as 384 Kbps or 500 Kbps. Faster speeds are more expensive.

EXAM TIP

Asymmetric indicates that something doesn't have balance or has differences, while *symmetric* indicates that it is similar in size and shape. Asymmetric DSL has differences; specifically, it has different speeds for uploads and downloads. Symmetric DSL has similarities; specifically, the upload and download speeds are the same.

DSL connections use a transceiver to send and receive data. This transceiver isn't technically a modem, but you'll often hear it referred to as a DSL modem.

A drawback with DSL is that users must be relatively close to the phone company's equipment. This limits DSL to large city areas.

Cellular

Cellular telephones have been around for a while, and you probably have one or know some-one who does. Traditionally, a cellular phone allowed you only to make phone calls using the phone company's cellular network. Many cellular networks are on the third generation (3G) and fourth generation (4G); cellular networks are spreading rapidly.

> **MORE INFO** **CHAPTER 9**
>
> Chapter 9 includes a comparison of different generations of cellular networks in the cel-lular connectivity section.

Telecommunications companies have been steadily upgrading their cellular towers and cellular networks to support data in addition to voice. It's now common to have a cellular phone that you can use to make traditional phone calls and access the Internet.

Cellular providers now sell devices that are specifically designed for mobile computers. For example, I have an air card modem from Verizon, shown in Figure 18-11 plugged into a laptop USB port. When I'm on the road, I plug it in, connect, and then I have Internet access. Just as you need a subscription for the cell phone, you also need a subscription for the wire-less Internet card.

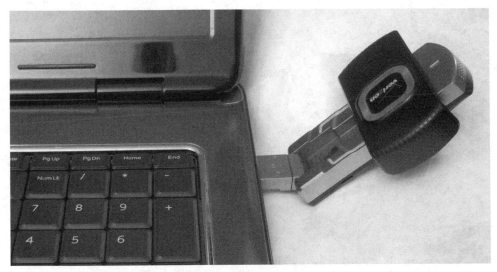

FIGURE 18-11 Wireless air card plugged into laptop computer.

Additionally, most smartphones have wireless capabilities built into them. For example, if you have a smartphone and a wireless network at your home, you can configure the smart-phone to connect to the Internet through the wireless network. Similarly, you can connect through public hotspots using wireless.

WiMAX

Worldwide Interoperability for Microwave Access (WiMAX) is a wireless standard that is expanding the range of many wireless networks. The goal is to deliver high-speed Internet access for large geographical areas without physical connectivity.

> **EXAM TIP**
>
> **WiMAX is not the same as a wireless network, commonly called Wi-Fi. Wi-Fi (covered in Chapter 23) includes several 802.11 standards used for wireless LANs (WLANs). WiMAX is used for long-range networks, such as a MAN.**

Figure 18-12 shows the basics of a WiMAX network. An ISP is connected to the Internet and has a wired connection to a WiMAX tower. The tower has a transmitter and receiver with a clear line of sight to another tower with another transmitter and receiver. Data is transmitted via microwave between the two towers.

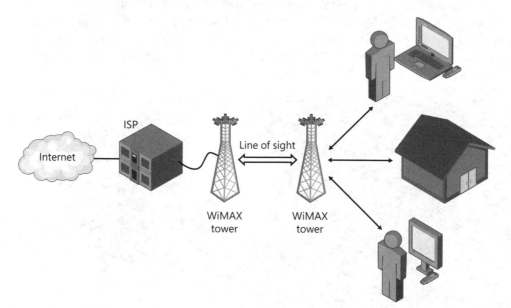

FIGURE 18-12 WiMAX network.

Users connect to the WiMAX network with subscriber stations. These are commonly *USB dongles,* which plug into a PC similarly to the air card shown in Figure 18-11. They act as a modem to connect to the WiMAX tower. Users can also use a gateway that can be installed outside the building or located close to a window. The gateway connects to the WiMAX tower and can provide a signal to multiple devices within the building.

Connections to the user systems or gateways do not require a line-of-sight connection.

Satellite

Another alternative available for users in rural areas is satellite access. This is sometimes a good alternative for users who don't have access to cable providers or don't have cellular access.

Figure 18-13 shows a typical configuration for a satellite-based Internet connection. The ISP maintains a satellite and has a connection to the Internet through its own satellite dish. Users have a satellite dish at their home with a satellite modem connected to their computer.

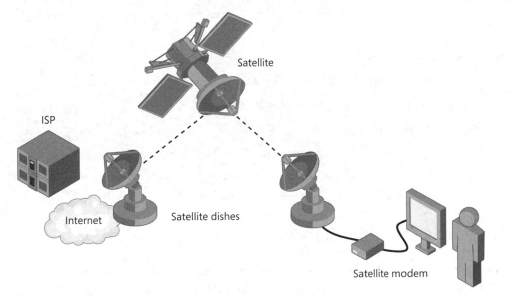

FIGURE 18-13 Satellite connection for a home user.

In older configurations, the user was required to have a phone connection and the user's satellite dish was able to only download data. That is, the user had a downlink from the satellite but not an uplink to the satellite. When a user clicked a link in a web browser, the signal was sent through the phone line to the ISP. The ISP then sent the data to the user through the satellite. In most current configurations, the user's equipment provides both an uplink and a downlink to the satellite.

Satellites are placed in a geostationary orbit. Even though the earth is spinning and the satellite is moving in space, the satellite always appears to be in the same location from any location on earth.

Users must have a clear line of sight to the satellite from their satellite dish. Obstructions from buildings and trees will block the connection. Additionally, moisture from rain and clouds can sometimes absorb the signal, reducing or blocking the connection.

Another drawback to satellites is that the signals have to travel so far. Satellites are over 22,000 miles above earth, and each signal must go up to the satellite and come back down. Then the reply has to travel up to the satellite and come back down. It's not unusual for a signal to take half a second or longer for a one-way trip. This results in high latency times for users. After a user clicks, it can take a second or longer to get a reply.

EXAM TIP

Satellite connections travel over the greatest distance compared to any other type of Internet connection, resulting in latency issues. The biggest limitation is that they require a clear line of sight between the satellite and each of the satellite dishes used for uplinks and downlinks.

✔ **Quick Check**

1. Considering Internet connectivity, what does broadband indicate?

2. What is unique to ADSL compared to SDSL?

Quick Check Answers

1. Greater bandwidth and higher speeds.

2. ADSL has different upload and download speeds. SDSL speeds are the same.

Standards Organizations

As you study networking topics, you'll come across some acronyms and names representing standards or standards organizations. You don't need to be an expert on them, but you should have a basic idea of what they are.

- **IEEE (Institute of Electrical Engineers).** This is a standards organization that has defined a wide assortment of standards. For example, IEEE 802.3 is a collection of standards for wired networks, and IEEE 802.11 is a collection of standards for wireless networks. It is commonly pronounced as "I Triple E."

- **ISO (International Organization for Standardization).** An international standards organization headquartered in Switzerland. Some standards are developed with the International Electrotechnical Commission (IEC) and designated as ISO/IEC. According to ISO, ISO is not an acronym but instead based on the Greek word *isos*, meaning equal.

- **IETF (Internet Engineering Task Force).** A standards organization that develops and promotes Internet standards. Its focus is on the TCP/IP protocol suite used on the Internet.

- **RFC (Request for Comment).** When the IETF develops standards, it first publishes them as an RFC with a number. For example, RFC 1918 defines what IP addresses should be reserved for private networks. An RFC is never modified after it is published. If a change is needed, a new RFC is published with a new number.

Chapter Summary

- A local area network (LAN) is a group of computers and other network devices connected together in a single location.

- Wide area networks (WANs) connect two or more LANs that are in separate geographical locations.

- A virtual private network (VPN) provides access to a private network over a public network such as the Internet. Tunneling protocols are used to protect data in a VPN.

- A personal area network (PAN) is a network organized around a person. Bluetooth-enabled devices are commonly used. A switch connects devices together in a network.

- A router connects networks together. Routers are needed to provide access from a network to the Internet and to connect networks together over a WAN.

- Network attached storage (NAS) is a network appliance that provides access to disk storage over a network.

- Voice over IP (VoIP) phones use network connections to make phone calls and can be used instead of a phone line.

- Network devices have link and activity lights that identify how they are working. Link lights are usually solid green to show a connection. Activity lights blink to show activity.

- A workgroup is a small group of computers in a network with separate account databases used for authentication.

- The maximum number of concurrent connections on Windows 7 is 20. On Windows XP Professional, the maximum is 10.

- A domain includes a centralized server used for accounts. In a Microsoft domain, a domain controller hosts Active Directory, which includes accounts. Users need to have only one account to access multiple computers.

- Broadband connections provide users with higher bandwidth and faster download times.

- Traditional dial-up connections use plain old telephone service (POTS) and a modem. The maximum speed is 56 Kbps.

- Digital subscriber lines (DSLs) provide faster speeds over phone lines than does traditional dial-up service. Asymmetric DSL has different speeds for uploads and downloads. Symmetric DSL uses the same speed for uploads and downloads.

- Cellular connections to the Internet use connections through cellular networks. Users can subscribe with a company and access the Internet with a phone, or they can use USB modems to connect to the cellular network.

- WiMAX is used for long-range wireless networks in MANs. Users connect with subscriber stations.

- Satellite Internet connections use satellite dishes for uploads and downloads. A drawback is that they require line-of-sight connections and have high latency times. Signals can be blocked by buildings, trees, and even rain.

Chapter Review

Use the following questions to test your knowledge of the information in this chapter. The answers to these questions, and the explanations of why each answer choice is correct or incorrect, are located in the "Answers" section at the end of this chapter.

1. You want to connect a network in one office to a network in an office in a separate city. What are you creating, and what device do you need to connect the two offices?

   A. You're creating a WAN, and you need routers.

   B. You're creating a WAN, and you need switches.

   C. You're creating a LAN, and you need routers.

   D. You're creating a PAN, and you need switches.

2. After replacing a faulty switch with an older switch on their 100-Mbps network, users complain that the network connections are slow. Of the following choices, what is the most likely problem?

   A. The switch is configured to use 1 Gbps.

   B. The switch's ports are disabled.

   C. The switch is not autosensing the speed of the network.

   D. The switch is running in WAN mode.

3. Computers connected on a network through a switch can no longer communicate with each other. You notice all the lights are steady. What should you do?

   A. Replace all the computers.

   B. Replace all the cables.

   C. Reboot the computers.

   D. Turn the switch off and then back on.

4. After adding a new computer to a network, you realize the computer is the only one that can't communicate with other devices on the network. You verified the cable to the switch is good. Of the following choices, what should you do next?

   A. Replace the NIC.

   B. Replace the computer.

   C. Verify the port on the switch is enabled.

   D. Power cycle the switch.

5. Which of the following Internet connections uses different speeds for uploads and downloads?

   A. DSL

   B. ADSL

   C. SDSL

   D. Dial-up

6. Which of the following connections requires a clear line of sight for devices?

   A. Dial-up

   B. ISDN

   C. Cellular

   D. Satellite

Answers

1. **Correct Answer: A**

   A. **Correct:** A wide area network (WAN) is two or more local area networks (LANs) located in separate locations. WANs are connected together with routers.

   B. **Incorrect:** This is a WAN, but routers are needed to connect the LANs.

   C. **Incorrect:** Each office network is a LAN, but when you connect them you're creating a WAN.

   D. **Incorrect:** A personal area network (PAN) is on or around a person and typically uses Bluetooth.

2. **Correct Answer: C**

   A. **Incorrect:** If it is configured to use 1 Gbps, it would try to run faster, not slower.

   B. **Incorrect:** Disabling ports on a switch will block all traffic, not slow it down.

   C. **Correct:** If a switch doesn't have autosense or auto-negotiation, it needs to be manually configured for the speed of the network. In this case, it's likely the switch is configured for a slower speed, such as 10 Mbps.

   D. **Incorrect:** There is no such thing as WAN mode for a switch. Additionally, routers are used to connect networks over a WAN.

3. **Correct Answer: D**

   A. **Incorrect:** It's unlikely all the computers suddenly developed faults at the same time.

   B. **Incorrect:** It's unlikely all the cables suddenly developed faults at the same time.

   C. **Incorrect:** Rebooting a computer is often a good troubleshooting step, but it's unlikely all the computers suddenly developed faults at the same time.

   D. **Correct:** The switch is the common point of failure here, and you can often correct a problem like this by power cycling the switch.

4. **Correct Answer: C**

   A. **Incorrect:** Replacing the network interface card (NIC) shouldn't be done first. A sound troubleshooting practice is to do the easy things first. If this answer was "Check the link light on the NIC," it would be easier than verifying the port on the switch, and a better answer.

   B. **Incorrect:** If network connectivity is the only problem, replacing the computer isn't necessary.

C. **Correct:** If the computer is the only one not working, the problem is with the computer's NIC, the cable, or the port on the switch. The cable has been checked, and it's easier to check the port than replace the NIC or the computer.

D. **Incorrect:** Power cycling the switch might be appropriate if all devices can't communicate. However, if other devices are working, this will interrupt their connectivity and is not appropriate in this scenario.

5. **Correct Answer:** B

A. **Incorrect:** There are different types of digital subscriber lines (DSLs) and not all of them use different speeds.

B. **Correct:** Asymmetric digital subscriber lines (ADSLs) have different speeds for uploads and downloads.

C. **Incorrect:** Symmetric digital subscriber lines (SDSLs) use the same speed for uploads and downloads.

D. **Incorrect:** Dial-up connections use the same speed for uploads and downloads.

6. **Correct Answer:** D

A. **Incorrect:** Dial-up uses cables and does not require a clear line of sight.

B. **Incorrect:** ISDN uses cables and does not require a clear line of sight.

C. **Incorrect:** Cellular uses radio frequency transmissions and does not require a clear line of sight.

D. **Correct:** Satellite connections require a clear line of sight from the satellite disk to the satellite. Obstructions such as buildings or trees block the connection. While not listed, Worldwide Interoperability for Microwave Access (WiMAX) requires a clear line of site between WiMAX towers.

CHAPTER 19

Exploring Cables and Connectivity

Chapter 18, "Introducing Networking Components," covers the basic hardware used in networks, such as network interface cards, switches, and routers. You connect this hardware together using cables. There are several different types of cables and connectors you can use depending on the characteristics of your network. Just as you can't put a square peg into a round hole, you can't put an RJ-45 connector into a fiber port, so it's important to know the differences, which you'll learn in this chapter.

Exam 220-801 objectives in this chapter:

- 1.7 Compare and contrast various connection interfaces and explain their purpose.
    - Physical connections
        - Other connector types: RJ-45, RJ-11
- 1.11 Identify connector types and associated cables.
    - Display Connector types
        - RJ-45
    - Display cable types
        - Coaxial
        - Ethernet
    - Device connectors and pin arrangements
        - RJ-45
    - Device cable types
        - Ethernet
        - Phone
- 2.1 Identify types of network cables and connectors.
    - Fiber
        - Connectors: SC, ST and LC

- Twisted Pair
    - Connectors: RJ-11, RJ-45
    - Wiring standards: T568A, T568B
- Coaxial
    - Connectors: BNC, F-connector
- 2.2 Categorize characteristics of connectors and cabling.
    - Fiber
        - Types (single-mode vs. multi-mode)
        - Speed and transmission limitations
    - Twisted pair
        - Types: STP, UTP, CAT3, CAT5, CAT5e, CAT6, plenum, PVC
        - Speed and transmission limitations
    - Coaxial
        - Types: RG-6, RG-59
        - Speed and transmission limitations
- 2.8 Identify various types of networks.
    - Topologies
        - Mesh
        - Ring
        - Bus
        - Star
        - Hybrid
- 2.10 Given a scenario, use appropriate networking tools.
    - Crimper
    - Punchdown tool
- 5.1 Given a scenario, use appropriate safety procedures.
    - Personal safety
        - Cable management

Exam 220-802 objectives in this chapter:

- 1.6 Setup and configure Windows networking on a client/desktop.
    - Network card properties
        - Half duplex/full duplex/auto

- 4.5 Given a scenario, troubleshoot wired and wireless networks with appropriate tools.
  - Tools
    - Punch down tools
    - Wire strippers
    - Crimper

Introducing Ethernet

You can't write a letter to a friend and throw it into the street hoping it will magically be delivered. You have to put the letter in an envelope, properly address it, and then put it into a mailbox with proper postage. I'm betting this is nothing new to you.

Networks also have requirements for transferring data. Devices connected together must use compatible protocols, speeds, cables, and connection modes. Ethernet provides the standards used by these devices.

Ethernet is a group of specifications used for most wired networks. These standards identify the speed supported by different types of cables and how the cables connect through devices like hubs, switches, and routers. Cable types used in Ethernet networks include twisted-pair, coaxial, or fiber optic cables.

Data travels over these cables as data bits, and Ethernet standards define how these bits are packaged together as packets or frames. At this stage of your career, you don't need to know the details of how a packet or frame is created, but you do need to know specifics about cables.

> **NOTE** A+ AND NETWORK+
>
> After taking and passing the A+ certification exams, many people pursue the Network+ exam. You'll find that much of the material you learn in the A+ exam will help you with the Network+ exam. The primary difference is that the Network+ exam covers the networking topics in more depth.

Safety and Environmental Issues

When working with cables and connectivity, you need to be aware of some basic safety and environmental issues. Much of cable management is just common sense, but some of the environmental issues, such as plenum-safe cables and interference, might be new to you.

Cable Management and Trip Hazards

Cable management is the process of keeping cables neat. This often makes it easier to troubleshoot connectivity issues, and it can also reduce safety hazards.

For example, imagine a computer with multiple devices connected via USB cables and ports. If one of the devices stops working, you might want to move the cable to another port to see whether the problem is with the device or the USB port. If the cables are in a tangled mess, this simple troubleshooting step can be a challenge. On the other hand, if the cables are neat, it will be easy to identify the right cable and check it.

> **EXAM TIP**
>
> Cable management techniques reduce troubleshooting times. Technicians can easily identify connections for specific devices. Cable management can also reduce injuries from trip hazards.

Cables should not be run across a floor where someone can trip over them. Unfortunately, some people run power cables across a floor to a surge protector instead of just buying another surge protector. They might be saving a little on the expense side, but they are adding significant risk from the potential trip hazard.

If you must run a cable across a floor, you should cover it with heavy tape. For example, in some temporary lab environments, cables on the floor are covered with duct tape. This isn't ideal, but it significantly reduces the trip hazard.

PVC vs. Plenum-Safe Jackets

Cables have a protective covering around them known as a *jacket*. The jacket is typically made of *polyvinyl chloride (PVC)*, a type of flexible plastic. PVC is sufficient for most installations. However, when PVC burns, it can give off toxic fumes that can cause problems if the cable is run through certain areas, such as a plenum.

A *plenum* is an open space between walls, floors, or ceilings of a building where air is forced through for heating and cooling. Cables don't take much space and won't interfere with airflow, so it's common to run cables through these plenum spaces. However, if a fire spreads or ignites in a plenum and PVC cable is present, it's a huge problem. The air system will send the toxic fumes from the burning PVC to all the spaces receiving heated or cooled air. Additionally, the cable provides a path for the fire to spread to other areas.

To avoid this safety hazard, all cable running through a plenum must be rated as plenum-safe. Plenum-safe cable is fire-resistant and does not emit toxic fumes if it burns.

EXAM TIP

Plenum-safe cable is required for any cable going through a plenum, such as a raised floor, a dropped ceiling, or space inside walls.

Understanding Interference and Crosstalk

Many cables and connections are susceptible to interference that can disrupt or degrade the signals. Before digging into the cable types, it's important to understand the different types of interference.

The two primary types of interference are commonly known as *electromagnetic interference* (*EMI*) and *radio frequency interference* (*RFI*). Additionally, *crosstalk*, which occurs when data from one cable crosses over to another cable, can also cause problems.

> **NOTE** **EMI AND RFI COMBINED PROTECTION**
>
> EMI and RFI are sometimes combined into the same type of interference, categorized as EMI/RFI. There are technical differences, but technicians commonly protect against both EMI and RFI with shielded cables. If you can identify the source of the interference, you might be able to remove it.

The solution to these problems is often to use shielded cable or cable that is not susceptible to EMI/RFI problems, such as fiber optic cable. In some cases, you might be able to identify the source of the problem and eliminate it. For example, you can avoid EMI from a power cable simply by not running a data cable next to a power cable.

EMI

Electromagnetic interference (EMI) comes from magnetic fields generated by a wide variety of sources. For example, power cables are carrying voltage, and as the power travels along the cable, it generates an EMI field around the cable.

You can't see the EMI field, but if you could, it would look similar to Figure 19-1. The power cable has three wires within it, and the EMI field extends outside of the cable. Many electricians have testers they place around power cables to measure the voltage. Think of putting your thumb and index finger around a cable and touching your fingertips. This tester is similar, but instead of fingers, it uses hinged metal arms to wrap around the cable. The metal arms measure the EMI field and can determine whether a cable is carrying a signal. This is certainly better than just cutting through a power cable to see if it's live.

EMI field
Power cable

Signal cable next to power cable

FIGURE 19-1 EMI field around a power cable.

On the right in Figure 19-1, you can see a signal cable next to a power cable. If you run a signal cable alongside a power cable, the EMI field can easily engulf the signal cable and disrupt the signal. Because of this, many organizations will not run power cables right next to signal cables, which is a simple but effective step to avoid EMI problems from power cables.

EXAM TIP

EMI can cause problems for signals if LAN cables and power cables are in close proximity to each other. You can avoid the problem by separating power cables and signal cables.

Other examples of potential sources of EMI include the following:

- **Magnets.** If they are too close, strong magnets can interfere with signals. This includes magnets from older CRT-based monitors and some uninterruptible power supplies (UPSs).

- **Motors.** This includes motors from electronic devices such as laser printers. If the motor is too close to other devices or cables, it can interfere with the signals.

- **Lights.** Many fluorescent lights emit EMI, which has caused problems in the past.

RFI

Radio frequency interference (RFI) is caused by *radio frequency (RF)* signal transmissions. As an example, an AM transmitter station in a field behind my home has sometimes boosted its power. These AM signals have leaked onto my phone lines and older TVs.

Some common examples in homes and offices are cordless phones and microwave ovens. They transmit frequencies in the 2.4-GHz range and can interfere with RF transmissions used on wireless networks. Chapter 23, "Exploring Wireless Networking," provides information about how you can use different channels to avoid problems from RFI.

Crosstalk

As mentioned earlier, crosstalk occurs when data from one cable crosses over to another cable. This can degrade the signals on each cable in some cases. At other times, it results in unauthorized users having access to data.

For example, Figure 19-2 shows how data can cross over from one cable to another. In this case, one cable is carrying secret data and the other is carrying unclassified data. If these two cables are right next to each other, secret data can cross over to the unclassified data cable.

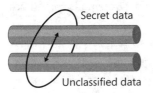

FIGURE 19-2 Crosstalk between two cables.

> ✔ **Quick Check**
>
> 1. What is the benefit of plenum-safe cables?
>
> 2. What type of interference can occur if you run data and power cables together?
>
> **Quick Check Answers**
>
> 1. They are fire-resistant and don't emit toxic fumes.
>
> 2. Electromagnetic interference (EMI).

Comparing Half-Duplex and Full-Duplex

Devices include a specification that identifies their capabilities for sending and receiving data at the same time. You should understand the following three terms:

- **Simplex.** *Simplex* allows traffic in only one direction, and one way only. That is, a connection can send data or receive data, but not both. This isn't common in a LAN today, but you might run across the term.

- **Half-duplex.** *Half-duplex* allows traffic in both directions, but in only one direction at a time. For example, walkie-talkies, push-to-talk radios, or press-to-talk cellular phones have this capability. You can listen or talk with the device, but while you're talking, you can't hear anyone else.

- **Full-duplex (also called duplex).** *Full-duplex* devices can send and receive at the same time. They include connections and cable support so that part of the cable is sending while part of the cable is receiving.

I've found that most people can easily grasp the meaning of these terms. Simplex is one-way only, half-duplex is two-way but only one direction at a time, and full-duplex is two-way simultaneous communications. However, connecting this concept to networking is sometimes challenging. Why is this important?

Imagine that I was using a walkie-talkie that allowed me to only talk or listen at any given time, and you were using a brand new cell phone that could also communicate on my walkie-talkie frequency. Your new phone allows you to talk and listen at the same time. However, if you start talking while I'm talking, I won't hear what you say. No matter how fancy your phone is, you still need to use it as a walkie-talkie when talking to me.

Similarly, to use full-duplex mode, all elements of a connection must support it. This includes both devices and the cable connecting them. For example, consider a brand new computer with a full-duplex network interface card (NIC) connecting to an older switch that uses only half-duplex. Because the switch can use only half-duplex, the computer must also use half-duplex.

Many older network devices use half-duplex. Because they can only send or receive at any given time, they are slower than full-duplex devices. Even if you connect a faster device using full-duplex, the faster device will use the slower half-duplex mode.

> **NOTE   LED COLOR SHOWS DUPLEX MODE**
>
> Network devices often display an amber LED for the connection if they are using half-duplex. In contrast, the network device will have a green light if it is running in full-duplex mode. This is different for different devices, but the device documentation will describe the meaning of the different lights.

Many newer network devices use *auto-negotiation* or *autosense* to automatically detect the capabilities of connected devices. For example, if you purchase a 1,000-Mbps switch that works in full-duplex mode, it will also work at 10 Mbps in half-duplex mode.

When you plug a device into a port, the switch senses the speed and mode of the other device. It will automatically adjust the settings for the port to connect at the fastest possible speed and fastest mode. If you plug in a newer 1,000-Mbps full-duplex device into a different port, the switch will sense its capabilities and adjust the port for the faster full-duplex mode. This won't affect communication on other switch ports.

Unfortunately, some older devices don't have auto-negotiation. To ensure maximum compatibility, they default to slower speeds. If you want to use the faster speed or the faster mode, you have to manually configure the device.

EXAM TIP

Full-duplex provides the fastest performance. If you suspect network devices are running slower than they should, check the mode and speed of the device. You might need to manually configure the device to use full-duplex mode and the fastest speed.

You can use the following steps to verify the duplex settings of a NIC on a Windows 7–based computer.

1. Click Start, and select Control Panel.

2. Type **network** in the Search Control Panel text box.

3. Select View Network Connections.

4. The NIC is commonly labeled Local Area Connection, but it might have been renamed. Right-click the connection and select Properties. Click Configure.

5. Click the Advanced tab. You'll see several of the NIC properties and assigned values. Different vendors use different property names, and when you select a property, it will show the current value of the property.

6. Select the property used for the connection speed and duplex settings. In the following graphic, this setting is named Connection Type, but you might see it named Speed & Duplex or something similar. To show the other available choices, click the arrow for the Value settings.

Intel 21140-Based PCI Fast Ethernet Adapter (Emulated) Propert...

General | Advanced | Driver | Details

The following properties are available for this network adapter. Click the property you want to change on the left, and then select its value on the right.

Property:

Burst Length
Connection Type
Extra Receive Buffers
Extra Receive Packets
Interrupt Mitigation
Memory Read Multiple
Network Address
Process Transmit First
Receive Buffers
Store And Forward
Transmit Threshold
Transmit Threshold 100Mbps
Underrun Max Retries
Underrun Threshold

Value:

AutoSense

100BaseFx
100BaseFx Full Duplex
100BaseT4
100BaseTx
100BaseTx Full Duplex
10BaseT (Twisted Pair)
10BaseT Full Duplex
AutoSense

OK   Cancel

7. Identify the setting used for autosense or auto-negotiation. In the graphic, it's named AutoSense, but you might see it listed as Auto Negotiation or something similar.

> *NOTE* **MAC ADDRESS**
>
> This graphic also shows how someone can change the media access control (MAC) address of a NIC. You can select Network Address and enter a new MAC address.

> ✔ **Quick Check**
>   1. What mode supports simultaneous communication?
>   2. What allows switches to automatically use the fastest speed and mode?
>
> **Quick Check Answers**
>   1. Full-duplex mode.
>   2. Autosense or auto-negotiation.

Comparing Bits per Second and Bytes per Second

Many speeds are listed as bits per second (bps), but you might also see speeds listed as bytes per second (Bps). Bits per second has a lowercase *b*, as in *bps*. Bytes per second has an uppercase *B*, as in *Bps*.

These two speeds are very different. Eight bits make up a byte, so 100 MBps indicates eight times more data than 100 Mbps. It's a subtle difference between *b* and *B*, but there is a huge difference in the meaning. It's important to be able to recognize the difference between the two.

Network connectivity is almost always listed in bits per second (bps). This includes the speed of a NIC, a switch, a router, and a connection to an Internet Service Provider (ISP). Unfortunately, some ISPs have listed download speeds with Bps, which confuses things.

Disk transfer speeds are sometimes listed in bytes per second, such as 150 MBps. You might also see disk transfer speeds listed in bits per second (bps), such as 3 Gbps. However, an uppercase *B* still means bytes, and a lowercase *b* still means bits.

Memory is always listed in bytes. For example, a 2-GB memory stick has two gigabytes (about 2 billion bytes) of memory storage capacity. It's incorrect to list this memory stick as 2 Gb, with a lowercase *b*.

Common Network Cables and Connectors

The most common type of cable you'll see in most networks today is twisted-pair. However, there are different types of twisted-pair cables and cables other than twisted-pair. In this section, you'll learn about the differences.

Ethernet Twisted-Pair

Twisted-pair cable used with Ethernet connections includes four twisted pairs of wires. Each pair has a specific number of twists per meter, with different pairs having a different number of twists. Even though the pairs are right next to each other in the same cable, these twists prevent signals from crossing over to each other. Additionally, the number of twists per meter determines the frequency capabilities of the cable. Higher frequencies allow the cable to transmit more data.

RJ-45 vs. RJ-11

Ethernet twisted-pair uses registered jack (*RJ-45*) connectors on both ends. These connectors are technically called 8P8C (eight pins eight contacts), but technicians call them RJ-45 connectors. However, 8P8C helps emphasize that the cable has eight wires as four pairs.

For example, one end can plug into the RJ-45 port of a computer's network interface card (NIC), and the other end can plug into a switch. Figure 19-3 shows the RJ-45 connector on the back of a computer.

 — RJ-45 port

FIGURE 19-3 RJ-45 connector on back of computer.

> *NOTE* **TWO LEDS**
>
> Figure 19-3 also shows two LEDs on the RJ-45 port. They aren't labeled, but the LED on the top right is the Link light used to show connectivity. The LED on the bottom right is the activity light, and it blinks when it detects activity on the port.

The RJ-45 connector is similar to the *RJ-11* connector used for phones. However, RJ-11 connectors are smaller than RJ-45 connectors. Also, phone cables using RJ-11 connections have only two pairs of wires, while Ethernet twisted-pair cables using RJ-45 connectors have four pairs of wires.

Figure 19-4 shows an example of a twisted-pair cable commonly used in Ethernet networks. One end of the cable is cut so that you can see the four pairs of twisted wires. The other end shows the RJ-45 connector common in Ethernet networks. In the figure, pin 8 is on the left and pin 1 is on the right. For comparison, an RJ-11 phone connector is shown next to the RJ-45 connector.

Pin 8

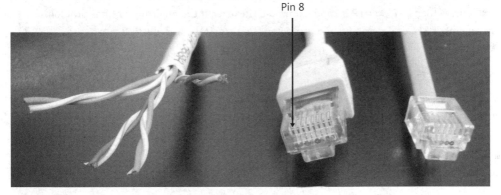

FIGURE 19-4 Twisted-pair cable with RJ-45 and RJ-11 connectors.

The length of twisted-pair cables is limited to 100 meters (about 328 feet). Therefore, the distance between a computer and a switch or between a switch and a router can't be more than 100 meters. If the distance between the devices is longer than 100 meters, you need to use a repeater. A repeater simply amplifies the signal so that it can go up to another 100 meters. Other cable types can also use repeaters, but their maximum distance is different from that of twisted-pair cables.

UTP vs. STP

Most Ethernet cable is *unshielded twisted-pair (UTP)*, similar to that shown in Figure 19-4. However, in some situations, EMI, RFI, or crosstalk can cause problems with unshielded cable. You can use *shielded twisted-pair (STP)* to prevent these problems.

Figure 19-5 shows a comparison of the different types of shielding. All types of twisted-pair have a covering, or jacket, over the pairs to protect them. STP cables also have a metallic shielding around the pairs to prevent interference and crosstalk. In simple STP, it has shielding only around all four pairs. In S/UTP, it has shielding around each of the pairs. In S/STP, it has shielding around each of the pairs and then again around all four pairs. Additional shielding provides additional protection.

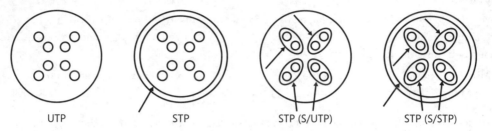

FIGURE 19-5 Four pairs in unshielded and shielded twisted-pair.

Comparing Categories

Twisted-pair is identified using different categories. Each category includes different specifications, and higher numbers indicate newer cables that can support faster speeds.

Each of these categories is commonly shortened to *CAT* and the number, as shown in Table 19-1. The table lists the maximum speeds of each, along with some comments. Each cable includes four pairs of wires and has a maximum length of 100 meters.

TABLE 19-1 Categories of Twisted-pair Cable

Category	Maximum Speed	Frequency	Comments
CAT 3	10 Mbps	16 MHz	Rarely used today
CAT 5	100 Mbps	100 MHz	Recommended maximum speed of 100 Mbps
CAT 5e	1,000 Mbps	100 MHz	Enhanced version of CAT 5
CAT 6	10 Gbps	250 MHz	Used with 10GBase-T

Notice that CAT 5 has a recommended maximum of 100 Mbps. The original specification for 1000BaseT indicated that you could use CAT 5 for 1,000 Mbps. However, in practice it often had problems with signal loss at 1,000 Mbps. CAT 5e is an enhanced version of CAT 5 and supports 1,000 Mbps without any problems.

EXAM TIP

You should know the category of cable required for different speeds. For example, if you are installing a Gigabit network, you must use at least CAT 5e cables.

T568A vs. T568B

A twisted-pair cable includes four pairs of wires, and each pair is twisted around each of the others as shown in Figure 19-4. It's not apparent from the black-and-white photo, but these pairs have matching colors. The colors of the four pairs are:

- Green, and white with a green stripe
- Blue, and white with a blue stripe
- Orange, and white with an orange stripe
- Brown, and white with a brown stripe

When building a twisted-pair cable, specific colored wires should go to specific pins in the RJ-45 connector. There are two standards in use: *T568A* and *T568B*. It doesn't matter which standard is used in a cable as long the same standard is used on both ends.

Table 19-2 shows the pinout for each of the standards. You can see that the differences are with the green pair and the orange pair. T568A has the green pair on pins 1 and 2 and the orange pair on pins 3 and 6. T568B has the green pair on pins 3 and 6 and the orange pair on pins 1 and 2.

TABLE 19-2 T568A and T568B Color Codes

T568A Color	RJ-45 Pin	T568B Color
White, green stripe	1	White, orange stripe
Green	2	Orange
White, orange stripe	3	White, green stripe
Blue	4	Blue
White, blue stripe	5	White, blue stripe
Orange	6	Green
White, brown stripe	7	White, brown stripe
Brown	8	Brown

Crossover Cable

Most twisted-pair cable is created as a *straight-through cable* using either the T568A or T568B standard. Pin 1 on one connector goes to Pin 1 on the other connector. This is required when connecting computers to network devices such as switches.

However, sometimes you need to connect similar network devices together, such as a computer with a computer, a switch with a switch, or even a router with a switch. In this case, specific pins of the cables need to be crossed over. Interestingly, if you wire one connector using T568A and the other connector using T568B, you've created a *crossover cable*.

> **NOTE** **CAT 6 USES AUTOSENSE**
>
> CAT 6 devices sense when a crossover cable is needed and automatically adjust the connection internally. Because of this, you don't need CAT 6 crossover cables.

The crossover cable allows one device to receive data transmitted by the other device. With a standard straight-through cable, the pins are wired so that similar devices would be transmitting on the same pins, effectively blocking the traffic.

Figure 19-6 shows an example. When connecting a computer to a switch, you'd use a regular straight-through cable. However, when connecting the switch to a router, you'd use a crossover cable.

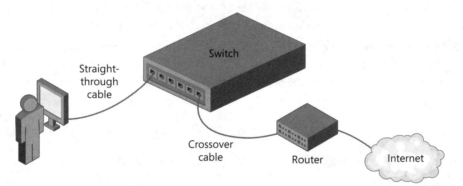

FIGURE 19-6 Crossover cable used to connect a switch and a router.

> **NOTE** **LABELING CABLES**
>
> Technicians commonly mark crossover cables with *X* to indicate that they are crossover cables. Additionally, you can place both of the clear plastic RJ-45 connectors side by side and look at the cables. If the colors of the wires are in the same order on both (such as orange, blue, and green), it is a straight-through cable. If the colors are in a different order on one of the connectors (such as green, orange, and blue), it is a crossover cable. There are more wires and more colors, but the solid orange, blue, and green wires stand out.

You can also connect two computers together with a crossover cable. It isn't common, but it does allow you to create a miniature network of two computers without a hub or a switch.

Many devices can dynamically modify the wiring within the port. These devices have a button labeled MDI/MDIX, short for medium dependent interface (MDI)/medium dependent interface crossover (MDIX). If you set it to MDIX, you can use a straight-through cable, but it wires the port as if a crossover cable were connected. Newer devices include an auto-MDIX capability. They don't have the MDI/MDIX button but can automatically sense the correct connection and select the correct mode.

Wire Strippers and Wire Crimper

You can purchase ready-made cables in many different lengths. However, if you're wiring several computers together, it's often cheaper to make your own cables, and it's relatively easy with the right tools. The two primary tools you need are the following:

- **Wire strippers.** The *wire strippers* are used to strip off the jacket and then to strip off the insulation on each wire.

- **Crimper.** A wire *crimper* squeezes the RJ-45 connector around the cable to hold it in place. You can buy basic crimpers for less than $10.

You strip off about 2 inches of the jacket and about 1/2 to 3/4 inch of the individual wires. Next, place the wires into the RJ-45 connector, matching them up to the correct pin. Be careful to untwist only what is absolutely needed to strip the wire and place it in the correct pin. If you untwist too much, it can reduce the frequency capabilities of the cable and result in errors when transmitting data at the highest speed. With everything in place, you use the crimper to squeeze the connector onto the wire.

> **NOTE   MAKE YOUR OWN CABLES**
>
> If you want to solidify some of this knowledge, here's a valuable project: buy some twisted-pair cable, some RJ-45 (8P8C) connectors, and a combo wire stripper/wire crimper tool. You can get it all for less than $30, and after making a few cables, you'll have a much deeper understanding of the wiring. And you'll be a step ahead for the Network+ exam.

Punchdown Tool

Cables sent through the walls to other rooms rarely have connectors. Instead, they are attached to jacks and punchdown blocks by using a *punchdown tool*.

Figure 19-7 shows the typical path of a cable in most organizations. Twisted-pair cable with RJ-45 connectors will run from the computers to RJ-45 jacks in the wall. Cables are attached to the other side of the jack inside the wall and then run to a punchdown block in a wiring room. Last, a short twisted-pair cable with two RJ-45 connectors is run from the other side of the punchdown block to a network device, such as a switch.

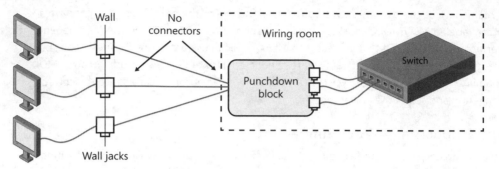

FIGURE 19-7 Cable path from computer to switch.

You use wire strippers and crimpers to create cables with the RJ-45 connectors. You use a punchdown tool to connect the cables to the back of the RJ-45 jacks and to the punchdown block.

A punchdown tool is a small handheld spring-loaded tool. A technician places a wire over the jack or in a slot in the punchdown block and then pushes the wire in with the punchdown tool. With a little pressure, the spring-loaded mechanism releases, stripping the wire and securing it in place.

Fiber Optic Cable

Fiber optic cable is made of a flexible glass material, and signals travel over fiber as light pulses. The many different types of connectors used for fiber include the following:

- **SC.** *SC* is short for *square connector*, and as you'd expect, it's shaped like a square.

- **LC.** *LC* is short for *Lucent Connector* because it was developed by Lucent Technologies. This is a miniaturized version of the SC connector and is becoming very popular in new installations.

- **ST.** *ST* is short for *straight tip*, and the connectors are round.

Fiber is more expensive and more difficult to work with than twisted-pair cables. It's rare to see it in small offices/home offices (SOHOs), but many larger organizations are using it more and more. Fiber has three important benefits over twisted-pair cable:

- **Signals can travel much farther.** Some types of fiber optic cable can carry signals as far as 10 kilometers (km), or over 6 miles, without a repeater. Compare this to the 100-meter limitation of twisted-pair cable.

- **It can carry more data.** Fiber cables have a larger bandwidth, allowing them to send and receive more data.

- **It's immune to EMI and RFI problems.** Because signals travel as light pulses, EMI and RFI interference doesn't affect the signal. Additionally, the light pulses can't cross over to other cables, so it's immune to crosstalk problems.

Fiber comes in two forms: *multi-mode fiber (MMF)* and *single-mode fiber (SMF)*. MMF allows multiple signals to travel in the same cable. SMF is used for only one signal, and data can travel farther on an SMF cable than it can on an MMF cable. Table 19-3 lists some MMF and SMF characteristics.

TABLE 19-3 MMF and SMF Characteristics

Characteristic	MMF	SMF
Size	Larger core	Smaller core
Max Distance	Up to 2 km	Up to 40 km
Max Speed	Up to 10 Gbps	Up to 10 Gbps
Core	Plastic core	Glass core

While the table shows the maximum distance and maximum speeds, MMF fiber cannot send data the maximum distance using the maximum speed. For example, it can transmit data at a rate of 100 Mbps up to 2 km or transmit data at a rate of 10 Gbps up to 300 meters, but it cannot transmit data at the maximum of 10 Gbps the maximum distance of 2 km.

Coaxial Cable

Coaxial cable is similar to the cable that you use to connect a TV to a VCR or DVD player, or even a TV to a cable TV connection. It includes a copper core, insulation, and shielding covered by a cable jacket. Many older networks used coaxial cable, but it has been replaced with twisted-pair or fiber cable, and it's rare to use coaxial cable in a local area network. However, it is commonly used for TV and cable TV connections and, in some cases, to network TV devices.

The two primary types of coaxial cables used with TV connections are *RG-59* and *RG-6*:

- **RG-59.** This was originally used with cable TV connections and is efficient when transmitting analog signals. It can be used to transmit data between video systems, such as between a DVD player and a TV. It was used in some early networks but can transmit only a limited amount of data. RG-59 uses a *BNC* connector, which uses a push and turn connection.

- **RG-6.** This cable has a larger center conductor than RG-59 does, and it has additional shielding. It has become the standard used with cable TV and satellite TV systems because it is more efficient when transmitting any digital signals, including High Definition (HD) signals. Networks using coaxial cable today will use RG-6. It uses an *F-type screw-on connector.*

Some cable companies have begun using coaxial cables between multiple boxes to create in-home networks. For example, DirecTV sells a Whole Home DVR that allows you to record television shows on a DVR room in one room and then play the shows from any DirecTV box in the house. It uses RG-6 cable with *F*-type connectors but will not work with the older RG-59 cable.

Older networks used RG-58 or RG-8 cable. For example, 10Base2 used RG-58 with BNC connectors and could transmit data at a rate of 10 Mbps up to 185 meters. 10Base5 used RG-8 with screw-on *N* connectors and could transmit data at a rate of 10 Mbps up to 500 meters.

✔ **Quick Check**

1. Name the two wiring standards used for twisted-pair cabling.
2. Name three common connectors used with fiber.

Quick Check Answers

1. T568A and T568B.
2. SC, LC, and ST.

Speeds and Specifications

Ethernet uses a specific naming convention. If you learn this format, you can usually identify the speed and what type of cable it is using. If you know the cable, you'll have an idea of the connector it needs.

The basic specification is *n*BASE-*x*, where *n* indicates the speed and *x* is an identifier for the cable. Table 19-4 shows some examples.

TABLE 19-4 Specification Examples

Specification	Speed	Cable and connector
10BASE2	10 Mbps	Coaxial cable using a BNC connector
100BASE-T	100 Mbps	Twisted-pair (notice the T) using an RJ-45 connector
1000BASE-LX	1,000 Mbps	Fiber cable using an ST or SC connector
10GBase-T	10 Gbps	Twisted-pair using an RJ-45 connector

You can see that if the first number is 10, it indicates the speed is 10 Mbps. If it's 100, it indicates a speed of 100 Mbps, and 1,000 indicates 1,000 Mbps (or 1 Gbps). The last item in the table uses 10G to indicate 10 Gbps.

EXAM TIP

There are many more identifier letters, and if you follow your studies into the Network+ exam, you'll dig deeper. However, if you can identify the speed and the cable type, you'll be prepped for the A+ exams. The speed is easy because it's just the first number. Identifying the cable is a little more challenging, but the identifier gives the clue. If it's 2, 5, or C, it's coaxial. If it starts with a *T*, it's twisted-pair. The rest are fiber.

Ethernet Speeds

Traditional Ethernet operates at 10 Mbps. That was certainly fast when it first came out, but it is relatively slow today. Most network devices can operate at speeds faster than 10 Mbps, with 1 Gbps common in most networks. Table 19-5 shows some common specifications used with traditional Ethernet.

TABLE 19-5 Some Common Ethernet Specifications

Cable type	Name	Comments
Coaxial	10Base2	Maximum distance 185 meters. Also called Thinnet.
Coaxial	10Base5	Maximum distance 500 meters. Also called Thicknet.
Twisted-pair	10BaseT	CAT 5 cable using two pair of a four-pair cable. Maximum distance 100 meters.
Fiber	10Base-FL	Can reach distances up to 550 meters (about 1,800 feet).

Fast Ethernet

Fast Ethernet improved the speed from 10 Mbps to 100 Mbps. Most Fast Ethernet cables are either twisted-pair or fiber, as shown in Table 19-6.

TABLE 19-6 Fast Ethernet Specifications

Cable type	Name	Comments
Twisted-pair	100Base-T	CAT 5 cable using two pairs in a four-pair cable.
Twisted-pair	100Base-Tx	Most common form of 100Base-T. Supports full-duplex mode.
Fiber	100Base-FX	Not compatible with 10Base-FL used in Ethernet.
Fiber	100Base-SX	Uses two strands of fiber: one for receiving and one for transmitting.

Gigabit Ethernet

Gigabit Ethernet is becoming much more common. Data can travel at 1 gigabit per second (1 Gbps), and it's commonly labeled as either 1,000 Mbps or 1 Gbps. Gigabit Ethernet requires all devices to use auto-negotiation and full-duplex mode.

A gigabit network can easily transfer broadcast quality video over a network. For example, home users can use one computer to store movies and TV and broadcast them to any TV in the home. Table 19-7 shows some common Gigabit Ethernet specifications.

TABLE 19-7 Gigabit Ethernet Specifications

Cable type	Name	Comments
Twisted-pair	1000Base-T	CAT-5E 6 cable using all four pairs of a four-pair cable. Max distance 100 m.
Single-mode Fiber	1000Base-LX	Max distance 5 km.
Single-mode Fiber	1000Base-ZX	Max distance 70 km.
Multi-mode Fiber	1000Base-SX	Max distance 550 m.
Multi-mode Fiber	1000Base-LX	Max distance 550 m.

The tables in these sections do not include all the possible specifications, but they do give you an idea of some common cables used with Ethernet. More specifically, they cover the specifications you can expect to see on an A+ exam.

10-Gigabit Ethernet

It isn't as common today, but 10-Gigabit Ethernet is being used in some networks. Just as the name implies, it can reach speeds of 10 Gbps. Twisted-pair using 10 Gigabit is identified as 10GBase-T, and it requires CAT 6 cable. Table 19-8 shows some of the 10-Gigabit standards.

TABLE 19-8 10-Gigabit Ethernet Specifications

Cable type	Name	Comments
Twisted-pair	10GBase-T	CAT-6 or enhanced CAT-6A cable. Max distance 100 m.
Single-mode Fiber	10GBASE-LR	LR indicates long range. Max distance 10 km.
Single-mode Fiber	10GBASE-ER	ER indicates extended range. Max distance 40 km.
Multi-mode Fiber	10GBASE-SR	SR indicates short range. Max distance 400 m.

Topologies

Computers can be organized within a network by using different network topologies. The *topology* refers to how the devices are logically connected, and the most common topology is the star topology. The following sections describe the different topologies in more detail.

EXAM TIP

Know the basics about the five basic topologies when preparing for the exam. These were not tested in previous versions of A+, but because they were added in this version, you can fully expect to see some questions related to them.

Star

A *star topology* has multiple devices connected to a central device such as a switch or hub. For example, Figure 19-8 shows a star topology. If you substitute the central device with a star, you can see how it got its name.

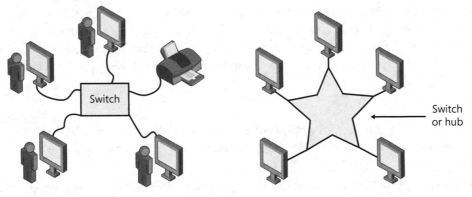

FIGURE 19-8 Star topology.

While this looks like a star when drawn, it does not indicate the physical layout. For example, imagine an Ethernet classroom with 20 computers. The computers would connect to RJ-45 jacks in the classroom walls. Cables run from the jacks to a punchdown block in a wiring room, and short cables run from the block to a switch, as shown in Figure 19-7.

A benefit is that each device has a direct line to the switch or hub, and if you use a switch, devices don't compete with each other to send traffic along the line. Also, if a connected device fails, it is the only device affected; it doesn't prevent other devices from working.

Bus

A *bus topology* has multiple devices connected to each other in a logical line. A unique characteristic of bus topologies is that both ends of the line must be terminated. When a signal travels along a cable, it will be reflected back without this terminator. This reflected signal results in data collisions and prevents any usable data transmissions.

Figure 19-9 shows a bus topology commonly used in older 10Base2 networks. Each device had a T connector, and devices were connected in a line with coaxial cable and BNC connectors. The devices on each end connected to a terminator instead of to another device.

FIGURE 19-9 Bus topology.

A bus topology is very simple to configure and uses less cable than a star topology. However, it is very problematic with 10Base2 networks. If a terminator is removed or if a cable anywhere on the bus is disconnected or faulty, all devices on the bus stop communicating. Not only that, but it's not a simple matter to identify the break. In contrast, when a single computer in a star network fails, it is the only one affected and the problem is with its cabling.

Ring

A *ring topology* has all computers logically configured in a single circle or a ring. Data travels around the ring to different devices. Most ring topologies use a logical token and are called *token ring networks*.

The token is a specially formatted set of bytes passed to devices in the ring. Devices can transmit data only when they have the token, and after they transmit their data, they pass the token on to the next computer.

A token ring network does not scale well. In other words, performance is seriously degraded as the number of devices increases. You can think of this as a single piece of paper passed around by a group of people, and each person can talk only when holding the piece of paper. This might work with 10 people in a room, but imagine if there were 100 or 1,000 people. Each person would have fewer opportunities to communicate. Similarly, ring topologies are effective only with a small number of devices.

Figure 19-10 shows different configurations of a ring topology. One of the problems discovered early with ring topologies is that if any single computer failed, it broke the ring and all traffic stopped. Many rings added a *multistation access unit* (*MAU*). The computers were still in a logical ring, but all devices sent and received data through the MAU. If a device failed, the MAU sensed the failure and didn't pass the token to the failed device.

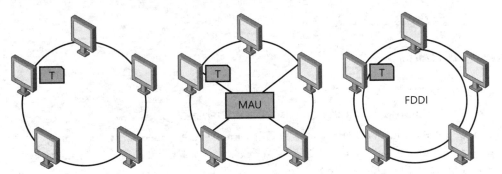

FIGURE 19-10 Ring topology.

> **NOTE HYBRID**
>
> A ring topology using an MAU is actually a hybrid of a ring and a star.

Fiber Distributed Data Interface (FDDI) is a type of token ring topology that uses fiber optic cable and two rings. The second ring provides a redundant path that can be used if the first path fails.

Mesh

A *mesh topology* is one where each device has a connection with all other computers in the network. It provides a high degree of redundancy, allowing devices to continue to communicate even if multiple connections fail. However, it is rarely used due to the expense.

Figure 19-11 shows an example of a mesh topology with five computers. Each computer needs four connections, and the network requires a total of 10 connections. If you had 10 computers, each computer would need nine connections, and the network would require a total of 45 connections.

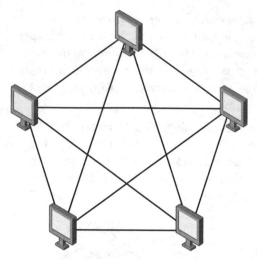

FIGURE 19-11 Mesh topology.

> **NOTE** **CALCULATING CONNECTIONS IN A MESH TOPOLOGY**
>
> You can calculate the number of connections in a mesh with the following formula: n x $(n\text{-}1) / 2$ where n is the number of devices. For example, with five devices, the formula is: $5 \times (5\text{-}1) / 2$ or 5 x 4 (20) divided by 2 (10).

Hybrid

A *hybrid topology* is a combination of any two or more of the other topologies, and many networks use a hybrid topology. For example, end user computers are commonly configured in a star topology. The same network can connect to servers using a high-speed FDDI topology.

> ✔ **Quick Check**
>
> **1.** What topology connects multiple devices using a central device such as a switch?
>
> **2.** What topology restricts communication until a device has a token?
>
> **Quick Check Answers**
>
> **1.** Star.
>
> **2.** Ring, or token ring.

Chapter Summary

- Ethernet is a group of specifications for networks. The standards identify speeds, cable types, and connections. Cables defined in Ethernet standards include twisted-pair, coaxial, and fiber optic cables.

- Cable management ensures that cables don't present a trip hazard and also results in easier troubleshooting.

- Plenum-safe cable is fire-resistant and does not emit toxic fumes when it burns.

- EMI comes from magnetic fields, including fields generated by power cables, magnets, lights, and motors.

- RFI comes from radio transmissions, including those from cordless phones and micro-wave ovens.

- Simplex transmissions go only one way on a cable. Half-duplex transmissions can be sent and received, but only one way at a time. Full-duplex transmissions can send and receive at the same time.

- Simplex is rarely used in networks anymore. Gigabit Ethernet devices all use full-duplex mode.

- LED lights on devices often indicate a device's speed and mode (such as full-duplex or half-duplex). Most devices automatically configure the fastest speed and mode, but older devices might need to be manually configured.

- Twisted-pair network cables include four pair of twisted wires. Each end of the cable has an RJ-45 connector, and they can plug into RJ-45 ports on devices.

- RJ-11 cables are smaller and carry voltages that can damage components if plugged into an RJ-45 port.

- Shielded twisted-pair (STP) provides protection against EMI and RFI.

- CAT 3 supports 10 Mbps but is rarely used today. CAT 5 supports 100 Mbps, CAT 5e supports 1 Gbps, and CAT 6 supports 10 Gbps. All are limited to 100 meters.

- Two standards used for wiring cables are T568A and T568B. The same standard must be used on both ends of the cable to create a straight-through cable.

- Crossover cables are used to connect network devices together, such as a switch and a router, or even two computers as a mini-network. Some devices include auto-MDIX capabilities to dynamically wire a port as if a crossover cable were connected.

- Wire crimpers clamp a prepared twisted-pair cable onto an RJ-45 jack. Punchdown tools connect twisted-pair wires to jacks or punchdown blocks.

- Fiber optic cable can carry signals farther than twisted-pair or coaxial cable without a repeater. It can also carry more data in smaller cables. Fiber is immune to EMI and RFI problems. Fiber cables commonly use SC, LC, or ST connectors.

- Coaxial cable is similar to cables used with TVs and DVD players. RG-59 cable uses BNC twist-on connectors. RG-8 cable uses a screw-on F-type connector.
- Ethernet cable specifications are commonly listed as *n*Base-*x*, where *n* is the speed, and *x* indicates the cable type.
- Original Ethernet used a speed of 10 Mbps. Fast Ethernet has speeds of 100 Mbps, and Gigabit Ethernet reaches speeds of 1,000 Mbps (or 1 Gbps).
- Topologies identify how devices are logically configured in a network. A star topology includes a central device such as a switch, a bus configures devices in a line, and a ring configures devices in a circle. A hybrid is a combination of any two or more topologies.

Chapter Review

Use the following questions to test your knowledge of the information in this chapter. The answers to these questions, and the explanations of why each answer choice is correct or incorrect, are located in the "Answers" section at the end of this chapter.

1. Of the following choices, what can a technician employ to easily identify connections for devices?

   A. Shielding

   B. Cable management

   C. Fiber optic cable

   D. Plenum-safe cable

2. What type of cable should you use in spaces used for air conditioning?

   A. Twisted-pair

   B. Fiber

   C. Coaxial

   D. Plenum-safe

3. What mode allows data to travel in both directions at the same time?

   A. Simplex

   B. Half-duplex

   C. Full-duplex

   D. MDIX

4. What type of connector will you find on a twisted-pair cable connected to a switch?

   A. RJ-11

   B. RJ-45

   C. BNC

   D. LC

5. Which category cable is the minimum recommended to support speeds of 1,000 Mbps?

   A. CAT 3

   B. CAT 5

   C. CAT 5e

   D. CAT 6

6. What type of cable would you use to connect two computers together that have RJ-45 ports?

   A. Twisted-pair crossover cable

   B. Twisted-pair straight-through cable

   C. Fiber crossover cable

   D. Fiber straight-through cable

7. What type of connector will you find on a fiber optic cable?

   A. RJ-11

   B. RJ-45

   C. BNC

   D. LC

Answers

1. **Correct Answer: B**

   A. **Incorrect:** Shielding can reduce problems from interference but won't help identify connections.

   B. **Correct:** Cable management ensures that cables are relatively neat and easy to trace. Cable management also reduces trip hazards.

   C. **Incorrect:** Fiber provides higher speeds and longer lengths without a repeater, but cables still need to be kept neat.

   D. **Incorrect:** Plenum-safe cable is fire-resistant and doesn't emit toxic fumes, but cables still need to be kept neat.

2. **Correct Answer: D**

   A. **Incorrect:** Twisted-pair can be used as long as it has a plenum-safe jacket.

   B. **Incorrect:** Fiber can be used as long as it has a plenum-safe jacket.

   C. **Incorrect:** Coaxial can be used as long as it has a plenum-safe jacket.

   D. **Correct:** Plenum-safe cable should be used in air-handling spaces because it is fire-resistant and doesn't emit toxic fumes.

3. **Correct Answer: C**

   A. **Incorrect:** Data can be only sent or only received when using a simplex connection.

   B. **Incorrect:** Half-duplex allows data to be sent or received on the same cable, but not at the same time.

   C. **Correct:** Data travels in both directions at the same time with full-duplex mode.

   D. **Incorrect:** Medium dependent interface crossover (MDIX) is a mode that allows a port to change connections as though it were connected with a crossover cable.

4. **Correct Answer: B**

   A. **Incorrect:** RJ-11 connectors are used for phone connections.

   B. **Correct:** RJ-45 connectors are used for twisted-pair cables connecting network devices, such as a switch.

   C. **Incorrect:** BNC connectors are used for coaxial cables.

   D. **Incorrect:** LC connectors are used for fiber cables.

5. **Correct Answer: C**

    A. **Incorrect:** CAT 3 is used for speeds up to 10 Mbps.

    B. **Incorrect:** CAT 5 is used for speeds up to 100 Mbps. It has errors when used at 1,000 Mbps, so CAT 5e is recommended instead.

    C. **Correct:** CAT 5e is an enhanced version of CAT 5, and it supports speeds up to 1,000 Mbps.

    D. **Incorrect:** CAT 6 is used for speeds up to 10 Gbps.

6. **Correct Answer: A**

    A. **Correct:** A twisted-pair crossover cable is used to connect two computers together directly through their RJ-45 ports.

    B. **Incorrect:** A straight-through cable is used to connect a computer to a switch but not to another computer.

    C. **Incorrect:** Fiber optic does not use crossover cables.

    D. **Incorrect:** Fiber optic does not use RJ-45 connectors but instead uses SC, LC, and ST connectors.

7. **Correct Answer: D**

    A. **Incorrect:** RJ-11 connectors are used for phone connections.

    B. **Incorrect:** RJ-45 connectors are used for twisted-pair cables.

    C. **Incorrect:** BNC connectors are used for coaxial cables.

    D. **Correct:** LC connectors are one type of connector used for fiber cables. Other common connectors are SC and ST.

CHAPTER 20

Understanding Protocols

Protocols provide the common language for devices to talk, and they also provide the rules for communicating. To put this into context, Chapter 18 covers devices such as routers, switches, and computers. Chapter 19 covers the different types of cables and how they connect the devices together. This chapter covers many of the common networking protocols.

Exam 220-801 objectives in this chapter:

- 2.3 Explain properties and characteristics of TCP/IP.
  - Client-side DNS
- 2.4 Explain common TCP and UDP ports, protocols, and their purpose.
  - Ports
    - 21 – FTP
    - 23 – TELNET
    - 25 – SMTP
    - 53 – DNS
    - 80 – HTTP
    - 110 – POP3
    - 143 – IMAP
    - 443 – HTTPS
    - 3389 – RDP
  - Protocols
    - DNS
    - LDAP
    - SNMP
    - SMB
    - SSH
    - SFTP
  - TCP vs. UDP

Introducing Network Protocols

Computers and other devices on a network must follow specific rules when communicating with each other. These rules are defined in a multitude of network protocols.

This is similar to how people communicate. If you're speaking English and I'm speaking Mandarin, we can talk all day long but we probably won't be communicating very well. Actually, even if two people are speaking English, they don't always communicate very well. If one person doesn't listen, filters the words, or changes the meaning, the result is miscommunication. Protocols provide the common language for network communication and help prevent miscommunication problems from occurring.

TCP/IP

Transmission Control Protocol/Internet Protocol (TCP/IP) is a full suite of protocols used on the Internet and on internal networks. It includes TCP, IP, and many more. You might see TCP/IP referred to as though it were a single protocol, but it's important to remember that it's just the name for the full suite.

It's easy to take this for granted because it works so effectively. However, there is a great deal of depth to what these protocols control.

For example, imagine that you wanted to mail all 1,440 pages of *War and Peace* to someone in London but that you could only paste a copy of one page at a time to the back of the postcard. You'd need to figure out a system to ensure that all pages were received and that your friend could put them back in order. If a page was lost in the mail, your friend would need to be able to identify the missing page and ask you to resend it.

Similarly, when you transfer files, TCP/IP ensures that it reaches the destination. If you include a 4-MB file of "War and Peace" as an email attachment, TCP/IP doesn't send it as a single 4-MB file. Instead, it breaks the file up into smaller pieces, transfers these smaller pieces, and puts them together on the other end. If any single piece doesn't make the trip successfully, TCP/IP senses the failure and requests the missing piece.

> **NOTE   PACKETS, FRAMES, AND SEGMENTS**
>
> Data transferred over a network are grouped together as individual packets. Packets are also called frames, segments, and protocol data units (PDUs) in different contexts, but in general they're called *packets*. Each packet includes the data and additional information. For example, it identifies where the packet came from and where the packet is going, using source and destination information in the packet. It also includes error checking information used to detect whether the packet has become corrupted.

Connectivity Protocols

Two core protocols used within TCP/IP are *Transmission Control Protocol (TCP)* and *User Datagram Protocol (UDP)*. Almost every connection uses either TCP or UDP.

The following sections cover both TCP and UDP, but for comparison, Table 20-1 summarizes important points related to them.

TABLE 20-1 Comparing TCP and UDP

TCP	UDP
Connection-oriented	Connectionless
Reliable, guaranteed delivery	Best effort delivery
Data receipt acknowledged	No acknowledgments
Uses three-way handshake	No handshake

To help clarify the comparison between connection-oriented and connectionless in Table 20-1, you can compare connection-oriented to making a phone call, and connectionless to sending a text message. The phone provides two-way communication before the message is sent. The text message is simply sent without a guarantee of delivery.

Imagine that a friend of yours just won the lottery. He wants to give you $10,000 if you pick him up at 8 a.m. tomorrow and give him a ride to pick up his winnings. If he calls and talks to you, he'd know that you received the message. The phone call provides two-way communication and guarantees delivery of the message.

On the other hand, if he sends you a text message, you will probably receive it, but it's not guaranteed. Text messages usually make it to the intended recipient without any problem. However, if your text message device was lost, stolen, or just run over by a bus, your friend wouldn't know. And you might lose $10,000.

TCP

Every TCP connection begins with a three-way handshake that verifies that both devices can connect. It's called a three-way handshake because three data packets are exchanged between the two systems.

For example, consider Figure 20-1. Lori is trying to connect to a server to access a file. Lori's system sends out a SYN (synchronize) packet, similar to asking, "Are you there?" The server responds with a SYN/ACK (synchronize/acknowledge) packet to acknowledge the connection attempt. Lori's system responds with an ACK packet that completes the TCP three-way handshake.

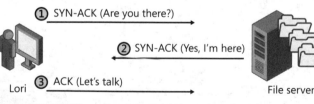

① SYN-ACK (Are you there?)

② SYN-ACK (Yes, I'm here)

Lori **③** ACK (Let's talk)   File server

FIGURE 20-1 DNS servers on internal network and on the Internet.

After the connection is established, the two systems exchange data. For example, Lori can download files from the file server. TCP uses additional checks to verify that all the data transfers successfully. If any of the data packets don't arrive, TCP sends a request for the missing packets. If any of the data packets arrive out of order, it arranges them in the original order.

EXAM TIP

TCP provides guaranteed delivery and is referred to as a connection-oriented protocol. It ensures that a logical connection exists before data is transferred. It uses acknowledgements to ensure that all data reaches the destination.

UDP

UDP does not use a three-way handshake and does not establish a connection before sending data. Instead, it just sends the data using its best effort. UDP is used with some protocols where some data loss is acceptable, or when the overhead of creating a connection isn't worth the effort. It is up to the application to provide error correction control.

For example, streaming audio and video often use UDP to provide best effort delivery. If some packets are lost, it's better to allow some gaps in the transmission rather than slow down the transmission. You've probably watched a video on the web where some of the transmission was lost. It skipped or paused for some of the video, but, overall, you were able to get the message.

EXAM TIP

UDP does not provide guaranteed delivery. It does not use a handshake to establish a connection or depend on acknowledgements when sending data.

✔ **Quick Check**

1. What protocol provides guaranteed delivery?

2. What protocol is connectionless?

Quick Check Answers

1. TCP.

2. UDP.

Introducing Ports

Chapter 21 covers IP addresses in greater depth. In short, every computer on a network using TCP/IP has an IP address. For example, my computer has an IP address of 192.168.1.10.

However, just because my computer has only one IP address doesn't mean it can process traffic for only one application at a time. I'm able to use Microsoft Outlook to send and receive email, use Internet Explorer to surf the Internet, and play music in the background streamed from a music site. Each of these applications is running at the same time, and my computer is using only a single IP address.

TCP/IP uses port numbers to identify specific protocols and services. When TCP/IP traffic reaches a computer, it uses the port number to determine which service or application will process the data.

Imagine entering a search on Bing.com with Internet Explorer. TCP/IP uses the IP address to get it to the Bing.com web server. The web server then looks at the port number to forward it to the application that will process the search query. In this case, it is an application on the web server that creates a webpage and sends it back to you.

Web browsers and web servers use Hypertext Transfer Protocol (HTTP) to transfer web traffic. Instead of using the words *Hypertext Transfer Protocol* in the packet, TCP/IP uses the port number *80* to identify HTTP.

> **NOTE** **LOGICAL VS. PHYSICAL PORTS**
>
> These port numbers are logical ports and do not relate to physical ports. In contrast, an RJ-45 port on a switch is a physical port that you can touch, and you can plug a twisted-pair cable into an RJ-45 port. You can't touch the port number 80 that represents HTTP.

Port Ranges

The number 80 isn't random. The Internet Assigned Numbers Authority (IANA), a part of the Internet Corporation for Assigned Names and Numbers (ICANN), has designated specific numbers to represent specific protocols. Table 20-2 shows the three ranges of ports.

TABLE 20-2 Port Ranges

Name	Port Range	Comments
Well-known	0 to 1023	Used by specific protocols or services and assigned by IANA.
Registered	1024 to 49,151	Companies use these to identify applications. Many are assigned by IANA.
Dynamic (or ephemeral)	49,152 to 65,535	Used by internal services and processes.

You don't have to remember which protocol or service maps to every one of these ports. However, you do need to know the number of several ports based on their protocol. As protocols are introduced in this chapter, you'll also see the port if it is relevant for the A+ exam. At the end of this chapter is a realistic example of how the ports are used. Most importantly for the A+ exam, Table 20-3 provides a summary of important port numbers to remember.

Ports and Firewalls

Chapter 22 covers firewalls in more depth, but in brief, a firewall can control the traffic in and out of a network. One of the ways it does so is by allowing or blocking traffic based on the port.

For example, if you want to allow users to visit websites, the firewall needs to allow HTTP traffic out. HTTP traffic uses port 80, so you need to allow outgoing traffic using port 80. On the other hand, if you want to prevent users from visiting any websites, you can block all outgoing traffic using port 80.

EXAM TIP

You create exception rules on firewalls to allow traffic. Most firewalls will block all traffic unless it has an exception to allow traffic. For example, if you want to allow HTTP traffic, the firewall must have an exception rule to allow traffic on port 80. This also known as *opening the port*.

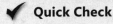 **Quick Check**

1. What does TCP/IP use to get a packet to a remote system?

2. What does TCP/IP use to get a packet to a specific service or application after it makes it to the remote system?

Quick Check Answers

1. IP address.

2. Port number.

Exploring Network Protocols

Many of the protocols used on networks and the Internet are very common. You need a basic understanding of them to be a successful technician and to pass the A+ exam. This section provides an overview of the commonly used protocols.

Encryption Protocols

It's relatively easy to capture data sent over a network. It can be tedious to analyze the data, but it is usually not difficult.

Administrators often use protocol analyzers (also called sniffers) to capture network traffic and analyze it. Attackers use the same tools to capture and analyze data. If data isn't protected, the attackers might be able to access secrets simply by listening on a network, just as an eavesdropper can listen in on conversations.

Encryption protocols scramble the data in such a way that it is not readable. More specifically, encryption creates cypher text that is not readable by unauthorized users. Authorized systems automatically decrypt the scrambled data to create readable text, but unauthorized systems or users cannot read it. Some common encryption protocols include the following:

- **Secure Shell (SSH).** SSH is often used within a network to encrypt traffic. Several protocols use it to encrypt traffic. For example, secure copy (SCP) uses it to copy files securely between two systems. SSH uses port 22 by default.

- **Secure Sockets Layer (SSL).** Many types of web traffic are encrypted with SSL. It often uses port 443 but may use other ports, depending on the protocol being encrypted.

- **Transport Layer Security (TLS).** TLS is the designated replacement for SSL. It can be used anywhere SSL is used.

Email Protocols

There are three primary protocols used for email. They are *Simple Mail Transfer Protocol (SMTP)*, *Post Office Protocol version 3 (POP3)*, and *Internet Message Access Protocol (IMAP)*.

- **SMTP.** This protocol is used to send email from user computers to email servers. SMTP uses port 25 by default. I often think of the "SM" in SMTP as "send mail" to remind me that SMTP is used to send email.

- **POP3.** This protocol is used to receive email from email servers. POP3 uses port 110 by default. Many POP email servers will delete the email after it has been downloaded by the user. I often imagine the email messages "popping" off the server as I receive them to help me remember that POP is used for receiving email.

- **IMAP.** This protocol is similar to POP except that messages are retained on the IMAP server in addition to being sent to users. IMAP uses port 143 by default, and the current version is IMAP4. IMAP provides more capabilities than POP, such as the ability to organize email in folders or to search through all the email for specific content.

EXAM TIP

SMTP uses port 25, and user computers use SMTP to send email to SMTP servers. POP3 uses port 110, and users receive email from POP3 servers. IMAP4 uses port 143, and it allows users to organize and search email on an IMAP4 server.

When you initially set up a computer for a user, you often need to configure the addresses of the SMTP, POP, and/or IMAP servers. The Internet Service Provider (ISP) will provide these addresses. For example, my ISP is Cox Communications and I have configured my email accounts with smtp.east.cox.net (to send email to their SMTP server) and pop.east.cox.net (to receive email from their POP3 server).

Chapter 9 introduces SMTP, POP3, and IMAP in the context of configuring tablet devices to send and receive email. Each protocol can be encrypted with SSL or TLS as *SMTPS*, *POP3S*, and *IMAPS*. The default ports for these are as follows:

- SMTPS: port 465
- IMAPS: port 993
- POP3S: port 995

✔ **Quick Check**

    1. What port and protocol are used for receiving email?

    2. What port and protocol are used for sending email?

Quick Check Answers

    1. POP3 uses port 110.

    2. SMTP uses port 25.

Web Browser Protocols

Web browsers display webpages formatted in a language called *Hypertext Markup Language (HTML)*. They retrieve HTML webpages from web servers using two primary protocols: *Hypertext Transfer Protocol (HTTP)* and *Hypertext Transfer Protocol Secure (HTTPS)*.

- **HTTP.** This is the primary protocol used to transfer data over the World Wide Web (WWW). HTTP uses port 80 by default.
- **HTTPS.** This protocol provides security for HTTP connections by encrypting the data. HTTPS uses port 443 by default, and it is secured with SSL or TLS.

EXAM TIP

HTTP uses port 80, and HTTPS uses port 443. SSL and TLS also use port 443 by default when used with HTTPS, and SSL and TLS can be used to encrypt other types of traffic. For example, virtual private network (VPN) connections sometimes use SSL over port 443.

Most web sessions don't need to be encrypted, so they use HTTP. However, some data needs to be encrypted to prevent unauthorized users from seeing it. For example, if you make a purchase with a credit card, you probably don't want anyone to be able to view your credit card data. Similarly, you wouldn't want others to see your user name and password as you log on to a website. In these situations, you want to ensure that you are using HTTPS.

Figure 20-2 shows an example of how you can tell whether you have a secure HTTPS connection with Internet Explorer. The first arrow points to the address line where https is listed (instead of http). The second arrow points to a lock icon indicating a secure connection. Different web browsers might put the lock icon in different places, but they will usually have a lock icon somewhere.

FIGURE 20-2 Verifying HTTPS is being used.

WWW and the Internet

The World Wide Web (WWW) and the Internet are not the same thing, although they are often confused. The WWW, commonly called the *web*, is used to transfer hypertext documents displayed in web browsers. The Internet is a network of networks that connects computers together from around the world.

Webpages are transferred over the Internet, but the Internet is also used to transfer much more. For example, email is transferred over the Internet by using SMTP and POP3 protocols. SMTP and POP3 aren't transferred over the web.

You can think of the Internet as a massive highway system. Trucks and cars travel over the highways, but the trucks and cars are not the highway. Similarly, webpages created by web servers make up the World Wide Web and send data over the Internet, but the webpages and web servers are not the Internet.

File Transfer Protocols

While many files are transferred over the Internet by using HTTP and HTTPS, this isn't always the best method. Files transferred with HTTP and HTTPS are displayed in a web browser, but sometimes you just want to upload or download files without displaying them.

FTP, TFTP, and SFTP

File Transfer Protocol (FTP) is used to upload and download files to and from FTP servers. FTP uses port 21 by default to send control signals to the FTP server and uses a second port for transferring data. The port number of the second port is dependent on the mode FTP is using. If it's using Standard (or passive) mode, FTP uses port 20 with port 21. If it's using Active mode, it dynamically assigns a second port number, up to port 65,535.

An FTP server is a server that is running FTP, but the server can be used for other purposes. It's common to have a web server also running as an FTP server.

For example, I manage some websites, and the servers hosting these websites run FTP. This allows me to upload and download files with an FTP application. I often use FileZilla, which is free (from Filezilla-project.org), efficient, and easy to use. Figure 20-3 shows a screen shot of FileZilla connected to a web server using FTP.

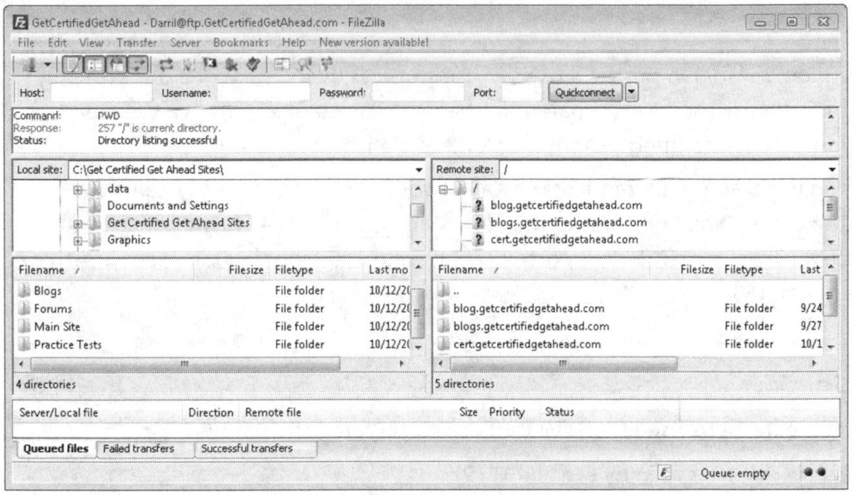

FIGURE 20-3 Using an FTP application.

Many operating systems include FTP. For example, Windows 7 includes an FTP client that you can access from the command prompt. Open the command prompt, type **FTP**, and press Enter to start it. The problem is that you need to know all the relevant FTP commands. The command prompt is useful in many situations, but for FTP, an application like FileZilla is easier. It allows you to upload and download files with just a few clicks.

EXAM TIP

Many firewalls block FTP traffic by default. To allow FTP traffic, you need to ensure that the firewall has port 21 open to allow outgoing FTP requests. This is also known as creating an exception on the firewall. Firewalls will allow return FTP traffic if outgoing FTP traffic is allowed. Therefore, you usually do not need to open the second port using FTP.

Trivial File Transfer Protocol (TFTP) is a streamlined, or "lite," version of FTP. TFTP uses port 69 by default. It uses the connectionless UDP, so it has less overhead than FTP, which uses the connection-oriented TCP.

Many network administrators use TFTP to upload or download files to routers or switches. For example, after configuring a router, they might use TFTP to download the configuration file as a backup. If the router ever fails, they can upload the configuration file and apply it rather than reconfiguring the router from scratch.

FTP traffic is normally sent over a network in clear text. This can sometimes include user names and passwords, along with associated data. If someone is using a sniffer, this data can easily be viewed.

Secure FTP (SFTP) uses SSH to encrypt the FTP traffic, including the user name, password, and data, so that it is not readable by unauthorized users. When secured by SSH, SFTP uses port 22 by default—the default port of SSH.

SMB

Server Message Block (SMB) is a protocol used to transfer files over a network. It is primarily used in Microsoft networks and is transparent to the user. For example, when a user sends a print job to a printer, the operating system uses SMB to transfer the data.

Similarly, when users access shared files over a network, Windows-based systems use SMB to create the connection and transfer the files. SMB typically uses Network Basic Input/Output System (NetBIOS) over TCP with ports 137, 138, and 139 by default. If used directly over TCP, it uses port 445.

> ### ✔ Quick Check
>
> 1. What are the ports used for HTTP traffic and encrypted HTTP traffic?
> 2. What are the ports used by FTP and TFTP?
> 3. What is used to encrypt web traffic displayed in Internet Explorer, and on what port?
> 4. What can you use to encrypt FTP traffic, and on what port?
>
> ### Quick Check Answers
>
> 1. HTTP uses port 80, and HTTPS uses port 443.
> 2. FTP uses port 20 (and sometimes port 21), and TFTP uses port 69.
> 3. HTTPS using port 443.
> 4. SSH on port 22.

Name Resolution Protocols

Most of us can remember names and words easier than numbers. However, computers work with numbers better than they do with names. Because of this, humans often identify computers with a name while the computers themselves use numbers.

The two types of computer names used with TCP/IP are as follows:

- **Host names.** Host names are used on the Internet and internal networks. Host names are often combined with a domain name to give a fully qualified domain name (FQDN). For example, a web server named www hosting a website for Margie's Travel has a FQDN of www.margiestravel.com. Similarly, a mail server named mail2 on an internal domain named contoso.com has an FQDN of mail2.contoso.com.

- **Network Basic Input/Output System (NetBIOS) names.** The NetBIOS name is usually the same as the host name. That is, the server with a host name of mail2 also has a NetBIOS name of mail2. NetBIOS names are used only on internal networks, not on the Internet.

The following sections describe how these names are resolved to IP addresses.

DNS

main Name System (DNS) is the primary method used to map host names to IP addresses. It you want to go to MSN.com, you simply type **msn.com** into your *uniform resource locator (URL)* address line. However, your computer can't reach MSN.com until it knows its IP address.

Your system will query a server running DNS (commonly called a DNS server) with the name, and the DNS server responds with an IP address. This is called name mapping or name resolution.

EXAM TIP

DNS maps host names to IP addresses. Systems can query the DNS server with a name, and the DNS server responds with an IP address. It is the primary method of name resolution on the Internet, and it is used on many internal networks.

Internet Service Providers (ISPs) host DNS servers, and many medium-to-large-size businesses have their own internal DNS servers. For example, consider the network shown in Figure 20-4. If internal users need to access systems on the internal network, they will query their internal DNS server. This server holds the mapping to all the names and IP addresses of internal systems.

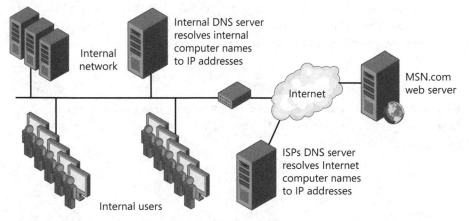

FIGURE 20-4 DNS servers on internal network and on the Internet.

If the users need to access an external site, they will still query the internal DNS server, but this server then queries the ISP's DNS server. The ISP's DNS server might know the answer, or it might need to query other DNS servers on the Internet. When it gets the answer, it gives it back to the internal DNS server and then to the user that requested it. All DNS traffic uses port 53 by default.

Many small office home office (SOHO) networks don't use an internal DNS server. A common configuration is with a wireless router (explained in Chapter 23) that uses the ISP's DNS server. The router forwards all DNS requests to the ISP's DNS server and returns the IP addresses to the user.

Client-Side DNS

Names can be resolved by the client without querying DNS. One of the ways is by adding names and IP addresses to a file named hosts. On Windows-based systems, this is located in the C:\Windows\system32\drivers\etc folder by default. If this file includes the name and IP address, the client does not query DNS; it uses the IP address in the file. NetBIOS names can be resolved by the client with a similar file called lmhosts.

Additionally, when a name is resolved by any method, it is placed in the host cache (sometimes called the DNS cache). If the name is in the cache, the client uses it instead of querying DNS again.

> **MORE INFO** CHAPTER 24
>
> Chapter 24 shows methods you can use to view and manipulate the cache with the ipconfig command.

WINS

Many internal networks use Windows Internet Name System (WINS) to resolve NetBIOS names to IP addresses. NetBIOS names and WINS servers are never used on the Internet. You'll see them only on internal networks, and their usage is dwindling.

> **NOTE** WINS IS NOT USED ON THE INTERNET
>
> Don't be fooled by the word *Internet* within Windows Internet Name Service. WINS has absolutely nothing to do with the Internet or resolving Internet names to IP addresses. It is used only to resolve NetBIOS names.

Remote Connectivity Protocols

There are two primary remote connectivity protocols relevant for an A+ technician. Both are used to create connections with remote systems. They are the Remote Desktop Protocol (RDP) and Telnet.

RDP

Remote Desktop Protocol (RDP) is used in Microsoft networks. Two primary applications that use RDP are Remote Desktop Connection and Remote Assistance. Both use RDP over a default port of 3389.

- **Remote Desktop Connection**. You can use this to connect to another system and log on. Administrators frequently use this to manage servers located in server rooms while they sit at a comfortable desk with a view out a window.

- **Remote Assistance**. This is used to provide assistance to other users. A novice can send out a remote assistance request, and a helper can use it to access the novice's computer from a remote location. If the novice grants permission, the helper can take control of the novice's computer and show how to accomplish specific tasks. As the helper moves the mouse and opens windows, the novice can view the activity. It even includes a chat window.

EXAM TIP

RDP uses port 3389. You need to ensure that this port is open on firewalls and routers between both systems. Otherwise, RDP traffic will be blocked.

Some users use RDP to access their home computers even when they're away. They enable port forwarding on their home router and configure it to allow the remote desktop session. Chapter 22 discusses port forwarding in more depth.

You can open Remote Desktop Connection on Windows 7 by clicking Start, typing in **mstsc**, and pressing Enter. You'll see a window similar to Figure 20-5. Type in the name of the computer you want to access, and if it's available and configured to accept remote desktop connections, you'll be prompted to enter a user name and password.

FIGURE 20-5 Using Remote Desktop Connection.

After you're connected, it works almost exactly like you just logged on while sitting in front of the computer. This can work with other computers besides your home computer. For example, you might be able to connect to your work computer from home. However, you should ensure that you're authorized to connect to the remote computer before trying. Additionally, ensure that you have permission to use RDP on a work computer before trying to use it to connect to a remote computer.

> **NOTE MSTSC**
>
> MSTSC is short for *Microsoft Terminal Services Connection*. Remote Desktop Services was previously called *Terminal Services*.

Telnet

Telnet is a command-line tool you can use to connect to remote systems. You can use this connection to execute commands through the telnet prompt. The default port used by Telnet is port 23. Telnet sends traffic in clear text making it easy for others to view the data with a sniffer. When security is needed, SSH is often used instead.

Technicians sometimes use Telnet for troubleshooting because it allows you to easily identify whether a system is listening and responding to traffic on a specific port.

For example, imagine a user is having problems with their email. You might want to verify that the email server (named mail2 in this example) is operational and listening for SMTP commands. You can enter the following command from the command prompt: **telnet mail2 25**.

The command will attempt to connect to the email server by using SMTPS default port 25. If successful, you'll have a blank screen waiting for you to enter SMTP commands. This tells you that the email server is operational and listening on port 25. If the mail server is not running, you'll get an error.

EXAM TIP

Telnet uses port 23 by default. You can use it to connect to remote systems using different ports and enter commands on the remote system.

The Telnet Client is not enabled by default on Windows Vista or Windows 7. You can use the following steps to enable it:

1. Click Start and select Control Panel.

2. Type **Feature** in the Search Control Panel text box.

3. Select Turn Windows Features On Or Off. If prompted by UAC, click Continue.

4. Select the check box for Telnet client, as shown in the following graphic.

5. Click OK. After the feature is installed, you can close Control Panel and open a command prompt to use Telnet.

MORE INFO   CHAPTER 14, "USING THE COMMAND PROMPT"

Chapter 14 covers the command prompt in greater depth, including how to open it. As with any command-line commands, you can get help on Telnet with the help switch. Type in telnet /?, and press Enter to view the help.

SNMP

Simple Network Management Protocol (SNMP) is used to communicate with and manage network devices such as routers and switches. There are three versions: SNMPv1, SNMPv2, and SNMPv3. SNMPv3 provides the highest level of security.

SNMP uses agents on each managed device. An agent is a software application that monitors a system for certain events (called traps) and reports them to a central SNMP monitoring system. The central system will often be running on a server within the network and it can send queries to SNMP agents.

LDAP

Lightweight Directory Access Protocol (LDAP) is used to interact with a special type of database called a directory. In this context, a directory has nothing to do with the folders used in Windows even though those folders are also called directories. Instead, a directory is a group of objects, such as users, computers, and groups, that are centrally managed and maintained.

For example, Microsoft uses Active Directory Domain Services (AD DS) to host all the objects within a domain. If a computer is joined to the domain, a computer object is created within AD DS. Similarly, when a user account object is created within AD DS, users can log in to the domain. LDAP is used to join computers to a domain, to log in users to accounts, and for any other type of interaction with AD DS.

> ✔ **Quick Check**
>
> **1.** What port must be opened to use Remote Desktop Connection?
>
> **2.** What is the Telnet command to connect to an HTTP server named Web1?
>
> **3.** What port does Telnet use by default?
>
> **Quick Check Answers**
>
> **1.** 3389.
>
> **2.** Telnet Web1 80.
>
> **3.** 23.

Summarizing Well-Known Ports

The first 1024 ports (0 to 1023) are called the well-known ports. There are several ports in this range that you should memorize for typical on-the-job work and the A+ exams. Table 20-3 summarizes the most important ports.

TABLE 20-3 Some Well-Known Ports

Protocol	Port	Protocol	Port
FTP	20, 21	HTTP	80
SSH	22	POP	110
SSH Port Forwarding	22	IMAP	143
Telnet	23	HTTPS	443
SMTP	25	SSL	443
DNS	53	SMTPS	465
TFTP	69	IMAPS	993
RDP	3389	POP3S	995

Without an explanation of how they're used, ports can be fuzzy concepts for many people. Sure, you can remember that HTTP uses port 80 and that SMTP uses port 25, but how does this really fit together? The following sections provide an example scenario that will help put it into context.

Sending an HTTP Query Using Ports

Kelly is using Internet Explorer to do a search through Bing.com. Imagine that her ISP has assigned her system an IP address of 70.160.136.10 and the IP address of Bing.com is 65.55.175.254. When she enters a search on Bing through her web browser, her system will create a data packet and send it to the Bing web server.

This packet includes destination and source data. In addition to the source and destination IP addresses, it also includes source and destination ports. The IP addresses are used to get the packet the computer. The ports are used to identify what to do with the packet when it arrives.

The Web server is using HTTP, so the destination port is 80. However, the port used by Kelly's system as the source port isn't as simple.

You might remember from earlier in the chapter that ports 49152 through 65,535 are dynamic ports. Systems map these ports to applications when needed. In this example, Kelly's system will assign 49,152 to Internet Explorer. If 49,152 were already mapped to another application or service, Kelly's system would use a different port, such as 49,153 or 49,154. When the packet returns from Bing, this port number tells her system that the data should be handled by Internet Explorer.

Figure 20-6 shows what this outgoing packet would look like. Again, TCP/IP uses the destination IP address to get the packet to the destination computer. When it arrives, TCP/IP uses the port number to get it to the right service on the computer.

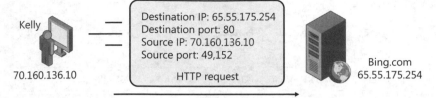

FIGURE 20-6 IP address and port information sent in a webpage request.

A Web Server Response Using Ports

The Bing server receives the packet with the destination port of 80. It knows that port 80 is used for HTTP, so it sends it to the application handling HTTP.

Bing uses Internet Information Services (IIS) as the web server application. IIS creates the webpage to answer Kelly's request. The bing.com server then readdresses the packet to Kelly's system by reversing the source and destination data.

Figure 20-7 shows the source and destination data for the response. It includes Kelly's IP address and the port of 49,152 as the destination, and it includes Bing.com's IP address and port 80 as the source. TCP/IP uses the IP address to get the packet to Kelly's computer.

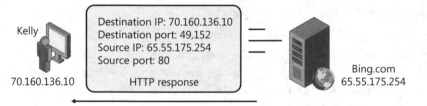

FIGURE 20-7 IP address and port information in the webpage response.

When the return packet arrives, Kelly's system knows that it mapped port 49,152 to Internet Explorer. It sends the HTTP response back to Internet Explorer, which displays the webpage.

> **NOTE** **VIEW OPEN CONNECTIONS**
> If you type *netstat -b* and press Enter at an elevated command line, you can see all of the current connections your system has open. (Chapter 14 explains how to open the command line with elevated permissions.) The -b switch will also identify the program or service using each of the open ports. If you have multiple Internet Explorer sessions open, you'll see several lines labeled with [iexplore.exe]. Close all Internet Explorer sessions, and rerun the command. You'll see that the connections are no longer there.

Last, it's worth mentioning that the well-known port numbers are the commonly used ports, but protocols can use different port numbers. You know that HTTP uses the well-known port of 80. If you type in www.bing.com as an address in Internet Explorer, it will actually use *http://www.bing.com:80*. Internet Explorer assumes this is an HTTP-based website and it assumes the default of port 80.

However, the bing.com administrators could configure their server using port 12345 for HTTP instead of port 80. Users would have to include the port number in order to reach the site like this: *http://www.bing.com:12345*. If a user typed in www.bing.com without the port of 12345, the browser would use the default port of 80 and the web server wouldn't respond.

Imagine if every website used a different port number. Not only would you have to remember the name of the website but also the port number. For most situations, it's best to use the well-known port number.

However, there are some times when different port numbers are used. Chapter 22 discusses proxy servers and how many companies use a single proxy server to provide shared Internet access to multiple users. Many proxy servers are configured to listen for HTTP queries on port 8080.

Chapter Summary

- Network protocols provide the rules that devices use to communicate with each other on a network.

- TCP/IP is a suite of protocols used on the Internet and on internal networks.

- TCP is a connection-oriented protocol that provides reliable, guaranteed delivery of data. TCP sessions begin with a three-way handshake.

- UDP is a connectionless protocol that gives a "best effort" to deliver data. It does not use a handshake but instead just sends the data.

- Ports are logical numbers used to identify protocols or services. Ports 0 to 1023 are well-known ports.

- Encryption protocols scramble data so that is unreadable to unauthorized users. SSH encrypts traffic within a network such as FTP. SSH uses port 22. SSL and TLS encrypt traffic on the Internet.

- Common email protocols are SMTP, POP3, and IMAP4. Systems use SMTP to send email over port 25. Users receive email from POP3 servers over port 110. IMAP4 allows users to manage email on a server, and it uses port 143. Each can be secured with SSL or TLS.

- HTTP and HTTPS are used to transfer files displayed in web browsers. HTTP uses port 80. HTTPS uses encryption to protect the data, and it uses port 443.

- FTP is used to upload and download files from FTP servers. FTP uses ports 21 and sometimes port 20. TFTP is used for smaller files, and it uses port 69. SFTP uses SSH to encrypt FTP traffic, and it uses port 22.

- DNS maps names to IP addresses. Systems query DNS with a name of a computer, and DNS responds with an IP address. DNS uses port 53.

- RDP is used by Remote Desktop Connection and Remote Assistance. Remote Desktop Connection can be started with mstsc, and it allows users to connect to remote systems. RDP uses port 3389.

- Telnet is used to connect to remote systems from the command prompt. It can be used to check whether ports are open on remote systems.

- SNMP is used to manage network devices such as routers and switches.

- LDAP is used to interact with directories such as Active Directory Domain Services.

Chapter Review

Use the following questions to test your knowledge of the information in this chapter. The answers to these questions, and the explanations of why each answer choice is correct or incorrect, are located in the "Answers" section at the end of this chapter.

1. Of the following choices, what is a difference between TCP and UDP?

   A. UDP provides guaranteed delivery, but TCP does not.

   B. TCP provides guaranteed delivery, but UDP does not.

   C. TCP is connection-oriented, but UDP does not use wires.

   D. UDP uses a three-way handshake, but TCP does not.

2. Which of the following protocols is used to receive email by a user?

   A. POP

   B. SMTP

   C. FTP

   D. RDP

3. Which of the following protocols uses port 143?

   A. IMAP

   B. SMTP

   C. POP

   D. HTTPS

4. Which of the following are the correct ports for HTTP and HTTPS?

   A. 22 and 25

   B. 80 and 143

   C. 80 and 443

   D. 443 and 3389

5. What protocol could you use to encrypt FTP traffic?

   A. HTTPS

   B. TFTP

   C. RDP

   D. SSH

6. What service provides the IP address of a computer when queried with the name of the computer?

   A. FTP

   B. SMTP

   C. DNS

   D. SSL

7. What port should be opened on a firewall to allow a user to connect to a system using RDP?

   A. 69

   B. 143

   C. 443

   D. 3389

8. You are troubleshooting an email problem for a user. The mail server is named mail, and you suspect that it is not answering SMTP queries. Which of the following commands can you use from the command prompt to test it?

   A. SMTP mail 23

   B. SMTP mail 25

   C. Telnet mail 23

   D. Telnet mail 25

Answers

1. **Correct Answer:** B

   A. **Incorrect:** UDP does not provide guaranteed delivery, but TCP does.

   B. **Correct:** TCP provides guaranteed delivery, and UDP uses a best effort to deliver data.

   C. **Incorrect:** TCP is connection-oriented and UDP is connectionless, but this does not refer to wires.

   D. **Incorrect:** TCP uses a three-way handshake, but UDP does not.

2. **Correct Answer:** A

   A. **Correct:** Post Office Protocol (POP) is used to receive email on port 110.

   B. **Incorrect:** Simple Mail Transfer Protocol (SMTP) is used to send email on port 25.

   C. **Incorrect:** File Transfer Protocol (FTP) is used to upload and download files from a file server, and it uses port 21.

   D. **Incorrect:** Remote Desktop Protocol (RDP) is used to connect to remote systems, and it uses port 3389.

3. **Correct Answer:** A

   A. **Correct:** Internet Message Access Protocol (IMAP) uses port 143.

   B. **Incorrect:** Simple Mail Transfer Protocol (SMTP) uses port 25.

   C. **Incorrect:** Post Office Protocol (POP) uses port 110.

   D. **Incorrect:** Hypertext Transfer Protocol Secure (HTTPS) uses port 443.

4. **Correct Answer:** C

   A. **Incorrect:** Secure Shell (SSH) uses port 22, and Simple Mail Transfer Protocol (SMTP) uses port 25.

   B. **Incorrect:** HTTP uses port 80, but Internet Message Access Protocol (IMAP) uses port 143.

   C. **Correct:** Hypertext Transfer Protocol (HTTP) uses port 80; Hypertext Transfer Protocol Secure (HTTPS) uses port 443.

   D. **Incorrect:** HTTPS uses port 443, but Remote Desktop Protocol (RDP) uses port 3389.

5. **Correct Answer:** D

   A. **Incorrect:** Hypertext Transfer Protocol Secure (HTTPS) secures webpages but not FTP traffic.

   B. **Incorrect:** Trivial File Transfer Protocol (FTP) is a scaled down version of FTP, but it does not encrypt FTP.

C. **Incorrect:** The Remote Desktop Protocol (RDP) is used to connect to remote systems, but it does not encrypt FTP.

D. **Correct:** Secure Shell (SSH) can be used to encrypt network traffic including File Transfer Protocol (FTP) traffic.

6. **Correct Answer:** C

    A. **Incorrect:** File Transfer Protocol (FTP) is used to upload and download files to and from an FTP server.

    B. **Incorrect:** Simple Mail Transfer Protocol (SMTP) is used to send email.

    C. **Correct:** Domain Name System (DNS) maps computer names to IP addresses and answers name resolution requests.

    D. **Incorrect:** Secure Sockets Layer (SSL) is used to encrypt HTTPS, and it uses port 443.

7. **Correct Answer:** D

    A. **Incorrect:** Trivial File Transfer Protocol (TFTP) uses port 69 and is unrelated to RDP.

    B. **Incorrect:** Internet Message Access Protocol (IMAP) uses port 143 and is unrelated to RDP.

    C. **Incorrect:** Hypertext Transfer Protocol Secure (HTTPS) uses port 443 and is unrelated to RDP.

    D. **Correct:** Remote Desktop Protocol (RDP) uses port 3389, so this port needs to be opened on the firewall.

8. **Correct Answer:** D

    A. **Incorrect:** There is no such command as SMTP.

    B. **Incorrect:** There is no such command as SMTP.

    C. **Incorrect:** This command will check to see whether Telnet was running on the mail server, because it is using port 23.

    D. **Correct:** The telnet command can connect to a server on specific ports. You want to check the mail server, so you should check the SMTP service on port 25.

CHAPTER 21

Comparing IPv4 and IPv6

One of the primary ways computers are identified in a TCP/IP network is with an IP address. As an A+ technician, you are very likely to come across the different types of IP addresses, and you might even need to troubleshoot some problems related to IP addressing. In this chapter, you'll learn about some of the basics both for IPv4 and for IPv6 addresses.

Exam 220-801 objectives in this chapter:

- 2.3 Explain properties and characteristics of TCP/IP.
    - IP class
        - Class A
        - Class B
        - Class C
    - IPv4 vs. IPv6
    - Public vs. private vs. APIPA
    - Static vs. dynamic
    - DHCP
    - Subnet mask
    - Gateway
- 2.4 Explain common TCP and UDP ports, protocols, and their purpose.
    - Protocols
        - DHCP
- 2.6 Install, configure, and deploy a SOHO wireless/wired router using appropriate settings.
    - NAT

Exam 220-802 objectives in this chapter:

- 1.6 Setup and configure Windows networking on a client/desktop.
    - Configuring an alternative IP address in Windows
        - IP addressing
        - Subnet mask
        - DNS
        - Gateway
    - Network card properties
        - Half duplex/full duplex/auto
        - Speed
        - Wake-on-LAN
        - PoE
        - QoS

REAL WORLD   **FIRST PRINTERS AND IP ADDRESSES**

My printer recently died, so I needed a new one. We have several computers in our house, so I wanted to make sure that everyone could use the printer. The solution was to purchase a network printer.

Setting up the new printer was relatively painless. I followed the quick-start directions to put it together, connected to my network, and used Windows 7 to locate and connect to it. This all went without a hitch, and I really didn't need to know anything about networking to get this network printer up and running.

But then we lost power for a short time, and suddenly no one could print. Did the printer go bad? Did I need to take it back and get another one? Or was there another problem?

I found that the problem was that the printer was assigned a new IP address after power came back on. I needed to take some steps to fix the immediate problem and prevent it from happening again. Taking these steps was a lot easier than exchanging the printer or calling in an A+ technician like you to come and fix it. Thankfully, I had the knowledge to fix it, and after you finish this chapter, you'll be prepared to help users who have the same common problem.

Examing IPv4 Addresses

Internet Protocol version 4 (IPv4) addresses have been around since the 1980s, and they are the most common IP addresses in use. You might also see IPv6 addresses (discussed later in this chapter), but you can count on seeing IPv4 addresses. With that in mind, you'll need to know some basics about IPv4 addresses.

Dotted Decimal Format

IPv4 addresses are created with 32 bits. However, it's not easy for us to read a string of 32 ones and zeros, so IPv4 addresses are commonly displayed in dotted decimal format. Each IP address has four decimal numbers separated by three dots, like this: 192.168.1.5.

Each decimal can be represented with eight bits (also called an octet). Four octets (or four sets of eight) add up to 32 bits. For example, the IP address of 192.168.1.5 can be represented as follows:

1100 0000 . 1010 1000 . 0000 0001 . 0000 0101

Most of us would rather work with decimal numbers, but it's worthwhile knowing that the IP address is composed of 32 bits with four octets of eight bits.

If all bits are a one in any octet (1111 1111), the value is 255. This is important to remember because an IPv4 address cannot have any decimals greater than 255. For example, the following IP address is not valid: 192.168.*256*.2 because the third decimal is 256. The decimal number of 256 can be displayed in binary as 1 0000 0000, but an octet in an IPv4 address has only eight bits.

EXAM TIP

Any IPv4 address with a number greater than 255 is not valid. IPv4 addresses can include only numbers between 0 and 255.

Two Parts of an IP Address

It is not apparent at first, but an IPv4 address has two parts. The first part is the network identifier, or network ID, and the second part is the host identifier, or host ID.

The network ID identifies the network, and all systems on the same network have the same network ID. Additionally, all systems on the same network have different host identifiers.

The Subnet Mask and the Network ID

IP addresses are matched with a subnet mask to identify the network ID and the host ID. Subnet masks are displayed in dotted decimal format similar to an IP address. The three most common subnet masks are as follows:

- 255.0.0.0
- 255.255.0.0
- 255.255.255.0

When the subnet mask is 255, that portion of the IP address is the network ID. When the subnet mask is 0, that portion of the IP address is the host ID.

> **NOTE** **SUBNET MASKS**
>
> As you continue in your IT career, you'll learn that the subnet mask can include numbers other than 255 or 0. However, for the A+ exam, you'll see subnet masks with the numbers of 255 or 0. This makes it much simpler to identify the network ID.

Consider Table 21-1, which shows an IP address of 192.168.1.5 and a subnet mask of 255.255.255.0.

TABLE 21-1 Identifying a Network ID

	First octet	Second octet	Third octet	Fourth octet
192.168.1.5	192	168	1	5
255.255.255.0	255	255	255	0
Network ID	192	168	1	0

In the first octet, the subnet mask is 255, so 192 is part of the network ID. The subnet mask is 255 in the second and third octets also, so 168 and 1 are also part of the network ID. However, the subnet mask is 0 in the last octet, so that portion of the network ID is 0.

Put together, you can see that the network ID is 192.168.1.0.

Host ID

The host ID is whatever is left over. Consider 192.168.1.5 with a subnet mask of 255.255.255.0. The network ID is 192.168.1.0, and the host ID is 5. The most important part of this is remembering that each system has different host IDs. More specifically, no two systems can have the same IP address. Because the network IDs must be the same, the host IDs must be unique on the network.

Consider what would happen if you and your neighbor both had the same mail address. How would the postal service know how to get the correct mail to you? Similarly, if two systems have the same IP address, TCP/IP is going to have problems getting the data to the correct system.

Network ID Challenge

Table 21-2 shows a list of IP address and subnet mask combinations. Test yourself and see whether you can determine the network ID for each.

TABLE 21-2 Determine the Network ID

	First octet	Second octet	Third octet	Fourth octet
192.168.7.15	192	168	7	15
255.255.255.0	255	255	255	0
Network ID	?	?	?	?
172.16.4.3	172	16	4	3
255.255.0.0	255	255	0	0
Network ID	?	?	?	?
10.5.3.5	10	5	3	5
255.0.0.0	255	0	0	0
Network ID	?	?	?	?

In the first combination (192.168.7.15, 255.255.255.0), the subnet mask is 255 for the first three octets. Only the first three numbers in the IP address are in the network ID. Therefore, the network ID is 192.168.7.0

In the second combination (172.16.4.3, 255.255.0.0), the subnet mask is 255 in the first two octets. Only 172 and 16 are in the network ID, so it is 172.16.0.0.

The last combination (10.5.3.5, 255.0.0.0) has a 255 in only the first octet. The network ID is 10.0.0.0.

A network ID is always displayed with trailing zeros. That is, it is not accurate to show the network ID as 192.168.7, 172.16, or 10. The trailing zeros must be included so that you have four decimal numbers as 192.168.7.0 or 172.16.0.0, or 10.0.0.0.

Network IDs in a Network

The following two important points about the network ID and the host ID are worth repeating:

- All computers within a network must have the same network identifier.
- All computers within a network must have unique host identifiers.

For example, consider Figure 21-1. It shows two networks, labeled as Network 1 and Network 2, separated by a router. Each of the computers on Network 1 must have the same network ID. However, one of them is incorrect. Can you see which one?

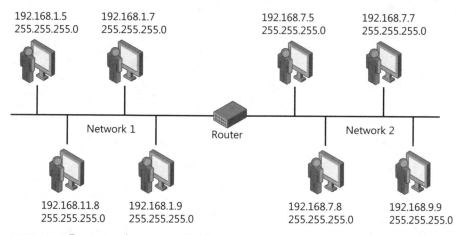

FIGURE 21-1 Two networks connected with a router.

Similarly, each of the computers on Network 2 must have the same network ID. However, one of these is also configured incorrectly. Can you see which one?

Most of the computers on Network 1 have a network ID of 192.168.1.0. However, the one on the bottom left has an IP address of 192.168.11.8, giving it a network ID of 192.168.11.0. This computer will be unable to communicate with any other system on the network.

The network ID on Network 2 for three of the computers is 192.168.7.0. However, the computer on the bottom right has a network ID of 192.168.9.0. This computer will be unable to communicate with other computers.

✔ **Quick Check**

1. What is wrong with the following IPv4 address: 192.257.2.5, 255.255.0.0?

2. What is the network ID of 192.168.24.6 with a subnet mask of 255.255.255.0?

Quick Check Answers

1. IPv4 addresses can't have numbers greater than 255 (such as 257).

2. 192.168.24.0.

Classful IP Addresses

A classful IP address has a predefined subnet mask based on the first number in the IP address. That is, just by looking at the IP address, you can identify the subnet mask. When you know the subnet mask, you should also be able to identify the network ID.

Table 21-3 shows the three classful IP addresses covered on the A+ exam. The first number of a Class A address is in the range of 1 to 126. An IP address of 10.1.2.3 has 10 as the first number. The number 10 is in the range of 1 to 126, so this is a Class A address and it has a subnet mask of 255.0.0.0. Further, the network ID is 10.0.0.0.

TABLE 21-3 Classful IP Addresses

Class	First octet range	Example	Subnet Mask
A	1 to 126	10.1.2.3	255.0.0.0
B	128 to 191	172.16.5.4	255.255.0.0
C	192 to 223	192.168.1.2	255.255.255.0

EXAM TIP

You should be able to easily identify the class of an IP address when you see it. For example, what class is 172.16.34.45? What is its subnet mask? What class is 192.168.7.3, and what is its subnet mask? 172.16.34.45 is a Class B address because the first number is 172 (in the range of 128 to 191), and the subnet mask is 255.255.0.0. 192.1687.7.3 is a Class C address because the first number is 192 (in the range of 192 to 223) and the subnet mask is 255.255.255.0.

Networks, Subnets, and LANs

I t's important to recognize the difference between a network and a local area network (LAN). A network includes all the computers connected together with the same network ID. A LAN includes two or more networks connected together in the same location. These networks are separated by one or more routers.

Subnetting is beyond the scope of the A+ exam, but in short, it divides classful IP networks into smaller subnetworks, or subnets. Each subnet has the same network ID, and each subnet is separated by one or more routers. A LAN includes two or more subnets, two or more networks, or a combination of subnets and networks.

You might hear many technicians refer to networks generically as subnets. It's common, but it isn't entirely accurate. Technically, a network is a subnet only if the classful IP address has been divided.

Loopback Addresses

You might notice a range of numbers missing between Class A and Class B addresses. The entire range of 127.0.0.0 through 127.255.255.255 is reserved for testing. However, there's really only one address used in this range for testing. It's called the *loopback address,* and the address is 127.0.0.1.

For example, you can use the following command from the command prompt to ping the loopback address:

```
Ping 127.0.0.1
```

You should see a response similar to this:

```
Pinging 127.0.0.1 with 32 bytes of data:
Reply from 127.0.0.1: bytes=32 time<1ms TTL=128
Reply from 127.0.0.1: bytes=32 time<1ms TTL=128
Reply from 127.0.0.1: bytes=32 time<1ms TTL=128
Reply from 127.0.0.1: bytes=32 time<1ms TTL=128
Ping statistics for 127.0.0.1:
    Packets: Sent = 4, Received = 4, Lost = 0 (0% loss),
Approximate round trip times in milli-seconds:
    Minimum = 0ms, Maximum = 0ms, Average = 0ms
```

EXAM TIP

You can also use the command ping localhost because systems resolve the name localhost to the IP address of 127.0.0.1. If the response is "Request timed out," it indicates a problem with TCP/IP on the local computer. As an A+ technician, you should make this one of the first things you check if you suspect a networking problem.

Ping sends four packets to the loopback address, and four replies are returned. This verifies that TCP/IP is installed and working correctly on the system. It doesn't check connectivity with other systems or verify that the hardware is working, but it does verify the TCP/IP protocols, also called the TCP/IP stack. It will succeed even if the network interface card (NIC) is disabled or unplugged from the network.

CIDR Notation

Another way that the IP address and subnet mask can be expressed is with Classless Inter-Domain Routing (CIDR) notation. CIDR notation identifies the number of bits that are one in the subnet mask, using /n. In this case, the n is the number of bits that are a one.

For example, consider a subnet mask of 255.255.255.0. The first octet is 255, representing eight ones (1111 1111). Similarly, the second octet is another eight ones, and the third octet is another eight ones. Therefore, the first 24 bits of the subnet mask are all ones. In this case, you can use /24 to represent the subnet mask.

Table 21-4 shows a few examples of CIDR notation.

TABLE 21-4 Expressing IP Addresses with CIDR Notation

IP Address	Subnet Mask	CIDR Notation
10.1.2.3	255.0.0.0	10.1.2.3 /8
172.16.1.2	255.255.0.0	172.16.1.2 /16
192.168.1.5	255.255.255.0	192.168.1.5 /24

There is no difference in the actual IP address or subnet mask when CIDR notation is used; it's just displayed differently. For example, the following two combinations represent the same IP address and subnet mask:

- 192.168.1.5, 255.255.255.0
- 192.168.1.5 /24

Unicast, Broadcast, and Multicast Addressing

IPv4 uses three primary types of addressing when sending traffic. The types are unicast, broadcast, and multicast.

- **Unicast** is one-to-one traffic. That is, the data is sent from one system to one other system.
- **Broadcast** is one-to-all traffic. One system sends the data to all other systems on the network. However, this is certainly not to all other systems in the world. Routers block broadcast traffic so that a broadcast is sent only to all the computers with the same network ID. A broadcast address is 255.255.255.255.

- **Multicast** is one-to-many traffic. A system can send data to multiple other systems. Multicast addresses are in the range of 224.0.0.1 through 255.255.255.254.

Only broadcast traffic stops at routers. Unicast and multicast traffic is routed to the correct destination through one or more routers.

✓ **Quick Check**

  1. What class is the following IP address: 10.192.168.5?
  2. How can you check the TCP/IP stack?

Quick Check Answers

  1. Class A.
  2. Ping the loopback address of 127.0.0.1.

TCP/IP Addressing in a Network

To communicate with other systems on the same network, every system in a network must have an IP address. Systems also need to have other information to communicate with systems in other networks.

You might remember that networks are separated by one or more routers. Each system needs to know the IP address of at least one adapter on a router so that it can reach other networks.

Default Gateway

A *gateway* is a path out of a network, and the default gateway identifies the default path out of a network. For example, if an internal system is trying to connect to the Internet, it goes through the default gateway. The default gateway is an interface on a router, and it has an IP address.

Figure 21-2 shows a network diagram with two default gateways identified in two different networks. Systems in Network 1 go through the default gateway with an address of 192.168.1.1. Systems in Network 2 go through the default gateway with an address of 192.168.7.1.

When a system transfers traffic from one computer to another, it first identifies the network ID of both systems. If the network IDs are the same, it knows that the computers are on the same network. If the networks IDS are different, it knows it needs to go through the default gateway.

While some people call the default gateway the router, you can see in Figure 21-2 that this isn't entirely accurate. It's like calling a car door a car. You use the door to get out of the car, but the door isn't the car. Similarly, you use the default gateway to get out of a network through the router, but the default gateway isn't the router.

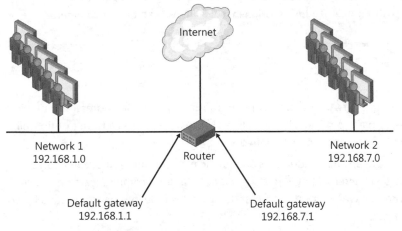

FIGURE 21-2 Default gateways for different networks.

Note that the default gateways for the networks are not the same. That is, each network has only one default path out of the network and only one default gateway.

It is very common to assign a default gateway with the first IP address in the network. It's not required, but it is common. For example, Network 1 has a range of IP addresses of 192.168.1.1 through 192.168.1.254, so you'll often see the default gateway assigned the address of 192.168.1.1.

EXAM TIP

The default gateway must have the same network ID as other systems in the network. If it has a different network ID, systems won't be able to communicate with it, and it won't be able to reach any systems outside of the network.

Public vs. Private IPs

Systems on internal networks use private IP addresses, and systems on the Internet use public IP addresses. Private IP addresses are formally defined in Request for Comments (RFC) 1918 as any address in one of the following ranges:

- 10.0.0.0–10.255.255.255 (Class A)
- 172.16.0.0–172.31.255.255 (Class B)
- 192.168.0.0–192.168.255.255 (Class C)

These are the only addresses you'll see on any internal network. Additionally, routers on the Internet will not route any traffic using these IP addresses as either a source or destination IP address.

NAT

Network Address Translation (NAT) is a protocol that translates private IP addresses to public and public IP addresses back to private. It is installed on a system such as a router or firewall located between the Internet and a private network.

Internal networks have private IP addresses and public networks have public IP addresses. However, computers on an internal network still need to be able to communicate on public computers on the Internet. NAT helps this process. It also helps hide internal computers from attackers on the Internet.

In smaller networks, a router with NAT would have one public IP address. In many larger networks, devices running NAT use multiple public IP addresses.

Figure 21-3 shows an internal network that accesses the Internet through a router with NAT. The internal network has private IP addresses, and NAT translates them to a public IP address when a user connects. For example, a user in a private network can access Bing.com on the Internet by using Internet Explorer. NAT translates the IP addresses so that the user in the private network can access the public website.

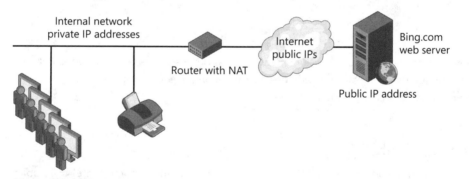

FIGURE 21-3 NAT translates private and public IP addresses.

> ✔ **Quick Check**
>
>   **1.** What identifies the default path out of a network for a system?
>
>   **2.** Is 198.162.5.1 a private address?

Static vs. Dynamic IP Addresses

Each computer on a network must have an IP address assigned. Most computers will receive the IP address dynamically or automatically, but you can also manually assign a static IP address.

Using DHCP for Dynamic IP Addresses

Dynamic Host Configuration Protocol (DHCP) is used to dynamically assign IP addresses and other TCP/IP configuration information to systems. A DHCP client is any system configured to receive TCP/IP information from a system running DHCP.

Large organizations use a DHCP server, but small offices and home offices (SOHOs) often have a wireless router that includes DHCP. When a DHCP client turns on, it sends a DHCP query, and if DHCP is running on the network, DHCP will provide TCP/IP configuration to the client.

DHCP commonly provides an IP address, subnet mask, and the default gateway. In many cases, DHCP will also provide the system with the address of a DNS server and a WINS server.

> **MORE INFO** **CHAPTER 20, "UNDERSTANDING PROTOCOLS," AND CHAPTER 23, "EXPLORING WIRELESS NETWORKING"**
>
> DNS and WINS are discussed in Chapter 20. As a reminder, DNS resolves host names to IP addresses and WINS resolves NetBIOS names to IP addresses. Chapter 23 covers wireless networks, including wireless routers.

APIPA Addresses

If a system can't reach a DHCP server, it will often assign itself an Automatic Private IP Address (APIPA). An APIPA address always starts with 169.254 and has a subnet mask of 255.255.0.0. The address can be anything in the range of 169.254.0.1 to 169.254.255.254.

Recalling the discussion earlier in this chapter about the network ID, do you know the network ID of the following address: 169.254.3.7 255.255.0.0? The network ID is always 169.254.0.0. Because of this, computers with APIPA addresses can communicate with each other without a DHCP server and without any manual configuration.

However, APIPA does not assign a default gateway, the address of a DNS server, or any other TCP/IP information. It assigns only the IP address and a subnet mask.

Chapter 24, "Connecting and Troubleshooting a Network," covers command-line tools such as ipconfig that you can use to identify a computer's assigned IP address. If you see an address starting with 169.254, you know that it is an APIPA address.

EXAM TIP

APIPA addresses are assigned if a DHCP client does not receive a response from DHCP. They always start with 169.254 and have a subnet mask of 255.255.0.0. They never assign a default gateway, address of a DNS server, or any other information. If you see an APIPA address, it's a clear indication of a DHCP-related problem. Troubleshooting steps would include identifying why the client can't reach DHCP and why DHCP is not responding.

Reserving IP Addresses

You can also use DHCP to reserve a specific IP address to a client. You do so by mapping the media access control (MAC) address of the DHCP client to a specific IP address. When the DHCP client turns on and requests an IP address, the DHCP server recognizes the client and gives it a specific IP address.

The Real World sidebar at the beginning of this chapter gives a perfect example. I recently purchased a network printer that ran as a DHCP client. When it first turned on, DHCP running on my wireless router assigned it an IP address of 192.168.1.114. I then configured other systems in my home network to use this printer with an IP address of 192.168.1.114.

At some point, we had a power outage. When the printer turned back on, DHCP assigned it an IP address of 192.168.1.123. At this point, none of my systems could print to the printer because they were trying to reach it with the IP address of 192.168.1.114.

After I realized the problem, I could have resolved it in one of two ways:

- Manually assign the IP address of 192.168.1.114
- Reserve the address of 192.168.1.114 to this printer

I chose to reserve the address. Figure 21-4 shows the DHCP reservation table from my wireless router. The table at the top shows all the clients currently assigned IP addresses from DHCP. The bottom table shows how I reserved the printer's MAC address (10:1F:74:00:9F:7D) to the IP address of 192.168.1.114.

Every time the printer turns on, it sends a DHCP query, and the wireless router assigns it an address of 192.168.1.114.

NOTE Ipconfig /all and MAC address

You can determine the MAC address of a system by entering ipconfig /all at a command prompt. The MAC address is listed as the physical address.

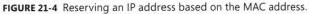

DHCP Reservation

Select Clients from DHCP Tables

Client Name	Interface	IP Address	MAC Address	Select
MyBookWorld	LAN	192.168.1.107	00:90:A9:82:4B:5F	☐
Pow er-PC	LAN	192.168.1.110	6C:62:6D:BA:73:6C	☐
Win7-1	LAN	192.168.1.111	00:03:FF:3A:94:42	☐
HP03997D	LAN	192.168.1.114	10:1F:74:03:99:7D	☐

Add Clients

Manually Adding Client

Enter Client Name	Assign IP Address	To This MAC Address	
	192 . 168 . 1. 0	00:00:00:00:00:00	Add

Clients Already Reserved

Client Name	Assign IP Address	To This MAC Address	MAC Address
Netw orkPrinter	192.168.1.114	10:1F:74:00:9F:7D	Remove

FIGURE 21-4 Reserving an IP address based on the MAC address.

Manually Assigning Static IP Addresses

Occasionally, you'll want to manually assign an IP address. In this case, you must type in all of the information needed by the system. You can assign static IP addresses for a server in a small office home office (SOHO) or a network printer. You won't need to do so very often, but you can also assign static IP addresses to client or desktop systems.

EXAM TIP

It's common either to manually assign an IP address for a network printer or to use a DHCP reservation to ensure that it always has the same IP address.

The process is different depending on what device you're configuring the IP address. Network printers usually have a menu-driven interface on the front panel that you can use. Operating systems allow you to configure the properties of the network interface card.

Accessing the NIC in Windows

Configuring the NIC is the same in Windows 7, Windows Vista, and Windows XP. However, the path to the NIC is a little bit different in these systems. You can use the following steps to access the NIC on each operating system.

Windows 7:

1. Click Start and type **Network and Sharing Center** in the Search Programs And Files text box.

2. Select Network And Sharing Center. Alternatively, you can open the Control Panel and select the Network And Sharing Center from the Network And Internet category.

3. On the left-pane menu, click Change Adapter Settings. You'll now see a list of available NICs on the system.

Windows Vista:

1. Click Start and type **Network and Sharing Center** in the Start Search text box.

2. Select Network And Sharing Center. Alternatively, you can open the Control Panel and select the Network And Sharing Center from the Network And Internet category.

3. On the left-pane menu, click Manage Network Connections. You'll now see a list of available NICs on the system.

Windows XP:

1. Click Start and select Control Panel.

2. If you're using Category View, select Network And Internet Connections and then Network Connections. If you're using Classic View, select Network Connections. You'll now see a list of available NICs on the system.

Assigning Static or Dynamic Addresses in Windows

After you've accessed the NIC, you use the following steps to manipulate the properties. These steps are for a Windows 7 computer, but they are the same on other Windows systems.

1. Right-click the network interface card (NIC) adapter and select Properties. The adapter is commonly named Local Area Connection.

2. Select Internet Protocol Version 4 (TCP/IPv4) and click Properties.

3. With the General tab selected, you can select Obtain An IP Address Automatically. With this selected, the computer will receive all of the TCP/IP configuration information from DHCP.

4. If you want to manually assign an IP address, select Use The Following IP Address.

5. Enter a valid IP address, subnet mask, and default gateway for your network. If your network has a DNS server, you can also enter its IP address here. Your display will resemble the following graphic.

Local Area Connection Properties

Networking

Connect using:

Intel 21140-Based PCI Fast Ethernet Adapter (Emulated)

Configure...

This connection uses the following items:

- ☑ Client for Microsoft Networks
- ☑ QoS Packet Scheduler
- ☑ File and Printer Sharing for Microsoft Networks
- ☑ Internet Protocol Version 6 (TCP/IPv6)
- ☑ Internet Protocol Version 4 (TCP/IPv4)
- ☑ Link-Layer Topology Discovery Mapper I/O Driver
- ☑ Link-Layer Topology Discovery Responder

Install...   Uninstall   Properties

Description

Transmission Control Protocol/Internet Protocol. The default wide area network protocol that provides communication across diverse interconnected networks.

OK   Cancel

Internet Protocol Version 4 (TCP/IPv4) Properties

General

You can get IP settings assigned automatically if your network supports this capability. Otherwise, you need to ask your network administrator for the appropriate IP settings.

○ Obtain an IP address automatically
◉ Use the following IP address:

IP address: 192 . 168 . 1 . 10
Subnet mask: 255 . 255 . 255 . 0
Default gateway: 192 . 168 . 1 . 1

○ Obtain DNS server address automatically
◉ Use the following DNS server addresses:

Preferred DNS server: 10 . 1 . 1 . 5
Alternate DNS server: . . .

☐ Validate settings upon exit   Advanced...

OK   Cancel

6. Click OK twice, and you're done.

Assigning Alternate IP Addresses in Windows

Mobile users sometimes need to have both a dynamic and a static IP address. For example, imagine Lori has a laptop that she uses at work and when she travels to customer locations. While at work, her computer is configured to obtain an IP address dynamically from DHCP. However, when she visits Lucerne Publishing, she needs a statically assigned IP address to access the Internet through their network. You could train Lori how to do this and have her manually make these changes, but there's an easier way: by configuring an alternate IP address.

If you followed the previous steps to assign an IP address in Windows, you might have noticed a subtle change when you selected Obtain An IP Address Automatically. Specifically, an additional tab named Alternate Configuration appears. This tab *disappears* when you select Use The Following IP Address.

Select this tab and you can configure the alternate configuration settings. Figure 21-5 shows this property page configured with an alternate IP address, subnet mask, default gateway, and DNS server. Normally, Automatic Private IP Address is selected.

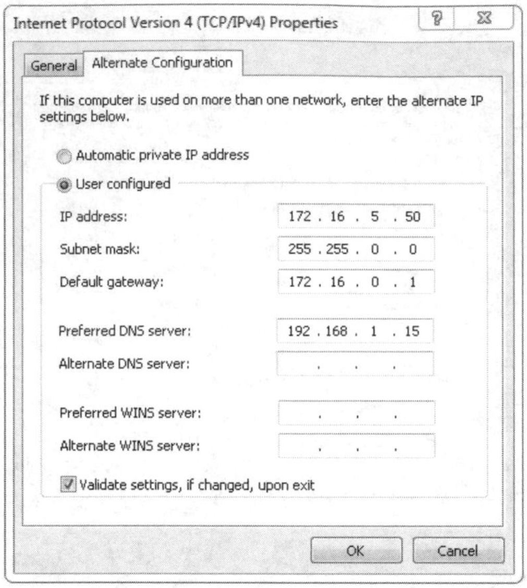

FIGURE 21-5 Assigning alternate configuration settings.

When Lori is at work, her computer receives the TCP/IP settings from DHCP. Lucerne Publishing doesn't have a DHCP server, so when she goes there, her computer never receives a DHCP response. Instead, it will assign itself the TCP/IP configuration settings from the Alternate Configuration tab.

EXAM TIP

By default, the Alternate Configuration is set to Automatic private IP address. Therefore, if a system doesn't receive a response from DHCP, it will assign itself an APIPA address.

Manipulating NIC Properties

Beyond the TCP/IP settings, the NIC has several other properties that you might need to manipulate. Chapter 19, "Exploring Cables and Connectivity," discusses this in the context of comparing half-duplex, full-duplex, and auto settings. A NIC is normally set to automatically configure the speed and duplex setting based on the connection, and you can use the steps in Chapter 19 to verify or modify the settings.

As a reminder, you can access these properties by right-clicking the NIC and selecting Properties. From the Properties page, click the Configure button and then click the Advanced tab. These properties are not standardized, so they usually have different names on different NICs.

Some of the other settings you can manipulate include the following:

- **Wake-On-LAN (WOL)**. This might be listed as WOL, Wake On Magic Packet, Wake On Pattern Match, Shutdown Wake-On-LAN, or something similar. A WOL packet (also called a magic packet) is a specially formatted packet that can cause a computer to turn on even if it is sleeping, hibernating, or completely turned off. Administrators use this to send updates to systems during non-business hours. This setting needs to be enabled on the NIC and in BIOS.

> **NOTE** **SLEEP AND HIBERNATE**
>
> Sleep is a low-power state, but the computer can wake up rather quickly. Hibernate copies the contents of RAM onto the disk as a file and turns the system off. When the system is turned back on, it copies the data from the disk back to RAM, returning the system to the same state it was in when it was turned off.

- **QoS (Quality of Service)**. This may be named QoS, Quality Of Service, Flow Control, or something similar. Some networks use QoS techniques to control the traffic by assigning different priorities to different types of traffic. For example, an administrator might want to cap the amount of streaming video that is allowed on a network and use QoS techniques to give streaming video traffic a very low priority. QoS is enabled on the NIC and configured on multiple devices throughout the network.
- **PoE (Power over Ethernet)**. Some NICs on mobile devices can be powered by voltages sent over an Ethernet cable. This is useful in devices located in remote areas where power isn't readily accessible. You need only to plug in a twisted-pair Ethernet cable into the RJ-45 port, and it powers the device. It isn't used for a desktop computer, but it is used from some wireless access points, IP phones, and IP cameras and can be configured on them.

> ✔ **Quick Check**
>
> 1. A system has an IP address of 169.254.5.6. What does this indicate?
> 2. What are the two ways IP addresses can be assigned?
>
> **Quick Check Answers**
>
> 1. It's an APIPA address, and the system is not receiving a response from DHCP.
> 2. Manually and with DHCP.

Examining IPv6 Addresses

An IPv6 address uses 128 bits instead of the 32 bits used by an IPv4 address. IPv6 addresses are typically displayed as eight groups of four hexadecimal characters. For example, the following is a valid IP address:

FC00:0000:0000:0076:0000:042A:B95F:77F5

You might remember from Chapter 1 that a hexadecimal number uses the characters 0–9 and A–F. Each hexadecimal number can be represented with four bits. For example, 8 is 1001 and F is 1111.

Why We Need IPv6

While IPv4 lasted quite a while, the Internet officially ran out of IPv4 addresses. The Internet Assigned Numbers Authority (IANA), which assigns IP addresses, issued the last batch of IPv4 addresses on February 3, 2011. Without IPv6, the Internet would need to stop growing.

IPv4 supports about 3.7 billion IP addresses on the Internet, using a 32-bit address space. In contrast, IPv6 uses 128 bits, so it can support more IP addresses. Specifically, IPv6 supports over 340 undecillion IP addresses. If you're like me, you probably don't use *undecillion* in everyday language. Here's where it comes in: million, billion, trillion, quadrillion, quintillion, sextillion, septillion, octillion, nonillion, decillion, undecillion.

This will be enough for everyone to have as many IP addresses for their own use as they need. Computers, printers, TVs, gaming devices, mobile phones, tablets, and more can all have their own IP address with IPv6, and you're not likely to run out.

With 340 undecillion IPv6 addresses, that works out to more than 3.7 billion IP addresses for every person on the planet. Therefore, everyone can have more addresses than are available with IPv4 on the entire Internet today. Actually, it's more: it works out to about 50 thousand trillion trillion IPv6 addresses per person. I just find it a little easier to comprehend numbers in the billions.

You might be wondering about IPv5. It was designed to use 64 bits for an IP address, but the designers realized that 64 bits wouldn't give them enough IP addresses. It never made it past the draft stages, and IPv6 was adopted to replace IPv4 instead.

Omitting IPv6 Leading Zeros

Each group of hexadecimal numbers in an IPv6 address includes four characters. However, if this number has leading zeros, you can omit them. This works the same in decimal. If I asked you to write down the number seven, you would write 7. You wouldn't typically write 007.

Similarly, the following IPv6 address can be written by omitting leading zeros in each of the groups:

- FC00:0000:0000:0076:0000:042A:B95F:77F5
- FC00:0:0:76:0:42A:B95F:77F5

Table 21-5 shows this with the hexadecimal groups labeled. You can see that leading zeros are omitted in the second, third, fourth, fifth, and sixth groups. An important point to make here is that we still have eight groups of hexadecimal numbers.

TABLE 21-5 Omitting Leading Zeros in an IPv6 Address

1st	2nd	3rd	4th	5th	6th	7th	8th
FC00	0000	0000	0076	0000	042A	B95F	77F5
FC00	0	0	76	0	42A	B95F	77F5

It's also important to point out that you can't omit trailing zeros. In the first group, FC00 cannot be shortened to just FC. Of course, this works the same in decimal. If I owed you 20 dollars, you wouldn't be very happy if I just gave you two dollars, saying that I decided to omit a zero.

IPv6 Zero Compression

IPv6 addresses often have a long string of zeros within them. You can include them, but you can also use a double colon (::) to indicate a string of zeros. Anyone that reads the address with the double colon knows to replace it with a string of zeros.

For example, the following two addresses are the same:

FC00:0000:0000:0076:0000:042A:B95F:77F5

FC00::76:0:42A:B95F:77F5

The second IPv6 address shows only six groups of hexadecimal numbers. Because you know that a full IPv6 has eight groups of numbers, you know that the double colon represents two groups of zeros.

An important rule is that you can compress only one string of zeros with a double colon. For example, the following is not valid:

FC00:0000:0000:0076:0000:042A:B95F:77F5

FC00::76::42A:B95F:77F5

You can see two strings of zeros in the original IPv6 address. Without seeing the original IPv6 address, you won't know how many zeros to assign to each double colon. It could be either of the following:

FC00:**0000:0000**:0076:0000:042A:B95F:77F5

FC00:0000:0076:**0000:0000**:042A:B95F:77F5

EXAM TIP

Valid IPv6 addresses include only hexadecimal numbers (0–9 and A–F). An IPv6 address can be expressed as eight groups of hexadecimal numbers separated by colons, or fewer groups with a single double colon. You can use only a single double colon in an IPv6 address.

IPv6 Prefixes

IPv6 addresses use prefixes to identify the network identifier. This is similar to how an IPv4 address uses an IP address and subnet mask to identify the network. However, IPv6 does not use a subnet mask. Instead, IPv6 uses prefix length notation. This is similar to CIDR notation used with IPv4 addresses.

For example, you might see an address like the following:

2001:0DB8:1234::5678:9ABC:DEF0:/48

The /48 prefix notation indicates that the first 48 bits are in the prefix. Similarly, the /64 in the following IPv6 address indicates that the first 64 bits are in the prefix:

2001:0DB8:1234::5678:9ABC:DEF0:/64

Peaceful Coexistence with IPv4

The IPv6 designers recognized that it wasn't feasible to require everyone in the world to switch over at the same time. Could you imagine someone picking an arbitrary date, such as February 3, 2011, and telling everyone in the world that they needed to switch over on that day? Some would be left behind with no Internet access.

Instead, they designed IPv6 so that it can interoperate with IP4. They can both operate on a network at the same time without any problems.

You'll find that most networks that are running IPv6 today are also running IPv4. At some point in the future, IPv4 will be phased out, but that's unlikely to happen anytime soon.

IPv6 Loopback Address

IPv6 has a loopback address similar to IPv4. As a reminder, you can ping the loopback address to verify that the TCP/IP stack is functioning properly. In this case, you can verify that the IPv6 portion of TCP/IP is functioning properly.

The IPv6 loopback IP address is ::1. This is using zero compression, indicating that it's a string of zeros with only a single one at the end. You can use the following command to test it from the command prompt:

```
Ping ::1
```

If successful, you should see the following results:

```
Pinging ::1 with 32 bytes of data:
Reply from ::1: time<1ms
Reply from ::1: time<1ms
Reply from ::1: time<1ms
Reply from ::1: time<1ms
Ping statistics for ::1:
    Packets: Sent = 4, Received = 4, Lost = 0 (0% loss),
Approximate round trip times in milli-seconds:
    Minimum = 0ms, Maximum = 0ms, Average = 0ms
```

Chapter Summary

- IPv4 addresses use 32 bits and are expressed in dotted decimal format like this: 192.168.1.5.

- The subnet mask is used to identify the network ID portion of an IP address. All computers on a network must have the same network ID.

- Classful IP addresses are identified by the first number in the IP address.

  - Class A: 1 to 126 as in 10.1.2.3,
    Subnet mask: 255.0.0.0

  - Class B: 128 to 191 as in 172.16.1.2
    Subnet mask: 255.255.0.0

  - Class C: 192 to 223 as in 192.168.1.2
    Subnet mask: 255.255.255.0

- The IPv4 loopback address is 127.0.0.1. Pinging this address verifies that the TCP/IP stack is functioning.

- The default gateway identifies the default path out of a network to other networks. It is the IP address of the router's NIC that is connected to the network. It is typically the first IP address on the network.

- Only private IP addresses should be used in a private network. Private IP address ranges are:

  - 10.0.0.0–10.255.255.255

  - 172.16.0.0–172.31.255.255

  - 192.168.0.0–192.168.255.255

- DHCP assigns TCP/IP configuration information to DHCP clients. This includes an IP address, subnet mask, default gateway, address of DNS, address of WINS, and more. A DHCP client receives DHCP information when it turns on.

- If a DHCP client doesn't receive a response from DHCP, it assigns itself an IP address starting with 169.254. This address is known as an APIPA address.

- An alternate address can be used with DHCP for a computer used in different locations. If DHCP doesn't respond, the alternate IP address will be used.

- IPv6 addresses use 128 bits and are expressed as eight groups of hexadecimal numbers separated by colons. Valid hexadecimal numbers are only 0–9 and A–F.

- Zero compression replaces zeros in IPv6 with two colons. You can use only one set of double colons in an IPv6 address.

- IPv4 and IPv6 are compatible with each other and can run on the same network without problems.

- The IPv6 loopback address is ::1.

Chapter Review

Use the following questions to test your knowledge of the information in this chapter. The answers to these questions, and the explanations of why each answer choice is correct or incorrect, are located in the "Answers" section at the end of this chapter.

1. Which of the following is a Class C IPv4 address?

   A. 10.1.2.3

   B. 127.0.0.1

   C. 172.16.5.4

   D. 192.168.1.21

2. Which of the following would be appropriate to assign to a client in a private network?

   A. 10.1.1.1

   B. 198.162.6.1

   C. 173.16.2.3

   D. 127.0.0.1

3. A system has an IP address and subnet mask combination such as the following:

   192.168.1.5

   255.255.255.0

   Which of the following would be a valid IP address for the default gateway?

   A. 255.255.255.255

   B. 192.168.1.1

   C. 192.168.15.1

   D. 192.168.1.0

4. A system is unable to access any network resources. You check the IP address and see that it includes the following information:

    IP address: 169.254.34.78

    Subnet mask: 255.255.0.0

    Default gateway: blank

    What is the most likely problem?

    A. DHCP

    B. IP address is wrong

    C. Subnet mask is wrong

    D. Default gateway is down

5. Which of the following would most often have manually assigned IP addresses?

    A. Windows 7–based computers in a SOHO

    B. Windows 7–based computers in a large domain

    C. Servers and network printers

    D. Servers and USB attached printers

6. Which of the following is a valid IPv6 address?

    A. FC00:0:0:76:0:0:042A:B95F:77F5

    B. FC00::0157:03CE::A47:52AF

    C. FC00:76::4234:BF:F5

    D. FC00:0000:1200:2076:0000:42A4:C95G:F523

7. Which of the following is the loopback address for IPv6?

    A. 127.0.0.1

    B. ::1

    C. 192.168.1.1

    D. 255.255.255.255

Answers

1. **Correct Answer: D**

   A. Incorrect: 10.1.2.3 is a Class A address, in the range of 1 to 126.

   B. Incorrect: 127.0.0.1 is the IPv4 loopback address.

   C. Incorrect: 172.16.5.4 is a Class B address in the range of 128 to 191.

   D. Correct: The first number in a Class C address is in the range of 192 to 223, and 192 is in this range.

2. **Correct Answer: A**

   A. Correct: Only valid private IP addresses should be assigned to computers in a private network. A private IP address should be in one of the following ranges: 10.0.0.0–10.255.255.255, 172.16.0.0–172.31.255.255, 192.168.0.0–192.168.255.255.

   B. Incorrect: An IPv4 address starting with 198 is public.

   C. Incorrect: An IPv4 address starting with 173 is public.

   D. Incorrect: This is the IPv4 loopback address.

3. **Correct Answer: B**

   A. Incorrect: This is a broadcast address and should not be assigned to the default gateway.

   B. Correct: The default gateway must have the same network ID as other clients on the network. In this case, the network ID of the system is 192.168.1.0. If the default gateway is 192.168.1.1, it also has a network ID of 192.168.1.0.

   C. Incorrect: An IP address of 192.168.15.1 gives the default gateway a network ID of 192.168.15.0, which is different from the system's network ID.

   D. Incorrect: 192.168.1.0 is the network ID and should not be assigned to a client.

4. **Correct Answer: A**

   A. Correct: An address starting with 169.254 is an Automatic Private IP Address (APIPA). A DHCP client will assign itself an APIPA address if it doesn't receive a response from DHCP.

   B. Incorrect: The IP address is correct as an APIPA address.

   C. Incorrect: The subnet mask is correct for APIPA.

   D. Incorrect: APIPA doesn't assign a default gateway.

5. **Correct Answer:** C

   A. **Incorrect:** Windows 7–based computers normally receive IP addresses automatically from DHCP.

   B. **Incorrect:** Windows 7–based computers normally receive IP addresses automatically from DHCP.

   C. **Correct:** Servers and network printers often have manually assigned IP addresses.

   D. **Incorrect:** A USB-attached printer does not use an IP address.

6. **Correct Answer:** C

   A. **Incorrect:** An IPv6 address has eight groups of hexadecimal numbers separated by seven colons, but this has nine groups separated by eight colons.

   B. **Incorrect:** An IPv6 can use one set of double colons for zero compression, but not two.

   C. **Correct:** This is a valid IPv6 address using zero compression and omitting leading zeros. The full IPv6 address is FC00:0076:0000:0000:0000:4234:00BF:00F5.

   D. **Incorrect:** IPv6 addresses use hexadecimal numbers (0–9 and A–F). G is not a valid hexadecimal number.

7. **Correct Answer:** B

   A. **Incorrect:** 127.0.0.1 is the IPv4 loopback address.

   B. **Correct:** The IPv6 loopback address is ::1.

   C. **Incorrect:** 192.168.1.1 is a valid IPv4 address but not the loopback address.

   D. **Incorrect:** 255.255.255.255 is the broadcast address.

CHAPTER 22

Network Security Devices

The only way to keep a computer 100 percent safe from attacks is to never turn it on. When you start using it, especially when it is connected to a network, the risk of attacks rises significantly. Defense-in-depth refers to the practice of using multiple layers of security to protect systems and networks. Digital security methods play a large role in network security. This chapter covers several digital security methods used on networks, with a strong focus on firewalls.

Exam 220-801 objectives in this chapter:

- 2.6 Install, configure, and deploy a SOHO wireless/wired router using appropriate settings.
    - Port forwarding, port triggering
    - Firewall
    - DMZ
    - Basic QoS
- 2.9 Compare and contrast network devices and their functions and features.
    - Firewall
    - Internet appliance

Exam 220-802 objectives in this chapter:

- 1.4 Given a scenario, use appropriate operating system features and tools.
    - Administrative
        - Windows firewall
        - Advanced security
- 1.5 Given a scenario, use Control Panel utilities (the items are organized by "classic view/large icons" in Windows).
    - Common to all Microsoft Operating Systems
        - Security center
        - Windows firewall

- 1.6 Setup and configure Windows networking on a client/desktop.
  - Proxy settings
  - Remote desktop
  - Home vs. Work vs. Public network settings
  - Firewall settings
    - Exceptions
    - Configuration
    - Enabling/disabling Windows firewall
- 2.1 Apply and use common prevention methods.
  - Digital security
    - Firewalls

Securing a Network

If you pay attention to the news, you've probably heard about many different types of IT attacks. Criminals are regularly looking for ways to break into networks and systems. Sometimes they're doing it for monetary gain, and other times they're attacking for revenge or espionage.

When they successfully hit large corporations, you hear about it on the news. When individuals or small business owners lose a few thousand dollars from an attack, you typically won't hear anything. However, these types of losses are happening every day.

Threats and Attacks

IT security professionals know that if a computer has a public IP address on the Internet, it's only a matter of time before it's discovered and probed looking for vulnerabilities.

Sometimes criminals can access systems remotely and scour the drives looking for data. Sometimes they use automated tools to launch attacks. Two common types of attacks are *denial of service (DoS)* and *distributed denial of service (DDoS)* attacks.

- **DoS.** This is an attack against a computer from one other computer. The goal is to disrupt the normal operation so that the computer can't provide service to users. For example, a DoS attack against a web server prevents it from answering requests for webpages in a timely manner.

- **DDOS.** This is a DoS attack from multiple attackers simultaneously. Botnets are frequently used to attack targets with thousands of zombie computers.

MORE INFO CHAPTER 26, "RECOGNIZING MALWARE AND OTHER THREATS"

Chapter 26 covers botnets and other threats. Some botnets have controlled more than a million computers at a time. The computers within the botnet act like zombies and do whatever the bot herder tells them to do.

It's important to be aware that threats are real. There are multiple digital security methods available that can help protect a computer, but when people ignore the threats, they often perceive the digital security methods as a hindrance and ignore them. One of the primary digital security methods that you'll find on almost every computer is a firewall.

Understanding Firewalls

Firewalls block or allow network traffic, with the goal of protecting networks and computers. The concept is similar to a firewall in a car, which separates the engine compartment from the passenger compartment. If the engine catches fire, the firewall protects the passengers by preventing the fire from reaching them.

Similarly, a computer firewall protects systems from malicious traffic. The most common source of malicious traffic is from the Internet, so it's important to use a firewall for any system connected to the Internet.

Firewalls are classified as either network-based or host-based.

- **Network-based firewall.** This controls traffic allowed in or out of the network. A network-based firewall can be a dedicated appliance that acts as only a firewall, or it can be another device, such as a router, that includes firewall capabilities.

- **Host-based firewall.** This is software running on a computer or host. Windows-based systems include the Windows Firewall, which is a Control Panel applet running within Windows, and many third-party software applications are also available.

Figure 22-1 shows a simple network using both network-based and host-based firewalls. The network firewall controls traffic to and from the Internet. The desktop computers and the server have host-based firewalls controlling traffic to and from each system.

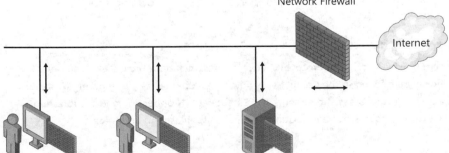

FIGURE 22-1 Network with network-based and host-based firewalls.

You might be wondering why there are so many firewalls being used. After all, if the network firewall is blocking malicious traffic from the Internet, why would you need firewalls on individual computers too? It's a common question.

The answer is based on a defense-in-depth philosophy of using multiple layers. It's very easy for a user to unknowingly bring in malicious software (malware) from his computer on a USB flash drive. After infecting his work computer, it could start crawling through the network to infect other computers. Host-based firewalls help protect against this type of scenario.

Exceptions

Most firewalls start with an implicit deny policy, meaning that they automatically block all traffic. Of course, you want to allow some traffic, so exceptions are allowed. For example, if you want to allow Hypertext Transfer Protocol (HTTP), you can configure a rule to identify the exception. The firewall will then block all traffic *except* for HTTP traffic.

Exceptions are identified as rules and stored in an *access control list (ACL)*. Firewalls will typically have many rules in place.

Packet-Filter Exceptions

A basic packet-filtering firewall can filter network packets based on the following components:

- **IP address.** A rule can be configured to block or allow traffic from a specific IP address such as 192.168.1.1 or from entire networks by using a network ID such as 192.168.1.0/24.

- **Ports.** Protocols are identified with ports, and traffic can be controlled by using these port numbers. For example, if you want to allow Simple Mail Transfer Protocol (SMTP) traffic, you can create an exception for port 25, the well-known port for SMTP.

MORE INFO CHAPTER 20, CHAPTER 21, AND CHAPTER 24

Chapter 20, "Understanding Protocols," covers ports, including the well-known ports specifically mentioned in the CompTIA A+ objectives. Chapter 21, "Comparing IPv4 and IPv6," covers IP addresses and network IDs. Chapter 24, "Connecting and Troubleshooting a Network," covers troubleshooting commands such as ping and tracert.

- **Protocol IDs.** Some protocols are identified with a protocol ID instead of a port. For example, the ping and tracert commands use Internet Control Message Protocol (ICMP), and ICMP traffic is identified with a protocol ID of 1. You can allow or block all ping and tracert traffic by using protocol ID 1.

- **A combination.** Packet rules can be created using any combination of these. For example, if an email server has an IP address of 192.168.1.10, you can create an SMTP rule that allows a computer to send port 25 packets only to 191.68.1.10. Port 25 packets with any other destination will be blocked.

EXAM TIP

As a PC technician, you might need to configure rules to allow or block specific types of traffic. The most common way this is done is by creating a port rule. This section has repeated that port 25 is used for SMTP traffic, but there are some other ports that you should memorize. Specifically, you should memorize the ports listed in Chapter 20, "Understanding Protocols," in Table 20-3.

Other Exceptions

Firewalls have become sophisticated over the years. Packet-filter firewalls are considered first generation firewalls, and newer files are called second generation and third generation. The advanced firewalls include the basic capabilities but add to them.

In addition to examining a single packet, these advanced firewalls can examine traffic from an entire network conversation between computers. Normal traffic follows specific patterns, but attackers use abnormal methods when attacking systems. These advanced firewalls can often detect abnormal traffic and block it.

Understanding DMZs

A *demilitarized zone (DMZ)* is a buffer zone that provides a layer of security protection. It is most commonly used to host Internet-facing servers and normally uses two firewalls.

Imagine a company that wants to host its own website. One method is to install *Internet Information Services (IIS)* on a Windows Server product such as Windows Server 2012. IIS works as a web server and is available for free on many Windows-based systems.

If the company places this server directly on the Internet, the server is highly susceptible to attacks. If the company puts it in its internal network, the Internet traffic adds risk to other computers on the internal network. Instead, the company places it in a buffer zone (the DMZ) between the Internet and the internal network, as shown in Figure 22-2.

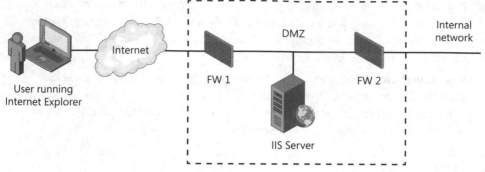

FIGURE 22-2 Hosting a web server in a DMZ.

The first firewall (FW1) provides access to the IIS server for Internet users. It also provides a layer of protection by controlling what traffic is allowed into the DMZ. The second firewall (FW2) provides an additional layer of protection for the internal network. Each firewall will have separate exception rules specifying what traffic is allowed.

> **NOTE THREE-LEGGED DMZ**
>
> It's common for a DMZ to have two firewalls, but there are other possible configurations. For example, a three-legged DMZ is a single firewall with three connections. One connection is for the Internet, another is for the web server, and the third is for the internal network. This is cheaper because only one firewall is used, but it is also more complex to configure.

> ✔ **Quick Check**
>   1. What is created in a firewall to allow traffic to pass?
>   2. How does a firewall identify SMTP traffic?
>
> **Quick Check Answers**
>   1. A rule or an exception.
>   2. By the use of port 25.

Port Forwarding

Most routers and firewalls support port forwarding. This allows specific traffic from the Internet to be forwarded to an internal system. Without port forwarding, Internet clients cannot access this internal system.

For example, imagine that you have a SOHO network protected by a firewall, as shown in Figure 22-3. The firewall is connected to the Internet with a public IP address, and the internal SOHO network has private IP addresses.

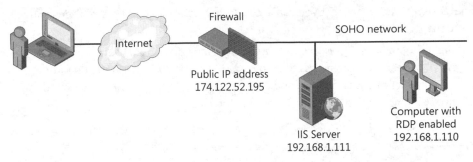

Public IP address
174.122.52.195

IIS Server
192.168.1.111

Computer with
RDP enabled
192.168.1.110

FIGURE 22-3 SOHO network with a web server and RDP-enabled computer.

If you had a laptop computer and you wanted to use it to connect to computers in your SOHO network while you were away, you could do so by enabling port forwarding on the firewall. The overall steps to do this with Remote Desktop are as follows:

1. Enable Remote Desktop Protocol (RDP) on the home computer. This includes ensuring that port 3389 is open on the computer's firewall.

2. Enable port forwarding on the firewall. You could use port 3389 so that any traffic on the Internet side of the firewall is forwarded to your home computer.

3. Start Remote Desktop Connection (mstsc) from an Internet location, and connect to the public IP address of your home firewall.

Remote Desktop Connection uses port 3389 by default. When you connect to the firewall by using port 3389, it will forward the traffic to your internal computer and you will have a remote connection.

> **MORE INFO**   **CHAPTER 20, "UNDERSTANDING PROTOCOLS"**
>
> Chapter 20 covers the remote connectivity protocols, including RDP and the Remote Desktop Connection. They are commonly used by administrators to remotely administer servers. The Windows Firewall section later in this chapter shows how to enable Remote Desktop exceptions on Windows-based systems.

You can also use port forwarding to access other systems. For example, if you configured a web server using IIS, you could forward traffic to it as well. A web server uses HTTP, and the default for HTTP is port 80, so you could configure the firewall to forward all traffic from the Internet to the internal web server by using port 80.

Configuring Port Forwarding

The steps you use to configure port forwarding on a router or firewall are dependent on the brand. You might need to dig out the manual to identify the steps. Many routers used in SOHOs have web-based pages that you can access from a computer, and these often include easy-to-use menus.

For example, Figure 22-4 shows the port forwarding page on a Cisco router. The router includes several pages, and I can access them by using *http://192.168.1.1* in the uniform resource locator (URL) of a web browser and then logging on. In the figure, I've selected the Applications & Gaming section, which includes port forwarding.

MORE INFO   CHAPTER 23, "EXPLORING WIRELESS NETWORKING"

Table 23-3 in Chapter 23 lists default IP addresses, administrator names, and passwords used to access the web-based pages in many routers. These passwords should be changed from the default to prevent anyone from accessing them.

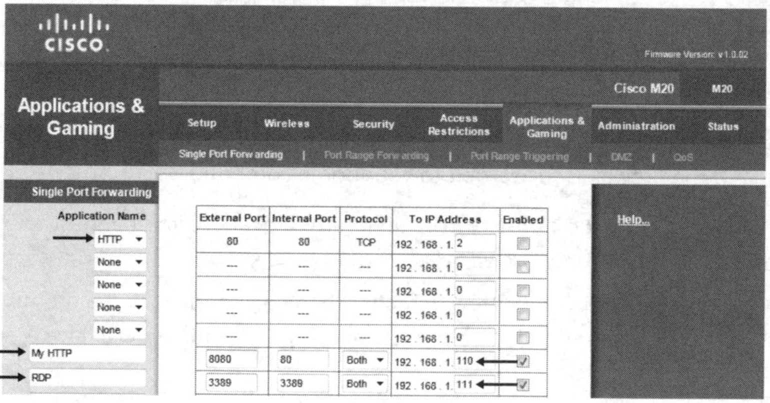

FIGURE 22-4 Configuring port forwarding on a router.

The default port for RDP is 3389. The RDP setting in Figure 22-4 is using this port as the trigger to forward traffic to the internal computer by using the IP address of 192.168.1.110.

I could have used the preconfigured HTTP setting. Notice that it uses the default port of 80 for the external IP address of the firewall and port 80 for the internal computer. If I used it, I would have entered 192.168.1.111 as the address of the internal web server and selected Enabled. A user from the Internet could use this URL *(http://174.122.52.195)*, and traffic would be forwarded to the web server.

However, just because port 80 is the default port of HTTP doesn't mean that you must use it on the external IP address for port forwarding. I instead chose to use port 8080 as the external port.

The My HTTP setting forwards all traffic using port 8080 to 192.168.1.111, port 80, which is the web server. If you wanted to access this from the Internet, you'd use the following URL: *http://174.122.52.195:8080*.

If the IP address is registered with Internet Domain Name System (DNS) servers, you can use the name instead of the IP address. For example, if Darrilgibson.com is registered with DNS and uses 174.122.52.195, you can enter the URL as *http://darrilgibson.com:8080*.

> **MORE INFO** **PORTFORWARD.COM**
>
> Figure 22-4 shows the port forwarding page for one router, but all routers are not the same. Port Forward (*http://portforward.com/*) includes multiple resources and guides that provide the steps for configuring port forwarding on hundreds of different routers.

Port Forwarding and IP Addresses

There's an important point to realize with port forwarding: the internal computers must always have the same IP addresses.

Internal desktop computers are typically assigned IP addresses with Dynamic Host Configuration Protocol (DHCP). When they are restarted, they can get a different IP address, and if the IP address is changed, port forwarding will no longer work for that computer.

> **EXAM TIP**
>
> The most common reason that port forwarding doesn't work is that it isn't configured correctly. It needs to be configured on the router with the correct ports, and the IP addresses of internal computers must not change.

Port Forwarding and SSH

Port forwarding is often associated with Secure Shell (SSH). SSH is an encryption protocol used to secure many different types of traffic, such as Secure File Transfer Protocol (SFTP) and Secure Copy (SCP). Both protocols use port 22.

When port forwarding is used to forward SSH traffic, it's common to use port 22 as the external port. Any external traffic using port 22 will be forwarded to an internal system configured to accept SSH traffic.

Port Triggering

Port triggering is used to open an incoming port in response to traffic on an outgoing port. The incoming port is normally closed and will close again a short while after the session is closed.

For example, imagine that you have an application that sends data out on port 5678 and receives data back on port 8765, as shown in Figure 22-5. You would configure the router to recognize outgoing port 5678 as the trigger, and when it received outgoing traffic on this port, it would open incoming port 8765.

Port 5678 ⟶

⟵ Port 8765

Internet

FIGURE 22-5 Using port triggering on a router.

EXAM TIP

Port triggering is used by internal clients only to open an incoming port. Port triggering is not used to open ports in response to triggers from an Internet computer.

Port triggering often uses port ranges. That is, the trigger range might be 5670 to 5680 and the input range might be 8760 to 8770. When the router receives outgoing traffic using any port between 5670 to 5680, it opens incoming ports 8760 to 8770.

One benefit is that port triggering isn't based on IP addresses. Therefore, internal clients can still use DHCP. The router returns data to the same IP address that sent the traffic that triggered the port.

A downfall is that only one internal client can use it at a time. If Joe started an application and triggered the port, it would work for him. If Holly then opened an application and triggered the port, either Joe's connection is lost or Holly's connection is refused. Some routers give preference to the first connection and won't close it. Other routers give preference to the most recent connection request.

Using Proxy Servers

Proxy servers are used in many networks to optimize and control Internet traffic. They are most commonly used with HTTP and Hypertext Transfer Protocol Secure (HTTPS), but they can be used with other protocols, such as File Transport Protocol (FTP).

Figure 22-6 shows a network with a proxy server. Computers configured to use the proxy server send URL requests to the proxy server instead of to the actual Internet web servers. The proxy server retrieves the webpage and returns it to the client.

The proxy server has one or more public IP addresses assigned to it and has direct access the Internet. The internal network has private IP addresses, and the proxy server uses network address translation (NAT) to translate the private IP addresses to public and the public IP address back to private.

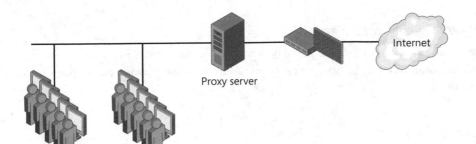

FIGURE 22-6 Network with a proxy server.

> **MORE INFO** CHAPTER 21
>
> Chapter 21 covers NAT in more detail. If a network isn't using a proxy server, it would usually run NAT on a router or firewall that is connected to the Internet. If NAT isn't used, all internal clients would need to have public IP addresses, which is expensive. In addition to saving money on public IP addresses, NAT also helps hide the internal clients.

Proxy Server Benefits

Proxy servers provide two important benefits: caching and content filtering. Caching reduces Internet bandwidth usage, and content filtering controls which sites users can access.

As an example of caching, imagine Joe uses his web browser to read some A+ blogs at *http://blogs.GetCertifiedGetAhead.com*. Joe's computer sends the URLs to the proxy server, and the proxy server retrieves the webpages. When the proxy receives the webpages, it stores a copy in an area of its memory called cache and also returns a copy to Joe's computer.

If another user tries to access any of these webpages, the proxy server returns the pages from cache rather than retrieving them from the Internet again. This reduces Internet bandwidth usage because the same pages don't need to be retrieved again.

Content filtering is used to restrict access to websites and block certain content. For example, an organization might decide that they do not want users to visit gambling websites from work computers.

Administrators configure the proxy server with a list of restricted websites, and if a user tries to access a site on the list, the user is redirected to another page. Many organizations display a page that indicates that access to the website is restricted and give information about the organization's security policy.

Proxy Exceptions

Proxy servers support the use of exceptions with proxy exception rules. For example, a proxy server could include the GetCertifiedGetAhead.com URL among its blocked domains. Administrators could then add proxy exception rules for a specific page within the domain or to an entire subdomain—for example, for the following URLs:

- *http://GetCertifiedGetAhead.com/aplus.aspx*
- *http://blogs.GetCertifiedGetAhead.com.*

After the exception rules are added, users will be able to access the Aplus page and the blog articles within the blogs subdomain, but all other access to the domain remains blocked.

Configuring Proxy Settings

The most common way that systems are configured to use a proxy server is from within the web browser. On Windows-based systems, you can access the Internet Explorer options through the Control Panel Internet Options applet.

MORE INFO **CHAPTER 13, "USING WINDOWS OPERATING SYSTEMS"**

Chapter 13 covers the Internet Options applet, including how to view and configure many of the other settings.

The following steps can be used to configure the Proxy settings for Internet Explorer via the Internet Options applet:

1. Click Start, Control Panel. If necessary, change the display to Large Icons or Classic View, depending on your operating system.

2. Select Internet Options. You can also access this through Internet Explorer. Press Alt+X to open the Tools menu, and select Internet Options.

3. Click the Connections tab.

4. Click the LAN Settings button.

5. In the proxy server area, select the Use A Proxy Server For Your LAN check box.

6. Enter the internal IP address of the proxy server and the port that the proxy server uses. You display will be similar to the following graphic. By default, these settings apply to all HTTP, HTTPS, and File Transfer Protocol (FTP) traffic, but you can click Advanced and configure different proxy servers for different protocols.

> **NOTE** **COMMON PROXY SERVER SETTINGS**
>
> It isn't a requirement, but proxy servers often use port 8080 instead of port 80 to listen for HTTP queries. The Bypass Proxy Server for Local Addresses is selected if the company has internal web servers. It allows computers to connect to internal web servers directly, without going through the proxy server.

Enforcing Proxy Server Use

When an organization has a proxy server in use, they often take steps to ensure that all Internet access is through the proxy. For example, users might realize that the proxy server is blocking access to a site and remove the proxy settings from the web browser.

A common way this is blocked is with a firewall rule. The rule will accept HTTP traffic from the proxy server but block all other HTTP traffic. If a user removes the proxy settings, this firewall rule blocks Internet access until the proxy settings are restored.

Some malware modifies or clears these settings when it takes over or hijacks a web browser. The malware author's goal is to allow the system to access malicious websites that wouldn't normally be accessible through the proxy. However, with the firewall rule in place, this modification effectively blocks all HTTP access for the infected system.

EXAM TIP

If a user has lost Internet access and a proxy server is in use, check the proxy server's settings. If they have been modified, the system might be infected with malware and a full scan should be run with up-to-date antivirus software. Similarly, if you've just cleaned a virus off a system but it still doesn't have Internet access, check these settings.

Basic QoS

Quality of Service (QoS) refers to techniques used to control traffic on a network. For example, users might regularly use computers to watch video from the Internet. Video is sent in a steady stream and can take up a lot of bandwidth. If too many users are streaming video at the same time, it has the potential to slow the network to a crawl.

QoS techniques can be used to give video traffic a lower priority. Streaming video is allowed, but if too many people are streaming videos at the same time, only their connections become slower. Other connections are unaffected, and the overall network performance remains high.

Another way QoS is used is to give higher priority to some traffic. For example, when Voice over Internet Protocol (VoIP) is used for phone calls or teleconferences, the voice data can be choppy if there isn't enough bandwidth. You might hear every other word a speaker says. Giving VoIP a higher priority helps minimize this problem.

QoS is implemented differently on different routers and firewalls. In general, you use rules but associate the rules with QoS. You then assign either a maximum bandwidth for the traffic or a priority.

✔ Quick Check

1. What is used to allow Internet access to an internal web server through a firewall?

2. What might cause proxy settings to be reconfigured without user interaction?

Quick Check Answers

1. Port forwarding.

2. Malware.

Windows Firewall

Windows-based systems since Windows XP have included the Windows Firewall. It's a host-based firewall running as software and can be accessed via the Control Panel.

In each operating system, the overall goal of Windows Firewall is the same: to control traffic and help protect the system from malicious traffic. However, criminals are constantly discovering new methods of attack, and security experts are constantly identifying newer and better methods of protection. Because of these improvements, there are some differences in Windows Firewall between different operating systems.

Home vs. Work vs. Public Network Settings

The Windows Firewall in Windows Vista and Windows 7 uses network locations to simplify settings. These are related to the risk level associated with the different locations, as follows:

- **Public risk.** If you connect to the Internet via a wireless network in an airport or coffee shop, you are connected in a public network. You really don't know who else is on the network, and your computer could be attacked. A public network represents the highest risk.

- **Home or work environment risk.** If you connect your computer to a network in your home or where you work, the risk is significantly reduced. It is much harder for an outsider to connect to these networks and launch attacks. Home and work networks are referred to as private networks.

The Windows Firewall is configured with stronger security when it is connected to a public network. This limits some usability but provides greater protection in high risk locations. When connected to a home or work network, the security settings are relaxed, providing increased usability.

Network Discovery

Network discovery is a group of network settings in Windows Vista–based and Windows 7–based computers that makes it easier for computers to locate each other when connected in a network. It is used in private (work and home) networks but disabled in public networks.

When network discovery is turned off, it effectively hides a computer from other devices on the network. It also prevents the computer from seeing other network devices. Network discovery should be turned off when a computer is in a public place.

Network Locations

The three primary network locations are as follows:

- **Home Network.** This is used for homes or SOHOs. Network discovery is enabled, making it easy for computers to see each other and share resources. Users running Windows 7 can create and join homegroups.

- **Work Network.** This is used in work environments and can be used for a SOHO. Network discovery is enabled, making it easy for computers see each other and share resources. However, users cannot create or join a homegroup when the work network location is selected.
- **Public Network.** This is used when the computer is connected to an untrusted location. It primarily refers to public locations, such as wireless networks in coffee shops, but should also be selected if a computer is connected directly to the Internet. This setting makes it difficult for other network devices to see the computer and also makes it difficult for the computer to see other network devices. The primary goal is to help protect the computer against malicious attacks.

If the computer is joined to a domain, administrators can force it to use a fourth choice called the Domain network location. It's not available to users as a choice, and when it's assigned, regular users cannot change it.

The first time that users connect to a new network, they are prompted to identify their current location. After they make a choice, network discovery and firewall settings are configured for that location.

You can view the current network from the Network and Sharing center. Additionally, you can change the network by clicking the link and selecting a different network. Figure 22-7 shows a system configured as a Home network and the network selection page that appears after clicking Home Network.

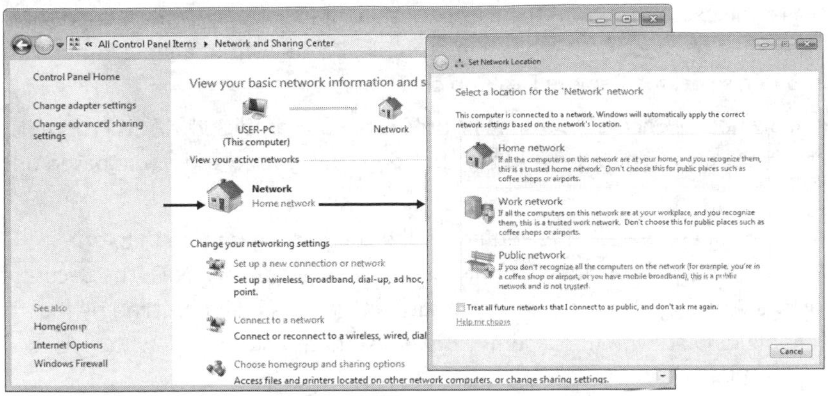

FIGURE 22-7 Network location choices.

Microsoft has a short video about choosing network locations, which you can view from here: *http://windows.microsoft.com/en-us/windows7/Choosing-a-network-location.*

Configuring Windows Firewall on Windows XP

You can start Windows Firewall on Windows XP from the Control Panel. Change the Control Panel view to Classic View, and double-click Windows Firewall. It has three tabs, as shown in Figure 22-8.

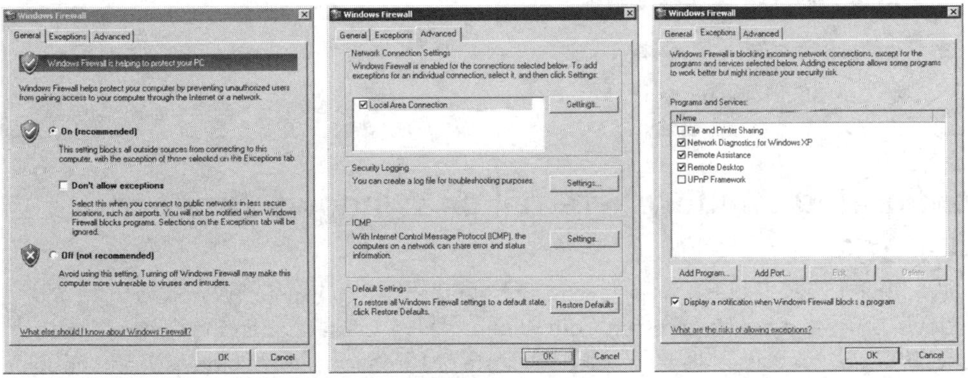

FIGURE 22-8 Windows XP Windows Firewall choices.

The General tab is used to enable or disable the firewall. It's recommended to leave it on, but if a third-party firewall is installed, you can use this page to turn it off. Windows XP doesn't use network locations, but the Don't Allow Exceptions choice is similar to the Public network location.

You can create firewall exceptions from the Exceptions tab. It includes five predefined rules that you enable or disable by checking the box. For example, if you want to enable Remote Desktop on a computer, select the Remote Desktop check box.

If you need to allow network access to a specific program, you can click the Add Program button and select a program. Clicking the Add Port button allows you to add a rule based on a port number alone.

The Advanced tab includes several other settings. If the computer has more than one network interface card (NIC), you can enable or disable the firewall for each NIC. The Security Logging setting allows you to enable logging. If you suspect traffic is being blocked by the firewall, you can enable logging with the Security Logging settings and then view the log to verify that the traffic is blocked.

By default, the Windows Firewall blocks ICMP traffic, including ping commands. Ping is useful for troubleshooting, and you might want to enable it. The ICMP settings page gives you several options to enable traffic used by ping and other ICMP-based tools.

✔ **Quick Check**

1. What network location should be used when connected to an unknown network?

2. What network location(s) supports homegroups?

Quick Check Answers

1. Public.

2. Only the Home network.

Configuring Windows Firewall on Windows Vista and Windows 7

The Windows Firewall applet can be accessed from the Control Panel in Windows Vista and Windows 7, just as it can be accessed from Windows XP. To start it, open the Control Panel, change the view to Classic View for Windows Vista or Large Icons for Windows 7, and double-click Windows Firewall.

Figure 22-9 shows the Windows Firewall on Windows 7. It's similar on Windows Vista, although you have more choices on Windows 7. The left pane includes several links to modify the settings, and the center pane provides information about its current configuration.

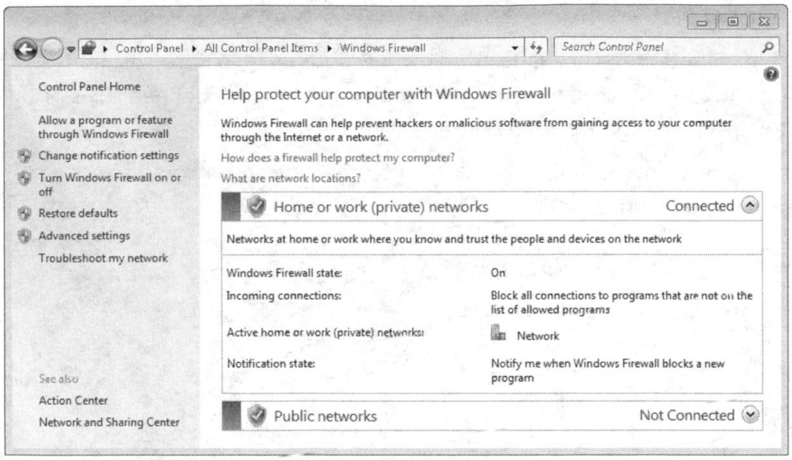

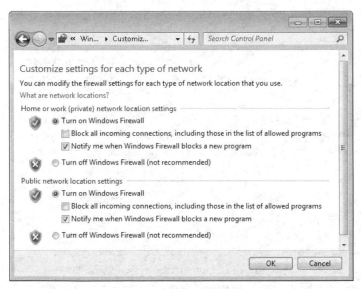

FIGURE 22-9 Windows 7 Windows Firewall choices.

Enable/Disable Windows Firewall

The Windows Firewall page includes a link labeled Turn Windows Firewall On Or Off. If you click it, you'll see a display similar to Figure 22-10. Notice that this gives you the option of manipulating the settings for the firewall in different network locations.

FIGURE 22-10 Enabling or disabling Windows Firewall on Windows 7.

If you suspect that the computer is infected with malware and connecting to external systems, you can select Block All Incoming Connections, Including Those In The List Of Allowed Programs. This will stop all traffic.

Enable Remote Desktop

The Windows Firewall page includes a link labeled Allow A Program Or Feature Through Windows Firewall. You can use this to enable or disable traffic by using predefined rules or by creating a new rule for specific programs or features.

For example, if you want to enable Remote Desktop, you can click the link and select Remote Desktop, as shown in Figure 22-11.

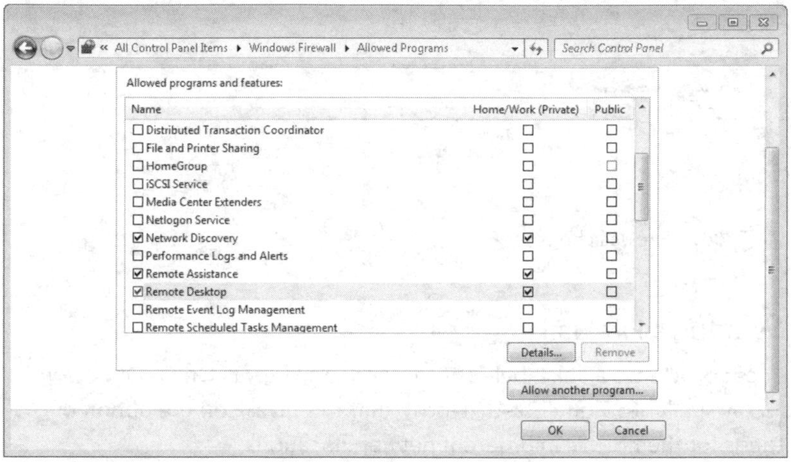

FIGURE 22-11 Enabling Remote Desktop on Windows 7.

Notice that it has separate selections for Home/Work and Public. As shown, Remote Desktop is enabled as long as the computer is connected to a Home or Work network location. However, if the computer is connected to a Public network location, Remote Desktop is disabled.

Windows Firewall has several predefined rules, but you can click Allow Another Program and select another program. This works similarly to how it works in Windows XP. You can't add rules based on ports from this page, but you can do so by using Windows Firewall With Advanced Security.

> *NOTE* **REMOTE DESKTOP CONNECTIONS**
>
> When Remote Desktop is enabled on a system, you can use Remote Desktop Connection (started with mstsc) to connect to most Windows-based systems. You cannot connect to Windows 7 Starter–based or Windows 7 Home Premium–based systems with Remote Desktop Connection. The following page has more details: *http://windows.microsoft.com /en-US/windows7/Remote-Desktop-Connection-frequently-asked-questions.*

Windows Firewall with Advanced Security

Windows Vista and Windows 7 include the Windows Firewall With Advanced Security applet. Settings in this applet apply to the Windows Firewall, but you have much more control over what you can accomplish.

You can create incoming rules for traffic coming into the computer and outgoing rules for traffic going out. The rules can be based on IP addresses, network IDs, ports, protocol IDs, or applications. You can also create rules for Home/Work network locations as Private, rules for the Public network location, and Domain rules.

To start this tool, open the Administrative Tools group in the Control Panel and double-click Windows Firewall With Advanced Security. It can also be started by entering wf.msc from the command prompt or in the Start, Search text box.

Figure 22-12 shows this tool open to the Inbound Rules section with the predefined rule for Remote Desktop open. This is the same Remote Desktop rule shown in Figure 22-11, but Windows Firewall allows you only to enable or disable it. With Advanced Security, you can view all of the properties, although many of the properties can't be changed in a predefined rule.

The Actions pane on the right in Figure 22-12 includes the New Rule link. Clicking this link with Inbound Rules selected opens the New Inbound Rule Wizard. If you select Outbound Rules and click New Rule, it opens the New Outbound Rule Wizard.

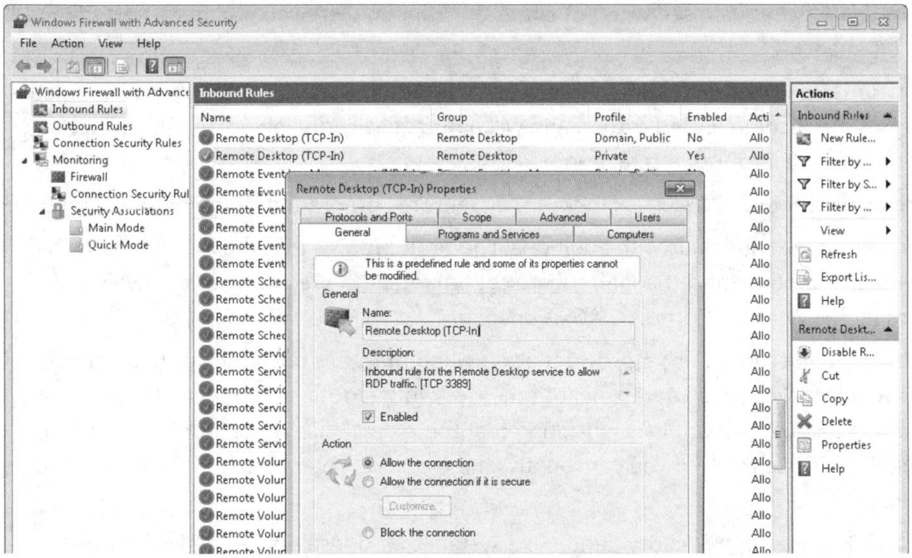

FIGURE 22-12 Enabling Remote Desktop by using Windows Firewall With Advanced Security.

Other Security Tools

In addition to Windows Firewall and Windows Firewall with Advanced Security, some other security tools are worth mentioning.

Security Center

Windows XP and Windows Vista use the Security Center applet to monitor a computer's security and provide feedback to users when unsafe settings are discovered. It regularly checks the following three items:

- **Firewall.** It checks to see whether either the Windows Firewall or a third-party firewall is enabled.

- **Automatic Updates.** It checks to see whether Automatic Updates is set to Automatic. This is the recommended setting and will automatically download and install updates without requiring user interaction.

- **Virus Protection.** This check looks for an antivirus program running on the computer.

Windows Vista expands this with additional checks. It ensures that the Internet security settings used when browsing the Internet are configured at the recommended levels and ensures that User Account Control (UAC) is enabled.

By default, the Security Center provides alerts when the system fails any of these checks. You'll see a red shield with a white X next to the clock in the notification area of the taskbar. Periodically, a text balloon appears indicating that there's an issue. If you double-click it, it opens the Security Center and you can identify the problem. You can also open it from the Control Panel.

Figure 22-13 shows the Security Center in a system that doesn't have any virus protection installed. An easy fix is to download and install Microsoft Security Essentials. Chapter 26 provides information about antivirus programs, including Microsoft Security Essentials, which is available for free to home users. You can read about it and download it from here: *http://windows.microsoft.com/mse*.

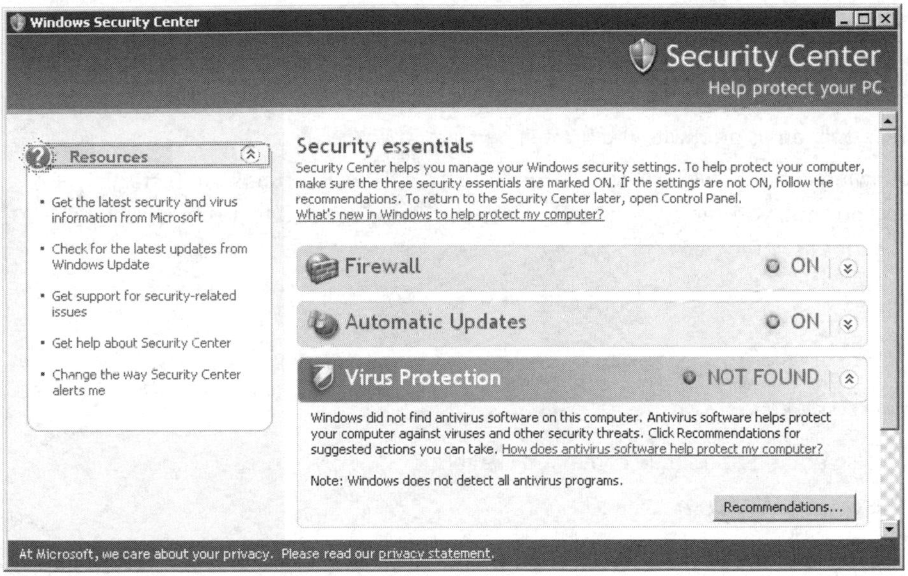

Security Center in Windows XP.

FIGURE 22-13 Security Center in Windows XP.

Action Center

The Security Center is replaced by the Action Center on Windows 7–based systems. It monitors the same settings as the Security Center but also monitors additional items in both Security and Maintenance categories.

- Security categories include the firewall, Windows Update, and antivirus checks similar to the Security Center. It also checks for spyware protection, security settings in Internet Explorer, and UAC settings.

- Maintenance categories provide information about recent problems and offer solutions if one is known. They also provide feedback if a system isn't being backed up or if Windows Updates need any attention.

The Action Center adds a flag in the notification area of Windows. You can click the flag to open it, or you can open the Action Center from the Control Panel.

EXAM TIP

You can disable notifications in both the Security Center and the Action Center. For example, if you're running third-party antivirus software that isn't recognized on a Windows 7–based computer, you can click Turn Off Messages About Virus Protection and the Action Center will no longer monitor the system for antivirus software.

Netsh

The net shell (netsh) is a powerful command prompt command that you can use to view and manipulate many settings. It is a shell command, meaning that it has multiple layers, but the focus here is only on using it with the firewall.

The following code shows how you can use it to view firewall settings. After starting a command prompt, you can type in the bolded text. The unbolded text shows how the prompt changes as you type in commands.

```
C:\>netsh

netsh>firewall

netsh firewall>show state
```

You can also enter it as a single command like this:

```
C:\>netsh firewall show state
```

The output shows the status of the firewall and includes a list of ports that are currently open on the firewall. For example, if you run this on Windows XP and Remote Desktop is enabled, it will list port 3389 as being open.

If you run the command on Windows 7, you'll see a message at the end indicating that you should use advfirewall instead of firewall. It includes a link (*http://support.microsoft.com/kb/947709*) to an article that shows comparable commands using advfirewall instead of firewall.

You can use the following commands to view some settings on Windows 7, but there isn't a netsh command that reliably shows the open ports:

```
C:\>netsh
netsh>advfirewall
netsh advfirewall>show currentprofile
```

You can also enter it as a single command, like this:

```
C:\>netsh advfirewall show currentprofile
```

Appliances

Within a network, the term appliance refers to a device that has built-in capabilities for a specific purpose. Appliances within a home, such as washing machines and toasters, make life simpler. You plug them in and they work. You don't have to understand how a toaster works, but you do understand that you can put bread in and get toast out.

Similarly, network appliances have a level of complexity in how they work, but they are simple to use. You might have to do some basic configuration, but for the most part, you plug them in and they work.

Network Security Appliance

Many organizations use network security appliances to streamline security. Firewalls and proxy servers can be quite complex, with a number of settings. If they're misconfigured, they might compromise security or make it more difficult for users to accomplish their jobs.

A network security appliance is a hardware device that runs specialized security software and simplifies installation and maintenance. Customers can plug them in, and they provide a wide range of security without requiring in-depth knowledge of their inner workings. Some of the services that a network security appliance can provide include the following:

- **Firewalls.** At their core, they are designed to control what traffic is allowed in or out of a network.

- **Proxy server content filtering.** Many include the same content-filtering capabilities of a proxy server. They can filter traffic based on URLs and block access to malicious websites.

- **Malicious software (malware) filtering.** They filter all traffic and can detect and block malicious software.

- **Spam filtering.** Many include the ability to detect and block spam before it reaches the user.

- **Intrusion detection systems (IDSs).** These monitor traffic and can detect attacks. They include a notification system to provide alerts when an attack is detected.

- **Intrusion prevention systems (IPSs).** These are an extension of IDSs and can prevent attacks. They are placed in line with the traffic to block malicious traffic before it reaches the network.

- **Network access control (NAC).** Clients are inspected to ensure that they meet certain requirements before access is granted. For example, a virtual private network (VPN) client might be inspected to ensure that it has up-to-date antivirus software before it is granted full VPN access.

> *NOTE* **UNIFIED THREAT MANAGEMENT (UTM)**
>
> Network security appliances that provide multiple security capabilities are commonly referred to as Unified Threat Management (UTM) solutions.

Some companies, such as Check Point Software, sell UTM solutions using their own hardware and software. Other companies bundle and configure someone else's software on an appliance. For example, nAppliance has a range of network appliances that use the Microsoft Forefront Edge Security suite.

Internet Security Services

Some companies sell Internet security services that an organization can use without purchasing any hardware or configuring software. These are very useful for SOHOs and small businesses that don't have the resources to purchase and maintain their own security appliance.

For example, Online Spam Solutions sells an email-filtering subscription service that blocks spam and malware. When you subscribe, your email is routed through their servers, where it is scanned and filtered before being sent to you. They have all the hardware, software, and supporting staff to maintain the service. You only have to authorize the payment.

Internet Appliance

An Internet appliance is a specialized device used for accessing the Internet by a single person. People use it to browse the Internet or access email, but it isn't designed to do much more.

EXAM TIP

Internet appliance is specifically listed in the CompTIA objectives, while other terms, such as network security appliance and Internet security services, aren't listed. An Internet appliance is not related to security, but because the term is so rarely used, people sometimes confuse it with a network security appliance or as an Internet security service.

Some of the devices, such as the Sony eVilla, use full-size monitors with a small form-factor computer. Other devices, such as the Nokia N810, are small handheld devices with a touch screen or keyboard. The features of these devices have been integrated into many mobile devices, such as smartphones and tablets, so you'll rarely hear the term anymore.

> ✔ **Quick Check**
>
> **1.** How will a user know whether the Windows Firewall is disabled on Windows 7?
>
> **2.** What command prompt command can you use to view firewall settings?
>
> **Quick Check Answers**
>
> **1.** Alerts from the Action Center remind the user.
>
> **2.** Netsh.

Chapter Summary

- Firewalls are classified as network-based or host-based firewalls. A network-based firewall controls traffic in and out of a network. A host-based firewall controls traffic in and out of a single computer.

- Firewalls use an implicit deny philosophy, blocking all traffic unless there is an explicit rule to allow it. Rules that allow traffic are called exceptions.

- A basic packet-filtering firewall can filter traffic based on IP addresses, ports, and protocol IDs. Most firewalls can filter traffic by using advanced methods.

- Port forwarding is configured on a router or firewall to allow Internet clients to access internal resources. For example, incoming traffic using port 3389 can be forwarded to a specific system that has Remote Desktop enabled.

- Port triggering is used to open an incoming port when a specific outgoing port is used. For example, if an internal system sends outgoing traffic by using port 6789, the port trigger on the firewall could be configured to open incoming port 9876.

- Proxy servers can reduce Internet bandwidth usage with caching and control Internet access with content filtering. Malware has been known to modify a web browser's proxy server settings.

- Windows Firewall is available in Windows XP, Windows Vista, and Windows 7. Windows Firewall with Advanced Security provides access to advanced firewall settings in Windows Vista and Windows 7.

- Windows Vista and Windows 7 use network locations. Home and Work network locations are considered private networks and have fewer firewall restrictions.

- The Public network location is used for unknown or public networks and has the most stringent firewall control. Network discovery is disabled in the public network location, making it more difficult for computers to see each other.

- All of the Windows Firewall versions include several predefined rules that can be enabled or disabled. You can also create additional rules based on ports or applications. Windows Firewall With Advanced Security provides the most options.

- The Security Center in Windows XP and Windows Vista performs basic security checks. Users are alerted if these settings are configured in a way that makes their computer less safe. The Action Center in Windows 7 replaces the Security Center and includes additional checks.

- Network security appliances that provide a bundled security solution in an easy-to-use device are available.

Chapter Review

Use the following questions to test your knowledge of the information in this chapter. The answers to these questions, and the explanations of why each answer choice is correct or incorrect, are located in the "Answers" section at the end of this chapter.

1. You are hosting a website on your home network, and you want to be able to access it when you're away from home. Of the following choices, what can you use to meet your goal?

    A. Port forwarding

    B. Port triggering

    C. A proxy server

    D. A Public network location

2. You successfully removed a virus from a user's computer, and a virus scan shows that it is clean. However, the user no longer has Internet access. What is the most likely reason?

    A. The Windows Firewall is enabled.

    B. The proxy settings for the browser are incorrect.

    C. Port forwarding has been disabled.

    D. The computer has been reconfigured for the Home location.

3. A user has configured four Windows 7 Professional–based computers in a SOHO but has not been able to get homegroups to work. Of the following choices, what is the most likely reason?

    A. Homegroups are not supported on Windows 7 Professional.

    B. The Windows Firewall is enabled on the computers.

    C. The Network location is set to Home.

    D. The Network location is set to Work.

4. You just connected to a wireless network in a coffee shop and plan on doing some work. You're prompted to choose a network location. What should you select?

    A. Home

    B. Work

    C. Public

    D. Private

5. You recently installed a program on a Windows 7–based computer that requires port 4545 to be opened on the firewall. What program would you use to configure it?

    A. Windows Firewall

    B. Remote Desktop

    C. Network Discovery

    D. Windows Firewall With Advanced Security

6. You are helping a small business owner increase network security. The owner is willing to purchase a product to protect against malicious Internet traffic but wants to minimize maintenance. What would you suggest to provide the greatest security?

    A. Install a router.

    B. Install a firewall.

    C. Install a network security appliance.

    D. Install an Internet appliance.

Answers

This section contains the answers to the chapter review questions in this chapter.

1. **Correct Answer:** A

    A. **Correct:** Port forwarding can forward requests from the Internet to an internal computer.

    B. **Incorrect:** Port triggering supports internal clients by opening an incoming port when an internal client uses a specific outgoing port.

    C. **Incorrect:** A proxy server provides centralized Internet access for internal clients.

    D. **Incorrect:** The Public network location blocks most network access and wouldn't help in this situation.

2. **Correct Answer:** B

    A. **Incorrect:** Users can access the Internet with the firewall enabled.

    B. **Correct:** Some malware modifies proxy settings, blocking Internet access.

    C. **Incorrect:** Port forwarding is not used to access the Internet from an internal computer.

    D. **Incorrect:** The Home network location would not block Internet access.

3. **Correct Answer:** D

    A. **Incorrect:** You can create homegroups on any edition of Windows 7 except Windows 7 Starter or Home Basic.

    B. **Incorrect:** Homegroups can work with the Windows firewall enabled.

    C. **Incorrect:** Homegroups are enabled in the Home network location, so this wouldn't block homegroups.

    D. **Correct:** Homegroups are disabled in the Work and Public network locations.

4. **Correct Answer:** C

    A. **Incorrect:** A home network is a private network.

    B. **Incorrect:** A work network is a public network.

    C. **Correct:** A coffee shop network is in a public place, and the Public network location should be selected.

    D. **Incorrect:** Private isn't a choice, but both Home and Work networks are considered private networks.

5. **Correct Answer:** D

    A. **Incorrect:** Windows Firewall on Windows 7 doesn't give you the option of creating rules based on ports.

    B. **Incorrect:** Remote Desktop is used to connect to remote systems, but it isn't used to open firewall ports.

    C. **Incorrect:** Network Discovery isn't a program but is instead a feature used to make it easier for computers to locate each other when it's enabled.

    D. **Correct:** Windows Firewall With Advanced Security includes the ability to create rules based on ports.

6. **Correct Answer:** C

    A. **Incorrect:** A router provides only basic protection.

    B. **Incorrect:** A firewall provides protection but isn't as effective as a network security appliance.

    C. **Correct:** A network security appliance provides a bundled solution, and many can be set up and maintained with minimal effort.

    D. **Incorrect:** An Internet appliance is a single-user device used for web browsing and email only.

CHAPTER 23

Exploring Wireless Networking

Wireless networks are very common today. They're easy to set up, and many home users, small offices, and home offices use them. You'll also see them in many medium-to-large organizations. As an A+ technician, you need to have a basic understanding of wireless components, wireless protocols, wireless security, and how to configure a wireless network. This chapter covers what you'll need for the A+ exams and on the job.

Exam 220-801 objectives in this chapter:

- 2.5 Compare and contrast wireless networking standards and encryption types.
  - Standards
    - 802.11 a/b/g/n
    - Speeds, distances and frequencies
  - Encryption types
    - WEP, WPA, WPA2, TKIP, AES
- 2.6 Install, configure, and deploy a SOHO wireless/wired router using appropriate settings.
  - MAC filtering
  - Channels (1 – 11)
  - SSID broadcast (on/off)
  - Wireless encryption
  - DHCP (on/off)
  - WPS (Wi-Fi Protected Setup)

Exam 220-802 objectives in this chapter:

- 2.5 Given a scenario, secure a SOHO wireless network.
  - Change default user-names and passwords
  - Changing SSID

- Setting encryption
- Disabling SSID broadcast
- Enable MAC filtering
- Antenna and access point placement
- Radio power levels
- Assign static IP addresses
- 4.5 Given a scenario, troubleshoot wired and wireless networks with appropriate tools.
  - Common symptoms
    - No connectivity
    - Intermittent connectivity
    - Slow transfer speeds
    - Low RF signal
  - Tools
    - Wireless locator

REAL WORLD   **WIRELESS HOME NETWORKS AND PORTABLE HOT SPOTS**

When I'm teaching classes and wireless topics come up, I frequently ask how many people have wireless networks where they live. Years ago, only about 25 percent of the people in the class had one. Today, 90 percent or more of the students usually say that yes, they have wireless networks.

Additionally, in several classes I've taught, students have their own portable Wi-Fi hot spots. They set the hot spot up, and it provides them with Internet connectivity for their laptops and other wireless devices. I don't mean to imply that everyone has to have a wireless network. However, because they are so popular, any A+ technician certainly needs to understand them.

Wireless Components

Wireless local area networks (WLANs) have become quite popular. They're easy to set up, and they provide a great deal of flexibility to users. For example, a homeowner can set up a wireless network without running any cables. Other people in the home can access the network from just about any room, or even on the porch.

The tradeoff is that a WLAN isn't always as fast or reliable as a wired network. WLANs are susceptible to interference, which can slow down performance. Additionally, users that are farther away from the wireless network have slower speeds.

WLANs have some basic components. It's important to understand what the components are before you can get a full idea of how they're configured on a network.

Wireless Access Point

A *wireless access point (WAP)* includes a transmitter and a receiver (called a *transceiver*) and acts as a bridge for wireless clients to a wired network. Organizations use WAPs to provide access to their network for wireless devices.

Wireless Router

A *wireless router* is a WAP with extra capabilities. It's common to find wireless routers used in home networks and small office/home office (SOHO) networks. It bridges wireless clients to a wired network just as a WAP does, but it often does much more. Some of the extra capabilities of a wireless router include the following:

- **Wired connections.** Many wireless routers include both wired and wireless capabilities.

- **Internet connectivity.** The wireless router is connected to the Internet. Any user connected to the router can access Internet resources.

- **Switch component.** The router also acts as a switch to connect devices to each other. For example, users can share data with others using a homegroup on Windows 7 systems.

- **Dynamic Host Configuration Protocol (DHCP).** DHCP provides IP addresses and other settings for the clients. It's common to provide the IP address of a router as the default gateway for clients and the IP address of a Domain Name System (DNS) server to resolve host names to IP addresses.

- **Network Address Translation (NAT).** The router issues private IP addresses to internal clients with DHCP, but the Internet uses public IP addresses. NAT translates the private IP addresses to public and public back to private for the clients. NAT also provides a layer of protection by hiding internal addresses.

■ **Firewall.** Many routers include basic firewalls. These allow you to create access control lists (ACLs) to allow or block certain types of traffic. Many routers also include port forwarding capabilities so that you can access internal clients from the Internet through the firewall.

Figure 23-1 shows a typical network configuration that uses a wireless router. Wired clients connect directly to the router by using cables, such as twisted-pair cable, and wireless clients connect using wireless network interface cards. The router provides a connection to the Internet through an Internet Service Provider (ISP) for all users.

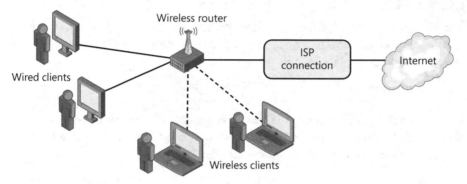

FIGURE 23-1 Wireless network.

The wired clients will have consistently high speed and reliability through the wireless router. In contrast, the wireless clients might have slower speeds or unreliable connections, depending on a variety of factors. For example, moving the wireless client farther away from the router will often degrade connection performance.

It's not apparent from Figure 23-1, but the clients can also communicate with each other through the wireless router. This is because wireless routers include a switch component.

NOTE WIRELESS ISOLATION MODE AND HOTSPOTS

To protect user privacy, many wireless hot spots prevent clients from communicating with each other. This is achieved by enabling wireless isolation mode on the wireless router.

Figure 23-2 shows a rear view of the same wireless router shown in Figure 23-1. The wired clients plug into the RJ-45 connections on the back of the router. Wireless clients connect using wireless transmissions. Figure 23-2 also shows the wide area network (WAN) connection found on many wireless routers. You connect the WAN port to the Internet.

The connection to the ISP can be different depending on how you connect to the Internet. For example, if you're using broadband cable, you need to install a modem between the wireless router and the ISP's connection. Some ISPs give users all-in-one devices that connect them to the ISP and also have wireless built right into them.

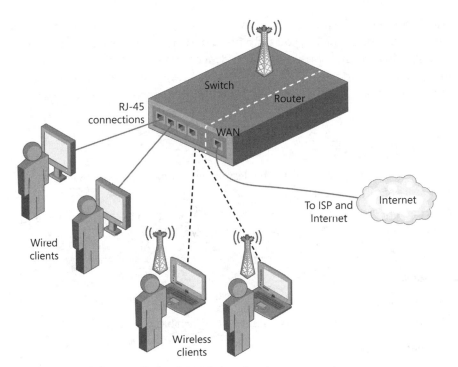

FIGURE 23-2 Wireless router showing switch and router components.

Wireless Device

Wireless devices are any devices that can connect to the network by using wireless technologies. In general, you can think of a wireless device as a laptop computer. However, there are more possibilities.

Many devices, such as wireless phones, tablets, and gaming systems, include wireless capabilities. For example, a Windows 7 Phone can connect to a cellular phone network for Internet access. However, when the phone is in range of a wireless network, you can configure it to connect to the Internet through the wireless network. It's often quicker and doesn't count against data limits for the phone.

You need to configure the wireless device by using the same configuration as the wireless router or WAP. This includes using the same wireless protocol and wireless security.

Infrastructure Mode vs. Ad-Hoc Mode

When you connect through a WAP or wireless router, as shown in Figure 23-1, you are using *infrastructure mode*. In contrast, an *ad-hoc* network is a wireless network without a WAP or router.

Ad-hoc is Latin for *as needed,* which is a good way of thinking about this. You create the network only when you need it. Imagine you and a friend both have wireless laptops and you want to connect the two computers together to share data or to play a game. One of you creates the ad-hoc network, and the other person joins the network. Similarly, if you have a wired Internet connection on one device, you can share it with someone else through an ad-hoc connection.

Wi-Fi and Wi-Fi Alliance

Wireless is often referred to as *Wi-Fi,* short for wireless fidelity. Generically, Wi-Fi is any WLAN based on one or more of the 802.11 standards.

Wi-Fi is also a trademark of the Wi-Fi Alliance. The Wi-Fi Alliance is a trade association that promotes standardization of wireless products and certifies wireless products.

✔ Quick Check

1. What's a benefit of a wireless network over a wired network?
2. When you compare a WAP and a wireless router, which has more capabilities?

Quick Check Answers

1. Flexibility in user locations and a lower cost.
2. A wireless router includes a WAP and also has additional capabilities, such as routing, DHCP, NAT, and firewall capabilities.

Wireless Standards

Common wireless networks use the *802.11* standards. When preparing for the A+ exam, it's important to know the wireless standards and some common characteristics. Three important characteristics of wireless standards are as follows:

- Maximum speed (data throughput)
- Frequency
- Range (distance)

Higher data throughputs result in faster downloads for the user. Wireless devices attempt to connect at the highest speed they can negotiate without errors. For example, if a wireless laptop is in the same room as a wireless router, it will probably connect at the highest speed possible. However, another laptop on a different floor or separated by walls will connect at a slower speed. Interference also results in slower connections.

Each device within the wireless network must use the same frequency range. The two frequency ranges used with 802.11 wireless networks are 2.4 GHz and 5.0 GHz.

Range refers to how far the wireless signal can travel. You'll find a wide assortment of distances quoted for the different wireless protocols. For example, some people say that 802.11a has a range of 150 feet and that 802.11g has a range of 300 feet. Others say that the ranges are 115 and 125 feet, respectively.

You can often modify the range by increasing the strength of the signal, modifying the position of the antenna, and eliminating interference in the environment. It isn't critical to know the exact range of any of the protocols, but you should know their ranges compared to each other.

> **NOTE DIRECTIONAL ANTENNAS EXTEND RANGE**
>
> You can also extend the range of a wireless network with a directional antenna. Most devices use omni antennas, which transmit and receive in all directions. A directional antenna transmits and receives in a single direction and has a much greater range. Attackers can use a cantenna (a simple can attached to a wire) as a directional antenna; they can use it to connect to wireless networks from far away.

Table 23-1 shows the maximum speed and frequency used by the common wireless protocols, and the approximate indoor distances. Notice that 802.11n has the highest speeds and the highest range. These two characteristics are primary reasons why 802.11n is becoming so popular today.

TABLE 23-1 802.11 Characteristics

Protocol	Maximum Speed	Frequency	Indoor Distances
802.11a	54 Mbps	5.0 GHz	Lowest range ~30 m (100 feet)
802.11b	11 Mbps	2.4 GHz	Medium range ~35 m (115 feet)
802.11g	54 Mbps	2.4 GHz	Medium range ~38 m (125 feet)
802.11n	600 Mbps 300 Mbps common	2.4 & 5.0 GHz	Highest range ~70 m (230 feet)

Many wireless devices support multiple protocols. For example, you can purchase an 802.11n wireless router and it will work with devices using 802.11a, b, and g. Today, most devices are either 802.11g or 802.11n, but you might run across some older devices using 802.11a or 802.11b.

802.11n uses *multiple-input multiple-output (MIMO)* technologies with multiple antennas. Instead of having a single powerful antenna to transmit and receive, MIMO devices use multiple antennas to transmit and receive data. It's common to see MIMO devices that support 300-Mbps speeds, but the speeds can be as high as 600 Mbps.

EXAM TIP

Know the maximum data throughput and frequencies used by each of the wireless protocols listed in Table 23-1. IEE 802.11n is the newest, and it uses MIMO to achieve higher
throughputs.

Antenna and Access Point Placement

Wireless devices use antennas to transmit and receive data, and how you position the antennas and access points affects these transmissions. First, it's important to realize that most
antennas are omni-directional. That is, they transmit or receive in all directions.

If you live in a single empty room, you would place the WAP in the middle to give you the
best performance throughout the room. Of course, it's highly unlikely that you live in a single
empty room. Instead, you probably live in a multiple-room residence, which might even have
more than one floor. Any physical objects such as walls, floors, ceilings, and furniture can
absorb the signal.

Wireless networks are also susceptible to interference from a wide variety of sources.
Electromagnetic interference (EMI) can come from equipment such as magnets and even
fluorescent lights. Radio frequency interference (RFI) can come from other transmitters.
Many cordless phones, baby monitors, and microwaves transmit on the same frequency that
wireless devices use, and they can interfere with the signal. It's best to place the WAP at least
three feet away from any of these devices.

Placing the antenna vertically or horizontally also affects the transmission. Point your
finger to the sky as if it were a vertically placed antenna. Positioned this way, an antenna
transmits the strongest outwards from you, but not as strongly up and down. This is good for
a one-floor residence. If you change the position so that it is horizontal, the signal is strongest
above and below. This works well for a multi-floor residence.

With all that in mind, where should you place the WAP? It often takes a little trial and
error if you want the signal to reach multiple locations. You can set up the WAP and then use
a wireless device to check the signal strength. For example, you can configure the WAP and
then use the signal strength meter in Windows to see the signal strength as someone else
moves the WAP or the antenna.

The steps in the Configuring Wireless Settings on Windows 7 later in this chapter show
how you can access the wireless signal strength meter and include a graphic of the meter.

Channels

802.11 protocols use frequency bands beginning with 2.4 GHz or 5.0 GHz. However, these are
starting frequencies, and each frequency includes multiple channels.

You normally don't have to change the channels. However, if you are experiencing excessive interference on one channel, you can switch to a different channel with less interference.

EXAM TIP

The stated frequency of wireless protocols identifies the beginning frequency, but each protocol includes multiple channels in the frequency range. You can change channels if there is excessive interference in a channel.

Figure 23-3 shows the options for changing the channel on a wireless router. This router chose channel 6 by default, which is common, but any of the channels can be selected.

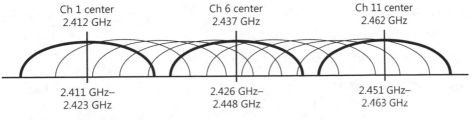

FIGURE 23-3 Changing the channel on a wireless router.

These channels work similarly to how a radio channel works. When you tune to a radio station's center frequency, you get the best reception, but you can often still hear a station if you tune it to a close frequency. Of course, radio stations are aware of this, and you'll rarely have two radio stations right next to each other, interfering with each other's broadcast. This isn't the case with the wireless channels.

The wireless channel frequencies shown in Figure 23-3 are the center frequency for each channel, and each channel is 22 MHz wide. Therefore, channel 6 is actually 2.426 GHz to 2.448 GHz, with a center frequency of 2.437 GHz. Figure 23-4 shows how the 22-MHz channels overlap with each other. Only channels 1, 6, and 11 are marked and highlighted. You can see that these channels do not overlap with each other.

Ch 1 center	Ch 6 center	Ch 11 center
2.412 GHz	2.437 GHz	2.462 GHz

2.411 GHz–	2.426 GHz–	2.451 GHz–
2.423 GHz	2.448 GHz	2.463 GHz

FIGURE 23-4 Wireless channels.

It's common for devices to default to channel 6. If you have multiple wireless devices in the same area, they might all be broadcasting on channel 6 and interfering with each other. They still work, but the interference forces them to retransmit traffic and can reduce performance. With that in mind, you can often improve wireless performance by changing to channel 1 or channel 11.

Many wireless devices will automatically scan the channels for wireless networks. That is, if you change the channel on a WAP or a wireless router, you usually don't have to change the channel on the wireless devices. For example, Windows 7 doesn't require you to manipulate the channel even if you've changed the channel on a wireless router.

EXAM TIP

If there are any other wireless networks near you, you can often improve the performance of your network by changing the channel. Channels 1, 6, and 11 are recommended for use because they do not overlap with each other. If other networks are using channel 6, you can change yours to 1 or 11 and avoid interference from the other networks.

Radio Power Levels

Many WAPs also include settings to adjust the radio power levels. All the devices transmit and receive radio frequency (RF) signals over the air to communicate. If you turn up the radio power of the WAP, you can increase the distance of the transmission.

Alternatively, if you don't want people outside the home or office to receive the signal, you can turn down the radio power levels. This limits the distance the signal travels, but it isn't a reliable security measure. A dedicated attacker can use a directional antenna to access the network.

NOTE LOWER POWER LEVELS EQUAL SLOW CONNECTIONS

Lowering the power level can affect users within your WLAN. Wireless devices connect to the WAP by using the fastest speed they can achieve without errors, and if the RF level is too low, it can result in intermittent connectivity or slow transfer speeds.

✔ **Quick Check**

    1. What is the maximum speed of 802.11g?

    2. What wireless protocol provides the greatest speed and range?

Quick Check Answers

    1. 54 Mbps.

    2. 802.11n.

Wireless Security

One of the most important concerns with wireless networks is security. Because data is transmitted over the air by using frequencies anyone can learn, the transmissions need to be protected. One of the most important security protections you can use is to configure the wireless network with a secure security protocol. Several wireless security measures are discussed in the following sections.

Encryption Types

Encryption scrambles data so that it can't be read or interpreted by unauthorized individuals. Encryption codes have been around since at least the time of Julius Caesar and the Roman Empire, but they are much better today than they were back then.

Wireless includes three security protocols, and they use different encryption types. The three available security protocols are as follows:

- **Wired Equivalent Privacy (WEP).** *WEP* is an older security protocol. It has been cracked and should not be used.

- **Wi-Fi Protected Access (WPA).** *WPA* was introduced as a short term replacement for WEP. It provided significant improvements over WEP and used existing hardware. Sometimes you have to upgrade the firmware on wireless devices to use WPA. When required, wireless device vendors usually provide free downloads that you can use to upgrade the device's capabilities and use WPA.

- **Wi-Fi Protected Access version 2 (WPA2).** *WPA2* is a permanent replacement for WEP and WPA. It requires more advanced hardware, but almost all hardware sold today supports WPA2.

EXAM TIP

WPA2 is the most secure wireless security protocol. If your wireless device shows support only for WEP, you can often upgrade the hardware's firmware to get support for WPA or WPA2. This is similar to upgrading the BIOS for a computer, but you're instead upgrading the firmware on a network interface card or wireless router.

The two encryption types used with wireless security protocols are as follows:

- **Temporal Key Integrity Protocol (TKIP).** WPA uses *TKIP*. It was designed so that WPA would be more secure than WEP while allowing users to use the same hardware. Even though legacy hardware supports TKIP, it sometimes requires a firmware upgrade for it to work.

- **Advanced Encryption Standard (AES).** WPA2 uses *AES*. It provides a stronger security combination than either WEP or WPA with TKIP. Beyond wireless, AES is used worldwide as an encryption standard in many different applications.

Table 23-2 summarizes the three wireless security protocols.

TABLE 23-2 Wireless Security Algorithms

Protocol	Strength	Comments
WEP	Weak	Don't use.
WPA	Stronger than WEP	Use only if hardware doesn't support WPA2. Might need to upgrade firmware. Uses TKIP.
WPA2	Strongest	Recommended for use today. Uses AES.

WPA and WPA2 also support Personal mode and Enterprise mode. Personal mode is simple to set up and used in most home networks and SOHOs. Enterprise Mode is used in larger organizations.

Wardriving

Wardriving is the practice of driving around looking for wireless networks. Attackers often use wardriving to discover wireless networks that are not secured or that are secured using easily beatable security such as WEP. When they discover a wireless network, they probe it to determine how far they can get in.

In some cases, attackers can access computers and resources in the wireless network. If the administrator password has not been changed on the wireless router, they can manipulate the settings and actually lock out the owner.

Personal Mode

Personal mode uses a preshared key or passphrase. Every wireless device must have the same passphrase as the wireless router. Figure 23-5 shows a setup page for a Linksys wireless router with the security mode set to WPA2 Personal and the shared key as IWillPa$$A+.

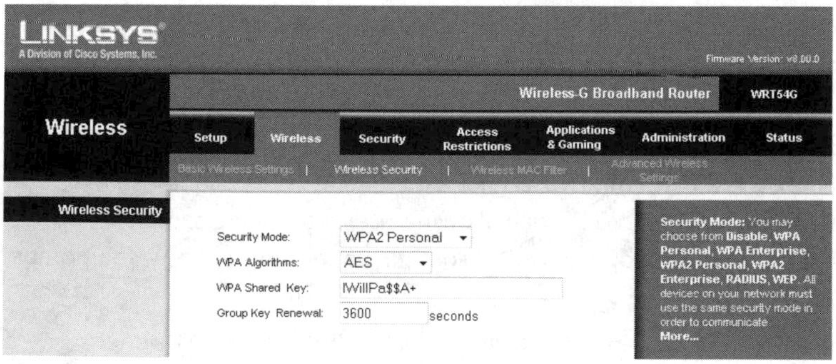

FIGURE 23-5 Wireless network.

The security mode is sometimes identified as security type, and the shared key is sometimes called a passphrase, network security key, or something similar. The important point to remember is that every wireless device must be configured with the same settings. In Figure 23-5, every device must be using WPA2 Personal with a key of IWillPa$$A+.

> **NOTE   PASSPHRASE**
>
> The passphrase or shared key should be strong so that it can't be easily guessed. Strong passphrases include a mixture of uppercase and lowercase letters, numbers, and symbols, and are at least eight characters long.

Enterprise Mode

Larger organizations sometimes use Enterprise mode. Enterprise Mode uses a Remote Authentication Dial-in User Service (RADIUS) server to authenticate clients. Users need a user name and password to access the wireless network.

MAC Filtering

Another security feature you can use is media access control (MAC) filtering. Each network interface card (NIC) has a theoretically unique MAC address assigned to it, and you can restrict access to a wireless network based on this address. I say theoretically unique because you are unlikely to see any two NICs with the same MAC address in the same network. However, manufacturers have a finite number of addresses and sometimes have to reuse them.

Figure 23-6 shows the Wireless MAC Filter page for a wireless router. As configured, it will allow only computers with the MAC address listed in MAC01 through MAC04 to connect. If a computer with a different MAC address tries to connect, the connection is blocked.

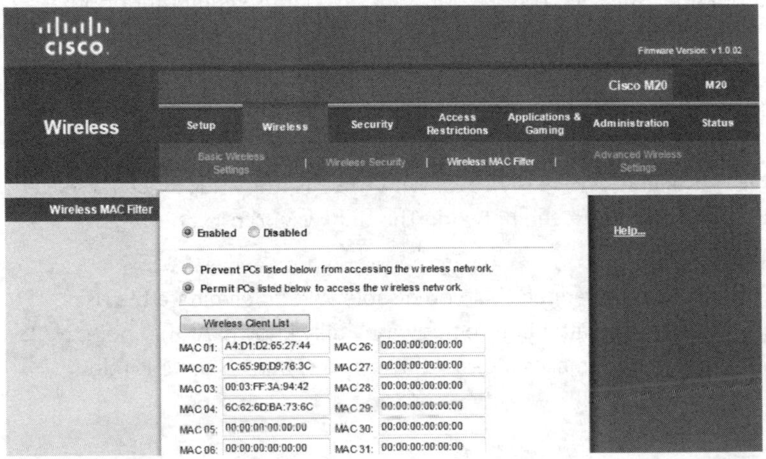

FIGURE 23-6 Filtering systems based on the MAC address.

On the surface, this might seem secure. After all, there are billions of MAC addresses and the possibility of someone guessing one of these is astronomically low. However, attackers can learn the MAC addresses that you're allowing and change their system to use the same MAC address.

It's relatively easy to change the MAC address for any NIC to match the MAC address of another NIC. Chapter 19, "Exploring Cables and Connectivity," includes steps to manipulate the duplex settings for a NIC and points out the setting for the MAC address.

In summary, you can use MAC filtering to restrict access, but be aware that a knowledge-able attacker can beat it. Additionally, if you have many computers on your wireless LAN, it might become an administrative burden to keep track of MAC addresses.

Wi-Fi Protected Setup

One of the challenges with wireless is that it can be complex to set up and create a secure environment. *Wi-Fi Protected Setup (WPS)* was developed by the Wi-Fi Alliance to make it easier for users to set up a secure wireless network. Two common WPS methods are as follows:

- **Push button.** Users press a button on the WAP and press a software button on the wireless device. The two devices communicate with each other and set up a secure connection. A complex preshared key is still used, but the user doesn't need to enter it.

- **PIN.** A PIN is assigned to a WAP and/or a wireless device. Users need to enter only the PIN of the other device to create a connection. For example, if the WAP has a PIN of 12345678, the user enters this PIN by using software on a laptop computer or other wireless device to make the connection. Just as with the push button method, a complex preshared key is still used for WPA2, but the user doesn't need to enter it.

While this sounds like it's a great resource to make the setup easier, it has a significant flaw. An open source software tool named Reaver that allows an attacker to easily discover the WPS PIN has been publicly available since early 2012. With the PIN, the attacker can discover the WPA or WPA2 passphrase and access the network. The only way to prevent this attack is to disable WPS on the WAP.

In the real world, it's highly recommended that you disable WPS to eliminate the risk. However, CompTIA objectives were created before this was widely known. At that point, WPS was recognized as a great feature that makes it easy for users to set up a secure wireless network.

✓ **Quick Check**

1. What security protocol is not secure and should not be used?

2. What security protocol is the most secure?

3. What can you enable to restrict which devices can connect?

Quick Check Answers

1. WEP.

2. WPA2.

3. MAC filtering.

SSID

Wireless networks are identified by the *service set identifier (SSID)*. The SSID is also known as the name of the wireless network. Many wireless routers have default SSIDs, such as Linksys or belkin54g, but some require you to give them a name when you're setting them up. All of them allow you to change the SSID, and an SSID can be up to 32 characters long.

Figure 23-7 shows a setup page for a Linksys wireless router. You can see that the Wireless Network Name (SSID) is identified as APlusCertified and that the SSID broadcast is set to Enable.

NOTE SSIDS ARE CASE-SENSITIVE

Because SSIDs are case-sensitive, an SSID of APlusCertified is not the same as apluscertified. If you don't enter the SSID exactly, it won't be recognized.

This device supports both 802.11b and 802.11g devices by selecting Mixed as the Wireless Network Mode. It also allows you to select a different wireless channel. In Figure 23-7, it's using channel 6 of the 2.4-GHz frequency range. If you're experiencing interference on a channel, you can change it to get better performance, as mentioned in the Channels section earlier in the chapter.

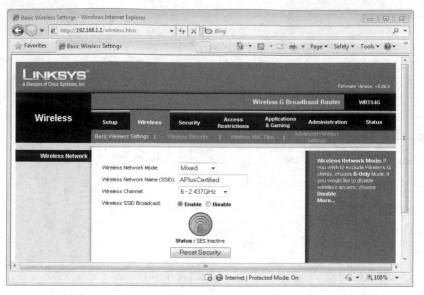

FIGURE 23-7 Linksys wireless router setup page.

Understanding SSID Broadcast

When SSID broadcast is enabled, the wireless router periodically sends out special packets that announce its presence. These broadcasts allow other wireless devices to easily see it and connect.

If you have a laptop, you might see other wireless networks from your neighbors. The SSID broadcast provides this information to advertise the wireless network.

Enabling or Disabling SSID Broadcast

As a general rule, it's recommended that SSID broadcast be enabled. That's not a typo. Wireless protocols are designed to work with WAPs and wireless routers advertising their presence with SSID broadcast enabled.

However, you might run across documentation indicating that SSID broadcast should be disabled to hide a wireless network. Other documentation indicates that disabling it provides no security. So, what's true?

The short answer is that disabling SSID broadcast doesn't provide any security. It does hide the network from some wireless devices. However, this reduces usability because it makes it difficult for some devices to connect. It does not hide the network from a knowledgeable attacker.

Many packets in standard wireless transmissions include the SSID, even if SSID broadcast is disabled. Free applications are available that anyone can install on a wireless-enabled laptop computer to capture these wireless transmissions. With just a few clicks, anyone can identify the SSID even if SSID broadcast is disabled. Therefore, disabling the SSID doesn't protect it from an attacker.

Some people might tell you that the SSID is the password, but this is not true. WEP, WPA, and WPA2 all support a passphrase. This is sometimes called a network security key or a shared key. However, this passphrase or key is different from the SSID.

However, CompTIA test writers don't necessarily understand that disabling the SSID doesn't provide security, or they might simply disagree with it. You might run across a test question that asks about hiding the wireless network. Disabling the SSID broadcast might be the best answer for the exam. However, it's important to remember that disabling the SSID doesn't provide any security.

EXAM TIP

The best way to protect a wireless network is by using a strong security protocol such as WPA2 and a strong passphrase that can't be easily guessed. You can hide a wireless network from some wireless devices by disabling the SSID, but this doesn't provide any security.

Renaming the SSID

From a security perspective, you should rename the SSID from the default. This reduces the amount of information available to anyone that can see your network.

For example, imagine that the default SSID for your wireless router is LinksysWRT54G. If you didn't change this, anyone that saw it would know you have a Linksys router with the model of WRT54G. They could download the manual from the Internet, and they might find a vulnerability. Then again, if you renamed the SSID to MyWiFi and someone saw it, they wouldn't have any information based on the name.

EXAM TIP

If the wireless router or WAP has a default SSID, you should rename the SSID after changing the administrator password.

Configuring Wireless Network

When you you're configuring a wireless network, the first step is to install and configure the WAP or wireless router. Most wireless devices provide a web-based interface, and you can use this to configure the settings. Additionally, most have default settings so that you can easily log in, but these defaults need to be changed.

From a macro perspective, here are the steps you'll follow to set up a network with a wireless router:

1. Turn on the wireless router.

2. Connect your computer to the wireless router.

3. Start a web browser and log on to the administration page.

4. Change the administrator password.

5. Configure the wireless protocol, the SSID, and the wireless security on the wireless router.

6. Configure wireless clients with a compatible wireless protocol, the SSID, and the same wireless security.

Changing Default User Names and Passwords

Table 23-3 shows some common administrator names, passwords, and IP addresses for many wireless routers. Anyone that has this book knows these defaults, and it's also easy to do a quick search on the Internet to discover them. With this in mind, it's important to change the default password and, if possible, change the default user names.

TABLE 23-3 Access Information for Wireless Routers

Vendor	Administrator name	Password	Starting IP
Belkin	Admin (or blank)	admin (or blank)	192.168.1.1
Dlink	Admin (or blank)	admin (or blank)	192.168.0.1
Linksys	Admin (or blank)	admin	192.168.1.1
Netgear	Admin	password	192.168.0.1

Wireless routers have an instruction manual or setup guide you can use. In short, you can either plug your computer directly into one of the RJ-45 connectors or use the wireless connection and connect using the defaults. After you're connected, you can open a web browser to access the administration page.

You enter the starting IP into the web browser to connect. This displays the administration page for the wireless router and prompts you to log in. Enter the default administrator name and password used for your router.

One of the first things you should do is change the default password for the administrator account. If you don't, an attacker or a practical joker can log in and start changing your settings. Some wireless routers include a reboot capability. If a malicious user can log in, they can interrupt connectivity by repeatedly rebooting it.

Figure 23-8 shows the page used to change the password on a Linksys router. I was able to access this page by clicking on the Administration menu item after logging in. Note that this is different from the security key or passphrase used for wireless security. Figure 23-5 showed the security key setting for this network.

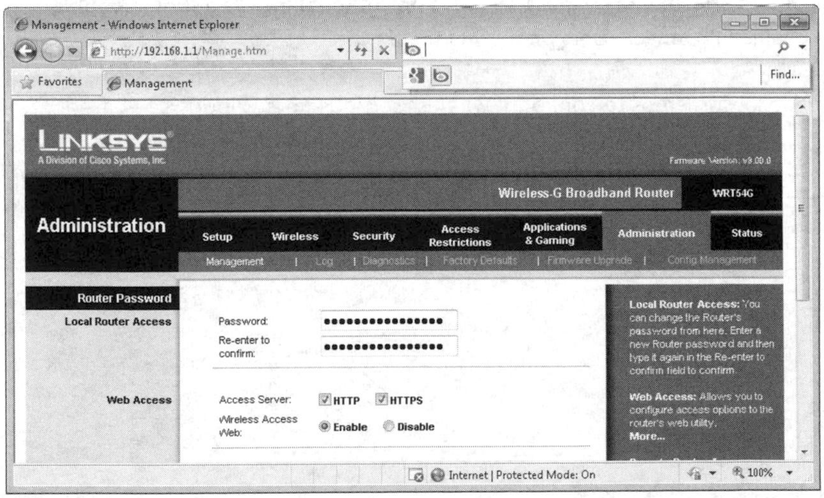

FIGURE 23-8 Changing the default password for the administrator account.

EXAM TIP

After configuring the wireless network, it's important to change the administrator password from the default. Otherwise, anyone that knows the default login information can log in to your wireless network and reconfigure it.

Next, you'd configure the wireless security with the passphrase. As mentioned in the Wireless Security section, WPA2 provides the best security, so it should be selected whenever possible. Additionally, you should use a strong passphrase or security key.

After you've configured security on the wireless router, you can configure the same security on any wireless network device.

Configuring Wireless Settings on Windows 7

Wireless devices have configuration menus that you can use to configure the wireless connection. The three primary pieces of information you need are as follows:

- SSID
- Security (such as WPA or WPA2)
- Passphrase or preshared key

EXAM TIP

If SSID broadcasting is enabled, you often don't need to enter the SSID or the security type. Instead, these will be automatically selected when you try to connect. However, the passphrase won't be available automatically. If you enter the incorrect passphrase on a wireless device, it won't be able to connect, so this is one of the things you should double-check if you're unable to connect after configuring the device.

You can use the following steps to configure wireless settings on a Windows 7–based computer:

1. Click Start, Connect To. You'll see a display similar to the following graphic on the far right of the taskbar. In the display, I'm hovering my mouse over one of the networks, and it shows details about the network.

NOTE **WIRELESS MIGHT NEED TO BE ENABLED**

If your system does not have wireless capabilities, you will not see the Connect To choice. If Connect To is not available, double-check to ensure that a wireless NIC is installed and enabled. Laptops commonly have a button or switch for wireless access that needs to be enabled.

2. Click the wireless network that you want to connect to, and click Connect.

3. If the network is not using security, you'll be connected automatically. If the network is secured, you'll be prompted to type in the network security key. Type it in and click OK.

IMPORTANT **ENSURE FIREWALL IS ENABLED**

If you are connecting to a wireless network that is not using security, you should ensure that your firewall is enabled and blocking all incoming connections. For example, on Windows 7, click Start, type in **Windows Firewall**, and select Windows Firewall within the Control Panel. Ensure that it's set to Public networks so that it blocks incoming connections.

You can also create a wireless connection manually. This is useful if you're not near the wireless network or the network is not broadcasting its SSID.

1. Click Start, Connect To. Click Open Network And Sharing Center.

2. Select Manage Wireless Networks from the menu on the left. If your system does not have wireless capabilities, you will not see the Manage Wireless Networks option.

3. Click Add.

4. Select Manually Create A Network Profile.

5. Enter the following information using the same information as you have on your wireless router or WAP:

   A. Enter the SSID as the Network Name.

   B. Select the Security Type used by the wireless network.

   C. Ensure the encryption type matches the wireless network.

   D. Enter the passphrase used on the wireless network as the Security Key. Your display will look similar to the following graphic.

NOTE **COMPARE PRECEDING GRAPHIC TO OTHER FIGURES**

The network joined in the graphic is the same network shown earlier. Figure 23-5 shows the wireless router configured using the Security Mode of WPA2 Personal, and the WPA Shared Key is IWillPa$$A+. Figure 23-7 shows the wireless router with an SSID of APlusCertified, and Wireless SSID Broadcast is set to Enable. The preceding graphic shows the settings on the Windows 7 system.

Configuring DHCP

Most wireless routers include DHCP for ease of use. After a wireless device connects, the wireless router gives it an IP address and other IP information such as the default gateway address and DNS. For most wireless devices, this is enabled automatically so that you don't need to configure anything.

The wireless router will issue clients with the following information:

- **IP address and subnet mask.** This will be on the same subnet as the router. If the router has an IP of 192.168.1.1 with a subnet mask of 255.255.255.0, all addresses it issues will start with 192.168.1 and use a subnet mask of 255.255.255.0.

- **Default gateway.** This is the address of the router and provides a path to the Internet. It is commonly 192.168.1.1, but it can be different.

- **DNS.** The router will typically receive one or more addresses of DNS servers from the ISP. It gives this information to the DHCP clients.

If you are using a WAP or a wireless router on an internal network, you might not want to use DHCP from the wireless device. It could be that your network has another DHCP server. Or you might want to manually assign the IP information.

If you decide to disable DHCP and you are manually assigning information, you need to ensure that each wireless device has a static IP on the same subnet. For example, if the router uses 192.168.1.1 with a subnet mask of 255.255.255.0 as its address, all other devices need to have an address in the range of 192.168.1.2 through 192.168.1.254, with the same subnet mask of 255.255.255.0. If you use different settings on any computer, it won't be able to communicate with other devices on the network.

EXAM TIP

If you disable DHCP on the router but don't have another DHCP server and do not manually assign an IP address, many computers will assign an Automatic Private IP Address (APIPA). APIPA addresses start with 169.254. If you see an address like 169.154.4.5, it's an APIPA address. This indicates that the client is configured to use DHCP but could not reach a DHCP server.

Troubleshooting Wireless Connections

When troubleshooting wireless connections, the first thing to check is whether you have the wireless connection configured correctly. This includes double-checking the following configurations:

- **SSID.** Remember, the SSID is case-sensitive.

- **Security type such as WPA or WPA2.** For example, if the WAP is using WPA2, all devices must use WPA2.

- **Passphrase or security key.** These are also case-sensitive.

Typo mistakes in any of these are easy to make, and typos will stop you from connecting.

Another common check is to verify that the wireless connection is available and enabled. Many laptops have switches that enable and disable wireless. If this switch is turned off, wireless connectivity won't work.

For example, I have an HP laptop that has a touchpad above the keyboard. I can turn sound on or off and modify the volume with a touch. It has touch areas to pause, play, fast forward, and fast reverse CDs and DVDs. On the far right is an area that I can use to enable or disable wireless capabilities simply by touching it (even if I didn't mean to touch it). Users sometimes disable wireless capabilities on a computer without realizing it, so this is an important check.

EXAM TIP

If your computer has wireless capabilities but wireless is not working, check to ensure that wireless capabilities have not been disabled on the computer.

Common Symptoms

Some of the common symptoms of wireless connection problems and their likely solutions are the following:

- **No connectivity when initially setting up device.** If you can't connect at all, the best thing to do is check the basics, such as the SSID, security type, and passphrase as mentioned previously. Check to see whether other wireless devices are working, and if so, you know that the WAP is working. You can also check the device to ensure that wireless is enabled.

- **No connectivity for a device that was connected.** If a wireless device previously worked but is not working now, it could be the WAP or the device. To verify that it is working, check to see whether other wireless devices can connect to the WAP. If the WAP is working, you can usually just reset the wireless connection. For example, restarting a Windows-based system solves many ills and will reset the connection.

MORE INFO CHAPTER 24, "CONNECTING AND TROUBLESHOOTING A NETWORK"

You can also try running Windows Network Diagnostics on the NIC. Chapter 24 includes the steps you can use to do this for both wired and wireless NICs in the Troubleshooting Network Problems section.

- **Intermittent connectivity.** Occasionally, problems can cause a device to periodically disconnect from the WAP. The user will likely complain about being disconnected from the Internet. You might need to modify the antenna and access point placement as mentioned earlier in this chapter. The problem can also be due to interference from other wireless networks, so changing the channel might help. Last, you might want to check the radio power level on the WAP and consider increasing it.

- **Slow transfer speeds.** Devices and WAPs connect using the fastest speed they can achieve without errors. If there is interference from any source, devices and WAPs will use slower speeds. Check the same items you would check for an intermittent connection.

- **Low RF signal.** As mentioned previously, many WAPs allow you to adjust the RF power level. You can lower it so that it is harder for people outside your home or office to connect. Of course, if you lower it too much, people within your wireless network might have problems. The solution is simple: turn the power level back up on the WAP. If that doesn't resolve the problem, reposition the WAP and antenna.

> **NOTE** **WIRELESS REPEATERS**
>
> Some large organizations use wireless repeaters. They extend the range of a wireless network so that the same network can reach a farther distance. If the RF signal is low but you can't reposition the WAP, a wireless repeater can help.

Wireless Locator

A wireless locator is a portable device with a directional antenna that you can hook up to a laptop computer. The primary legitimate purpose is to locate rogue WAPs. For example, an attacker can hook up a WAP to a network and transmit the information wirelessly to capture it. A technician using the wireless locator will be able to detect this rogue WAP and pinpoint its location.

War drivers also use wireless locators. They can use the directional antenna and connect into networks even if they are well beyond the traditional broadcast range of the WAP.

> ✔ **Quick Check**
>
> 1. What is the first security change you should make when configuring a wireless router?
> 2. What three items are needed to configure a wireless device?
>
> **Quick Check Answers**
>
> 1. Change the default administrator password.
> 2. SSID, security type, and passphrase or preshared key.

Chapter Summary

- A wireless access point (WAP or access point) bridges wireless clients to a wired network.
- Wireless routers include a WAP and have additional capabilities. It's common for a wireless router to include DHCP, NAT, and a firewall.
- Infrastructure mode uses a WAP or a wireless router to connect devices. In ad-hoc mode, wireless devices connect without a WAP or wireless router.

- 802.11a uses 5 GHz and has a maximum speed of 54 Mbps.

- 802.11b uses 2.4 GHz and has a maximum speed of 11 Mbps.

- 802.11g uses 2.4 GHz and has a maximum speed of 54 Mbps.

- 802.11n uses 2.4 and 5 GHz and has a maximum speed of 600 Mbps. 802.11n uses MIMO for increased speed.

- The distance wireless signals travel is affected by many factors. You can adjust the antenna and access point placement, use a different channel, or adjust power levels to improve the reception. Devices typically use channel 6 by default, so you can select channel 1 or channel 11 to avoid interference from other networks using channel 6.

- WEP is an older security protocol and should not be used.

- WPA2 is the strongest security protocol and recommended for use today. WPA is better than WEP and should be used if hardware doesn't support WPA2.

- You can sometimes upgrade the firmware of wireless devices to support WPA or WPA2.

- Personal Mode uses a shared key or passphrase. Anyone with the key can access the WLAN.

- Enterprise mode uses an authentication server, and each user must have an account to access the WLAN.

- Wi-Fi Protected Setup (WPS) allows users to configure security for a wireless network by pressing a button or entering a PIN.

- The SSID is the network name. The default SSID should be renamed.

- You can disable SSID broadcast to hide the network from some wireless devices, but this does not provide security.

- When configuring a wireless router, one of the first steps is to change the defaults, such as the default administrator password.

- The three items you need when configuring a wireless device are: the SSID, the security type (such as WPA2-Personal), and the passphrase or shared key. If you can't connect, double-check these items.

- Most laptops include a switch that can disable wireless access. Check this if a wireless device can no longer connect to a WLAN.

- Technicians can use a wireless locator to locate rogue wireless networks. War drivers also use them when searching for wireless networks.

Chapter Review

Use the following questions to test your knowledge of the information in this chapter. The answers to these questions, and the explanations of why each answer choice is correct or incorrect, are located in the "Answers" section at the end of this chapter.

1. What is the maximum speed of 802.11g?

    A. 11 Mbps

    B. 54 Mbps

    C. 300 Mbps

    D. 600 Mbps

2. Which of the following protocols uses multiple input multiple output (MIMO) antennas?

    A. 802.11a

    B. 802.11b

    C. 802.11g

    D. 802.11n

3. Which of the following protocols operate at 2.4 GHz? (Choose all that apply.)

    A. 802.11a

    B. 802.11b

    C. 802.11g

    D. 802.11n

4. Users regularly connect to a WLAN by using 802.11g. However, excessive interference is seriously degrading the connection. What can they do to improve performance?

    A. Disable the SSID broadcast

    B. Upgrade the network to 802.11b

    C. Configure the wireless router to use WPA2

    D. Change the channel used by the wireless router

5. You are configuring a wireless router. Which security type provides the highest level of security?

    A. WEP

    B. WPA

    C. WPA2

    D. 802.11n

6. You want to restrict which computers can access a wireless network. What can you do?

   A. Enable MAC filtering

   B. Change the default SSID

   C. Enable SSID broadcast

   D. Upgrade the firmware on the wireless network

7. What can you do to partially hide a wireless network?

   A. Disable WEP

   B. Disable WPA2

   C. Disable MAC filtering

   D. Disable SSID broadcast

8. You have just installed a wireless router for a new wireless network. Of the following choices, what should be one of the first things you do?

   A. Check the range of the wireless network

   B. Change the channel used by the router

   C. Change the default administrator password

   D. Upgrade the firmware

Answers

1. **Correct Answer:** B

   A. **Incorrect:** 802.11a has a maximum speed of 11 Mbps.

   B. **Correct:** The maximum speed of 802.11g is 54 Mbps.

   C. **Incorrect:** 802.11n has a typical speed of 300 Mbps.

   D. **Incorrect:** 802.11n has a maximum speed of 600 Mbps.

2. **Correct Answer:** A

   A. **Incorrect:** 802.11a does not use MIMO.

   B. **Incorrect:** 802.11b does not use MIMO.

   C. **Incorrect:** 802.11b does not use MIMO.

   D. **Correct:** 802.11n uses multiple input multiple output (MIMO) antennas.

3. **Correct Answer:** B, C, D

   A. **Incorrect:** 802.11a operates at 5.0 GHz.

   B. **Correct:** 802.11b operates at 2.4 GHz.

   C. **Correct:** 802.11g operates at 2.4 GHz.

   D. **Correct:** 802.11n operates at both 2.4 and 5.0 GHz.

4. **Correct Answer:** D

   A. **Incorrect:** The SSID broadcast doesn't impact interference on a network.

   B. **Incorrect:** Changing to 802.11b is a downgrade not an upgrade, with a speed of 11 Mbps compared 54 Mbps for 802.11g. Additionally, it operates on 2.4 GHz so it will have similar problems with interference.

   C. **Incorrect:** WPA2 is a strong security algorithm, but changing security won't affect interference.

   D. **Correct:** If a WLAN has excessive interference on one channel, you can change to a channel with less interference.

5. **Correct Answer:** C

   A. **Incorrect:** WEP is weak and should not be used.

   B. **Incorrect:** WPA can be used if devices don't support WPA2.

   C. **Correct:** WPA2 provides the highest level of security for wireless networks.

   D. **Incorrect:** 802.11n does not provide security.

6. **Correct Answer:** A

   A. **Correct:** MAC filtering can be used to restrict access to a WLAN to computers with specific MAC addresses.

   B. **Incorrect:** Changing the default SSID is a good security practice, but it does not restrict access.

   C. **Incorrect:** Enabling SSID broadcast is good for usability, but it does not restrict access.

   D. **Incorrect:** Upgrading the firmware is sometimes useful when a device doesn't support WPA or WPA2, but it won't restrict access.

7. **Correct Answer:** D

   A. **Incorrect:** WEP is a legacy security protocol that shouldn't be used, and it doesn't hide a WLAN.

   B. **Incorrect:** WPA2 is a secure security protocol that should be used, but it doesn't hide the WLAN.

   C. **Incorrect:** MAC filtering can restrict which computers can connect to a WLAN, but it doesn't hide it.

   D. **Correct:** Disabling the SSID hides the WLAN from some wireless devices, but it isn't a reliable security measure.

8. **Correct Answer:** C

   A. **Incorrect:** You can check the range after setting up the router, but this isn't always necessary.

   B. **Incorrect:** You can change the channel if the default channel has interference, but this isn't always necessary.

   C. **Correct:** One of the first steps you should take is to change the default administrator password.

   D. **Incorrect:** You can upgrade the firmware to get extra capabilities, such as to use WPA or WPA2, but if it's a new router, this is probably unnecessary.

CHAPTER 24

Connecting and Troubleshooting a Network

Previous chapters in this network section covered the basics of networking. In this chapter, the pieces are tied together, showing you common components for a small office home office (SOHO) network. It also includes some basic tools you can use for troubleshooting.

Exam 220-801 objectives in this chapter:

- 2.3 Explain properties and characteristics of TCP/IP.
  - Client-side DNS
- 2.10 Given a scenario, use appropriate networking tools.
  - Toner probe
  - Cable tester
  - Loopback plug

Exam 220-802 objectives in this chapter:

- 1.3 Given a scenario, use appropriate command line tools.
  - Networking
    - PING
    - TRACERT
    - NETSTAT
    - IPCONFIG
    - NET
    - NSLOOKUP
    - NBTSTAT
- 1.6 Setup and configure Windows networking on a client/desktop.
  - Establish networking connections
    - VPN

- Dialups
  - Wireless
  - Wired
  - WWAN (Cellular)
- HomeGroup, file/print sharing
- Network shares/mapping drives
- 2.6 Given a scenario, secure a SOHO wired network.
  - Change default usernames and passwords
  - Enable MAC filtering
  - Assign static IP addresses
  - Disabling ports
  - Physical security
- 4.2 Given a scenario, troubleshoot common problems related to motherboards, RAM, CPU and power with appropriate tools.
  - Tools
    - Loopback plugs
- 4.5 Given a scenario, troubleshoot wired and wireless networks with appropriate tools.
  - Common symptoms
    - No connectivity
    - APIPA address
    - Limited connectivity
    - Local connectivity
    - IP conflict
  - Tools
    - Cable tester
    - Loopback plug
    - Toner probes
    - PING
    - IPCONFIG
    - TRACERT
    - NETSTAT
    - NBTSTAT
    - NET

Install and Configure a SOHO Network

Previous chapters have given you the information you need to install and configure a small office/home office (SOHO) network. For clarity, this section puts everything together. These are the steps you'd commonly take to install and configure a SOHO network today. You can also use these same steps to configure a network in your home.

The primary reasons to create a network are to share resources and to provide access to the Internet. With this in mind, you'll need different devices, cables, and protocols.

Figure 24-1 shows a typical SOHO network. Refer to this figure as you read through the following sections.

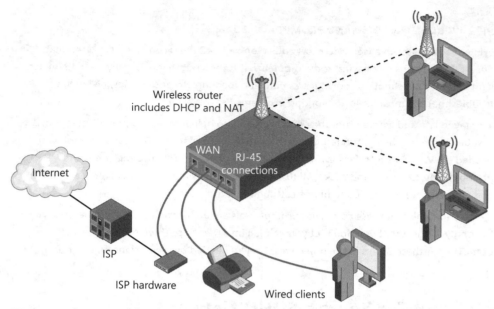

FIGURE 24-1 Components in a SOHO network.

Devices

A network that has Internet access requires the following hardware devices:

- **Internet access hardware.** This is typically provided by the Internet Service Provider (ISP). For example, you might have a broadband connection, and the ISP will lease or sell you a broadband modem. It could also be via a fiber connection, ISDN, DSL, or even through a satellite.

- **Wireless router.** The ISP connection plugs into the WAN connection of the wireless router, and the router provides connectivity for all internal clients. The wireless router has multiple components.

  - **Wireless access point (WAP).** The WAP provides access to wireless clients using Radio Frequency (RF) signals.

  - **Switch functionality.** Internal systems can communicate with each other through the switch capability of the wireless router.

  - **Wireless capability.** It's common to have a wireless router to provide connectivity for wireless clients. This isn't a requirement, but it does provide greater flexibility.

- **Network interface cards (NICs).** Each wired client needs a NIC. Common NICs have RJ-45 connectors for twisted-pair cable. A printer is shown as a wired client, but you can have a wireless printer instead.

- **Wireless adapters.** Wireless clients need to have wireless adapters that can communicate with the WAP. These are commonly built into laptops. It's also possible to purchase wireless adapter cards for desktop computers, or USB adapters that can plug into any open USB port.

Cables

Wired clients need to be connected with cables. Chapter 19, "Exploring Cables and Connectivity," covers a wide range of cables and connectivity, but a SOHO will typically use twisted-pair cable. Unshielded twisted-pair (UTP) cable with RJ-45 connectors is the most commonly used cable in SOHOs.

Three important points with the twisted-pair cable are as follows:

- If the devices support speeds of 1 Gbps or greater, you'll need to use at least CAT 5e cable.

- If the environment has an excessive amount of interference, you might need to use shielded twisted-pair (STP) cable.

- If the cables run through a plenum, you'll need to ensure that you're using plenum-safe cable.

EXAM TIP

CAT 5e or CAT 6 cable is required for Gigabit Ethernet. Plenum-safe cable is fire resistant and doesn't emit toxic fumes if it burns.

The wired clients connect to the wireless by router using straight-through cable. The connection from the WAN port of the wireless router to the ISP hardware often uses a crossover cable. If a device has an MDI/MDIX button, you can select MDIX instead of using a crossover cable.

MDI/MDIX is short for medium dependent interface (MDI)/medium dependent interface crossover (MDIX). Selecting MDIX mimics a crossover cable. Additionally, many newer devices will automatically sense the need for a crossover cable and automatically select MDIX for this connection.

Protocols

The Internet uses the Transmission Control Protocol/Internet Protocol (TCP/IP) suite, so all internal devices need to support TCP/IP.

Additionally, the wireless router will typically have the following protocols running:

- **Dynamic Host Configuration Protocol (DHCP).** DHCP provides internal clients with TCP/IP configuration. This includes an IP address, subnet mask, default gateway, and address of a Domain Name System (DNS) server.

- **Network Address Translation (NAT).** NAT translates public and private IP addresses. This allows internal clients to have private addresses but share the public IP address provided by the ISP.

- **Wireless protocols.** Wireless clients need to be running compatible wireless protocols. IEEE 802.11n is the fastest and is compatible with 802.11g. Therefore, you can have an 802.11n wireless router and a mixture of 802.11g and 802.11n wireless clients.

The wireless router usually acts as a DHCP client and a DHCP server. The WAN port connected to the ISP is configured as a DHCP client, and it receives TCP/IP configuration from the ISP. This includes a public IP address and the address of a DNS server on the Internet.

As a DHCP server, the wireless router provides internal clients with private IP addresses. It will also provide these internal clients with the address of the DNS server provided by the ISP.

VoIP

While it's not a requirement, many SOHOs also have basic Voice over Internet Protocol (VoIP) applications. These applications allow users to use the network connection for voice communications and multimedia sessions.

For example, users can subscribe to a service that allows them to use the Internet connection to make long-distance phone calls. In other cases, applications support video teleconferencing. Users can have meetings and conferences using the Internet connection.

Securing a SOHO Wired Network

In addition to making sure everything works, security is also an important consideration. The following key steps can be used to secure a SOHO wired network:

1. **Change default user names and passwords.** If computers or network devices have default user names and passwords, these should be changed. This is stressed in Chapter 23, "Exploring Wireless Networking," in the context of wireless networks, and the same steps should be followed with a wired network.

2. **Enable MAC filtering.** You can restrict which computers can access a network based on their MAC address. Chapter 23 shows how to do this on a wireless router, and the same concepts apply to a wired network.

3. **Assign static IP addresses.** You can statically assign IP addresses instead of using Dynamic Host Configuration Protocol (DHCP) to dynamically assign them. This makes it more difficult for unauthorized systems to access your network but requires more effort. Chapter 21, "Comparing IPv4 and IPv6," shows how to assign static IP addresses to Windows-based systems.

4. **Disable ports.** You should enable only the firewall ports needed by the SOHO. By disabling unneeded ports, you ensure that unauthorized traffic over these ports is blocked. Chapter 20, "Understanding Protocols," introduces the concepts of ports, and chapter 22, "Network Security Devices," discusses ports in the context of firewalls.

5. **Ensure physical security.** Physical security includes any security that you can touch. Ideally, computing devices such as servers and routers should be protected in a locked closet. Similarly, portable disk drives and other media with valuable data should be locked up when not in use.

✔ **Quick Check**
   1. What do most wireless routers include to provide systems with IP addresses?
   2. What type of cable is used for a SOHO with Gigabit Ethernet?

Quick Check Answers
   1. DHCP.
   2. CAT 5e or CAT 6.

Establish Networking Connections

One of the great strengths of computers today is the ability to connect to a network and share resources. Many of the methods have been described in general terms within the Networking chapters. This section provides a review and includes some steps you'd take to connect to specific types of networks.

Wired

When connecting a client or desktop system to a wired network, you need to ensure that the system is physically connected and configured with the proper TCP/IP settings. Most internal networks use twisted-pair cable, so you'd connect the cable from the computer's NIC to a hub, router, or switch in the network.

The two ways of configuring TCP/IP are statically or dynamically. Chapter 21 includes details about both methods. If the wired network is using DHCP, simply configure the computer to get the settings dynamically. If the network is not using DHCP, assign the settings manually with an available IP address used within the network.

Wireless

The primary difference between connecting to a wireless network or a wired network is that the wireless network doesn't use cables. You need to ensure that a wireless access point (WAP) is functioning within the network and configure the client to connect to it.

Chapter 23 covers the wireless requirements. As a reminder, you'll need the following information:

- The wireless standard (802.11a, b, g, or n) supported by the WAP
- The Service Set Identifier (SSID), which is the name of the wireless network
- The security method used by the WAP, such as Wi-Fi Protected Access version 1 (WPA) or 2 (WPA2)
- The passphrase or shared secret used by the security method

You configure TCP/IP on the wireless NIC just as you'd configure it on the wired NIC. It is more common to use DHCP, but you can statically assign them if desired.

Dial-Up Connections

A dial-up connection requires a modem, a connection to a phone line, and an Internet Service Provider (ISP) that supports a dial-up connection. You can use the following steps to create a dial-up connection on a Windows 7 computer:

1. Click Start and select Control Panel.

2. Select Network And Sharing Center.

3. Select Set Up A New Connection Or Network.

4. Select Set Up A Dial-Up Connection and click Next. The system will try to detect a modem in your system. If it isn't detected, you can still complete the steps. Click Set Up A Connection Anyway.

5. Enter the information required by your ISP. This includes the phone number used to connect to the ISP, your user name, and a password. You can rename the connection or leave it as Dial-up Connection.

6. Select the Allow Other People To Use This Connection check box or leave it unchecked. If the box is left unchecked, only the account used to create the connection will be able to use it. Your display will look similar to the following graphic.

7. Click Create and click Close.

At this point, you can click Connect To A Network from the Network And Sharing Center and select this dial-up connection.

WWAN (Cellular)

The steps that you'd use to connect to a cellular network are dependent on the cellular provider. For example, I have a wireless air card that I purchased from Verizon Wireless with a cellular contract. They have an application called VZAccess Manager that I use with this modem.

> **MORE INFO** **CHAPTER 18, "INTRODUCING NETWORKING COMPONENTS"**
>
> Chapter 18 included a section on cellular phone connections with a picture of a wireless air card. These are sometimes called USB dongles.

Figure 24-2 shows the VZAccess Manager in action. When I want to connect, I plug the card into my system, start the application, and click Connect. This application also gives an indication of the connection type (4G LTE) and the signal strength using bars.

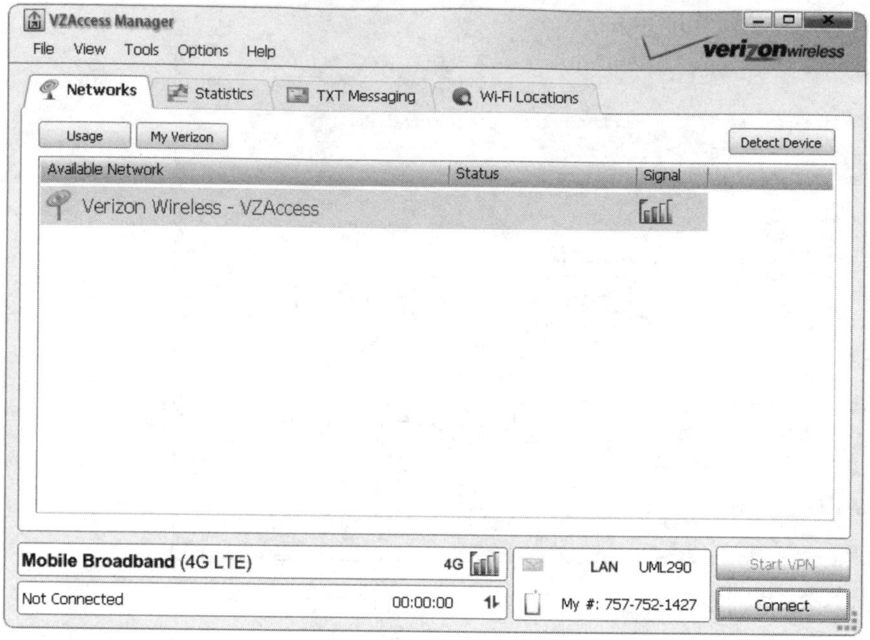

FIGURE 24-2 Connecting to cellular service.

VPN

A virtual private network (VPN) allows a user to connect to a private network over a public network. In most cases, the public network is the Internet. After a user is connected to the Internet, the user can connect to the private network.

For example, consider Figure 24-3. The user connects to the ISP using *Point-to-Point Protocol (PPP),* and the ISP provides access to the Internet. After connecting to the Internet, a VPN connection creates a tunnel to the VPN server or to a firewall that forwards traffic to the VPN server. Users connected to the VPN server have access to any internal resources that they could normally access. For example, they can check their mail or access files.

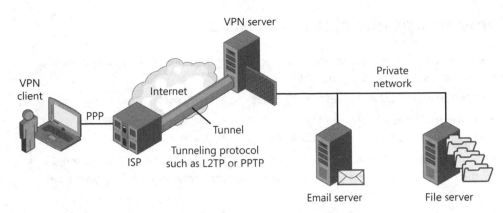

FIGURE 24-3 Connecting to a VPN server.

Several types of VPN tunneling protocols are in use. Two common ones are Layer Two Tunneling Protocol (L2TP) and *Point to Point Tunneling Protocol (PPTP)*. One of the challenges when sending data over a public network is that data can be intercepted, so most VPNs are encrypted. For example, L2TP uses *Internet Protocol security (IPsec)* to encrypt the data in the tunnel.

You can use the following steps to create a VPN connection on a Windows 7–based computer:

1. Click Start and select Control Panel.

2. Select Network And Sharing Center.

3. Select Set Up A New Connection Or Network.

4. Select Connect To A Workplace and click Next.

5. Select Use My Internet Connection (VPN). If your organization is hosting a remote access server with a modem, you can select Dial Directly. However, this direct dial connection is not considered a VPN.

6. Enter the IP address of the VPN server. You can get this from the company that is hosting the VPN. Click Next.

7. Enter a user name, password, and domain name (if required) that are authorized to connect to the VPN server. Click Connect.

8. The computer will try to connect to the VPN server by using all of the available tunneling protocols. When it finds a tunneling protocol that is accepted by the VPN server, it will use it.

Homegroups and Network Places

One of the reasons to create a network is to share network resources. Accessing these shared resources depends on the operating system version.

- **My Network Places.** In Windows XP, users can access resources via My Network Places.
- **Network.** Network replaced My Network Places in Windows Vista and Windows 7. The functionality is similar, although it looks a little different.
- **Homegroup.** Homegroups were introduced in Windows 7. This provides a simpler method of sharing and accessing resources on small networks, such as those used in SOHOs.

EXAM TIP

Homegroups are supported only on Windows 7–based computers. You can create a home-group on a SOHO network that includes Windows XP and Windows Vista computers, but only Windows 7 computers will be able to join it.

Accessing My Network Places and Network

You can access My Network Places on Windows XP with the following steps:

1. Click Start and select My Computer.

2. In the left pane under Other Places, select My Network Places.

   A. If the left pane is not showing, click the Tools drop-down menu and select Folder Options.

   B. On the General tab, select Show Common Tasks In Folders in the Tasks section. Click OK.

3. Click View Workgroup Computers.

This will show you all devices on your network, and you can double-click any of these devices. You'll be able to see any shared folders that you have permissions to access.

With Windows Vista and Windows 7, you don't use the term My Network Places, but you can access network locations on these systems with the following steps:

1. Click Start and select Computer.

2. Select Network.

NOTE DYNAMIC MENU

When you select Network, the choices on the menu ribbon change to give you additional options. They include the Network And Sharing Center, Add A Printer, and Add A Wireless Device selections.

3. The following graphic shows what you'll see on a Windows 7 computer. If you double-click any of these, you'll see a listing of resources shared by that system.

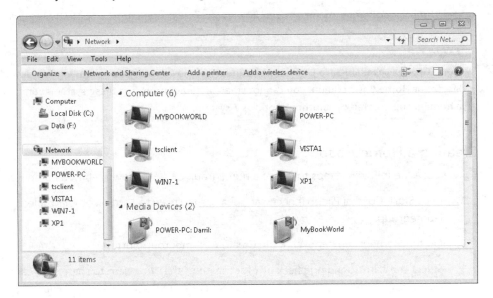

Understanding Homegroups

Windows 7 introduced *homegroups* as a simpler way to share resources in a network. Users can share any of their libraries with other users in the network.

> **MORE INFO** **CHAPTER 13, "USING WINDOWS OPERATING SYSTEMS"**
>
> Chapter 13 covers libraries in more depth. As a reminder, users can group common files into a library even if the files are stored in different locations.

The following three primary steps are related to using homegroups.

1. Create a homegroup on one Windows 7 computer in the network. This user also decides which libraries to share.

2. Other users running Windows 7–based systems join the homegroup. Users decide which libraries to share from their computer.

3. All users can now access resources shared on other systems.

The following sections describe the process of creating, joining, and using homegroups. You might also want to check out the videos on the following Microsoft sites:

- *http://windows.microsoft.com/en-us/windows7/Access-files-and-printers-on-other-homegroup-computers*
- *http://windows.microsoft.com/en-US/windows7/Join-a-homegroup*
- *http://windows.microsoft.com/en-US/windows7/help/videos/sharing-files-with-homegroup*

Additionally, Microsoft has created a comprehensive start-to-finish page on homegroups that you can check out if want to dig a little deeper:

- *http://windows.microsoft.com/en-US/windows7/help/homegroup-from-start-to-finish*

EXAM TIP

HomeGroup is available in all editions of Windows 7. However, if you're running Windows 7 Starter or Home Basic edition, you cannot create a homegroup, but these systems can join a homegroup created on another Windows 7 system.

Creating a Homegroup

You can use the following steps to create a homegroup on a Windows 7–based computer.

1. Click Start, Control Panel. If necessary, change the view to Large Icons and select Homegroup.

2. On the Homegroup page, click the Create A Homegroup button.

3. Select the corresponding check box for the items that you want to share. You can share pictures, documents, music, and videos that are stored on your system. Selecting any of these check boxes will share your library in that category. You can also share printers configured on your computer. Click Next.

4. Windows 7 will create the homegroup and display a password. You can share this password with other users so that they can join the homegroup.

5. Click Finish.

6. The Change Homegroup Settings page appears. You can use this to change what is shared, view the password, change the password, and leave the homegroup.

NOTE SHARING FOLDERS

In addition to your libraries, you can share folders within the homegroup. Use Windows Explorer to browse to the folder you want to share. Right-click the folder and select Share With. Select Homegroup (Read) to give other users read access. Select Homegroup (Read/Write) to give other uses the ability to read and write to the folder.

Joining a Homegroup

If another user has created a homegroup in your network, you can join it, share your libraries, and access other users' shared files.

1. Click Start, Control Panel. If necessary, change the view to Large Icons and select Homegroup.

2. Windows 7 will check the network for the existence of a homegroup. If one exists, it will display homegroup information and prompt you to join it.

3. Click Join Now to join the homegroup.

4. Select the corresponding check box for the items that you want to share from your computer on the homegroup. You can share pictures, documents, music, printers, and videos that are stored on your system. Click Next.

5. Enter the password of the homegroup and click Next.

6. A page will appear indicating that you have joined the homegroup. Click Finish.

> **NOTE TROUBLESHOOTING HOMEGROUPS**
>
> Occasionally, homegroups develop problems, stopping other users from joining. The homegroup troubleshooter can sometimes correct the problems. If this doesn't work, another fix that often works is to leave the homegroup on each of the systems and then re-create it.

Viewing Homegroup Resources

After you've created and joined a homegroup, any user that has joined the homegroup can access resources on other homegroup systems. You can use the following steps on any computer in the homegroup:

1. Click Start and select Computer.

2. Select Homegroup in the left pane. Your display will resemble the following graphic. The graphic shows one other computer (Power-PC) in the workgroup hosted by a user named Darril. Darril is sharing the Documents, Music, Pictures, and Videos libraries from his system, and the Windows 7 Videos folder is opened. Any other user in the workgroup can copy or view these videos or any other shared files.

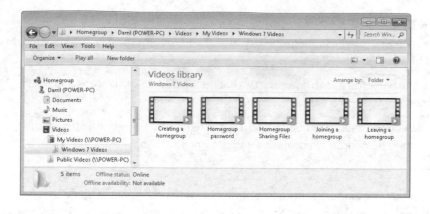

EXAM TIP

Windows 7–based systems support up to 20 concurrent connections. That is, a Windows 7–based computer can share files in a homegroup, and up to 20 other users at a time can connect to this system to access the files. In contrast, Windows XP Professional supports up to 10 concurrent connections.

Mapping Drives

When you share a folder on a computer, it can be accessed by other users as long as they know the *Universal Naming Convention (UNC)* path. A UNC path is in the format of \\ComputerName\ShareName. For example, if your computer was named Success and you shared a folder named Notes, other users could connect to it by using the UNC path of \\success\notes. UNC paths are not case-sensitive.

Users can enter the UNC path from the command prompt, the Run line, or the Search Programs And Files text box in Windows 7.

While the UNC path will connect users to the share, it's often confusing to users. Instead of requiring users to remember the UNC path, you can map a drive letter to the path. The drive will appear in Windows Explorer and can be accessed with a simple drive letter.

Mapped drives can be created from Windows Explorer in any Windows-based system. The following steps show how to map a drive on Windows 7.

1. Click Start and select Computer. This starts Windows Explorer.

2. Select Map Network Drive from the Tools drop-down menu. If the menu bar isn't showing, you can click Organize, Layout, Menu Bar to display it. Alternatively, you can click Map Network Drive on the menu along the top.

3. You can change the drive letter or leave it as is. Enter the UNC path in the Folder text box in the format of \\ComputerName\ShareName.

4. Select Reconnect At Logon to ensure that the mapped drive appears each time the user logs on. Your display will look similar to the following graphic.

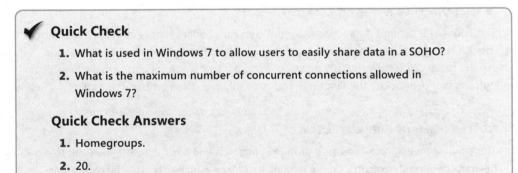

5. Click Finish.

The graphic also shows how a mapped drive appears in Windows Explorer after it has been created. This network includes a server named archive used for file sharing. It includes folders named public and APlusNotes. Public is mapped to the Z drive, and the previous steps will map the APlusNotes folder to the Y drive.

> ✔ **Quick Check**
>
> 1. What is used in Windows 7 to allow users to easily share data in a SOHO?
>
> 2. What is the maximum number of concurrent connections allowed in Windows 7?
>
> **Quick Check Answers**
>
> 1. Homegroups.
>
> 2. 20.

Command Prompt Tools

You can often troubleshoot connectivity issues from the command prompt and quickly identify a network problem. As with any tool, the key is to know which tool to use for which problem. This section provides an overview of common command prompt tools you can use, along with information about how to use them.

As a quick reminder, you can start the command prompt on a Windows 7 system by clicking Start, typing **command** in the Search Programs And Files text box, and selecting command prompt.

MORE INFO CHAPTER 14, "USING THE COMMAND PROMPT"

The command prompt is covered in Chapter 14. It shows how to start and use the command prompt, including how to start it with administrative privileges when needed. If you get an error indicating that the command requires elevation, it means that you must run it from a command prompt with administrative privileges.

The following sections describe these tools in more depth. As a short introduction, the following is a summary of the important tools:

- **Ping.** Checks connectivity with a device on a network and identifies response times.
- **Ipconfig.** Displays TCP/IP configuration assigned to network interface cards.
- **Tracert.** Checks connectivity with a device and shows routers in the path.
- **Nslookup.** Verifies that DNS can resolve a host name to an IP address. It can verify that a record exists in DNS.
- **Netstat.** Shows network statistics, including a list of inbound and outbound connections for a system.
- **Nbtstat.** Shows statistics for NetBIOS.
- **Arp.** Shows MAC address to IP address mappings.
- **Net Use.** Used to map drives to remote shares.

The command prompt is easier to learn through experience. That is, don't just read about it—do it. I strongly encourage you to type each of the commands covered in this section to see the results. You will probably make some typos. That's natural and actually helpful. If everything works perfectly the first time, you probably won't remember it as easily.

NOTE COMMAND-LINE REFERENCE

This chapter covers some command prompt commands and basic usage. If you want to dig deeper, check out Microsoft's Command-line Reference, which covers all the commands you have available, at *http://technet.microsoft.com/library/cc754340*.

Ping

Ping is an invaluable tool for checking connectivity between two devices. For example, if you're having trouble connecting to another computer, you can use ping to verify that you have network connectivity.

The basic syntax is as follows:

```
Ping target
```

The target can be either the IP address or the name of a destination computer. For example, if the IP address of your default gateway is 192.168.1.1, you can use the following command to check connectivity:

`Ping 192.168.1.1`

If you instead want to check connectivity with a server named mail1 in your network, you can use the following command:

`Ping mail1`

Ping will resolve the name of the server (mail1) to an IP address. It usually does so by querying DNS.

Figure 24-4 shows an example of the ping utility in action. The first command (ping getcertifiedgetahead.com) pings the website by the name, and the second command (ping 174.122.52.195) pings the website by using the website's IP address. Both commands sent four pings to the server and successfully received four replies, indicating that the site is reachable.

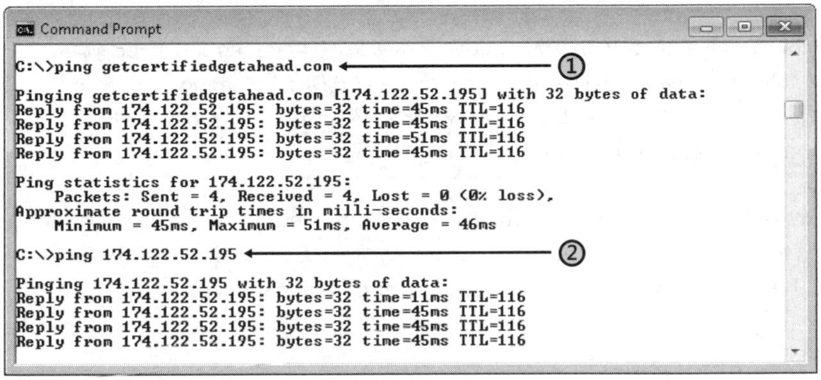

```
Command Prompt                                                      _ □ ✕

C:\>ping getcertifiedgetahead.com  ◄─────────────────── ①

Pinging getcertifiedgetahead.com [174.122.52.195] with 32 bytes of data:
Reply from 174.122.52.195: bytes=32 time=45ms TTL=116
Reply from 174.122.52.195: bytes=32 time=45ms TTL=116
Reply from 174.122.52.195: bytes=32 time=51ms TTL=116
Reply from 174.122.52.195: bytes=32 time=45ms TTL=116

Ping statistics for 174.122.52.195:
    Packets: Sent = 4, Received = 4, Lost = 0 (0% loss),
Approximate round trip times in milli-seconds:
    Minimum = 45ms, Maximum = 51ms, Average = 46ms

C:\>ping 174.122.52.195  ◄─────────────────── ②

Pinging 174.122.52.195 with 32 bytes of data:
Reply from 174.122.52.195: bytes=32 time=11ms TTL=116
Reply from 174.122.52.195: bytes=32 time=45ms TTL=116
Reply from 174.122.52.195: bytes=32 time=45ms TTL=116
Reply from 174.122.52.195: bytes=32 time=45ms TTL=116
```

FIGURE 24-4 Using ping.

Notice that the first example resolves the name to an IP address. The first line after the command (Pinging getcertifiedgetahead.com [174.122.52.195]) shows that it identified the address of the site as 174.122.52. 195. This also verifies that it was able to query DNS to get the IP address of the web server.

You can also see in the figure that ping shows the approximate roundtrip time. This gives you an indication of the response time of the remote computer. These times are shown in milliseconds, and for reference, 1,000 msec equals one sec.

> **MORE INFO**   **CHAPTER 21, "COMPARING IPV4 AND IPV6"**
>
> Chapter 21 briefly introduces ping in the context of TCP/IP. It shows how you can use the ping command with the loopback address (as ping 127.0.0.1) to check the TCP/IP stack. You can also ping the name localhost (as ping localhost), because systems automatically resolve the name localhost to the loopback address.

If ping cannot reach a computer, you'll see a "Request timed out" error listed four times instead of four Reply From messages. This does not necessarily mean that the other computer is not operational. Many firewalls block ping requests, so a system can be operating but be configured so that it does not respond to pings.

Windows-based systems send four ping packets out and expect to receive four packets back. In contrast, Linux systems will constantly ping a system until you press Ctrl+C to stop the command.

You can use the -t switch on Windows systems so that the ping command has the same functionality as it does on Linux systems. For example, if you think a problem might be related to a loose connection in a cable, you might want to wiggle the cable around to see whether your symptoms change. You can use the following command and then watch the display as you manipulate the cable:

```
ping 192.168.1.1 -t
```

EXAM TIP

Ping is used to check connectivity with other network devices. If you ping the name, your system must be able to resolve the name to an IP address, and DNS is commonly used to resolve names to IP addresses. You can use the -t switch on Microsoft systems to cause ping to continuously repeat until you press Ctrl+C keys.

Table 24-1 shows common switches used with the ping command. The help for ping shows switches listed with a dash (-). However, you can use any of the switches with a dash or a forward slash. This is the same for many other command prompt commands.

TABLE 24-1 Common Ping Switches and Examples

Switch and Example	Usage
-? ping -?	View help on the ping command.
-t ping 192.168.1.1 -t	Continue sending until stopped. You can stop the ping by pressing Ctrl+C.
-l nn ping 192.168.1.1 -l 16	Modify the buffer size with a lowercase L and a number. The example changes the buffer size to 16 bytes.
-4 ping server1 -4	Force ping to use IPv4. It will first resolve the name to an IPv4 address and then ping it with the IPv4 address.
-6 ping server1 -6	Force ping to use IPv6. This resolves the name to an IPv6 address and then pings the IPv6 address.

Ping and Sonar

The late Mike Muus wrote the original ping program and named it after the sound that sonar makes. Sonar sends a sound wave to another object, and when the sound wave hits the object, it returns. Based on how long it takes for the wave to return, it's possible to identify the distance between the two objects. Similarly, the ping program can measure the time it takes for a packet to travel to and from a remote system.

Submarines use sonar all the time. In war time, they send these sound waves to locate enemies, and enemies can also locate submarines using sonar. If you've watched any submarine movies, such as *Hunt for Red October*, you've probably heard the "ping" sound when a sound wave hits the hull of the submarine.

Ipconfig

Ipconfig (short for IP configuration) is an easy tool you can use to view the TCP/IP configuration on a system. Ipconfig is both simple and complex. When you use it without any switches, it gives you a quick indication of the configuration. However, you can also use ipconfig with switches to do much more.

As a simple example, the following code shows what you'll see if you enter ipconfig on a Windows 7–based system:

```
C:\>ipconfig
Windows IP Configuration
Ethernet adapter Local Area Connection:
   Connection-specific DNS Suffix  . :
   IPv4 Address. . . . . . . . . . . : 169.254.8.51
   Subnet Mask . . . . . . . . . . . : 255.255.0.0
   Default Gateway . . . . . . . . . :
```

This computer is unable to communicate on the network. Do you know why?

Chapter 21 introduces IP addressing, including Automatic Private IP Addressing (APIPA). As a reminder, an APIPA address always starts with 169.254. Additionally, APIPA addresses are assigned to DHCP clients when they do not receive a response from a DHCP server.

You don't necessarily know why you can't reach DHCP. However, this is the problem you'd need to pursue.

On the other hand, if ipconfig shows a valid IP address and the default gateway, you could then use the ping command. You could do any of the following:

- Ping the default gateway to determine connectivity
- Ping the IP address of the NIC to verify that it can respond
- Ping the loopback address to verify the TCP/IP stack

When troubleshooting connectivity issues, ping and ipconfig are two of the most commonly used tools. You can often identify a problem by first checking the TCP/IP configuration with ipconfig and then checking connectivity with ping.

Table 24-2 shows some of the common switches used with the ipconfig command, along with sample usage.

TABLE 24-2 Common Ipconfig Switches and Examples

Switch and Example	Usage
-? ipconfig /?	View help on the ipconfig command. This provides a listing of all switches available.
/all ipconfig /all	View full TCP/IP configuration information. This identifies the host name, the media access control (MAC) address, the address of a DNS server, the address of a DHCP server address (if it is a DHCP client), and more.
/release ipconfig /release	Release the IPv4 address. Use this on DHCP clients to remove all DHCP assigned information.
/renew ipconfig /renew	Renew the IPv4 address. Use this on DHCP clients to renew all DHCP assigned information.
/release6 ipconfig /release6	Release the IPv6 address. Use this on DHCP clients to remove all IPv6 assigned settings.
/renew6 ipconfig /renew6	Renew the IPv6 address. Use this on DHCP clients to renew IPv6 DHCP assigned settings.

If a client can't reach DHCP, DHCP clients assign themselves an APIPA address. After repairing the problem, you can use ipconfig /renew to get a new IP address from DHCP. If you want to get a new IP address from DHCP, use ipconfig /release and then ipconfig /renew.

Many Unix-based systems also support ifconfig in addition to ipconfig. The ifconfig command has more capabilities than ipconfig, and technicians use it to configure the network interface card.

Client-Side DNS and Ipconfig

Chapter 20 discusses client-side DNS. As a reminder, the hosts file (located in the C:\Windows\System32\drivers\etc folder by default) includes name-to-IP address mappings used by a computer. If a host name is in this file, the computer will always use that IP address instead of querying DNS.

Some viruses have modified the hosts file, causing problems for computers. For example, some viruses have modified them by giving a bogus IP address for Microsoft's Windows Update website. When a user attempts to update the operating system, the system goes to the bogus IP address instead of the Windows Update site. The result is that the system cannot be updated.

You can detect problems like this by using the following two additional ipconfig switches:

`ipconfig /displaydns`

`ipconfig /flushdns`

The first command (/displaydns) displays the contents of the host cache (sometimes called the DNS cache). These cached entries come from the hosts file and from recent responses from DNS.

You can remove all the cached entries from DNS responses with the /flushdns switch. However, this command does not remove entries from the hosts file. If you flush the cache and then immediately display the cache, you'll see entries that originate from the hosts file.

Tracert

Tracert is another tool you can use to check connectivity between two devices. However, tracert goes a step further. It will trace the path or route (think of it as trace route) showing all the routers between the two devices. The basic command is:

`tracert target`

Similar to the ping command, the target can be either the IP address or the name of a destination computer. Therefore, if a file server named File1 has an IP address of 192.168.15.19, you can use either of the following commands:

`tracert 192.168.15.19`

`tracert file1`

For example, consider Figure 24-5, which shows a network with multiple routers. Imagine that Gail is unable to reach the file server. Gail can ping the default gateway (on Router 1), and this succeeds, but she finds that she cannot ping the file server. Where is the problem?

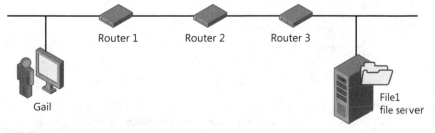

FIGURE 24-5 Network with multiple routers.

EXAM TIP

Tracert checks connectivity just as ping does but is much more useful if you have multiple routers in the network. If a faulty router is in the path, ping fails without any indication of why. Tracert helps the technician identify the router that is likely the problem.

Tracert will trace the path through each of the routers and identify where the path stops. In this context, the routers are often referred to as hops, and tracert can evaluate the hops.

You can also use tracert to trace the path to a site over the Internet. For example, if you want to identify all the routers between you and a site named Getcertifiedgetahead.com, you could use the following command:

```
tracert getcertifiedgetahead.com
```

You probably aren't going to be troubleshooting Internet problems very soon. However, if you were, tracert might be one of the tools you'd use to identify Internet router problems. Table 24-2 lists some switches and examples.

TABLE 24-2 Common Tracert Switches and Examples

Switch and Example	Usage
-d Tracert darrilgibson.com -d	Do not resolve addresses to host names. Only IP addresses are listed.
-4 Tracert darrilgibson.com -4	Use only IPv4 in the trace.
-6 Tracert darrilgibson.com -6	Use only IPv6 in the trace.

✔ **Quick Check**

1. Name two commands you can use to check connectivity between two systems.

2. List the two commands used to get a new IP address from a DHCP server.

Quick Check Answers

1. Ping and tracert.

2. Ipconfig /release and ipconfig /renew.

Nslookup

Nslookup (short for name server lookup) is often used to troubleshoot name resolution problems with DNS. It queries DNS and can verify that records exist in DNS to resolve host names to IP addresses. It can help you determine whether a system can map a host name to an IP address by querying DNS.

MORE INFO CHAPTER 20, "UNDERSTANDING PROTOCOLS"

Chapter 20 covers name resolution and name resolution protocols in more depth. In short, DNS is used to resolve host names to IP addresses. Host names are used on the Internet and in many internal networks.

Nslookup is a *shell* command, which means that if you type just **nslookup** and press Enter, you'll start the shell and see a prompt of ">". You'll then be able to enter nslookup commands from the shell. However, you can also enter nslookup commands directly from the command prompt. The basic command is as follows:

```
nslookup hostname
```

For example, suppose you have problems reaching the Getcertifiedgetahead.com site. You might want to determine whether DNS can resolve the name to an IP address. You can use the following command:

```
nslookup getcertifiedgetahead.com
```

When I run this command on my system, I get the following result:

```
Server:  cdns1.cox.net
Address:  68.105.28.11
Non-authoritative answer:
Name:    getcertifiedgetahead.com
Address:  174.122.52.195
```

The DNS server providing the response is identified in the first two lines as cdns1.cox.net, along with its IP address (68.105.28.11). The last two lines show that the DNS server can resolve the site to the IP address of 174.122.52.195.

NOTE NON-AUTHORITATIVE ANSWERS

A non-authoritative answer indicates that the DNS server doesn't host the record to map the computer to an IP address. However, it can query other DNS servers to get the answer. If the DNS server hosts the record, it will not include the line "Non-authoritative answer" in the response.

Netstat

Netstat (short for network statistics) is a useful command you can use to view inbound and outbound TCP/IP connections. It allows you to quickly view network activity and identify what is generating the activity. Table 24-3 shows some common switches used with netstat.

TABLE 24-3 Common Netstat Switches and Examples

Switch and Example	Usage
-? netstat -?	View help on netstat.
-a netstat -a	Show all connections and ports. This is very useful for viewing Internet connections.
-b netstat -b	List the application associated with each connection. You can combine this with the -a switch (netstat -b -a).
-s netstat -s	Show statistics for protocols. This will list statistics for TCP, UDP, and IP statistics for both IPv4 and IPv6.

NOTE **USING NETSTAT TO DETECT CONNECTIONS**

Netstat can sometimes identify activity caused by virus infections. For example, if a system was joined to a botnet after a virus infection, netstat will show connections to Internet systems with public IP addresses even if web browser sessions aren't active.

For a quick exercise to see netstat in action, try the following steps:

1. Close all applications that have Internet access.

2. Open a command prompt, run the following command to list all of the current connections, and write the information into a file named Connections.txt:

   Netstat -a > connections.txt

3. Enter the following command to open up the text file you just created in Notepad:

   notepad connections.txt

4. Open Internet Explorer, and visit an Internet website.

5. With Internet Explorer still open, run the following command at the command prompt:

   Netstat -a

6. If you compare the output with the connections.txt file, you can see the connections your system created when you visited the website. Many websites create multiple connections.

Nbtstat

Nbtstat is a command-line tool used to troubleshoot Network Basic Input/Output System (NetBIOS) name resolution. NetBIOS names are primarily resolved to an IP address by a WINS server and used only on internal networks. Nbtstat is one of the few commands that use case-sensitive switches. That is, nbtstat -r is different from nbtstat -R.

When a Windows Internet Name System (WINS) client is turned on, it contacts the WINS server and registers its name and IP address. Other clients can then query the WINS server with the name, and the WINS server responds with the IP address. Clients can also use broadcasts to resolve NetBIOS names.

> **MORE INFO** **CHAPTER 20, "UNDERSTANDING PROTOCOLS"**
>
> Chapter 20 covers name resolution and name resolution protocols in more depth. In brief, WINS is used to resolve NetBIOS names. NetBIOS names are used only on internal networks, and some internal networks use only host names, In contrast, host names are resolved by DNS and used on the Internet and in internal networks.

Nbtstat is short for NetBIOS over TCP/IP statistics. Table 24-4 shows some common switches used with nbtstat, with some examples.

TABLE 24-4 Common Nbtstat Switches and Examples

Switch and Example	Usage
-c nbtstat -c	Lists known system names and their IP addresses. These are placed in cache after being resolved to an IP.
-r nbtstat -r	Lists all the names resolved by broadcast and via WINS.
-R nbtstat -R	Purges and reloads the remote cache name table from the lmhosts file (if it exists).
-RR nbtstat -RR	Release/Refresh. This first releases the name registration with WINS and then refreshes the name registration. This is useful if WINS has the incorrect IP address registered for the client.

Arp

Arp is a command-line tool you can use to show MAC and IP address mapping. Before seeing what it does, it helps to understand some background information.

As discussed in Chapter 21, NICs have MAC addresses assigned to them. The MAC address is sometimes called a physical address. A MAC address is 48 bits long and is shown as six hexadecimal pairs, like this: 68-7f-74-ae-8b-de.

Additionally, NICs have IP addresses assigned. In many situations, TCP/IP has an IP address of another system but it needs to know the MAC address. The Address Resolution Protocol (ARP) is used to identify the MAC address from the IP address. Each time a system needs to know the MAC address of another system, it broadcasts the IP address, essentially asking, "Who has this IP address?"

The system with the IP address responds with its MAC address. The first system then stores the results in a short-term memory cache called the ARP cache, which brings us to the arp command. You can view the contents of the ARP cache with the *arp -a* command as follows:

```
C:\>arp -a
Interface: 192.168.1.111 --- 0xa
  Internet Address     Physical Address     Type
  192.168.1.1          68-7f-74-ae-8b-de    dynamic
  192.168.1.107        00-90-a9-82-4b-5f    dynamic
. . .
```

This first shows the IP address of the NIC listed as Interface. If your system has more than one interface, it will list the mappings for each. For brevity, I've shortened the output, but as you can see, the command lists the Internet address (the IP address), the physical address (the MAC address), and the type of storage.

If the result is from an ARP query, it is listed as dynamic and stays in cache for just a few minutes. If the mapping was added manually or by the operating system, it is listed as static.

Resolving Names, IPs, and MACs

You might have noticed that TCP/IP uses several resolution processes. You and I use words and names, but computers use numbers. Moreover, computers use different types of numbers in networking. Overall, here's the process:

- Computers have names. People commonly use names to identify the computers.

- DNS resolves computer names (host names) to IP addresses. You can use the ns-lookup name command to verify that DNS can resolve a name to an IP address. In some cases, WINS is used to resolve NetBIOS names to IP addresses.

- NICs are assigned IP and MAC addresses. MAC (or physical) addresses are often burned into the card, but IP addresses are changed frequently.

- ARP resolves IP addresses to MAC addresses. You can use the arp -a command to show the addresses that ARP has resolved and is currently storing in cache.

Net

The *net* command has multiple uses. One of the common uses related to networking is the net use command. It allows you to map a drive to a shared folder on a remote system. The basic syntax is as follows:

```
net use driveLetter UNCPath
```

In the "Mapping Drives" section earlier in this chapter, you saw how you could map a drive to a UNC path with Windows Explorer. The net command does the same thing, but from the command prompt. For example, imagine that your network includes a server named DC1 and that this server is sharing a folder named Data. The UNC path is \\dc1\data.

One way you could connect to this share from a Windows 7–based system is by entering \\dc1\data in the Search Programs And Files text box. However, you can also map the share to a drive so that it is accessible in Windows Explorer. You'd do so with the following command:

```
net use p: \\dc1\data
```

This command maps the P drive letter to the share. When viewed in Windows Explorer, it would resemble Figure 24-4.

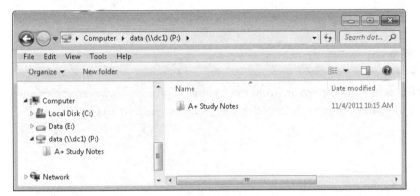

FIGURE 24-6 Viewing a mapped drive in Windows Explorer in Windows 7.

When a share is mapped this way, users can access the data just as if it were a folder on their system. If you want to delete the mapping, you can use the following command:

```
Net use p: /delete
```

This doesn't delete the share on the server. It deletes only the mapping so that is no longer visible in Windows Explorer.

Table 24-5 shows some other common net commands you might find useful.

TABLE 24-5 Common Net Commands

Command	Usage
Net use	Shows mapped drives.
Net view	Shows a list of remote shares known to the system. These are often listed in the Network area of Windows Explorer.
Net share	Lists all files shared on the local system.
Net statistics workstation	Shows basic statistics on data sent and received.
Net statistics server	Shows connections for a system sharing folders, including how many files have been accessed in the current session.

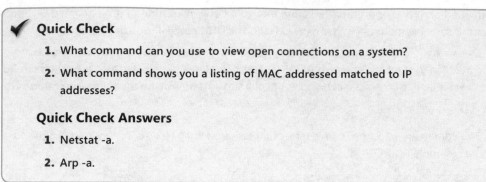

Hardware Tools

Many of the easy troubleshooting steps are from the command prompt. However, you might need to use one of the hardware tools described in this section to help when troubleshooting network problems.

Cable Tester

Cable testers are handy tools used to ensure that cables are wired correctly and that there aren't any breaks in the cable. Most cable testers allow you to plug in both ends of the cable to verify that each of the wires within the cable is connected.

Some cable testers have LED displays that show a picture of the connection. For example, if you plug a crossover cable into both connectors, it will show you a display with the wires crossed over. Plug in a straight-through cable, and it shows the wires going to the same pins on both connectors. If you plug in a faulty cable, it will show the wires that are broken or not connected.

Loop Back Plugs

A *loop back plug* is a small plug that you can plug into a jack that loops output signals back into the device. For example, an RJ-45 loop back plug is just a connector that loops signals from output pins to input pins. It simulates plugging the NIC into a network.

After plugging in the loop back plug, you can ping the IP address of the computer. This will verify the NIC is functional.

Toner Probe

Sometimes you'll need to trace a cable from one room to another. For example, imagine that you have 50 identical white wires going from room 101 to room 405. You've located wire 22 in room 101. You now need to locate wire 22 in room 405. How can you do it?

In some cases, you can manually trace a cable or wire by using the hand-over-hand method. This can be tedious, and it isn't always feasible, especially if you have to trace a cable between floors. A better option is a toner probe.

Toner probes have two elements. One creates a tone and has alligator clips that you can use to connect it to a wire. When you connect it and turn on the tone, the signal travels down the wire. The second element usually has a speaker and a probe that you can use to touch a cable or wire. In this example, you'd connect the tone to the wire in room 101. You'd then go to room 405 and connect the speaker probe to each of the wires until you heard the tone. When you hear the tone, you've found the wire.

> ✓ **Quick Check**
> 1. What tool can you use to verify that a cable is not wired incorrectly?
> 2. After plugging in a loop back plug, what can you ping to verify that the NIC is working?
>
> **Quick Check Answers**
> 1. Cable tester.
> 2. The IP address assigned to the NIC.

Troubleshooting Network Problems

This section provides a short summary of actions you can take to resolve some common networking problems. The goal in this section is to put the networking topics into context for common on-the-job networking problems.

Cannot Communicate on the Network

The most common symptom is that a system cannot communicate at all. Use the following quick checks to narrow down the problem:

1. Use **ipconfig** to determine the system configuration.
   A. If the IP address is an APIPA address (starting with 169.254), it indicates that it's a DHCP client but that it can't reach a DHCP server.
   B. If it isn't an APIPA address, note the IP address and subnet mask.
2. Verify that the IP address and subnet mask are correct for the network. Chapter 21 describes how to determine the network ID.
   A. If the information was manually assigned, it might have been entered incorrectly. Use **ipconfig /all**. If it does not show a DHCP server in the listing, it indicates that the information was manually assigned.

B. If possible, use **ipconfig** on a system that is working and compare the configuration. Enter an IP address and subnet mask using the correct network ID if necessary.

3. Ping the loopback address (127.0.0.1). If this fails, it indicates a problem with the TCP/IP stack within the operating system. A reboot might resolve the problem.

4. Ping the IP of the NIC. This will verify that the NIC is functional. You might also choose to use a loopback plug and ping the NIC to eliminate any issues on the network as possible causes.

Cannot Get out of Network

In some cases, a system can access resources on the network but not any resources on other networks. For example, a user might be able to print to a network printer but can't access the Internet.

In this case, check the default gateway with the following steps:

1. Use **ipconfig** to determine the IP address of the default gateway.

   A. Verify that an IP address for the default gateway is assigned. If not, correct the IP configuration for the NIC.

   B. Verify that the default gateway is on the same network as the computer. Both share the same subnet mask and need to have the same network ID.

2. Ping the default gateway.

   A. If successful, the problem is probably with the router or somewhere after the router.

   B. If pings to the default gateway are not successful, the problem might be with the cabling between the switch and the router.

3. Verify that a valid IP address is assigned for the DNS server. You can check this with **ipconfig /all**. Without a valid DNS address, the system won't be able to access systems beyond the default gateway by using host names. You will be able to ping remote systems with IP addresses, but pings to remote systems using their host names will fail. For example, the following will fail:

   ```
   ping getcertifiedgetahead.com
   ```

   But this will succeed:

   ```
   ping 174.122.52.195
   ```

Remember the Lights

Networking devices have LEDs that provide a quick indication of connectivity and activity. This includes network interface cards, switches, and routers. If you're troubleshooting a problem, a quick look at the lights can help you identify problems.

These indicators are discussed in Chapter 18, "Introducing Networking Components," and Chapter 19, "Exploring Cables and Connectivity." To summarize, possible indicators include the following:

- **No light.** Indicates no connection, either because the cable is faulty or because one of the devices is faulty.

- **Steady activity light.** The activity light should be blinking, so if it is steady, there is no network activity. Resetting the device might help. For example, if all the lights on a switch are steady green, power cycling the switch might clear the problem.

- **Different colored light (duplex mode).** Many devices show one color (such as green) when the device is running in full-duplex mode and another color (such as amber) when the device is running in half-duplex mode.

- **Different colored light (speed).** Many devices show one color for one speed and another color for a different speed.

If you see different-colored lights for any connection, verify that both devices support the faster mode and speed. You should also verify that autosense is enabled. If autosense is not enabled or not a feature of the device, you might need to manually configure the faster mode or speed.

Use Windows Network Diagnostics

Another tool that is sometimes useful is the Windows Network Diagnostics included with Windows 7. For example, if you're having problems with connectivity, you might be able to just click a couple of buttons and let Windows resolve the problem. You can start Windows Network Diagnostics for a NIC with the following steps:

1. Click Start, Control Panel. If necessary, switch to Large Icons view.

2. Select Network And Sharing Center from the Control Panel list.

3. Select the connection in the View Your Active Networks section. This is commonly named Local Area Connection.

4. Your display will resemble the following graphic. Click the Diagnose button. Windows will run through a series of diagnostics and attempt to resolve the problem.

Local Area Connection Status

General

Connection

IPv4 Connectivity: Internet
IPv6 Connectivity: No Internet access
Media State: Enabled
Duration: 2 days 11:57:37
Speed: 100.0 Mbps

Details...

Activity

Sent ———   ——— Received

Bytes: 12,492,762 | 16,708,455

Properties   Disable   Diagnose

Close

Common Symptoms

The previous section described methods used to troubleshoot network problems. In summary, the following list shows common symptoms and the likely causes:

- **No connectivity.** This indicates a problem with the NIC or the connection. Check the link lights, cables, and connections.

- **APIPA address.** An address starting with 169.254 is a clear indication that the system is a DHCP client but that it was not able to reach DHCP.

- **Local connectivity.** This indicates that the client can communicate with systems on the same local subnet but not on any other subnets. Ensure that the default gateway is configured correctly and that the router is functioning.

- **Limited connectivity.** This indicates that the client can connect to some devices or networks but not to all of them. If the client can't connect to only a specific device, such as a server in the network, check that device. Routers are used to provide connectivity to other networks, so if you can't reach another network, check the routers in the path.

- **IP conflict.** If two devices on the same network have the same IP address, it results in an IP address conflict. If a Windows-based system detects that it has the same IP address as another system, it assigns itself an IP address of 0.0.0.0, allowing the first device that has the duplicated address to function. Additionally, you'll see error messages on Windows-based systems, indicating that there is a conflict. The solution is to identify the devices and change one of the IP addresses.

Chapter Summary

- A SOHO network with Internet access includes hardware to connect to the ISP, a router (commonly a wireless router), and NICs on internal systems.

- Common networks use twisted-pair cabling. Gigabit Ethernet networks require at least CAT 5e twisted-pair.

- TCP/IP is required for a network connected to the Internet. Additionally, internal networks commonly use DHCP to assign IP addresses, and NAT to translate public and private IPs.

- Windows XP uses My Network Places to access many network resources.

- Windows 7 uses homegroups to share and access resources on other Windows 7–based systems. Homegroups are supported on all Windows 7–based systems but cannot be created on Windows 7 Starter or Home Basic editions.

- A mapped drive assigns a drive letter to a shared folder on another system.

- Ping is used to check connectivity with systems and identify response times. Pinging the loopback address (127.0.0.1) verifies the TCP/IP stack.

- Ipconfig is used to view IP configuration information. The /release switch can be used to release an IP address assigned by DHCP, and the /renew switch requests a new IP address from DHCP.

- Tracert traces the path through all routers between two systems. It checks connectivity with each of these routers.

- Nslookup verifies that host names can be resolved by a DNS server.

- Netstat shows network statistics and can also identify which application is using specific network connections.

- Nbtstat helps troubleshoot NetBIOS name resolution issues.

- Arp shows MAC address to IP address mappings.

- Net use can map drive letters to UNC paths.

- Hardware tools include cable testers, loop back plugs, and toner probes. A cable tester can verify that a cable is wired correctly. A loop back plug can be used when troubleshooting NICs. Toner probes help you locate both ends of a wire using a tone and a speaker.

Chapter Review

Use the following questions to test your knowledge of the information in this chapter. The answers to these questions, and the explanations of why each answer choice is correct or incorrect, are located in the "Answers" section at the end of this chapter.

1. What should be enabled on a wireless router to ensure that all internal users are assigned IP addresses?

   A. DNS

   B. DHCP

   C. NAT

   D. VoIP

2. You are managing a network with 15 Windows 7 Home Basic and Windows 7 Professional–based systems. You are trying to create a homegroup on a Windows 7 Home Basic–based system, but it is not working. Why not?

   A. Homegroups cannot be created on networks with more than 10 systems.

   B. Homegroups can be created only on Windows XP systems.

   C. You cannot create homegroups on networks that include Windows 7 Home Basic.

   D. You cannot create a homegroup on a Windows 7 Home Basic–based system.

3. Which of the following commands can you use to check connectivity with a remote system? (Choose all that apply.)

   A. Ping

   B. Tracert

   C. Ipconfig

   D. Net use

4. You're troubleshooting a computer, and you want to verify that the computer can connect to another system on the network. Which of the following would you use?

   A. Ping 127.0.0.1.

   B. Ping loopback.

   C. Ping the address of the default gateway.

   D. Ping the address of the subnet mask.

5. You suspect that DHCP has assigned a user's system an IP address that is used by another system on the network. Which of the following commands can you use to force the system to get a new IP address from DHCP?

    A. Ping dhcp -4

    B. DHCP /force

    C. Ipconfig /release and ipconfig /renew

    D. Ipconfig /force

6. A user is unable to connect to a remote server in a large network with several routers. What tool can you use to list all the routers between the user's system and the server?

    A. Tracert

    B. Ping

    C. Arp

    D. Net Trace

7. Which of the following commands will show the following result?

    192.168.1.1   68-7f-74-ae-8b-de   dynamic

    A. Ping DC1

    B. Ipconfig /all

    C. Arp -a

    D. Netstat -a

8. Which of the following commands can map a drive to a share on a remote computer?

    A. Netstat

    B. Net use

    C. Nslookup

    D. Arp

9. You have connected a computer with a switch. However, you don't have any connectivity and the LED lights are not lit on either the NIC or the switch. You've verified that the switch and the computer are functioning. What tool would you use as the next step?

    A. Nslookup

    B. Tracert

    C. Homegroup

    D. Cable tester

Answers

1. **Correct Answer:** B

   A. **Incorrect:** DNS helps systems resolve names to IP addresses but does not assign IP addresses.

   B. **Correct:** DHCP provides internal users with IP addresses and other TCP/IP configuration information.

   C. **Incorrect:** NAT translates public and private IP addresses, but it does not assign IP addresses.

   D. **Incorrect:** Some applications use VoIP to transmit voice over an IP network, but VoIP does not assign IPs.

2. **Correct Answer:** D

   A. **Incorrect:** There are no limitations to how many systems are on a network using homegroups. However, Windows 7–based systems do not support more than 20 concurrent connections.

   B. **Incorrect:** Windows XP–based systems do not support home groups.

   C. **Incorrect:** Windows 7 Home Basic–based systems can join a homegroup, but they cannot create homegroups.

   D. **Correct:** Homegroups cannot be created on Windows 7 Home Basic–based systems.

3. **Correct Answer:** A, B

   A. **Correct:** Ping will check connectivity with a remote system.

   B. **Correct:** Tracert will check connectivity with a remote system and also list all routers in the path.

   C. **Incorrect:** Ipconfig shows the TCP/IP configuration of a system.

   D. **Incorrect:** Net use can map drive letters to shares on remote systems.

4. **Correct Answer:** C

   A. **Incorrect:** Pinging the loopback IP address (127.0.0.1) verifies that the TCP/IP stack is installed but does not verify network connectivity.

   B. **Incorrect:** Pinging the loopback name is the same as pinging the loopback IP address.

   C. **Correct:** Pinging the address of the default gateway will verify network connectivity with another system. In this case, it verifies connectivity with the router.

   D. **Incorrect:** It is not possible to ping the subnet mask.

5. **Correct Answer:** C

    A. **Incorrect:** This command will try to ping a host named dhcp using IPv4. However, ping does not request a new IP.

    B. **Incorrect:** There is no such command as DHCP /force.

    C. **Correct:** The ipconfig /release command releases a DHCP assigned IP address, and the ipconfig /renew command requests a new IP address.

    D. **Incorrect:** Ipconfig does not have a /force switch.

6. **Correct Answer:** A

    A. **Correct:** The tracert command will trace the route between two systems and list all routers in the path.

    B. **Incorrect:** Ping can check connectivity, but you've already verified that you cannot connect to the remote server, so this will fail without giving any extra help.

    C. **Incorrect:** Arp lists MAC-to-IP address mappings.

    D. **Incorrect:** Net Trace includes many commands but not a Net Trace command.

7. **Correct Answer:** C

    A. **Incorrect:** The ping command checks connectivity with systems and shows the result of these attempts.

    B. **Incorrect:** The ipconfig /all command shows all of the TCP/IP configuration information of a system.

    C. **Correct:** The arp -a command shows IP address to MAC address mappings.

    D. **Incorrect:** The netstat -a command displays a listing of inbound and outbound connections.

8. **Correct Answer:** B

    A. **Incorrect:** Netstat shows network statistics, including inbound and outbound connections.

    B. **Correct:** The net use command can be used to map a drive to a share. After it is mapped, the share is viewable in Windows Explorer with the mapped drive letter.

    C. **Incorrect:** Nslookup can verify whether a DNS server can resolve a host name to an IP address.

    D. **Incorrect:** The Arp -a command shows information about MAC address and IP address mappings.

9. **Correct Answer: D**

   A. **Incorrect:** Nslookup verifies that DNS can resolve a host name but would not work if you don't have connectivity.

   B. **Incorrect:** Tracert lists routers in the path between two systems but would not work without connectivity.

   C. **Incorrect:** Homegroups are used to share files between Windows 7–based systems but wouldn't work without connectivity.

   D. **Correct:** If you've verified that the switch and computer are functioning correctly, the next step is to verify that the cable between the two is functioning, and a cable tester does that.

CHAPTER 25

Understanding IT Security

Information Technology (IT) security includes multiple elements all designed to minimize losses. Digital security methods ensure that users are uniquely identified and authenticated before they are granted permission to access resources. Valuable data can be further protected with encryption. When disposing of media at the end of its life cycle, secure methods are used to erase the data. When necessary, the media is destroyed.

Exam 220-802 objectives in this chapter:

- 1.4 Given a scenario, use appropriate operating system features and tools.
  - Administrative
    - Users and groups
    - Local security policy
- 1.5 Given a scenario, use Control Panel utilities (the items are organized by "classic view/large icons" in Windows).
  - Common to all Microsoft Operating Systems
    - User accounts
- 1.8 Explain the differences among basic OS security settings.
  - User and groups
    - Administrator
    - Power user
    - Guest
    - Standard user
  - NTFS vs. Share permissions
    - Allow vs. deny
    - Moving vs. copying folders and files
    - File attributes
  - Shared files and folders
    - Permission propagation
    - Inheritance

- User authentication
  - Single sign-on
- 2.1 Apply and use common prevention methods.
  - Physical security
    - Lock doors
    - Biometrics
    - Badges
    - Key fobs
    - RFID badge
    - RSA token
    - Retinal
  - Digital security
    - User authentication/strong passwords
    - Directory permissions
  - User education
  - Principle of least privilege
- 2.3 Implement security best practices to secure a workstation.
  - Setting strong passwords
  - Requiring passwords
  - Restricting user permissions
  - Changing default user names
  - Disabling guest account
  - Screensaver required password
- 2.4 Given a scenario, use the appropriate data destruction/disposal method.
  - Low level format vs. standard format
  - Hard drive sanitation and sanitation methods
    - Overwrite
    - Drive wipe
  - Physical destruction
    - Shredder
    - Drill
    - Electromagnetic
    - Degaussing tool

Prevention

Security models commonly follow a prevent/detect/respond model. First, methods are implemented to prevent any security incidents from occurring. Incidents still occur, so other methods are used to detect them and respond as quickly as possible to contain the damage from an incident. Two methods that are important in the realm of prevention are user education and the principle of least privilege.

User Education

A core tenet of security is educating users about risks. The better users understand the risks, the more likely they are to comply with the security requirements.

User education might be done formally in gatherings or via online training sessions. Additionally, education is often done informally by an educated PC technician sharing knowledge with users. To share your knowledge, you first need to ensure that you have it.

Security-conscious PC technicians understand the different authentication methods and the importance of strong passwords and password management. They understand the importance of least privilege and how groups are often used in its implementation. They recognize the risks related to different types of malicious software (malware) and understand the importance of running up-to-date antivirus software on up-to-date computers. They are well aware of various methods used by attackers, including social engineering attacks, and are willing to share their knowledge.

> **MORE INFO**   **CHAPTERS 15 AND 26**
>
> Chapter 15, "Configuring Windows Operating Systems," covers Windows Update and patch management techniques. Chapter 26, "Recognizing Malware and Other Threats," covers different types of malware, antivirus software, and social engineering.

Principle of Least Privilege

The principle of *least privilege* is an important security concept used in IT systems and networks of all sizes. Users should be given only the rights and permissions that they need to do their jobs and no more. This prevents them from accidentally causing problems such as accidentally deleting key system files. It also protects IT resources if a faithful worker becomes a disgruntled employee.

If usability is your only concern, you can give everyone full administrative access. Everyone will be able to access any resource and perform any task. In practice, this is rarely used because of the significant security risks. Instead, most organizations implement the principle of least privilege by identifying what privileges users need to perform their jobs and grant them only those privileges.

Authentication

Authentication occurs when users prove their identity. The most common way this occurs is when a user claims an identity with a user name and proves the identity with a password. However there are several possible authentication methods, known as *authentication factors*. The three authentication factors are as follows:

- **Something you know.** This includes passwords or personal identification numbers (PINs).
- **Something you have.** This includes items you can physically hold, such as some types of badges and smart cards.
- **Something you are.** Biometric methods such as fingerprints or retinal scans are in this factor category.

Something You Know

Passwords are by far the most common method of authentication. They are also the weakest compared with the other factors. Ideally, users should create strong passwords so that they can't easily be guessed. This is common knowledge among IT professionals, but many regular users don't realize the importance of using a strong password or even how to create a strong password.

> **MORE INFO** **CREATING STRONG PASSWORDS**
>
> Microsoft hosts the Safety And Security Center, which provides a wealth of information about computer security, digital privacy, and online safety. It includes the following page, which provides information about creating strong passwords: *http://www.microsoft.com /security/online-privacy/passwords-create.aspx*. You can use the following page to test the strength of a password: *https://www.microsoft.com/security/pc-security/password -checker.aspx*.

Elements of Strong Passwords

Many systems apply a set of rules that users must follow when they create a password. This is commonly called a password policy, and it helps ensure that users create a strong password. If users don't follow the password policy rules, the password or password change is rejected.

A strong password includes the following elements, and any or all of these rules can be a part of a password policy:

- **Uses at least eight characters.** If you use a single lowercase alphabet letter password such as *a* or *b*, it only takes 26 guesses to discover it. If you use two characters, it takes 676 guesses (26^2). Guessing a password with eight lowercase alphabet letters requires over 208 billion guesses (26^8). Some people suggest a password should be 12 or more characters.

- **Uses all four character types.** Passwords should include uppercase letters, lowercase letters, numbers, and special characters such as $ or @. Instead of just 26 possible characters, there are 95 possible characters—26 lowercase letters, 26 uppercase letters, 10 numbers, and 33 characters. An 8-character password using all four character types has over 6 quadrillion (95^8) possible combinations.

- **Does not use your name.** Passwords shouldn't include your user account name, your actual name, the name of your company, or other names that can be easily guessed.

- **Is different from other passwords.** If you have a password of IP@ssedA+, you shouldn't use another password that's similar, such as IP@ssedA+2 or IP@ssedA+3. After the first password is discovered, the others are easily guessed.

EXAM TIP

Strong passwords should be used with any desktop user account. Strong passwords use at least three character types, and four character types are commonly recommended.

Using Passphrases

A common method used to create a strong password is with a passphrase. There are multiple ways you can do this, such as the following:

1. Start with a sentence such as **I am A+ certified.**

2. Capitalize the first letter of each word—**I Am A+ Certified.**

3. Remove all the spaces—**IAmA+Certified.**

4. Replace some letters with characters (for example, replace *i* with *!*, or *a* with @)—**IAmA+Cert!f!ed.**

5. Add numbers or replace some letters with numbers (for example, replace *I* with *1* or *e* with *3*)—**1AmA+Cert!f!ed.**

At this point, you have a strong 12-character password that is easy to remember. Later in your IT career, you can replace it with **1AmNet+Cert!f!ed** and then **1AmSec+Cert!f!ed**.

✔ Quick Check

1. What is the weakest type of authentication?
2. What is included in a strong password?

Quick Check Answers

1. Passwords.
2. At least eight characters and multiple character types.

Something You Have

All of the methods in the something-you-have authentication factor are items that you can hold in your hand. Often these items serve dual purposes. For example, a user can wear a badge when walking around the building and then use the badge to log on. In this case, the badge would also include smart-card components.

Badges and Smart Cards

A *smart card* is about the same size as a credit card. It includes data about the user and some cryptographic information to help keep it secure. Smart card readers are connected to a computer or part of the keyboard. When users want to log on, they insert the card into the reader and enter a PIN or password to authenticate.

A risk with smart cards is that they can be lost or misplaced. Anyone who finds the card can potentially use it to impersonate the user. However, by combining it with another method of authentication, such as a PIN or password, the user reduces that risk. It's the same concept used with automated teller machine (ATM) cards and PINs.

> **NOTE MULTIFACTOR AUTHENTICATION**
>
> When more than one factor of authentication is used, it's called multifactor authentication. Multifactor authentication must include one element in two or more different factors. Using both a PIN and a password is not multifactor authentication because PINs and passwords are both in the something-you-know factor, but a PIN and a smart card is multifactor authentication.

In many cases, the smart card is also used as a badge. It includes the user's picture and other information about the user. Some organizations use stronger physical security within secure areas and require employees to wear these badges at all times except for when they use the badge to log on to their computer.

> **EXAM TIP**
>
> Device drivers for smart card readers often must be installed separately. If you add a keyboard that includes a smart card reader, you might need to install device drivers. If the smart card reader is part of the computer, it can often be enabled or disabled in the BIOS.

RFID Badges and Physical Security

One way you can provide physical security for a secure area is by keeping the entry doors locked. This is useful for smaller areas, such as a wiring closet that houses network devices like routers and switches. It isn't as useful for a high-traffic area where people frequently go in and out.

Radio Frequency Identification (RFID) badges are sometimes used to automatically open doors. Users simply wave their badge in front of a badge reader and the door unlocks. This is similar to how you can wave some credit cards in front of a credit card reader to purchase items.

Both use the same type of electronics. The card reader includes a special type of magnet, and when the card is passed close to the reader, the magnet charges the card, providing it with power. The card then broadcasts information received by the reader. For RFID badges, the broadcasted information can be a simple code to open the door. It can also include information about the user to record the user's access.

Key Fobs and RSA Tokens

A *key fob* is a small device that displays a number and can easily be attached to a key chain. The number changes periodically and is synchronized with an authentication server. Key fobs are most commonly used when authenticating with a website.

For example, a company can issue key fobs to traveling employees so that they can log on to a company website. Figure 25-1 shows how this works. The user accesses the company server over the Internet, and the server responds with a login page. The user enters a valid user name, password, and the number displayed in the key fob, and then the user clicks the Log In button. The server validates this data, and if everything is correct, the user is authenticated.

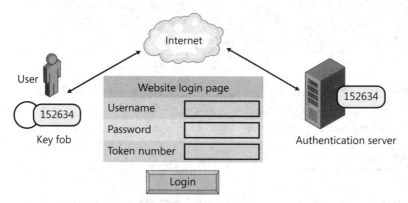

FIGURE 25-1 Authenticating with a key fob.

Typically, the number displayed in the key fob changes every 60 seconds. The authentication server knows what should be displayed in the key fob at any given time, so a number previously used won't work. Users must have the key fob in their possession. RSA SecureID is a popular key fob, and it is sometimes just called RSA token. These are sold by EMC Corporation.

> **NOTE RSA IS NOT AN ACRONYM**
>
> RSA is the name of a company that is now a security division of EMC Corporation. The letters are derived from the founders of RSA: Rivest, Shamir, and Adleman.

Something You Are

The third factor of authentication is something you are. This factor is proven with *biometrics*. The most common method uses fingerprints. Users register their fingerprints with the biometric system and authenticate later with the fingerprint.

Fingerprints can be used for both identification and authentication. For example, police use fingerprints for identification. If they find a fingerprint at a crime scene and can match it to another fingerprint, they can identify an individual.

Authentication systems can use fingerprints for authentication or identification. When used for authentication, a user enters a user name to claim an identity and then uses a fingerprint to prove the identity. This method is less susceptible to errors.

Retinal scans are the most accurate and often the most expensive form of biometrics. The retina is at the rear of the eye and includes a complex network of blood vessels. The pattern of these blood vessels is unique and normally stays the same for a person's entire lifetime. The retina is scanned with an infrared light as a person looks into an eyepiece.

EXAM TIP

Biometric authentication systems are susceptible to errors. They can falsely reject an authorized user and falsely accept an unauthorized user. Retinal biometric systems are the most accurate.

Other biometric methods used for authentication are iris scans (scanning the iris instead of the retina), facial recognition, and voice recognition.

Behavioral biometrics aren't used as often, but it is possible to identify individuals based on actions. This includes signature verification (identifying someone from their signature) and keystroke dynamics (measuring speed and pressure as an individual types).

✔ **Quick Check**

1. What is displayed in a key fob?
2. What is the strongest type of biometric authentication?

Quick Check Answers

1. A number synchronized with an authentication server.
2. Retinal scans.

Single Sign-On

Single sign-on (SSO) technologies allow a user to log on once and access multiple resources without logging on again. Chapter 18, "Introducing Networking Components," compares workgroups and domains. Often, the reason an organization creates a domain instead of a workgroup is to support SSO.

Figure 25-2 compares a workgroup and a domain. In a workgroup, each computer has its own security accounts manager (SAM) database, which includes user names and passwords. Tom can log on to his computer because his user name and password are in the SAM on his computer. If Tom wants to log on to Kim's computer, the SAM on Kim's computer needs to have a separate account for Tom. If Tom needs to log on to all four computers, each SAM would have separate entries and he'd need to remember four separate user names and passwords.

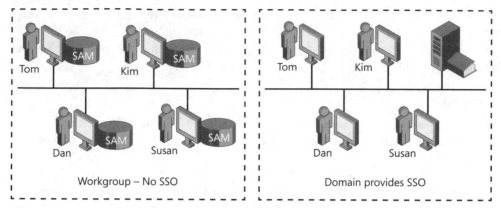

FIGURE 25-2 Authentication in workgroup and in domain.

In comparison, a Microsoft domain adds a domain controller running Active Directory Domain Services (ADDS). Each user has one account within ADDS and can use this account to log on once. For example, Tom can use his domain account to log on to any of the four computers.

EXAM TIP

Users have a single account to access multiple resources with SSO. When users are required to remember multiple passwords, they are more likely to write them down, decreasing overall security.

Requiring Password with the Screen Saver

Another security step you can take is to enable a password-protected screen saver on the computer. This requires users to log in after a screen saver starts.

Screen savers are designed to protect monitors from screen burn-in. For example, if the same image is displayed in a plasma monitor, the image can be burned in and remain visible even when the power is turned off. The screen saver starts after a period of inactivity and prevents the burn-in.

On Windows 7, you can enable the screen saver by right-clicking the desktop, selecting Personalize, and then clicking Screen Saver. Figure 25-3 shows the Screen Saver Settings page. After configuring the screen saver, select the On Resume, Display Logon Screen check box. After the screen saver starts, the user must enter credentials to get back into Windows.

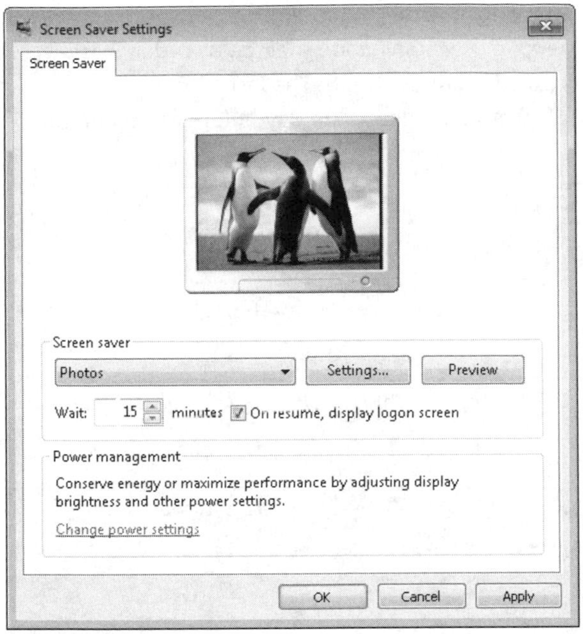

FIGURE 25-3 Enabling password protection with the screen saver.

It's not recommended, but it's possible to have a Windows user account without a password. If the user account isn't using a password, the screen saver doesn't require one.

> **IMPORTANT   BEWARE OF VIRUSES**
>
> Windows includes several built-in screen savers, and you can find more online. However, many screen savers available online are infected with malware. When you install the screen saver, you're also installing the malware. Whenever malware is hidden within an apparently legitimate program, it's called a Trojan, or Trojan horse.

Local Security Policy

The Local Security Policy applet includes hundreds of settings that administrators commonly use to help secure a computer. Many of these settings aren't accessible anywhere else.

You can start it from the Administrative Tools group within Control Panel. You can also start it by entering **secpol.msc** from a command prompt or in the Start, Search text box.

Requiring Strong Passwords

One way the Local Security Policy is often used is to configure a password policy. When configured, it applies to all computer accounts on the local system and enforces the password policy.

Figure 25-4 shows the Local Security Policy open with Account Policies expanded and the Password Policy selected. These settings require users to change their password at least every 42 days and use a complex password at least 12 characters long. The last 24 passwords are remembered for the account, and the user must wait at least one day before changing the password again.

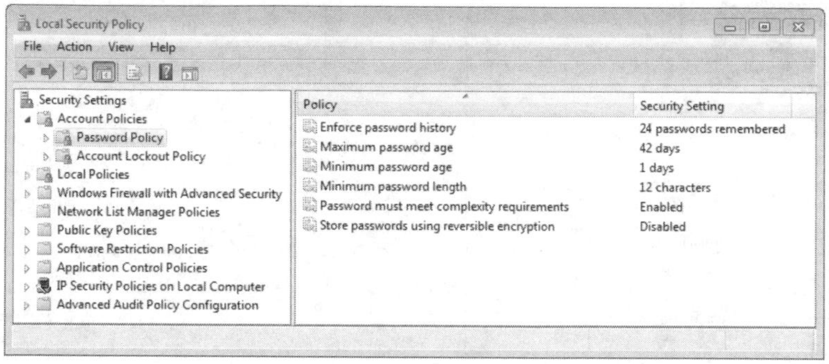

FIGURE 25-4 Using Local Security Policy to require a strong password.

NOTE POLICY SET BY DOMAIN POLICY IN A DOMAIN

Administrators commonly configure domain-wide policies that apply to all computers and users in the domain. If the computer is joined to the domain, domain policies take precedence over the policy set on the local computer.

Group Policy and Local Security Policy

Group Policy is a powerful tool used by administrators to configure a setting once and apply it to multiple computers in a domain. For example, if users need to use strong passwords, an administrator can configure one Group Policy setting and all users in the domain will be required to comply with the policy.

You can start the Group Policy editor for a local system by entering **gpedit.msc** from the command prompt or in the Start, Search text box. You can also create your own Microsoft Management Console (MMC) and add the Group Policy Object Editor snap-in by using procedures from Chapter 13, "Using Windows Operating Systems."

Figure 25-5 shows the Group Policy editor open on a Windows 7–based system. The dotted-line box is highlighting some key security settings, and if you compare them to those in Figure 25-4, you can see that they are the same settings available in the Local Security Policy tool.

Group Policy has thousands of configuration settings, including hundreds of security settings that can be accessed with the Local Security Policy. You certainly aren't expected to know all of the settings that are available in Group Policy, but it is valuable to know that it is commonly used to manage computers in a domain.

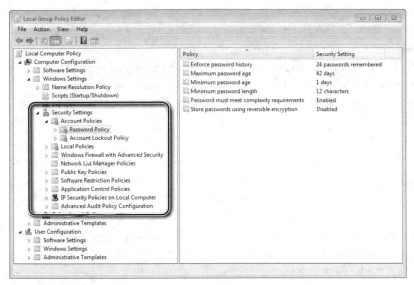

FIGURE 25-5 Viewing Security Settings in the Group Policy Editor.

✓ **Quick Check**

1. What allows users to use a single user name and password?

2. What tool is used to force users to create strong passwords?

Quick Check Answers

1. Single sign-on (SSO).

2. Local Security Policy (or Group Policy in a domain).

Users and Groups

Microsoft systems support users and groups as a primary method of authentication and *authorization*. Users authenticate by providing a user name and password. They are then authorized to perform tasks based on rights and permissions granted to this account.

It's common to assign rights and permissions with groups. For example, you can add a user account to the Administrators group, granting the user full administrative privileges.

> **NOTE RIGHTS, PERMISSIONS, AND PRIVILEGES**
>
> Rights refer to the ability to take an action, such as the right to change the time.
> Permissions refer to the ability to access a resource, such as the permission to read or
> modify a file. Privileges include both rights and permissions. For example, administrative
> privileges imply that the account has full rights and permissions on a system.

User Accounts

When Windows is first installed, a user account is created for the primary user. There are additional user accounts created by default, and you can also add additional accounts with different tools.

When a user tries to access a resource, the operating system verifies that the user is authorized. Administrators often enable security logging to show when users access resources. These logs record the activity of the user based on the user account.

If someone else used your account and deleted data or modified entries, log entries recording the action would record that you did it. With this in mind, users should have individual user accounts with their own password. Additionally, users should never give out their password to anyone else.

Default User Accounts

Windows-based systems include default user accounts. The following two default user accounts, both disabled by default, are in Windows XP, Windows Vista, and Windows 7:

- **Administrator.** The Administrator account has full rights and permissions to do anything and everything on the system. It is often referred to as the local administrator account because when you use it, you can manipulate resources only on the local system, not on other computers.

- **Guest.** The Guest account is disabled by default and is created for temporary use only. For example, if you want to let someone use your computer to browse the Internet, you can enable the Guest account. The user can log on with this account and run basic applications, including a web browser. This way you don't have to create an account that you won't need after the user is done.

> **EXAM TIP**
>
> The Guest account provides a user with basic access to programs. It is disabled by default and should be kept disabled unless it's needed.

Windows XP also the following two additional user accounts by default. They are not in Windows Vista or Windows 7:

- **HelpAssistant.** This account is used for providing Remote Assistance.
- **SUPPORT_388945a0.** This is used for the Help And Support Service.

Standard User vs. Administrator

In Windows Vista and Windows 7, accounts are identified as standard user accounts or administrator accounts. The account created during the installation of Windows is an administrator account.

- **Standard user.** Users can run most software with this account, and they can modify some system settings that do not apply to other users. They cannot modify security settings.
- **Administrator.** Administrators have full privileges on the computer and can modify any settings.

In Windows XP, accounts are identified as limited or computer administrator. The limited account is similar to a standard user account, and a computer administrator account is the same as an administrator account in Windows Vista and Windows 7.

UAC and Access Tokens in Windows Vista and Windows 7

User Account Control (UAC) is used in Windows Vista and Windows 7 as a method to prevent unauthorized changes. For example, malware can sometimes make changes in Windows XP without the user's knowledge. UAC in Windows Vista and Windows 7 blocks this malware.

Anytime a user is logged on with an administrator account, the user is assigned two access tokens: a standard user access token and an administrator access token. These are directly related to the standard user and administrator account types.

Most of the time, only the standard user access token is used, and the user can do anything that a standard user can do. If the user tries to do something that requires administrative privileges, UAC switches into Admin Approval Mode. By default, UAC dims the screen and prompts the user to approve the action. The dimmed screen prevents software from automatically approving the action and requires the user to answer the prompt.

> ***MORE INFO*** **CHAPTER 11, "INTRODUCING WINDOWS OPERATING SYSTEMS"**
>
> Chapter 11 describes UAC in more depth and includes steps you can use to view and modify UAC settings.

User Accounts Applet

There are two ways you can create user accounts—with the User Accounts applet and with the Local Users And Groups snap-in that is a part of the Computer Management console. This section shows how to use the User Accounts applet, and Local Users And Groups is covered later.

You can start the User Accounts applet in Windows XP, Windows Vista, and Windows 7 by clicking Start and selecting Control Panel. Change the view to Classic View on Windows XP and Windows Vista, or Large Icons on Windows 7. Double-click User Accounts.

Figure 25-6 shows User Accounts in Windows XP on the left and Windows 7 on the right. In Windows XP, User Accounts shows all users, and you can click an individual account to change its settings. In Windows Vista and Windows 7, User Accounts starts with the focus on the currently logged in user's account settings, and you can click Manage Another Account to show all accounts.

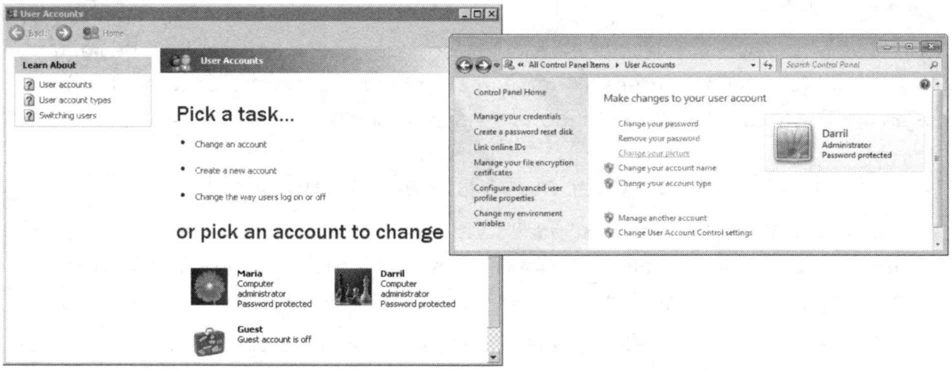

FIGURE 25-6 User Accounts applet in Windows XP and Windows 7.

Notice that the User Accounts applet tells you whether the account is an administrator type of account. When Computer Administrator or Administrator is not listed, it indicates that it is a limited or standard user type of account. If Password Protected is not included in the description, it indicates that a password is not configured.

You can use the User Accounts applet to create new accounts and to change the account type, passwords, and pictures. However, the Local Users and Groups applet provides more options.

Changing Default User Names

As a security best practice, it's recommended that you change the default user names. In Windows XP, Windows Vista, and Windows 7, the default accounts are Administrator and Guest. By changing the default user names, you make it more difficult for malware or an attacker to use these accounts.

For example, you can change the name of the Administrator account to Newadmin. If others try to log on by using Administrator, error messages will indicate that either the user name or the password is wrong. No matter how many times they try to guess the password, they'll never succeed. Similarly, you can change the name of Guest to Newguest, making it more difficult to use this account.

Understanding Groups

Windows-based systems use groups to manage privileges and include some built-in groups. Instead of assigning privileges to an individual account, a best practice is to add a user to a group and assign the rights and permissions to the group.

Figure 25-7 shows user accounts for Holly and Joe. Holly's account is added to the Administrators group, and Joe's account is added to the Users group. The Administrators group has full access to the computer, so Holly can access the \Windows\System32 folder. If Joe tried to do so, he would be blocked because neither his account nor the Users group has permission to access this folder.

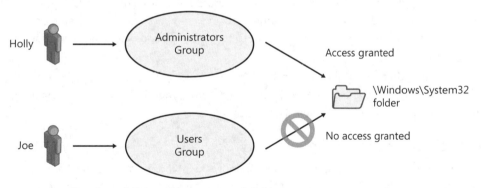

FIGURE 25-7 Granting privileges with group membership.

Default Groups

Windows-based systems include several default groups when Windows is first installed. Some of these built-in groups include the following:

- **Administrators.** This group has full privileges on the local computer. The administrator is a member of this group, which is how the administrator account gets its privileges. Similarly, when you create an administrator account on Windows Vista and Windows 7 or a computer administrator account on Windows XP, the account is placed into this group.

- **Power Users.** This group has more privileges than a regular user but not as many as an administrator. For example, users in this group can install a printer or add a different printer driver. However, administrative privileges are required to install applications and device drivers, and the Power Users group does not have these privileges.

> **NOTE POWER USERS GROUP NOT NEEDED IN WINDOWS VISTA AND WINDOWS 7**
>
> The Power Users group is needed in Windows XP so that users can run some legacy applications that require some advanced privileges. Due to how User Account Control (UAC) is used in Windows Vista and Windows 7, the Power Users group isn't needed in those operating systems, but it's kept for backward compatibility.

- **Users.** Regular users are in this group. They can run typical applications but don't have privileges to make system changes.
- **Backup Operators.** Users in this group can back up and restore files.
- **Remote Desktop Users.** Users in this group are authorized to connect to the system by using Remote Desktop.

There are additional groups in different operating systems. For example, Windows Vista and Windows 7 include the Event Log Readers and Performance Monitor Users groups, which give users privileges to use the Event Viewer and Performance Monitor.

If there is a default group that provides the appropriate privileges a user needs, the user account should be placed in that group. In large networks, administrators often create additional groups. They assign appropriate privileges to these groups and place the user accounts into the groups.

For example, a company might have a sales department with multiple salespeople. An administrator might create a group called Sales, assign it privileges needed by the salespeople, and add the salespeople user accounts to this group.

Using Local Users and Groups

The Local Users And Groups tool is available in Windows XP, Windows Vista, and Windows 7 as a snap-in in the Computer Management tool. You can start Computer Management by clicking Start, Control Panel, changing to Classic View or Large Icons, opening the Administrative Tools group, and double-clicking Computer Management.

Figure 25-8 shows Computer Management open on a Windows 7–based computer, with Users selected under Local Users And Groups. The Darril Gibson account was created when Windows 7 was first installed, and the other two accounts (Administrator and Guest) are default accounts.

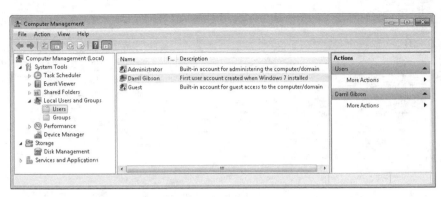

FIGURE 25-8 Local Users and Groups on Windows 7.

The Administrator and Guest accounts both have an icon of a down arrow in a circle. This is letting you know that these accounts are disabled, which is the default in Windows 7. On the right, you can see the Actions pane, which includes links to additional wizards. You can use these links to create new user accounts or to change passwords of existing accounts.

Figure 25-9 shows the three property tabs of an account. You can use the General tab to manipulate password rules and disable or enable an account. The Member Of tab shows group membership for a user account, and you can use it to view, add, or remove group membership. The Profile tab provides a method for changing the profile location.

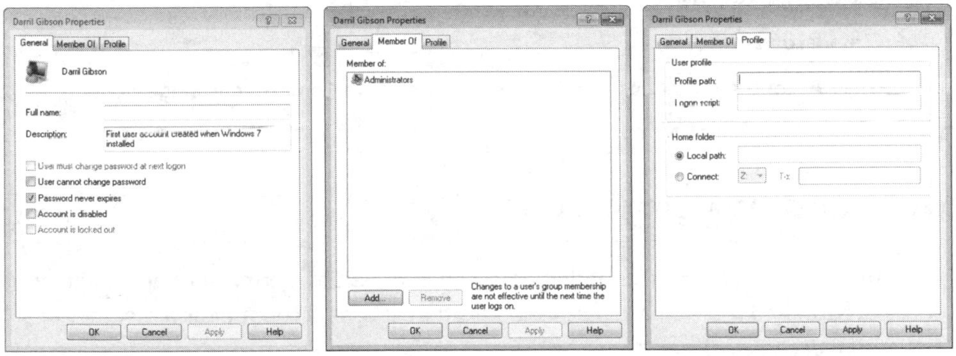

FIGURE 25-9 Viewing user properties from Local Users And Groups.

> **NOTE** **GROUP MEMBERSHIP CHANGES AREN'T REFLECTED IMMEDIATELY**
>
> A user's group membership is checked only when the user first logs on. If you make a change to the user's group membership, the user needs to log off and then back on before the changes apply to the account.

Figure 25-10 shows the groups within a Windows 7–based system with the Administrators group property page opened. You can double-click any group to view its properties. Using this property page, you can view, add, or remove individual users from a group.

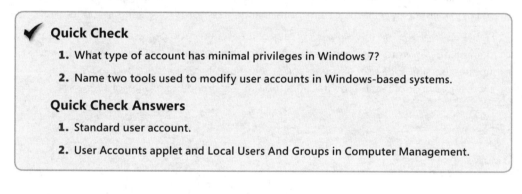

FIGURE 25-10 Viewing group properties in Local Users And Groups.

Understanding Permissions

You can control who can access files and folders with permissions. Permissions are assigned to users or groups, and if users have permission from their user account or as a member of a group, they can access the resource.

For example, if you want someone to be able to read a file, you can grant read permission on the file. Permissions can be assigned to New Technology File System (NTFS) files, folders, or shares.

> **NOTE** **AUTHENTICATION VS. AUTHORIZATION**
>
> Users prove their identity with a password or some other method of authentication. This allows a user to log on. However, just because users can prove an identity doesn't mean they are automatically granted access to all resources. Instead, users are authorized access through rights and permissions assigned to their account or through group membership.

NTFS Permissions

NTFS permissions are available only on NTFS drives and not on file allocation table (FAT) drives. You can access the NTFS permissions for any file or folder through Windows Explorer by right-clicking the item, selecting Properties, and clicking the Security tab.

Figure 25-11 shows permissions assigned to a folder named A+ Study Notes on an NTFS drive. You can edit permissions by clicking the Edit button, and you'll see the dialog box shown on the right in the figure.

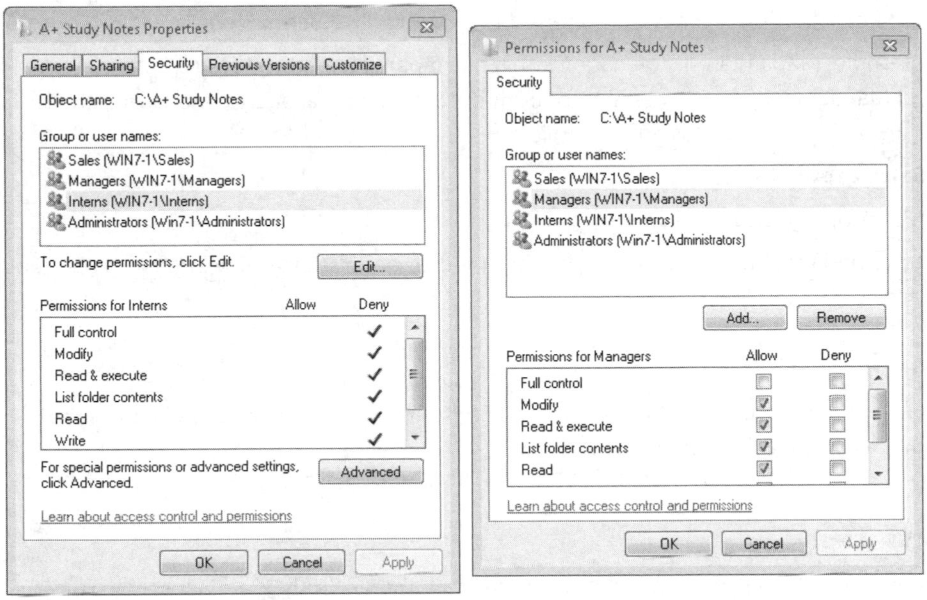

FIGURE 25-11 Viewing NTFS permissions.

> **NOTE** **ALLOW VS. DENY**
>
> Permissions can be assigned as Allow or Deny. In Figure 25-11, on the left, the Interns group is selected, and you can see that it is assigned Deny permissions on this folder so their access is blocked. On the right, the Managers group is selected, and you can see that it is assigned Allow permissions, granting access for members of this group.

The basic types of NTFS permissions are as follows:

- **Read.** Users can open files and read the contents. This does not give permission to save changes to a file.

- **Write.** Write allows a user to modify the contents of a file. It is normally assigned with the Read permission.

- **Read & Execute.** Programs require a user to have this permission to run them. It is not needed for files that are opened by a user.

- **Modify.** This is similar to read and write, with a significant addition: users can also delete files.
- **Full Control.** Full control allows the user to do anything and everything to the file. This includes the ability take ownership of files and change permissions on the files.

Combining NTFS Permissions

Permissions are most often assigned to groups, and a user can be a member of multiple groups. When this happens, the user is granted a combination of all the permissions assigned to all of the groups. This is commonly referred to as cumulative permissions.

For example, Maria is a sales manager within a company that has created groups called Sales and Managers. Maria is a member of both the Sales and Managers groups, and the permissions for a folder are assigned as follows:

- **Sales group.** Read.
- **Managers group.** Modify.

Because Maria is in both groups, she has both sets of permissions, allowing her to read and modify files within the folder.

EXAM TIP

Permissions are cumulative. When a user is granted permissions from multiple groups, the user has a combination of all the permissions.

Allow vs. Deny

In addition to granting permission with Allow, you can also explicitly block access by assigning Deny. If Deny is assigned for a user or group, it takes precedence and overrides allowed permissions.

For example, suppose a company hires sales interns and puts their user accounts in the Sales group. These users now have access to all the same data as anyone else in the Sales group. If the company wants to block the interns from accessing some files, it can assign the Deny permission for the Interns group. It would apply to users in the Interns group but to no one else.

If you look again at Figure 25-11, you'll see that the Interns group is assigned Deny for the A+ Study Notes folder. Even if one of the interns was added to the Managers group, which is granted access, the Deny takes precedence and will block the intern's access.

Permission Inheritance and Permission Propagation

Children inherit genes and sometimes huge fortunes from their parents. Permissions use inheritance as a metaphor to show that permissions assigned to parent folders are inherited by children folders and by any files within a parent folder.

Imagine that you create a folder named Study Notes. Any files or folders you create inside this folder are children, and any permissions you assign to the parent are automatically inherited by the children. This is also called permission propagation because the parent folder permissions are propagated to the children.

Figure 25-12 shows the A+ folder as a child of Study Notes and Network+ as another child of Study Notes. Similarly, the A+ folder includes several files that are children of the A+ folder. If you granted a group Full Control to the A+ folder, group members would automatically have access to all the files in that folder through permission inheritance.

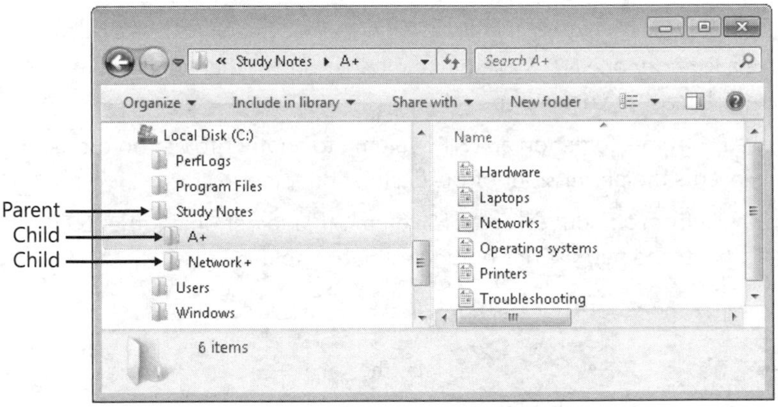

FIGURE 25-12 Inherited permissions from parent folder.

This does not give them access to the Network+ folder because the A+ and Network+ folders are both on the same level as children of the Study Notes folder. A brother doesn't inherit genes from a brother, and a child folder doesn't inherit permissions from another child folder.

What would you do if you wanted to give someone access to both the A+ and Network+ folders? One way is to assign permissions individually to each folder. An easier way is to assign permissions to the parent Study Notes folder. If you grant access to the Study Notes folder, access is granted to both the A+ and Network+ folders through inheritance.

Effect on Permissions When Copying and Moving Files

When you assign permissions directly to a file, it's important to understand how the operating system handles these permissions when you move or copy the file. For example, if you give Holly Read permission to a file named Study.doc, will she still have Read permission if you copy or move the file?

There is only one situation that results in the directly assigned permissions staying the same: when you move a file on the same partition or volume. Any other time, the permissions are inherited from the target location.

EXAM TIP

A short way to remember this is with either of the following phrases: "Move on same retains and everything else inherits" or "Move on same stays the same and everything else inherits."

Figure 25-13 shows all of the following possibilities:

- When you move a file (drag and drop) from one folder to another folder on the same NTFS volume, the file retains the permissions. This is the only time the original permissions are retained.

- When you move a file from one NTFS volume to a folder on another volume, the file inherits the permissions of the destination folder.

- When you copy a file from a folder on an NTFS volume to another folder on the same volume, the file inherits the permissions of the destination folder.

- When you copy a file from a folder on an NTFS volume to a folder on another NTFS volume, the file inherits the permissions of the destination folder.

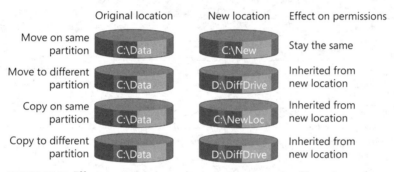

FIGURE 25-13 Effect on permissions when moving or copying files.

EXAM TIP

The only time that directly assigned permissions stay the same is when the file is moved on the same partition or volume. Remember that a partition and a volume refer to the same thing. Moving a file from C:\Data to C:\New can be referred to as moving a file on the same partition or moving a file on the same volume. Permissions are not supported on FAT volumes, so if you move or copy a file to a FAT volume, all permissions are lost.

File Attributes

Files have attributes that describe them such as hidden, read-only, and system. These work in conjunction with permissions, but they aren't the same.

For example, if a file is marked as read-only, the operating system prevents anyone from making modifications to the file. If you remove the read-only attribute, it can be modified.

In contrast, permissions are more selective. You can assign one group Read and Write permission for a file and assign another group only Read permission. Attributes apply to all users universally, but permissions can be applied to users and groups differently.

> **MORE INFO   CHAPTER 14, "USING THE COMMAND PROMPT"**
>
> Chapter 14 shows how to use the attrib command to view and modify attributes from the command prompt.

Share Permissions

Shares are folders on other network computers that are accessible over the network. You can assign permissions to these shares, and they interact with NTFS to allow or block access.

> **MORE INFO   CHAPTER 16, "UNDERSTANDING DISKS AND FILE SYSTEMS"**
>
> Chapter 16 covers shares in more depth, including administrative shares and regular shares. Only folders can be shared. When shared, all the files and subfolders within the share are accessible over the network by using a Universal Naming Convention (UNC) path in the format of *ServerName**ShareName.*

There are only three Share permissions, described in the following list, and each can be assigned as Allow or Deny:

- **Full Control.** This is the same as the NTFS Full Control permission. Users with full control permission can do anything with files within the share.
- **Change.** This is similar to the NTFS Modify permission. It allows users to read and modify files.
- **Read.** When a share is created, this is the default permission assigned.

Share permissions are cumulative, just as they are with NTFS. If a user is granted Read and Change permissions, the user has Change permission that includes Read. The permissions don't cancel each other.

The exception is when Deny is assigned. Just as Deny takes precedence in NTFS, Deny takes precedence with Share permissions. If a user is assigned Deny Read, it doesn't matter how many groups grant the user Allow Read. Deny overrides the Allow permission, and access is blocked.

Shares are accessed only over a network. If you access the folder on your local computer, you are accessing the folder, not the share. If you access the folder, the Share permissions do not apply.

Combining NTFS and Share Permissions

When you access a file within a share that is on an NTFS drive, both the NTFS and the Share permissions apply. In this case, the permissions are not cumulative. You can use the following three simple steps to determine what the ultimate permissions are for a file within the share:

1. **Identify the combined NTFS permissions.** For example, if a user is a member of multiple groups and is granted Read permission as a member of one group and Full Control permissions as a member of the second group, the user is granted a combination of both Read and Full Control permissions. In this case, Full Control includes Read, so it's appropriate to say that the combined NTFS permissions are Full Control.

2. **Identify the combined share permissions.** Similarly, if a user is a member of multiple groups granting the user Read as a member of one group and Change as a member of the second group, the user is granted a combination of both Read and Change permissions. In this case, Change includes Read so it's appropriate to say that the combined share permissions are Change.

3. **Identify the lower permission of the two.** Which provides less access? Full Control from the combined NTFS permission or Change from the combined Share permissions? Change is less than Full Control, and that's the ultimate permission.

The default permission when you create a share is Read for the Everyone group. Unless you change this, users will be able to only read the files in the share. It doesn't matter what type of NTFS permissions they have. A user with Full Control NTFS permissions and Read share permissions is granted only Read permission when accessing files through the share.

> *NOTE* **LEAST RESTRICTIVE AND MOST RESTRICTIVE**
>
> Combining NTFS and Share permissions is often described as using the least restrictive and most restrictive permissions. First, you combine the NTFS permissions to identify the least restrictive NTFS permission, which is Full Control in the preceding explanation. Next, you combine the Share permissions to identify the least restrictive Share permission, which is Change in the explanation. Last, you identify which is most restrictive between the two. Change is more restrictive than Full Control, so Change is the applied permission.

> ✔ **Quick Check**
>
> 1. What permissions will a user have when the user is a member of two groups?
> 2. When do permissions stay the same when a file is moved or copied?
>
> **Quick Check Answers**
>
> 1. A combination of permissions from both groups.
> 2. Only when moved on the same partition or volume.

Understanding Encryption

Encryption is the process of converting plain text data into cipher text that is unreadable. Decryption converts cipher text back into plain text so that it is readable. The primary goal is to keep secret data secret. Security professionals refer to this as preventing loss of confidentiality by preventing unauthorized access.

The two primary times when encryption methods are applied are as follows:

- **Data at rest.** Whenever data is stored on media, it is at rest. This includes data stored on hard drives, optical media, and USB flash drives. You can encrypt individual files and folders with NTFS Encrypting File System (EFS). Similarly, you can encrypt entire partitions with BitLocker.

- **Data in motion.** When data is transferred over a network, it is in motion. Network protocols such as Secure Shell (SSH), Secure Sockets Layer (SSL), and Transport Layer Security (TLS) are used to encrypt data in motion. Wireless networks also use encryption to protect some transmitted data.

The Advanced Encryption Standard (AES) is commonly used in many different security applications to encrypt both data at rest and data in motion. It has replaced the older Data Encryption Standard (DES), which is no longer considered secure.

> **MORE INFO   CHAPTER 20 AND CHAPTER 23**
>
> Chapter 20, "Understanding Protocols," covers encryption protocols. For example, SSH is used with Secure File Transfer Protocol (SFTP) and Secure Copy (SCP) to encrypt data sent over a network. Chapter 23, "Exploring Wireless Networking," covers the wireless protocols used to encrypt data.

Encrypting Files with EFS

Windows operating systems using NTFS include *Encrypting File System (EFS)*, which you can use to encrypt files and folders. When an authorized user accesses an encrypted file, the operating system automatically decrypts the file and opens it. When a user saves a file that was originally encrypted, the operating system automatically encrypts it again.

You can use the following steps to encrypt a folder on a Windows 7 NTFS drive:

1. Open Windows Explorer by clicking Start, Computer.

2. Browse to the drive and folder that you want to encrypt.

3. Right-click the folder you want to encrypt and select Properties. If necessary, click the General tab.

4. Click Advanced. Select Encrypt Contents To Secure Data. Your display will look similar to the following graphic. Click OK.

> **NOTE** **ENCRYPT OR COMPRESS**
>
> Files and folders can be encrypted *or* compressed, but they cannot be encrypted *and* compressed at the same time. Only one choice is allowed at a time.

5. Click OK again. On the Confirm Attribute Changes dialog box, ensure that Apply Changes To This Folder, Subfolders And Files is selected and click OK. This ensures that all folders within the folder will also be encrypted.

The folder appears green in color. Any new files you create in this folder and any files that you copy or move into it will also be encrypted. If you set compression instead of encryption, the folder will be blue. Files can be green, indicating that they're encrypted, or blue, indicating that they are compressed, but they can't be both green and blue at the same time. More specifically, they can't be compressed and encrypted at the same time.

EFS uses certificates in the encryption and decryption process. The operating system automatically creates a certificate the first time a user encrypts a file, and this certificate includes cryptographic keys. The certificate is accessible only to the user, and when the user opens a file, the operating system retrieves the certificate to decrypt it.

This brings up an important point. If you move encrypted files from one computer to another, they can't be decrypted unless you also move the user's certificate. You need to export the certificate from the original computer and then import it on the new computer.

On Windows 7, you can use the User Accounts applet and click Manage Your File Encryption Certificates to access wizards to help with the process. Technet includes an article, "Manage Certificates," which includes information about exporting a certificate from one computer and importing it on another computer. You can access it here: *http://technet. microsoft.com/library/cc771377*.

Offline Files Encryption

The Offline Files feature allows users to access files even when users are away from the network, and it is useful for laptop users. Imagine that Server1 hosts files within a share, and Holly uses her laptop computer to access the files when her laptop computer is connected to the work network.

When the Offline Files feature is enabled, the files are also copied onto Holly's laptop. She can access these files even when she's away from work and not connected to the network.

If these files include sensitive data, they can be protected with encryption. If the user's laptop is lost or stolen, encryption helps prevent unauthorized individuals from viewing the data.

The Offline Files feature includes the ability to encrypt offline files but requires different steps to access them on different operating systems.

- On Windows XP, start the Folder Options applet from the Control Panel. Click the Offline Files tab and click Encrypt Offline Files To Secure Data.

- On Windows Vista, start the Offline Files applet from the Control Panel. Click the Encryption tab and click Encrypt.

- On Windows 7, start the Sync Center from the Control Panel and click Manage Offline Files. Click the Encryption tab and click Encrypt.

BitLocker Drive Encryption

BitLocker Drive Encryption is a Windows feature that can encrypt the entire volume. This makes it difficult for unauthorized individuals to access data if they are able to steal a hard drive.

If you protect files on a drive by using NTFS permissions, they can't easily be accessed. However, an administrator can take ownership of the files and change the permissions. With this in mind, a thief can be an administrator on a computer he owns. He can install a stolen hard drive as a second drive on his computer, take ownership of the files, and change their permissions.

Disk drives protected with BitLocker Drive Encryption are protected from this type of attack. When the drive is moved to another system, they remain encrypted and unreadable.

BitLocker uses a Trusted Platform Module (TPM) when available. A TPM is a chip on the motherboard, and it often needs to be enabled in the BIOS. If a TPM is not available,

BitLocker can be used with a PIN that the user enters when the computers starts or with a USB flash drive that includes a startup key and is inserted when the computer is started.

BitLocker To Go is a feature available in Windows 7 that allows you to encrypt data on removable disks, such as a USB flash drive. It uses AES and provides strong encryption.

> **MORE INFO** **BITLOCKER**
>
> If you want to dig a little deeper into BitLocker, check out the following links:
>
> - BitLocker Drive Encryption: *http://windows.microsoft.com/en-us/windows-vista/BitLocker-Drive-Encryption-Overview.*
> - Windows BitLocker Drive Encryption Step by Step Guide: *http://go.microsoft.com/fwlink/?LinkId=53779.*
> - BitLocker and BitLocker To Go video: *http://technet.microsoft.com/en-us/windows/bitlocker-and-bitlocker-to-go.aspx.*

✔ **Quick Check**

1. What is used to encrypt individual files?
2. What is required to support BitLocker?

Quick Check Answers

1. EFS, which is part of NTFS.
2. A TPM. As an alternative, you can use a PIN or a USB.

Destruction and Disposal of Data and Media

When media such as hard drives, backup tapes, CDs, and DVDs reach the end of their life cycle, they should be destroyed or disposed of properly. This includes when a computer is donated, recycled, returned to the vendor at the end of a lease, or simply thrown away. The primary goal is to ensure that the data doesn't fall into the wrong hands.

Sanitization is the process of removing all usable data from media. The ultimate form of sanitization is physical destruction.

There are many different methods of sanitizing media, and organizations commonly have procedures in place for destruction and disposal. The sensitivity of the data often dictates which method is used. For example, you might need to destroy a disk drive that has highly classified material but only need to erase data from another drive.

Hard Drive Sanitization

If you need to dispose of a hard drive, you should ensure that it does not have any data that could be valuable to someone else. In some cases, you can use software tools to sanitize a hard drive. Software tools overwrite the drive to remove all remnants of the data. Hardware tools are used to destroy the drive.

Deleting Files

It's relatively easy to delete files in Windows. You can browse to the file by using Windows Explorer, right-click the file, and select Delete. However, even though you've selected Delete, the file isn't actually deleted.

Most people know about the Recycle Bin available in Windows. If you accidentally delete a file, you can go into the Recycle Bin, locate the file, right-click it, and select Restore.

However, even when it's deleted from the Recycle Bin, the file is not actually totally deleted. File systems use a table to identify the location of files. When you delete a file, you're deleting only the entry in the table. This is similar to the index in the back of a book that you can use to find a topic. If the index entry is deleted, the topic still remains in the book; it's just a little harder to find.

Many undelete tools are available that can locate deleted files and add them back to the file system table. If you have data that you don't want anyone else to access, you need to do more than just delete it. Other tools are available to completely remove the files.

Overwrite and Drive Wipe Tools

Data is written as magnetized fields on a hard drive, and even when a file is deleted and over-written, some magnetism of the original data remains. This is often called data *remanence*. Specialized forensics tools can locate and recover this data.

Software tools are available that will overwrite deleted files to remove all data remnants. For example, Unix includes a utility called *shred* that can overwrite individual files or entire disk drives. It overwrites the file at least three times with multiple patterns.

Some tools write a pattern of 1s and 0s (such as 1001 1100) in the first pass and then write the complement of the pattern (0110 0011 in this example) in a second pass. The last pass writes random bits.

EXAM TIP

Deleting a file doesn't truly erase it. Overwriting a file multiple times with different bit patterns is a secure method of deleting a file.

Low-Level Format vs. Standard Format

Hard drives start as platters with ferromagnetic material that isn't organized in any way. Manufacturers perform a low-level format of the hard drives at the factory to define the positions of the tracks and sectors. Later, users perform a standard format to prepare the disk with a file system like NTFS.

It's unlikely that you'll ever perform a true low-level format of a hard disk drive. However, the process of writing zeros onto the disk will erase the disk and is often referred to as a low-level format.

A zero-fill program sanitizes a disk drive by filling every sector with zeros. The dd command in Unix is used for copying data at the bit level, and it can be used as a zero-fill program.

> **NOTE** **LOW-LEVEL FORMAT VS. WRITING ZEROS**
>
> Over 20 years ago, end users occasionally needed to perform low-level formats due to disk aging problems. These problems never occur on current disks, so the low-level format performed at the factory never needs to be repeated. However, applications that write zeros (zero-fill programs) are sometimes referred to as low-level format programs. These are not the same as the factory low-level format, but they will erase all data on the drive.

Hard drive manufacturers often provide hard drive utilities that include a zero-fill utility. For example, Western Digital offers utilities that work with its drives. The knowledge base article titled "How to low level format or write zeros (full erase) to a WD hard drive or Solid State drive" describes the full process and includes download links. You can view it here: *http://wdc.custhelp.com/app/answers/detail/a_id/1211*.

A standard format prepares the hard drive for file storage and is performed by users within an operating system. For example, you can format a hard drive by using Disk Management or the format command.

> **MORE INFO** **CHAPTER 16, "UNDERSTANDING DISKS AND FILE SYSTEMS"**
>
> Chapter 16 provides steps for formatting a disk drive by using Disk Management and the format command. A standard format can be either quick or full. The full format checks the sectors and marks faulty sectors as bad so that they aren't used. It is not a low-level format.

Just as there are undelete tools that can undelete files, there are also unformat tools that can unformat hard drives. An important point to realize is that a standard format is not an effective method of sanitizing a drive.

Physical Destruction

Although many of the methods for sanitizing media can be effective, they are all susceptible to problems or errors. For example, an undetected software bug might prevent the complete erasure of data or the person running the program might make a mistake.

When media holds extremely sensitive or top secret data, an organization often chooses to eliminate any of these risks. Instead of using tools to erase the data, the organization destroys the media.

Shredder

Shredders are commonly used to destroy paper and can also be used to destroy some media. Some small shredders used in small offices/home offices (SOHOs) might be able to shred a CD, but they are rarely good enough to shred a thicker DVD or Blu-ray disc.

Some companies, such as Shred-it, have mobile trucks with industrial-sized shredders inside the truck and they can shred materials at the customer's location. In addition to paper, these companies can also shred any type of hard drive from desktop and laptop computers, magnetic tapes, floppy disks, and optical media.

> **NOTE CROSSCUT SHREDDERS**
>
> A simple strip shredder cuts paper into strips and is not suitable for destruction. A dumpster diver can retrieve the strips from the garbage and put them back together. Crosscut or confetti shredders cut in more than one direction to create small pieces of paper similar to confetti. Higher-quality crosscut shredders create extremely small particles of paper.

Degaussing Tool (Magnet and Electromagnetic)

Hard drives store data by magnetizing ferromagnetic material on the platters. A *degaussing tool* exposes the drive to a strong magnetic field, scrambling the data. Similarly, degaussing tools erase data from magnetic tapes. There are two types of degaussing tools:

- **Permanent magnet.** A strong permanent magnet is used to create the magnetic field.
- **Electromagnetic.** Electricity is sent through a coil to generate strong magnetic fields.

Degaussing is an effective method of sanitizing damaged hard drives, but you shouldn't use it on a drive that you want to use again. The magnetic fields that erase the data will also destroy the hard drive.

> **EXAM TIP**
>
> Degaussing is an effective method of sanitizing hard drives and tapes, but it has no effect on non-magnetic media. You cannot use it on optical media such as CDs and DVDs.

Drilling, Sanding, and Grinding

Drills, sanders, and grinders are sometimes used to destroy media. Drilling several holes through the platters makes a disk unusable and is sometimes considered a suitable method of destroying the media. Electric sanders and grinders completely remove all of the magnetic material, ensuring that there is nothing left on the disk.

> ✔ **Quick Check**
>
> 1. What type of format erases data on a disk?
> 2. Name two methods of physical destruction.
>
> **Quick Check Answers**
>
> 1. A low-level format or writing zeros.
> 2. Shredding, degaussing, and drilling are possible answers.

Chapter Summary

- Security methods attempt to prevent incidents, detect them when they occur, and respond to quickly contain them. User education is an important prevention method.

- The principle of least privilege ensures that users are granted only the privileges they need for their job.

- Users prove who they are with authentication. Passwords are used most often but are the weakest form of authentication. Tools such as the Local Security Policy ensure that users create strong passwords with multiple character types.

- Badges and smart cards provide strong authentication when combined with another authentication method, such as a PIN or a password. Biometric authentication is the strongest method, and retinal scans are the strongest form of biometric authentication.

- Single sign-on allows users to log on once and access multiple resources without logging on again.

- Windows XP includes a limited user account and a computer administrator account. Similarly, Windows Vista and Windows 7 use a standard user account and an administrator account.

- You can create and modify accounts with the User Accounts applet or the Local Users And Groups snap-in available in Computer Management.

- Privileges are granted to users when the account is added to a group. Users can be in multiple groups and have a combination of all the privileges assigned to the groups.

- NTFS permissions are assigned on NTFS volumes. When assigned to a folder, the folder is the parent and the permissions are inherited by files and subfolders with the parent folder.

- Permissions can be assigned as Allow or Deny. When a user is assigned multiple Allow permissions, the result is a combination of all. When Deny is assigned, it takes precedence and blocks any Allow permission.

- Share permissions apply to shared folders only when the share is accessed over the network. They do not apply when the folder is accessed locally.

- Files and folders can be encrypted with EFS. An encrypted file appears green. If EFS files are copied to another computer, the EFS certificate should also be copied.

- BitLocker Drive Encryption encrypts entire hard drives. It can be used with a TPM, a PIN, or a USB flash drive.

- Media should be sanitized prior to disposal. One method of sanitizing media is by using programs that overwrite it with repeating patterns of bits. Media can also be destroyed by using shredders, by using degaussing tools, and by drilling holes in the media.

Chapter Review

Use the following questions to test your knowledge of the information in this chapter. The answers to these questions, and the explanations of why each answer choice is correct or incorrect, are located in the "Answers" section at the end of this chapter.

1. Which one of the following passwords is the strongest?

   A. apluscertified

   B. IPassedAPlus

   C. IPa$$ed!!

   D. IPa$$ed801

2. Which of the following provides the strongest authentication?

   A. Strong passwords

   B. Retinal scans

   C. Smart cards

   D. RSA tokens

3. A user was first assigned as a member of the Sales group and later added to the Managers group. What are the effective permissions of the user?

   A. Only permissions assigned to the Sales group.

   B. Only permissions assigned to the Managers group.

   C. A combination of permissions from both groups.

   D. Only permissions granted to both groups.

4. Of the following choices, when will directly assigned permissions stay the same?

   A. When a file is copied to a new location on a volume.

   B. When a file is copied to a different volume.

   C. When a file is moved to a new location on a volume.

   D. When a file is moved to a different volume.

5. What is the benefit of encrypting data with NTFS?

   A. It helps prevent unauthorized users from viewing it.

   B. It helps prevent unauthorized users from copying it.

   C. It ensures that the data stays hidden.

   D. It ensures that the data is not modified.

6. Which of the following methods provides the strongest sanitization of a hard disk?

   A. Formatting the disk with the format command.

   B. Low-level format writing zeros.

   C. Physical destruction.

   D. Deletion of individual files.

Answers

This section contains the answers to the chapter review questions in this chapter.

1. **Correct Answer:** D

    A. Incorrect: apluscertified uses only one character type (lowercase) and is the weakest.

    B. Incorrect: IPassedAPlus uses only two character types.

    C. Incorrect: IPa$$ed!! uses only three character types.

    D. Correct: IPa$$ed801 is the strongest because it uses all four character types (uppercase, lowercase, special characters, and numbers).

2. **Correct Answer:** B

    A. Incorrect: Passwords are the weakest form of authentication.

    B. Correct: A retinal scan is a biometric method of authentication, and it is the strongest.

    C. Incorrect: Smart cards are strong when combined with a second method but are not very strong when used alone.

    D. Incorrect: RSA tokens are strong when combined with a second method but are not very strong when used alone.

3. **Correct Answer:** C

    A. Incorrect: It does not matter when permissions are granted. The fact that the user was added to the Sales group first is not relevant.

    B. Incorrect: Permissions are not limited to just one group.

    C. Correct: When a user is a member of multiple groups, the user has a combination of permissions from all groups.

    D. Incorrect: Permissions are not limited if a user is added to another group.

4. **Correct Answer:** C

    A. Incorrect: Permissions are inherited from the new location when a file is copied to a new location.

    B. Incorrect: Permissions are inherited from the new location when a file is copied to a different volume.

    C. Correct: The only time directly assigned permissions stay the same is when files are moved on the same volume.

    D. Incorrect: Permissions are inherited from the new location when a file is moved to a different volume.

5. **Correct Answer: A**

   A. **Correct:** Encryption scrambles data so that unauthorized users are unable to view it.

   B. **Incorrect:** Encryption doesn't prevent copying.

   C. **Incorrect:** Encryption doesn't hide data.

   D. **Incorrect:** Encryption doesn't stop authorized users from modifying data.

6. **Correct Answer: C**

   A. **Incorrect:** An operating system format does not sanitize a drive because the process can be reversed.

   B. **Incorrect:** A low-level format writing zeroes is a strong method of sanitization but not as strong as destruction.

   C. **Correct:** Physical destruction is the ultimate form of sanitization.

   D. **Incorrect:** Deleting files isn't reliable unless a tool is used to overwrite the files multiple times.

CHAPTER 26

Recognizing Malware and Other Threats

It's rare for any of today's computers to never access the Internet, and the Internet is a dangerous place. An unprotected computer will quickly become infected with one or more of the many types of malicious software. However, it isn't that hard to keep a computer protected. You can usually find reliable free software to protect your systems, and when a system becomes infected, there are some simple steps you can take to clean it. Beyond the digital security methods used to protect systems, there are also several physical security methods that provide an additional layer of protection.

Exam 220-802 objectives in this chapter:

- 1.7 Perform preventive maintenance procedures using appropriate tools.
  - Best practices
    - Antivirus updates
- 2.1 Apply and use common prevention methods.
  - Physical security
    - Tailgating
    - Securing physical documents/passwords/shredding
    - Privacy filters
  - Digital security
    - Antivirus
    - Antispyware
- 2.2 Compare and contrast common security threats.
  - Social engineering
  - Malware
  - Rootkits
  - Phishing
  - Shoulder surfing
  - Spyware

- Viruses
  - Worms
  - Trojans
- 2.3 Implement security best practices to secure a workstation.
  - Disable autorun
- 4.6 Given a scenario, troubleshoot operating system problems with appropriate tools.
  - Common symptoms
    - Spontaneous shutdown/restart
- 4.7 Given a scenario, troubleshoot common security issues with appropriate tools and best practices.
  - Common symptoms
    - Pop-ups
    - Browser redirection
    - Security alerts
    - Slow performance
    - Internet connectivity issues
    - PC locks up
    - Windows updates failures
    - Rogue antivirus
    - Spam
    - Renamed system files
    - Files disappearing
    - File permission changes
    - Hijacked email
    - Access denied
  - Tools
    - Anti-virus software
    - Anti-malware software
    - Anti-spyware software
    - Recovery console
    - System restore
    - Pre-installation environments
    - Event viewer
  - Best practices for malware removal
    - Identify malware symptoms

- Quarantine infected system
- Disable system restore
- Remediate infected systems: Update anti-virus software, Scan and removal techniques (safe mode, pre-installation environment)
- Schedule scans and updates
- Enable system restore and create restore point
- Educate end user

REAL WORLD   **SECURITY LESSONS—THE EASY WAY AND THE HARD WAY**

Criminals have become very proficient at tricking people and separating them from their money. I recently worked with a business owner who almost lost $10,000 after falling prey to a criminal's tactics.

The owner received an official-looking email from his bank explaining a problem that urged him to verify some information to avoid losing access to his account. While the owner was normally tech-savvy, this email came to him at the end of a long problem-solving day, and he wearily looked at it as another problem he needed to solve. He clicked, logged on, and provided some other information.

What he didn't realize right away was that this was a phishing email and that he was providing information to a criminal. A little voice nagged at him that something didn't seem right, and he ended up calling the bank the next afternoon as a follow-up.

He learned three things. First, the email was not from his bank and his account did not have any problems. Second, someone withdrew almost $10,000 from his account. Third, if he didn't report this within three business days, the money from this business account would not be retrievable. (You have more time with personal accounts.) Thankfully, he reported it in time and did not lose the money.

He later explained to me what happened and asked what additional steps could be taken to prevent similar problems. I was able to help him increase both digital and physical security for his business, but what I found interesting was that he wasn't receptive to these recommendations before. I was reminded of how some lessons are learned easily while others are learned the hard way—such as after almost losing $10,000. This chapter has some important information that can help you avoid losses before they occur.

Exploring Malware

Malicious software (malware) is software with malicious intent. Many criminals write malware to infect systems for personal gain. In some cases, the malware can gather information about users to steal their identity or to access their bank accounts. Other times, a criminal wants to remotely take over the computer. Sometimes the malware will simply cause damage to the computer, making it unbootable or unusable.

EXAM TIP

Some people use the term *virus* when they're talking about any type of malware. This isn't technically accurate. When preparing for the A+ exams, you should have a good understanding of the different types of malware, such as viruses, worms, and Trojan horses.

Historically, malware has been designed to cause damage to a user's computer by deleting files or corrupting data. Sometimes it just harmlessly displayed a message like "Legalize Marijuana" and disappeared.

However, criminals have found they can make money with malware, and this has become the bigger threat. That is, today's malware usually doesn't damage the computer so that it's unusable. Often, the modifications aren't even detectable by a regular user. Instead, the malware infects the system so that the criminal can use it to steal money.

One of the biggest ways criminals make money with malware is with botnets.

Botnets

The term *botnet* is short for *robot network*. It implies a group of computers acting together on a network to perform certain tasks. Within the context of malware, a botnet is a group of computers that work together as zombies to do the bidding of a *bot herder*. Some terms related to botnets are:

- **Bot herder.** A criminal who controls a botnet. The bot herder manages one or more command and control servers and sends commands to all the computers in the botnet.

- **Command and control server.** The command and control server hosts software that can communicate with members of the botnet. The bot herder manages the command and control server.

- **Zombies.** Computers in the botnet are called *zombies* or sometimes just *bots*. They periodically check in with the command and control server. Just like a zombie in the movies, these bot zombies will do whatever they are directed to do. This often includes downloading and installing additional malware.

Bot herders sometimes rent out access to their botnet to other criminals. Malware from the other criminals can direct the zombies to send spam email to others, start attacks, or participate in other malicious actions. In many cases, the command and control server downloads remote control software. This gives the bot herder full access to the user's computer from a remote location over the Internet.

Botnets are huge. It's not uncommon for a botnet to include tens of thousands of zombie computers. Several botnets have included more than a million computers.

User's systems often join a botnet after becoming infected with malware. If antivirus (AV) software doesn't detect the infection, the users won't know. However, one sign of a botnet infection is unusual network activity when a user is not accessing the Internet.

Virus

A *virus* is malicious code that attaches itself to another host file, similar to how a flu virus attaches itself to a cell of a person. When a file is infected, the malicious code runs when the file is executed.

This provides an important distinction for a virus: it must have a host file to run. Viruses come in many forms, including the following:

- **Program or application.** It infects the executable application file, and when the file is run, the virus runs.

- **Boot sector.** It infects the boot sector of the hard drive and loads when the computer is booted.

- **Polymorphic.** The virus morphs, or changes, to prevent detection from AV software.

- **Stealth.** The virus uses different methods to hide itself from AV software.

- **Multipartite.** A multipartite virus has several components. For example, it can include elements that infect applications and the boot sector.

Viruses can infect files on just about any type of media. This includes disk drives (internal and external), USB flash drives, writable optical drives (CDs and DVDs), and tapes.

Consider the following scenario as an example of how a virus can infect a system and spread to other computers. This scenario assumes that the users are not running antivirus software with up to date definitions.

1. Mark visits a malicious website, and his system is infected with a virus. Mark doesn't know his system is infected.

2. Lori asks for a copy of a file from Mark and gives Mark her USB flash drive. As soon as Mark inserts the USB flash drive, his system detects the new hardware and infects Lori's USB flash drive with the virus.

3. Lori inserts the USB flash drive into her system. When her system accesses the USB, the virus infects Lori's system.

4. Kim asks for a file from Lori and gives Lori her USB flash drive. It infects Lori's USB flash drive, and then later Lori's system, and on and on.

A virus will usually have three goals: replicate, activate, and take action. It will try to replicate by infecting other files and other systems. At some point, it will activate to achieve an objective. It rarely activates immediately, to ensure that the virus has time to replicate. After it activates, it takes some type of action. It might join a botnet, grant an attacker remote access to the infected system, or do anything else the attacker codes into the virus.

EXAM TIP

Up to date AV software and secure settings on computers can prevent many of these infections. However, if security on systems is weakened and they are not running AV software, any of these actions can spread the virus.

Worm

A *worm* is malware that does not need a host file to run. Instead, it travels over the network by using network protocols and attempts to infect systems running specific services or applications.

EXAM TIP

A primary difference between a virus and a worm is that a worm self-replicates without user interaction. A virus requires a host file and is run after some type of user interaction.

Trojan Horse

A *Trojan horse* (sometimes called simply a *Trojan*) is malicious code that looks like something useful or fun but that is actually something else. It will often look harmless, but it can cause damage.

For example, a user might download a free registry scanner, thinking they are getting a tool that can make their system run quicker. However, when they install and run the scanner, it also runs the malicious code. It will often install a separate virus on the user's system. Even if the user later decides to uninstall the original software, the virus remains.

EXAM TIP

It's common for pirated software offered for free to actually be a Trojan horse. Users think they're getting a full version of software for free, and that might be true. However, they're often getting a little something extra. It could be a keylogger, which records their keystrokes and sends it to a criminal, or a remote access program that gives a criminal full access to their computer.

Rogueware

Rogueware (also called *rogue antivirus*, *scareware* or *ransomware*) is a form of a Trojan horse. Here's how it works.

A user visits a website and sees a pop-up window indicating that the user's computer is infected. In other cases, the webpage displays a button or a link to "free" software to scan the user's system. It then encourages the user to download and install the free software. If the user downloads and installs it, the free software "detects" viruses or other issues.

The software often includes a button or link to "clean the computer" or "remove viruses." If the user clicks the button, the rogueware then tells the user that the free version won't fix the problems. However, for only $69.95 (or some other price), the user can upgrade to the full version with all the capabilities.

In addition to getting the initial $69.95, criminals often use or sell the credit information for fraudulent charges. They are reportedly making over $30 million a month with this! As if this isn't enough, the rogueware often installs other malicious code as a Trojan horse.

> **IMPORTANT   ROGUEWARE CAN COME DISGUISED AS A FRIEND**
>
> Security Essentials is a well-known rogueware program. This is not the free Microsoft Security Essentials program, but the criminals have developed it to look similar to the Microsoft one. If you want Microsoft Security Essentials, ensure that you get it from the Microsoft.com site.

Figure 26-1 shows a valid alert from Microsoft Security Essentials. Some of the error messages from rogueware will look similar. The big difference is that Microsoft Security Essentials won't charge you to clean the virus. Click the Apply Actions button in Microsoft Security Essentials, and the virus will be gone.

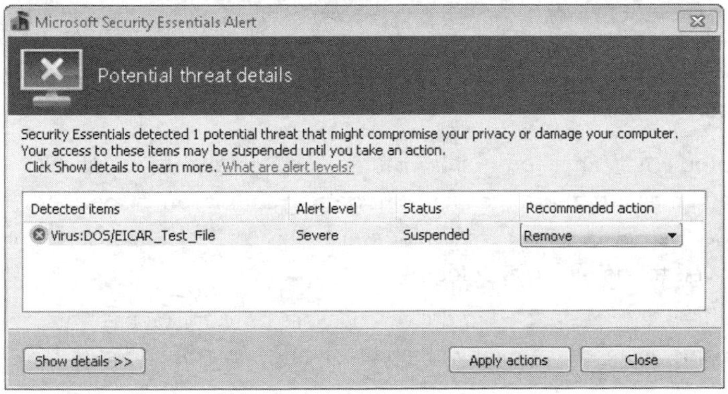

![Microsoft Security Essentials Alert window. Title bar reads "Microsoft Security Essentials Alert". Heading "Potential threat details". Text: "Security Essentials detected 1 potential threat that might compromise your privacy or damage your computer. Your access to these items may be suspended until you take an action. Click Show details to learn more. What are alert levels?" A table with columns Detected items, Alert level, Status, Recommended action. Row: Virus:DOS/EICAR_Test_File, Severe, Suspended, Remove. Buttons: Show details >>, Apply actions, Close.](image)

FIGURE 26-1 Microsoft Security Essentials on Windows 7.

Rootkits

A *rootkit* is a special type of malware that takes over root or administrative access on a computer. After it is installed, it can hide its presence. It controls what a user and antivirus software can view, making the rootkit difficult to detect and remove.

Antivirus software applications often include statements indicating that they can detect and remove rootkits. Unfortunately, malicious rootkits often require extraordinary measures to remove them. For example, one rootkit infects the master boot record (MBR) of a disk and write-protects it. Even if you try to reformat the disk, the virus protects the MBR and the rootkit remains present.

Spyware

Spyware is software that installs itself on the user's system, or modifies the system, without the user's knowledge or consent. The purpose is often to gain information about the user and the user's habits.

In some cases, the spyware will collect data and periodically send it back to a server on the Internet. For example, it can send a list of websites visited by the user after retrieving the list from the web browser history.

EXAM TIP

Spyware often modifies the user's web browser settings. It sometimes changes the user's home page, and other times it installs web browser add-ins or toolbar helpers. Legitimate software can do this as well, but it prompts the user before doing so.

Adware is sometimes referred to as spyware. It observes system activity and presents targeted advertisements to users. In many cases, the adware displays unwanted pop-up windows with advertisements. It can target the advertisements based on information gained about the user.

Spam and Malware

Spam is unwanted or unsolicited email. Email programs include a junk email folder and will automatically move suspected email into this folder. If you're getting spam from a specific sender, you can add the sender's email to a junk email sender list. This causes all that sender's email to be automatically moved to the junk mail folder.

While spam isn't malware itself, it is often used to deliver malware or to trick a user into clicking a link. Malware can come as an attachment with an email or as an embedded script.

Often, spam includes a link to a website that attempts to steal the user's money or download malware. For example, many websites advertise pharmaceutical drugs, but the websites never ship the drugs or the drugs that they ship are not authentic. Other times, a user can just click the link to a malicious website and become infected with a *driveby* download. A driveby download automatically downloads and installs itself on the user's system without the user's knowledge.

Infected computers that have joined a botnet will often be directed to send out spam. If a computer is sending out spam without any user interaction, this is a clear indication that the system is infected and is a member of a botnet.

Phishing

The *phishing* email tries to trick users into providing their user name, password, or other personal information. It looks like it's from a legitimate source, but it's not. Attackers often send massive amounts of spam that include phishing attacks.

A phishing email often includes three elements. First, it lists a problem, such as suspicious activity on an account. Second, it includes a sense of urgency, such as a warning that your account will be locked out. Last, it includes a call to action, such as replying to an email with specific information or clicking a link and providing the information via a website.

For example, an attacker can send an email that looks like it's from PayPal or eBay, even using the same graphics as PayPal or eBay, but the email is completely fake. Another example is a notification that the user has won the lottery. To claim the winnings, the user needs to send back their address, phone number, and bank account number so that the winnings can be deposited into the account. Instead, the bank account is emptied.

> **NOTE NEVER GIVE OUT YOUR PASSWORD**
>
> Legitimate companies never request that their users validate passwords in an email. Any requests for sensitive information should be considered suspicious. An excellent basic security rule to follow is to never give out your password to anyone. When you start making exceptions, you can inadvertently give it out to a criminal. Another basic rule is to not click email links. If you want to check an account, type the address into the web browser so that you know you're going to the actual site.

> ✔ **Quick Check**
>   1. What type of malware requires a host?
>   2. What type of malware does not require a host?
>
> **Quick Check Answers**
>   1. Virus.
>   2. Worm.

Digital Security

 Digital security refers to the technical methods used to protect systems. Antivirus and antispyware software are two primary digital security methods, but there are additional methods.

EXAM TIP

Security has become an important part of the A+ exams. The second domain of the 220-802 exam is titled "Security" and makes up 22 percent of the exam. This reflects the importance of security to organizations and how much they value security-conscious employees.

Antivirus Software

The best protection against malware is up-to-date antivirus (AV) software. *AV software* helps to prevent infections and to detect them when they occur.

AV software can detect multiple types of malware, not just viruses. For example, it's common for AV software to include the ability to detect viruses, worms, Trojan horses, adware, spyware, and other types of malware.

There are many AV software vendors. Some offer their products for free, and some companies sell their AV software. There's no requirement to get any specific version for any specific operating system.

However, you should consider it a security requirement to have some type of AV software running on every system you have. The only exception is a computer that never accesses the Internet, is not on a network, and never accepts files from external sources such as USB flash drives. A computer matching this description is rare, but if you have one, you might be able to do without AV software. Otherwise, you need it.

EXAM TIP

AV software should be installed and running on a computer before it connects to the Internet. Attackers are constantly scanning the Internet looking for unprotected systems.

AV Definitions and Updates

Malware has specific characteristics that AV software uses to identify the malware. For example, malware might be a specific size, have specific names, or have other characteristics that can identify them. These characteristics are stored in definition files used by the AV software.

AV software scans files and compares them against the definitions in the definition file. When a file has the same characteristics as a definition, the AV software identifies the malware and takes action to isolate it.

Definition files should be regularly updated. Criminals are constantly creating new malware and even different versions of old malware. If the definition file doesn't include the definition of a new virus, the AV software won't detect it. Years ago, IT professionals recommended updating the definitions once a week. Vendors now recommend updating them daily. Many AV programs will automatically check for updates several times a day and will download the updates when they're available.

EXAM TIP

You should check for updated definition files regularly. Many AV applications automatically check for updates one or more times a day. Also, it's common for AV software to include an option to automatically check for new definitions before running a scheduled scan.

Malware sometimes prevents a computer from receiving definition updates or system updates. If this is the case, you can often start the computer by using Safe Mode With Networking and retrieve the updates in this mode. You might also be able to download the definitions on another computer and copy them to the infected computer.

Antivirus Actions

When malware is detected, the AV software attempts to isolate it as quickly as possible, usually immediately. It suspends the activity of the malware and sends an alert to the user.

The alert can come in the form of a pop-up dialog box indicating the file is infected. Many Windows AV programs display a notification in the notification area that is on the far right of the taskbar. For example, Figure 26-2 shows an alert from Windows Defender.

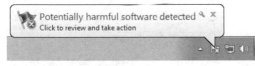

FIGURE 26-2 Windows Defender alert.

The alert usually provides a recommendation, such as blocking the activity, but the user can override the recommendation.

IMPORTANT TAKE AV RECOMMENDATIONS SERIOUSLY

Ignoring the recommendation can result in the malware running and infecting the user's system. Unless you're positive that the AV software is incorrect, you should not override the recommendation.

The two most common actions for AV software are as follows:

- **Quarantine.** A quarantined item is prevented from running and is often moved to a special location. Quarantined items can't cause damage to the system, but users can later restore the item if they determine that it is safe to do so.

- **Remove.** This deletes the item from the system. In some cases, the item can't be deleted immediately. Instead, the AV software quarantines it and the item is removed during the next restart cycle.

In many cases, the AV software allows the user to configure automatic actions. That is, instead of notifying the user of all activity, the AV software automatically takes the action.

For example, Figure 26-3 shows the settings for Microsoft Security Essentials. The default is normally "Recommended action" for each of these alerts. However, I changed the settings to show some of the different actions available.

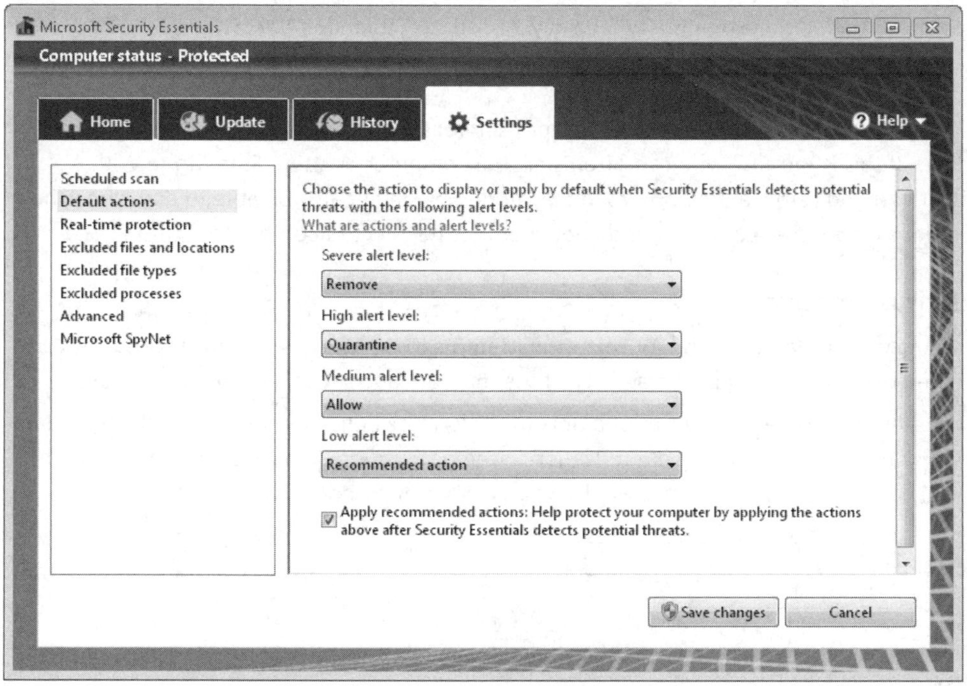

FIGURE 26-3 Microsoft Security Essentials settings on Windows 7.

Antivirus Protection

Most AV software provides protection on different levels, including the following:

- **Real-time protection.** The AV software constantly monitors any files that the user downloads or opens. For example, if a user downloads a file or opens a document, the AV software will scan it to determine whether it is malware. It also monitors system activity, looking for any suspicious actions.

- **Scheduled scans.** A scheduled scan runs at a specific time, such as every week at 1 AM on Sunday morning. It will start and run without user interaction. If the AV software doesn't include the ability to run a scheduled scan, you can sometimes schedule it with the Windows Task Scheduler.

- **On-demand scans.** If users or technicians suspect malicious activity is occurring, they can start a scan immediately to check the system.
- **Automatically update definitions.** This is usually built into the software. In some cases, the AV software will periodically check for updates, such as once or twice a day, and download updates only when there are changes. In other cases, the software checks based on a schedule, such as once a day.

Microsoft Security Essentials

Microsoft Security Essentials is free for home users and small businesses with up to 10 computers. It provides protection against many types of malware, including viruses, Trojan horses, worms, spyware, and more.

To get Microsoft Security Essentials, go to the Microsoft download site (*http://www.microsoft.com/download/*) and search on Windows Security Essentials. There are 32-bit and 64-bit versions. Make sure that you download the version that matches your CPU architecture.

In addition to providing real-time protection, Microsoft Security Essentials will also automatically check for updated definitions. During periods of high activity for new malware, it can update the definitions several times a day.

Figure 26-4 shows a screen shot of Microsoft Security Essentials in action after detecting a virus. You can click the Clean Computer button and it will take a recommended action based on the definition file. In most cases, it will remove the malware.

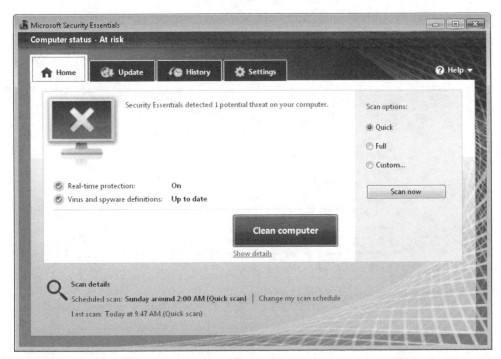

FIGURE 26-4 Microsoft Security Essentials alerting about malware.

Other AV Software

Just because Microsoft has free AV software available doesn't mean you have to use it. You might be running a non-Microsoft operating system, or you might choose to use AV software from another vendor. There are many reputable companies that offer AV software that you can purchase or download for free.

> **IMPORTANT** **WATCH OUT FOR ROGUEWARE**
>
> The biggest warning related to free AV software is to beware of rogueware. Criminals have been known to post positive reviews of their rogueware on other sites. Therefore, just because someone posts a positive review on the Internet doesn't necessarily mean the software is valid. Trust your friends and reputable sources.

Microsoft systems recognize many AV software applications, but not all of them. If you install AV software that is not recognized by Windows, it will show notifications indicating that the system is unprotected. However, you can let Windows know that you do have AV software installed and tell it to stop the notifications.

Figure 26-5 shows the Windows Action Center in Windows 7. If you've installed legitimate AV software but the Action Center indicates that your system doesn't have any AV software, you can click Turn Off Messages About Virus Protection. The display will change to Currently Not Monitored For Virus protection.

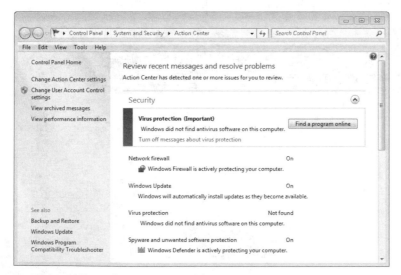

FIGURE 26-5 Microsoft Security Essentials Action Center.

> **NOTE** **WINDOWS SECURITY CENTER NOW ACTION CENTER**
>
> The Action Center was called the Windows Security Center in Windows XP and Windows Vista.

Automatically Starting AV Software

For AV software to be helpful, it needs to be running. Most AV software will automatically start when the system starts. However, malware sometimes changes these settings. You can use the System Configuration tool to verify that AV software is set to start automatically.

You can start the System Configuration tool by entering **msconfig** from the command prompt in any Windows-based system. Figure 26-6 shows this with the Startup tab selected. You can see that the Microsoft Security Client (which starts Microsoft Security Essentials) is deselected. A cool feature that's available with this is the Date Disabled column. You can use this to determine when it was disabled, and you might be able to connect it to the infection.

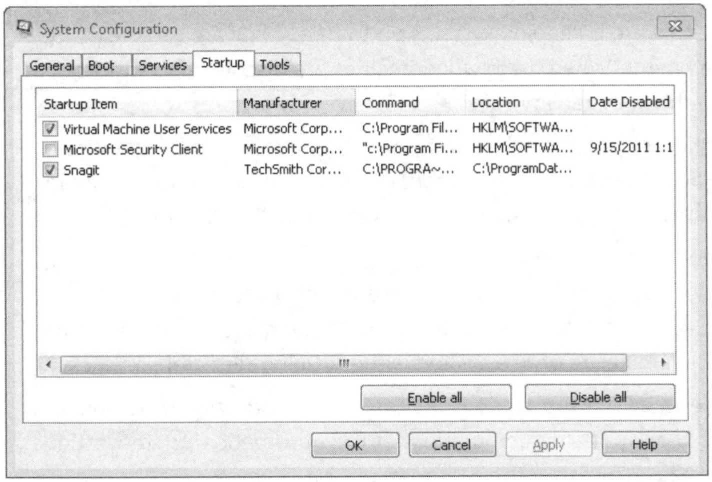

FIGURE 26-6 Verifying AV software set to start automatically.

In other cases, the service running the antivirus software might have been disabled. You can click the Services tab of the System Configuration utility and see whether any of the services are set to disabled. You can also view the running services from the Services applet available through the Control Panel.

Antispyware

Antispyware is software that is designed to look specifically for spyware. For example, Windows Defender is a free antispyware tool that is included with Windows Vista and Windows 7. It's also available as a free download for Windows XP. It attempts to prevent, remove, or quarantine spyware.

Many antivirus applications include antispyware capabilities. You can have separate antivirus and antispyware applications, but they can interfere with each other. Because of this, antivirus vendors often recommend that you do not run separate applications.

> **TIP   WINDOWS SECURITY ESSENTIALS COVERS FOR WINDOWS DEFENDER**
>
> If you are running Microsoft's Windows Security Essentials, Windows Defender won't run. Windows Security Essentials includes the capabilities of Windows Defender, so using both is unnecessary.

Just as other AV software has definitions that need to be updated, Windows Defender uses updates. If you want to watch a short video showing how this is done, check out the following link: *http://windows.microsoft.com/en-us/windows7/keep-windows-defender-definitions-up-to-date*.

Keeping Systems Up to Date

Another protection against malware is keeping systems up to date. Malware often exploits vulnerabilities in operating systems. When these vulnerabilities are discovered, vendors release updates to eliminate the vulnerability.

For example, Microsoft releases patches and updates on the second Tuesday of every month (commonly called "Patch Tuesday"). Systems configured to apply updates automatically will download the updates and apply them without user action. It's also possible to configure a system to apply the updates manually.

Of course, these updates are useful only when they are applied. If the update is not applied, the system remains vulnerable. Malware authors love finding these systems, as the authors are often able to install malware onto a system without being detected.

Criminals are aware of the value of keeping a system up to date and have sometimes included code in malware to block updates. If you find that the Automatic Updates settings have changed or that you can't get updates, the system might be infected.

> **MORE INFO   CHAPTER 15, "CONFIGURING WINDOWS OPERATING SYSTEMS"**
>
> Chapter 15 covers Windows Update, how to enable Automatic Updates, and the importance of patch management practices used in organizations. If a system is not kept up to date against known security problems, it becomes an easy target.

Disabling Autorun

The terms autorun and AutoPlay are often used interchangeably, but Microsoft makes a distinction between the two. A help article available in Windows 7, "What's the difference between AutoPlay and autorun?," defines the differences.

Autorun is a technology that automatically starts an application when media is inserted. For example, when you insert a CD, an application on the CD automatically starts. Autorun looks for a file named Autorun.inf, and if it is there, autorun reads it to identify which program to start. Autorun originally worked on any type of media, including optical discs, USB flash drives, and external hard drives.

> **MORE INFO** **UPDATE INFORMATION ABOUT AUTORUN AND AUTOPLAY**
>
> Microsoft Security Advisory 967940 (*http://technet.microsoft.com/security/advisory/967940*) discusses an update to autorun and AutoPlay. Specifically, it prevents AutoPlay from working with USB flash drives, external hard drives, or network shares on Windows XP and Windows Vista. This matches the functionality in Windows 7.

AutoPlay is a feature within Windows that allows you to define default actions. Instead of automatically starting the application defined in the Autorun.inf file, it gives the user additional choices.

While autorun was useful, criminals found ways to exploit it. They could add malware to the media and add or modify the Autorun.inf file. When the media was inserted into the system, autorun automatically installed the malware on the system. Before it was disabled on USB flash drives in Windows-based systems, malware was often spread from system to system with the help of autorun.

Here's a scenario that frequently occurs on unprotected systems. First, a single computer is infected. Among other tasks, the malware waits for a USB flash drive to be plugged in. When the flash drive is plugged in, the malware writes a virus file on the drive and also adds or modifies the Autorun.inf file to automatically start the virus when the drive is plugged into another system. When this USB flash drive is plugged into any other unprotected system, autorun installs the virus on the new system.

There are two primary ways that you can protect systems. First, ensure that all systems have up-to-date antivirus software running. Second, ensure that AutoPlay is not configured to automatically run applications from USB drives or from any other media.

On Windows XP, you can access AutoPlay settings from Windows Explorer. Right-click an optical disc drive, select Properties, and click the AutoPlay tab.

On Windows Vista and Windows 7, you can access the AutoPlay applet in Control Panel from a list view.

Figure 26-7 shows a typical pop-up (on the left) that appears when you insert an optical disc in a drive. This disc came with an HP printer. I can click Run Setup.exe and it will run the install program. It's possible to select Always Do This For Software And Games, although it isn't recommended. If you ever want to change the settings, you can start AutoPlay (shown on the right).

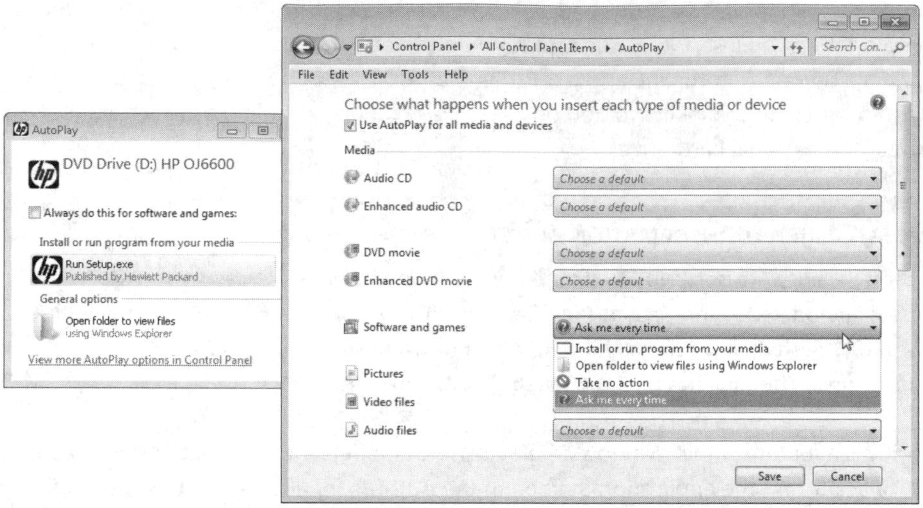

FIGURE 26-7 Viewing AutoPlay settings.

EXAM TIP

As a security best practice, autorun should be disabled. Any setting except Install or Run Program From Your Media will prevent an application from automatically starting.

Each of the settings includes a drop-down box, and for security reasons, the default setting for Software And Games is Ask Me Every Time. This prevents potentially malicious software from running automatically. If you want to completely disable it, select Take No Action.

Figure 26-7 shows the Use AutoPlay For All Media And Devices setting selected. This does not include USB flash drives or hard drives. It does include devices such as cameras, tablets, and MP3 players.

Quick Check

1. How often should AV definitions be updated?
2. What tools can you use to verify that your antivirus software is set to start automatically?

Quick Check Answers

1. Regularly, such as once a day, but not less than once a week.
2. System Configuration (msconfig) and Services.

Symptoms of an Infection

When a computer is infected with malware, the system will give you a variety of different indications. The following list describes many of the common symptoms of an infection:

- **Security alerts.** One of the primary symptoms is a report from antivirus or antispyware software of the infection. It's common for antivirus software to show a pop-up window indicating that the system is infected. You might also see errors in the Event Viewer (covered in Chapter 17, "Troubleshooting Windows Operating Systems").

- **Random pop-up advertisements.** The malware is often trying to get you to click a link which will likely take you to a malicious web site.

- **Slow performance.** Malware activity can often consume system resources. It can cause random disk or network activity and consume processor and memory.

EXAM TIP

Unusual disk activity could be from a virus spreading on your computer, but it could also be due to other issues. It might be that AV software is scanning your system, your disk is fragmented and needs to be defragmented, or you don't have enough RAM and your system has excessive paging.

- **Spontaneous shutdown/restart.** When the malware interferes with the operating system, it can cause the system to restart itself. At other times, it can stop and show a stop error.

- **PC locks up.** Instead of restarting, the system might just stop responding to keyboard or mouse input.

- **Won't perform familiar tasks.** For example, an application might stop running or no longer start. In some cases, a user might no longer be able to access a familiar website.

- **Changes to files.** Malware can rename system files, delete files, or modify permissions without user interaction. If a user is authorized to access a file or folder but sees an Access Denied message when accessing it, it can be an indication that malware has modified the permissions.

- **Can't access hardware.** In some cases, the malware will interfere with accessing some disk drives, printers, or other hardware.

- **Windows Update failures.** Malware sometimes modifies the system configuration settings to prevent updates.

- **Browser redirection.** When you try to access a known site, the system takes you to a different website.

- **Browser modifications.** Some malware resets the home page, modifies the proxy settings, and/or installs unauthorized add-ins.

- **Internet connectivity issues.** Often, malware will modify the web browser proxy server settings. Instead of accessing the Internet through the proxy server, the system tries to access the Internet through other paths. This can bypass security protections from the proxy server, or it might block Internet access for the system until the settings are restored.

- **Antivirus software disabled.** Malware often tries to disable antivirus software so that the malware can run unimpeded.

- **Access denied or other unusual error messages.** Error messages might be from the operating system reporting errors. They might also be from the malware itself trying to trick the user into clicking a link. If malware is trying to install software on its own, User Account Control (UAC) will block it with an Access Denied error.

EXAM TIP

When you clean an instance of malware on a system, it will often try to reinstall itself from a temporary location. Windows 7 includes checks to block this. It might give an Access Denied error with a title of RunDLL. In other cases, UAC might prompt you to approve an installation even though you aren't installing anything.

- **Unusual network activity.** Some malware tries to infect other systems over the network. If the computer has joined a botnet, it will check in with the botnet herder for instructions and might start attacks on others.

- **Files with double extensions.** File extensions like .txt.exe or .jpg.exe are not normal. Malware sometimes overwrites existing files and just adds the extra extension. For example, Figure 26-8 shows Windows Explorer without extensions on the left and with extensions on the right. The Sunrise.JPG.vbs file is a malicious Visual Basic script. A user might be fooled into thinking that the .vbs file is a .jpg file. If a .vbs file is double-clicked, the malicious script will run.

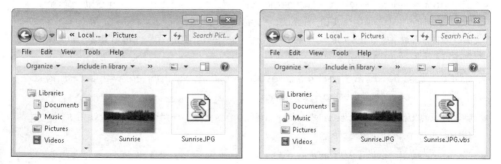

FIGURE 26-8 Viewing files with and without extensions.

MORE INFO   CHAPTER 13, "USING WINDOWS OPERATING SYSTEMS"

You can modify how extensions are viewed by using the Folder Options applet in Control Panel. Chapter 13 includes steps for modifying these settings.

This is certainly not an all-inclusive list. The key to recognizing malware is recognizing unusual or suspicious activity. If you detect anything out of the ordinary, it's worth your time to update the definitions and run a virus scan.

Removing Malware

Antivirus software is often unable to remove a virus, so you need to remove it manually. When this is the case, antivirus software vendors often have step-by-step instructions for how to remove all elements of the virus.

Some organizations have a policy of completely reimaging a computer after an infection rather than trying to clean it. In some extreme cases, you also need to completely reformat the disk and reinstall the operating system. However, there are other steps you can take to clean and remove some malware.

EXAM TIP

Criminals often write very sophisticated malware, but there are many talented professionals that dissect it to learn how it works and how to remove it. When standard steps for removing malware aren't effective, the best source for additional information is antivirus websites. Microsoft also maintains some sites with valuable security information. For example, the Malware Protection Center (*http://www.microsoft.com/Security/portal/*) includes timely information on current threats.

Delete Temporary Files

Malicious software often hides itself within temporary files stored on your hard drive. Malware often stores a copy of itself there, and if the original is discovered and deleted, it later restores itself.

You can delete these files by using the web browser settings. For example, if you're running Internet Explorer 9, you can use the following steps:

1. Start Internet Explorer.

2. Click Tools, and select Internet Options.

3. Ensure that the General tab is selected. Click the Delete button.

4. On the Delete Browsing History page, ensure that Temporary Internet Files is selected, as shown in the following graphic. Click Delete. When the file deletion completes, click OK.

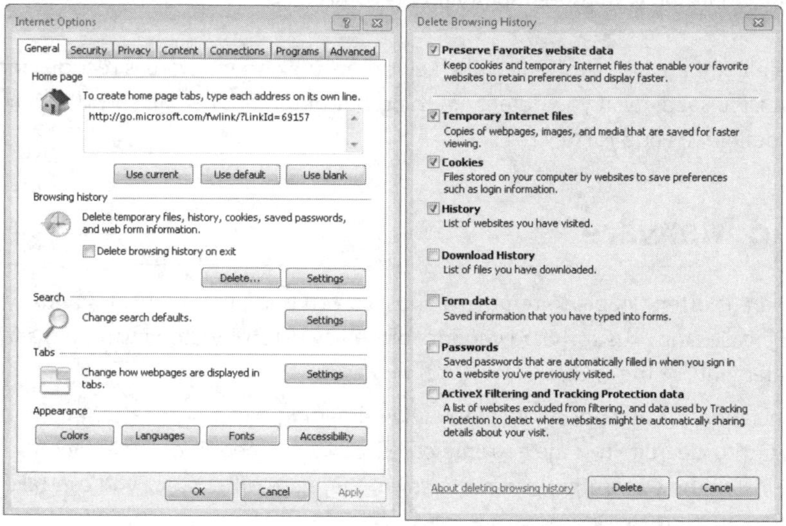

You can also use the Disk Cleanup tool in Windows-based systems to delete temporary files. The following steps show how:

1. Start Windows Explorer.

2. Right-click the C drive and select Properties.

3. Click Disk Cleanup.

4. Ensure that Temporary Internet Files is selected. You might also want to select the Temporary Files selection, but you'll have to scroll down to see it.

5. Click OK. A pop-up window will ask whether you're sure you want to permanently delete the files. Click Delete Files.

6. After a moment, the Disk Cleanup page will appear. Click OK.

Using Safe Mode

Safe Mode can be very useful when removing malware. Sometimes the antivirus software can't remove the software normally, but when you run it in Safe Mode, it can remove the malware. Other times you might need to delete a file, but you'll be able to do so only from Safe Mode.

EXAM TIP

If the system prevents you from deleting a file and reports that the file is in use, you can usually delete the file from Safe Mode. There are other tools that you can also use. For example, you might be able to use the del (delete) command with the /f switch to delete a file, or you might use a third-party tool.

Because Safe Mode starts with a minimal set of drivers and services, the malware usually won't be started and can't protect itself. Chapter 17 talks about Safe Mode in greater depth, but in brief, you can access Safe Mode on Windows-based systems with the following steps:

1. Reboot your system.

2. Press F8 as the computer starts but before the Windows logo appears. This will give you access to the Advanced Options menu.

3. Select Safe Mode.

EXAM TIP

If you need to update definitions for your AV software, you'll need to select Safe Mode With Networking.

Using Preinstallation Environments

In some cases, Safe Mode can't detect or remove all malicious software, and you might need to use a preinstallation environment (PE). Windows PE is used during the installation of Windows and during some Windows recovery operations. For example, if you run Windows memory diagnostics, it runs in a Windows Recovery Environment, which is an enhanced Windows PE.

A preinstallation environment with antivirus tools is often referred to as an offline scanning kit. Microsoft has published the Infrastructure Planning and Design Malware Response document, and Appendix C of that document includes steps that you can use to create an offline scanning kit. This document also includes detailed steps and flow charts that you can use to troubleshoot an infected computer. You can access the download here: *http://go.microsoft .com/fwlink/?LinkId=93108*.

EXAM TIP

You can boot into any alternate operating system and then run antivirus software to remove malware. This is often effective when removing malware that is embedded in the boot sector or the master boot record. Alternate operating systems can be a preinstallation environment, a basic operating system on a 3.5-inch floppy drive, or an operating system booted from a CD or DVD.

If you already have an alternate operating system, a good tool to have is Microsoft's Malicious Software Removal Tool. You can get a free copy from Microsoft. The following page provides more information about the tool, including a link to download it: *http://www.microsoft.com/security/pc-security/malware-removal.aspx.*

Using Recovery Console and Windows RE

In some cases, you might need to use the Recovery Console on Windows XP or the Windows Recovery Environment (Windows RE) on Windows Vista or Windows 7. This is especially useful if the malware has modified the disk.

You can use commands such as fixboot to repair an infected boot sector or fixmbr to repair a damaged master boot record (mbr) from the Recovery Console. Similarly, you can use the bootrec /fixboot and bootrec /fixmbr commands from the Windows RE.

> **MORE INFO**   **CHAPTER 17**
>
> Chapter 17 covers many troubleshooting tools, including the Recovery Console and the Windows RE.

System Restore

In some cases, you can remove malware by restoring your system to a previous state with System Restore. Use the procedures described in Chapter 15 to use System Restore.

Best Practices for Malware Removal

There are several steps you can take that are considered best practices for malware removal on Windows systems. The following steps outline these practices:

1. **Identify malware symptoms.** The list in the "Symptoms of an Infection" section earlier in this chapter identifies common symptoms.

2. **Quarantine infected system.** You quarantine a system by isolating it from other systems. Most computers are on networks today, and if you can disconnect a computer from the network, you have quarantined it. This is as simple as unplugging the network cable.

EXAM TIP

When removing malware, it's often useful to isolate the system by removing its Internet access. You can do this by removing the network cable to the computer or by disabling the network interface card.

3. **Disable system restore.** While removing malware, you will likely make modifications that would normally be captured by system restore. By disabling system restore, you ensure that a user can't accidentally reinfect the system by applying a restore point.

4. **Remediate infected system.** Ensure that the antivirus software is up to date. If necessary, you might need to copy definition files from an uninfected system, but you do not want to connect the infected system to the network or to the Internet. Next, use tools to scan and remove the malware. You might need to use Safe Mode or a preinstallation environment.

5. **Schedule scans and updates.** After cleaning the system, ensure that the antivirus software is configured to regularly retrieve updates and scan the system for malware.

6. **Enable system restore and create restore point.** This normalizes the system and provides a known clean restore point. If the system develops a different problem later, you can use this restore point. If you use an earlier restore point, it's possible that you will re-infect the system again.

7. **Educate end user.** End users often do not understand the risks related to computers and can easily fall prey to common criminal tactics. You can help prevent a reoccurrence of many problems and also help end users avoid suffering from personal losses with just a little education. Users aren't always as receptive to this information prior to an incident, but they become very interested after one.

✔ **Quick Check**

1. Name two ways you can delete temporary files.
2. What mode can you use if antivirus software can't clean malware when started normally?

Quick Check Answers

1. By using Disk Cleanup and through the web browser options.
2. Safe Mode or Safe Mode with Networking.

Recognizing Other Security Threats

The first part of this chapter covers malware, but there are some other common security threats that you should know about. Most organizations have become much more security-conscious, and they realize that one of the best prevention tactics against threats is to have knowledgeable employees.

Employees who understand these threats are less likely to be tricked by them. Additionally, these employees are more likely to support the policies designed to thwart attackers and criminals.

Social Engineering

Social engineering is a fancy way of saying that attackers or criminals attempt to fool people by using social methods. The attacker uses trickery and conniving to get people to do something they wouldn't normally do.

For example, if a stranger asks you to give him your password, you probably wouldn't. On the other hand, imagine the following scenario.

An employee named Sally receives a phone call from someone identifying himself as an IT professional within the company. He tells Sally that her system is infected with a virus that will destroy all her data and that she needs to turn her computer off. Someone from IT will be around to fix her computer within a week.

Instead of doing without a computer for a week, Sally says, "Wait. I need my computer. Isn't there another way this can be fixed?"

The IT professional (who is actually a criminal impersonating an IT professional) says, "Well, I can fix your system over the network. I have to use your account and password. Don't tell anyone I'm doing this for you because everyone will want me to do it for them too." Sally then gladly gives this social engineer her user name and password.

This is just one example of social engineering, but criminals use many more. Some examples of social engineering tactics are as follows:

- If a stranger asks you to give him money for bogus software or to install a virus in your system, you probably wouldn't. Yet rogueware tricks people into taking both of these actions.

- Most people wouldn't give a stranger their user names and passwords for bank accounts. However, carefully worded phishing emails and sophisticated lookalike websites regularly trick people into giving up this information.

- Criminals impersonating bank employees have called people to verify account information. What they're actually doing is collecting account information so that they can empty the account.

- Employees wouldn't normally allow strangers into internal company locations. However, a criminal impersonating a phone company employee or pest control technician might be granted free and unsupervised access.

Some criminals use a social engineering attack as part of a more sophisticated point. For example, a criminal might call and trick employees into giving up information about executives. The criminal can then launch a *whaling attack*, which is a phishing attack targeted at executives.

Physical Security

Physical security includes securing anything you can touch, such as by locking doors or shredding documents. There are some specific threats related to security that PC technicians should understand, along with basic methods of preventing problems.

Tailgating

Many organizations control access to workspaces by using electronic badges or cipher locks. They swipe their badge across a reader and it opens the door, or they enter the code in the cipher lock to open the door. The locked door keeps unauthorized people out, but attackers can bypass it with a simple practice known as *tailgating*.

An attacker can follow closely behind an employee, and when the employee opens the door, the attacker simply follows behind. The attacker doesn't need a badge or the cipher code. If an attacker is wearing a bad-guy mask, employees are less likely to allow this practice. However, instead of a mask, attackers often have a friendly, disarming smile.

Educating employees about tailgating helps stop it. Another method is to have turnstiles that allow only one person to pass through at a time.

Securing or Shredding Physical Documents

Printed documents can include a great wealth of data, and if left unsecured, the information can easily be stolen. Many organizations implement a clean desk policy that requires employees to secure physical documents. They might lock the documents in a drawer or safe, but the documents aren't left where anyone can see them. Similarly, passwords should never be written down and left in plain sight.

Dumpster diving is the practice of looking through trash to find information. People often throw away papers that have valuable information, and a criminal can just look through the trash to get the data. A simple way of preventing criminals' success is by shredding documents instead of throwing them away. Many home users have recognized the importance of this and have home shredders.

Shoulder Surfing and Privacy Filters

Shoulder surfing is the practice of looking over someone's shoulders to view what they're typing on the screen or to watch what they type on the keyboard.

For example, employees might process sensitive data on their computer. The data is protected from unauthorized access with permissions, but if criminals can just look over someone's shoulders and get the information, they don't have to take the time and effort to hack into a system.

A simple protection against shoulder surfing is the use of privacy filters. They limit the viewing angle of the monitor and can reduce the success of shoulder surfers.

> **MORE INFO** CHAPTER 6, "EXPLORING VIDEO AND DISPLAY DEVICES"
>
> Privacy and antiglare filters are mentioned in Chapter 6. They can be used to reduce eyestrain and to increase security.

Chapter Summary

- Malicious software (malware) is software written by malicious users with the intent to cause harm or damage.

- Criminals run botnets, which are groups of infected computers acting as zombies. These zombies do whatever they're commanded to do.

- Different types of malware have different behaviors and intended outcomes.

  - A virus requires a host file. When the host file executes, the malicious code in the virus executes.

  - A worm does not require a host file. It self-replicates over a network without user interaction.

  - A Trojan appears to be one thing but is something else.

  - Rogueware is fake antivirus software offered for free but used to collect money from unsuspecting users.

  - Rootkits take over the system from users and antivirus software.

  - Spyware installs itself on a user's system or modifies a user's system without the user's knowledge or consent.

  - Spam is unwanted email. Malware is often spread through the Internet as email attachments.

  - Phishing is malicious email sent to a large group of people trying to trick them. It often tries to get the user to give up personal information such as a user name and password.

- Antivirus software is the best protection against malware. Most AV software protects against multiple types of malware, not just viruses.

- AV software identifies viruses by using definitions. Definitions should be updated regularly, such as once a day.

- AV software will try to remove or quarantine malware. Quarantined files can be retrieved if desired.

- Most AV software will start automatically when the system starts, but malware sometimes tries to change this behavior. You can use msconfig to verify that the AV software starts automatically.

- Systems should be kept up to date to avoid infections. This includes keeping antivirus software up to date with current definitions and keeping the operating system up to date.

- Any type of unusual activity can indicate an infection. Run AV software to verify that the system is not infected.

- Deleting temporary files can often remove malware remnants on a system and prevent reinfections.

- Safe Mode is useful for removing malware that can be removed normally. If you need to download up-to-date definitions, use Safe Mode With Networking.
- Social engineers attempt to trick users into giving up information or taking actions that they wouldn't normally take.
- Physical security methods help prevent attacks such as tailgating, dumpster diving, and shoulder surfing.

Chapter Review

Use the following questions to test your knowledge of the information in this chapter. The answers to these questions, and the explanations of why each answer choice is correct or incorrect, are located in the "Answers" section at the end of this chapter.

1. Which of the following can spread without user interaction?

   A. Virus

   B. Worm

   C. Trojan horse

   D. Botnet

2. After installing a free game, a user's system began acting erratically. It showed unusual errors and was randomly rebooting. What does this describe?

   A. Worm

   B. Rogueware

   C. Trojan horse

   D. Spam

3. Lori received an email that indicates it's from her bank, saying there is a problem with her account. The email asks her to verify her account information. What best describes this?

   A. Trojan horse

   B. Spyware

   C. Adware

   D. Phishing email

4. A user hasn't connected to the Internet in several weeks. The user was recently infected with a virus from a USB even though the user has AV software installed. What should be done?

   A. Purchase newer AV software.

   B. Reinstall the operating system.

   C. Update the AV software definitions.

   D. Enable the Windows Firewall.

5. A user has AV software installed, and the software previously ran all the time. However, it no longer starts automatically. What's the likely reason?

   A. The software has been removed.

   B. The service is set to disabled.

   C. It's configured to start only in Safe Mode.

   D. Windows Defender is running.

6. A user's system is infected with a virus, and the virus is preventing the AV software from obtaining up-to-date definitions for installed AV software. What should be done? (Choose all that apply.)

   A. Start in Safe Mode and download the definitions.

   B. Start in Safe Mode With Networking and download the definitions.

   C. Download the definitions on another computer and copy them to the infected computer.

   D. Use System Restore to return your system to a previous state.

7. You have discovered a malicious file on your computer. When you try to delete it, the system reports that the file is in use and prevents the deletion. What should you do?

   A. Start the Action Center and delete it from there.

   B. Delete the file from the command prompt.

   C. Boot into BIOS and disable password protection.

   D. Boot into Safe Mode and then delete the file.

Answers

This section contains the answers to the chapter review questions in this chapter.

1. **Correct Answer:** B

    A. Incorrect: A virus attaches itself to an application and requires user interaction to spread.

    B. Correct: A worm is self-replicating and will spread without user interaction.

    C. Incorrect: A Trojan horse is a type of malware that appears to be one thing but also includes something else that is malicious.

    D. Incorrect: Computers can join a botnet after becoming infected with a virus, but the botnet itself doesn't spread.

2. **Correct Answer:** C

    A. Incorrect: A worm is self-replicating, so it is not installed with a game.

    B. Incorrect: Rogueware is fake AV software.

    C. Correct: A Trojan horse looks like one thing (such as a free game) but also installs something malicious.

    D. Incorrect: Spam is unwanted email.

3. **Correct Answer:** D

    A. Incorrect: The user might be tricked into installing a Trojan horse after clicking a link in a phishing email, but the email itself is not a Trojan horse.

    B. Incorrect: Spyware will try to collect information about users, but this can't be done just from the email.

    C. Incorrect: Adware pops up advertisements, but it does not send email to users.

    D. Correct: A phishing email purports to come from a legitimate company and tries to trick the user into giving up personal information. Legitimate companies do not ask users to verify account information in this way.

4. **Correct Answer:** C

    A. Incorrect: The existing AV software might be adequate if it has up-to-date definitions.

    B. Incorrect: It is not necessary to reinstall the operating system.

    C. Correct: If the computer hasn't connected to the Internet in several weeks, the virus definitions are out of date and should be updated.

    D. Incorrect: The Windows Firewall won't block viruses.

5. **Correct Answer:** B

   A. **Incorrect:** The scenario says it is installed.

   B. **Correct:** One way that malware protects itself is by disabling the service for AV software. If the service previously started automatically, this should be checked.

   C. **Incorrect:** Applications are not configured to start only in Safe Mode.

   D. **Incorrect:** Windows Defender does not prevent AV software from running.

6. **Correct Answer:** B, C

   A. **Incorrect:** Safe Mode without networking won't provide access to the Internet.

   B. **Correct:** Starting Safe Mode With Network will allow you to connect to the Internet to download the definitions.

   C. **Correct:** Updating definitions on another computer and then copying them to the infected computer will work.

   D. **Incorrect:** System Restore repairs many problems, but it does not update malware definitions.

7. **Correct Answer:** D

   A. **Incorrect:** The Action Center reports on current security settings, but it doesn't include the ability to delete files.

   B. **Incorrect:** If the file is protected because it's in use, you won't be able to delete it from the command prompt.

   C. **Incorrect:** BIOS password protection can protect the BIOS, but it doesn't affect how files are protected when the system is booted.

   D. **Correct:** Safe Mode uses minimal drivers and services. You can often delete files in Safe Mode that you can't delete normally.

Glossary

Numbers and Symbols

802.11 Group of wireless protocols. 802.11a uses 5.0 GHz and has a maximum speed of 54 Mbps. 802.11b uses 2.4 GHz and has a maximum speed of 11 Mbps. 802.11g uses 2.4 GHz and has a maximum speed of 54 Mbps. 802.11n uses 2.4 and 5.0 GHz and has a maximum speed of 600 Mbps.

A

A/V (Audio Video) A combination of sound (audio) and gr aphics (video). Camcorders can capture A/V.

AC voltage Alternating current used by commercial power to transmit electricity to buildings. AC voltage is available at common electrical wall outlets, and power supplies convert AC to DC.

accelerometer A chip in many mobile devices used to detect the orientation of the device and change the display. A basic use is to change the display to landscape or portrait mode based on the orientation. It is often combined with a gyroscope chip.

access point Same as wireless access point.

ACL (access control list) A list of rules or exceptions used in routers and firewalls.

ACPI (advanced configuration power interface) An open standard used by operating systems to change the power state of devices to conserve power.

ACT (activity) An LED on a network interface card that indicates network activity.

active partition A partition that is bootable. On an MBR disk, one of the primary partitions is marked as active.

actuator Used on hard disk drive to move position read/write heads over specific tracks.

ad-hoc mode A wireless network created without a WAP or wireless router. In contrast, infrastructure mode uses a WAP or wireless router.

Administrative Tools A group of tools available in the Control Panel, used by administrators and advanced users.

ADSL (asymmetrical digital subscriber line) A specific type of DSL. ADSL uses different speeds for uploads and downloads.

adware Software that presents unwanted advertisements to users.

Aero A graphics feature that first appeared in Windows Vista and was improved in Windows 7. It includes translucent effects and animations. Windows 7 Aero supports features such as Snap, Peek, and Shake.

AES (Advanced Encryption Standard) A strong encryption standard used worldwide in many applications, including with WPA2.

AGP (accelerated graphics port) An expansion card standard dedicated to a graphics card. It has been replaced with PCIe in most systems today.

AMD (Advanced Micro Devices) One of the two primary manufacturers of CPUs. Intel is the other.

analog Signals that are transmitted with a sine wave. In contrast, digital data is transmitted as 1s and 0s.

Android An open source operating system used in many mobile devices. It is associated with Google but was created by a consortium of organizations. Users of Android-based devices commonly purchase applications from Google's Google Play. .

antivirus software Software used to detect, block, and remove viruses and other malware.

APIPA (Automatic Private Internet Protocol Addressing) Address type used for DHCP clients when they don't receive a response from DHCP. An APIPA address always starts with 169.254.

APM (advanced power management) An older standard used to conserve power. It has been replaced by ACPI.

Application log One of the logs in the Event Viewer. It records events from applications.

arp A command-line program that shows MAC-to-IP address mapping. ARP is also an acronym for Address Resolution Protocol, used to resolve IP addresses to MAC addresses. The arp command shows the result of ARP activity for a system.

ATA (advanced technology attachment) A standard for disk drive interfaces. It was derived from IDE.

ATAPI (advanced technology attachment packet interface) An enhancement of the ATA standard to support other drives such as CD-ROM and DVD-ROM drives.

ATM (asynchronous transfer mode) A method of transferring data over a network by using fixed-size cells instead of Ethernet packets.

attrib Command used to view and manipulate file attributes including hidden, system, and read-only attributes.

ATX (Advanced Technology Extended) A common motherboard specification. ATX motherboards are 12 inches by 9.6 inches. ATX also defines power requirements associated with ATX-based power supplies.

authentication Proving an identity. The three factors of authentication are something you know (such as a

password), something you have (such as a smart card), or something you are (using biometrics).

authorization Providing access to a resource. Authenticated users are granted authorized access to resources if they have appropriate permissions.

Automatic Updates A feature within Windows that automatically checks for updates. It can be configured to download and install updates without user intervention.

autosense (or auto-negotiation) A feature on many network devices, including NICs, that automatically detects the speed and duplex mode of the connection.

B

back side bus The connection between the CPU and its internal cache memory.

backlight A light used in LCD monitors to shine through LCD crystals. If the backlight fails, the LCD monitor is dim or doesn't display anything at all. Some backlights use LEDs.

basic disk The most common type of disk used in Windows-based systems. The alternative is dynamic disks.

bcd (boot configuration data) A file in Windows Vista–based and Windows 7–based systems in place of the Boot.ini file in Windows XP. It identifies the location of operating systems.

BD-R (Blu-ray disc Recordable) An optical Blu-ray disc that can be written to once.

BD-RE (Blu-ray disc Recordable Erasable) A Blu-ray disc that can be rewritten to multiple times.

binary A numbering system using a base of two. It uses only 0 and 1 as valid digits.

biometric devices Devices that can read biometric characteristics, such as fingerprints. They are used for identification and/or authentication.

biometrics A method of authentication. The most common method is with fingerprints, and the strongest method is with retinal scans.

BIOS (Basic Input/Output System) Firmware stored on a chip on the motherboard. It stores the instructions for starting the computer and includes a program used to change some settings. Current systems commonly store this on flash memory. BIOS is updated by a process called flashing.

bit A single binary digit. Bits are either 0 or 1.

blackout A complete loss of power. Systems protected with an UPS will continue to run during a blackout, at least for a short period of time.

Bluetooth A wireless protocol used for personal area networks (PANs). Class 2 devices have a range of about 33 feet.

Blu-ray A newer standard for optical discs. A single-layer BD-R holds 25 GB of data, and a dual-layer disc holds 50 GB of data.

BNC (Bayonet Neill-Concelmen or British Naval Connector) Connector type used with coaxial cable.

boot partition The location of the operating system files. On Windows systems this is usually C:\Windows. Compare this to the system partition that holds the boot files and is normally located at the root of the C: drive.

Boot.ini A file used in Windows XP as part of the boot process. It is not used in Windows Vista or Windows 7.

bootcfg A command available in the Windows XP Recovery Console that can be used to rebuild the Boot.ini file.

bootrec A command available in the Windows RE on Windows Vista and Windows 7 to repair the BCD and hard disk problems.

botnet Short for robot network. Group of computers, or bots, controlled by a bot herder for malicious purposes.

broadcast Data sent from one computer to all other computers in the same network. The IPv4 broadcast address is 255.255.255.255.

brownout A temporary reduction in power. It often causes lights to flicker and can cause systems to reboot.

Systems protected with an UPS are not affected by brownouts.

BSOD (blue screen of death) A stop error screen that sometimes appears when a Windows-based system is unable to boot. The BSOD screen includes failure codes that indicate the source of the problem.

BTX (Balanced Technology Extended) A motherboard form factor designed by Intel as an alternative to the ATX. Intel stopped using it in 2006. ATX is the most common standard.

bus topology A logical network topology where devices are connected in a logical line. Both ends must be terminated.

bus The connection between devices on a computer used to transfer data. A computer has multiple busses.

byte A group of 8 bits. Many values in computers are expressed in bytes, such as 2 GB of memory or 650 GB of hard drive space.

C

cable lock A physical lock used to secure laptops.

cable select A jumper selection for IDE/PATA drives. When selected for both drives, the drive connected to the black connector on the end of the ribbon cable is the master, and the drive connected to the middle gray connector is the slave.

cable tester A hardware tool used to test for correct wiring and possible wiring breaks within a cable.

cache An area used for fast access of data. CPUs use L1, L2, and sometimes L3 cache. Similarly, hard drives include RAM as cache to improve their read and write performance. Cache can also be an area on a hard drive where files are stored temporarily.

CAPTCHA (Completely Automated Public Turing Test To Tell Computers and Humans Apart) A method used to prevent webpage automated entries. Text is displayed as a distorted image that cannot be interpreted by a program. A person enters the text, proving that a person is making the entry.

CAT Short for *category* when describing twisted-pair cable types. CAT 3 can be used for 10 Mbps, CAT 5 for 100 Mbps, CAT 5e for 1 Gbps, and CAT 6 for 10 Gbps.

CD (compact disc) An early version of optical discs. A CD can hold up to 700 MB of data.

cd Command used to change a directory.

CDFS (compact disc file system) A file system used on optical discs and widely supported by different operating systems.

CD-R (compact disc-recordable) A CD that can be written to once. This is sometimes referred to as a WORM disc.

CD-ROM (compact disc read-only media or compact disc read-only memory) CDs released by manufacturers that have data on them. Data can be read from these discs, but it is not possible to write to them.

CD-RW (compact disc-rewritable) A CD that can be written to multiple times.

chain of custody A document that tracks how evidence has been protected since the time it was collected. It helps verify that collected evidence has been controlled, preventing anyone from tampering with it.

charging The step in the seven-step laser imaging process where the imaging drum is charged with a high voltage. See also processing, exposing, developing, transferring, fusing, and cleaning.

chipset One or more integrated circuit (IC) chips on the motherboard that provide an interface between the CPU and the rest of the system. Compare to north bridge and south bridge.

chkdsk A command-line tool used to check the integrity of disks. It can also fix errors and recover files.

classful IP address An address with a predefined subnet mask based on the first number in the IPv4 address.

Class A: 1 to 126, as in 10.1.2.3.
The Class A subnet mask is 255.0.0.0.

Class B: 128 to 191, as in 172.16.1.2.
The Class B subnet mask is 255.255.0.0.

Class C: 192 to 223, as in 192.168.1.2.
The Class C subnet mask is 255.255.255.0.

cleaning The step in the seven-step laser imaging process where the imaging drum is cleaned. See also processing, charging, exposing, developing, transferring, and fusing.

closed source Indicates that software code is not freely available. The developer views the code as a trade secret and it is not freely available. Apple's iOS is closed source.

cluster A group of sectors on a disk. Clusters are also known as allocation units. File systems use clusters to identify the location of files.

cmd Command used to open the command prompt.

CMOS (complementary metal oxide semiconductor) Storage area for BIOS settings that can be changed by the user. Most current systems do not include an actual CMOS chip but instead store this information on the same flash memory where BIOS is stored.

CNR (Communications and Networking Riser) A small slot in the motherboard used for some add-on communications and networking devices such as modems or network interface cards. These features are often included in the chipset instead of by using a CNR card.

coaxial Cable type used in older Ethernet networks. It is similar to cable used to connect TVs to VCRs and DVD players. See RG-8 and RG-59.

cold cathode fluorescent lamp (CCFL) A type of backlight used in LCD monitors.

Command Prompt A text-based window you can use to enter MS-DOS–based commands. The application is cmd.exe, and it can be launched normally or with administrative permissions.

compact flash (CF) A common type of memory used with camera and digital recorders. SD is a similar type.

Computer Management One of the tools in the Administrative Tools group. It includes several snap-ins, organized in three groups: System Tools, Storage, and Services And Applications.

COMx (communication port) (x=port number) A designation for a serial port, such as COM1, COM2, and so on.

Control Panel A central repository of mini-programs or applets. Applets vary in different operating systems.

convert A command-line tool used to convert a FAT-based file system to NTFS without losing any data.

copy Command used to copy files. An extended version is xcopy, which has many more capabilities.

core Refers to a processor within a CPU. A single CPU can have multiple cores that simulate multiple processors.

CPU (central processing unit) The primary processor within a computer. It does the majority of the computing work.

CRIMM (Continuity Rambus Inline Memory Mode) A special circuit card used with RDRAM. RDRAM must be installed in pairs, and if the second card doesn't have memory, a CRIMM is used.

crimper A hardware tool used to attach cables to connectors. A crimper is used to connect twisted-pair cable to RJ-45 connectors.

crossover cable A cable created to connect similar devices, such as a computer to a computer or a switch to a switch. Compare to a straight-through cable.

CRT (cathode-ray tube) A type of display monitor. It is heavy, large, and power-hungry. CRTs have been replaced by flat panel displays in most situations.

D

DAC (discretionary access control) An access control model where users are owners of their files and make changes. NTFS uses the DAC model.

daisy chain A method of connecting devices in sequence with each other. An alternative would be having each device connect directly to a controller.

DB-25 (parallel communications D-shell connector, 25 pins) A D-shaped connector with 25 pins. A DB-25

port on a computer that has holes instead of pins is a parallel port.

DB-25 (serial communications D-shell connector, 25 pins) A D-shaped connector with 25 pins. A DB-25 port on a computer that has pins instead of holes is a serial port.

DB-9 (9-pin D shell connector) A D-shaped connector with nine pins. The DB-9 port on a computer is known as the serial port.

DC voltage Direct current voltages supplied to electrical components. Power supplies convert AC to DC.

DDoS (distributed denial of service) A DoS attack against a system from multiple attackers.

DDR RAM (double data-rate random access memory) A shortened acronym for DDR SDRAM.

DDR SDRAM (double data-rate synchronous dynamic random access memory) An improvement over SDRAM that doubles the clock rate by using both the leading and trailing edge of the clock. DDR2 and DDR3 are upgrades to DDR.

default gateway The default path out of a network for TCP/IP traffic. It is the IP address of a router's interface card on the same network as a client.

defrag A command-line tool used to defragment a hard drive. It works like Disk Defragmenter.

degaussing tool A tool used to sanitize media. Degaussing tools have strong magnetic fields that erase data and destroy hard drives.

del Command used to delete files in a directory.

developing The step in the seven-step laser imaging process during which the toner is applied to the imaging drum. See also processing, charging, exposing, transferring, fusing and cleaning.

device driver Software that provides instructions for an operating system to use a piece of hardware.

Device Manager A tool used to manage devices and device drivers. You can use it to disable devices and to update, uninstall, and roll back drivers.

DHCP (dynamic host configuration protocol) A protocol used to dynamically assign IP addresses and other TCP/IP configuration information.

digital Signals that are transmitted as 1s and 0s. In contrast, analog data is transmitted with a sine wave.

DIMM (dual inline memory module) A circuit card that holds RAM. Laptops use SODIMMs instead.

DIN (Deutsche Industrie Norm) The German Institute for Standardization. DIN standardized the mini-DIN connections.

DIP (dual in-line package) An integrated circuit (IC) chip. DIP chips can be plugged into DIP sockets or soldered onto a board.

dir Command used to view a listing of files in the current directory.

Direct Media Interface (DMI) bus The connection between the CPU and newer chipsets instead of the front side bus.

directory MS-DOS–based name of a folder. In Windows Explorer, folders are called folders, but at the command prompt, they are called directories.

Disk Cleanup A Windows utility that can identify and remove unneeded files on a system.

Disk Defragmenter A GUI tool used to analyze and defragment hard drives.

Disk Management A GUI tool used to manage disks and volumes. Some common tasks include creating, formatting, resizing, and deleting volumes. Diskpart is a command-line equivalent.

disk thrashing Activity indicating that a hard drive is constantly busy. You can hear the actuator constantly seeking and see the LED constantly blinking. It can be due to a fragmented hard drive or not enough memory.

diskpart A command-line tool that can do many of the same tasks as the Disk Management GUI.

DisplayPort A display interface developed by VESA. The connector is rectangular with a cut-off corner.

DLL (dynamic link library) A file that includes reusable code within Windows-based systems.

DLP (Digital Light Processing) A technology used in some TVs and projectors. It is a trademark owned by Texas Instruments.

DLT (Digital Linear Tape) A self-contained tape cartridge used for backups. DLT can transfer data as fast as 60 MB/s, and 800-GB cartridges are available. It is being replaced by LTO.

DMA (direct memory access) Data transfers between memory and a device without using the CPU.

DMZ (demilitarized zone) A buffer zone used to protect systems that are accessible on the Internet without putting the system directly on the Internet.

DNS (Domain Name System) Used to map computer names to IP addresses. Systems query DNS with a name, and it responds with the IP address. DNS resolves host names. In comparison, WINS resolves NetBIOS names.

docking station A small case into which a laptop can be plugged. It extends the capabilities of the laptop.

domain A network with centralized authentication. In Windows, a domain includes a domain controller. The domain controller hosts Active Directory, and users have a single account they can use to log on to the domain.

DoS (denial of service) An attack against a system by a single attacker designed to disrupt service provided by the system. Compare with DDoS.

double pumping A method used to double the clock rate by using both the leading edge and trailing edge of a clock. DDR RAM types and most CPU clocks use double pumping.

double-sided DIMM Also known as double rank. Data on the DIMM is divided into two groups or ranks, and only one rank can be accessed at a time. DIMMs with chips on both sides can be single, dual, or quad rank. Compare to single-sided DIMM.

dpi (dots per inch) A printing term that identifies the resolution or clarity of the output. Higher numbers provide a higher resolution and a better-quality printout.

DRAM (dynamic random access memory) A type of RAM that uses capacitors to hold data. It is cheaper than SRAM but not as fast because the capacitors need to be refreshed regularly. Compare to static RAM and synchronous dynamic RAM.

DSL (digital subscriber line) A connection through a public switched telephone network (PSTN) to connect to the Internet. Asymmetric DSL (ADSL) uses different speeds for uploads and downloads. Symmetric DSL (SDSL) uses the same speed for uploads and downloads.

dual channel DRAM RAM that is accessed in two separate 64-bit channels. It can transfer twice as much data as single channel. Compare to single channel and triple channel.

dual-boot A system that can boot into more than one operating system. For example, a computer that can boot into Windows XP and Windows 7 is a dual-boot system.

dual-layer DVD A DVD with 8.5 GB of storage rather than the 4.7 GB of standard DVDs. A double-sided dual-layer DVD holds 8.5 GB on each side, for a total of 17 GB.

duplexing assembly A component in printers that allows them to print on both sides of a sheet of paper.

DVD (digital video disc or digital versatile disc) An optical disc standard introduced after CDs. A DVD can hold 4.7 GB of data.

DVD-R (digital video disc-recordable) A DVD that can be written to once. This is sometimes referred to as a WORM disc.

DVD-RAM (digital video disc-random access memory) An alternative to DVD-RW. It is not widely used.

DVD-ROM (digital video disc read-only media or read-only memory) DVDs released by manufacturers that have data on them. Data can be read from these discs, but it is not possible to write to them.

DVD-RW (digital video disc-rewritable) A DVD that can be written to multiple times.

DVI (digital visual interface) An interface used with displays. It includes DVI-A for analog displays, DVI-D for digital, and DVI-I integrated for both analog and digital.

dxdiag The command that starts the DirectX Diagnostic Tool. It can diagnose problems with video and sound devices.

dynamic disk A special type of disk supported in Windows-based systems. Dynamic disks can be used to create striped, mirrored, and spanned volumes. The alternative is basic disks.

E

ECC (error correction code) A method used to detect and correct memory errors on high-end servers. Desktop systems typically use non-ECC RAM.

ECP (extended capabilities port) An interface used with older printers via the parallel port. It supports two-way data transfers and is quicker than the plain parallel port.

EEPROM (electrically erasable programmable read-only memory) A chip on the motherboard used to store BIOS on older systems. It can be erased and reprogrammed with a software program by using a process commonly called flashing. Most current systems store BIOS on a type of flash memory similar to what is used with a thumb drive. See ROM, PROM, and EPROM.

EFS (encrypting file system) Part of NTFS used to scramble data. Encryption is the process of converting plain text data into cipher text data so that it cannot be read.

EIDE (enhanced integrated drive electronics) An enhancement of the IDE standard. It is commonly referred to as PATA.

EMI (electromagnetic interference) Interference from magnetic fields, such as from power cables, motors, and magnets.

EMP (electromagnetic pulse) A burst of electromagnetic radiation from an explosion. An EMP pulse can damage electronic equipment.

EPP (enhanced parallel port) An interface used with older printers via the parallel port. It is similar to ECP except that it supports direct memory access.

EPROM (erasable programmable read-only memory) PROM that can be erased. It has a small window, and data can be erased by shining ultraviolet light into the window. The program is typically rewritten by using specialized hardware. See ROM, PROM, and EEPROM.

eSATA (external serial ATA) An external connection for SATA devices. eSATA cables have additional shielding and can be as long as 2 meters.

eSATAp (external serial ATA powered) A combination of an eSATA port and a USB port that can provide power to external SATA devices. It requires a special 5-V cable to carry 5 V of power or a special 12-V cable to carry 5 V and 12 V.

ESD (electrostatic discharge) Static electricity that can build up and discharge causing damage to electronic components. Antistatic devices help prevent ESD damage.

Ethernet Group of specifications for most wired networks in use today. It includes specifications for cables, communication devices, and how data is transferred.

EVDO (evolution data optimized or evolution data only) A wireless standard used with broadband Internet access.

Event Viewer One of the tools in the Administrative Tools group. It provides access to view Windows logs, such as the Application log, the Security log, and the System log.

EVGA (extended video graphics adapter/array) A display device resolution of 1024 × 768.

expansion card A circuit card that can be installed in an available expansion slot to add additional capabilities to a system. Common expansion cards use PCIe.

Explorer Also known as Windows Explorer, used for browsing through files and folders on Windows-based systems. It is not the same as Internet Explorer.

exposing The step in the seven-step laser imaging process where the laser writes the image onto the imaging drum. See also processing, charging, developing, transferring, fusing, and cleaning.

ExpressCard An expansion card used in laptop computers. Cards come in two versions: ExpressCard/34 and ExpressCard/54. Both can plug into the same type of ExpressCard slot.

extended partition A partition type on basic MBR disks that supports multiple logical drives. Only one extended partition can be used on a disk. Compare to primary partition.

F

FAT (File Allocation Table) A basic file system used to format disks. FAT16 (commonly called just FAT) and FAT32 are the two common versions. NTFS is recommended instead of FAT for most implementations due to better performance and security.

F-connector A connector used with RG-6 coaxial cable. It is commonly found on TV cable coming from a cable company.

FDD (floppy disk drive) A small disk drive that accepts 3.5-inch floppy disks. They are rarely used today.

fdisk An old program used to partition a disk from the command prompt prior to installing an operating system.

feeder An alternative to a paper tray used in printers. Feeders are normally on top of a printer.

fiber Cable type used in Ethernet networks. Data travels as light pulses along the cable. Common connectors are SC, LC, and ST.

FireWire A standard used for high-speed serial bus transfers. FireWire 400 supports speeds of up to 400 Mbps, and FireWire 800 supports speeds of up to 800 Mbps.

firmware Software that is written into a hardware device. BIOS is considered firmware.

first response Within IT, refers to actions taken by the first person that observes prohibited content or activity.

Three important steps include identifying the incident, reporting the incident, and preserving data or devices from the incident.

fixboot A command available in the Windows XP Recovery Console to fix a boot sector.

fixmbr A command available in the Windows XP Recovery Console to fix the master boot record.

flashing Process of upgrading BIOS.

Fn key (Function key) A key used on laptop computers to provide additional uses for traditional function keys.

Folder Options A Control Panel applet used to control views in Windows Explorer.

format Process of preparing a disk for use. Disks are formatted with a file system such as FAT32 or NTFS. Formatting an existing disk deletes the data on the disk.

FPM (fast page-mode) An early asynchronous version of DRAM. It has been replaced with synchronous versions of DRAM.

FQDN (fully qualified domain name) A combination of a host name and a domain name. FQDNs are commonly used to address servers on the Internet.

FRU (field replaceable unit) Any component that can be replaced by a technician without returning it to a manufacturer.

FSB (front side bus) The connection between the CPU and the supporting chipset. Newer chipsets use a Direct Media Interface (DMI). Compare to back side bus.

FTP (File Transfer Protocol) Used to upload and download files to and from FTP servers. It uses port 21 and sometimes port 20. It can be encrypted with SSH.

full-duplex Data transmission mode specifying that data can be sent or received at the same time. Compare to simplex and half-duplex.

function keys Keys labeled F1 through F12 that provide shortcuts within applications. For example, F1 opens Help.

fuser assembly The component used in laser printers that melts the toner onto the paper.

fusing The step in the seven-step laser imaging process where the toner is melted onto the paper. See also processing, charging, exposing, developing, transferring, and cleaning.

G

gadgets Mini-programs that can run on the desktop of Windows 7 or in a sidebar in Windows Vista.

game pad A joystick replacement used with many games. It includes at least one analog stick to simulate a joystick and multiple buttons.

Gb (gigabit) About 1 billion bits; specifically, 1,073,741,824 bits.

GB (gigabyte) About 1 billion bytes; specifically, 1,073,741,824 bytes.

GDI (graphics device interface) A video card. The interface is used to send graphics to a display monitor.

geotracking Some mobile devices record the location of the device at different times and store the information in a file on the device. Anyone who can read this file can track past locations of the device (and by implication, the owner).

GHz (gigahertz) Frequency speed commonly referring to a computer clock. One hertz (Hz) indicates that a signal can complete one cycle a second. One GHz indicates that it can complete 1 billion cycles a second.

Globally Unique Identifier (GUID) Partition Table (GPT) A type of disk that supports disks larger than 2 TB. Windows 7 supports up to 128 partitions on a GPT disk. Compare to MBR.

GPS (Global Positioning System) A feature on many mobile devices that identifies the exact location of the device. Many applications use GPS, and it can be used to locate a lost device.

GPU (graphics processing unit) A processor on a video card used to create graphics. It takes the load off the CPU.

GSM (Global System for Mobile Communications) A standard used for cellular phones. GSM is incorporating 4G standards.

GUI (graphical user interface) An interface that allows users to interact by pointing and clicking rather than by using text commands.

gyroscope A chip in many mobile devices used to detect the orientation of the device and change the display. It is often combined with an accelerometer chip.

H

HAL (hardware abstraction layer) Part of the operating system that hides hardware differences from other parts of the operating system.

half-duplex Data transmission mode specifying that data can be sent or received, but not at the same time. Compare to simplex and full-duplex.

HAV (Hardware Assisted Virtualization) A feature included with most CPUs to support virtualization on a system. It often has to be enabled in the BIOS.

HCL (hardware compatibility list) A list of hardware devices that have been verified to work with different versions of Windows. It is currently known as the Windows Logo'd Products List (LPL).

HDD (hard disk drive) The most common type of hard drive in computers. It includes spinning platters and read/write heads.

HDMI (high definition media interface) A digital interface used with display monitors. It includes video and 8-channel audio.

heat sink A specially designed piece of metal that draws heat away from chips, such as the CPU. Heat sinks typically have flared fins, allowing more air through.

hexadecimal A numbering system using a base of 16. Valid characters are the numbers 0 through 9 and the letters A through F. A hexadecimal number can be expressed with four binary numbers.

hibernate A power-saving state. Data from RAM is written to the hard disk, and the system is turned off.

homegroup A Windows 7 feature that allows users to easily share libraries in small networks. One user creates the homegroup and others can join it.

host name A type of computer name used on networks and on the Internet. DNS resolves host names to IP addresses.

hot-swappable Indicates the device can be removed without powering a system down. For example, devices connected with USB, FireWire, SATA, and eSATA connections are hot-swappable.

HTML (hypertext markup language) A language used to format webpages. HTML pages are retrieved from web servers by using HTTP or HTTPS.

HTPC (home theater personal computer) A PC configured to work as a digital video recorder (DVR) for television, audio player for music, and video player for movies. It is often contained in a special form factor case also called HTPC.

HTTP (Hypertext Transfer Protocol) The primary protocol used to transfer data over the web. It uses port 80.

HTTPS (Hypertext Transfer Protocol Secure) An encrypted version of HTTP. It uses port 443.

hub A basic network device used to connect computers together. Data going into any port goes out all ports. Many organizations replace hubs with switches.

hybrid topology A logical network topology using any two of the other types of topologies.

hyperthreading Technology (HT) An Intel technology that allows each core within a CPU to process two threads at a time. It is often combined with multiple CPUs.

HyperTransport A technology used by AMD to increase the speed of the front side bus.

hypervisor Associated with virtualization, the software running on the physical host, acting as the virtual machine manager for the guest virtual machines.

I

I/O (input/output) The process of providing an input and getting an output. Many computer components provide I/O services.

ICMP (internet control message protocol) A protocol used for diagnostics and troubleshooting. Ping and tracert commands use ICMP. ICMP traffic is often blocked by firewalls.

ICR (intelligent character recognition) An advanced implementation of OCR that can read handwriting.

IDE (integrated drive electronics) An early implementation of hard drive interfaces that moved drive controller electronics onto the drive. It was later upgraded to EIDE, standardized as ATA, and commonly referred to as PATA.

IDS (Intrusion Detection System) A system designed to monitor traffic and detect attacks.

IEEE (Institute of Electrical and Electronics Engineers) Pronounced as "I triple E." A standards organization that has defined a wide assortment of standards for networks.

IEEE 1394a Also known as FireWire 400. See FireWire.

IEEE 1394b Also known as FireWire 800. See FireWire.

IIS (Internet Information Services) A web server service included in Microsoft server products.

image A file that contains a snapshot of all the files of a system. The image can be applied to a new computer with all of the same settings.

imaging drum A round cylinder covered with photo-sensitive material and used in laser printers.

IMAP (Internet Message Access Protocol) Used with email servers. It allows users to organize email in folders on the server and to search the email. IMAP uses port 143.

IMAPS (Internet Message Access Protocol Secure) An encrypted version of IMAP. It can be encrypted with SSL or TLS and uses port 993 by default.

impact printer A printer that prints by pushing print head pins against an ink ribbon pressing ink onto paper. It is commonly used to print multipart forms.

infrastructure mode A wireless network created with a WAP or wireless router. In contrast, in ad-hoc mode devices connect to each other without a WAP or wireless router.

inkjet printer A color printer popular with home users that prints by injecting ink onto a piece of paper.

Integrated graphics processing unit (GPU) Indicates that the GPU is included either within the chipset or within the CPU. An integrated GPU is not as powerful as a dedicated graphics card.

Intel One of the two primary manufacturers of CPUs. AMD is the other.

Internet Explorer A web browser built into Windows. It is not the same as Windows Explorer, which is used for browsing through files and folders.

Internet Options A Control Panel applet used to manipulate settings for Internet Explorer.

Internet Protocol security (IPsec) An encryption protocol used on internal networks and on the Internet. It is often used in virtual private network (VPN) tunnels.

inverter Used in laptop computers with LCD displays. It converts DC voltage to AC voltage for the CCFL backlight.

iOS The primary operating system used on Apple-based mobile devices. It is a closed source, vendor-specific operating system. Apple doesn't license its use on any devices other than Apple products. Users of iOS-based devices can purchase and download applications from Apple's App Store.

IP (internet protocol) A protocol in the TCP/IP suite. It defines how packets are sent across a network.

IP address A numerical address assigned to a computer. An IPv4 address uses 32 bits and is expressed in dotted decimal format, such as 192.168.1.1. An IPv6 address uses 128 bits and is expressed in eight groups of hexadecimal characters, such as FC00:0000:0000:0076:0000:042A:B95F:77F5.

ipconfig A command-line program used to view IP configuration information on a system. It includes multiple switches, including the /release and /renew switches used to release and renew information from a DHCP server.

IR (infrared) A line-of-sight wireless standard. It allows devices to transmit and receive data using LEDs and IR sensors, similarly to how TV remote controllers work.

IrDA (Infrared Data Association) An organization that develops and maintains IR standards.

IRQ (interrupt request) A number assigned to a device that allows it to get the attention of the CPU. IRQs are automatically assigned with plug and play.

ISA (industry standard architecture) An older expansion card standard using 8 bits or 16 bits. It was replaced with Extended ISA (EISA) and then the different PCI standards. It is not used in current systems.

ISDN (integrated services digital network) A special type of dial-up connection to the Internet that uses a telephone network. ISDN uses terminal adapters in place of modems.

ISO (International Organization for Standardization) An international standards organization. According to the ISO, ISO is not an acronym but instead is based on the Greek word *isos*, meaning equal.

ISP (Internet service provider) A company that provides Internet access to businesses and home users.

J

JBOD (just a bunch of disks or just a bunch of drives) Refers to multiple disks operating independently. In some usages, it indicates a spanned volume.

K

Kb (kilobit) About 1,000 bits; specifically, 1,024 bits.

KB (kilobyte) About 1,000 bytes; specifically, 1,024 bytes.

key fob An authentication device. Key fobs display a number that is synchronized with an authentica-

tion server. Users can enter the number as a part of an authentication process.

kill Unix-based command used to terminate a process.

KVM (keyboard video mouse) A switch that allows multiple computers to share a single keyboard, video display, and monitor.

L

L1 cache Cache used by a CPU for short-term storage of data and instructions. It is the fastest and closest to the CPU.

L2 cache Cache used by a CPU for short-term storage of data. It is used second after L1 cache and is slower than L1.

L3 cache Cache used by a CPU for short-term storage of data. It isn't always used, but when it is available, it is used after L1 and L2 cache.

LAN (local area network) A group of computers and other devices connected together. Users can share resources when connected in a LAN.

land grid array (LGA) A specific type of CPU socket where the socket has pins instead of holes. The chip also has small pins created as bumps or pads. Compare to PGA.

laptop A portable computer. Very small laptops are often called netbooks. High-performance laptops have as much power as a desktop computer.

laser printer A popular printer for businesses. It uses a seven-step imaging process and creates high quality outputs.

LBA (logical block addressing) A scheme used for specifying locations of blocks on a hard disk.

LC (Lucent connector) Connector used with fiber cables. It was developed by Lucent Technologies and is a miniaturized version of the SC connector.

LCD (liquid crystal display) A flat panel display. It is thinner and lighter than a CRT monitor and consumes significantly less power.

LDAP (lightweight directory access protocol) Used to access directory services databases, such as Active Directory Domain Services used in a Microsoft domain.

least privilege Security principle that restricts access. Users are granted rights and permissions for what they need to perform their job but no more.

LED (light emitting diode) A small electrical component that emits light. LEDs are commonly used on computers as indicators. For example, the power LED lights up when the computer is turned on.

li-ion (lithium-ion) A battery type commonly used in laptops.

loadstate One of the two commands included with the User State Migration Tool (USMT). Loadstate loads files and settings onto a new installation. Scanstate must be run first to capture the information from the original installation.

LoJack A feature available on some laptops that can be enabled in the BIOS. It uses a transceiver that helps locate a stolen laptop similar to the way LoJack is used to recover stolen automobiles.

loopback plug A connector that loops output pins back to input pins. RJ-45 loopback plugs can help test NICs that have RJ-45 jacks.

loopback address A predefined address used to test the functionality of TCP/IP. The IPv4 loopback address is 127.0.0.1. The IPv6 loopback address is ::1.

LPD/LPR (line printer daemon/line printer remote) A UNIX-based protocol used to print to printers over a network.

LTO (Linear Tape-Open) A self-contained tape cartridge used for backups. LTO-5 can transfer data at 140 MB/s, and cartridges can hold as much as 1.5 TB. LTO is replacing DLT.

LVD (low voltage differential) Sometimes called LVD signaling (LVDS), a standard that transmits data as the difference in voltages between two wires in a pair. It is used by SATA, FireWire, AMDs HyperTransport, and PCIe.

M

MAC (mandatory access control) An access control model that uses labels to determine access. NTFS uses DAC instead of MAC.

malware Malicious software that includes viruses, Trojan horses, worms, and more.

MAN (metropolitan area network) Type of network that connects multiple networks together over a large metropolitan area. Worldwide Interoperability for Microwave Access (WiMAX) is used for many MANs.

MAPI (messaging application programming interface) An interface used by application developers to create programs that can send and receive email.

Master Boot Record (MBR) A type of disk that supports disks as large as 2 TB and up to four partitions. Compare to Globally Unique Identifier (GUID) Partition Table (GPT).

master On PATA drives, the IDE drive that is designated as the first device. Compare to slave.

MAU (multistation access unit) A device used in ring networks. All devices communicate through the MAU but in a logical ring.

Mb (megabit) About 1 million bits; specifically, 1,048,576 bits.

MB (megabyte) About 1 million bytes; specifically, 1,048,576 bytes.

MBR (master boot record) An area on a hard disk. It includes code to locate the active partition and to load boot sector code.

MBSA (Microsoft Baseline Security Analyzer) A tool available as a free download that can check one or more systems for potential security issues.

md Command used to make a directory.

mesh topology A logical network topology where each device is connected to all other devices in the network.

MFD (multifunction device) Any device that performs more than one function. Multifunction printers that can print, scan, copy, and fax are common MFDs.

MFP (multifunction product) See MFD.

MHz (megahertz) Frequency speed commonly referring to a computer clock. One hertz (Hz) indicates that a signal can complete one cycle a second. One MHz indicates that it can complete 1 million cycles per second.

micro-SD The smallest version of SD flash card memory used in cameras and digital recorders.

MIDI (musical instrument digital interface) connector The DB-15 connection found on older sound cards for MIDI-enabled devices or joysticks. MIDI devices can play music by using .mid files, but they commonly connect with USB ports today.

MIME (multipurpose internet mail extension) The standard format used to send email messages.

MIMO (multiple-input multiple-output) Technology used by 802.11n wireless devices. They use multiple antennas to transmit and receive resulting in higher speeds.

Mini-DIN A round connection used for many devices. The PS/2 ports are 6-pin mini-DIN ports. Other mini-DIN ports can have 3–9 pins.

mini-SD A smaller version of SD flash card memory used in cameras and digital recorders. It is larger than micro-SD.

mirrored volume See RAID-1.

MMC (Microsoft Management Console) An empty console that can be populated with snap-ins to manage Windows.

MMX (multimedia extensions) An instruction set used with Intel processors. AMD has a similar instruction set named 3DNow!.

modem A modulator-demodulator that converts analog signals to digital signals and digital signals to analog signals. Modems can provide access to the Internet

via a phone line. Special modems are used to provide access to the Internet by cable TV companies.

Molex A common power connector included with internal power supplies. It provides 5 V and 12 VDC to different devices, such as Parallel Advanced Technology Attachment (PATA) disk drives.

mp3 (Moving Picture Experts Group Layer 3 Audio) A file extension used for audio files.

mp4 (Moving Picture Experts Group Layer 4) A file extension used for files that include digital video with audio.

MPEG (Moving Picture Experts Group) A group that defines standards for audio and video compression.

msconfig (Microsoft configuration) The command used to open the System Configuration tool. This can be used to view and manipulate what services and applications start automatically.

MSDS (Material Safety Data Sheet) A document that identifies the contents, characteristics, and first aid responses for different materials used in a work space.

msinfo32 Command to start the System Information tool. Can be used to identify BIOS version, amount of RAM installed, processor type and speed, and much more.

mstsc A command-line program, short for Microsoft Terminal Services Connection. It is used to open Remote Desktop Connection.

MUI (multilingual user interface) A system that can display information in different languages. When additional language files are installed, Windows can display wizards, dialog boxes, menus, and help topics in different languages.

multiboot Similar to dual-boot but includes systems that can boot to more than two operating systems.

multimeter A meter that can take different types of measurements. Multimeters are commonly used to measure voltages provided by a power supply.

multi-mode fiber (MMF) A fiber optic cable used to transmit multiple signals at the same time. It cannot transmit signals as far as SMF can.

multitouch A feature on tablets that senses when a user touches more than one location at a time. It is commonly used for pinch and spread gestures.

N

NAC (network access control) A group of technologies used to inspect network clients prior to granting network access.

NAS (network attached storage) A dedicated computer system used to provide disk storage on a network. It's often a small device that is easy to plug in and use.

NAT (Network Address Translation) A protocol that translates private IP addresses to public and public IP addresses to private. It allows multiple internal clients to access the Internet with a single public IP address.

native resolution The resolution that should be used with LCD monitors. Different resolutions distort the display.

nbtstat A command-line tool related to NetBIOS over TCP/IP Statistics. It works with NetBIOS names instead of host names.

net A command-line command. It's used for many purposes, including mapping drives with the net use command.

NetBIOS (Network Basic Input/Output System) name A type of computer name used on internal networks. WINS servers resolve NetBIOS names to IP addresses.

netstat A command-line program used to view network statistics and view inbound and outbound connections.

NIC (network interface card) Used to provide connectivity with a network. PCs commonly have built-in NICs that use an RJ-45 connector and twisted-pair cable.

NiCd (nickel cadmium) A battery type used in older laptops.

NiMH (nickel metal hydride) A battery type used in older laptops.

NLX (New Low-profile Extended) A motherboard form factor used by several vendors in low-profile cases. It has been superseded by Micro-ATX and Mini-ITX form factors.

NNTP (network news transfer protocol) Used to transmit newsgroup messages between systems. Newsgroups have largely been replaced by web-based forums, so NNTP is not used often.

north bridge Part of the CPU chipset. It provides the primary interface for high-speed devices such as the CPU, RAM, and a dedicated graphics slot and is sometimes called the memory controller hub (MCH). North bridge functions have been taken over by the CPU on newer CPUs. Compare to south bridge.

Notepad A basic text editor. You can use it to create and modify batch files.

nslookup A command-line program used to verify the existence of records on a DNS server. It can also verify whether a DNS server can resolve a name to an IP address.

NTFS (New Technology File System) A file system used on Windows-based systems. It is more efficient and provides much more security than do FAT-based file systems.

NTLDR (new technology loader) A file used in the boot process for Windows XP. NTLDR uses Boot.ini to load Windows.

NTP (Network Time Protocol) Used to synchronize computer clocks over the Internet.

O

OCR (optical character recognition) Software that can identify characters from documents. Scanners often include OCR software that can scan a document and convert contents to editable text.

OEM (original equipment manufacturer) Any company that resells another company's product using its own name and branding. For example, Dell uses motherboards it has purchased from Intel to build computers that Dell sells. These are marketed as Dell computers, and Dell is the OEM.

offline files A feature in Windows-based systems that provides access to shared files when a user is disconnected from a network. Offline files are cached on a user's system.

OLED (Organic Light Emitting Diode) A newer type of flat panel display that can emit light without a backlight.

open source Software code that is freely available. The Android operating system is open source.

operating system Software that interacts with the hardware and hosts applications. Windows is the most common operating system in use on desktops.

P

paging file A file stored on the hard drive that is used as virtual memory.

PAN (personal area network) A network around a single person. Bluetooth is commonly used to connect mobile devices such as smartphones and ear pieces in a PAN.

parallel Refers to sending data as multiple bits at the same time. Before USB became popular, parallel ports were faster than serial ports.

parity A method used to detect errors. RAM comes in parity and non-parity versions, but desktop systems rarely use parity RAM. Parity is also used in some RAID configurations.

partition A usable portion of a disk. A single physical disk can be a single partition or divided into multiple partitions. A partition is the same as a volume.

PATA (parallel advanced technology attachment) The common name for IDE/EIDE drives. It is being replaced by SATA.

patch management Practices and procedures used to keep systems up to date with current patches.

PC (personal computer) Any computer used by an individual.

PCI (peripheral component interconnect) An expansion card standard. It has largely been replaced by PCIe but is still used in some systems today.

PCIe (peripheral component interconnect express) The primary expansion card standard used in systems today. It uses multiple lanes to transfer data and is identified by how many lanes it supports. A PCIe card can have 1, 2, 4, 8, 16, or 32 lanes (designated as x1, x2, x4, x8, x16, and x32).

PCI-x (peripheral component interconnect extended) An early enhancement for PCI primarily used on servers. Most systems use PCIe instead. PCIe and PCI-x are sometimes confused, but there are significant differences between the two.

PCL (printer control language, or printer command language) A protocol used to send print jobs to a printer.

PCMCIA (Personal Computer Memory Card International Association) A standardization organization that defines standards for laptop computers. It defined the older PC Card standard and the newer ExpressCard standard.

PDA (personal data assistant) A handheld device that can include contact lists, an address book, calendar, appointment lists, and more. Many mobile devices include PDA features.

Performance Monitor A Control Panel applet used to measure system performance.

peripheral Any device that you connect to a computer. Devices can be connected using existing ports, or expansion cards can be added to provide the connectivity.

permissions The ability to access a resource. For example, a user can be given Read permission on a file. Compare to rights and privileges.

PGA (pin grid array) A specific type of CPU socket in which the socket has holes and the CPU has pins. Compare to LGA.

phishing Spam sent by attackers in an attempt to get users to click a link or provide personal information.

photosensitive surface A surface that reacts to light. A laser printer imaging drum uses a photosensitive surface.

pickup rollers Rollers in a printer used to pick up paper from a paper tray. They are used with separator pads.

PII (Personally Identifiable Information) Information that can be used to identify an individual. PII should be protected as sensitive data.

PIN (personal identification number) A number used for authentication. It is often combined with another method, such as with a smart card.

ping A command-line program that can check network connectivity with other systems and their response times.

pixel A pixel element. Display monitors display a pixel by using a combination of red, green, and blue dots.

PKI (public key infrastructure) A group of technologies used to create, manage, and distribute certificates. Certificates are used for several cryptographic methods, including encryption and authentication.

platter Used in hard disk drives. They are circular and covered in ferromagnetic material used to hold data. Hard drives typically have multiple platters.

plenum Area between floors, walls, and ceilings in buildings where air is forced through for heating and cooling. Cable run through plenums must be fire-resistant and rated as plenum-safe. Non-plenum-safe cables emit toxic fumes.

PnP (plug and play) A feature in Windows that automatically installs and configures device drivers.

POP3 (Post Office Protocol version 3) Used to receive email from email servers. POP3 uses port 110.

POP3S (Post Office Protocol version 3 Secure) An encrypted version of POP3. It can be encrypted with SSL or TLS and uses port 995 by default.

port replicator A connection plugged into a laptop to provide additional ports. Compare to docking station.

PoS (Point of Sale) The location where a purchase is completed. Thermal printers are often used as POS locations to create receipts.

POST (power-on self test) A basic test routine included in the BIOS that is run when the computer first starts. Failures are indicated by displayed errors and specific beep codes.

POST card An expansion card that can be used to view POST cards as a system boots. They are available in PCI and PCIe versions and include an LED display to show the boot progress.

POTS (plain old telephone service) A standard telephone service available in most parts of the world. Users can use POTS and a modem for Internet access.

power plans A feature in Windows Vista and Windows 7 that has configured power saving settings for hardware. The balanced plan is used for laptops when plugged in to a power source, and the power saver plan is used when laptops run on battery power.

power supply tester A testing device used to measure power supply voltages for power supplies that are not plugged into a motherboard.

PPM (pages per minute) A printing term that identifies the speed of a printer. Faster printers have a higher PPM.

PPP (point-to-point protocol) A protocol often used when a system connects to the Internet via an ISP.

PPTP (point-to-point tunneling protocol) A tunneling protocol used with VPNs.

previous versions Part of System Protection that keeps copies (previous versions) of user data. It's also called shadow copy.

PRI (primary rate interface) PRI is associated with ISDN and includes 23 64-Kbps data channels and one 16-Kbps signal channel. In North America, it's called a T1 line.

primary partition A partition type used on disks. Basic MBR disks support up to four primary partitions, or three primary partitions and one extended partition.

private IP address An address assigned to a computer in a private network. Private IPv4 addresses are formally defined in the following ranges:

```
10.0.0.0–10.255.255.255
172.16.0.0–172.31.255.255
192.168.0.0–192.168.255.255
```

privileges A combination of rights and permissions.

processing The step in the seven-step laser imaging process during which the raster image is processed. See also charging, exposing, developing, transferring, fusing, and cleaning.

processor Typically refers to the central processing unit (CPU). However, graphics cards also have a processor called the graphics processing unit (GPU).

PROM (programmable read-only memory) Read-only memory that can be programmed. It is used for firmware, which is software code written into a hardware chip. See ROM, EPROM, and EEPROM.

PS/2 (personal system/2 connector) A mini-DIN connector. The green port is for the mouse, and the purple port is for the keyboard.

PSTN (public switched telephone network) The network of telephone communications companies.

PSU (power supply unit) An internal component within a computer case that converts AC voltage to DC voltages used by a computer.

public IP address Addresses assigned on the Internet. Compare this to private IP addresses.

punchdown tool A hardware tool used to attach cables to jacks or punchdown blocks. It is used to attach twisted-pair cable to the back of jacks and to punchdown blocks in wiring rooms.

PVC (permanent virtual circuit) A dedicated circuit link between two facilities. It is used with ATM networks.

PVC (polyvinyl chloride) A protective covering around cables, commonly called a *jacket*. PVC can give off toxic fumes if it burns, so it is not used in plenum spaces.

PXE (preboot execution environment) Refers to a client that can boot from a NIC. PXE-enabled clients include a NIC and BIOS that can be configured to boot from the NIC instead of a hard drive. It is often used to allow clients to download images.

Q

QoS (Quality of Service) A group of technologies used to control traffic on a network.

R

RAID (redundant array of independent—or inexpensive—disks) Storage method that combines multiple hard disks. RAID configurations include RAID-0, RAID-1, RAID-5, and RAID-10.

RAID-0 A RAID configuration of two or more disks combined as a single volume. Used for read and write enhancements but no fault tolerance. Also called a striped volume.

RAID-10 A RAID configuration of four or more disks. Also called a stripe of mirrors because it combines RAID-0 and RAID-1. It always has an even number of disks.

RAID-1 A RAID configuration of two disks created for fault tolerance. Data written to one disk is also written to the other. Also called a mirrored volume.

RAID-5 A RAID configuration of three or more disks. The equivalent of one drive holds parity data used for fault tolerance. Also called a striped volume with parity.

RAM (random access memory) Memory used in a computer for short-term storage of applications and data.

RAS (remote access service) Microsoft service used for connecting to other systems. It is used with Remote Assistance and with Remote Desktop Connection.

raster image processor (RIP) A processor on a laser printer used to create a raster image. The image is then transferred to the page as the printout.

raster image A combination of dots used to create a printout on a laser printer. It is created by a raster image processor.

RCA A type of single connection jack used with some audio and video. The Radio Corporation of America created it, but RCA is not an acronym.

rd Command used to remove or delete a directory.

RDP (Remote Desktop Protocol) Used in Microsoft networks to connect to remote systems. Remote Desktop Connection and Remote Assistance use RDP over port 3389.

RDRAM (rambus dynamic random access memory) A type of RAM that can be used instead of DDR SDRAM.

real-time clock A clock running on the motherboard that keeps track of the current time and date. It's powered by the motherboard battery (sometimes called the CMOS battery) when the system is turned off.

recovery console A command prompt–based environment used in Windows XP. It includes commands such as fixboot and fixmbr.

Recovery Environment A special command prompt environment available in Windows Vista–based and Windows 7–based systems. It includes access to bootrec commands that can fix boot problems.

recovery partition A partition added by a computer reseller on a disk drive. It is often invisible but can be used to return a system to the state it was in when it was sold.

refresh rate Identifies how many times the display is rewritten in a display monitor.

regedit/regedt32 Commands used to start the registry editor.

registry A database of settings used by Windows-based systems. It can be viewed and modified with the registry editor (regedit).

regsvr32 A file used to register or unregister DLLs.

remanence Data that remains on media, even after the data is supposedly deleted or overwritten. Sanitization methods are used eliminate any data remanence.

Remote Assistance A built-in service within Windows-based systems. It allows novices to request help. Helpers can connect remotely and show users how to accomplish tasks within Windows.

Remote Desktop Connection This is a Microsoft application used to connect to remote systems. You can start it with the mstsc command.

resolution Describes the width and height of a display in pixels. Higher resolution results in a crisper display.

restore point Part of System Protection. It can be used to revert a system to a previous state.

retinal scan A strong method of biometric authentication.

RF (radio frequency) Refers to signals transmitted over the air without wires.

RFI (radio frequency interference) Interference caused from radio transmissions, such as from cordless phones and microwaves.

RG-59 A coaxial cable that uses BNC connectors. It is used for analog data and can be used between a TV and DVD player.

RG-6 A coaxial cable that uses F-type screw-on connectors. It is used for digital data, such as from a cable TV company.

RGB (red green blue) Three separate analog signals used for some video displays.

right The ability to perform an action. For example, a user can be given the right to change the computer time. Compare to permissions and privileges.

RIMM (rambus inline memory module) The circuit card used to hold RDRAM instead of a DIMM.

ring topology A logical network topology where devices are connected in a logical circle. Most ring topologies are token ring, using an electronic token to restrict communication.

RIP (routing information protocol) A protocol used by routers to share routing information.

RIS (remote installation service) An older service used to deploy images in Microsoft networks.

RISC (reduced instruction set computer) A computer or CPU that uses a small number of optimized instructions rather than a large number of specialized instructions.

RJ (registered jack) A standard used for cables and connectors. RJ-11 is used with phones, and RJ-45 is used with networks.

RJ-11 (registered jack function 11) Connector used for phone connections. It is smaller than the RJ-45 connector used in network cables.

RJ-45 (registered jack function 45) Connector used for twisted-pair cable in Ethernet networks. RJ-45 connectors are larger than RJ-11 connectors.

RMA (returned materials authorization) An authorization from a company to return a product for a refund or repair.

robocopy Robust file copy tool. It includes the capabilities of copy and xcopy but can also copy metadata such as permissions.

rogueware Fake antivirus software. Also called scareware or ransomware.

ROM (read-only memory) Memory that can only be read. It is used for firmware, which is software code written into a hardware chip. See PROM, EPROM, and EEPROM.

rootkit Malware that takes control of a system at the root or administrative level. It hides its activities from users and from antivirus software.

router A network device that connects networks together. A router is needed to get to other networks, including the Internet. In contrast, a switch connects individual computers together in a network.

rpm (revolutions per minute) Indicates the speed of hard drive platters. Common speeds are 5,400, 7,200, 10,000, and 15,000 rpm.

RS-232 or RS-232C (recommended standard 232) A standard used for serial communications. It isn't common with desktop computers but is still used in some situations.

S

shoulder surfing Practice of looking over someone's shoulders to gain information.

S.M.A.R.T. (self-monitoring, analysis, and reporting technology) A feature introduced in ATA-3 that allows drives to monitor reliability indicators. They can detect potential problems with a drive before an actual failure. It is used with both PATA and SATA.

SAN (storage area network) A network of storage devices used in large organizations. Smaller organizations use networked attached storage (NAS).

sanitization Erasing data from media. Overwriting a file or disk with repeating patterns of bits is one method of sanitizing a drive.

SAS (Serial Attached SCSI) A SCSI interface that uses a serial connection similar to SATA.

SATA (Serial Advanced Technology Attachment) A newer hard drive technology that is replacing PATA. SATA connectors have a distinctive L shape.

SATA1 The first generation of SATA. SATA1 has a bit speed of 1.5 Gbits/s or 150 MBps.

SATA2 The second generation of SATA. SATA2 has a bit speed of 3 Gbits/s or 300 MBps.

SATA3 The third generation of SATA. SATA3 has a bit speed of 6 Gbit/s or 600 MBps.

SC (square connector) Square connector used with fiber cables.

scanner A device that can scan documents and photos, creating a digital file. Multifunction printers often include scanning capabilities.

scanstate One of the two commands included with the User State Migration Tool (USMT). Scanstate is run on a computer to capture files and settings. Loadstate is later run on the new installation to load the information captured from scanstate.

SCP (secure copy or secure copy protection) Used to copy files between two systems in an encrypted format. SCP uses SSH.

SCSI (small computer system interface) A drive interface that can be used instead of PATA or SATA. It is rarely used in desktop systems.

SCSI ID (small computer system interface identifier) A number from 0 to 15 that identifies a SCSI device. SCSI ID 7 is the highest priority and usually assigned to the SCSI controller.

SD (Secure Digital) A common type of flash memory used with cameras, digital recorders, and other portable devices.

SDRAM (synchronous dynamic random access memory) An improvement over DRAM, using a clock to synchronize data transfers. All DDR RAM is SDRAM.

SEC (single edge connector) An older method used to mount CPUs. The CPU and cache were mounted on a circuit board and plugged into a CPU slot.

sector Portion of a track on a hard disk drive platter and also known as a track sector. Clusters are made up of multiple sectors.

secure desktop A feature of User Account Control (UAC) that dims the desktop and prevents any other activity until the user responds to a dialog box. The secure desktop prevents malicious software from bypassing UAC prompts.

Security log One of the logs in Event Viewer. It records security events, such as when users enter incorrect passwords.

separator pads Reverse turning rollers that work with the pickup roller to ensure that only one sheet of paper is picked up.

serial Refers to sending data 1 bit at a time. High-speed serial technologies such as USB and FireWire are common. Low-speed technologies such as RS-232 are not used as often.

Services A Control Panel applet used to manipulate services.

sfc The System File Checker command is used to verify and repair system files.

SFF (small form factor) A motherboard form factor used in small mobile devices. Pico-ITX is an example.

SFTP (Secure FTP) An encrypted version of FTP. It is encrypted with SSH over port 22.

SGRAM (synchronous graphics random access memory) A type of RAM used in some older video cards.

shadow copy A feature within Windows Vista and Windows 7 that creates copies of user data. It's also called previous versions.

share A folder that is available to other users over a network. Files within a share are accessible to users that have access to the share.

shutdown Command used to shut down, restart, or log off from a system.

Sidebar A feature in Windows Vista that allowed users to add gadgets, or mini programs, to their desktop. Sidebar is not included in in Windows 7, but users are still able to add gadgets to their desktop.

SIMM (single inline memory module) An older circuit card used to store RAM. It is replaced with DIMMs.

simplex Data transmission mode specifying that data is transferred in one direction only. Compare to half-duplex and full-duplex.

single channel DRAM RAM that is accessed in a single 64-bit channel. Compare to dual channel and triple channel.

single-sided DIMM Also known as single rank. A single-sided DIMM can access all RAM on the DIMM as a single group, or rank, of RAM. Single rank DIMMs almost always have chips on only one side of the DIMM. Compare to double-sided DIMM.

single-mode fiber (SMF) A fiber optic cable with a smaller core than multimode fiber. It is used to transmit one signal and transmit it farther than multimode fiber.

slave On PATA drives, the IDE drive that is designated as the second device. Compare to master.

sleep/suspend A power-saving state. RAM contents are retained, and the CPU runs very slowly. The system can return from a sleep or suspend state very quickly.

SLI (scalable link interface) A method used by NVIDEA to link multiple GPUs on two or more video cards.

smart card A credit-card sized card used for authentication. Users often use it with a PIN when authenticating.

SMB (Server Message Block) A protocol used to transfer files over a network. Unlike FTP, SMB is transparent to users.

SMTP (Simple Mail Transfer Protocol) SMTP is used to send email from clients to email servers. SMTP uses port 25.

SMTPS (Simple Mail Transfer Protocol Secure) An encrypted version of SMTP. It can be encrypted with TLS or SSL and uses port 465 by default.

SNMP (simple network management protocol) A protocol used to communicate with and manage network devices such as routers and switches.

social engineering Methods used to trick people into revealing information or taking actions that they wouldn't normally do.

socket The holder for a CPU on a motherboard. The two popular types of sockets are PGA and LGA.

SODIMM (small outline dual in-line memory module) A smaller version of a DIMM used in smaller devices such as laptop computers and some printers.

SOHO (small office/home office) A small business office with between 1 and 10 users.

south bridge Part of the CPU chipset. It provides the interface to low speed devices and is often called the I/O Controller Hub (ICH). Compare to north bridge.

SP (service pack) A collection of patches and updates released since the operating system was released. The first SP is referred to as SP1, the second as SP2, and so on.

spam Unwanted or unsolicited email.

spanned volume A single volume that includes more than a single physical disk. Spanned volumes do not provide any performance gains.

SPDIF (Sony-Philips digital interface format) A connection for specific sound systems. It uses a single connection to deliver all digital sound channels.

SPGA (staggered pin grid array) A type of CPU socket similar to PGA. Instead of using uniform rows, the pins are staged to fit more pins.

spike A quick, sharp increase in AC voltage which can damage unprotected equipment. Surge suppressors prevent spikes from damaging equipment and are included in most UPS systems.

spyware Software that installs itself or modifies a user's system without the user's knowledge or consent.

SRAM (static random access memory) A fast type of RAM typically used in CPU L1, L2, and L3 cache. Bits are stored by using switching circuitry, but this increases the cost. Compare to dynamic RAM and synchronous dynamic RAM.

SSD (solid state drive) A drive that functions as a traditional hard disk drive but has no moving parts.

SSH (Secure Shell) An encryption protocol. It is commonly used to encrypt traffic within a network, such as FTP transmissions. SSH uses port 22.

SSID (service set identifier) The name of an 802.11 wireless network. It can be up to 32 characters long and is case-sensitive.

SSL (secure sockets layer) An encryption protocol. It is commonly used to encrypt traffic on the Internet, such as HTTP (as HTTPS). It uses port 443 when encrypting HTTPS.

ST (straight tip) Round connector used with fiber cables.

standby A power saving state similar to sleep or suspend.

star topology A logical network topology where devices are connected with a central device such as a hub or a switch.

STP (Shielded twisted-pair cable) Helps protect against EMI and RFI. Compare to UTP.

straight-through cable A twisted-pair cable with wires attached to the same pins on both connectors. Compare to crossover cable.

striped volume See RAID-0.

surge suppressor A power strip with extra components that protects electronic systems from power surges or spikes.

surge A short-term increase in power. It can sometimes cause lights to shine brighter. A surge suppressor prevents damaging surges from reaching equipment.

SVGA (super video graphics array) A display device resolution of 800 × 600.

S-Video (Separate Video) A 4-pin DIN used for analog video. It transmits video over two channels.

switch A network device used to connect computers and other network devices together. Switches are more efficient than hubs. They can direct traffic to specific ports instead of sending data to all ports, as a hub does.

SXGA (super extended graphics array) A display device resolution of 1280 × 1024.

Sysprep A system preparation tool used before imaging a Windows computer. Sysprep removes unique settings on a computer, such as the security identifier (SID).

System Configuration A tool used to view and manipulate what services and applications start automatically. It can be opened with the msconfig command.

System Information A tool used to provide an overview of Windows. It is opened with the msinfo32 command.

System log One of the logs in Event Viewer. It records system events, such as when a service fails to start.

system partition The location of files used to boot the computer. This is usually the root of the C: drive on the computer. Compare this to the boot partition that holds the system files and is normally located at C:\Windows on Windows systems.

System Protection A feature in Windows that creates restore points. On Windows Vista and Windows 7, it also captures previous versions of user files.

System An applet within Control Panel. It provides a snapshot of the Windows configuration and includes links to tools to configure other settings.

T

T568A/T568B Two wiring standards used for twisted-pair cables. They identify specific pins for specific colored wires. Straight-through cables should use one standard or the other on both connectors for a cable.

tablet A small handheld computing device with a touch screen. The Apple iPad is an example. Tablets are not upgradable or serviceable by technicians in the field.

Task Manager A tool used to view and manipulate running tasks. It can be used to end unresponsive applications.

Task Scheduler A Control Panel applet used to schedule tasks.

tasklist Command used to list running tasks or processes on a system. It was previously called tlist.

TB (terabyte) About 1 trillion bytes; specifically, 1,099,511,627,776 bytes.

TCP (Transmission Control Protocol) A connection-oriented protocol. It uses a three-way handshake to establish a connection and provides reliable, guaranteed delivery of data.

TCP/IP (Transmission Control Protocol/Internet Protocol) A full suite of protocols used on the Internet and in internal networks.

Telnet A command prompt application you can use to connect to remote systems. It is sometimes used to check whether remote systems are operating on specific ports. Telnet uses port 23.

TFTP (Trivial File Transfer Protocol) A streamlined version of FTP. It uses port 69.

thermal paste A special compound used between CPUs and heat sinks. It fills in microscopic gaps and helps draw heat from the CPU into the heat sink where it is dissipated.

thermal printer A printer used for cash register receipts. It prints by heating a special type of paper.

thick client A computer system that includes typical applications needed by a user. Compare to a thin client.

thin client A computer system that has minimum applications installed. Instead, a user accesses the applications over a network. Compare to a thick client.

TKIP (Temporal Key Integrity Protocol) An encryption standard used with WPA. WPA with TKIP was an effective upgrade from WEP, but at this point, WPA2 with AES is recommended.

tlist Command used to list running tasks or processes on a system. It has been renamed to tasklist.

TLS (Transport Layer Security) The designated replacement for SSL. It can be used anywhere SSL is used.

toner An extremely fine powder that includes carbon and plastic. It is transferred to paper and melted into the paper by a fusing assembly in the laser imaging process.

topology Identifies how computers and other devices are logically connected. Primary topologies covered in A+ exam are: star, ring, bus, hybrid, mesh.

touch flow A feature on tablets that senses when a user moves a finger across a tablet screen. It is commonly used with drag, pan, and flick gestures.

touchpad A pad used on laptop computers instead of a mouse.

TPM (Trusted Platform Module) A chip on the motherboard used with software applications for security. It can be used with Windows BitLocker Drive Encryption to provide full-disk encryption and to monitor for system tampering.

tracert A command-line program used to trace the route between two systems, listing all of the routers in the path.

track A circular area around a disk drive platter. Platters have multiple tracks, and tracks are divided into sectors.

tractor feed A method of feeding continuous-feed paper through impact printers. Most printers use feeders and/or paper trays.

transfer belt A component used in some color laser printers. Colors are applied to the belt and then applied to the paper.

transfer roller A component in a laser printer that electrically charges paper to attract the toner.

transferring The step in the seven-step laser imaging process during which the paper is charged and the toner is transferred to the paper. See also processing, charging, exposing, developing, fusing, and cleaning.

triple channel DRAM RAM that is accessed in three separate 64-bit channels. It can transfer three times as much data as single channel. Compare to single channel and dual channel.

Trojan Application that appears to do one thing but does something else, usually malicious.

TRS (tip ring sleeve) connector A common connector used with speakers, headphones, and other sound components.

TV tuner Expansion card that allows a system to play and record television.

twisted-pair cable Common cable type used in Ethernet networks. Twisted-pair includes four pairs, uses RJ-45 connectors, and comes in shielded and unshielded versions.

U

UART (universal asynchronous receiver transmitter) An individual chip or built-in feature in a Super I/O chip on a motherboard. It is used to translate data between serial and parallel.

UDF (universal disk format or universal data format) A file system format used for DVDs.

UDF (user-defined functions) Part of a program that performs a specific task. Programming languages provide many built-in functions, but application developers can create their own. A function created by a developer is a UDF.

UDMA (ultra direct memory access) A faster interface for hard drives, introduced with ATA-4.

UDP (User Datagram Protocol) An alternative to TCP. It is connectionless and uses a best effort to deliver data.

UNC (universal naming convention) A path used to connect to a share on another system. The format is \\computer\share.

unicast Data sent from one computer to one other computer.

UPS (uninterruptible power supply) A battery backup system that provides short-term power to systems when commercial power is lost. Most UPS systems include a surge suppressor.

URL (uniform resource locator) A pointer to a web resource. For example, *http://www.bing.com* is a URL pointing to the Bing search engine.

USB (universal serial bus) A common method of connecting external peripherals. A single USB port can connect as many as 127 devices. USB 2.0 supports speeds of up to 480 Mbps, and USB 3.0 supports speeds of up to 5 Gbps.

User Account Control (UAC) A security feature in Windows Vista and Windows 7 that ensures users are informed when system changes occur and helps to prevent unauthorized changes. It uses two account tokens.

USMT (User State Migration Tool) A tool used to migrate user data and settings. It includes two commands. Scanstate captures user's data and settings, and loadstate loads the captured information onto the new installation.

UTP (Unshielded twisted-pair cable) Common twisted-pair cable without shielding. Compare to STP.

UXGA (ultra extended graphics array) A display device resolution of 1600 × 1200.

V

VESA (Video Electronics Standards Association) A standards organization that has created standards for SVGA displays and video peripherals.

VFAT (virtual file allocation table) A feature in Windows that supports long file names.

VGA (video graphics array) A display device resolution of 640 × 480. A VGA interface uses a 3-row DB-15 connector.

virtualization Running operating systems or applications in a virtual environment within a physical host. For example, one physical computer (called the *host*) can run multiple virtual machines (called *guests* or *VMs*) without requiring multiple computers. A hypervisor is an application that manages the virtual systems.

virus Malware that attaches itself to another host file. When the other file executes, the malware executes.

VM (Virtual Machine) A guest operating system on a system using virtualization. The host system runs hypervisor software and can manage one or more VMs at a time.

VoIP (Voice over Internet Protocol) A protocol used for voice and multimedia sessions over an IP network.

VoIP phone A Voice over Internet Protocol (VoIP) phone is used to make phone calls over an IP network instead of traditional plain old telephone service (POTS) lines.

volume A usable portion of a disk. A single physical disk can be a single volume or divided into multiple volumes. A volume is the same as a partition.

VPN (virtual private network) A VPN provides access to an internal private network over a public network such as the Internet. VPNs use tunneling protocols to protect data transmitted over the public network.

VRAM (video random access memory) A type of RAM used in older video cards.

W

WAN (wide area network) Two or more local area networks (LANs) connected together but in different geographic locations.

WAP (Wireless Application Protocol) Protocol used to send web-based content such as webpages to mobile devices.

watt A measure of power calculated by multiplying voltage and amperage. Power supplies are rated in watts.

webcam A camera attached to a computer to provide real-time video. It is often used with phone calls.

Well-known ports Port numbers 0 to 1023 used to identify protocols and services.

WEP (Wired Equivalent Privacy) Legacy security protocol used with wireless networks. It should not be used today.

Wi-Fi (wireless fidelity) A WLAN using 802.11-based wireless technologies. It is a trademark of the Wi-Fi Alliance.

WiMAX (Worldwide Interoperability for Microwave Access) A wireless technology used to connect metropolitan area networks (MANs). It requires line-of-sight connectivity between towers.

Windows Anytime Upgrade A feature in Windows 7 that allows users to a purchase an upgrade to a higher edition of Windows 7. Users purchase a license key and can upgrade the system without the installation DVD.

Windows Easy Transfer A tool used to transfer files and settings between two computers as part of a migration. It's included in Windows 7, and free downloads are available that can be installed on Windows XP–based and Windows Vista–based systems.

Windows Memory Diagnostic A tool in Windows Vista and Windows 7 that is used to test physical memory.

Windows RE (Recovery Environment) A preinstallation environment used for troubleshooting Windows.

Windows Update A service provided by Microsoft to provide updates to Windows systems.

Windows 7 Upgrade Advisor A free tool used to determine whether a system is compatible with Windows 7. It checks the hardware and existing applications for compatibility issues and provides a report for the user.

Windows XP Mode A feature in Windows 7 that allows you to run applications from within a virtual Windows XP environment. It is useful if you want to migrate to Windows 7 but have an older legacy application that won't run on Windows 7. The legacy application can run in Windows XP Mode within Windows 7.

WINS (Windows Internet Name System) Used to resolve NetBIOS names to IP address on internal networks. In comparison, DNS is used to resolve host names on the Internet and on internal networks.

wire strippers A hardware tool used to strip covering off of wires.

wireless access point (WAP) Device that acts as a bridge for wireless clients to a wired network. WAP is also an acronym for Wireless Application Protocol.

wireless router A WAP with routing capabilities. Wireless routers often have other capabilities, such as DHCP, NAT, and a firewall.

WLAN (wireless local area network) A local area network using wireless technologies.

workgroup A small network that does not have centralized authentication. Each computer has a separate database holding user accounts.

WORM (write-once read-many) Indicates that a disc can be written to only once. Discs designated with R (such as DVD-R) can be written to once and are sometimes referred to as WORM discs.

worm Malware that can travel over a network without a host file and without user interaction.

WPA/WPA2 (Wi-Fi Protected Access) Newer security protocols used with wireless networks. WPA2 is the newest and the most secure.

WPS (Wi-Fi Protected Setup) A feature with many wireless devices that allows users to configure wireless security with a push button or a PIN. When enabled, it is vulnerable to attacks using free open source software.

WUXGA (wide ultra extended graphics array) A display device resolution of 1920 × 1200.

X

x64 Indicates a 64-bit processor supporting a 64-bit operating system. 64-bit versions of Windows can run on x64-based systems.

x86 Indicates a 32-bit processor supporting a 32-bit operating system. On a 64-bit Windows operating system, 32-bit application files are stored in the C:\Program Files (x86) folder by default, and 64-bit program files are stored in the C:\Program Files folder by default.

xcopy The extended copy command is used to copy files and folders. It can do everything copy can do, but it has many more capabilities.

xD An older type of flash memory card used in some digital cameras. Newer cameras have switched to SD.

XGA (extended graphics array) A display device resolution of 1024 × 768.

Z

ZIF (zero-insertion-force) A feature often used with PGA sockets to lock a CPU into place. LGA sockets often use a locking flip-top case instead.

zip (zigzag inline package) A file extension used for compressed files and folders.

Index

Symbols

A

B

D

O

Q

R

S

X

Z

About the Author

DARRIL GIBSON has been an author and trainer for many years. He's authored or coauthored more than 25 books, including books about CompTIA A+, Network+, and Security+ certifications. He has a wide range of certifications, including in the certifications just mentioned, as well as in CASP; (ISC)2 SSCP and CISSP; and Microsoft MCT, MCTS, MCITP, MCSA, and MCSE. Darril tweets daily exam tips on Twitter (*http://twitter.com/DarrilGibson*).

Contact the Author

I regularly post blog articles at *http://blogs.GetCertifiedGetAhead.com,* and I often answer questions from people studying for certifications on various public forums. If you'd like to contact me directly, you can send me an email at *darril@GetCertifiedGetAhead.com.* I especially love hearing from people who have used one of my books to successfully take and pass an exam and become certified.

What do you think of this book?

We want to hear from you!

To participate in a brief online survey, please visit:

microsoft.com/learning/booksurvey

Tell us how well this book meets your needs—what works effectively, and what we can do better. Your feedback will help us continually improve our books and learning resources for you.

Thank you in advance for your input!